Expanding Our Horizons

Jeff Jones, Publisher

January 1, 2020, marks our sixth year at Waterway Guide Media after taking the helm of this distinguished brand from the Dozier family, who owned and operated the company for 12 years. Prior to that, Waterway Guide had several other owners–both family-run and corporate–since its founding in 1947.

Along the way, the *Waterway Guide* content has been continuously reviewed, updated and improved upon with the sole purpose of helping boaters navigate safely and enjoyably to their destinations. We know it is timely and accurate content that brings readers back to Waterway Guide year after year. This is the heart and soul of the Waterway Guide business model and what continues to drive us today.

The next decade holds exciting horizons for the boating industry. As new technologies emerge, the way we boat, navigate, communicate and just plain enjoy our beautiful waterways will change. Our ongoing commitment is to provide valuable information to boaters on multiple media platforms using the same solid content that we have become so well known for over the last 73-plus years.

Yes, we will remain committed to our popular print publications, including the 10 *Waterway Guide* editions and the annual *Explorer Magazine*, and these publications will interface more efficiently with our digital offerings, including the online Waterway Explorer (waterwayguide.com), our Waterway Guide Marinas app, various Waterway Guide partner apps (i.e., iNavX, AquaMap) and our weekly electronic newsletter. There is so much more to come.

We will continue to update and expand our print and digital offerings. You can rely on Waterway Guide Media to provide current and accurate information on navigation alerts, fuel prices, marinas and service facilities, bridge and lock schedules and anchorages, whether you are doing the Great Loop or weekend sailing on your favorite body of water.

So, as you look ahead to your next boating adventure, we hope you will keep Waterway Guide Media at the ready to assist in your planning, safety and enjoyment. And look for us on the water because, like you, we love an adventure.

Thanks again for making this lifestyle possible,

Jeff Jones, Publisher

Staying Connected to the Internet While Cruising

Retreating to the boat and escaping from our daily lives sounds good, but how many of us would really leave our phones on the dock and go for an extended cruise? Like it or not Internet connectivity is ingrained in modern life. While I certainly advocate for turning phones off at certain times particularly on the boat, I also understand the importance of being able to stay connected. As an owner of a small business and a boat, I appreciate being able to get away on the boat but sometimes need to remain connected. Onboard Internet allows me to spend more time on the boat while continuing to keep business going. Tablets, phones and laptops help boaters like me make reservations at marinas, check fuel dock locations/prices, monitor weather, conduct business, communicate with friends and family and post to social media when there is a working Internet signal.

Wave WiFi provides easy to use connectivity solutions for all sizes and types of boats that help keep boats online. Their basic systems combine an ethernet converter and antenna in one housing which allows boaters to gain access to WiFi from further away. Their Graphic User Interface makes it easy to identify and connect to WiFi hot spots by showing their name, signal strength, frequency and whether they are encrypted or open. Systems like the Rogue Wave PRO DB (Dual Band) that I have used both on my boat and on recent deliveries, connects to both 2.4GHZ and 5GHZ providing access to the fastest connection available. The PRO works well plugged directly into my laptop via an Ethernet cable or can be connected to a router like the MBR 550, an onboard wireless router with a built-in universal SIM slot. The PRO connects into the MBR550 and then multiple devices can connect wirelessly to the Internet simultaneously. In a marina on an island that has notoriously bad cell coverage, and limited WiFi service, I was able to connect to the strongest 5GHZ connection in the marina. Multiple user aboard could not only get on the Internet but place voice over Internet calls since they had no cell coverage. When we left the marina and were out of WiFi range, the MBR 550 seamlessly transitioned to cellular, and with an optional external cellular antenna was able to pick up signal in areas where our phones could not.

If Internet connectivity is needed aboard your boat, Wave WiFi has a host of practical and effective solutions that can keep you connected so you can cruise more. When you want to listen to the waves and relax you can always turn the Internet off!

The adventure of a lifetime
America's Great Loop

2+ Countries • 14+ States and Provinces • 100+ Locks • 5,250+ Miles...
... all aboard your own boat!

America's Great Loop Cruisers' Association

AGLCA is a group of over 6,000 people who share a passion for the Great Loop. We provide information and inspiration that help our members move the Great Loop from their bucket list to reality. Whether you're brand new to the idea of the Great Loop, you're actively planning for it, or you're ready to drop the dock lines and head out now, AGLCA offers something for you!

Membership includes:

- Events
- Discounts
- Newsletters
- Podcasts
- Camaraderie
- Blogs
- Cost Calculators
- and so much more!

Visit our website:
www.GreatLoop.org

500 Oakbrook Lane,
Summerville, SC 29485
Tel: 877-GR8-LOOP

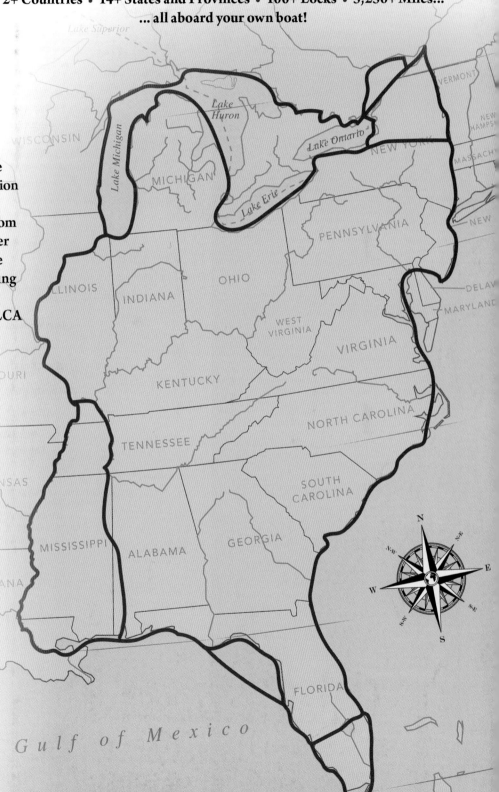

WATERWAY GUIDE OFFICES

Corporate/Production Office
16273 General Puller Hwy.
P.O. Box 1125
Deltaville, VA 23043
804-776-8999
804-776-6111 (fax)
www.waterwayguide.com

BOOK SALES

waterwayguide.com/shipstore
800-233-3355

FOUNDED IN 1947

Publisher	**JEFF JONES** jjones@waterwayguide.com
General Manager/ Editor-in-Chief	**ED TILLETT** etillett@waterwayguide.com
Managing Editor	**JANI PARKER** jparker@waterwayguide.com
Graphic Design/ Production Manager	**SCOTT MCCONNELL** scott@waterwayguide.com
Product Manager	**HEATHER SADEG** heather@waterwayguide.com
Marketing & Advertising Traffic Manager	**SANDY HICKEY** sandy@waterwayguide.com
Book Sales Manager	**LINDA JERNIGAN** linda@waterwayguide.com
Business Development & National Sales Manager	**GRAHAM JONES** graham@waterwayguide.com
Comptroller	**ARTHUR CROWTHER** acrowther@waterwayguide.com
Senior Advisor/ Skipper Bob Editor	**TED STEHLE** tstehle@waterwayguide.com
News Editor	**LISA SUHAY** lisa@waterwayguide.com
Web Master	**MIKE SCHWEFLER**
Office Assistant	**LEON HOLZMAN**

NATIONAL SALES

GRAHAM JONES   graham@waterwayguide.com

REGIONAL MARKETING REPRESENTATIVES

KELLY CROCKETT   kelly@waterwayguide.com

PETE HUNGERFORD   pete@waterwayguide.com

JOE LOWREY   joe@waterwayguide.com

REGIONAL CRUISING EDITORS

BAHAMAS	MARK BAKER LUCY & MATT CLAIBORNE DEB & DENNIS JANSMA
SOUTHERN, FLORIDA KEYS, WESTERN GULF COAST, ATLANTIC ICW, CHESAPEAKE BAY & NORTHERN	MARK BAKER SCOTT RICHARD BERG MICHAEL CAMERATA LUCY & MATT CLAIBORNE TOM DOVE CAPT. GEORGE & PAT HOSPODAR DEB & DENNIS JANSMA CAPT. DENA HANKINS & JAMES LANE BOB SHERER (ICW CONTRIBUTING EDITOR) ELIZABETH A. STOLTZ (CONTRIBUTING EDITOR)
GREAT LAKES	CAPT. JOHN JOHNSTON MICHAEL O'REILLY & ANN PHILLIPS MARY & THERON RODRIGUEZ
CUBA	ADDISON CHAN NIGEL CALDER (CONTRIBUTING EDITOR)

@Waterway Guide   @WaterwayGuide   @waterway_guide

Atlantic ICW Coverage

ATLANTIC ICW COVERAGE

WATERWAY GUIDE
THE CRUISING AUTHORITY
www.WaterwayGuide.com

Ch 1
Ch 2
Ch 3
Ch4
Ch 5
Ch 6
Ch 7
Ch 8
Ch 9
Ch 10

VIRGINIA
NORTH CAROLINA
NORTH CAROLINA
SOUTH CAROLINA
SOUTH CAROLINA
GEORGIA
GEORGIA
FLORIDA

Chesapeake Bay
Cape Henry
Norfolk
Virginia Beach
MILE 0
Rudee Inlet
Coinjock
MILE 50
Elizabeth City
Edenton
Albemarle Sound
MILE 80
Manteo
Oregon Inlet
Belhaven
Washington
Pamlico River
Pamlico Sound
Cape Hatteras
New Bern
Oriental
Ocracoke
Hatteras
Neuse River
MILE 185
Hatteras Inlet
Ocracoke Inlet
Morehead City
Beaufort
MILE 205
Adams Creek
Swansboro
Cape Lookout
Beaufort Inlet
Wilmington
Wrightsville Beach
Masonboro Inlet
Cape Fear River
MILE 309
Southport
Cape Fear River Inlet
Myrtle Beach
Georgetown
Waccamaw River
Winyah Bay Entrance
Bull Bay
Isle of Palms
MILE 456
Charleston
MILE 467
Charleston Inlet
MILE 536
Beaufort
Stono River
MILE 475
Savannah
Port Royal Sound
Hilton Head Island
Tybee Roads Inlet
Ossabaw Sound
MILE 475
MILE 615
St. Catherines Sound
St. Simons Sound
MILE 686
Jekyll Island
St. Marys
MILE 716

Atlantic Ocean

N

Atlantic ICW Coverage

Contents

2020 Atlantic ICW Edition, Volume 73, No. 1

Before you can begin your journey down the ICW, you must traverse the 10-mile stretch through the Hampton Roads area. This is the home to the world's largest naval base and is one of the busiest harbors on the ICW. The "official" beginning of the ICW is at Mile Zero in Norfolk, VA. At Mile 7.3 you must choose one of two very different routes south: the Albemarle-Chesapeake Canal or the Dismal Swamp Canal. The two routes converge on the southern side of the Albemarle Sound. North Carolina's sounds (Inner Banks) and the Outer Banks are rewarding side trips and are unlike any other regions along the Mid-Atlantic coast. The barrier islands extend in a crescent from the Virginia state line, then swing back at Cape Hatteras.

After passing through the sister cities of Beaufort and Morehead City (Mile 205), the ICW follows the open Bogue Sound and New and Cape Fear Rivers to an area known as "The Ditch." The dredged channel cuts through low marshy islets, across several small rivers and finally through a long land cut that ends in Charleston Harbor. This is where the Cooper and Ashley Rivers meet and is a favorite destination for cruisers.

It's 244 miles along the ICW from Charleston to Florida's state line. During this stretch of the ICW, you will wend your way across wide river mouths, through a series of sounds and past numerous coastal inlets. The banks are lined with woods, moss-covered live oaks and marshland. You may even glimpse the ocean. When you leave Georgia, you will notice a change from open sounds and rivers to creeks connected by narrow land cuts.

How to Use This Guide

Marina listings and locator maps

Dockage/mooring and anchorage details

Mile-by-mile navigation

Detailed Goin' Ashore for select ports with locator map and key featuring attractions, shopping and dining

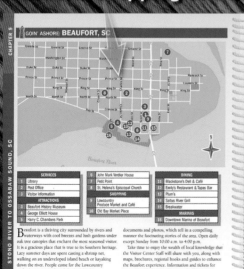

Includes Skipper's Handbook with bridge schedules, selected inlets, GPS waypoints, customs procedures and more!

NEW Maine Yacht Center
Portland, ME

Wentworth By The Sea Marina
New Castle, NH

NEW Newburyport Harbor Marina
Newburyport, MA

NEW Hilton's Marina
Newburyport, MA

NEW Windward Yacht Yard
Newburyport, MA

NEW Newburyport Boat Basin
Newburyport, MA

Nantucket Boat Basin
Nantucket, MA

NEW Star Island Yacht Club
Montauk, NY

Oakdale Yacht Club
Oakdale, NY

Harbor East Marina
Baltimore, MD

Osprey Point Marina
Rock Hall, MD

Mears Point Marina
Grasonville, MD

Mears Marina Annapolis
Annapolis, MD

Eastport Yacht Center
Annapolis, MD

Port Annapolis Marina
Annapolis, MD

Shipwright Harbor Marina
Deale, MD

Herrington Harbour North
Tracy's Landing, MD

Herrington Harbour South
North Beach, MD

The Inn at Herrington Harbour
North Beach, MD

Nanticoke River Marina
Blades, DE

Ocean City Fishing Center
Ocean City, MD

Sunset Marina
Ocean City, MD

Spring Cove Marina
Solomons, MD

Zahniser's Yachting Center
Solomons, MD

Deltaville Marina
Deltaville, VA

Atlantic Yacht Basin
Chesapeake, VA

Morningstar Marinas | Kings Point
Cornelius, NC

River Dunes Marina
Oriental, NC

Homer Smith Docks and Marina
Beaufort, NC

Marina at St James Plantation
Southport, NC

Lightkeepers Marina
Little River, SC

Harborwalk Marina
Georgetown, SC

Hazzard Marine
Georgetown, SC

Charleston Harbor Marina
Mount Pleasant, SC

Harborage at Ashley Marina
Charleston, SC

Windmill Harbour Marina
Hilton Head Island, SC

Shelter Cove Marina
Hilton Head Island, SC

Harbour Town Yacht Basin
Hilton Head Island, SC

Hinckley Yacht Services
Savannah, GA

Morningstar Marinas | Bahia Bleu
Savannah, GA

Morningstar Marinas | Golden Isles
St Simons Island, GA

Brunswick Landing Marina
Brunswick, GA

St. Augustine Municipal Marina
St. Augustine, FL

Palm Coast Marina
Palm Coast, FL

New Smyrna Beach City Marina
New Smyrna Beach, FL

Boat Tree Marina
Sanford, FL

Westland Marina
Titusville, FL

Harbortown Marina Canaveral
Merritt Island, FL

Ocean Club Marina
Port Canaveral, FL

Suntex Marina at Vero Beach
Vero Beach, FL

Harbour Isle Marina
Fort Pierce, FL

Causeway Cove Marina
Fort Pierce, FL

Fort Pierce City Marina
Fort Pierce, FL

Harborage Yacht Club & Marina
Stuart, FL

Sailfish Marina
Stuart, FL

Hinckley Yacht Services
Stuart, FL

Admirals Cove Marina
Jupiter, FL

The Bluffs Marina
Jupiter, FL

Loggerhead Marina
Palm Beach Gardens, FL

Soverel Harbour Marina
Palm Beach Gardens, FL

Twelve Oaks Marina
North Palm Beach, FL

Old Port Cove Marina
North Palm Beach, FL

North Palm Beach Marina
North Palm Beach, FL

New Port Cove Marine Center
Riviera Beach, FL

Loggerhead Marina | City Marina
Riviera Beach, FL

Sailfish Club of Florida
Palm Beach, FL

Palm Beach Yacht Club
West Palm Beach, FL

Suntex Marina at Lantana
Lantana, FL

Suntex Marina at South Lantana
Lantana, FL

The Seagate Yacht Club
Delray Beach, FL

New River / Downtown Docks
Fort Lauderdale, FL

Cooley's Landing Marina
Fort Lauderdale, FL

Las Olas Marina
Fort Lauderdale, FL

Bahia Mar Yachting Center
Fort Lauderdale, FL

NEW Port 32
Fort Lauderdale, FL

Seahaven Superyacht Marina
Dania Beach, FL

Suntex Marina at Hollywood
Hollywood, FL

Suntex Marina at Aventura
Aventura, FL

NEW Sunset Harbour Yacht Club
Miami Beach, FL

Miami Beach Marina
Miami Beach, FL

Marlin Bay Yacht Club
Marathon, FL

Conch Harbor Marina
Key West, FL

City Marina at Garrison Bight
Key West, FL

Key West Bight Marina
Key West, FL

Esplanade Marina
Marco Island, FL

Marco Island Marina
Marco Island, FL

Port of the Islands Marina
Naples, FL

Legacy Harbour
Fort Myers, FL

Fort Myers Yacht Basin
Fort Myers, FL

Marina Jack
Sarasota, FL

Longboat Key Moorings
Longboat Key, FL

Cove Sound Moorings
Cortez, FL

Riviera Dunes Marina
Palmetto, FL

Tierra Verde Marina Resort
Tierra Verde, FL

Suntex Marina at St. Petersburg
St. Petersburg, FL

Pasadena Yacht & Country Club Marina
Gulfport, FL

Home Port Marina
Palm Harbor, FL

Bay Street Marina
Nassau, Bahamas

Highbourne Cay Marina
Exumas, Bahamas

Soldier Cay
Exumas, Bahamas

Little Halls Pond Cay
Exumas, Bahamas

Compass Cay
Exumas, Bahamas

Wild Tamarind Cay
Exumas, Bahamas

Cruising Editors

Waterway Guide's on-the-water Cruising Editors bring us firsthand information about the navigation, news and trends along the waterways we cover. In addition to contributing to the annual guide, they provide daily updates on the Waterway Explorer at waterwayguide.com. We are pleased to introduce you to our crew.

Southern, Florida Keys, Western Gulf Coast & Bahamas

Matt and Lucy Claiborne currently cruise the U.S. East Coast and the Bahamas full time on their 38-foot sailboat *Dulcinea*. Starting in South Florida and the Keys, they've owned boats ranging from a 38-foot sailing catamaran and 19-foot runabouts to kayaks and paddleboards. Matt and Lucy both hold SCUBA certifications, FAA pilot certificates and USCG Master licenses. They love everything about the cruising lifestyle from sailing the Sea of Abaco to sundowners with friends on the Chesapeake Bay.

Mark Baker and his partner, **Ann**, have been avid "part-time liveaboards" since purchasing their 37-foot, shoal-draft, racer/cruiser 10 years ago. Since that time they have put over 4,000 nautical miles under the keel and have personally made all repairs and upgrades to their sailboat. They enjoy meeting new folks in the towns and cities along the way and also seeking out secluded spots to enjoy the natural world and to experience some good ol' gunkholing. Ann is a talented birdwatcher and Mark enjoys underwater photography and the study of geology. Both being former teachers, they are practitioners of life-long learning.

Debi and Dennis Jansma both have a long-lived love of the sea and boating. Dennis began sailing as a teenager on a Hobie Cat in Hingham, MA, while Debi grew up in marinas along the Erie Canal. The two met in high school in Rumson, NJ, and sailed together on the Navesink River. In 2005, Debi and Dennis moved to the Miami area, seeking a longer sailing season, and became very active on the CGSC Race Committee. In 2012, they began building their dream boat, a kit catamaran from Australia called a Fusion 40 (*XYZZY*) on the west coast of Florida. Launched in 2015, they have cruised the US East Coast north as far as Maine, and spent several winters in the Bahamas and Eastern Caribbean. Both Debi and Dennis are SSCA members.

Tom Dove began sailing in 1955, created popular programs for Annapolis Sailing School in the 1960s (including the world's first flotilla cruises) and has cruised on a variety of sailboats in the U.S. and various other parts of the world. He has been writing about boating for books, national and regional magazines and television for the past 30 years. In 2017, he chose a more "age appropriate" vessel and now ambles happily along the Atlantic coast with his wife, Kathy, on *SNOWBIRD*, a renovated 1977 Grand Banks 32 trawler.

Atlantic ICW

Capt. George and Patricia Hospodar have been boaters for over 46 years and have cruised more than 46,000 miles together aboard two sailboats and their 48-foot Symbol motor yacht, *Reflection*. Since 2008 they have traveled up and down the Atlantic ICW numerous times between their home on Barnegat Bay in Brick, NJ, and their "adopted" home at Banana Bay Marina in Marathon, FL, and have completed the America's Great Loop journey twice, as well as the Triangle Loop through the waterways of the U.S. and Canada. George and Pat are Platinum lifetime members of the America's Great Loop Cruisers' Association, as well as members the Marathon Yacht Club. Together he and Pat (a retired music teacher and choral director) have authored two popular boating books: *Reflection on America's Great Loop* and *The Great Loop Experience from Concept to Completion*, and they are often featured speakers at boat shows, TrawlerFests, AGLCA Rendezvous, and other nautical events. George and Patricia are also Cruising Editors for the Northern, Chesapeake, and Atlantic ICW editions of *Waterway Guide*.

Long-time skipper **Bob Sherer** is a contributing editor at *Waterway Guide*. Bob (better known in cruising circles as "Bob 423") focuses on navigational alerts along the Atlantic ICW. Bob and his wife, Ann, just completed their eighth trip down the ICW from Poughkeepsie, NY, to Key West. Bob is best known for his activity on numerous cruising forums and the couple has a popular blog at fleetwing.blogspot.com. Bob and Ann spend 9 months of the year aboard *Fleetwing*, a Beneteau 423, with four-legged crew member, Hoolie, a Brittany.

Chesapeake Bay & Northern

Capt. Dena Hankins and **James Lane** moved aboard their first boat in Seattle, WA, in 1999, and their travels since under sail have spanned two oceans and countless sounds, bays, rivers and waterways. After starting aboard a 48-foot Seawolf ketch, they've been struck by two-foot-itis in reverse several times, downsizing for the ease and freedom of a smaller boat. Since seaworthiness is key, they currently live on and sail a Baba 30 named *Cetacea*. Since independence is another non-negotiable requirement, *Cetacea* is outfitted with an off-the-grid electrical system and a composting head. Dena and James have contributed to the Northern, Chesapeake, ICW and Southern editions of *Waterway Guide* and

have been covering Maine since 2015. Dena is a multi-published novelist and short-story author who writes best in quiet anchorages. James is an inspired photographer and storyteller who finds grist for both mills in his everyday life aboard.

Scott Richard Berg is a lifelong boater and full-time cruiser with five decades of experience on a range of vessels from el Toro prams to a 135-foot Baltic Trader. He operated Chardonnay Boatworks, a full-service marine repair company, for many years from a series of cruising sailboats (all named Chardonnay). He is the immediate past president of the SSCA, an ABYC-Certified Master Technician and holds an Amateur Extra Class radio license. Scott is Waterway Guide's on-the-water Cruising Editor for the Potomac River.

Michael Camarata started his sailing/boating life in the early 1970s when he decided to buy a Sunfish-type sailboat with his future wife, Carol Zipke. A few years later they bought a larger sailing dinghy with TWO sails. This was to set a pattern of larger and more complicated sailing vessels that continued to the vessel they now own and live aboard, a 44-foot sailing catamaran, *Infinite Improbability*, which Michael says is their last upgrade. Michael and Carol's cruising area originally ranged from New York City to Nantucket and north of the Cape Cod Canal. Now, having sold all of their "dirt-based property" the couple roams from southern New England to the Florida Keys and the Bahamas. They live in Mystic, CT, in the summer and Marathon, FL, in the winter.

Great Lakes

Michael O'Reilly and Ann Phillips came to sailing by first messing about with canoes and kayaks while living on the Canadian shore of Lake Superior. Sailing replaced the smaller boats, and over the last 15-plus years they have enjoyed many extended summer cruises. Most recently they completed a cruise through four of the five Great Lakes and currently plan on exploring Lake Ontario, the St. Lawrence Seaway down to Newfoundland and beyond. Mike is a long-time freelance journalist, writing mostly about the sciences. With the transition to this new watery life, Mike now spends most of his work time writing about traveling, destinations and cruising. Ann is an accomplished photographer. Together they are chronicling their life afloat.

Mary and Tharon Rodriguez enjoy cruising the Great Lakes in Michigan Summers and Florida Keys/Bahamas the remainder of the year. Their fleet includes *Fuzz*, an S2 7.3, located on the Great Lakes, and *Tipsy Gypsy*, a 36-foot Hinterhoeller Nonsuch, located in Florida. They are both digital nomads working and cruising full-time and sharing their adventures through writing blog posts, taking pictures for Instagram and uploading videos on YouTube. They are fun-loving, adventure-seeking, mid-westerners with a whole lot to offer our team. Learn more about them by visiting maryandtharon.com.

Captain John "JJ" Johnston is our Cruising Editor for the Erie Canal and the New York State Canal System. He is originally from Pittsburgh, PA, but calls Fairport, NY, his home canal town. Capt. JJ retired from Kodak's motion picture division in 2007 and became a captain on *Sam Patch*, a popular Erie Canal tour boat. He also served as Executive Director of CANAL NY, a destination marketing organization, traveling on his 29-foot diesel inboard C Dory, *Penguin*, across the State of New York, promoting the waterway and learning about its history, operation and navigation. He's motored all 524 miles of the NY State Canal System, been up and down all 57 locks and overnighted in 45 canal communities. Look for Captain JJ and *Penguin* when you cruise through Fairport.

Cuba

Addison Chan is the Cruising Editor for the Cuba edition of *Waterway Guide*. He and his wife, Pat, have cruised from the U.S. to Cuba and The Bahamas multiple times aboard their 42-foot sailboat, *Threepenny Opera*. Addison has a popular Facebook group called *Cuba, Land and Sea*, which is a clearinghouse of current information about cruising and traveling in Cuba. The Cuba cruising guide addresses questions posed there that encompass not only the boating aspects of Cuba but the other aspects of experiencing Cuba as well. Addison's world travel, seamanship, navigation skills and spirit for adventure all combined to offer what we consider to be the most experienced view of Cuba's culture, its people and insight for anyone taking their boat there.

Other Contributors

Waterway Guide gathers information and photos from a variety of sources, including boaters, marinas, communities and tourism divisions. We would like to thank everyone who contributed to this edition, with special thanks to:

The Albemarle Loop (albemarleloop.com)
Crystal Coast (crystalcoastnc.org)
Rudy & Jill Sechez
Bill Hezlep
VanessaK Photography/Charleston Aerials

Marinas	**Services**	**Anchorages**	**Bridges & Locks**	**Nav Alerts**	**Fuel**

6 Waterway Explorer provides different icons that overlay on the maps as modes

Modes

Info Pane with details

*Plan your time on the water with **Explorer***

www.waterwayguide.com

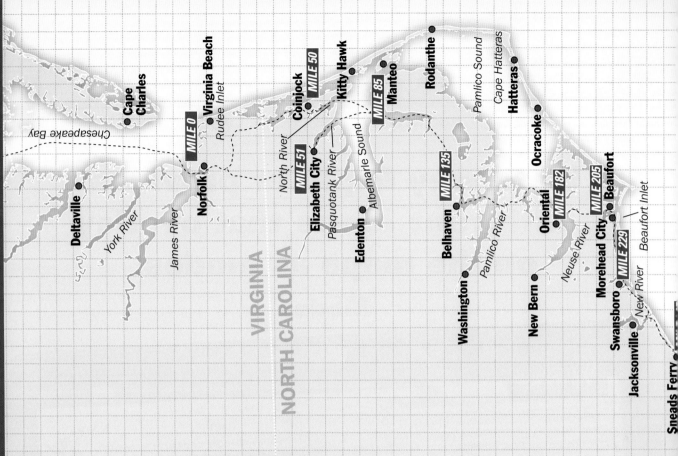

Inside-Route Distances
from Norfolk, Virginia, to Fernandina Beach, Florida

STATUTE MILES

Diagonal locations (with coordinates):

- Norfolk, VA — 36°50.9' N, 76°17.9' W.
- Elizabeth City, NC — 36°18.1' N, 76°13.0' W.
- Hertford, NC — 36°11.6' N, 76°28.0' W.
- Columbia, NC — 36°55.0' N.
- Edenton, NC — 36°03.3' N, 76°36.6' W.
- Plymouth, NC — 35°51.8' N, 76°45.6' W.
- Manteo, NC — 36°54.6' N, 75°40.2' W.
- Belhaven, NC — 35°32.1' N, 76°37.4' W.
- Washington, NC — 35°32.6' N, 76°03.7' W.
- Ocracoke, NC — 35°06.8' N, 75°59.1' W.
- Oriental, NC — 35°01.5' N, 76°41.8' W.
- New Bern, NC — 35°06.1' N, 76°40.2' W.
- Beaufort, NC — 34°43.1' N, 76°40.2' W.
- Morehead City, NC — 34°42.8' N, 76°41.8' W.
- Swansboro, NC — 34°41.0' N, 77°07.3' W.
- Jacksonville, NC — 34°44.7' N, 77°26.3' W.
- Wrightsville, NC — 34°13.1' N, 77°48.8' W.
- Wilmington, NC — 34°14.0' N, 77°57.0' W.
- Southport, NC — 33°54.8' N, 78°01.0' W.
- Little River, SC — 33°52.2' N, 78°36.6' W.
- Bucksport, SC — 33°39.0' N, 79°05.6' W.
- Georgetown, SC — 33°21.4' N, 79°16.9' W.
- McClellanville, SC — 33°04.7' N, 79°27.6' W.
- Charleston, SC — 32°47.2' N, 79°55.2' W.
- Beaufort, SC — 32°25.6' N, 79°55.2' W.
- Savannah, GA — 32°05.0' N, 80°40.2' W.
- Thunderbolt, GA — 32°01.5' N, 81°02.8' W.
- Brunswick, GA — 31°08.0' N, 81°29.7' W.
- Fernandina Beach, FL — 30°40.3' N, 81°28.0' W.

Upper-right portion of chart (reading across, distances from each origin):

```
89* 102 102 113 121  92 138 180 151 184 207 204 205 230 266 283 314 308 344 377 405 430 467 536 585 583 685 717
     45  55  64  45  91 131 105 136 160 154 157 182 217 235 266 260 296 329 358 382 419 488 536 535 636 669
         30  40  48  53  91 132 112 137 160 158 158 184 219 236 267 261 298 330 358 383 421 489 537 536 638 670
             29  38  52  90 131 110 136 159 157 157 182 217 235 266 260 296 329 357 382 419 488 536 535 636 669
                 16  62 100 142 120 145 168 166 167 191 227 245 276 270 306 338 366 391 429 497 547 545 645 678
                     70 109 150 130 154 178 175 175 201 237 254 285 280 315 349 376 402 438 506 556 555 656 688
                         81 121  70 105 127 127 127 152 186 205 236 231 267 299 326 352 388 457 506 505 606 639
                             45  49  49  72  70  70  96 131 150 181 175 211 243 270 296 334 402 451 450 551 582
                                 69  64  87  85  85 110 146 163 194 189 224 258 285 311 348 417 465 464 565 597
                                     47  71  68  68  93 129 147 178 173 208 241 268 293 331 399 449 448 549 580
                                         26  25  25  51  86 105 136 130 166 198 226 251 289 357 406 405 506 537
                                             44  44  69 105 123 154 148 184 216 245 270 307 376 425 423 525 557
                                                  3  28  63  81 112 107 143 175 203 229 266 334 383 382 483 514
                                                     25  61  79 110 105 140 173 200 226 264 331 381 380 481 512
                                                         36  53  84  79 115 147 175 200 238 306 356 353 453 487
                                                             55  86  81 116 148 177 203 239 308 357 356 457 489
                                                                 31  25  60  93 121 146 184 253 302 300 400 434
                                                                     24  60  93 121 146 183 252 300 299 402 433
                                                                         36  69  97 122 159 228 276 275 376 409
                                                                             32  61  86 123 192 241 239 341 373
                                                                                 28  53  91 159 208 206 308 339
                                                                                     28  64 133 183 181 283 314
                                                                                         37 106 155 153 255 287
                                                                                             69 120 119 220 251
                                                                                                 49  47 150 181
                                                                                                     16 117 150
                                                                                                        101 133
                                                                                                             40
```

Lower-left portion of chart (reading across, distances from each origin):

```
 77*
 89  39
 89  39  26
 98  48  35  25
105  56  42  33  14
 80  39  46  45  54  61
120  79  79  78  87  95  70
156 114 115 114 123 130 105  39
131  91  97  96 104 113  61  43  60
160 118 119 118 126 134  91  43  56  41
180 139 139 138 146 155 110  63  76  62  23
177 134 137 136 144 152 110  61  74  59  22  38
178 136 137 136 145 152 110  61  74  59  22  38   3
200 158 160 158 166 175 132  83  96  81  44  60  24  22
231 189 190 189 197 206 162 114 127 112  75  91  55  53  31
246 204 205 204 213 221 178 130 142 128  91 107  70  69  46  48
273 231 232 231 240 248 205 157 169 155 118 134  97  96  73  75  27
268 226 227 226 235 243 201 152 164 150 113 129  93  91  69  70  22  21
299 257 258 257 266 274 232 183 195 181 144 160 124 122 100 101  53  52  31
328 286 287 286 294 303 260 211 224 209 172 188 152 150 129 129  82  81  60  28
352 311 310 318 327 283 248 233 246 233 196 213 177 174 152 154 105  84  53  24
374 332 333 332 340 349 306 257 270 255 218 235 199 196 174 176 128 127 106  75  46  24
406 364 366 364 373 381 337 290 302 288 251 267 231 229 207 208 160 159 138 107  75  56  32
466 424 425 424 432 441 397 349 362 347 310 327 290 288 266 268 220 219 198 167 138 116  92  60
508 466 467 466 475 483 440 392 404 390 353 369 333 331 309 310 262 261 240 209 181 159 135 104  43
507 465 466 465 474 482 439 391 403 389 352 368 332 330 309 261 260 239 179 157 133 103  41  14
595 553 554 553 562 570 527 479 491 477 440 456 420 418 396 397 349 349 327 296 268 246 222 191 130 102  88
623 581 582 581 589 598 555 506 519 504 467 484 447 445 423 425 377 376 355 324 295 273 249 218 157 130 116  35
```

ICW Planning Map

Grid is approximately 5 nm. For planning purposes only.
Not to be used for navigation.

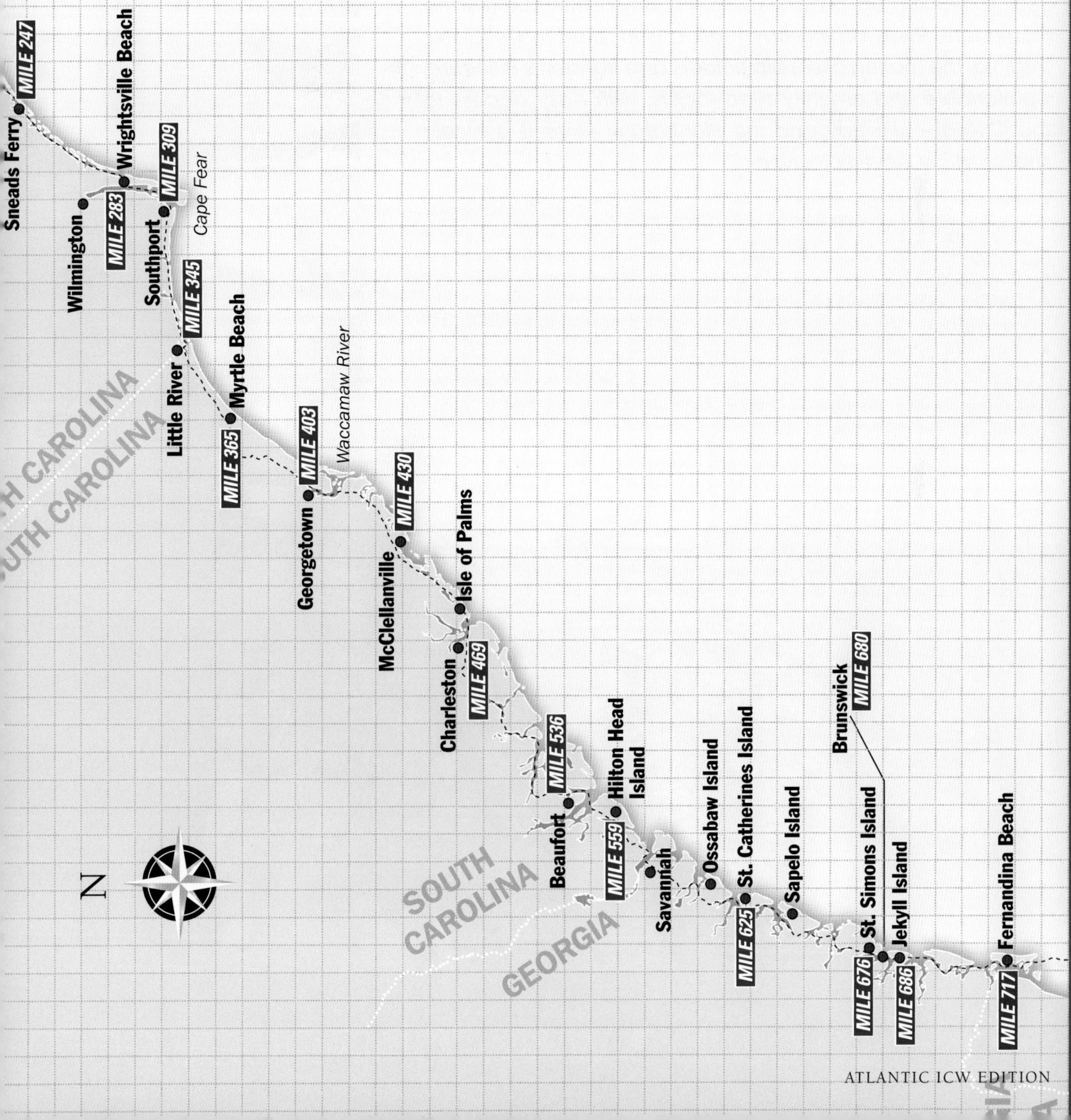

MILE 247
Sneads Ferry
Wrightsville Beach
MILE 309
Wilmington
MILE 283
Southport
Cape Fear
MILE 345
Little River
Myrtle Beach
Waccamaw River
MILE 365
MILE 403
Georgetown
MILE 430
McClellanville
Isle of Palms
Charleston
MILE 469
NORTH CAROLINA
SOUTH CAROLINA
MILE 536
Hilton Head Island
Beaufort
MILE 559
Savannah
Ossabaw Island
St. Catherines Island
Sapelo Island
Brunswick
MILE 680
St. Simons Island
Jekyll Island
Fernandina Beach
MILE 625
MILE 676
MILE 686
MILE 717
SOUTH CAROLINA
GEORGIA

N

Fishing Bay Marina
DELTAVILLE, VIRGINIA

519 Deagles
Deltaville, VA 230
Phone: (804) 776-68
Fax: (804) 776-88
info@fishingbay.co

On the beautiful deep waters of Fishing Bay at the mouth of the Piankatank River, Fishing Bay Marina is located in Deltaville, Virginia. The marina offers slip holders and transients a secure, comfortable and amenity-filled facility, with easy access to the Chesapeake Bay and the Piankatank River. It is nicely sheltered by Stove Point Neck.

- Transient Slips accommodating vessels larger than 200ft.
- Approach/Dockside Depth: 18 / 15 ft.
- Tide Range: 1.5 ft.
- Fuel Dock with ValvTect Marine Fuel – gas and diesel (including high-speed)
- Pump-out and water services
- Virginia Clean Marina
- Full service boatyard adjacent to our marina: ChesapeakeBoatWorks.com

- Olympic size swimming pool
- Clean, air-conditioned bathhouses
- Laundry washer and dryer
- Captain's Lounge
- Ice, Grills, and Bicycles
- FREE WiFi High-Speed Internet
- Courtesy Car
- Horseshoe Pits & Volleyball Court
- Close proximity to town

804-776-6800 • www.fishingbay.com

SKIPPER'S HANDBOOK

Rules of the Road

Anyone planning to cruise our waterways should make themselves familiar with the rules of the road. *Chapman Piloting: Seamanship and Small Boat Handling* and *The Annapolis Book of Seamanship* are both excellent on-the-water references with plentiful information on navigation rules. For those with a penchant for the exact regulatory language, the Coast Guard publication *Navigation Rules: International–Inland* covers both international and U.S. inland rules. (Boats over 39.4 feet are required to carry a copy of the U.S. Inland Rules at all times.) These rules are also available online at navcen.uscg.gov. Click on NavRules on the top menu bar.

The following is a list of common situations you will likely encounter on the waterways. Make yourself familiar with them, and if you ever have a question as to which of you has the right-of-way, let the other vessel go first. Sailors need to remember that a boat under sail with its engine running is considered a motorboat.

Passing or being passed:

■ If you intend to pass a slower vessel, try to hail them on your VHF radio to let them know you are coming.

■ In close quarters, BOTH vessels should slow down. Slowing down normally allows the faster vessel to pass quickly without throwing a large wake onto the slower boat.

■ Slower boats being passed have the right-of-way and passing vessels must keep clear of these slower vessels.

■ As you pass a slower boat, take a look back to see how they were affected by your wake. Remember: YOU are responsible for your wake. It is the law to slow down, and it is common courtesy.

At opening bridges:

■ During an opening, boats traveling with the current go first and generally have the right-of-way.

■ Boats constrained by their draft, size or maneuverability (e.g., dredges, tugs and barges) also take priority.

■ Standard rules of the road apply while circling or waiting for a bridge opening.

Tugs, freighters, dredges and naval vessels:

■ These vessels are usually constrained by draft or their inability to easily maneuver. For this reason, you will almost always need to give them the right-of-way and keep out of their path.

■ You must keep at least 100 yards away from any Navy vessel. If you cannot safely navigate without coming closer than this, you must notify the ship of your intentions over VHF Channel 16.

■ Keep a close watch for freighters, tugs with tows and other large vessels while offshore or in crowded ports. They often come up very quickly, despite their large size.

■ It is always a good practice to radio larger vessels (VHF Channel 13 or 16) to notify them of your location and your intentions. The skippers of these boats are generally appreciative of efforts to communicate with them. This is especially true with dredge boats on all the waterways.

In a crossing situation:

■ When two vessels under power are crossing and a risk of collision exists, the vessel that has the other on her starboard side must keep clear and avoid crossing ahead of the other vessel.

■ When a vessel under sail and a vessel under power are crossing, the boat under power is usually burdened and must keep clear. The same exceptions apply as per head-on meetings.

■ On the Great Lakes and western rivers (e.g., the Mississippi River system), a power-driven vessel crossing a river shall keep clear of a power-driven vessel ascending or descending the river.

Power vessels meeting any other vessel:

■ When two vessels under power (either sailboats or powerboats) meet "head-to-head," both are obliged to alter course to starboard.

■ Generally, when a vessel under power meets a vessel under sail (i.e., not using any mechanical power), the powered vessel must alter course accordingly.

■ Exceptions are vessels not under command, vessels restricted in ability to maneuver, vessels engaged in commercial fishing or those under International Rules, such as a vessel constrained by draft.

Two sailboats meeting under sail:

■ When each has the wind on a different side, the boat with the wind on the port side must keep clear of the boat with the wind on the starboard side.

■ When both have the wind on the same side, the vessel closest to the wind (windward) will keep clear of the leeward boat.

■ A vessel with wind to port that sees a vessel to windward but cannot determine whether the windward vessel has wind to port or starboard will assume that windward vessel is on starboard tack and keep clear.

VHF Communications

Skippers traveling the U.S. inland waterways use their VHF radios almost every day to contact other vessels and bridgetenders, make reservations at marinas, arrange to pass other vessels safely and conduct other business. *Waterway Guide* has put together the following information to help remove any confusion as to what frequency should be dialed in to call bridges, marinas, commercial ships, or your friend anchored down the creek. Remember to use low power (1 watt) for your radio transmission whenever possible. If you are within a couple of miles of the responding station (bridge, marina or other craft) there is no need to broadcast at 25 watts and disturb the transmissions of others 25 miles away.

Channel Usage Tips

■ VHF Channel 16 (156.8 MHz) is by far the most important frequency on the VHF-FM band. VHF Channel 16 is the international distress, safety and calling frequency.

■ If you have a VHF radio on your boat, FCC regulations require that you to maintain a watch on either Channel 09 or 16 whenever you are underway and the radio is not being used to communicate on another channel. Since the Coast Guard does not have the capability of announcing an urgent marine information broadcast or weather warning on VHF Channel 09, it recommends that boaters normally keep tuned to and use VHF Channel 16, but no conversations of any length should take place there; its primary function is for emergencies only.

■ The Coast Guard's main working channel is VHF Channel 22A, and both emergency and non-emergency calls generally are switched to it in order to keep VHF Channel 16 clear. Calling the Coast Guard for a radio check on VHF Channel 16 is prohibited.

■ Radio-equipped bridges in SC, GA and FL use VHF Channel 09, with a few exceptions.

■ Recreational craft typically communicate on VHF Channels 68, 69, 71, 72 or 78A. Whenever possible, avoid calling on VHF Channel 16 altogether by prearranging initial contact directly on one of these channels. No transmissions should last longer than 3 minutes.

Coast Guard radio communication radar tower

■ The Bridge-to-Bridge Radio Telephone Act requires many commercial vessels, including dredges and tugboats, to monitor VHF Channel 13. VHF Channel 13 is also the frequency used by bridges in several states.

Distress Calls

MAYDAY: The distress signal "MAYDAY" is used to indicate that a vessel is threatened by grave and imminent danger and requests immediate assistance.

PAN PAN: The urgency signal "PAN PAN" is used when the safety of the ship or person is in jeopardy.

SÉCURITÉ: The safety signal "SÉCURITÉ" is used for messages about the safety of navigation or important weather warnings.

VHF Channel 16 is the distress call frequency. The codeword "MAYDAY" is the international alert signal of a life-threatening situation at sea. After a MAYDAY message is broadcast, VHF Channel 16 must be kept free of all traffic, other than those directly involved in the rescue situation, until the rescue has been completed. If you hear a MAYDAY message and no one else is responding, it is your duty to step in to answer the call, relay it to the nearest rescue organization and get to the scene to help. Remember, a MAYDAY distress call can only be used when life is threatened. For example, if you have run on the rocks but no one is going to lose their life, that is NOT a MAYDAY situation.

Note: The Coast Guard has asked the FCC to eliminate provisions for using VHF Channel 09 as an alternative calling frequency to VHF Channel 16 when it eliminates watch-keeping on VHF Channel 16 by compulsory-equipped vessels.

VHF Channels

09	Used for radio checks and hailing other stations (boats, shoreside operations). Also used to communicate with drawbridges in Florida.
13	Used to contact and communicate with commercial vessels, military ships and drawbridges. Bridges in several states monitor VHF Channel 13.
16	*Emergency use only.* May be used to hail other vessels, but once contact is made, conversation should be immediately switched to a working (68, 69, 71, 72, 78A) VHF channel.
22	Used for U.S. Coast Guard safety, navigation and Sécurité communications.
68 69 71 72 78A	Used primarily for recreational ship-to-ship and ship-to-shore communications.

How to Make a Distress Call

Hello All Ships. MAYDAY! MAYDAY! MAYDAY!

This is: Give your vessel name and call sign.

Our position is: Read it off the GPS, or give it as something like "two miles southwest of Royal Island." (Your rescuers must be able to find you!)

We are: Describe what's happening (e.g., on fire/hit a reef/sinking)

We have: Report how many people are on board

At this time we are: Say what you're doing about the crisis (e.g., standing by/abandoning ship)

For identification we are: Describe your boat: type, length, color, etc. (so your rescuers can more readily identify you)

We have: List safety equipment you have e.g., flares/smoke/ocean dye markers/EPIRB

We will keep watch on Channel 16 as long as we can.

Port Security

In the U.S., the U.S. Coast Guard and Customs and Border Patrol–both components of the Department of Homeland Security–handle port security. Local law enforcement agencies and the FBI also have a role in port security at the local and regional level. Each year, more than 11 million maritime containers arrive at our seaports. At land borders, another 11 million arrive by truck and 2.7 million by rail. Homeland Security is responsible for knowing what is inside those containers, whether it poses a risk to the American people and ensuring that all proper revenues are collected.

As an example, one in five food items is now imported. American consumers demand fresh limes and blueberries all year round and, as a result, during the winter months in the U.S., nearly 80 percent of the fresh fruits and vegetables on our tables come from other countries. With the ever-increasing amount of trade, the agricultural risks to the United States grow. The threat to crops and livestock is real.

In response to this threat and others, the U.S. Coast Guard has established "protection zones" around all U.S. naval vessels, tank vessels and large-capacity cruise vessels, even when underway. U.S. Navy bases, U.S. Coast Guard bases and some shoreside facilities, such as nuclear power plants, are also in protection zones. Non-military vessels (this means YOU) are not allowed within 100 yards of these protection zones. To do so can rack up serious civil penalties and even imprisonment. These protection zones vary from port to port and from facility to facility, but ignorance of the protection zones is not a viable excuse. Having said that, law-abiding boaters sometimes find themselves unable to comply with the letter of the law without hitting a jetty, for example. In such cases, common sense and good communication should prevail.

America's Waterway Watch Program

Government officials view the recreational boating community as an ally. We can do our part (and perhaps stave off more stringent regulations and surveillance measures) by becoming familiar with the Coast Guard's

America's Waterway Watch program. Think of it as a neighborhood watch program for the waterways.

It is not the intent of America's Waterway Watch to spread paranoia or to encourage spying on one another, and it is not a surveillance program; instead, it is a simple deterrent to potential terrorist activity. The purpose of the program is to allow boaters and others who spend time along the water to help the authorities counter crime and terrorism. To report suspicious behavior, call the National Response Center at 877-249-2824 (877-24WATCH). For immediate danger to life or property, call 911, or call the Coast Guard on Marine VHF-FM Channel 16.

This section includes a list of ports and places that require a little forethought and vigilance on your part. Following the steps in the action plan below will help ensure a trouble-free journey and keep you and your crew out of the headlines.

Prepare:

■ Before you leave, check the current charts for the area in which you will be traveling and identify any security areas. Security zones are highlighted and outlined in magenta with special notes regarding the specific regulations pertaining to that area.

■ Check the latest *Local Notice to Mariners* (available online at navcen.uscg and posted at some marinas) and identify any potential security areas that may not be shown on the chart.

■ Listen to VHF Channel 16 for any Sécurité alerts from the Coast Guard (departing cruise ships, U.S. Navy vessels, fuel tankers, etc.) for the area you will be cruising prior to your departure.

■ Talk to other boaters in your anchorage or marina about the areas where you will be traveling. They may have tips and suggestions on any potential security zones or special areas they may have encountered on their way.

Stay Alert While Underway:

■ Mind the outlined magenta security areas noted on your charts.

■ Look for vessels with blue or red warning lights in port areas and, if approached, listen carefully and strictly obey all instructions given to you.

■ Keep your VHF radio switched to VHF Channel 16 and keep your ears tuned for bulletins, updates and possible requests for communication.

■ Avoid commercial port operation areas, especially those that involve military, cruise line or petroleum facilities. Observe and avoid other restricted areas near power plants, national monuments, etc.

■ If you need to pass within 100 yards of a U.S. Navy vessel for safe passage, you must contact the U.S. U.S. Navy vessel or the Coast Guard escort vessel on VHF Channel 16 to let them know your intentions.

■ If government security or the U.S. Coast Guard hails you, do exactly what they say, regardless of whether or not you feel their instructions have merit.

Additional Resources
Department of Homeland Security: dhs.gov
U.S. Customs and Border Protection: cbp.gov
Local Notice to Mariners: navcen.uscg.gov (then click on "LNMS" on the top menu bar)
Atlantic Intracoastal Waterway Association: atlintracoastal.org
America's Waterway Watch: americaswaterwaywatch.org
Virginia Port Authority: portofvirginia.com
North Carolina Port Authority: ncports.com
South Carolina Port Authority: scspa.com
Georgia Port Authority: gaports.com

U.S. Coast Guard

The Coast Guard stands watch at all times to aid vessels of all sizes and the persons on board. The Coast Guard locations listed below cover the areas included in this edition of *Waterway Guide*. In some areas, you can reach the Coast Guard quickly by dialing *CG on a cellular phone. If you have a question of a non-emergency nature, the Coast Guard prefers that you telephone the nearest station. As always, if there is an emergency, initiate a "MAY DAY" call on VHF Channel 16.

■ FIFTH COAST GUARD DISTRICT

District Office: Federal Building, 431 Crawford St., Portsmouth, VA 23704
757-398-6441 or 800-334-8377

VIRGINIA (SECTOR HAMPTON ROADS)

4000 Coast Guard Blvd., Portsmouth, VA 23703
757-483-8567

NORTH CAROLINA (SECTOR NORTH CAROLINA)

735 Medical Center Dr., Wilmington, NC 28401
910-343-3880

Field Office Cape Hatteras: 252-441-0300

Field Office Fort Macon: 252-247-4583

Station Elizabeth City: 252-335-6360

Station Emerald Isle: 252-354-2462

Station Hatteras Inlet: 919-986-2175/-2176

Station Hobucken: 252-745-3131

Station Oak Island: 910-278-1133

Station Ocracoke: 252-928-4731 (seasonal)

Station Oregon Inlet: 252-441-6260

Station Wrightsville Beach: 910-256-4224/-4015 (emergencies)

■ SEVENTH COAST GUARD DISTRICT

District Office: Brickell Plaza Federal Building, 909 SE 1st Ave., Miami, FL 33131
305-415-6860

SOUTH CAROLINA/GEORGIA (SECTOR CHARLESTON)

196 Tradd St., Charleston, SC 29401
843-724-7683

Station Georgetown: 843-546-2742

Station Charleston: 843-720-7727

Station Brunswick: 912-267-7999

Station Tybee Island: 912-786-5440

For more information: uscg.mil

Coast Guard Requirements

In addition to aiding boaters in distress, the Coast Guard also enforces maritime law and conducts safety inspections. While a Coast Guard boarding can be unnerving, if you are responsible and prepared, it will only take 15 to 30 minutes and will be a non-event. First, have your boat in order. This includes having your vessel documentation, registration and insurance documents on hand, as well as your passport. Organize this in a binder and keep it in the nav station so you don't have to fumble around looking for documents and paperwork. You will need to acknowledge the location of any weapons on board and show a permit (when required by state law).

As they begin to inspect your boat, the officers will focus on areas with the largest safety concerns, including the following.

Life Jackets: One Type I, II, II, or V per person plus one Type IV throwable device is required. PFDs must be U.S. Coast Guard-approved, wearable by the intended user and readily accessible. The Type IV throwable device must be located such that it is immediately available.

Visual Distress Signals: All vessels 16 feet and over must be equipped with minimum of 3 day-use and 3 night-use or 3 day/night combination pyrotechnic devices. Non-pyrotechnic substitutes: orange flag (for day use) and electric S-O-S signal light (for night use). Flares must be up to date (e.g., not expired).

Sound Producing Devices: A whistle, horn, siren, etc. capable of a 4-second blast audible for 0.5 mile must be on board for use during periods of reduced visibility. Boats 65 feet and over must have a bell and one whistle or horn required to signal intentions.

Navigation Lights: All boats over 16 feet must have working navigational lights and an independent all-around anchor light. Sailboats under power are considered powerboats and must follow "power" rules.

Fire Extinguisher: U.S. Coast Guard-approved, marine-type fire extinguishers are required on any boat with enclosed fuel or engine spaces, enclosed living spaces, or permanent (not movable by one person) fuel tanks. They must be in good working condition and readily accessible. (Number of units required depends on vessel length.)

Ventilation: Boats built after August 1, 1980, with enclosed gasoline engines must have a powered ventilation system with one or more exhaust blowers.

Backfire Flame Arrester: All gasoline-powered inboard/outboard or inboard motor boats must be equipped with an approved backfire flame arrester.

Pollution Placard: It is illegal to discharge oil or oily waste into any navigable waters of the U.S. Boats over 26 feet must display a durable oily waste pollution placard of at least 5 by 8 inches in a prominent location.

MARPOL Trash Placard: It is illegal to dump plastic trash anywhere in the ocean or navigable waters of the U.S. Boats over 26 feet must display a durable trash placard at least 4 by 9 inches in a prominent location.

Navigation Rules: Boats 39.4 feet and over must have a copy of current Navigation Rules on board. You can download a copy at uscgboating.org.

Marine Sanitation Devices: The discharge of treated sewage is allowed within 3 nm of shore except in designated "No Discharge Zone" areas. The Coast Guard will check that overboard discharge outlets can be sealed (and are sealed, if within 3 nm of shore).

These requirements are detailed in a **downloadable boater's guide** at uscgboating.org/images/420.PDF. State and local requirements are also considered. If there is a minor violation, they may give you a written warning explaining what needs to be fixed to be in compliance. If you are found with a small violation and correct it quickly, then this will merely be a chance to interact with those whose goal is to keep you as safe as possible on the water.

Customs Reporting Procedures: Arrival in the U.S.

Operators of small pleasure vessels, arriving in the U.S. from a foreign port are required to report their arrival to Customs and Border Patrol (CBP) immediately. The master of the vessel reports their arrival at the nearest Customs facility or other designated location. These reports are tracked in the Pleasure Boat Reporting System. An application to lawfully enter the U.S. must be made in person to a CBP officer at a U.S. port-of-entry when the port is open for inspection.

CBP has designated specific reporting locations within the Field Offices that are staffed during boating season for pleasure boats to report their arrival and be inspected by CBP. The master of the boat must report to CBP telephonically and be directed to the nearest Port of Entry to satisfy the face-to-face requirement, or report to the nearest designated reporting location, along with the boat's passengers for inspection.

You may be required to rent a car or take a cab to the nearest airport or federal office several miles away for the inspection. These offices are often closed on weekends. If your arrival is after working hours, you are required to stay on board and clear in the next morning. You must, however, clear in within 24 hours of your arrival. Everyone on board, regardless of nationality, has to report in person. U.S. nationals must take their passports or passport cards. All non-U.S. Nationals should take their passports with valid visas and a Green Card, if held. Take your boat papers, either U.S. documentation or state registration with state decal number. You should also present a list of firearms and ammunition on board.

Exceptions to Face-to-Face Reporting

Alternative Inspection Systems (AIS) satisfy the boat operator's legal requirement to report for face-to-face inspection, but boaters must still phone in their arrival. There are currently five exceptions to the face-to-face inspection at a designated reporting location: ROAM, NEXUS and Canadian Border Boat Landing Permit (I-68). Participation in any of the programs does not preclude the requirement for physical report upon request by U.S. Customs and Border Protection.

Designated Ports of Entry		
Virginia *(Report to individual station or call 757-533-4218 after hours.)*		
Norfolk-Newport News	101 E. Main St., Norfolk, VA	757-533-4200
North Carolina *(After-hours service is by advance appointment only. If arriving outside of regular hours, tie-up/anchor and hoist "Q" flag. No one should board or leave the vessel until inspected.)*		
Morehead City–Beaufort	534 N. 35th St., Ste. H, Morehead City, NC	252-726-5845
Wilmington	721 Medical Center Dr., Ste. 200, Wilmington, NC	910-772-5900
South Carolina		
Myrtle Beach Int'l. Airport	1100 Jetport Rd., Myrtle Beach, SC	843-916-0438
Charleston	200 East Bay St., Charleston, SC	843-579-6500
Georgia		
Savannah	1 East Bay St., Savannah, GA	912-447-9400
Brunswick	700 Gloucester St. (2nd floor), Brunswick, SC	912-262-6692

For more information: cbp.gov/travel/pleasure-boats-private-flyers

Reporting Offsite Arrival–Mobile (ROAM)

In September 2018, the U.S. Customs and Border Patrol introduced the Reporting Offsite Arrival–Mobile (ROAM) app as the official replacement for the Local Boater Option (LBO) and Small Vessel Reporting System (SVRS) programs that have been used over the years. These programs required an initial interview to get in but usually resulted in a quick phone call instead of a face-to-face meeting to re-enter the U.S. With ROAM, travelers arriving by boat into many popular U.S. ports can now check into the country on their phones or tablets.

To download the ROAM app, just search the Apple App Store or the Google Play Store on your device. If you have a Login.gov account, you can log into the app immediately. If you need a password, the app directs you to the website, then walks you through the steps, including entering the specifics for each person on board and for your vessel. Once you've entered all of the details and submitted it for a review, an officer may initiate a video call to discuss the trip or to ask any necessary questions. All of this happens directly inside the app.

Now that the app has been implemented on a larger scale, travelers entering by boat in the Great Lakes; most of the East Coast (Delaware to Florida); Texas and San Diego, CA; and the U.S. territories in the Caribbean can use the app. New locations are continually being added, and because the program is new, it's probably a good idea to call your port of arrival to ensure they are using the ROAM app.

Of course, there may still be instances where in-person reporting is required. If you require an I-94, need to pay customs fees or duties, or need to obtain a cruising permit, you will still need to appear in person. Boaters are also still required to have a current fee decal onboard.

NEXUS (entry from Canada)

This joint Canada-U.S. initiative offers facilitated customs and immigration clearance for recreational low-risk boaters entering either country through registration into the program. NEXUS is valid for 5 years and satisfies the boat operator's legal requirement to report to a port-of-entry for face-to-face inspection, but boaters must still phone in their arrival.

Canadian Border Boat Landing Permit (I-68)

Under this program, applicants for admission into the U.S. by small pleasure boats are inspected and issued an I-68 permit for the entire boating season. The I-68 permit allows boaters to enter the U.S. from Canada for recreational purposes with only the need to report to CBP by telephoning in their arrival.

Float Plan

BoatU.S.

1. Phone Numbers

Coast Guard:_____

Marine Police:_____

Local TowBoatU.S. Company:_____

2. Description of the Boat

Boat Name:_____Hailing Port:_____

Type:_____Model Year:_____

Make:_____Length:_____Beam:_____Draft:_____

Color, Hull:_____Cabin:_____Deck:_____Trim:_____Dodger:_____

Other Colors:_____# of Masts:_____

Distinguishing Features:_____

Registration No:_____Sail No:_____

Engine(s) Type:_____Horsepower:_____Cruising Speed:_____

Fuel Capacity, Gallons:_____Cruising Range:_____

Electronics/Safety Equipment Aboard

VHF Radio:_____Cell Phone:_____CB:_____SSB:_____

Frequency Monitored:_____Loran:_____SatNav:_____

Depth Sounder:_____Radar:_____GPS:_____

Raft:_____Dinghy:_____EPIRB:_____A/B/C/406M
(Indicate Type)

3. Trip Details

Owner/Skipper (Filing Report):_____

Phone:_____Age:_____

Address:_____

Additional Persons Aboard, Total:_____

Name:_____Age:_____

Address:_____Phone:_____

Boating Experience:_____

Name:_____Age:_____

Address:_____Phone:_____

Boating Experience:_____

Name:_____Age:_____

Address:_____Phone:_____

Boating Experience:_____

Name:_____Age:_____

Address:_____Phone:_____

Boating Experience:_____

Name:_____Age:_____

Address:_____Phone:_____

Boating Experience:_____

Departure Date/Time:_____Return No Later Than:_____

Depart From:_____

Marina (Home Port):_____Phone:_____

Auto Parked At:_____

Model/color:_____Lic. #_____

Destination Port: _____

_____ETA:_____No Later Than:_____

Phone:_____

Anticipated Stopover Ports:_____

_____ETA:_____No Later Than:_____

Phone:_____

_____ETA:_____No Later Than:_____

Phone:_____

_____ETA:_____No Later Than:_____

Phone:_____

_____ETA:_____No Later Than:_____

Phone:_____

_____ETA:_____No Later Than:_____

Phone:_____

Plan Filed With:_____

Name:_____Phone:_____

Get in the habit of filing a Float Plan. It can assure quicker rescue in the event of a breakdown, stranding or weather delay. Fill out the permanent data in Sections 1 and 2. Then, make enough copies to last for the season. If you file a Float Plan with someone not at your home, such as a harbormaster or boating friend, be sure to notify them as soon as you return. Don't burden friends or authorities with unnecessary worry and responsibility if you are safe.

Check your *BoatU.S. Towing Guide*. Some listed companies will accept a verbal Float Plan via telephone or VHF.

SKIPPER'S HANDBOOK

Anchoring Doesn't Have to be a Drag

Excerpt from *ANCHORING–A Ground Tackler's Apprentice*

As you seek anchorages along the coasts or in the various waterways, you will encounter a variety of sea beds. Add to that Mother Nature's quirky sense of humor, throwing at you a wide range of wind speeds, currents, and wave conditions…it's no wonder that anchoring is looked upon as a challenge. However, it doesn't have to be, and here are a few suggestions to ease the challenge.

Sand, mud, and weeds are the types of sea bottoms cruisers will most likely encounter, and as there won't always be a choice, cruisers should outfit with anchors that will enable them to securely anchor in all three.

SuperMax, Spade, Delta, Bruce, Fortress and other general-purpose anchors, in addition to Fisherman-style anchors, all work well in sand. However, anchors with a 45-degree fluke angle do not do well in sand; if they do set, once the wind picks up they usually do not hold.

For "sand" anchors, unless the manufacturer suggests differently, the anchor sizes listed in the manufacturer's sizing chart are adequate for wind speeds from 0 to around 25 knots; gale force winds usually require an increase of at least one size, and storm force winds, two sizes.

Any anchor that works in sand will most likely work in mud, but the holding power of the anchor will be less in mud than in sand–as little as one-sixth. Therefore, an anchor used in mud, regardless of whether it has a 45-degree fluke angle–the optimum angle for mud–will need to be bigger than that used in sand, at the very least one size bigger than that mentioned above.

In weeds, general-purpose anchors usually just hook into the weeds instead of the seabed, often pulling out once the wind picks up. For an anchor to hold well in a weedy bottom, it must have the weight to crush down to the seabed and have palms or flukes long enough to dig below the weeds into the seabed. The one anchor that can do this reliably is the Fisherman-style anchor. Having one of these anchors onboard, such as a Luke take-apart anchor, not only broadens your choices of anchorages, if sized appropriately (two pounds per foot of boat), it also makes for a great storm anchor.

A fourth type of bottom is the "solid bottom," either rock or coral. With little or no soil for the anchor to dig into deep enough, when you try to set the anchor or as the wind rises the anchor will just drag along the bottom or may catch and release. In this type of bottom, unless the vessel is moored to a massive-enough weight or to an augured-in anchor, as the wind speed rises the wise captain will seek an anchorage with better holding.

It is Mother Nature that dictates the amount of rode that must be deployed, and as the wind rises a scope of at least 10:1 may be needed. When calculating for scope, add together the *depth of the water*, *height of the freeboard*, and any *additional tide*. But if the wind is expected to rise toward gale force levels or higher, also include the *depth that the anchor buries*, *height of the waves*, and the *height of any storm surge*. Adequate scope is also important, so when high winds are expected, don't skimp; if there isn't enough room to let out enough rode, move the boat to where there is.

There are also times when more than one anchor may be required, but not just any anchor is suitable for this job. Additional anchors must also be sized for the wind speed encountered and be of a design that is compatible with the type of seabed. Multiple anchors are not the time to use "ill-sized" or "ill-suited" anchors.

Use appropriate anti-chafe techniques and don't break your windlass….When setting or breaking out your anchor, use a stopper. One type, for chain only, is a formed metal "chain" stopper. For use with rope or chain rodes or for those who "hand" their rodes, a soft stopper is more practical. A soft stopper is simply a short length of rope only long enough to be belayed to a strong point at one end with the other end roller hitched to the rode. Also, when laying to your anchor, employ a snubber or bridle.

If your current ground tackle does not conform to the above recommendations, upgrade it. Also, don't forget to follow the applicable "rules" concerning the display of day-shapes and anchor lights.

Rudy and Jill Sechez are the authors of *ANCHORING–A Ground Tackler's Apprentice*. To read more, order a copy of this book through waterwayguide.com or call 800-233-3359. Rudy and Jill are Trawler Training and Anchoring Consultants, providing one-on-one onboard sessions, consultations, and group seminars. They are also available to talk to groups and clubs; to arrange to have them speak to your organization, contact them at rudyandjill@yahoo.com.

Navigation and Weather Briefings for ICW Boaters

If you are transiting the ICW in the spring or fall you should plan your schedule to be near Southport Marina to attend one of Hank Pomeranz's nightly navigation and weather briefings. Since 2014 Hank has developed and presented navigation and weather briefs geared toward vessels on the ICW.

Retired U.S. Navy meteorologist, cruising sailor and owner of Carolina Yacht Care, Hank hosts the daily discussions complete with graphics, handouts and insight into what to expect on the next leg of your journey.

The briefings include the latest U.S. Army Corps of Engineers surveys, *Local Notice to Mariners*, recent fellow cruiser postings, direct cruiser feedback and local knowledge to help you safely navigate the ICW problem areas.

On the weather side, Hank reviews current advisories, watches and warnings, analyses and forecast charts and discusses the forecasts for winds and seas, precipitation, temperatures, fog and severe weather potential for the Carolina coast, and the Pamlico and Albemarle Sounds.

Spring briefings for northbound vessels from Southport (ICW Mile 309) to Norfolk, VA (ICW Mile 0) are held from April 15 through Memorial Day. Fall briefings are scheduled from October 15 through December 15 and focus on the stretch of the AICW from Southport to Savannah, GA.

The briefings are held nightly at Southport Marina at 6:00 p.m. and are sponsored by Southport Marina and Zimmerman Marine. There is no charge to attend.

Talking About the Weather

Every day on the water can't entail balmy breezes, abundant sunshine and consistently warm weather; however, staying out of bad weather is relatively easy if you plan ahead. The National Weather Service (NWS) provides mariners with continuous broadcasts of weather warnings, forecasts, radar reports and buoy reports over VHF-FM and Single Side Band (SSB) radio. Reception range for VHF radios is usually up to 40 miles from the antenna site, although Florida stations are frequently picked up in the near Bahamas. There are almost no areas on the U.S. coast where a good quality, fixed-mount VHF cannot pick up one or more coastal VHF broadcasts. Also, there is no substitute for simply looking at the sky, and either stay put or seek shelter if you don't like what you see.

SSB Offshore Weather

SSB reports are broadcast from station NMN in Chesapeake, VA, and from station NMG in New Orleans, LA. The broadcasts are not continuous, so refer to the latest schedules and frequency lists (see sidebar) to catch them. SSB reports provide the best source of voice offshore weather information. Two major broadcasts alternate throughout the day. The High Seas Forecast provides information for mariners well offshore, including those crossing the North Atlantic Ocean. Coastal cruisers will be more interested in the Offshore Forecast, which includes information on waters more than 50 miles from shore. The forecast is divided into regions.

Weather Apps
Boating Weather (FREE)
Buoy Weather (FREE)
Marine Weather by AccuWeather (FREE)
NOAA SuperRes Radar HD ($3.99)
PredictWind (FREE)
Storm Radar with NOAA Weather (FREE)
Weather Underground (FREE)
Windfinder (FREE)
Windy (FREE)

Weather Online
Accuweather (accuweather.com)
Windfinder (windfinder.com)
Buoy Weather (buoyweather.com)
National Hurricane Center (nhc.noaa.gov)
National Weather Service (weather.gov)
NOAA Marine Forecasts (nws.noaa.gov/om/marine)
Passage Weather (passageweather.com)
Predict Wind (predictwind.com)
Sailflow (sailflow.com)
The Weather Channel (weather.com)
Weather Underground (wunderground.com/MAR)

SSB Weather Frequencies

UTC	Chesapeake, VA NMN Frequencies (kHz)	New Orleans, LA NMG Frequencies (kHz)
0330 (Offshore)	4426.0, 6501.0, 8764.0	4316.0, 8502.0, 12788.0
0515 (High Seas)	4426.0, 6501.0, 8764.0	4316.0, 8502.0, 12788.0
0930 (Offshore)	4426.0, 6501.0, 8764.0	4316.0, 8502.0, 12788.0
1115 (High Seas)	6501.0, 8764.0, 13089.0	4316.0, 8502.0, 12788.0
1530 (Offshore)	6501.0, 8764.0, 13089.0	4316.0, 8502.0, 12788.0
1715 (High Seas)	8764.0, 13089.0, 17314.0	4316.0, 8502.0, 12788.0
2130 (Offshore)	6501.0, 8764.0, 13089.0	4316.0, 8502.0, 12788.0
2315 (High Seas)	6501.0, 8764.0, 13089.0	4316.0, 8502.0, 12788.0

(UTC, or Coordinated Universal Time, is equivalent to Greenwich Mean Time)

VHF-FM/NOAA Weather Frequencies

WX1	162.550 MHz
WX2	162.400 MHz
WX3	162.475 MHz
WX4	162.425 MHz
WX5	162.450 MHz
WX6	162.500 MHz
WX7	162.525 MHz

Lightning Safety

Water and metal are excellent conductors of electricity, making boating in a thunderstorm a risky prospect. Several coastal Florida cities are among the most lightning-prone in the U.S., according to the World Meteorological Organization (WMO). Some of the cities that made the "Top 10" and average number of thunderstorms per year are: Fort Myers (88 days), Tampa (82.7 days), Tallahassee (82.5 days), West Palm Beach (76.8 days), Daytona Beach (73.4 days) and Miami (72.3 days). But Florida isn't alone in this dubious honor: Lake Charles, Louisiana, also made the top of the list (75.8 days), as did Mobile, Alabama (75.5 days). While the odds of a given boat being hit are small, the consequences are severe and deadly. Do not try and play the odds!

The best advice if you are out on the water and skies are threatening is get back to land and seek safe shelter, but that's not always practical for cruisers who live aboard or are not near land.

Reading the Skies

Thunderstorms occur when air masses of different temperatures meet over inland or coastal waters. An example of this would be when air with a high humidity that is warm near the ground rises and meets cooler air, which condenses and creates water droplets. This releases energy, which charges the atmosphere and creates lightning. This is why thunderstorms are a daily occurrence between March and October near southern waterways.

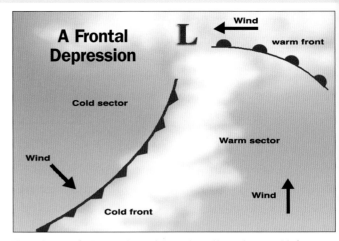

A Frontal Depression

The trigger of change is a depression. Here, in a cold front, a counterclockwise flow of cold air comes in from the northwest. Warm air is sucked in from the south, which rises above the cold air, causing wind sheer and rain. The wind veers. A falling barometer is one of the warnings of a developing front.

A tell-tale sign of a thunderstorm is cumulonimbus clouds: those tall clouds with an anvil-shaped (flat) top. Thunderstorms can also precede even a minor cold front. Keep in mind that thunderstorms generally move in an easterly direction so if you see a storm to the south or southwest of you, start preparing!

Don't Wait Until It's Too Late

Almost all lightning will occur within 10 miles of its parent thunderstorm, but it can strike much farther than that. Also, the current from a single flash will easily travel for long distances. Because of this, if you

see lightning or hear thunder, you CAN get struck! The ability to see lightning will depend on the time of day, weather conditions and obstructions, but on a clear night it is possible to see a strike more than 10 miles away. Thunder can also be heard for about 10 miles, provided there is no background noise, such as traffic, wind or rain.

If you see lightning, you can determine the distance by timing how long it takes for you to hear the thunder. The old rule that every 5 seconds of time equals 1 mile of distance works well. So if it takes 20 seconds to hear thunder after you see lighting, then the storm is 4 miles away. This is the time to drop anchor and "hunker down."

Safety Tips

Lightning tends to strike the tallest object and boats on the open water fit this profile to a tee. The lightning will try to take the most direct path to the water, which is usually down the mast on a sailboat or the VHF antenna on a powerboat. However, both sailboats and powerboats with cabins–especially those with lightning protection systems properly installed–are relatively safe, provided you keep a few things in mind:

If You Are Struck

1. **Check people first.** Many individuals struck by lightning or exposed to excessive electrical current can be saved with prompt and proper cardiopulmonary resuscitation (CPR). Contrary to popular belief, there is no danger in touching persons after they have been struck by lightning.

2. **Check the bilge** as strikes can rupture through-hull fittings and punch holes in hulls. Props and rudders are natural exit points on power boats.

3. **Check electronics and the compasses.** Typically everything in the path of the lightning is destroyed on the way down to the water, including instruments, computers and stereos.

4. **Consider a short haul** to check the bottom thoroughly. Lightning strikes sometimes leave traces of damage that may only be seen when the boat is out of the water.

■ Before the storm strikes, lower, remove or tie down all antennas, fishing rods and flag poles.

■ Stay down below and in the center of the cabin. Avoid keel-stepped masts and chain plates (on sailboats) and large metal appliances, such as microwaves or TVs. Remove any metal jewelry.

■ Disconnect the power and antenna leads to all electronics, including radios. Do not use the VHF radio unless absolutely necessary.

■ If you are stuck on deck, stay away from metal railings, the wheel, the mast and stays (on sailboats) or other metal fittings. Do not stand between the mast and stays as lightning can "side-flash" from one to the other.

■ Stay out of the water. Don't fish or dangle your feet overboard. Salt water conducts electricity, which means that it can easily travel through the water toward you.

■ Don't think your rubber-soled deck shoes will save you; while rubber is an electric insulator, it's only effective to a certain point. The average lightning bolt carries about 30,000 amps of charge, has 100 million volts of electric potential and is about 50,000°F.

Don't Rush Back Out

Because electrical charges can linger in clouds after a thunderstorm has passed, experts agree that you should wait at least 30 minutes after a storm before resuming activities. And remember: If you can hear thunder, you can still be struck by lightning!

NOAA National Severe Storms Laboratory: nssl.noaa.gov

Hurricanes

While all coastal areas of the country are vulnerable to the effects of a hurricane (especially from June through November), the Gulf Coast, Southern and Mid-Atlantic states typically have been the hardest hit. But northern locales aren't immune; several destructive hurricanes have dealt a blow to areas in New England over the last 100 years, including Hurricane Sandy in 2012 and Matthew in 2016. While hurricanes can create vast swaths of devastation, ample preparation can help increase your boat's chances of surviving the storm.

According to the National Weather Service, a mature hurricane may be 10 miles high with a great spiral several hundred miles in diameter. Winds are often well above the 74 mph required to classify as hurricane strength, especially during gusts. Hurricane damage is produced by four elements: tidal surge, wind, wave action and rain.

- Tidal surge is an increase in ocean depth prior to the storm. This effect, amplified in coastal areas, may cause tidal heights in excess of 15 to 20 feet above normal. Additionally, hurricanes can produce a significant negative tidal effect as water rushes out of the waterways after a storm.

- Wind gusts can exceed reported sustained winds by 25 to 50 percent. So, for example, a storm with winds of 150 mph might have gusts of more than 200 mph, according to the National Weather Service.

- Wave action is usually the most damaging element of a hurricane for boaters. The wind speed, water depth and the amount of open water determine the amount of wave action created. Storm surges can transform narrow bodies of water into larger, deeper waters capable of generating extreme wave action.

- Rainfall varies but hurricanes can generate anywhere from 5 to 20 inches or more of rain.

If your boat is in a slip, you have three options: Leave it where it is (if it is in a safe place); move it to a refuge area; or haul it and put it on a trailer or cradle. Some marinas require mandatory evacuations during hurricane alerts. Check your lease agreement, and talk to your dockmaster before a hurricane if you are uncertain. Keep in mind that many municipalities close public mooring fields in advance of the storm. In some localities, boaters may be held liable for any damage that their boat inflicts to marina piers or property; check locally for details. Because of this, rivers, canals, coves and other areas away from large stretches of open water are best selected as refuges.

Consult your insurance agent if you have questions about coverage. Many insurance agencies have restricted or canceled policies for boats that travel or are berthed in certain hurricane-prone areas. Review your policy and check your coverage, as many insurance companies will not cover boats in hurricane-prone areas during the June through November hurricane season. Riders for this type of coverage are notoriously expensive.

Natural Seasickness Remedies

Take slow, deep breaths. This helps with upset stomach and dizziness.

Focus on the horizon. Keep your body still and head facing forward and watch a stationary object. Taking the helm always helps.

Ginger can help. Eat ginger snaps, drink ginger tea or ginger ale or digest ginger in capsule form ahead of time.

Peppermint works too. Sucking on a peppermint candy, drinking peppermint tea or breathing in peppermint oil dabbed on a cloth can help with stomach issues.

Acupuncture wristbands apply pressure to specific points in your wrist and can reduce nausea.

Hurricane Categorization

CATEGORY	PRESSURE	WIND SPEED	SURGE
1	Above 980 mb (Above 28.91 in.)	64–82 knots (74–95 mph)	4–5 ft. (1–1.5 m)
Visibility much reduced. Maneuvering under engines just possible. Open anchorages untenable. Danger of poorly secured boats torn loose in protected anchorages.			
2	965–979 mb (28.50–28.91 in.)	83-95 knots (96–110 mph)	6–8 ft. (1.5–2.5 m)
Visibility close to zero. Boats in protected anchorages at risk, particularly from boats torn loose. Severe damage to unprotected boats and boats poorly secured and prepared.			
3	945–964 mb (27.91–28.50 in.)	96–113 knots (111–130 mph)	9–12 ft. (2.5–3.5 m)
Deck fittings at risk and may tear loose, anchor links can fail and unprotected lines will chafe through. Extensive severe damage.			
4	920–944 mb (27.17–27.91 in.)	114–135 knots (131–155 mph)	13–18 ft. (3.5–5.4 m)
Very severe damage and loss of life.			
5	Below 920 mb (Below 27.17 in.)	Above 135 knots (131–155 mph)	Above 18 ft. (Above 5.4 m)
Catastrophic conditions with catastrophic damage.			

Preparing Your Boat

- Have a hurricane plan made up ahead of time to maximize what you can get done in amount of time you will have to prepare (no more than 12 hours in some cases). You won't want to be deciding how to tie up the boat or where to anchor when a hurricane is barreling down on you. Make these decisions in advance!

- Buy hurricane gear in advance (even if there is no imminent storm). When word of a hurricane spreads, local ship stores run out of storm supplies (anchors and line, especially) very quickly.

- Strip everything that isn't bolted down off the deck of the boat (canvas, sails, antennas, bimini tops, dodgers, dinghies, dinghy motors, cushions, unneeded control lines on sailboats), as this will help reduce windage and damage to your boat. Remove electronics and valuables and move them ashore.

- Any potentially leaky ports or hatches should be taped up. Dorades (cowls) should be removed and sealed with deck caps.

- Make sure all systems on board are in tip-top shape in case you have to move quickly. Fuel and water tanks should be filled, bilge pumps should be in top operating condition and batteries should be fully charged.

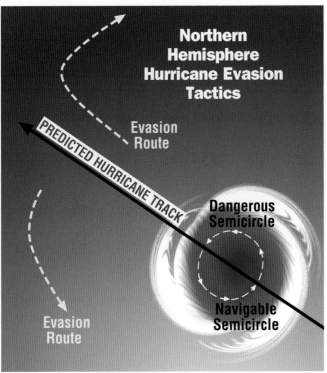

Northern Hemisphere Hurricane Evasion Tactics

Evasion Route

PREDICTED HURRICANE TRACK

Dangerous Semicircle

Navigable Semicircle

Evasion Route

You will need many lengths of line to secure the boat; make certain it is good stretchy nylon (not Dacron). It is not unusual to string 600 to 800 feet of dock line on a 40-foot-long boat in preparation for a hurricane. If you can, double up your lines (two for each cleat), as lines can and will break during the storm. Have fenders and fender boards out and make sure all of your lines are protected from chafe.

- If you are anchored out, use multiple large anchors; there is no such thing as an anchor that is too big. If you can, tie to trees with a good root system, such as mangroves or live oaks. Mangroves are particularly good because their canopy can have a cushioning effect. Be sure mooring lines include ample scope to compensate for tides 10 to 20 feet above normal.

- Lastly, do not stay aboard to weather out the storm. Many people have been seriously injured (or worse) trying to save their boats during a hurricane. Take photos of the condition in which you left your boat and take your insurance papers with you.

Returning Safely After the Storm

- Before hitting the road, make sure the roads back to your boat are open and safe for travel. Beware of dangling wires, weakened docks, bulkheads, bridges and other structures.

- Check your boat thoroughly before attempting to move it. If returning to your home slip, watch the waters for debris and obstructions. Navigate carefully as markers may be misplaced or missing.

- If your boat is sunk, arrange for engine repairs before floating it, but only if it is not impeding traffic. Otherwise, you will need to remove it immediately. Contact your insurance company right away to make a claim.

NOAA Hurricane Resource Center:
hurricanes.noaa.gov

National Hurricane Center:
nhc.noaa.gov

BoatU.S. Hurricane Resource Page:
boatus.com/hurricanes

Ditch Bag Checklist

Rescue Items

- [ ] Functioning, registered EPIRB
- [ ] Handheld VHF radio (waterproof or in sealed pouch, with extra batteries)
- [ ] Sea anchor, drogue and line
- [ ] Manual inflation pump
- [ ] Selection of flares (parachute and handheld) and smoke signals
- [ ] Strobe light (may be present in inflatable PFD)
- [ ] Flashlight & batteries (headlamp is ideal)
- [ ] Whistle (may be present in inflatable PFD)
- [ ] Signal mirror
- [ ] Handheld GPS or compass (for position)
- [ ] Small pair of binoculars (to confirm a boat or plane spotting before using flares)

Survival Items

- [ ] Sponges and bailer (with handle)
- [ ] Patch kit for inflatable dinghy or life raft (or emergency clamps)
- [ ] Water (individually sealed or in collapsible containers)–at least 2 gallons per person
- [ ] Emergency food rations and can opener (if needed)
- [ ] Power Bars
- [ ] Prescription medications
- [ ] Seasickness medications/remedies
- [ ] First aid kit
- [ ] Multipurpose tool or sailor's knife
- [ ] Waterproof matches

Other Items

- [ ] Solar blanket
- [ ] Heavy-duty coated gloves
- [ ] Duct tape
- [ ] Sewing kit
- [ ] Simple fishing gear (line, jigs, hooks, etc.)
- [ ] Polypropylene line
- [ ] Waterproof sunscreen and zinc oxide
- [ ] Bug repellent
- [ ] Ziploc bags (gallon size)
- [ ] Paper and pen in Ziploc bag
- [ ] Spare prescription glasses and sunglasses (polarized to reduce glare)
- [ ] Laminated copies of passports or license
- [ ] Cash ($50 in small bills)
- [ ] Copy of the yacht's papers (including insurance)

Reference Materials

NOAA Charts & Corrections

Paper Charts: Updated weekly and available from NOAA-certified print agents. For a complete list, see: nauticalcharts.noaa. gov/publications/print-agents.html#paper-charts.

Electronic Nautical Charts (ENCs)/Booklet Charts: Updated weekly with *Notice to Mariner* corrections..

1. Go to Chart Locator at: https://www.charts.noaa. gov/InteractiveCatalog/nrnc.shtml.
2. Click on Paper Charts (RNC&PDF) tab.
3. Pan and Zoom and select the chart of interest. It will be highlighted in yellow.
4. On the right, under "Available Products" click on the appropriate link for the product you need.
5. Download to your local computer.

USCG *Local Notice to Mariners*: Provides timely marine safety information for the correction of all U.S. Government navigation charts and publications from a wide variety of sources, both foreign and domestic. Divided by district. Updated weekly and available as a PDF at navcen.uscg.gov. (Select LNMs tab at top of page.)

Navigation

- *NAVIGATION RULES, INTERNATIONAL— INLAND*, U.S. Dept. of Homeland Security. The U.S. Coast Guard requires all vessels over 12 meters [39 feet] carry this book of the national and international rules of the road. Can be downloaded as a PDF at navcen.uscg.gov.

- *U.S. Coast Pilot (1-5)*, NOAA. Includes piloting information for coasts, bays, creeks and harbors. Also includes tide tables and highlights restricted areas. Updated weekly and can be downloaded as a PDF at nauticalcharts.noaa.gov/nsd/cpdownload.htm.

- *A Boaters Guide to the Federal Requirements for Recreational Boats*, U.S. Coast Guard. Can be downloaded as a PDF at uscgboating.org.

> ***NOAA Chart No 1. Symbols, Abbreviations and Terms, NOAA/DoD can be downloaded as a PDF at nauticalcharts.noaa.gov.***

Maintenance

- *Boatowner's Mechanical & Electrical Manual* (4th Edition), Nigel Calder
- *Boatowner's Illustrated Electrical Handbook*, Charlie Wing
- *Boat Mechanical Systems Handbook*, David Gerr

Seamanship

- *The Annapolis Book of Seamanship* (4th Edition), John Rousmaniere
- *The Art of Seamanship*, Ralph Naranjo
- *Boater's Pocket Reference*, Thomas McEwen
- *Chapman Piloting & Seamanship* (68th Edition), Charles B. Husick
- *Eldridge Tide and Pilot Book* (annual), Robert E. and Linda White
- *Heavy Weather Sailing* (7th Edition), Peter Bruce
- *Nigel Calder's Cruising Handbook*, Nigel Calder
- *Offshore Cruising Encyclopedia*, Steve and Linda Dashew
- *World Cruising Essentials*, Jimmy Cornell
- *Anchoring: A Ground Tackler's Apprentice,* Rudy and Jill Sechez

First Aid & Medical

- *Advanced First Aid Afloat* (5th Edition), Dr. Peter F. Eastman
- *DAN Pocket Guide to First Aid for Scuba Diving*, Dan Orr & Bill Clendenden
- *First Aid at Sea*, Douglas Justin and Colin Berry
- *Marine Medicine: A Comprehensive Guide* (2nd Edition), Eric Weiss and Michael Jacobs
- *On-Board Medical Emergency Handbook: First Aid at Sea*, Spike Briggs and Campbell Mackenzie

Onboard Waste & No-Discharge Zones

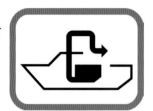

Up until the late 1980s, many boaters simply discharged their untreated sewage overboard into the water. After a revision to the Clean Water Act was passed in 1987, the discharge of untreated sewage into U.S. waters within the three-mile limit was prohibited. Shortly thereafter, pump-out stations became a regular feature at marinas and fuel docks throughout the U.S. waterways.

Simply stated, if you have a marine head installed on your vessel and are operating in coastal waters within the U.S. three-mile limit (basically all of the waters covered in the guide you are now holding), you need to have a holding tank, and you will obviously need to arrange to have that tank pumped out from time to time.

While your overboard contribution to the waterways may seem small in the grand scheme of things, similar attitudes among fellow boaters can quickly produce unsavory conditions in anchorages and small creeks. The widespread availability of holding tank gear and shoreside pump-out facilities leaves few excuses for not doing the right thing.

No-Discharge Zones

■ No-Discharge means exactly what the name suggests: No waste, even waste treated by an onboard Type I marine sanitation device (MSD), may be discharged overboard. All waste must be collected in a holding tank and pumped out at an appropriate facility.

■ Keep in mind that there are some areas that forbid overboard discharge of any waste, including gray water from showers or sinks. Familiarize yourself with local regulations before entering new areas to ensure you don't get hit with a fine.

■ No-Discharge Zones in Florida include Destin Harbor, the Florida Keys National Marine Sanctuary and the City of Key West.

The Law

■ If you have a marine head onboard and are operating on coastal waters within the U.S. three-mile limit (basically all of the waters covered in this guide), you need to have an approved holding tank or Type I MSD. In a No-Discharge area even a Type I MSD system must have a holding tank.

■ All valves connected to your holding tank or marine head that lead to the outside (both Y-valves AND seacocks) must be wire-tied, padlocked or absent of the valve handle and in the closed position. Simply having them closed without the (non-releasable) wire ties will not save you from a fine if you are boarded.

■ You may discharge waste overboard from a Type I MSD in all areas except those designated as No-Discharge Zones. A Type I MSD treats waste by reducing bacteria and visible solids to an acceptable level before discharge overboard.

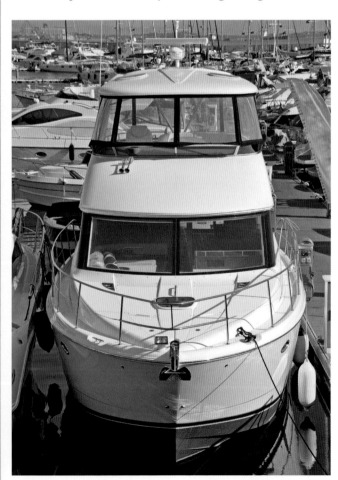

While small and inconvenient for most cruisers, "Port-A-Potties" meet all the requirements for a Type III MSD, as the holding tank is incorporated into the toilet itself.

Marine Sanitation Devices

Florida Statute 327.53 requires that vessels 26 feet or longer with an enclosed cabin and berth facilities must have one of the three types of MSDs described below on board when in state waters.

■ Type I MSD: Treats sewage before discharging it into the water using maceration. The treated discharge must not show any visible floating solids and must meet specified standards for bacteria content. Raritan's Electro Scan and Groco's Thermopure systems are examples of Type I MSDs. Not permitted in No-Discharge Zones.

■ Type II MSD: Type II MSDs provide a higher level of waste treatment than Type I units and are larger as a result. They employ biological treatment and disinfection. These units are usually found on larger vessels due to their higher power requirements. These may not be discharged in No-Discharge Zones.

■ Type III MSD: Regular holding tanks store sewage until the holding tank can either be pumped out to an onshore facility or the "Y" valve can be open to legally discharge directly overboard when offshore (3 miles or more–oceans only). When not offshore, "Y" valve must be closed.

Additional Resources
BoatU.S. Guide to Overboard Discharge:
boatus.com/foundation/guide/environment_7.html

EPA Listing of No-Discharge Zones:
epa.gov/vessels-marinas-and-ports/no-discharge-zones-ndzs-state

Inside Route Distances - Norfolk, Virgina to Fernandina Beach, Florida
(nautical and statute miles)

	Fernandina Beach, FL	Brunswick, GA	Thunderbolt, GA	Savannah, GA	Beaufort, SC	Charleston, SC	McClellanville, SC	Georgetown, SC	Bucksport, SC	Little River, SC	Southport, NC	Wilmington, NC	Wrightsville, NC	Jacksonville, NC	Swansboro, NC	Morehead City, NC	Beaufort, NC	New Bern, NC	Oriental, NC	Ocracoke, NC	Washington, NC	Belhaven, NC	Manteo, NC	Plymouth, NC	Edenton, NC	Columbia, NC	Hertford, NC	Elizabeth City, NC	Norfolk, VA
Norfolk, VA	623	595	507	508	466	406	374	352	328	299	268	273	248	231	20	178	177	180	160	131	156	120	80	105	98	89	89	77*	•
Elizabeth City, NC	581	553	465	466	424	364	332	311	286	257	226	231	204	189	158	136	134	139	118	91	114	79	39	56	48	39	39	•	89
Hertford, NC	582	554	466	467	425	366	333	311	287	259	227	232	205	190	160	137	137	139	119	97	115	79	46	42	35	26	•	45	102
Columbia, NC	581	553	465	466	424	364	332	310	286	257	226	231	204	189	158	136	136	138	118	96	114	78	45	33	25	•	30	45	102
Edenton, NC	589	562	474	475	432	373	340	318	294	266	235	240	213	197	166	145	144	146	126	104	123	87	54	14	•	29	40	55	113
Plymouth, NC	596	570	482	483	441	381	349	327	303	274	243	248	221	206	175	152	152	155	134	113	130	95	61	•	16	38	48	64	121
Manteo, NC	555	527	439	440	397	337	306	283	260	232	201	205	178	162	132	110	110	110	91	61	105	70	•	70	62	52	53	45	92
Belhaven, NC	506	479	391	392	349	290	257	235	211	183	152	157	130	114	83	61	61	63	43	43	39	•	81	109	100	90	91	91	138
Washington, NC	519	491	403	404	362	302	270	248	224	195	164	169	142	127	96	74	74	76	56	60	•	45	121	150	142	131	132	131	180
Ocracoke, NC	504	477	389	390	347	288	255	233	209	181	150	155	128	112	81	59	59	62	41	•	69	49	70	130	120	110	112	105	151
Oriental, NC	467	440	352	353	310	251	218	196	172	144	113	118	91	75	44	22	22	23	•	47	64	49	105	154	145	136	137	136	184
New Bern, NC	484	456	368	369	327	267	235	213	188	160	129	134	107	91	60	38	38	•	26	71	87	72	127	178	168	159	160	160	207
Beaufort, NC	447	420	332	333	290	231	199	177	152	124	93	97	70	55	24	3	•	44	25	68	85	70	127	175	166	157	158	154	204
Morehead City, NC	445	418	330	331	288	229	196	174	150	122	91	96	69	53	22	•	3	44	25	68	85	70	127	175	167	157	158	157	205
Swansboro, NC	423	396	307	309	266	207	174	152	128	100	69	73	46	31	•	25	28	69	51	93	110	96	152	201	191	182	184	182	230
Jacksonville, NC	425	397	309	310	268	208	176	154	129	101	70	75	48	•	36	61	63	105	86	129	146	131	186	237	227	217	219	217	266
Wrightsville, NC	377	349	261	262	220	160	128	106	82	53	22	27	•	55	53	79	81	123	105	147	163	150	205	254	245	235	236	235	283
Wilmington, NC	376	349	260	261	219	159	127	105	81	52	21	•	31	86	84	110	112	154	136	178	194	181	236	285	276	266	267	266	314
Southport, NC	355	327	239	240	198	138	106	84	60	31	•	24	25	81	79	105	107	148	130	173	189	175	231	280	270	260	261	260	308
Little River, SC	324	296	208	209	167	107	75	53	28	•	36	60	61	116	115	140	143	184	166	208	224	211	267	315	306	296	298	296	344
Bucksport, SC	295	268	179	181	138	79	46	24	•	32	69	93	94	148	147	173	175	216	198	241	258	243	299	349	338	329	330	329	377
Georgetown, SC	273	246	157	159	116	56	24	•	28	61	97	121	122	177	175	200	203	245	226	268	285	270	326	376	366	357	358	358	405
McClellanville, SC	249	222	133	135	92	32	•	28	53	86	122	146	147	203	200	226	229	270	251	293	311	296	352	402	391	382	383	382	430
Charleston, SC	218	191	103	104	60	•	37	64	91	123	159	183	184	239	238	264	266	307	289	331	348	334	388	438	429	419	421	419	467
Beaufort, SC	157	130	41	43	•	69	106	133	159	192	228	252	253	308	306	331	334	376	357	399	417	402	457	508	497	488	489	488	536
Savannah, GA	130	102	14	•	49	120	155	183	208	241	276	300	302	357	356	381	383	425	406	449	465	451	506	556	547	536	537	536	585
Thunderbolt, GA	116	88	•	16	47	119	153	181	206	239	275	299	300	356	353	380	382	423	405	448	464	450	505	555	545	535	536	535	583
Brunswick, GA	35	•	101	117	150	220	255	283	308	341	376	402	402	457	456	481	483	525	506	549	565	551	606	656	647	636	638	636	685
Fernandina Beach, FL	•	40	133	150	181	251	287	314	339	373	409	433	434	489	487	512	514	557	537	580	597	582	639	688	678	669	670	669	717

SKIPPER'S HANDBOOK

Distances: Outside (Coastwise) Route– Norfolk, VA to Key West, FL

Coastwise Distances – Norfolk, Virginia to Key West, Florida
(nautical miles)

	Straits of Florida	Key West, FL	Miami, FL	Port Everglades, FL	Port of Palm Beach, FL	Stuart, FL	Fort Pierce, FL	Cape Canaveral, FL	St. Augustine, FL	Jacksonville, FL	Fernandina Beach, FL	Brunswick, GA	Savannah, GA	Port Royal, SC	Charleston, SC	Georgetown, SC	Wilmington, NC	Southport, NC	Morehead City, NC	Diamond Shoals, NC	Norfolk, VA	Chesapeake Bay Entrance
Chesapeake Bay Entrance 36°56.3'N., 75°58.6'W.	942	881	743	720	678	666	647	612	557	560	533	527	476	465	402	365	336	315	222	117	27	-
Norfolk, VA 46°50.9'N., 76°17.9'W.	969	908	770	747	705	693	674	639	584	587	560	554	503	492	429	392	363	342	249	144	-	
Diamond Shoals, NC 35°08.0'N., 75°15.0'W.	825	764	626	603	561	549	530	495	440	443	416	410	359	348	285	248	219	198	105	-		
Morehead City, NC 34°42.8'N., 76°41.8'W.	772	711	573	550	509	497	476	438	377	379	352	346	295	284	220	184	154	133	-			
Southport, NC 33°54.8'N., 78°01.0'W.	707	646	508	485	443	423	407	367	296	294	265	260	206	191	130	87	21	-				
Wilmington, NC 34°14.0'N., 77°57.0'W.	728	667	529	506	464	444	428	388	317	315	286	281	227	212	151	108	-					
Georgetown, SC 33°21.4'N., 79°16.9'W.	671	610	472	449	407	391	368	324	246	247	216	210	154	141	79	-						
Charleston, SC 32°47.2'N., 79°55.2'W.	633	572	434	411	369	353	329	283	199	197	166	156	102	90	-							
Port Royal, SC 32°22.3'N., 80°41.6'W.	605	544	406	383	341	324	298	251	157	152	120	110	51	-								
Savannah,GA 32°05.0'N., 81°05.7'W.	604	543	405	382	340	324	298	251	152	145	115	104	-									
Brunswick,GA 31°08.0'N., 81°29.7'W.	549	488	350	327	285	268	242	195	90	82	50	-										
Fernandina Beach, FL 30°40.3'N., 81°28.0'W.	526	465	327	304	262	242	216	169	61	53	-											
Jacksonville, FL 30°19.2'N., 81°39.0'W.	523	462	324	301	256	240	214	167	56	-												
St. Augustine, FL 29°53.6'N., 81°18.5'W.	475	414	276	253	211	192	167	120	-													
Cape Canaveral, FL 28°24.6'N., 80°36.5'W.	374	313	175	152	110	91	69	-														
Fort Pierce, FL 27°27.5'N., 80°19.3'W.	316	255	117	94	52	32	-															
Stuart, FL 27°12.2'N., 80°15.6'W.	300	239	101	78	36	-																
Port of Palm Beach, FL 26°46.1'N., 80°03.0'W.	267	207	68	46	-																	
Port Everglades, FL 26°05.6'N., 80°07.0'W.	226	165	27	-																		
Miami, FL 25°47.0'N., 80°11.0'W.	211	151	-																			
Key West, FL 24°33.7'N., 81°48.5'W.	73	-																				
Straits of Florida 24°25.0'N., 83°00.0'W.	-																					

GPS Waypoints

The following list provides selected waypoints for the waters covered in this book. The latitude/longitude readings are taken from government light lists and must be checked against the appropriate chart and light list for accuracy. Some waypoints listed here are lighthouses and should not be approached too closely as they may be on land, in shallow water or on top of a reef. Many buoys must be approached with caution, as they are often located near shallows or obstructions. The positions of every aid to navigation should be updated using the Coast Guard's *Local Notice to Mariners*, which is available online at: navcen.uscg.gov/lnm.

The U.S. Coast Guard will continue to provide Differential GPS (DGPS) correction signals for those who need accuracy of 10 meters or less, even though most GPS receivers now come with an internal capability for receiving differential signals.

> *Prudent mariners will not rely solely on these waypoints to navigate. Every available navigational tool should be used at all times to determine your vessel's position.*

Albemarle Sound to Neuse River

LOCATION	LATITUDE	LONGITUDE
Albemarle Sound Entrance Light AS	N 36° 03.733'	W 075° 56.133'
Albemarle Sound North Light N	N 36° 06.100'	W 075° 54.750'
Albemarle Sound South Light S	N 36° 01.083'	W 075° 57.617'
Pasquotank River Entrance Light PR	N 36° 09.367'	W 075° 58.650'
Pungo River Junction Light PR	N 35° 22.667'	W 076° 33.583'
Goose Creek Light 1	N 35° 20.400'	W 076° 35.750'
Bay Point Light	N 35° 10.350'	W 076° 30.317'
Bay River Light 1	N 35° 09.800'	W 076° 32.017'
Neuse River Junction Light	N 35° 08.783'	W 076° 30.183'
Whittaker Creek Light 2	N 35° 01.383'	W 076° 41.150'
Smith Creek (Oriental) Channel Light 1	N 35° 00.900'	W 076° 41.467'
Adams Creek Light 1AC	N 34° 58.500'	W 076° 41.767'

Oregon Inlet to Cape Lookout

LOCATION	LATITUDE	LONGITUDE
Oregon Inlet Jetty Light	N 35° 46.433'	W 075° 31.500'
Hatteras Inlet Light	N 35° 11.867'	W 075° 43.933'
Diamond Shoal Lighted Buoy 12	N 35° 09.083'	W 075° 17.550'
Ocracoke Light	N 35° 06.533'	W 075° 59.167'

Hampton Roads to Rudee Inlet

LOCATION	LATITUDE	LONGITUDE
Little Creek Entrance Lighted Buoy 1LC	N 36° 58.083'	W 076° 10.067'
Lynnhaven Roads Fishing Pier Light	N 36° 55.000'	W 076° 04.717'
Cape Henry Light	N 36° 55.583'	W 076° 00.433'
Rudee Inlet Lighted Whistle Buoy RI	N 36° 49.783'	W 075° 56.950'

Beaufort Inlet to Florida Border

LOCATION	LATITUDE	LONGITUDE
Beaufort Inlet (NOTE: This is not the location of a particular buoy.)	N 34° 38.000'	W 077° 41.000'
Masonboro Inlet (NOTE: This is not the location of a particular buoy.)	N 34° 10.000'	W 077° 47.000'
Frying Pan Shoals Lighted Buoy 16	N 33° 28.783'	W 077° 35.083'
Cape Fear R. Ent. Lighted Whistle Buoy CF	N 33° 46.283'	W 078° 03.033'
Oak Island Light	N 33° 53.567'	W 078° 02.100'
Little River Inlet Lighted Whistle Buoy LR	N 33° 49.817'	W 078° 32.450'
Winyah Bay Lighted Whistle Buoy WB	N 33° 11.617'	W 079° 05.183'
Charleston Ent. Lighted Buoy C	N 32° 37.083'	W 079° 35.500'
North Edisto Rvr. Ent. Lig. Whistle Buoy 2NE	N 32° 31.350'	W 080° 06.850'
South Edisto Rvr. Approach Lig. Buoy A	N 32° 24.717'	W 080° 17.700'
St. Helena Sound Entrance Buoy 1	N 32° 21.667'	W 080° 18.450'
Port Royal Sound Lighted Whistle Buoy P	N 32° 05.133'	W 080° 35.033'
Calibogue Sound Entrance Daybeacon 1	N 32° 02.850'	W 080° 50.533'
Tybee Lighted Buoy T	N 31° 57.883'	W 080° 43.167'
Wassaw Sound Lighted Buoy 2W	N 31° 51.550'	W 080° 53.017'

Beaufort Inlet to Florida Border continued

LOCATION	LATITUDE	LONGITUDE
Ossabaw Sound Ent. Lighted Buoy OS	N 31° 47.800'	W 080° 56.200'
St. Catherines Sound Lighted Buoy STC	N 31° 40.217'	W 081° 00.200'
Sapelo Sound Buoy S	N 31° 31.200'	W 081° 03.900'
Doboy Sound Lighted Buoy D	N 31° 21.233'	W 081° 11.400'
Altamaha Sound Shoal Light	N 31° 18.867'	W 081° 15.333'
St. Simons Sound Lig. Buoy STS	N 31° 02.817'	W 081° 14.417'
St. Andrew Sound Outer Ent. Buoy STA	N 30° 55.550'	W 081° 18.967'
St. Marys Rvr. Approach Lighted Buoy STM	N 30° 42.900'	W 081° 14.650'

Bridge Basics

Bridges have to be factored in when planning a trip. Depending on where you cruise, you may be dependent on bridge openings; a particular bridge's schedule can often decide where you tie up for the evening or when you wake up and get underway the next day. While many are high (over 65 feet), and some usually remain open (such as railroad bridges), others are restricted for different hours in specific months, closed during rush hours and/or open on the quarter-hour, half-hour or even at 20 minutes and 40 minutes past the hour. To add to the confusion, the restrictions are constantly changing. Just because a bridge opened on a certain schedule last season does not mean it is still on that same schedule. (See the Bridges & Locks section in this guide or waterwayguide.com for the most current schedules.) Changes are posted in the Coast Guard's *Local Notice to Mariners* reports, which can be found online at navcen.uscg.gov. It is also a good idea to check locally to verify bridge schedules before your transit.

Most bridges monitor VHF Channel 09, designated by the Federal Communications Commission as the "bridgetender channel." Bridges in NC and VA still answer on VHF Channel 13, as do the locks in the Okeechobee. In any waters, it is a good idea to monitor both the bridge channel and VHF Channel 16–one on your ship's radio and one on a handheld radio, if your main set doesn't have a dual-watch capability–to monitor oncoming commercial traffic and communications with the bridgetender.

When using VHF, always call bridges by name and identify your vessel by name and type (such as sailing vessel or trawler) and whether you are traveling north or south. If you are unable to raise the bridge using VHF radio, use a horn signal. (For further information, see the *Coast Pilot 4, Chapter Two: Title 33, Navigation Regulations, Part 117, Drawbridge Regulations.*) If the gates do not come down and the bridge does not open after repeated use of the radio and the horn, call the Coast Guard and ask them to call the bridgetender on the land telephone line, or you may be able to call the bridge directly. Phone numbers for many bridges are given in the following Bridges & Locks section, although some of the numbers are not for the actual bridgetender, but for a central office that manages that bridge. Some bridges are not required to open in high winds. If you encounter a bridge that won't open, it is prudent to drop the hook in a safe spot until the situation is resolved.

Swing Bridges:
Swing bridges have an opening section that pivots horizontally on a central hub, allowing boats to pass on one side or the other when it is open.

Lift Bridges:
Lift bridges normally have two towers on each end of the opening section that are equipped with cables that lift the road or railway vertically into the air.

Most bridges carry a tide board to register vertical clearance at the center of the span. (Note that in Florida waters the tide board figure–and the one noted on the chart–is generally for a point that is 5 feet toward the channel from the bridge fender.) In the case of arched bridges, center channel clearance is frequently higher than the tide gauge registers. So check your chart and the tide boards and, unless it specifically notes that vertical clearance is given "at center," you may be able to count on a little extra height at mid-channel, under the arch of the bridge. Some bridges may bear signs noting extra height at center in feet.

Because many bridges restrict their openings during morning and evening rush hours to minimize inconvenience to vehicular traffic, you may need to plan an early start or late stop to avoid getting stuck waiting for a bridge opening.

Pontoon Bridges:

A pontoon bridge consists of an opening section that must be floated out of the way with a cable to allow boats to pass. Do not proceed until the cables have had time to sink to the bottom.

Bascule Bridges:

This is the most common type of opening bridge you will encounter. The opening section of a bascule bridge has one or two leaves that tilt vertically on a hinge like doors being opened skyward.

Bridge Procedures:

■ First, decide if it is necessary to have the drawbridge opened. You will need to know your boat's clearance height above the waterline before you start. Drawbridges have "clearance gauges" that show the closed vertical clearance with changing water levels, but a bascule bridge typically has 3 to 5 feet more clearance than what is indicated on the gauge at the center of its arch at mean low tide. Bridge clearances are also shown on NOAA charts.

■ Contact the bridgetender well in advance (even if you can't see the bridge around the bend) by VHF radio or phone. Alternatively, the proper horn signal for a bridge opening is one prolonged blast (four to six seconds) and one short blast (approximately one second). Bridge operators sound this signal when ready to open the bridge, and then usually the danger signal–five short blasts–when they are closing the bridge. The operator of each vessel is required by law to signal the bridgetender for an opening, even if another vessel has already signaled. Tugs with tows and U.S. government vessels may go through bridges at any time, usually signaling with five short blasts. A restricted bridge may open in an emergency with the same signal. Keep in mind bridgetenders will not know your intentions unless you tell them.

■ If two or more vessels are in sight of one another, the bridgetender may elect to delay opening the bridge until all boats can go through together.

■ Approach at slow speed and be prepared to wait, as the bridge cannot open until the traffic gates are closed. Many ICW bridges, for example, are more than 40 years old and the aged machinery functions slowly.

■ Once the bridge is open, proceed at no-wake speed. Keep a safe distance between you and other craft, as currents and turbulence around bridge supports can be tricky.

■ There is technically no legal right-of-way (except on the Mississippi and some other inland rivers), but boats running with the current should always be given the right-of-way out of courtesy. As always, if you are not sure, let the other boat go first.

■ When making the same opening as a commercial craft, it is a good idea to contact the vessel's captain (usually on VHF Channel 13), ascertain his intentions and state yours to avoid any misunderstanding in tight quarters.

■ After passing through the bridge, maintain a no-wake speed until you are well clear and then resume normal speed.

Locks and Locking Through

Many rivers in North America are a series of pools created by dams. When the dams also include locks, navigation is possible beyond the dam. Locks are watertight chambers with gates at each end. They raise and lower boats from one water level to the next. Many cruisers find locking through a pleasant experience and part of the adventure of boating.

Lock Types

- Conventional lift locks are single chambers that raise and lower boats.

- Flight locks are a series of conventional lift locks.

- Hydraulic lift locks have water-filled chambers supported by rams or pistons that move in opposite directions. The movement of one chamber forces the movement of the other via a connected valve. The chamber in the upper position adds sufficient water to cause it to drop, forcing the lower chamber to rise. The chambers have hinged gates fore and aft that contain the water and allow boats to enter or leave.

- Marine railways convey boats over obstacles, usually a landmass, by containing boats in a gantry crane that moves over the land and deposits the boat on the other side of the obstruction.

River locks are usually conventional lift locks. The dam deepens water around shoals, and the lock allows vessels to bypass the dam. Conventional lift locks work by gravity alone. Water passively flows into or out of the lock. When the lock is filling, the valve at the upper end of the lock is opened, and water flows in. The downstream lock gate is closed, preventing the escape of the water. This is the time of greatest turbulence in the locks and the time of greatest vigilance for boaters. When the upper water level is reached, the upper lock gate opens to allow boats to exit or enter.

When the lock empties, both lock doors are closed, a valve on the lower end of the lock is opened, and water exits. This creates a surge of water outside the lock, but inside the lock, the water recedes like water in a tub. When the water level in the lock is the same as the lower river level, the lower lock gate opens and vessels leave.

Locking Protocol

1. Call ahead on the VHF (Channel 13 or sound three blasts) for permission to lock through. Indicate whether you are northbound (upbound) or southbound (downbound). Your presence and communication indicate to the locktender your desire to lock through.

2. Wait a safe distance from the lock, or find an anchorage nearby and within sight of the lock.

3. Prepare for locking by placing large fenders fore and aft and having lines ready. Fender boards are useful because they protect your fenders and provide a skid plate against the dirt and algae on the lock wall.

4. When approaching the lock, stay back to allow outbound vessels to clear the lock. Do not enter until signaled to do so. Signals vary. Look for a telephone/pull rope at the lock wall; listen for a whistle blast–one long and one short blast, or three

blasts; look for a "traffic" light–green, yellow or red. Follow directions given by the locktender. The order of priority is:

U.S. Military
Mail boats
Commercial passenger boats
Commercial tows
Commercial fishermen
Pleasure craft

5. When the locktender turns on the green light or calls for you to enter, enter in the order that boats arrived at the lock. The longest waiting boat goes first, unless directed by the locktender, who may call boats in according to size and the configuration of the lock. Do not jump the line; do not scoot in front of others; defer to faster boats so you do not have them behind you after you leave the lock.

6. When entering the lock, leave no wake, heed instruction, and respect other boaters. If they are having trouble and appear unsettled, stand by until they are secure. Listen to the directives of the locktenders. Some lock systems require all line handlers to wear personal flotation devices (PFDs). Crew members on the bow should wear PFDs.

7. You will be directed by the locktender to a place along the lock wall. You will find an inset mooring pin (floating bollard), vertical cable or a rope. If there is a floating bollard, secure the boat to the pin via a center cleat by wrapping the line around the pin then back to the boat cleat. If there is a vertical cable, wrap the line around the cable, and bring it back to the boat; the loop will ride up or down the cable. If there is a drop-down line, bring the line around a cleat, and hold it. DO NOT TIE LINES! If you are asked to provide a line, throw it to the locktender. After the locktender has secured it, take the bitter end and wrap, but do not tie, around a cleat. Attend the bow and the stern, and adjust the line(s) as the boat rises or falls in the lock chamber.

8. In crowded locks, move forward as far as you can to make room for others coming in behind you. Small boats may raft to bigger boats. Set adequate fenders for fending off another vessel.

9. Inside the lock chamber, turn off engines when secure. Exhaust fumes contained in the lock chamber are an irritant to people in small, open boats. Attend the lines at all times. Be prepared for turbulence when the lock fills. Never use hands or feet to fend a boat off a lock wall. Stay alert to other boats. Be prepared to quickly cut a line if needed.

10. When the lock reaches its determined depth/height, the locktender will loosen the line and drop it to you if you are using a line attached at the top of the lock. After receiving a whistle blast by the locktender, recover any lines used, and prepare to exit. Leave the lock in the same order as entering. Do not rush ahead of those in front of you.

Lock Fees
Unlike locks in other countries (including Canada), there is no fee for transiting locks managed by the Army Corps of Engineers.

Bridge & Lock Schedules

KEY:

Statute Miles from ICW Mile 0
Vertical Clearance

Drawbridge clearances are vertical, in feet, when closed and at Mean High Water in tidal areas. Bridge schedules are subject to schedule changes due to repairs, maintenance, events, etc. Check Waterway Explorer at waterwayguide.com for the latest schedules or call ahead.

East Coast ICW

VA BRIDGES MONITOR ((VHF)) CHANNEL 13

2.6 / 6' — **Belt Line Railroad Lift Bridge:** Usually open. When the bridge closes for any reason, the controller will announce 30 min. in advance, 15 min. in advance, and immediately proceeding the actual lowering over VHF Channel 13. Remote operation. 757-271-1741

2.8 / 145' — **Jordan Hwy. Bridge:** Fixed

3.6 / 10' — **Norfolk & Western Railroad Lift Bridge:** Usually open. Clearance of 9 feet or less has been reported. 757-494-7371

5.8 / 35' — **Gilmerton Lift Bridge:** Opens on signal, except from 6:30 a.m. to 8:30 a.m. and 3:30 p.m. to 5:30 p.m., Mon. through Fri. (except federal holidays), when the draw need not open. Draw will not open if adjacent railroad bridge is closed. 757-485-5488/-5567

5.8 / 7' — **Norfolk & Southern #7 Railroad Bascule Bridge:** Usually open. Remote operation. 757-924-5320

7.1 / 65' — **I-64 Hwy. Bridge:** The draw will open on signal if at least 24-hour notice is given.

8.9 / 95' — **Veterans Bridge:** Fixed

11.3 — **Great Bridge Lock:** Opens on request, but coordinates with Battlefield Blvd. Bridge. 757-547-3311

12.0 / 8' — **Battlefield Blvd. Bascule Bridge:** Opens on signal, except 6:00 a.m. to 7:00 p.m. daily, when the draw need only open on the hour. The drawtender may delay the hourly opening up to 10 min. past the hour for approaching vessels. Timed to open with Great Bridge Lock. 757-482-8250

13.0 / 65' — **Chesapeake Expressway (SR 168 Bypass) Bridge:** Fixed

13.9 / 7' — **Albemarle & Chesapeake Railroad Lift Bridge:** Usually open.

15.2 / 4' — **Centerville Turnpike (SR 170) Swing Bridge:** Opens on hour and half-hour, except Mon. through Fri. from 6:30 a.m. to 8:30 a.m. and 4:00 p.m. to 6:00 p.m. (except federal holidays and weekends), when the draw need not open. The drawtender may delay the hourly opening up to 10 min. past the hour for approaching vessels. 757-547-3631/-3632

NC BRIDGES MONITOR ((VHF)) CHANNEL 13

20.2 / 6' — **North Landing Swing Bridge:** Opens on signal, except from 6:00 a.m. to 7:00 p.m., when the draw need only open on the hour and half-hour. 757-482-3081

28.3 / 65' — **Pungo Ferry Bridge:** Fixed

49.9 / 65' — **Coinjock (U.S. 158) Bridge:** Fixed

Dismal Swamp

10.5 — **Deep Creek Lock:** Opens at 8:30 a.m., 11:00 a.m., 1:30 p.m. and 3:30 p.m. 757-487-0831

11.1 / 4' — **Deep Creek (U.S. 17) Bascule Bridge:** Openings coordinated with lock operation. 757-487-0831

28.0 / 0' — **Dismal Swamp Canal Visitors Center Foot Bridge:** Usually open. This is a floating pontoon bridge. 252-771-6593

31.5 / 65' — **U.S. 17 Hwy. Bridge:** Fixed

32.6 / 4' — **South Mills Bascule Bridge:** Openings coordinated with lock operation. 252-771-5906

32.7 — **South Mills Lock:** Opens at 8:30 a.m., 11:00 a.m., 1:30 p.m. and 3:30 p.m. 252-771-5906

47.7 / 3' — **Norfolk & Southern Railroad Swing Bridge:** Usually open. (Note: Bridge is hand operated.) 866-527-3499 (emergencies only)

50.7 / 2' — **Elizabeth City (U.S. 158) Bascule Bridge:** Opens on signal, except from 7:00 a.m. to 9:00 a.m. and 4:00 p.m. to 6:00 p.m., Mon. through Fri., when the draw need only open at 7:30 a.m., 8:30 a.m., 4:30 p.m. and 5:30 p.m. if vessels are waiting to pass. 252-331-4772

East Coast ICW (cont.)

84.2 / **14'** — **Alligator River (U.S. 64) Swing Bridge:** Opens on signal. (Note: Bridge may not open if wind speed exceeds 34 knots.) 252-796-7261

113.9 / **65'** — **Fairfield (NC 94) Bridge:** Fixed

125.9 / **64'** — **Wilkerson (U.S. 264) Bridge:** Fixed (Also known as the **Walter B. Jones Bridge**.) (Note: This bridge is lower than the authorized 65-foot fixed vertical clearance.)

157.2 / **65'** — **Hobucken (NC 33/304) Bridge:** Fixed

195.8 / **65'** — **Core Creek (NC 101) Bridge:** Fixed

203.8 / **65'** — **Beaufort Channel (U.S. 70) Hwy. Bridge:** Fixed

203.8 / **4'** — **Beaufort Channel Railroad Bascule Bridge:** Usually open.

206.7 / **65'** — **Atlantic Beach Bridge:** Fixed (Note: Clearance may be 2 or 3 feet lower than charted.)

226.0 / **65'** — **Cedar Point Hwy. Bridge:** Fixed (Also known as the Emerald Isle Bridge.)

240.7 / **12'** — **Onslow Beach Swing Bridge:** (Use northwest draw.) Opens on signal, except from 7:00 a.m. to 7:00 p.m., when the draw need only open on the hour and half hour. You MUST signal, even though the operator may see you waiting. 910-440-7376

252.3 / **64'** — **U.S. 210 Hwy. Bridge:** Fixed (Note: This bridge is lower than the authorized 65-foot fixed vertical clearance.)

260.7 / **65'** — **Surf City (NC 50) Bridge:** Fixed

278.1 / **20'** — **Figure Eight Island Swing Bridge:** Opens on the hour and half-hour. Clearance may be higher than charted. (Note: Bridge may not open if wind speed exceeds 30 mph.) 910-686-2018

283.1 / **20'** — **Wrightsville Beach (SR 74) Bascule Bridge:** Opens on the hour 7:00 a.m. to 7:00 p.m. Schedule may change during special events. (Note: Actual clearance is lower than charted. May be as low as 14 feet.) 910-256-2886

295.7 / **65'** — **Snows Cut (U.S. 421) Hwy. Bridge:** Fixed

311.8 / **65'** — **Oak Island Bridge:** Fixed

316.8 / **67'** — **Middleton St. Bridge:** Fixed

323.6 / **65'** — **Holden Beach (NC 130) Bridge:** Fixed

333.7 / **65'** — **Ocean Isle (NC 904) Bridge:** Fixed

337.9 / **65'** — **Mannon C. Gore (Sunset Beach) Bridge:** Fixed

SC BRIDGES MONITOR CHANNEL 09

347.2 / **65'** — **Nixon Crossroads Hwy. Bridge:** Fixed

347.3 / **7'** — **Captain Archie Neil "Poo" McLauchlin Swing Bridge** (formerly **Little River Swing Bridge**): Opens on signal. 843-280-5919

349.1 / **65'** — **Robert Edge Pkwy. Bridge:** Fixed (Also called the **North Myrtle Beach Connector Bridge**.)

353.3 / **31'** — **Barefoot Landing Swing Bridge:** Opens on signal. 843-361-3291

355.5 / **65'** — **Conway Bypass (U.S. 17) Twin Bridges:** Fixed

357.5 / **65'** — **Grande Dunes Bridge:** Fixed

360.5 / **65'** — **Grissom Pkwy. Bridge:** Fixed

365.4 / **16'** — **SCL Railroad Bascule Bridge:** Usually open.

365.4 / **65'** — **U.S. 501 Hwy. Bridge:** Fixed (Referred to with adjacent railroad bridge as **Combination Bridges**.)

366.4 / **65'** — **Fantasy Harbor Bridge:** Fixed

371.0 / **11'** — **Socastee Swing Bridge:** (Use southeast draw.) Opens on signal. 843-347-3525

SC BRIDGES MONITOR ((VHF)) CHANNEL 09

371.3 **65'**
Socastee (SC 544) Hwy. Bridge: Fixed
(Note: Clearance as low as 60 feet has been observed.)

372 **65'**
Carolina Bays Parkway (SC 31) Bridges: Fixed
(Under construction at press time in summer 2019 with no estimated completion date. This construction will necessitate some waterway restrictions/closures. These will be announced in the *Local Notice to Mariners*.)

402.1 **65'**
Lafayette (U.S. 17.) Bridge: Fixed

411.5 **0'**
Estherville-Minim Canal Swing Bridge: Usually open, except when a vehicle needs to cross (infrequent). Watch for flashing yellow lights on sign. The bridge rests against the east bank of the river when in the open position. This is a floating swing bridge.

458.9 **65'**
Isle of Palms Connector Bridge: Fixed
(Note: Clearance may be lower than charted.)

462.2 **31'**
Ben Sawyer Memorial (SR 703) Swing Bridge: Opens on signal, except from 7:00 a.m. to 9:00 a.m. and from 4:00 p.m. to 6:00 p.m., Mon. through Fri. (except federal holidays), when the draw need not open. On Sat., Sun. and federal holidays from 9:00 a.m. to 7:00 p.m. the draw need open only on the hour. Use the west span. 843-883-3581

469.9 **67'**
James Island Expressway (SR 30) Bridge: Fixed

470.8 **33'**
Wappoo Creek (SR 171) Bascule Bridge: Opens on signal, except from 6:00 a.m. to 9:29 a.m. and 3:31 p.m. to 7:00 p.m., Monday through Friday, (except federal holidays), when the draw need not open. Between 9:30 a.m. and 3:30 p.m., Monday through Friday (except federal holidays), when the draw need only once an hour on the half hour. 843-852-4157

479.3 **65'**
John F. Limehouse Hwy. Bridge: Fixed

501.3 **65'**
McKinley Washington Jr. (SR 174) Bridge: Fixed
(Note: Clearance may be lower than charted.)

536.0 **30'**
Ladies Island (U.S. 21) Swing Bridge (officially the **Richard V. Woods Memorial Bridge**): Opens on signal, except from 6:30 a.m. to 9:00 a.m. and 3:00 p.m. to 6:00 p.m., Mon. through Fri. (except federal holidays), when the draw need not open to navigation; and from 9:00 a.m. to 3:00 p.m., when the draw need open only on the hour. During the months of Apr., May, Oct. and Nov., Mon. through Fri. (except federal holidays), the draw will open on signal except from 7:00 a.m. to 9:00 a.m. and from 4:00 p.m. to 6:00 p.m., when the draw need not open to navigation; and from 9:00 a.m. to 4:00 p.m., when the draw need open only on the hour and half-hour. 843-521-2111

539.7 **65'**
J.E. McTeer Memorial Hwy. Twin Bridges: Fixed
(Also called **Ladys Island Dr. Twin Bridges.**)

557.5 **65'**
J. Wilton Graves (U.S. 278) Hwy. Twin Bridges: Fixed

GA BRIDGES MONITOR ((VHF)) CHANNEL 09

579.9 **21'**
Causton Bluff (Sam Varnedoe) Bascule Bridge: Opens on signal, except 6:30 a.m. to 9:00 a.m. and 4:30 p.m. to 6:30 p.m., Mon. through Fri. (except federal holidays), when the draw need only open at 7:00 a.m., 8:00 a.m. and 5:30 p.m. (Note: Clearance may be higher than charted.) 912-897-2511

582.8 **65'**
State of Georgia Memorial (U.S. 80) Bridge: Fixed
(Also called **Thunderbolt Bridge**.)

592.9 **65'**
Diamond Causeway (Skidaway) Bridge: Fixed

674.5 **65'**
F.J. Torras Causeway Bridge: Fixed

684.4 **65'**
Jekyll Island (SR 520) Bridge: Fixed

Inlets: Norfolk, VA to St. Marys, GA

Cruising the "inside waterway" (the ICW) is a bit like driving down I-95. There are areas where every amenity and convenience you need is but an exit away (especially in FL), and then there are stretches with only marsh and woods as far as the eye can see (mostly in SC and GA). And like I-95 there is constant construction, many speed-restricted areas and several bridges to pass under. (The lowest bridge clearance on the ICW is the Julia Tuttle Causeway at Mile 1087.1 in Miami, which is 56 feet.) The main difference between the highway and the waterway is the "road maintenance." With federal funding for dredging being scarce, shoaling has been more commonplace on the ICW and the "projected depths" on the NOAA charts can no longer be considered valid. This, alone, will drive (pun intended) some vessels to take the offshore (Atlantic Ocean) route.

Offshore Runs: Some boaters choose the offshore run to save time or to get a break from the bridge openings and speed restrictions. Many sailboats will take this option to turn off the engine and unfurl the sails. You may be forced to take the offshore route due to vessel draft or vertical clearance. Regardless of your reasons for exiting the ICW, there are numerous inlets along the coast that will allow you to duck in or back out should the weather turn. Keep in mind that not all inlets are navigable and some are treacherous under certain conditions.

This section will assist you in recognizing those but it is still important to study the charts, pay attention to the weather and seek current local knowledge before proceeding on an offshore run.

Overall Mileage: Heading north or south, many skippers mistakenly assume that they will shorten their trips by going out to sea and running down the coast. The distances shown here–both inside (ICW) and outside (from inlet to inlet)–demonstrate that this is not necessarily true. Keep in mind that even if outside distances from sea buoy to sea buoy are virtually the same as the ICW distances, the mileage in and out to the buoys adds to the total coastwise figure.

Cautions and Warnings: Before you begin an offshore passage, take an honest accounting of your vessel, your crew and yourself. Is each of you up to the task? Is the vessel properly outfitted? Do you have the necessary safety equipment, charts, long distance communications gear such as single sideband radio (SSB), an Emergency Position Indicating Radio Beacon (EPIRB) and life raft? Do you and your crew have adequate experience in boating and navigation to attempt an offshore coastal passage?

Check the weather using as many sources as possible. If you have access to weather routing services, they are a good option, particularly for longer offshore passages. You are seeking a weather window with enough space on each side to get you safely out and back in, with room for unexpected contingencies.

Of course, always file a float plan with a reliable person. A sample float plan is provided in this guide. You might also look into the free app BoatSafe Free, which allows you to create a float plan and email it to participants or emergency contacts.

Entering & Exiting: Plan your trip so that you enter in daylight, with the tide, particularly if your boat is slow or underpowered. Remember that wind against tide can create short, steep waves in an inlet that can quickly make even a ship channel impassable for slower boats. If conditions are bad when you reach the sea buoy for an inlet, you may find yourself being driven ashore by wind or waves and unable to find the inlet buoys. It may be better to remain well offshore in rough conditions, possibly continuing to a better inlet.

Be advised that the markers at some inlets are moved on a regular basis and the buoys should be honored. Should you find yourself at an inlet and needing direction, a call on VHF Channel 16 for local knowledge is likely to bring you a response. Sea Tow and TowBoatU.S. are two other knowledgeable sources. The Coast Guard may also be able to assist you, but only if it is indeed an emergency.

Resources: Prior to your voyage, there are a number of online sources that can familiarize you with the inlets, including the following:

- **Waterway Explorer** (waterwayguide.com)–Website provides chart and satellite views of the inlets plus cruising details from local boaters.

- **United States Coast Pilot** (nauticalcharts.noaa. gov)–Nine-volume annual publication distributed by the Office of Coast Survey (NOAA) to supplement nautical charts.

- **Local Notice to Mariners** (navcen.uscg.gov, then select the LNMs tab)–Weekly updates provided by The U.S. Coast Guard to provide corrections to navigational publications and nautical charts.

- **Tide Tables** (tidesandcurrents.noaa.gov)–Provided by NOAA to provide tidal predictions (highs and lows) for specific areas.

Norfolk, VA to St. Marys, GA Entrances & Inlets

Recommended (big ship) inlets in this section are denoted with this symbol:

Inside vs. Outside Mileage

 Entrance & Inlet Distances

Hampton Roads to Beaufort Inlet:
222 nm (outside)/204 sm (ICW)

Beaufort Inlet to Cape Fear River Entrance:
115 nm (outside)/105 sm (ICW)

Cape Fear River Entrance to Winyah Bay Entrance:
65 nm (outside)/97 sm (ICW)

Winyah Bay Entrance to Charleston Harbor Entrance:
46 nm (outside)/58 sm (ICW)

Charleston Harbor Entrance to Port Royal Sound Entrance:
57 nm (outside)/85 sm (ICW)

Port Royal Sound Entrance to Tybee Roads Entrance:
10 nm (outside)/27 sm (ICW)

Tybee Roads Entrance to St. Simons Sound Entrance:
62 nm (outside)/102 sm (ICW)

St. Simons Sound Entrance to St. Marys Entrance:
21 nm (outside)/36 sm (ICW)

Note: In keeping with standard NOAA conventions, outside (ocean) distances are measured in nautical miles (nm), while ICW distances are measured in statute miles (sm):

1nm = 1.15 sm

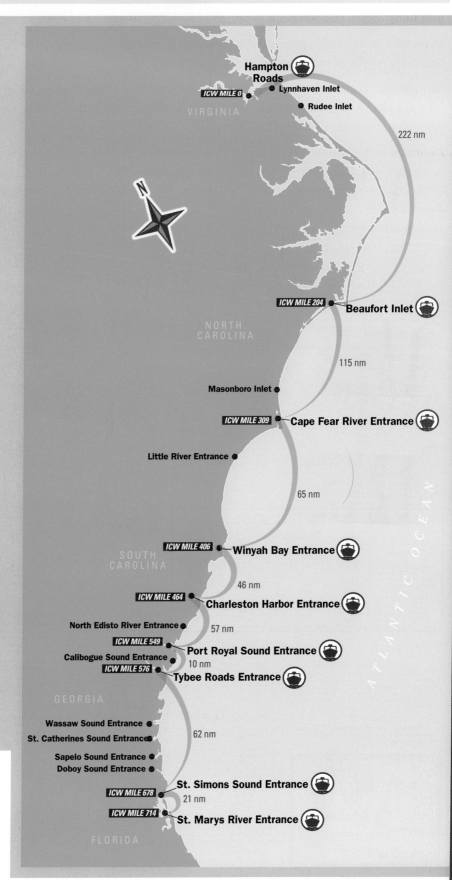

Hampton Roads
ICW MILE 0
Lynnhaven Inlet
Rudee Inlet
VIRGINIA
222 nm
ICW MILE 204
Beaufort Inlet
NORTH CAROLINA
115 nm
Masonboro Inlet
ICW MILE 309
Cape Fear River Entrance
Little River Entrance
65 nm
ICW MILE 406
Winyah Bay Entrance
SOUTH CAROLINA
46 nm
ICW MILE 464
Charleston Harbor Entrance
North Edisto River Entrance
57 nm
ICW MILE 549
Port Royal Sound Entrance
Calibogue Sound Entrance
ICW MILE 576
10 nm
Tybee Roads Entrance
GEORGIA
Wassaw Sound Entrance
St. Catherines Sound Entrance
62 nm
Sapelo Sound Entrance
Doboy Sound Entrance
St. Simons Sound Entrance
ICW MILE 678
21 nm
ICW MILE 714
St. Marys River Entrance
FLORIDA
ATLANTIC OCEAN

INLETS: NORFOLK, VA TO ST. MARYS, GA

Hampton Roads (Norfolk), VA

Sea buoy: None. Use waypoint N 36° 58.113'/W 76° 19.980'.

Overview: Strategically situated at Mile Zero, the "official" beginning of the ICW, Norfolk offers nearly every type of marine service and equipment.

Navigation: From the waypoint, follow the well-marked Thimble Shoal Channel east and south to flashing red "2C" off Cape Henry, where the mouth of the Chesapeake Bay meets the Atlantic Ocean. Along this stretch, you will pass through or over the 17-mile-long Chesapeake Bay Bridge-Tunnel,

Cautions and hazards: This is a busy port. Naval Station Norfolk, the largest naval installation in the world, is homeport for the U.S. Navy's Atlantic Fleet, encompassing aircraft carriers, cruisers, destroyers, frigates, support ships, nuclear submarines and admiral's barges. The world's merchant fleet loads and unloads cargo at the Hampton Roads as well.

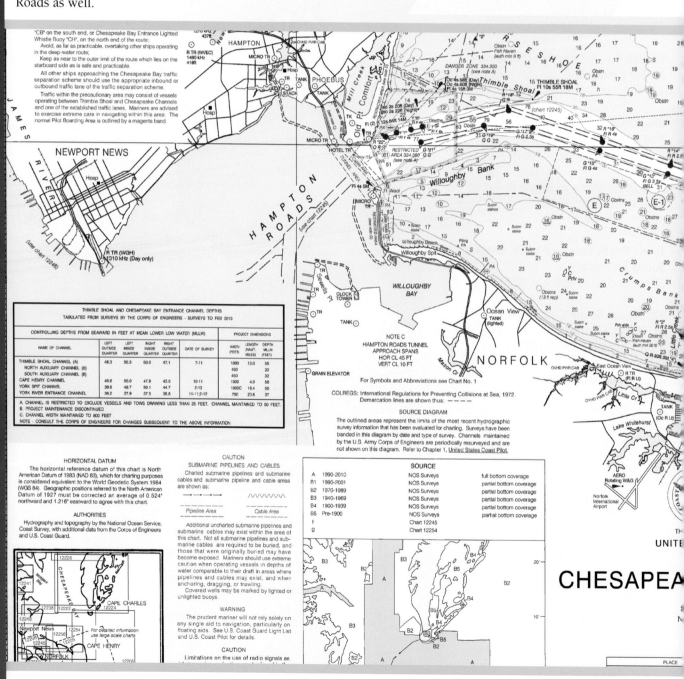

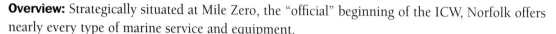

Depth: See interactive charts on Waterway Explorer at waterwayguide.com.

ICW connection: Norfolk is located at Mile Zero (the beginning) of the ICW.

Nearest recommended inlet: The next big ship inlet is Beaufort Inlet, NC, which is 222 nm.

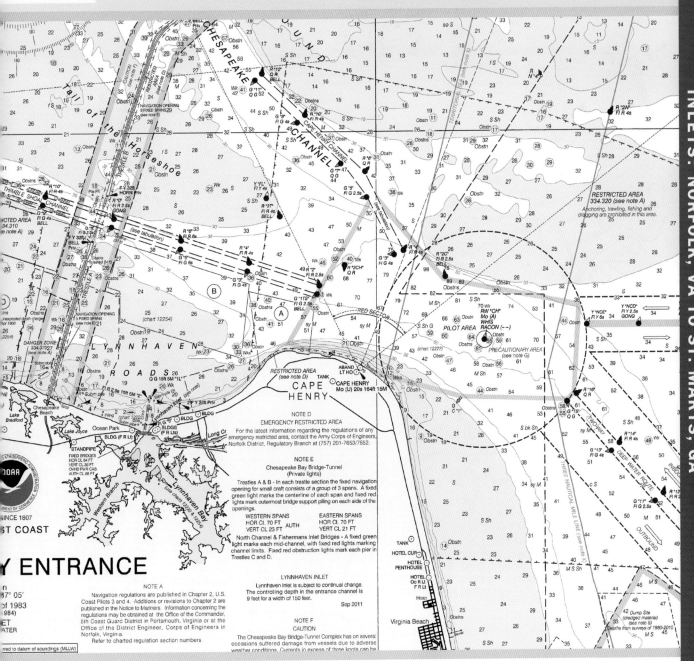

Lynnhaven Inlet, VA

Sea buoy: No sea buoy here. Use waypoint N 36° 55.350'/W 76° 05.370'.

Overview: Provides easy and fast access to the Atlantic Ocean, Chesapeake Bay or the ICW. Marinas catering to sportfishermen abound. Located just southeast of the Chesapeake Bay Bridge Tunnel, inside Cape Henry. This is not a jettied inlet like many others.

Navigation: From the waypoint, proceed 0.25 nm on a heading of 196° M to green "IL." Follow the markers in just past red nun "6" where you will encounter the fixed Lesner Bridge with a vertical clearance of 45 feet. Note that there are fixed bridges with 20- to 36-foot clearances to negotiate to the south, which eventually leads to Broad Bay. There are anchoring possibilities in Broad Bay.

Cautions and hazards: The straight, dredged entrance channel runs through a series of fixed and floating markers before passing under the 45-foot vertical clearance fixed bridge. Other than the height restriction, there are no other hazards, except a fairly strong current through the bridge.

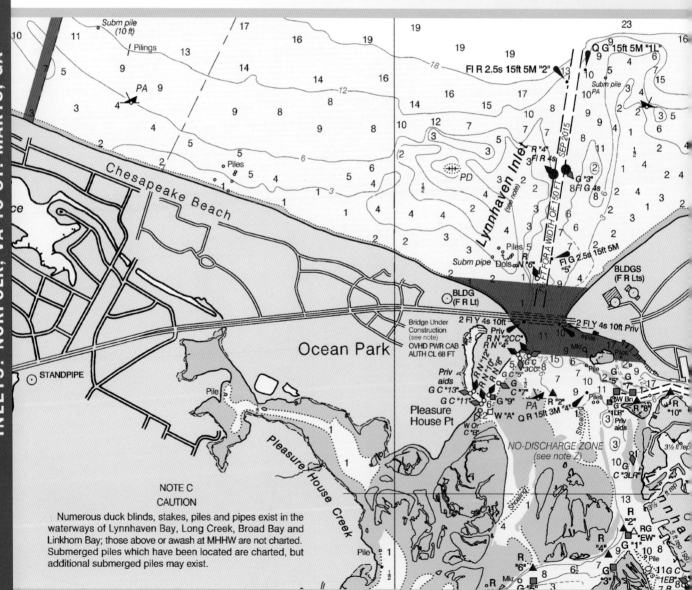

Depth: The area was last dredeged in spring 2019. See interactive charts on Waterway Explorer at waterwayguide.com.

ICW connection: None.

Nearest recommended inlet: If you cannot clear the bridges in Lynnhaven, you can proceed to Hampton Roads, 13 nm to the west, or proceed out and around Cape Henry to the south for about 14 nm to Rudee Inlet. Note that Rudee Inlet also does not connect with the ICW.

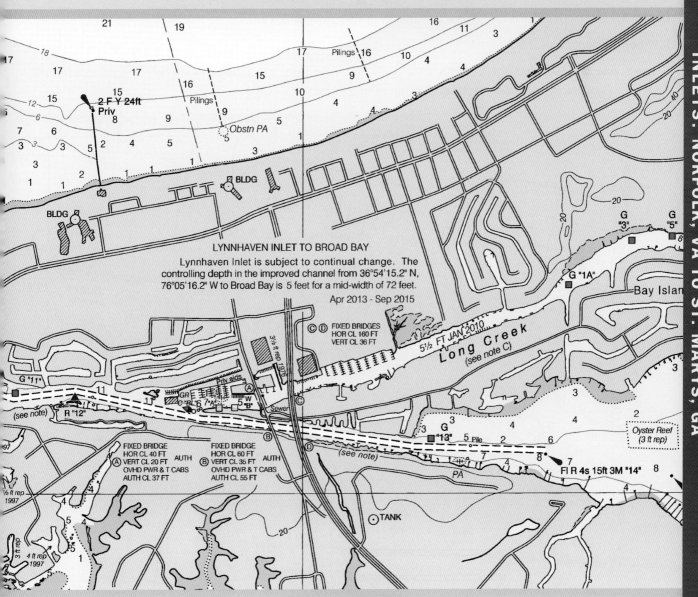

LYNNHAVEN INLET TO BROAD BAY

Lynnhaven Inlet is subject to continual change. The controlling depth in the improved channel from 36°54'15.2" N, 76°05'16.2" W to Broad Bay is 5 feet for a mid-width of 72 feet.

Apr 2013 - Sep 2015

Use Chart 12254

Rudee Inlet, VA

Sea buoy: Lighted red and white Morse (A) whistle buoy "RI" located at N 36° 49.790'/W 75° 56.950' (1 nm east-northeast of the jetties).

Overview: Two jetties protect the inlet, which offers easy access to the Atlantic. Quick access to the Atlantic Ocean has made Rudee Inlet a haven for sportfishing boats.

Navigation: Dredged channel leads between the jetties to a basin just inside, then westward to a safety area about 0.2 nm above the entrance. Lake Rudee is to the north and Lake Wesley to the south. Two fixed highway bridges with a vertical clearance of 28 feet cross the arm of the inlet leading to Lake Rudee. Several overhead power and telephone cables with charted vertical clearances of 54 feet cross east of the bridge. The depths at the inlet and in the lakes can be 7 feet at MLW. Vessels that cannot get under the bridge can dock at Lake Wesley to the south.

Cautions and hazards: Dredged frequently but shoals quickly across the south side of the channel, starting from the outer edge to the centerline, beginning approximately 40 feet east of the east end of the South Jetty and extending out eastward approximately 230 feet. Deeper draft vessels should seek local knowledge before attempting to enter.

Depth: See interactive charts on Waterway Explorer at waterwayguide.com.

ICW connection: None.

Nearest recommended inlet: About 66 nm to the south is Oregon Inlet, NC, recommended only in good weather and calm seas. Cape Henry is 5.5 nm north at the entrance to the Chesapeake Bay.

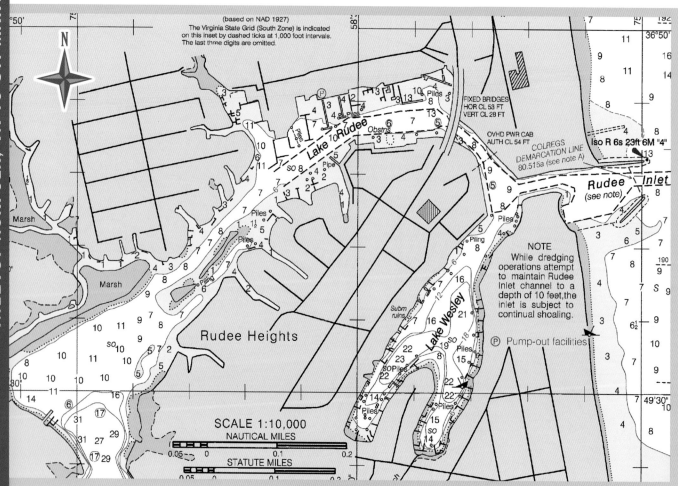

Use Chart 12205

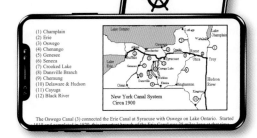

Beaufort Inlet, NC

Sea buoy: Lighted red and white Morse (A) (RACON) whistle buoy "BM" located at N 34° 34.830'/ W 76° 41.550' (5 nm out).

Overview: Wide, deep and very well marked. Farthest "northerly" inlet recommended for transient recreational boaters. To the north lie the Outer Banks; rounding them entails a long passage in Atlantic Ocean waters.

Cautions and hazards: Areas of shoaling have been identified throughout the Beaufort Inlet and Harbor; however, dredging in 2019 should alleviate some of those issues. Current runs 2 knots on the flood. Mariners are urged to use extreme caution when transiting the area.

Navigation: As this is a big ship entrance, you can forgo the sea buoy, which is more than 5 nm out, and start your approach from flashing green buoy "9" and flashing red bell buoy "10," which are just southwest of N 34° 40.000'/W 76° 40.000'. From here, follow the markers and stay in the center on a course slightly east of north to quick flashing red buoy "16" on Shackleford Point, then bear west of north. Shoaling was reported at quick flashing red buoy "16."

If you are headed for Beaufort itself, take the channel leading to the east side of Radio Island, taking care to round quick flashing red buoy "2." Don't cut flashing red buoy "20" short; it is very shallow out of the channel. If your destination is Morehead City, bear to port at flashing green buoy "21," and then continue to follow the big ship markers under the bridge.

Depth: This area was last dredged in spring 2019. See interactive charts on Waterway Explorer at waterwayguide.com.

ICW connection: Proceed to the turning basin (ICW Mile 204) and bear to port if you are heading south on the ICW. If heading north, continue through the Beaufort Channel Railroad Bridge (4-foot closed vertical clearance, usually open), followed by the fixed Beaufort Channel Bridge (65-foot vertical clearance) immediately ahead of you.

Nearest recommended inlet: Barden Inlet is about 6 nm to the east at Cape Lookout, and even though it is no longer considered navigable for cruising vessels, a sheltered anchorage can be found behind Cape Lookout. Bogue Inlet is 20 nm to the southwest. Masonboro Inlet at Wrightsville Beach, a popular passage choice in settled weather, is about 65 nm distant.

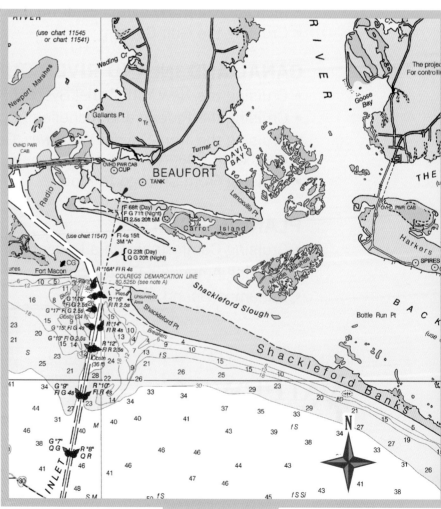

Use Chart 11544

Masonboro Inlet, NC

Sea buoy: Lighted red and white Morse (A) whistle buoy "A" at N 34° 10.600'/ W 77° 47.870'.

Overview: Uncomplicated entrance protected by jetties on both sides and with good depths within. Popular with sportfishermen. Coast Guard Station Wrightsville Beach is just past red daybeacon "10."

Navigation: From the sea buoy, jetties lie to the northwest and are unmarked. Once inside, if you are headed to Wrightsville Beach, bear to starboard at green and red daybeacon "WC" and then turn to port at Motts Channel a bit farther up. If Masonboro is your destination, continue straight ahead.

Cautions and hazards: There are no particular difficulties with this inlet, although a southeasterly wind can cause difficult conditions for smaller boats.

Depth: See interactive charts on Waterway Explorer at waterwayguide.com.

ICW connection: ICW Mile 285 lies straight ahead past Shinn Creek.

Nearest recommended inlet: Masonboro is a good inlet for faster boats or for early-rising sailors or trawler skippers wanting to get off the ICW to or from Beaufort, NC, which is just under 65 nm to the northeast. Some slow-boat skippers make this an overnight passage, arriving at either end shortly after sunrise. Carolina Beach Inlet is 6 nm to the south, but a wiser and quicker course is to continue on the ICW from Masonboro, enter the Cape Fear River through Snows Cut, catch the outgoing tide and proceed to Southport (or detour upriver to visit Wilmington).

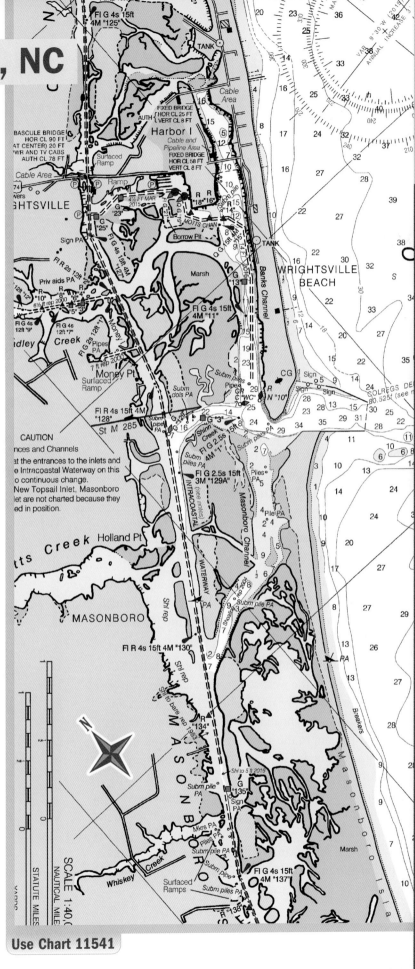

Use Chart 11541

Cape Fear River Inlet, NC

Sea buoy: Lighted red and white Morse (A) (RACON) whistle buoy "CF" at N 33° 46.280'/W 78° 03.020' (5 nm out).

Overview: Well-marked big ship channel protected from the north and an easy entrance day or night.

Navigation: Cruisers can approach using the waypoint N 33° 50.370'/W 78° 01.780', which is close to red buoy "8" where the surrounding waters begin to shallow. From flashing red buoy "8," proceed slightly east of north to quick flashing red buoy "10" and then to quick flashing red buoy "12,"(flashing green "11" may be missing) where you can pick up the Bald Head Shoal Range. For those headed north, we advise you stay on the ICW here to avoid a significant detour around Frying Pan Shoals, which extend 30 nm out into the Atlantic.

Cautions and hazards: Daytime entrances are straightforward. As this is a busy inlet, keep a constant watch posted for big ships. The current is very strong; time your entrance to take advantage of the tides. Northbound in slower boats would be well-advised to check the tides before attempting the Cape Fear River's strong currents.

Depth: See interactive charts on Waterway Explorer at waterwayguide.com.

ICW connection: Connects with the ICW at Mile 308.5. Heading north, the ICW follows the big ship channel toward Wilmington. To head south on the ICW, bear to port at Southport.

Nearest recommended inlet: Little River Inlet, SC, is about 24 nm to the west-southwest and takes you past the Lockwood's Folly and Shallotte Inlets, which are known for severe shoaling. The best option is Winyah Bay, SC (65 nm to the sea buoy), with its well-marked shipping channel. The drawback is that rejoining the ICW to continue south involves coming back north over 8 miles into the inlet, or 15 miles if Georgetown is your destination. Any northbound coastal passage requires rounding Frying Pan Shoals. The most prudent path is to continue northward on the ICW and use Masonboro Inlet at Wrightsville Beach, NC, as your jumping-off point to go offshore to Beaufort NC.

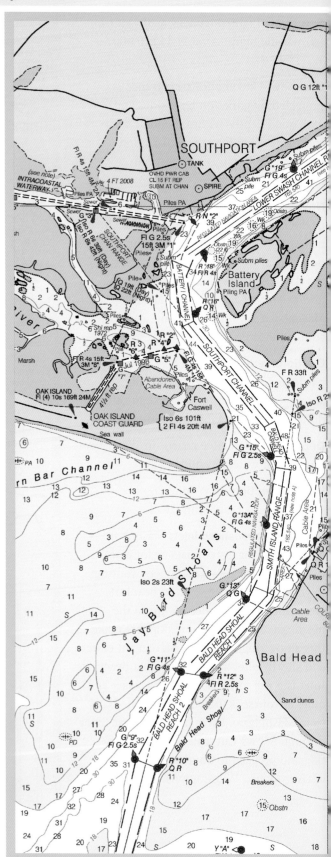

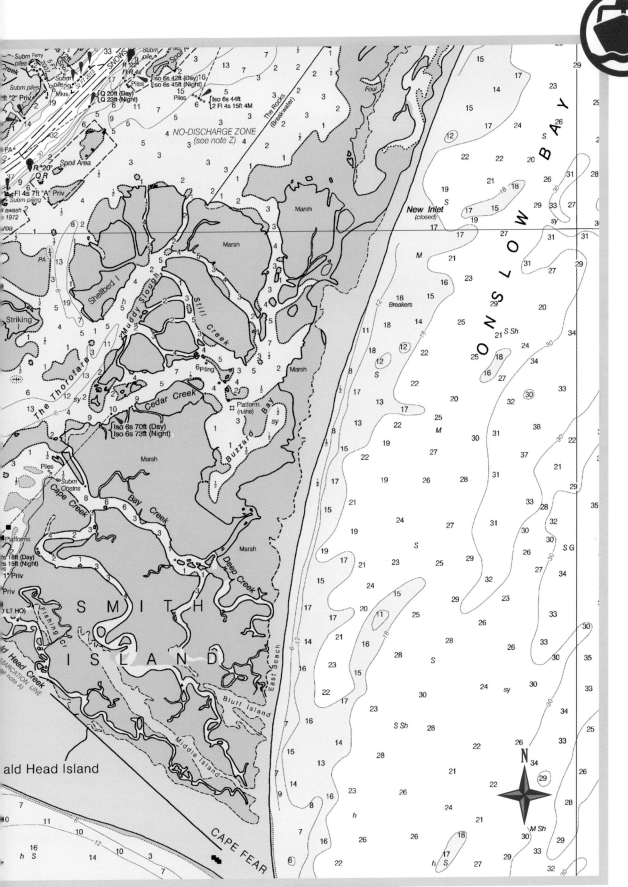

Use Chart 11537

Little River Inlet, SC

Sea buoy: Lighted red and white Morse (A) whistle buoy "LR" in position N 33° 49.890'/W 78° 32.430'.

Overview: Deep, wide and busy, with a steady flow of tourist and fishing boats. Presents little difficulty in most conditions.

Navigation: From the sea buoy, proceed to the entrance markers on the ends of the twin breakwaters, keeping clear of the shoal to your northeast. The inlet then sweeps west. The channel is well marked with a controlling depth of 10 feet MLW and should present no difficulties.

Cautions and hazards: There is a 5-foot shoal just off the east jetty (starboard on entry) that is awash with breaking waves in the right conditions. The chart shows three submerged wrecks near the entrance.

Depth: See interactive charts on Waterway Explorer at waterwayguide.com.

ICW connection: Connects to the ICW a little more than 1 nm to the north at Mile 343.

Nearest recommended inlet: The sea buoy for Winyah Bay lies 47 nm to the southwest. The Cape Fear River entrance is 24 nm to the east. Both are well marked and deep. Remember that all ICW markers have either a yellow square or a yellow triangle on them.

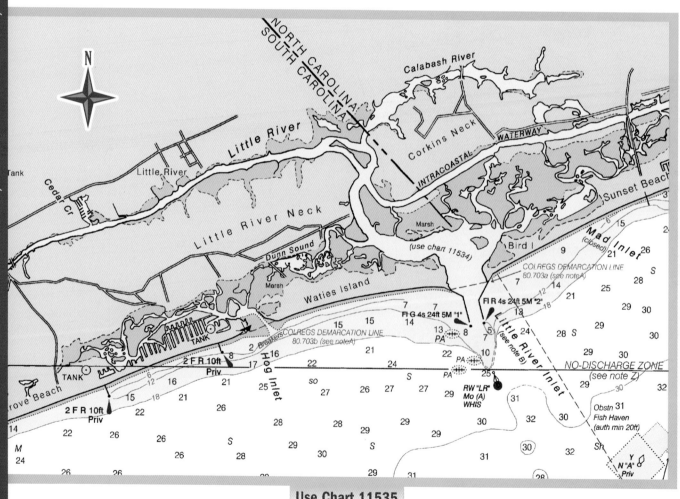

Use Chart 11535

Winyah Bay Entrance, SC

Use Chart 11532

Sea buoy: Lighted red and white Morse (A) whistle buoy "WB" in position N 33° 11.620'/W 79° 05.180'.

Overview: Well marked and deep. Presents a challenge for underpowered vessels with its strong currents. It pays to watch the tide here and enter or leave with the current. Nighttime entry is feasible due to well-marked ranges.

Navigation: Georgetown Light, 85 feet above the water, shines from a white cylindrical tower on the north side of Winyah Bay entrance. Smoke from one or another of the stacks in Georgetown can often be seen from well offshore. The sea buoy is well out; recreational vessels can safely approach waypoint N 33° 11.570'/W 79° 07.040', which is just east of red buoy "4." From the waypoint, entry is straightforward on a heading of due west, turning to northwest at red buoy "8" and north-northwest after that.

Cautions and hazards: Conditions can be particularly bad at the ends of the jetties when tide opposes wind. Also, much of the south jetty is visible only at low water. Northbound vessels need to be aware of the shoals to the south and west of the channel and not stray west of the waypoint. Anything under 20 feet MLW indicates you are too far west on your approach.

Depth: See interactive charts on Waterway Explorer at waterwayguide.com.

ICW connection: Connects to the ICW at Mile 406 (9 nm). Southbound traffic coming from offshore will want to leave the main shipping channel sooner, veering to port at flashing green buoy "17" to enter the ICW via the Western Channel.

Nearest recommended inlet: Murrells Inlet, a good secondary inlet with no connection to the ICW, is 19 nm to the north. The entrance to Cape Fear is 65 nm to the northeast. The entrance to Charleston is 46 nm to the southwest. The latter two are big-ship channels.

Charleston Harbor Entrance, SC

Sea buoy: Lighted red and white Morse (A) (RACON) whistle buoy "C" located at N 32° 37.070'/W 79° 35.490'.

Overview: Heavily used ship channel with a great deal of commercial traffic day and night.

Navigation: This is a Class A inlet for big ships with lots of deep water all about. The sea buoy is 10 nm farther out than necessary for recreational craft. A waypoint at N 32° 42.86'/W 79° 47.550' between green buoy "15" and red buoy "16" saves considerable time although southbound vessels need to be aware of the shoaling to the north and guide their course appropriately, coming in on a southwesterly heading. Several lighted buoys are missing or off station in this inlet. Follow the existing markers in, and if continuing south on the ICW, bear to the west on the South Channel Range. Those northbound or heading for the Cooper River continue, using the Mount Pleasant Range and following it out of the channel, watching for flashing red buoy "1" about 0.25 mile to the east marking the entrance to the northbound ICW.

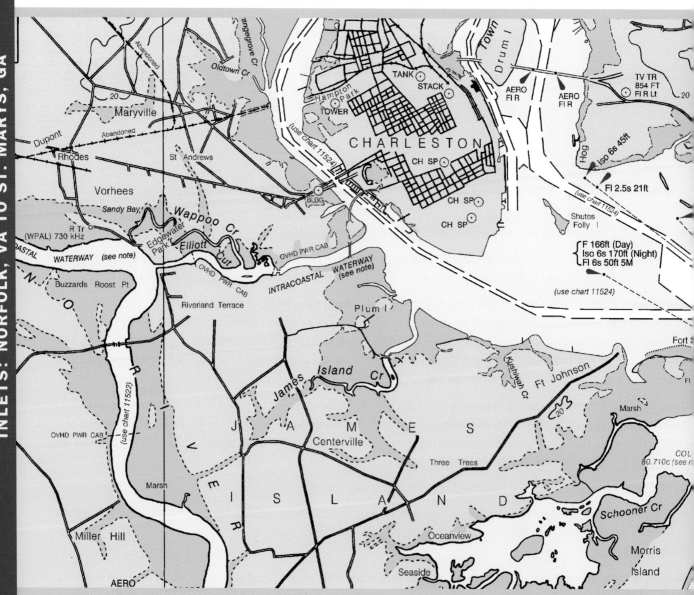

Cautions and hazards: Smaller vessels are advised to stay to the edge of the channel until reaching the inlet jetties. There is a ship anchorage to the north of the channel farther out, but it is not a place for smaller vessels. Be aware of the partially submerged jetties north and south of the channel at quick flashing green buoy "17" and quick flashing red buoy "18." After clearing the jetties, do not proceed onto the charted Middle Ground without a harbor chart (NOAA Chart 11524) that provides expanded coverage. This inlet can be very confusing for nighttime entries due to the many lights both on the water and land, and the considerable traffic you'll encounter at all hours.

Depth: See interactive charts on Waterway Explorer at waterwayguide.com.

ICW connection: Southbound ICW intersects at Mile 464.1.

Nearest recommended inlet: The Winyah Bay entrance is 46 nm to the northeast. For the southbound cruiser, North Edisto is a fair weather-only inlet 21 nm to the southeast. Port Royal Sound, 57 nm to the southeast, is deep and well marked but has a great disadvantage for slow moving craft: The entrance channel begins 9 nm offshore as a cut through shallow banks.

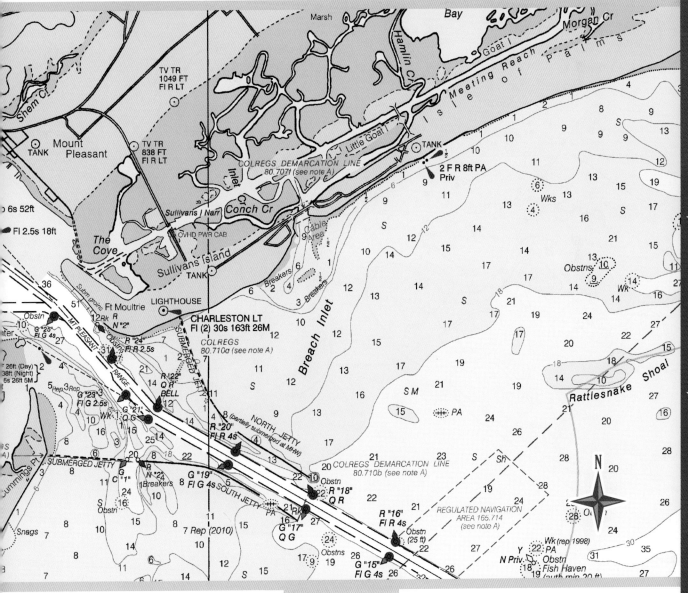

Use Chart 11521

North Edisto River Inlet, SC

Sea buoy: Flashing red whistle buoy "2NE" located at N 32° 31.360'/W 80° 06.850'.

Overview: Entrance is a straight shot, with shoals to the west and breakers to the northeast.

Navigation: Proceed on a course of 286° M, leaving flashing red buoy "6" to starboard (red nun buoy "4" is close by), turning to 325° M, picking up green can buoy "7" before lining up with the charted range that leads you close alongside flashing green buoy "9."

Cautions and hazards: The chart shows a 5-foot-deep section near flashing red buoy "6," which will not be a problem provided you keep the marker to starboard on entering.

ICW connection: Connects to the ICW approximately 7.5 nm from the inlet at White Point (Mile 496.7).

Depth: See interactive charts on Waterway Explorer at waterwayguide.com.

Nearest recommended inlet: The entrance to Charleston Harbor is 21 nm to the northeast. For southbound vessels, the entrance to Port Royal Sound is 35 nm to the southwest; Tybee Roads, GA and the Savannah River are 46 nm away.

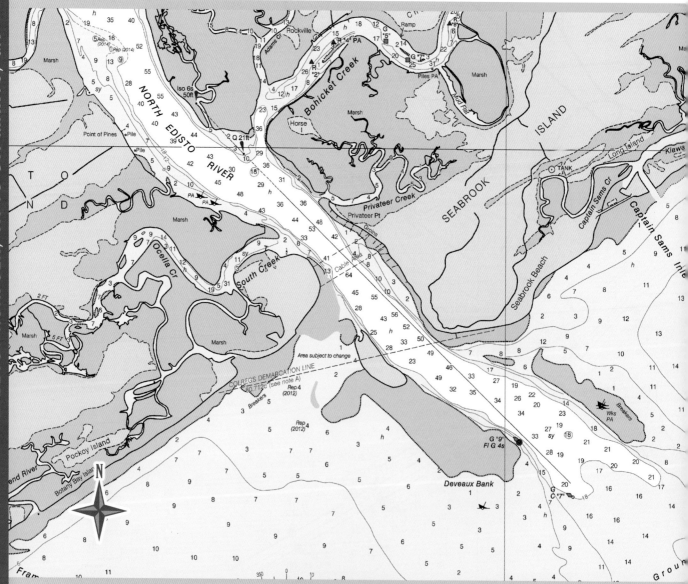

Use Chart 11521

Port Royal Sound Entrance, SC

Sea buoy: Lighted red and white Morse (A) whistle buoy "P" located at N 32° 05.140'/W 80° 34.960'.

Overview: Wide, deep and very long. If headed south offshore, this is not the best option as a point of entry, as you will backtrack some distance to re-enter the ocean.

Navigation: From the sea buoy, head north and follow the range to flashing red buoy "14," then veer to the west to quick flashing green buoy "25," where you can head west as noted to the southbound ICW and Hilton Head Island, or north to Beaufort, SC. There are ranges northbound to quick flashing green buoy "37" on the Beaufort River.

Cautions and hazards: If you are going northbound after dark, there are land-based lights that can confuse even the best navigator. Also, if there is any sort of wind against tide, or you are bucking the current, things are likely to get a bit rough.

Depth: See interactive charts on Waterway Explorer at waterwayguide.com.

ICW connection: Connects to the ICW after quick flashing green buoy "25" at approximately Mile 548.6.

Nearest recommended inlet: To the northeast, about 21 nm away, begins the channel into St. Helena Sound. The North Edisto entrance is 36 nm away and Charleston, SC, 57 nm. Southbound, the Tybee Roads, GA, entrance to the Savannah River and Hilton Head, SC, is about 10 nm away on a southerly course.

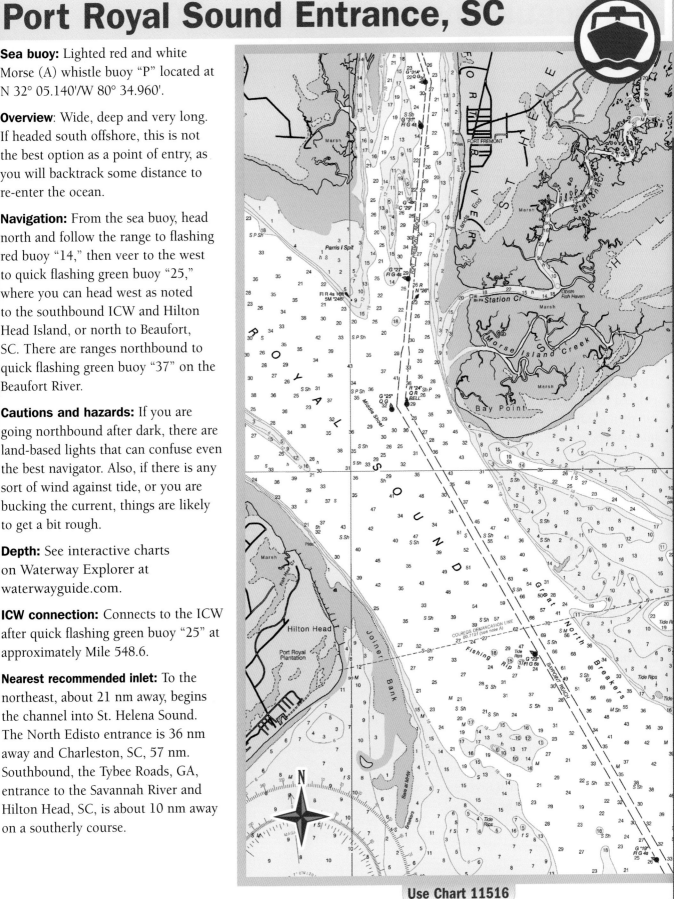

Use Chart 11516

Calibogue Sound Entrance, SC

Sea buoy: Use the sea buoy for Tybee Roads, lighted red and white Morse (A) (RACON) buoy "T" located at N 31° 57.700'/W 80° 43.100'.

Overview: Alternative to Tybee Roads, this entrance leads to Calibogue Sound and Hilton Head Island.

Navigation: For South Hilton Head Island via Calibogue Sound, use the sailing directions for entering the Savannah River but stay on Bloody Point Range after flashing red buoy "14," passing the lower range light and leaving green daybeacon "1" well to port. Next, keep clear of the 5- to 6-foot deep shoal at the back Bloody Point Range, and then turn north toward quick flashing green buoy "3." Depths will briefly fall to 8 to 10 feet MLW from 14 feet, then rise again as you pass quick flashing green buoy "3." At quick flashing green buoy "3," turn due north, and proceed to flashing green buoy "5," where you can then follow the remaining channel markers into Calibogue Sound.

Cautions and hazards: Coming from the north, mariners need to be aware of Gaskin Banks, an extensive shoal area extending nearly 8 nm out from Hilton Head Island. There is also a submerged breakwater north of the Tybee Roads channel that is roughly parallel to flashing red buoys "12" and "14," which must be avoided if one is heading toward Calibogue Sound. Entering this inlet needs your full attention when transiting.

Depth: See interactive charts on Waterway Explorer at waterwayguide.com.

ICW connection: Connects to the ICW at the Cooper River (Mile 564).

Nearest recommended inlet: At night or in heavy seas, forgo Calibogue Sound and continue on Tybee Roads to the Savannah River entrance. Port Royal Sound is 10 nm to the northeast.

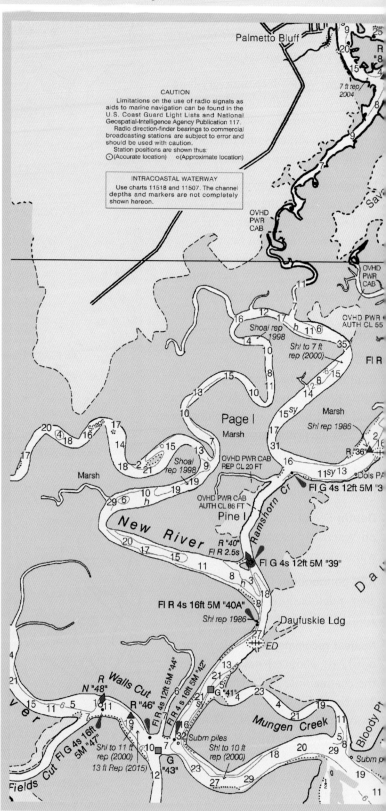

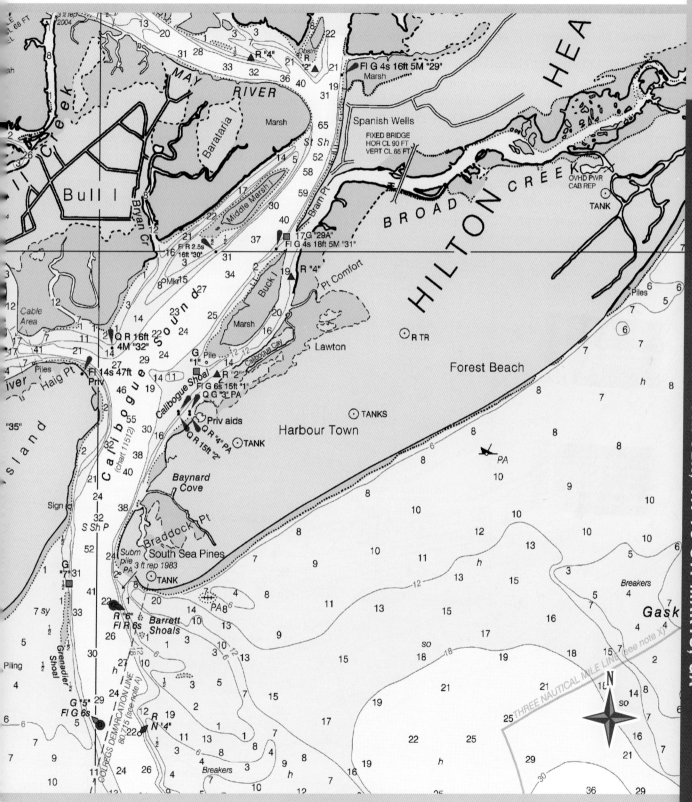

Tybee Roads Inlet, GA

Sea buoy: Lighted red and white Morse (A) (RACON) buoy "1" located at N 31° 57.700'/W 80° 43.100'.

Overview: Big ship entrance, offering entry to Savannah via the Savannah River.

Navigation: Entering the channel from the sea buoy, follow the Tybee range to quick flashing red bell buoy "8," turning north to follow the Bloody Point Range to flashing red "14." Turning to port here, follow the Jones Island Range to flashing red buoy "18," and then turn slightly southwest and continue in on Tybee Knoll Cut Range to flashing red buoy "24." Here, you will have Oyster Bed Island to your north and Cockspur Island to the south. Pick up New Channel Range and follow the channel markers. Note the partially submerged breakwater that begins just past flashing red buoy "18," which is marked by a flashing white light, noted as "Fl 4s 16ft 5M" on your chart.

Cautions and hazards: Coming from the north, mariners need to be aware of Gaskin Banks, an extensive shoal area extending nearly 8 nm out from Hilton Head. Also to be avoided is a submerged breakwater north of and roughly parallel to flashing red buoy "12" and flashing red buoy "14."

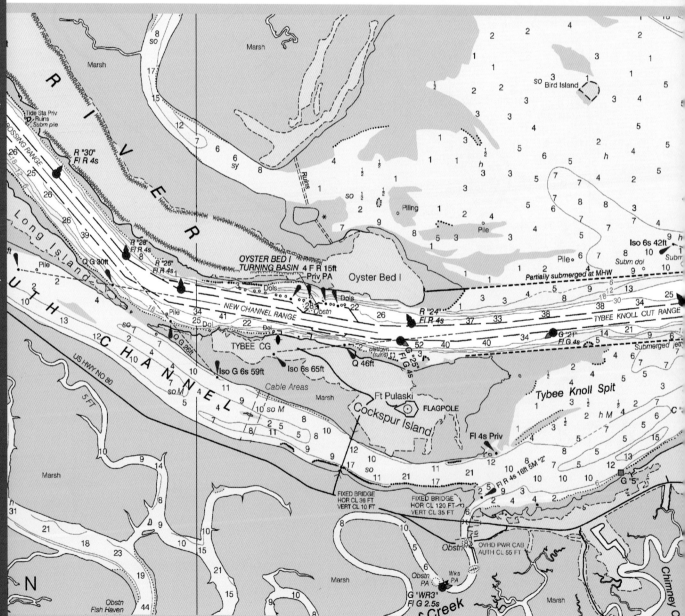

Depth: See interactive charts on Waterway Explorer at waterwayguide.com.

ICW connection: Savannah River crosses ICW at Fields Cut (Mile 575.7), directly opposite flashing green buoy "35."

Nearest recommended inlet: Northbound cruisers heading for Hilton Head may detour from Tybee Roads to make Calibogue Sound, with an entrance that is usable by day and in settled weather. From Tybee Roads, the sea buoy for Port Royal Sound is 10 nm to the northeast. If southbound, Wassaw Sound, 10 nm to the southwest, is another strictly fair-weather, daylight entrance. Ditto for St. Catherines Sound, 22 nm away.

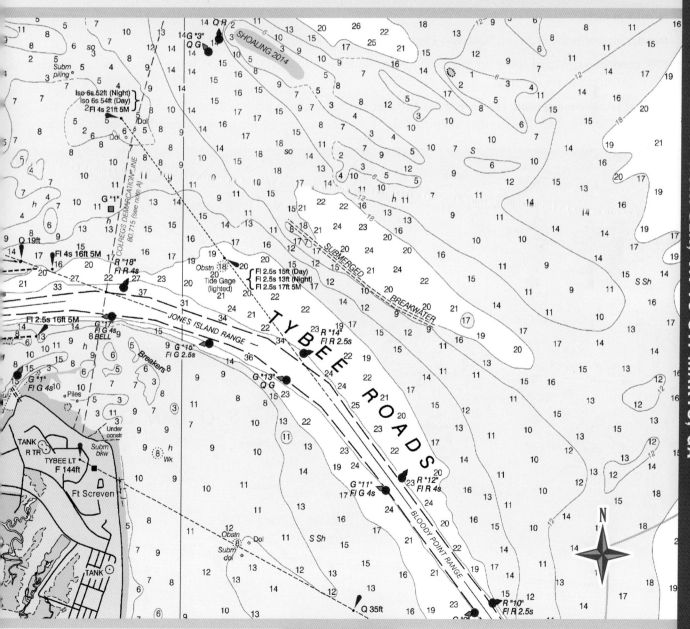

Use Chart 11512

Wassaw Sound Entrance, GA

Sea buoy: Flashing red buoy "2W" located at N 31° 51.560'/W 80° 53.000'.

Overview: Popular local inlet, but not one for dark and stormy arrivals without local knowledge, as it is poorly marked and surrounded by shoals nearly 5 nm out from the entrance.

Navigation: Current and trustworthy local knowledge required. The entrance to Wassaw Sound changes continually, so red buoys "4," "6" and "8" are not charted. Before beginning this inlet, mark a boundary line on your chart running due south from flashing red buoy "10." From flashing red buoy "2W," head west-northwest and curve to the north around the shoal to starboard until you reach the above noted line from flashing red buoy "10." Head due north to green can buoy "9" and turn northwest to follow the markers; depths will be 20 feet MLW or better. Stay to the center of Wilmington River until you turn to the north after flashing red "22" and then stay to the east side of the river for deep water.

Cautions and hazards: The 2 nm from the sea buoy to the first markers are tricky, with shoals on both sides, breakers and no markers. Just east of green can "9" and flashing red can "10" there is extensive shoaling. If you draw more than 5 feet, think twice before entering this inlet. The inlet has no lighted markers until you are inside, and it would be foolhardy to enter at night.

Depth: See interactive charts on Waterway Explorer at waterwayguide.com.

ICW connection: Wilmington River meets the ICW at Skidaway Narrows (Mile 585.5), about 3.5 nm north of flashing red buoy "20" at the river's entrance.

Nearest recommended inlet: The deep water entrance to the Savannah River at Tybee Roads, GA is 10 nm to the northeast. Southbound, fair-weather inlets include St. Catherines at 12.5 nm away and Sapelo Sound at 22 nm.

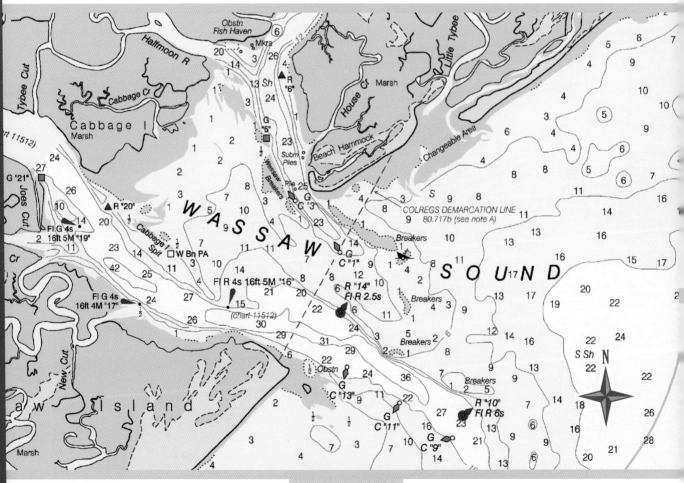

Use Chart 11509

St. Catherines Sound Entrance, GA

Sea buoy: Lighted red and white Morse (A) (RACON) buoy "STC" located at N 31° 40.198'/W 81° 00.235'.

Overview: Wide, uncomplicated entrance with good depths within.

Navigation: Heading west from the sea buoy, turn in between green can "1" and flashing red "2" and head north to flashing green "5" in no less than 12 feet at MLW. (Or head straight from RW "STC" to flashing green "5" where you may see 9-foot MLW depths.) The channel turns west toward green can "7."

Cautions and hazards: The charted Middle Ground Shoal is to the southwest of green can "7." Be sure to stay well off to the north.

Depth: See interactive charts on Waterway Explorer at waterwayguide.com.

ICW connection: St. Catherines Sound Entrance intersects the ICW at Mile 618, about 3nm from flashing green "5" at the entrance.

Nearest recommended inlet: The Wassaw Sound Entrance is 12 nm to the north, while the Sapelo Sound Entrance is 9.5 nm to the south.

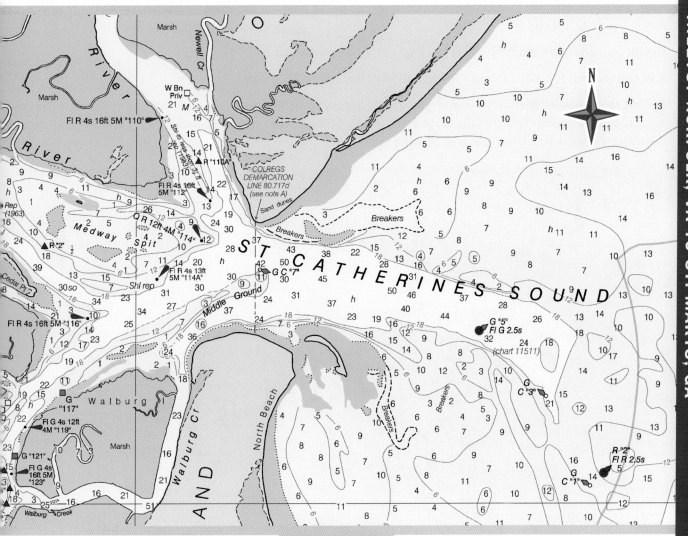

Use Chart 11509

Sapelo Sound Entrance, GA

Sea buoy: Red and white call buoy "S" located at N 31° 31.210'/W 81° 03.890'.

Overview: Used by fishermen and shrimpers, not to mention legendary pirate Edward Teach ("Blackbeard"). (You will pass just north of Blackbeard Island and Blackbeard Creek while transiting this inlet.) Southbound cruisers hoping to avoid the Georgia ICW rarely use the inlet, preferring to jump offshore through the big ship channels at Charleston, Port Royal or Savannah.

Navigation: Current and trustworthy local knowledge required. From the sea buoy, proceed first to red nun buoy "2" and then head slightly south of west to green can buoy "3." Depths will drop from more than 20 feet down to 12 feet MLW along the way. If you see 10-foot MLW depths, you are in trouble and need to reverse course. At green can buoy "5," you will see 20-plus-foot MLW depths return, and it is a simple matter of following the red buoys in until you meet up with the ICW past red nun buoy "10."

Cautions and hazards: Not the best inlet in rougher weather, due to extensive shoals to the north and south of the inlet. Sound is quite wide and the aids to navigation are unlighted, making it unfavorable for nighttime passage except by the well experienced. Depths between green can buoy "3" and green can buoy "5" drop to 12 feet MLW in places, and there are breaking shoals to the north of the channel; otherwise, depths typically run to over 20 feet MLW. Do not be tempted to cut corners. Once in the sound, be aware of the shoal by green daybeacon "143" and stay at least 100 feet off.

Depth: See interactive charts on Waterway Explorer at waterwayguide.com.

ICW connection: Junction of Sapelo Sound and ICW is at Mile 632.

Nearest recommended inlet: Northbound, you should bypass St. Catherines Sound (9.5 nm) and continue to Wassaw Sound (22 nm) if conditions are calm or, best yet, go on to Tybee Roads to the Savannah River (31 nm). Southbound, the ship channel at St. Simons Sound is 29.5 nm away.

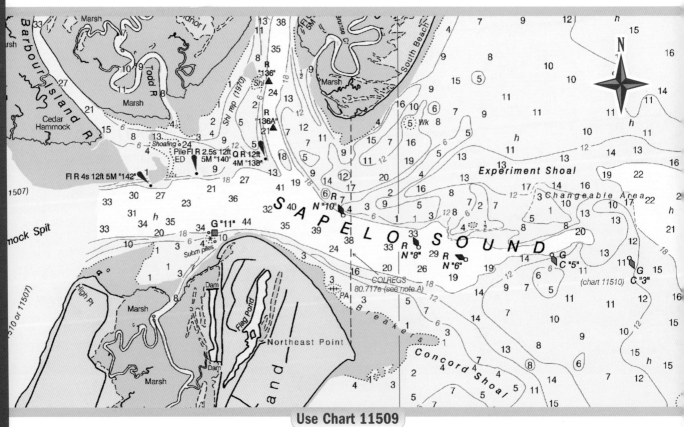

Use Chart 11509

Doboy Sound Entrance, GA

Sea buoy: Lighted red and white Morse (A) buoy "D" located at N 31° 21.230'/ W 81° 11.390'.

Overview: Uncomplicated and breakwaters may give some protection from south-setting waves.

Navigation: Heading slightly north of west from the sea buoy, continue in past the breakwaters to the north of red nun buoy "4." The channel shoals to 7 feet MLW approaching green can "3," then deepens again. Continue to red nun "8" on the northerly point of land in 20- to 40-foot depths. Once in the sound, keep an eye out for shoaling.

Cautions and hazards: Breakwaters to the north and a long easterly shoal on the south side are the main hazards here. Aside from the sea buoy and flashing red "8," all of the aids to navigation in this inlet are unlighted, making it a difficult, if not dangerous, nighttime passage.

Depth: See interactive charts on Waterway Explorer at waterwayguide.com.

ICW connection: About 2.5 nm from the inlet proper, Doboy Sound intersects the ICW just above Commodore and Doboy Islands at Mile 649. The ICW runs around the north and west sides of Doboy Island.

Nearest recommended inlet: The big ship channel of St. Simons Sound is 18 nm to the south. Wassaw Sound, a good fair-weather inlet, is 35 nm to the north, while the shipping channel at Tybee Roads (to the Savannah River) is past Wassaw, 44 nm distant.

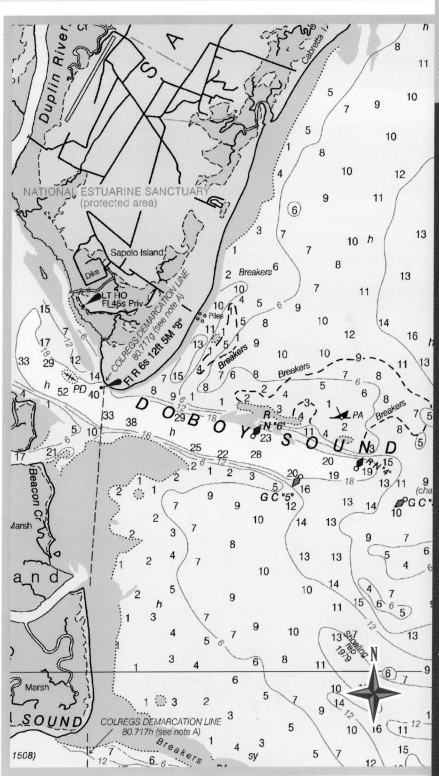

Use Chart 11509

St. Simons Sound Entrance, GA

Sea buoy: Lighted red and white Morse (A) (RACON) whistle buoy "STS" located at N 31° 03.200'/W 81° 15.100'.

Overview: All-weather, big ship entrance to Brunswick.

Navigation: Entrance is straightforward. From the sea buoy, proceed northwesterly to quick flashing red buoy "16" on the range, then turn to port and pick up Plantation Creek Range.

Cautions and hazards: Start from the sea buoy due to shallows that extend quite far from shore. Channel shallows very rapidly outside of the markers, and ebb current is quite strong at the mouth of the inlet. Busy entrance; keep watch for big ships transiting the inlet.

Depth: See interactive charts on Waterway Explorer at waterwayguide.com.

ICW connection: ICW is immediately inside inlet at Mile 678.

Nearest recommended inlet: The fair weather inlet at Doboy Sound, GA, is 18 nm to the north. To the south, the big ship channel at the St. Marys Entrance is 21 nm away.

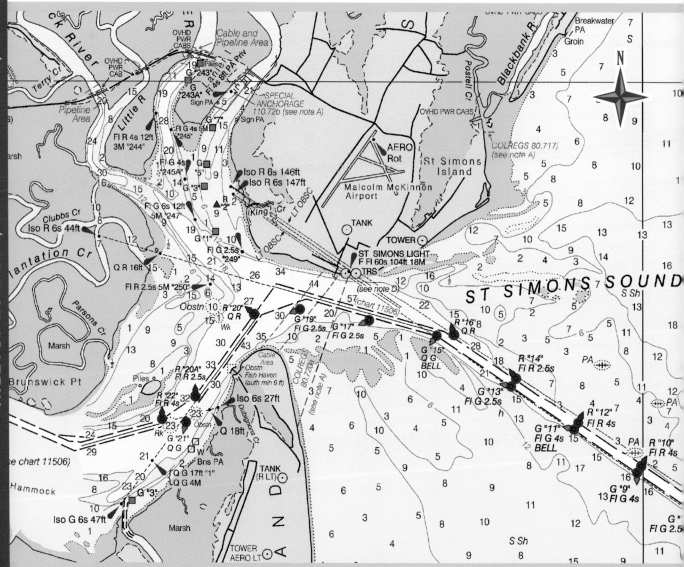

Use Chart 11502

WATERWAY EXPLORER
RATINGS & REVIEWS

***Waterway Explorer** has ratings and reviews. See what others say about Marinas, Anchorages, Bridges/Locks and Navigation Alerts!*

1 Mar **Marathon Ma**

Max Length: 125

Total/Transient

2 Caloo **Resort**

Be the first to review this marina

Max Length: 65
Total/Transient Slips: 32/5
Approach/Dockside Depth: 5.0/6.0

Diesel | Gas | Repairs

3 Hawks Cay Resort Marina

Be the first to review this marina
Max Length: 110
Total/Transient Slips: 85/52
Approach/Dockside Depth: 5.0/5.0

Yellow stars indicate the rating that this marina got from reviewers

No stars indicate that this marina is awaiting a review

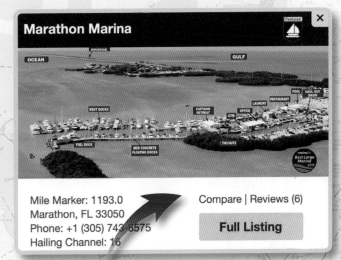

Marathon Marina

Mile Marker: 1193.0
Marathon, FL 33050
Phone: +1 (305) 743-6575
Hailing Channel: 16

Compare | Reviews (6)

Full Listing

Be the first to review and rate – or add your comments to the list!

- **Fill out the review form and post your rating**
- **No log in required**
- **No private information shared**

Waterway Guide staff and editors validate and verify postings and content to ensure accuracy

Reviews: Marathon Marina

These are observations from the boating community. Waterway Guide information is verified regularly and all efforts will be made to validate any new updates submitted here. Thank you for taking the time to share comments

Waterway Guide reserves the option of editing reviews and comments for grammar, clarity and the removal of defamatory or potentially slanderous language. When appropriate, reviews are forwarded to businesses for response prior to being made public. We will make every effort to be objective and impartial when posting reviews, but do not publicize details of disputes between parties.

View in Waterway Explorer

Marathon Marina

1021 11th Street Ocean
Marathon, FL 33050
AIWW, Boot Key Harbor 1193.0 47.5

Lat / Lon: N 24° 42.246' / W 081° 06.733'
Hours: 8am - 5pm Daily
Contact: Susan Prichard
VHF Monitored: 16
VHF Working: 10
Phone: (305) 743-6575; 8:00 am - 5:00 pm daily
Fax: (305) 743-5509
Email: susanp@marathonmarinaandresort.com
Website: www.marathonmarinaandresort.com

 (6)
5 out of 5 stars

Review for Marathon Marina

Reviewed by: Eddie Tuttle on Apr 2, 2019
Boat Type: Power
LOA: 46'
Draft: 4.5'
Rating:

Review This Business

Name *(Displayed)*
Reviewer Name

Email *(Not Displayed)*
Email

Vessel Name Display?
Vessel Name

LOA (ft): | Draft (ft): | Boat Type:
| | Sail Power

Rating:

Comments:

Type review here. How was the service?

St. Marys Entrance

Sea Buoy: No sea buoy. Steer to a waypoint of N 30° 42.630'/W 81° 14.630' (2.5 nm seaward of the channel). Then steer to N 30° 42.690'/W 81° 21.520' to access the center of the channel at red marker "10."

Overview: Big ship and military ship inlet. Most northerly of the Florida inlets located between Cumberland Island (GA) and Fort Clinch State Park.

Navigation: Very straightforward and well marked. From red marker "10" proceed due west into Cumberland Sound.

Cautions and hazards: Some shoal sections to the north of the channel inside the jetty. Current is very strong and dictates appropriate boat handling to compensate. Slower boats are well advised to time their passages for slack water or a favorable tide. The inlet also serves the Kings Bay Submarine Base so be on the lookout for any military craft that might be in the area. The Coast Guard has established regulated navigation areas (RNAs) covering the St. Marys Entrance Channel, portions of the Cumberland Sound and the Atlantic Ocean that will be in effect whenever any

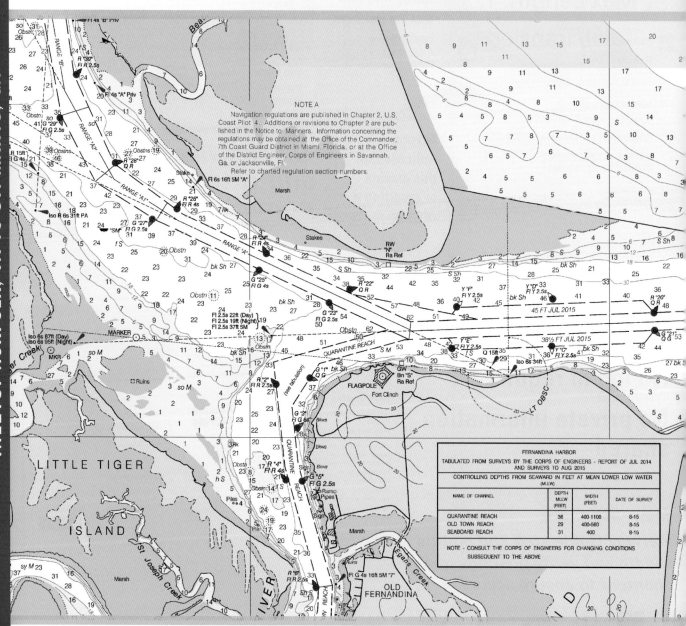

Navy submarine (foreign or domestic) is escorted by the Coast Guard. These RNAs are necessary to help ensure the safety and security of submarines, their Coast Guard escorts and the public. No person or vessel may enter or remain within the security zone without the permission of the Coast Guard.

Depth: Refer to the most recent NOAA charts or your onboard navigation device.

ICW connection: ICW crosses the inlet at Mile 714. For either north or south, follow the banks, which remain deep outside of the channel.

Nearest recommended inlet: It is approximately 30 nm to the big ship inlet at the St. Marys (Cumberland Sound) Entrance.

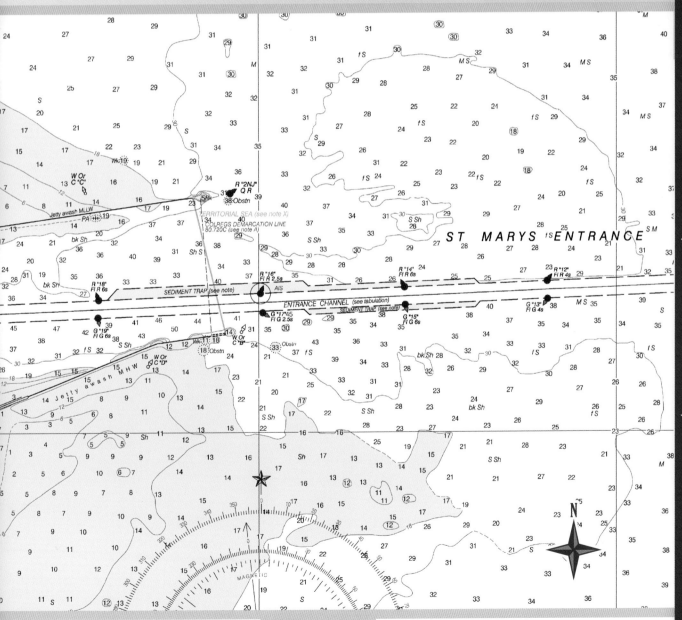

Use Chart 11503

Skipper's Notes

Norfolk, VA to New Bern, NC

■ HAMPTON, NORFOLK & PORTSMOUTH, VA   ■ VIRGINIA CUT & DISMAL SWAMP ROUTES, VA/NC
■ SIDE TRIP: THE ALBERMARLE & ROANOKE SOUNDS, NC   ■ ALBEMARLE SOUND TO THE NEUSE RIVER, NC
■ SIDE TRIP: THE PAMLICO SOUND & OUTER BANKS, NC

Chesapeake Bay
95
Cape Henry
MILE ZERO
Norfolk
Virginia Beach
Rudee Inlet
VIRGINIA
TH CAROLINA
MILE 50
Coinjock
Elizabeth City
Kitty Hawk
Edenton
Albemarle Sound
MILE 85
Manteo
Pamlico Sound
Pamlico River
Ocracoke
New Bern
Oriental
MILE 182
Neuse River
N
Morehead City
Beaufort
MILE 205
Swansboro
MILE 229
Cape Lookout
Beaufort Inlet
Bardens Inlet
Bogue Inlet

Visit Waterway Explorer at waterwayguide.com

Norfolk, VA to New Bern, NC

For southbound boats, the first 200-mile-long stretch of the Atlantic Intracoastal Waterway (ICW) between Mile Marker 0 at Norfolk and Mile Marker 205 at Morehead City/Beaufort, NC, presents a diverse array of navigational challenges while offering equally diverse natural beauty, fascinating sights, side trips and ports of call. Boaters often start the trip south after anchoring in Hampton, Portsmouth or Norfolk. The route passes through a lock (or two depending on the route you choose), canals, land cuts and open-water sounds along the way. Some of the open water offers the challenges associated with long fetches, shallow depths and choppy wave action when the wind kicks up. Sailors will consider minimizing motoring time by sailing from sound to sound.

Once you have begun the journey south from Norfolk, VA, depending on the route you take, the eerie beauty of the Great Dismal Swamp or the Albemarle and Chesapeake Canal morphs into the broad and fascinating waters of two large Sounds. From the Albemarle and Pamlico Sounds, side trips to waterside villages such as Elizabeth City, Belhaven, Washington, and Oriental offer diversions from the ICW proper. Meanwhile, to the east of the ICW, you will find the famous wilds of North Carolina's Outer Banks, with isolated beaches, massive dunes and excellent bird-watching opportunities. On

These boats in Oriental Harbor, NC, on Racoon Creek are ready for the summrner. Long known as "The Sailing Capital of North Carolina," Oriental is blessed with wide waters, steady winds and easy access to dozens of creeks and estuaries.

Croatan Sound, which connects the Albemarle and Pamlico Sounds, boaters can put in to the friendly little port town of Manteo, NC, on Roanoke Island, where one of the earliest American settlements was established and from which the same settlement mysteriously vanished (now known as the Lost Colony).

Cruising Conditions

In much, but not all of North Carolina (and sporadically in other ICW states), the Army Corps of Engineers has placed signs just outside the channel marking each 5 statute-mile increment along the route. Note that the numbers on these signs do not necessarily correspond to the "Mile Markers" on the charts. Some are the same, some are different by a hundred yards or so, and some by as much as 1 mile. If you are using the actual signs to determine your location in relation to a timed bridge or marina location, you may find yourself a lot closer or farther away than you thought. Use the charts for this information, but make sure you have the most current edition. When in doubt, seek local knowledge, but keep in mind that the channel markers are in place for a reason. They are the first source of information you follow. Also be sure to visit waterwayguide.com for daily news and navigational updates.

Bridges/Distances
(Approximate Statute Miles from Mile Zero, Norfolk, VA)

NORFOLK

LOCATION	MILE	CLEARANCE
Beltline Railroad Lift Bridge	2.6	6''
Jordan Highway Bridge	2.8	145'
Norfolk & Western Railroad Lift Bridge	3.6	10'
Gilmerton Lift Bridge	5.8	35'
Norfolk & Southern #7 Railroad Bridge	5.8	7'
Interstate 64 Highway Bridge	7.1	65'
Veterans Bridge	8.9	95'

VIRGINIA CUT ROUTE

LOCATION	MILE	CLEARANCE
Great Bridge Lock	**11.3**	
Great Bridge Bascule Bridge	12.0	8'
Chesapeake Expressway	13.0	65'
Albemarle & Chesapeake RR Bridge	13.9	7'
Centerville Turnpike Swing Bridge	15.2	4'
North Landing Swing Bridge	20.2	6'
Pungo Ferry Bridge	28.3	65'
Coinjock Bridge	49.9	65'

DISMAL SWAMP ROUTE

LOCATION	MILE	CLEARANCE
Deep Creek Lock	**10.5**	
Deep Creek Bascule Bridge	11.1	4'
Dimsal Swamp Visitor Center Bridge	28.1	0'
Dismal Swamp Canal Highway Bridge	31.5	65'
South Mills Bascule Bridge	32.6	4'
South Mills Lock	**32.7**	**65'**
Albemarle & Chesapeake RR Bridge	47.7	3'
Elizabeth City Highway Bridges	50.7	2'

ICW ROUTE SOUTH

LOCATION	MILE	CLEARANCE
Alligator River Swing Bridge	84.2	14'
Fairfield Bridge	113.9	64'
Wilkerson Bridge	125.9	64'
Hobucken Bridge	157.2	65'
Core Creek Bridge	195.8	65'
Beaufort Channel Hwy. Bridge	203.8	65'
Beaufort Channel RR Bascule Bridge	203.8	4'

Clearance is vertical, closed, in feet. Bridges and locks in bold type have restricted openings.

Hampton, Norfolk & Portsmouth, VA

ICW Mile Zero–Mile 7   **VHF** VA Bridges: Channel 13

CHARTS NOAA 12206, 12222, 12253

■ HAMPTON ROADS

Before you can begin your journey down the Atlantic Intracoastal Waterway (AICW), you must traverse the 10-nm stretch through the Hampton Roads area.

Hampton Roads (roads means a roadstead, which is a body of water where ships can lie reasonably at anchor) is home to the world's largest naval base, a major shipbuilder and several great commercial ports. Hampton Roads Harbor begins at the line between Old Point Comfort on the north shore and Willoughby Spit to the south. Sitting on a little island in the middle of the harbor's entrance is Fort Wool, which along with Fort Monroe at Hampton's Old Point Comfort, guarded the entry. Hampton Roads is the site of the famous *Monitor* and *Merrimack* naval battle of 1862, which ended in a draw between the ironclads and is one of the world's greatest natural harbors.

Mariners must find their way carefully among all the vessels and aids to navigation in this impressive nautical crossroads. Many of us cruising the waters covered by the many *Waterway Guides* will never experience a busier harbor than Hampton Roads. It is as busy, if not busier, than New York Harbor. Stay tuned to VHF Channel 16 and, if your radio scans, also to VHF Channel 13, the channel on which commercial traffic communicates. If you don't have a scanner, hopefully you have a second VHF or a handheld to monitor VHF Channel 13. Remember that you are in deep water in this harbor, and you can safely run alongside the channel (and outside it) to provide ample space between you and the many 1,000-foot container ships, submarines, aircraft carriers and commercial vessels that move through here.

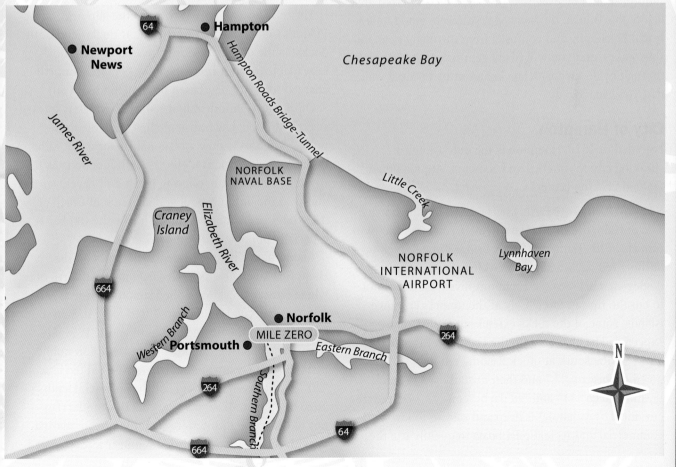

At Old Point Comfort a conspicuous historical brick landmark is the former Chamberlin Hotel (now now a senior services community) marking the north side of the entrance to Hampton Roads Harbor. Fort Monroe and Hampton University are on the eastern side of Hampton Harbor. The City of Hampton, just west of Old Point Comfort, is located on both sides of the short, busy Hampton River.

NAVIGATION: Use NOAA Chart 12222. Twin 3-mile-long bridge–tunnels join the north and south sides of Hampton Roads (from Hampton to Norfolk) between Old Point Comfort and Willoughby Spit (detailed in the Chesapeake Bay edition of this guide.) Channels over the tunnels are well marked, but they also serve as bottlenecks through which all boat and big ship traffic must pass. Tidal currents are usually strong here.

Proceeding south through Hampton Roads Harbor, give ships at the Norfolk Naval Station a wide berth. This area is constantly patrolled, and it is advisable to favor the west side of the channel or even just outside the channel, where there is still adequate water depth. In fact, all military and commercial ships must be given a wide berth–500 yards when possible–as dictated by the Homeland Security Act. This is not a No-Wake Zone but caution should be exercised through this congested area. Before this transit, tie down as if you were going to sea. It will be choppy and confused from the many boat and ship wakes, and you will likely get rocked on your way through by an inconsiderate boater or by residual wakes that you can't avoid.

City of Hampton

Founded in 1610, Hampton is the oldest English-speaking city in America and is one of Virginia's main seafood packing centers.

NAVIGATION: Use NOAA Chart 12222. On the north side of Hampton Roads Harbor, after you cross the twin tunnels of the Hampton Roads Bridge-Tunnel, pick up flashing red daybeacon "2" marking the start of the dogleg channel into the Hampton River. Take care not to cut the rip-rap too closely at the tunnel's entrance islands; some of the rocks extend out farther than expected. The channel into the Hampton River makes a turn to the south at quick flashing red light "6" and green daybeacon "7," and then to starboard at quick flashing green "11" and red daybeacon "12." Despite the curviness, the channel is deep and easy to follow. Both commercial and recreational boats frequently use the

channel. All of the marinas are located before the 29-foot fixed vertical clearance **Settlers Landing Bridge**. See additional information about the town of Hampton in our Chesapeake Bay edition of *Waterway Guide*.

Dockage: The first three of Hampton's marinas are on Sunset Creek, which leads off to the west from the main Hampton River channel. Bluewater Yachting Center spans the southwest corner of the Hampton–Sunset Creek fork and features 200 floating slips for vessels up to 200 feet. They have three separate high-speed fueling stations, along with complimentary water shuttle service to downtown. They also have high-speed WiFi and a common area with grills, picnic tables and corn hole boards. Bluewater Yacht Yards is located beyond on Sunset Creek and also has space available for transients at its floating docks. They have 100- and 50-ton lifts and offer all types of marine services, gas and diesel. Bluewater also manages the Bluewater Outer Banks Yard in Wanchese (described in more detail in Manteo section). At the end of the navigable portion of Sunset Creek is Sunset Boating Center, which may also have transient slips and sells all fuels.

Back on the main river, the Hampton Yacht Club holds a few spots for transients who are members of reciprocating yacht clubs.

The tour boat to Fort Wool uses the slip next to the Visitor's Center. Farther upstream, at the far end of the docks, is the dinghy docking area. Short-term dockage is available for four hours. Stay longer, and you will be charged for a full day, based on the length of your boat

Old Point Comfort Military Marina, which is located at Fort Monroe, has transient slips available to the public. The fort is now a National Historic Site rather than an active base. The officer's club functions as the Paradise Ocean Club, offering meals and beverages to guests at the outdoor pool and a stretch of beach at daily rates or by membership. The on-site tiki bar is especially popular.

Anchorage: There are three anchorages on the Hampton River. One is at Cedar Point, just north of where Sunset Creek joins the Hampton River at Mile 196.2. It has good holding in 7 to 8 feet MLW in mud but is open to the northeast, south and ICW wakes. Another is opposite the downtown Hampton public piers. Boats may anchor anywhere past red daybeacon "20" on the red-marker side of the channel. Depths are 6 to 15 feet MLW; use your depth sounder. Do not block traffic or interfere with the private marina or with the city dock. This is no longer a "designated

Norfolk Waterfront

anchorage area" so be sure to use appropriate day-shape and anchor lights.

Boats that can get under the 29-foot fixed vertical clearance of the Settlers Landing Bridge at the end of the channel can find good anchorage upstream, in 8 to 10 feet MLW with good holding and plenty of swing room. As always, exercise caution in shoal areas.

The dinghy dock moves but will be either at the up-river end of the pier or next to the Head & Tour boat slip. Look for the sign.

■ MILE ZERO: ELIZABETH RIVER

Strategically situated at Mile Zero, the "official" beginning of the AICW, Hampton, Norfolk and Portsmouth offer nearly every type of marine service and equipment and are especially good fitting-out places in preparation for a cruise south or north. They're also exciting places to visit, with rejuvenated waterfronts filled with shops, restaurants, hotels, museums and historic sites.

The world's merchant fleet loads and unloads cargo at the Hampton Roads and Elizabeth River piers. Colliers fill their holds with 100,000 tons of coal at a time. Even so, the military presence is still larger than the commercial. Naval Station Norfolk, the largest naval installation in the world, is homeport for the U.S. Navy's Atlantic Fleet, encompassing aircraft carriers, cruisers, destroyers, frigates, support ships, nuclear submarines and admiral's barges. The Joint Expeditionary Base at Little Creek is a few miles east over land and is the world's largest amphibious base. Most of the Navy's operational aircraft are stationed at Naval Air Station Oceana in Virginia Beach. There is also a large Navy training center at Dam Neck and the Army operates Fort Story at Cape Henry. Across Hampton Roads Harbor is Langley Air Force Base. The Marines have several camps in the area. Even NATO has a headquarters in the area. All in all, this area, by far, is the largest military complex in the world.

There are multiple daily bus tours of Naval Station Norfolk in summer months (for a fee). The 45-minute tour departs from the Naval Tour and Information Center located at 9079 Hampton Blvd., next to Gate 5. Bus tours conducted by Navy personnel take you past aircraft carriers, destroyers, frigates, amphibious assault ships and the busy airfield. The tour passes through "Admiral's Row," a group of historic homes from the 1907 Jamestown Exposition that have been restored and are now quarters for the admirals and generals stationed here. A picture ID is required for all adults and schedules are subject to change; call 757-444-7955 before going.

The Confederate ironclad *Merrimack*, which famously dueled with the Union's *Monitor* in 1861, was built in

Hampton River, VA

		Largest Vessel Accommodated	VHF Channel Monitored	Transient Berths / Total Berths	Approach / Dockside Depth (reported)	Floating Docks	Gas / Diesel	Groceries, Ice, Marine Supplies, Snacks	Repairs: Hull, Engine, Propeller	Lift (tonnage), Crane, Rail	Min/Max Amps	Laundry, Pool, Showers, Courtesy Car	Pump-Out Station	Nearby: Grocery Store, Motel, Restaurant
HAMPTON AREA				**Dockage**				**Supplies**			**Services**			
1. Bluewater Yachting Center ▱ WiFi	757-723-6774	200	16	60/200	12/12	F	GD	IMS	HEP	L100	30/100	LPS	P	GR
2. Bluewater Yacht Yards ▱ WiFi	757-723-0793	80	16	60/200	12/8	F	GD	IMS	HEP	L100	30/50	LPS	P	GR
3. Sunset Boating Center WiFi	757-722-3325	34	16/68	10/38	10/8	F	GD	IMS	–	L20	30/50	LS	P	GR
4. Hampton Yacht Club WiFi	757-722-0711	100	–	call/192	10/8	F	–	MS	–	C5	30/50	S	P	GMR
5. Customs House Marina WiFi	757-636-7772	50	–	call/60	12/11	–	–	–	–		30/50	PS	–	GMR
6. Downtown Hampton Public Piers ▱ WiFi	757-727-1276	130	16/68	27/27	12/11	F	–	I	–		30/100	LPS	P	GMR
OLD POINT COMFORT														
7. Old Point Comfort Marina ▱ WiFi	757-788-4308	50	16/68	10/314	20/13	F	GD	IS	–	C6	30/50	LS	P	GR

▱ Internet Access WiFi Wireless Internet Access **WG** Waterway Guide Cruising Club Partner ⬤onSpot dockside WiFi facility

See WaterwayGuide.com for current rates, fuel prices, web site addresses, and other up-to-the-minute information. *(Information in the table is provided by the facilities.)*

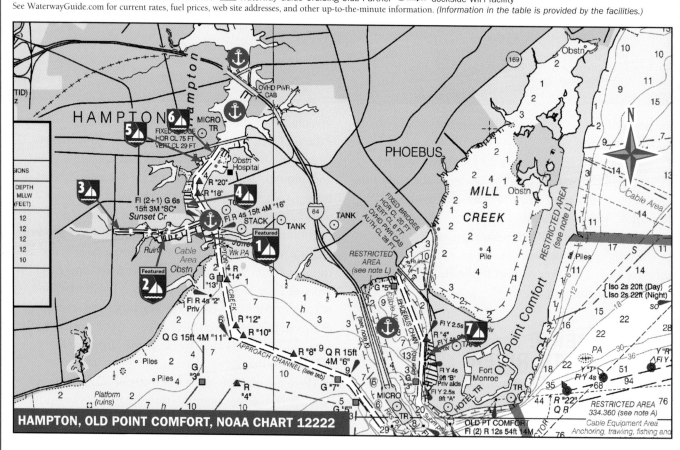

HAMPTON, OLD POINT COMFORT, NOAA CHART 12222

Jordan Hwy. Bridge

Beltline Railroad Bridge

the Norfolk Naval Shipyard in Norfolk's harbor on the Elizabeth River. The turret of the *Monitor* is housed in the world-famous Newport News Mariners' Museum, located to the north on the James River. Close by is Newport News Shipbuilding, the largest private shipyard in the nation, which is capable of building nuclear-powered supercarriers.

The Norfolk–Portsmouth-Chesapeake area is a good centralized spot for sightseeing in the surrounding countryside, for picking up or dropping off guests and for flying in to join a boat. Limousine/cab service to and from Norfolk's airport is easy to arrange. If you are in Hampton or Newport News, you should also consider the Newport News/Williamsburg International Airport. It is about 25 minutes north of Hampton on I-64.

NAVIGATION: Use NOAA Chart 12222, 12253 or 12206. Chart 12253 provides an inset of Norfolk Harbor and the Elizabeth River at 1:10,000 scale. Use the Hampton Roads Tide Table. For high tide, add 18 minutes; for low tide, add 15 minutes. Be sure to access updated NOAA charts or the Waterway Explorer (waterwayguide.com), as there are constant updates and new bathymetry along the entire Norfolk waterfront.

Elizabeth River quick flashing red buoy "36," just east of Hospital Point, marks Mile 0 and the beginning of the 1,243-mile-long Atlantic ICW. Located on the western side of the main Elizabeth River channel, south of the

Reminder: All mileage on the Norfolk-to-Florida segment of the ICW is measured in **statute** rather than nautical miles.

Western Branch junction, Hospital Point is home to a huge naval hospital, the nation's oldest and largest.

Even with all its commercial and military activity, navigating through Norfolk Harbor is relatively easy during daylight hours. If southbound from Hampton Roads, pick up the marked channel past Sewells Point at the western end of Willoughby Bay and continue on into the Elizabeth River. Southbound past Sewells Point, you will see a great array of naval vessels to the east, from aircraft carriers to submarines. The harbor itself begins at Craney Island, where you can switch to NOAA Small Craft Chart 12206. At night, navigation can be a bit more difficult with all the illumination ashore, making aids to navigation more difficult to detect. You will be much happier and enjoy the sights a lot more doing this in daylight.

As in other large harbors, it is recommended you run alongside or outside the marked channel if ship traffic is heavy. Depths alongside the channel are good. The main hazard is flotsam, which can be in the form of wooden planks or piles the size of telephone poles. If you choose to run outside the channel, use the western side until you are past the Norfolk Naval Base and port operations to the east. Patrol boats and security barriers line the Restricted Area (shown as a purple shaded area on your NOAA chart) on the eastern side of the channel. From Craney Island southward, remain inside the channel to avoid shallows and military or port facilities.

The current can be strong here and discourteous boaters may throw a wake that will roll you, so be aware and prepared. Expect less current as you proceed from

ICW Mile 0 southward. Heavy commercial traffic, bridge schedules and lock openings can also sometimes cause marked delay in arrival time, so planning ahead is a good idea before proceeding southward.

Western Branch, Elizabeth River

NAVIGATION: Use NOAA Chart 12206. The Western Branch of the Elizabeth River leads off to starboard to the south of the bend in the main channel at Lamberts Point. Note the magenta restricted area on the NOAA chart east of Lovett Point on your approach to Western Branch. The 45-foot fixed vertical clearance **West Norfolk Bridge**, located just west of Lovett Point, makes it impossible for some sailboats to pass farther upstream. Those who can clear the fixed bridge will find depths of 15 to 20 feet all the way to the Churchland (High St.) Bridge, with a 38-foot fixed vertical clearance.

Dockage: Western Branch Diesel Inc., conveniently located on the north side before the 45-foot fixed West Norfolk Bridge, offers installation, service and parts for vessels of all sizes and a 35-ton boat lift, in addition to transient space. They are on site 24/7 and also offer mobile parts and service. Virginia Boat & Yacht Service,

also located on the north side of Western Branch, may have some transient space and offers some repairs.

City of Norfolk

For two centuries, Norfolk has been a Navy town and to this day it is flanked on north and south by ships in gray livery. Well before the U.S. Navy was established, merchant ships and sailors called Norfolk home, and cargo vessels of all types with international crews still call to load, discharge and undergo repairs.

Anyone arriving in Norfolk by boat from either direction, whether from the isolated small towns of the Chesapeake Bay or from the cypress-bound sounds of North Carolina, is in for re-entry shock. It begins with the visual stimulation of the sheer volume of water traffic and intense industrial activity on both banks of the Elizabeth River and culminates with immersion into a vibrant city. Enjoy it because when you leave, in either direction, you will go a long way before encountering anything like it again.

By itself, Norfolk, with a population approaching 250,000, is the second largest city in Virginia. The urban sprawl it forms with the surrounding cities

Elizabeth River, VA

		Largest Vessel Accommodated	VHF Channel Monitored	Approach / Dockside Depth (reported)	Transient Berths / Total Berths	Floating Docks	Gas / Diesel	Groceries, Ice, Marine Supplies, Snacks	Repairs: Hull, Engine, Propeller	Lift (tonnage), Crane, Rail	Min/Max Amps	Laundry, Pool, Showers, Courtesy Car	Pump-Out Station	Nearby: Grocery Store, Motel, Restaurant
LAFAYETTE RIVER				**Dockage**			**Supplies**		**Services**					
1. Norfolk Yacht and Country Club WiFi	757-423-4500	–	–	call/200	11/	F	GD	S	–	–	30/50	PS	P	R
WESTERN BRANCH														
2. Western Branch Diesel, Inc.	**757-673-7100**	100	–	4/62	12/7	–	–	M	E	–	30/50	–	–	–
3. Virginia Boat & Yacht Service	757-673-7167	150	–	5/62	12/8	–	–	M	HEP	L35	30/50	LS	–	GMR
NORFOLK														
4. Nauticus Marina 0	757-664-1000	60	–	15/15	45/20	F	–	IS	–	–	30/50	LS	P	MR
5. Waterside Marina 🖳 WiFi 0	**757-625-3625**	270	16/68	50/50	45/20	F	–	GI	EP	–	30/100	S	P	GMR
PORTSMOUTH														
6. Portsmouth Boating Center 🖳 WiFi 0	757-397-2092	80	16	10/40	8/10	–	GD	IMS	HEP	L70	30/50	LS	P	GMR
7. Tidewater Yacht Marina 🖳 WiFi 0	**757-393-2525**	300	16/68	100/300	12/11	F	GD	IMS	–	–	30/200+	LPS	P	GMR
8. Ocean Yacht Marina 🖳 WiFi .6	**757-321-7432**	350	16/09	25/122	45/30	F	GD	IMS	HEP	L80	30/100	LS	P	GMR
9. Ocean Marine Yacht Center	757-399-2920	235	–	–	–	–	GD	M	HEP	L1250,R	–	–	–	GMR

🖳 Internet Access WiFi Wireless Internet Access WG Waterway Guide Cruising Club Partner onSpot dockside WiFi facility

See WaterwayGuide.com for current rates, fuel prices, web site addresses, and other up-to-the-minute information. *(Information in the table is provided by the facilities.)*

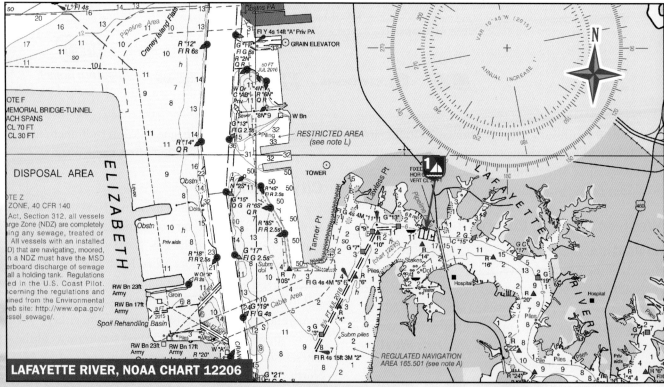

LAFAYETTE RIVER, NOAA CHART 12206

Norfolk Waterfront

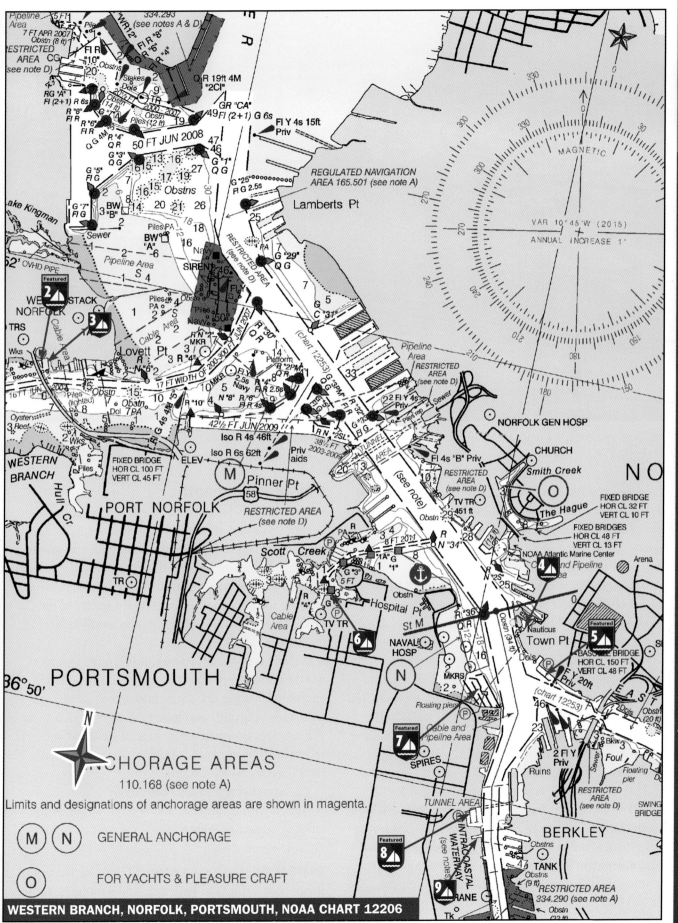

WESTERN BRANCH, NORFOLK, PORTSMOUTH, NOAA CHART 12206

of Virginia Beach, Chesapeake, Suffolk, Portsmouth, Hampton, Newport News, Poquoson and Williamsburg is the largest in the state. It is not surprising that Norfolk supports many of the cultural and recreational outlets associated with bigger cities. It has a symphony orchestra, several museums, professional sports teams and a downtown shopping mall full of high-end retail stores.

Dockage: There is a wave screen directly in front of the 60-slip Waterside Marina to provide protection for vessels moored there. Transient space is available at floating slips with access to restrooms and showers. Overnight slip holders can get transportation for provisioning arranged by the dockmaster on request. The deep-water marina can accommodate vessels to 400 feet. Waterside Marina is part of the City of Norfolk's Waterside District, which has undergone a multimillion dollar renovation. The marina is well protected and within easy walking distance of downtown venues.

There is a smaller marina facility (15 slips) for overflow close by at Nauticus, a museum and park (see Goin' Ashore for details). Call Waterside Marina for information and reservations for the Nauticus Marina. You may tie up for 2 hours at no charge if you are visiting the museum. Nauticus Marina can only accept

vessels that do not exceed 24 feet vertical clearance due to a walking bridge that spans the opening.

City of Portsmouth

Portsmouth has long served as a key point at the beginning or end of a passage through the ICW. For many years before the city began construction on the new face it now presents to the Elizabeth River, it was a place to only to take aboard fuel and provisions before running for the less threatening open spaces of the Bay or the ICW. Today, it is a destination worth exploring for its own sake.

Directly across from Portsmouth, America's largest warships and support vessels are often berthed in enormous floating dry docks undergoing refits. Upstream, shipyards and industrial piers stretch as far as you can see. Downstream, towers of glass and concrete in Norfolk's business district loom above the harbor. The river itself teems with traffic.

The waterfront area has been largely rebuilt. High St.t is vibrant with commerce, and several museums and cultural centers provide distractions enough to fill a visit of several days.

NAVIGATION: Use NOAA Chart 12206. Use Hampton Roads Tide Table. For high tide, add 9 minutes; for low tide, add 10 minutes. Located directly on "Mile Zero" of the ICW, Portsmouth is a convenient location to regroup for the journey south or to recoup from the rigors of "the ditch" when heading north. Pedestrian ferry service to Norfolk is available at both North Landing Dock and High Street Landing. The 150-passenger Elizabeth River Ferry drops off and picks up every 30 minutes at Waterside in Norfolk for $2.00 (one way). There are discounts and multi-day passes available.

Dockage: Dockage on the Portsmouth side of the Elizabeth River is available on Scotts Creek at the full-service Scott's Creek Marina and at Portsmouth Boating Center, known for its high-speed diesel pumps and reasonable fuel prices (as well as a 70-ton boat lift).

Directly opposite Norfolk's Town Point, on the southwest side of the Elizabeth River, the full-service Tidewater Yacht Marina has 100 deep-water slips available for transients on their floating docks, as well as diesel and gas fueling stations, substantial lift and repair facilities and a well-stocked ship store with charts, clothing and groceries. To reach the fuel dock, pass behind the breakwater from the river, then turn southeast down the first fairway. The large pumps on the outermost dock are only for ferries and other large vessels. The marina offers a floating swimming pool, a laundry, multiple bathhouses and conference facilities. The restaurant is situated above the marina store and office, with a commanding view of the harbor.

Ocean Yacht Marina, a sister marina to Tidewater Yacht Marina, is 0.5 miles south with transient space on floating docks and amenities that include laundry, storage, recycling, a ship store, pump-out services and gasoline. On site is Ocean Marine Yacht Center, one of the largest yacht service yards on the east coast, capable of servicing yachts up to 235 feet. The facilities are adjacent to the Union Bank & Trust Pavilion, where big name entertainers regularly perform, and to the ferry landing at High Street. The Olde Towne Portsmouth historic district is within walking distance, with numerous shops and restaurants.

Both North Harbor Landing and High Street Landing offer free short-term dockage for vessels 40 feet and under (36-hour limit; no more than 3 days in any 30-day period). There are no utilities. This is where the Elizabeth River Ferry drops off and picks up. A city-owned, free pump-out facility is available at the North Harbor Inlet. Boaters should check in at the kiosk across from the High Street Landing for a list of rules and regulations. Call the Visitor Center (757-393-5111) for more information.

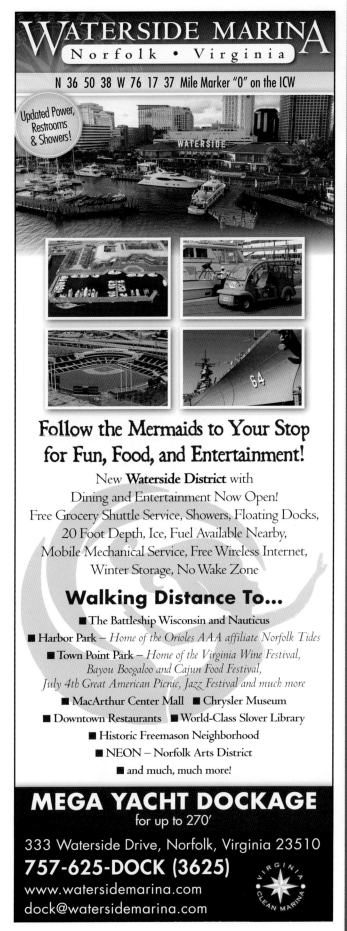

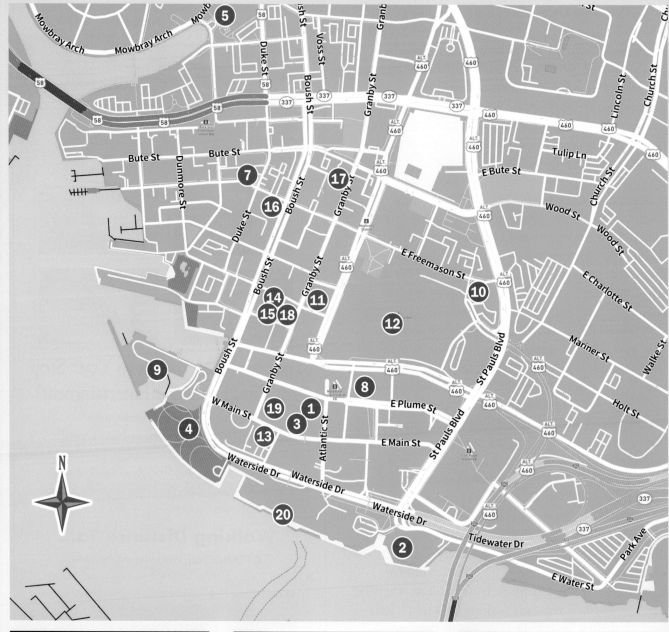

GOIN' ASHORE: NORFOLK, VA

SERVICES	
1	Library
2	Post Office
3	Visitor Information
ATTRACTIONS	
4	Armed Forces Memorial
5	Chrysler Museum of Art
6	Harbor Park
7	Hunter House Victorian Museum
8	MacArthur Memorial

9	Nauticus
10	Norfolk History Museum
11	Wells Theatre
SHOPPING	
12	MacArthur Center
13	Prince Books
DINING	
14	Big Easy Grill & Oyster Bar
15	Byrd & Baldwin Bros. Steak House
16	Freemason Abbey

17	Rama Garden
18	Granby Bistro & Deli
19	Hilton Norfolk The Main
20	Waterside District
MARINAS	
9	Nauticus Marina
20	Waterside Marina

Norfolk, home of the world's largest naval base, has roots that begin at the waterfront and are entwined with it throughout history. In 1801 the Continental Navy established its first Navy Yard here. During the Civil War, Norfolk's strategic location made it the focus of the attention of both sides, which took turns destroying much of it until the city surrendered to the Union Army in 1862. This was shortly after the significant but inconclusive Battle of Hampton Roads between the ironclads *Monitor and Merrimack*, which ushered in a new era of naval warfare. Connected to the north by Chesapeake Bay, to the west by railroads and to the south by the Albemarle and Chesapeake Canal (which opened in 1859) and the Dismal Swamp Canal, it soon became, according to the city's official history, the world's largest seaport.

At its heart, Norfolk is still a seaport and a naval base, and the rejuvenation of its city center has been highly successful in the downtown area of Town Point, where Norfolk's waterfront basks in light reflected off high-rise office buildings and hotels. It is here that visiting boaters will tie up within walking distance of many of Norfolk's must-sees. Walk a couple of blocks up Main St. to the Visit Norfolk Tourist Information Center (232 E. Main St.) to learn more about local attractions, look over restaurant menus or grab a Norfolk map.

Getting Around: As in most larger cities, you will have no problem locating and accessing provisions and entertainment. Hampton Roads Transit connects with destinations beyond downtown and with all the cities in the Hampton Roads area via bus, light rail and ferry. Norfolk's light-rail transit system (The Tide) connects the city center with points west and east, including the waterfront baseball field at Harbor Park. It operates in connection with the bus system so you can switch back and forth. Call 757-222-6100 or visit gohrt.com for details.

Attractions: Nauticus is a fusion of science museum, game arcade and theme park, centered around humankind's historic engagement with the ocean and its denizens. In the same building, the Hampton Roads Naval Museum showcases the U.S. Navy's 200-year association with the Hampton Roads region. Berthed alongside is the *Wisconsin BB-64*, a veteran of three wars. She was the last of four Iowa Class Battleships built for the Navy. They were the largest and last battleships before the Navy switched to aircraft carriers. All are museums and open to the public. Tours by bus or boat provide a close-up view of active-service ships at Naval Station Norfolk. Call 757-664-1000 for operating hours and information.

A city whose lifeblood is the military must necessarily cope with death. Several memorials remind visitors of the ultimate price our warriors pay. The MacArthur Memorial, where Gen. Douglas MacArthur and his wife are laid to rest, is both a celebration of his life and achievements and a tribute to the millions of men and women who served in America's wars, from the Spanish-American War to Korea. It is located downtown next to the MacArthur Center mall. Admission is free and it is well worth an hour of your time. More evocative at a personal level, the Armed Forces Memorial in Town Point Park tells its story through examples of letters written home by servicemen and women who subsequently died in action. A good time to visit is in late afternoon, when warm light and long shadows highlight the messages, each one borne on cast bronze sheets and displayed as though strewn across the plaza by the wind.

Energetic walkers can follow the marked Cannonball Trail, which loops through the downtown area, taking in many city sights including Town Point, the Freemason Historic District, St. Paul's Church and the MacArthur Memorial. Those who care to make a morning or afternoon of it will find abundant opportunities for refreshment along the way.

Norfolk has multiple museums on varying subject matter. Here's just a sampling: Chrysler Museum of Art (245 W. Olney Rd., 757-664-6200); Norfolk History Museum at the Willoughby-Baylor House (601 E. Freemason St., 757-333-6283); and Hunter House Victorian Museum (240 W. Freemason St., 757-623-9814). A little farther afield the Norfolk Botanical Garden (757-441-5830) and the Virginia Zoo (757-441-2374) provide windows on the plants and animals that call this area home.

As you walk around, you can't help but notice the over two dozen mermaids. These city mascots are all dressed in different outfits depicting different themes. There is even one at the Naval Base dressed in Navy Uniform. They are fun, colorful, fanciful and very photogenic.

There's nothing quite like a baseball game on a summer night and no better place to see one than at the waterfront Harbor Park, home of the Norfolk Tides, a AAA farm team for the Baltimore Orioles. The park opened in 1993 and is known for its outstanding views from the stands.

For something more cultural, the Virginia Stage Company (757-627-1234) is based in the Wells Theater at 108 E. Tazewell St., which is a restored Beaux Arts landmark that opened in 1913 as a vaudeville theater. The Virginia Symphony (757-892-6366) plays at several venues in the Hampton Roads area in the course of its 42-week season, which runs from September through June. The Virginia Opera (866-763-7282) performs at the Harrison Opera House, located on the corner of Virginia Beach Blvd. and Llewellyn Ave., about 1.5 miles from Waterside.

Town Point Park hosts cultural and musical festivals throughout the summer. The annual Harborfest has its origins in Operation Sail, the tall ship tour that was part of America's Bicentennial celebrations in 1976. It is held in early June and is a major week-long celebration focused around the waterfront with food concerts, sail parades, and the like. Working Chesapeake watermen bring their deadrise workboats to town and race for bragging rights for the coming year. The homeport of the victor takes great pride in the recognition. The Norfolk Waterfront Jazz Festival is a great summertime party with top-notch performers. Check the calendar as the schedule moves from year to year. If you are at Waterside Marina you have a ringside berth. See details at festevents.org.

Shopping: You can easily walk to MacArthur Center from the waterfront, which is three stories of department stores, small shops, restaurants and a theater complex. A variety of stores line the streets in between. One example is Prince Books at 109 E. Main St. (757-622-9223), where the discriminating bibliophile can browse a broad and eclectic selection of books and partake of a restorative coffee and a muffin in the on-site Lizard Café.

In the nearby residential neighborhood of Ghent you will find a variety of eclectic shops, bistros, restaurants and historic homes. Visit the new NEON district.

Dining: Restaurants in downtown Norfolk serve every gastronomic taste from meatballs to highballs. The newly renovated Market of the Waterside District is made up of an abundance of restaurants offering a wide variety of world cuisines along with bars featuring a full array of beers, ales, wines and cocktails in an open pavilion walk-around food court setting.

As in all cities, restaurants come and go, so forage along Granby St. and its neighboring side streets for options. Hilton Norfolk The Main (757-763-6200) has two restaurants and a beer garden that always delight. You can almost see your boat at Waterside Marina from the roof garden. You might want to try Granby Bistro & Deli (225 Granby St., 757-622-7003) or Thai cuisine at Rama Garden (441 Granby St., 757-616-0533).

Freemason Abbey (209 Freemason St., 757-622-3966) is housed in a former church that is over 135 years old. They offer fine dining with American cuisine. The prime rib is a specialty. Byrd & Baldwin Bros. Steak House (116 Brooke Ave., 757-222-9191) is top-rated and their prime beef is aged on site. Norfolk Seafood Company & Big Easy Oyster Bar (111 W. Tazewell St., 757-227-6222) has seafood covered.

These are just a few suggestions from our on-the-water Cruising Editors; every continent is represented here, and the restaurants are numerous. Visit downtownnorfolk.org for an up-to-date list of restaurants, many of which are within easy walking distance of your boat. When you're ready to embark, use visitnorfolk.com as your online guide to the city. Norfolk is the best of the old and new. Enjoy!

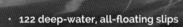

Anchorage: Late arrivals and those who prefer to anchor normally use the harbor's small-boat anchorage (Hospital Point), south and west of the channel at flashing red buoy "36," between the large brick naval hospital and Tidewater Yacht Marina. Anchor in 8 to 9 feet MLW in mud. Holding is only fair, so don't skimp on scope, though the anchorage is popular and usually holds numerous boats. The no wake zone in the harbor keeps you relatively calm (other than occasional tug wakes or inconsiderate boaters), but strong winds in summer storms can funnel down the river.

Dinghy dockage and use of some facilities is available at the Tidewater Yacht Marina adjacent to the Portsmouth side of the river for a fee. You can also take the dinghy to the Waterside Marina on the Norfolk waterfront across the river and make fast inside (for a small fee or no fee depending on your negotiating skills and destination), if there is space.

Eastern Branch, Elizabeth River

Beyond Mile 0, Town Point on the Norfolk side marks the mouth of the Elizabeth River's Eastern Branch. Commercial traffic can be heavy in this area, with tugs passing through and large commercial vessels maneuvering into and out of the docks. It is a good idea to monitor VHF Channel 13 and to call any tug or other vessel whose intentions are unclear. Sometimes, though, listening is enough. Always yield to commercial traffic in this area.

The Eastern Branch of the Elizabeth River curves around Norfolk's Waterside development to port, while the Southern Branch (AICW) bears to starboard around Portsmouth.

⚠️ Before reaching Town Point, study your NOAA chart carefully. Many mariners mistakenly continue along the Eastern Branch thinking it is the AICW, only to turn around 2 miles later at its end. The AICW route follows the Southern Branch of the Elizabeth River.

There are no aids to navigation in this area, and none are needed, as the water is deep to the shoreline. Four bridges cross this stretch: two bascule bridges, one with a 48-foot and one with a 4-foot closed vertical clearance; one fixed with a 65-foot vertical clearance; and one railroad swing bridge with a 6-foot vertical clearance. The bascule and swing bridges have restricted closures. Check the Explorer at waterwayguide.com for complete schedules when planning to navigate this river.

Southern Branch, Elizabeth River (AICW)

Norshipco is the yard on the Norfolk side with the huge dry docks that mark the intersection of the Southern and Eastern Branch. Leave this facility to port heading south to enter the Southern Branch. Large Naval and cruise ships can normally be seen in the dry docks. The Norfolk Naval Shipyard is farther along the Southern Branch of the Elizabeth River heading south on the Portsmouth (west) side. As many signs warn, no landings are permitted. Navy and Coast Guard patrol boats guard the naval vessels docked along both sides of the river. We know of cruisers who have been stopped and searched after getting too close and taking photos.

NAVIGATION: Use NOAA Chart 12206. Proceeding southward on the Southern Branch of the Elizabeth River, you will encounter a 7-mile-long congested stretch with a 6-mph speed limit (enforced) and six bridges. Be sure to monitor VHF Channel 13, where all commercial vessels communicate and bridge traffic is handled, as well as VHF Channel 16. Most bridges open promptly, except during restricted hours. Northbound vessels leaving the lock at Great Bridge at the same time are usually required to bunch together for openings of all the bridges in this stretch, whether the vessels are fast or slow, power or sail.

The two railroad lift bridges on either side of the fixed 145-foot vertical clearance **Jordan Hwy. Bridge** (the **Belt Line Railroad Lift Bridge** at Mile 2.6 and the **Norfolk & Western Railroad Lift Bridge** at Mile 3.6) are usually open, but closures do occur. Note that a closed vertical clearance of less than 9 feet has been observed at the Norfolk & Western Railroad bridge, despite the published 10-foot clearance. The Belt Line Railroad Bridge is operated remotely.

The **Gilmerton Lift Bridge** (35-foot closed vertical clearance) at Mile 5.8 opens on signal, except from 6:30 a.m. to 8:30 a.m., and from 3:30 p.m. to 5:30 p.m., Monday through Friday (except federal holidays), when the bridge need not open. The adjacent **Norfolk and Southern #7 Railroad Bridge** is normally open. Note that it is unmanned and does not respond to VHF calls. It is important to note that the Gilmerton Bridge will not open unless the railroad bridge is open. Openings of the railroad bridge are announced on VHF Channel 13, and it is operated remotely with light, horn and audio signals when opening and closing. Be sure both bridges are open completely before you start through.

GOIN' ASHORE: **PORTSMOUTH, VA**

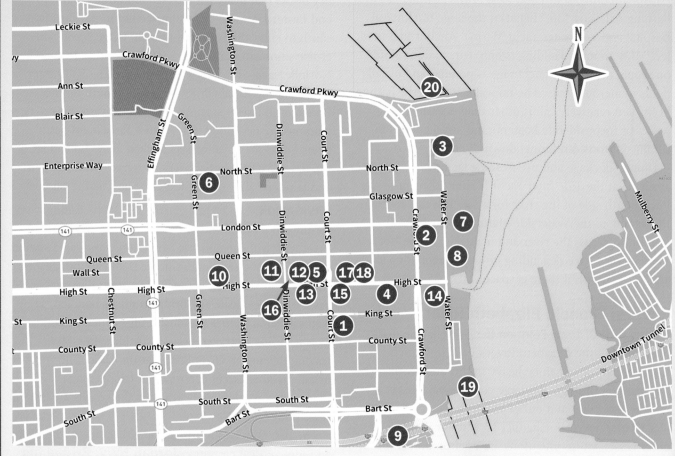

SERVICES	
1	Library
2	Post Office
3	Visitor Information
ATTRACTIONS	
4	Children's Museum of Virginia
5	Courthouse Galleries
6	Emanuel AME Church
7	Lightship Museum

8	Naval Shipyard Museum
9	Railroad Museum of Virginia
SHOPPING	
10	Skipjack Nautical Wares
DINING	
11	Baron's Pub
12	Bier Garden
13	Commodore Theatre
14	Legend Brewing Depot

15	Lobscouser Restaurant
16	Longboards
17	Roger Brown's Restaurant and Sports Bar
18	The Coffee Shoppe
MARINAS	
19	Ocean Yacht Marina
20	Tidewater Yacht Marina

Portsmouth was founded as a town in 1752 on 65 acres of land on the shores of the Elizabeth River. The town was founded by William Crawford, a wealthy merchant and ship owner. The 65 acres were part of Colonel Crawford's extensive plantation and were constituted as a town by an enabling act of the General Assembly of Virginia. The town was named after the English naval port of the same name, and many of the streets of the new town reflects the English heritage. During the Revolutionary War, squabbles between groups with differing loyalties led to parts of the town being burned, but the defeat of Lord Dunmore at Great Bridge spared the town from the utter destruction that the English had wrought on Norfolk.

After the war, the town continued to grow along with the new nation's expanding international trade and in support of the Navy charged with protecting it. In 1827, the U.S. Navy chose Fort Nelson for the site of the first naval hospital. Naval Medical Center Portsmouth is the Navy's oldest continually operating hospital.

In 1833, the Navy expanded the Gosport Navy Yard in Portsmouth, but named the facility the Norfolk Naval Shipyard so that it wouldn't be confused with the Portsmouth Naval Shipyard in Kittery, ME. The nation's first dry dock was built then and is still in use today. Other firsts for the Norfolk Naval Shipyard include building the Navy's first steel ship, the battleship *Texas*, the first fast cruiser *Raleigh* and the conversion of the collier *Jupiter* to the first aircraft carrier, *USS Langley*. At the same time, the Portsmouth and Weldon Railroad came to town connecting the canal system of the Roanoke River with the port facilities adjacent to Hampton Roads.

Attractions: A significant number of Portsmouth's attractions–whether culinary, cultural or recreational–are within easy walking distance of both downtown marinas.

In the Olde Towne Historic District, one block from the waterfront, scores of historically and architecturally important structures line leafy streets that still follow the original grid pattern laid out in 1752. Stop in at the Visitor Center (6 Crawford Pkwy.) and pick up the Olde Towne walking tour brochure to assist in your exploration.

Some buildings are as interesting for their social significance as for their age. Emanuel AME Church at 637 North St. was built in 1857 to replace one on Glasgow St. that burned in 1856. It is not only the second oldest church building in the town, it was also built by Portsmouth's oldest black congregation, which itself dates to the 1730s.

Resurgent and pre-resurgent neighborhoods everywhere are sometimes recolonized by the arts fringe drawn to the creative opportunities presented by antique buildings available for low rent. Portsmouth's Olde Towne is no exception and has been a magnet for artists in all media. Their works are on display and on sale in a number of cooperative galleries and workspaces, as well as in businesses that welcome the color and cachet they add to the neighborhood. More formal exhibits appear in regular sequence in the Portsmouth Art & Cultural Center (757-393-8543), housed in the architecturally impressive and historically significant 1846 courthouse on the corner of High St. and Court St.

On the waterfront at the foot of High St. is the Lightship Museum (757-393-8591), which is housed in a refurbished lightship. Nearby on the waterfront is a first-order Fresnel lens from a lighthouse. Two blocks away is the Children's Museum of Virginia (221 High St., 757-393-5258). A Key Pass is available that gives access to the museums and the Courthouse Galleries.

The Railroad Museum of Virginia (757-335-2284) is at Crawford Pkwy. and Pavilion Dr. and is open Friday and Saturday from 10:00 a.m. to 4:00 p.m.

A pedestrian ferry connects the Norfolk waterfront to downtown Portsmouth across the Elizabeth River, so whichever side you moor your boat you will have access to the amenities of both. And because you are in a city, taxicabs and rental cars are available to take you farther afield. Norfolk International Airport is a mere 5 miles from downtown.

Both the town and its various civic and cultural organizations put on events year-round, most of them centered on Olde Towne and the waterfront. An annual Memorial Day Parade gets summer off to a spirited start and fireworks off the riverfront punctuate the sky on Independence Day. Various art and musical festivals and gatherings fill in the gaps between.

Live concerts by recognized musicians in many genres draw crowds all summer long to the Union Bank and Trust Pavilion (757-393-8181) on the waterfront behind Ocean Yacht Marina.

Shopping: Shopping, whether for provisions or for fun, is found on the first seven blocks of High St. and its tributaries. You will find art, antiques, a pharmacy and specialty stores all within a comfortable walk. Skipjack Nautical Wares at 620 High St. (757-399-5012) maintains a fantastic inventory of nautical gifts and artwork. Plan some time for a visit...Skipjack is a joy to rummage through. For the galley, visit the Kitchen Coop at 638 High St. for spices, cookware and more (757-399-4475).

For provisioning, there is a Food Lion supermarket and all the usual associated stores, about 2 miles out (a cab ride) on London Blvd. Also at that end of town, there is a Kroger supermarket or Harris Teeter Market. A Dollar General is on High St.

Dining: A stroll along High St. will take you past a variety of eateries with offerings for breakfast, lunch, cocktails and dinner as well as baked goods or ice cream. Perhaps the most unusual is the Art Deco-style Commodore Theatre (421 High St., 757-393-6962). A fully-appointed dining room occupies the main

auditorium of this restored movie theater built in 1945 and listed on both the National Register of Historic Places and the Virginia Landmarks Register. Dine while watching first-run movies screened in all their digital and Dolby glory, but be sure to call ahead or visit commodoretheatre. com for schedules and reservations.

Sports fans and pool players will enjoy the big screens and billiard room at Roger Brown's Restaurant and Sports Bar at 316 High St. (757-399-5377). Visit Legend Brewing Depot at 1 High St. (757-998-6733) Try the Portsmouth Pale Ale, brewed on premises. Wings, burgers and beer are on the menu at Longboards at 440 High St. (757-399-4010). They also have a daily happy hour between 2:00 p.m. and 9:00 p.m.

For a more family-friendly atmosphere and extremely modest prices try the Lobscouser Restaurant at 337 High St. (757-397-2728). (Closed on Sunday.)

At the Baron's Pub (500 High St., 757-399-4840), you can get the best burgers in town along with great drinks and other dishes.

At the Bier Garden (438 High St., 757-393-6022), you can enjoy home-cooked German cuisine with your choice of over 400 beers from around the world.

To get a java fix and a vibe on the Olde Towne social scene in an artsy atmosphere, try The Coffee Shoppe at 300 High St. (757-391-9191).

To avoid a delay of up to 3 hours while idling in river currents, plan departures and arrivals carefully. Situated on a bend in the river, these bridges are hard to see until you are nearly upon them. Yield to commercial traffic and listen to the radio for their intentions. If you have any questions about their movement, contact them using VHF Channel 13 and be clear and direct in your communications.

⚠️ Do not mistake St. Julian Creek at Mile 4.9, for the ICW. (This is easier to do northbound than southbound, when it is just north and to port of the Gilmerton Bridge.) A 45-foot-high overhead power cable crosses this creek. Beacons warning of the power cable were placed at the mouth of St. Julian Creek after several vessels were dismasted.

You cross **Mile 0** on the Atlantic ICW with little fanfare. There is no line in the water as seen on the screen during an America's Cup race, nor is there a starting horn blast. The line–were it to exist–would be located at N 36° 50.540'/W 76° 17.540' and would cross the waterway between Town Point and Tidewater Yacht Marina. From this "starting line" the ICW stretches 1,243.8 statute miles (1,080.8 nm) south to Key West, FL.

Anchorage: Boats often anchor south of the Gilmerton Bridge and just north of the ICW behind the red buoy "24," where there is 9 to 13 feet MLW, good holding and protection all around. Boats often anchor here to wait out railroad bridge closures (and sometimes stay all night), where they are safely out of the waterway.

■ CRUISING OPTIONS: TWO ROUTES

Those traveling south from Norfolk on the ICW must now choose between two routes into North Carolina: either the Dismal Swamp Canal or the Albemarle-Chesapeake Canal, also known as the Virginia Cut. Each has its advantages, but careful consideration must be given to this decision. Both routes are described in detail in the following chapter.

Virginia Cut & Dismal Swamp Routes, VA/NC

 ICW Mile 7–Mile 50

 VA Bridges: Channel 13/NC Bridges: Channel 13

CHARTS NOAA 12206

At Mile 7.3, almost immediately south of the high-level I-64 Hwy. Bridge, cruisers must choose one of two very different routes south to Albemarle Sound: the Virginia Cut route (officially the Albemarle-Chesapeake Canal) to North Landing River or the Great Dismal Swamp Canal route to Elizabeth City, NC. An Army Corps of Engineers sign, positioned on the west side of the waterway just south of the turn for Deep Creek, points the way to each route. It also states whether the canal at Dismal Swamp is open or closed and gives its controlling depth.

The Virginia Cut has deeper water and only one lock to negotiate, while the Dismal Swamp has a controlling depth of 6 feet and two easy locks. During periods of low water, the Dismal Swamp Canal may be closed to navigation or have limited lock/bridge openings to protect the water levels in the Great Dismal Swamp Wildlife Refuge. It can sometimes be closed due to drought conditions, but this hasn't been an issue for the past few years. Call the Army Corps of Engineers to confirm canal status before proceeding (757-201-7500, Option 3). The Dismal Swamp Canal Welcome Center (877-771-8333) and the Waterway Explorer (waterwayguide.com) are also good sources of information on the status of the canal.

The Virginia Cut route winds 13 miles to the headwaters of North Landing River, on to Currituck Sound, into Coinjock Bay and then to the town of Coinjock, NC, on the North Carolina Cut. From Coinjock, it follows the North River into Albemarle Sound. The Dismal Swamp route runs 30 miles to the headwaters of North Carolina's Pasquotank River, and then to Elizabeth City and on to the broad expanse of Albemarle Sound.

The two routes rejoin near Mile 79 (after crossing Albemarle Sound) at the mouth of the Alligator River. Side trips east to the river towns of Albemarle Sound or west to visit the Outer Banks are covered in the "Side Trips: The Albemarle Sound & Roanoke Sounds" chapter of this guide.

■ VIRGINIA CUT (ICW) ROUTE

Virginia Cut, the primary ICW route, is well marked and always open for navigation. The Army Corps of Engineers ICW project depth is 12 feet with a channel width of 90 feet. This route begins almost east–west, and then turns north–south. The fresh-to-brackish waters have no tide, but they may rise or fall with the wind. A strong northerly lowers the water, and southerlies can raise it, both by as much as 2 feet, so tie your lines

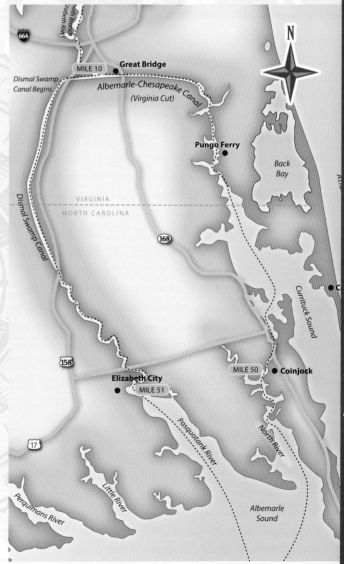

Great Bridge Dock

as if you'll have that much tide. Suffice it to say that no matter how well you plan, you will be delayed by bridges and locks along this section, and it will take longer than you planned or thought. It is just a fact of life along this stretch. Relax and enjoy the journey.

NAVIGATION: Use NOAA Chart 12206. The **I-64 Hwy. Bridge** at Mile 7.1 has a 65-foot closed vertical clearance. An opening for taller vessels requires 24-hours advance notice. The **Veterans Bridge** at Mile 8.9 has a fixed 95-foot vertical clearance.

   Dockage: Top Rack Marina at Mile 8.8 has very reasonably-priced dockage and fuel and receives high marks for its clean facilities, although it is more of a dry stack facility. They also offer very good fuel prices. The on-site restaurant, The Amber Lantern (757-227-3057), offers fine dining with nice views of the river, and there is a deli (open seasonally) and a ship store on the premises.

Great Bridge Lock–ICW Mile 11.3

The **Great Bridge Lock** is the only lock on this route. The lock raises or lowers boats 2 to 3 feet with little turbulence. Delays can occur at Great Bridge Lock, especially during periods of heavy traffic. Many recreational craft lock through at once when traffic is heavy. If the line is long, late arrivals should not push ahead.

   The lock opens on request, but coordinates with the **Battlefield Blvd. Bridge** (8-foot closed vertical

clearance) just east of the lock, which opens on the hour from 6:00 a.m. to 7:00 p.m., and on request at all other times. The lock is 600 feet long, 72 feet wide and can handle tows up to 530 feet long. Since commercial traffic has first preference in locking through, it is not a good idea to push ahead of a tug, as you will probably have to wait for the vessel once you arrive. Government and commercial vessels have precedence, while fuel barges and vessels transporting hazardous materials are locked through alone. The lockmaster monitors VHF Channel 13 (757-547-3311) and can provide information on the route ahead if needed.

   If the lock cannot accommodate all the boats waiting, and you are at the back of the line, prepare for a delay. There is room to maneuver or anchor as you wait on the west end of the lock. On the west side of the bridge, on the south side of the canal, is a face dock where you can tie up to wait. Note that this dock is between the bridge and the lock. It is a good spot from which to visit Great Bridge, and 24-hour dockage is allowed.

   If you are northbound and waiting at the east end of the lock and bridge, you will find a face dock

Note: Anyone who gets off the boat at Great Bridge Lock is required to wear a **personal flotation device**.

on the north bank that holds half a dozen boats and allows 24-hour dockage. This is the Great Bridge Battlefield and Waterways Park and Visitors Center (gbbattlefield.org). Keep the radio on VHF Channel 13, as the lockmaster may wish to contact you. There is another free dock on the opposite side of the bridge on the opposite shore.

Vessels tied to the face docks on either side of the bridge should be prepared for possible commercial traffic and a rise and fall in the water level from the displacement effect of these vessels. It is not a good idea to leave your boat unattended at these docks. There are no facilities, except trash receptacles at the west docks. Both docks are within easy walking distance of stores and restaurants but be aware that vehicular traffic is always heavy on the road here.

A speed limit of 3 mph (actively enforced by the Virginia Marine Police) applies on the waterway until you are past the lock and bridge. It is a good idea to continue at that speed until you are well past the long face dock at the yacht basin on the south bank, east of the bridge. If you think you are about to miss the opening of the lock and bridge, do not speed. The bridgetender can delay the opening for 10 minutes if notified ahead of time on VHF Channel 13. Otherwise, the canal has no speed limit, but the standard rule applies here as elsewhere: You are liable for damage caused by your wake. If yours is a big boat, remember to allow for the "canal effect," a tendency of the stern to swing in toward the bank in narrow waters.

Atlantic Yacht Basin offers a free ice advisory service for mariners traveling during the weather months. Call 757-482-2141 for information about ice conditions along the upper freshwater stretches of either the Virginia Cut or Dismal Swamp routes.

NAVIGATION: Use NOAA Chart 12206. As you approach the lock, you will see either a red or a green signal light. Call the lockmaster on VHF Channel 13 to request an opening, but do not approach closer than 300 feet until the light turns green. Should your VHF call go unanswered, the horn signal for opening is two long and two short blasts. Even in cases where boats are already in line ahead of you for an opening, you should call the lockmaster and give him your boat name so that he knows how many boats are ready to lock through. If there are a lot of boats, he will direct who goes where on the lock walls.

Tannins Explained

The amber-colored water of the Dismal Swamp is preserved by tannins from the bark of the juniper, gum and cypress trees, which prohibit the growth of bacteria. Before the days of refrigeration, water from the Swamp was a highly prized commodity on sailing ships. It was stored in kegs and stayed fresh for extended periods. Some folks believed in the magical qualities of the tea-colored water, which was believed to prevent illness and promote long life if consumed on a regular basis. Since incoming tides bring clear ocean water inland through inlets, and outgoing tides pull the brown water from inland canals out, the "schedule" of the tannin-tinged water naturally varies with the tides. It can be the color of tea or as dark as strong coffee. Tannins are also responsible for the trademark brown "mustache" that many ICW boats sport on their bow. If you are looking to remove your "boat mustache," try lemon juice if you don't have access to common hull cleaner sold in marine supply stores.

Virginia Cut, VA

Largest Vessel Accommodated
VHF Channel Monitored
Transient Berths / Total Berths
Approach / Dockside Depth (reported)
Floating Docks
Gas / Diesel
Groceries, Ice, Marine Supplies, Snacks
Repairs: Hull, Engine, Propeller
Lift (tonnage), Crane, Rail
Laundry, Pool, Showers, Courtesy Car
Min/Max Amps
Pump-Out Station
Nearby: Grocery Store, Motel, Restaurant

GREAT BRIDGE			Dockage					Supplies		Services				
1. Top Rack Marina 🖵 WiFi 8.8	757-227-3041	75	16	10/22	20/12	F	GD	IMS	HE	–	30/50	S	P	GR
2. Atlantic Yacht Basin, Inc. 🖵 onSpot 12.2	757-482-2141	120	16/68	100/200	12/10	–	GD	IMS	HEP	L60,C30,R99	30/100	LS	P	GMR
3. Centerville Waterway Marina WiFi 15.2	757-547-4498	34	13	6/32	12/5	–	GD	IMS	EP	L	30/50	LS	P	GMR

🖵 Internet Access WiFi Wireless Internet Access WG Waterway Guide Cruising Club Partner onSpot dockside WiFi facility
See WaterwayGuide.com for current rates, fuel prices, web site addresses, and other up-to-the-minute information. *(Information in the table is provided by the facilities.)*

Enter at idle speed with bow and stern lines and fenders ready to moor as directed by the lockmaster. If there are only a few boats to pass through, you will be directed to the north or (more likely) the south side of the lock. The rubber fender system on the south side of the Great Bridge Lock is excellent, which is why the lockmasters are now requesting that all recreational craft choose that side. There are cleats and bollards to loops lines around, but there are no lock attendants to help on this side.

When there is an overload of recreational vessels, some will be asked to use the lock's north side. In this case, lock attendants will usually assist in getting your lines looped around the bollards. Be aware that you will definitely need your own fenders and long dock lines when on the steel and concrete of the north side. Also, be prepared to tend your lines during the locking process, especially the stern lines as the stern may want to swing toward the center of the lock as the water level adjusts.

Vessels traveling northbound from Great Bridge Lock will usually be required to group together for the Gilmerton Bridge opening north of the lock.

Great Bridge to North Landing River– ICW Mile 12 to Mile 20

In Great Bridge, you will find the Chesapeake City Hall and other municipal buildings. Stores, numerous restaurants, shopping centers, banks, a library and a liquor store are all within a short walk of the ICW. Buses run to downtown Norfolk, and a taxi ride to Norfolk International Airport takes around 30 minutes.

The Great Bridge Battlefield & Waterways Park pays tribute to the Battle of Great Bridge in 1775 and includes a large stone monument (visible from the ICW) commemorating the Patriot soldiers who fought and died here. A new Visitor Center and Museum is in the planning stages. See details at gbbattlefield.org.

NAVIGATION: Use NOAA Chart 12206. The **Chesapeake Expressway (VA 168 Bypass) Bridge** (65-foot fixed vertical clearance) crosses the channel at Mile 13.0. The **Albemarle & Chesapeake Railroad Lift Bridge** (7-foot closed vertical clearance) at Mile 13.9 is usually open unless a train is approaching. The **Centerville Turnpike (VA 170) Swing Bridge** (4-foot closed vertical clearance) at Mile 15.2 opens on signal from 6:30 a.m. until 8:30 a.m. and between 4:00 p.m. and 6:00 p.m., Monday through Friday (except federal holidays), from 8:30 a.m. to 4:00 p.m. the draw need only open on the hour and half-hour. The drawtender may delay the opening by up to 10 minutes to accommodate approaching vessels. Call on VHF Channel 13 to announce your intentions.

The **North Landing Swing Bridge** (SR 165) at Mile 20.2 has 6-foot closed vertical clearance and opens on signal, except from 6:00 a.m. to 7:00 p.m., when the draw need only open on the hour and half-hour. The 5-mile distance between the Centerville and North Landing Bridges is slightly beyond the speed of most sailboats or slower trawlers to make neatly synchronized openings, so you might as well take your time.

⚠ At times of low water, use caution in the areas on either side of the Centerville and North Landing swing bridges. Stakes mark the outer limits of stumps, which go almost halfway across on the west side but not as far on the east. Occasionally, stumps are unseen, unmarked and uncharted, posing a constant threat to vessels. In 2019 the North Landing Swing Bridge had numerous closures due to mechanical and electrical problems. You may want to call the bridge ahead of time at 575-482-3081 to check if it is operational.

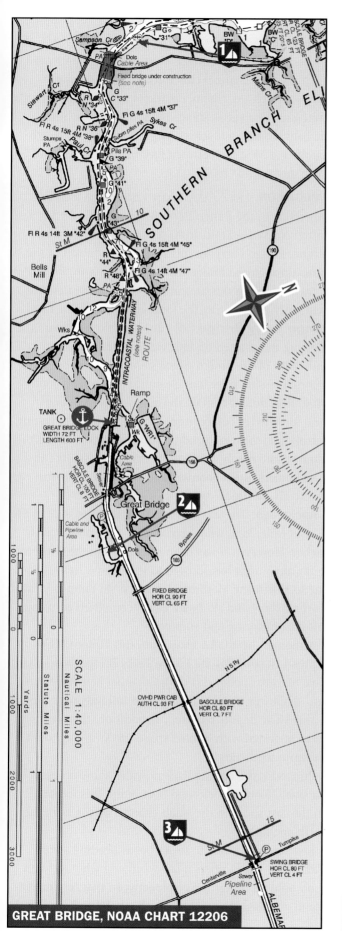

GREAT BRIDGE, NOAA CHART 12206

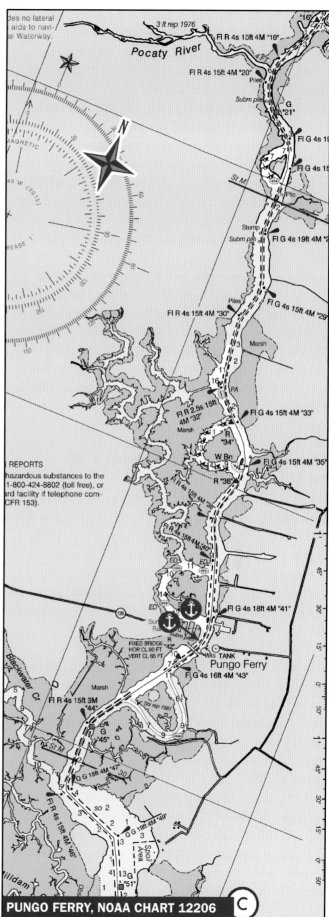

PUNGO FERRY, NOAA CHART 12206 Ⓒ

The first marker north of the North Landing Swing Bridge is flashing green "1," beginning the numbering system from Great Bridge to the Alligator River entrance.

Dockage: Just east of the Great Bridge Bascule Bridge, Atlantic Yacht Basin, Inc. is a full-service boatyard with a well-stocked marine store. This facility's long dock is along the canal (be aware of your wake in this area), and a large protected work and storage basin is behind the wharf. If the courtesy car is not available, both local supermarkets may give you and your groceries a lift to the boatyard but check with the cashier before you start shopping. There are many restaurants within a short walk from the marina, and the town of Chesapeake is very visitor friendly.

On the northwest side of the Centerville Turnpike Swing Bridge is the Centerville Waterway Marina. They sell marine supplies and all fuels, provide engine and propeller repairs and offer canvas repair. The CITGO station (208 Battlefield Blvd.), two blocks south of the ICW, refills propane. Near that same intersection, you will find the Great Bridge Shopping Center, which includes a very nice grocery, a pharmacy and other specialty shops.

North Landing River–ICW Mile 20 to Mile 41

About 8 miles beyond Great Bridge, the heavily wooded and sparsely populated land-cut stretch makes into the headwaters of North Landing River. From here to the Pungo Ferry Bridge, you will notice side sloughs and bypassed bends of the river, which look like secluded anchorages. Do not be tempted! All these old river loops are either silted in or may have spoil banks, submerged pilings or wrecks across them.

The poles and lines seen along the sides of the channel are catfish lines. Watch for snags and flotsam and stay to mid-channel. Over the years, wakes have eroded the banks, leaving wide shallows off the channel with stumps just below the surface. What looks like a small limb might actually be attached to a tree trunk suspended just below the surface; give any suspect debris a wide berth.

Along the Virginia Cut, recreational boat traffic increases significantly during the transient seasons in fall and spring. The cut is narrow in some areas, making it almost impossible for three vessels to pass through at once. Be mindful of other vessels and not just your own schedule. Wakes are especially dangerous in narrow channels. Barges and tugs use the cut and often travel at night.

The North Landing River winds leisurely southward, and a dredged channel cuts through its widening waters. Watch the channel markers in the lower Virginia stretch of the river as shoals tend to encroach from the banks. The route leaves Virginia and enters North Carolina at Mile 34, between flashing green "61" and green daybeacon "63."

NAVIGATION: Use NOAA Chart 12206. The area on either side of the Pungo Ferry Bridge at Mile 28.3 is a posted No-Wake Zone, from the location of the now-defunct Pungo Ferry Marina immediately north of the spans through the bridge fenders to the south. Be sure to travel through this area at idle speed. Note that it is frequently patrolled by the local authorities. The fixed **Pungo Ferry Bridge** (SR 726) has two tide boards, showing the charted 65-foot vertical clearance, on both sides of the bridge. Some sailboats, however, have reported less than 64-foot clearance here after a south wind. If in doubt, contact the authorities or obtain local knowledge before proceeding. (We suggest hailing northbound vessels for tide board readings.) During the summer, the beach north of the bridge is usually full of swimmers, knee-boarders and swarms of personal watercraft, so proceed slowly.

Anchorage: There is an oxbow on the west side of the ICW at Mile 28.5, where boats have been observed to anchor. However, it has been reported that the entrance to the anchorage has shoaled to less than 4 feet MLW due to Hurricane Matthew. A charted ski ramp is located on the oxbow and ski boats have been observed using this area in spring and summer.

Although the NOAA chart indicates 10-foot MLW depths just south of the Pungo Ferry Bridge, boats that have tried to anchor out of the channel here have run into shallower water and very poor holding, with around 5-foot MLW depths reported. In addition, this area is very congested with limited space (no swinging room) on warm weekends.

Pungo Ferry Landing Park provides shore access via small floating docks and boat ramp. It is located on the east shore in the small channel across from the north anchorage.

Just south of Mile 30, to starboard heading south, Blackwater Creek offers a fair-weather anchorage with good holding. Enter the creek between that tiny marsh island and flashing red "46." A shoal of 4 to 5 feet MLW has been reported at the entrance. The charted point shown on the north side at the entrance is usually under water with just a couple of tuffs of grass showing. Favor the southern bank on entering. If you can navigate it, you should find 6- to 10-foot MLW depths once inside and up the creek. Local outboard-powered boats rushing up and down the creek on weekends may bother you. Winds from the north quadrant can blow the water out of this spot and leave vessels firmly aground. There is little swinging room for boats longer than 35 feet.

Currituck Sound–ICW Mile 42 to Mile 49

This stretch is generally placid, but Currituck Sound can develop an unpleasant chop. There is little tide, but strong winds can affect water levels and create stiff currents. Government snag-boats check the cuts periodically, but, as always, look out for floating debris.

NAVIGATION: Use NOAA Chart 12206. Once in Currituck Sound, observe intermediate daybeacons carefully. A hedge of submerged pilings on the east side protects the narrow dredged channel, and a beam wind from the west can push you right up on them. These may be closer to the marked channel than indicated by the NOAA chart. This stretch is subject to shoaling. It is important to stay in the center of the channel and to check astern, as well as ahead, to track your progress. The centerline channel is charted to carry 12 feet. Prolonged strong northerly winds will lower the depths here by as much as 2 or 3 feet, but tugs and barges drawing more than 9 or 10 feet regularly transit this sound with few problems.

Between flashing green "79" near Mackay Island to red daybeacon "122" at Piney Island, the lowest depth observed was 11 feet. The most recent NOAA chart shows marker "91" (Mile 40) as a daybeacon, but it is actually a small can. Most of the way it ranges between 12 and 13 feet MLW. Also in the area, be alert for the ferry from Currituck, which crosses the ICW on its route to Knotts Island. Next to flashing green "111," there is a warning daybeacon with a white diamond-shaped daybeacon reading "Danger: Shoal." Locals report that this is only one area of persistent shoaling from the east (green) side of the ICW in the south end of Currituck Sound. The narrowest and most difficult part of this

stretch is between flashing green "111" and flashing red "118." Wind-driven current will also try to push you out of the channel throughout Currituck Sound.

Coinjock to Albemarle Sound– ICW Mile 49 to Mile 65

About 1 mile south of shallow Coinjock Bay, the quiet hamlet of Coinjock, at Mile Marker 50, announces itself with an array of marine facilities that cater to transients. Centered on a particularly lonely stretch of the ICW, the conveniences here are welcome for those in need of a secure place to rest, plug in, take on reasonably priced fuel and restore basic supplies. Coinjock, named by the Indians for the berries still growing in the area, includes a hardware store, barbershop and Post Office.

NAVIGATION: Use NOAA Chart 12206. Watch for submerged logs or stumps in the channel in the stretch of Coinjock Bay between Long Point and the entrance to the North Carolina Cut, especially in the narrow cut at Long Point. Shoaling has been reported to be

North Carolina Cut, NC

COINJOCK			Dockage				Supplies		Services				
	VHF Channel Monitored	Largest Vessel Accommodated	Approach / Dockside Depth (reported)	Transient Berths / Total Berths	Floating Docks	Gas / Diesel	Groceries, Ice, Marine Supplies, Snacks	Repairs: Hull, Engine, Propeller	Lift (tonnage), Crane, Rail	Laundry, Pool, Showers, Courtesy Car	Min/Max Amps	Pump-Out Station	Nearby: Grocery Store, Motel, Restaurant
1. Midway Marina & Motel ▢ (WiFi) 49	252-453-3625	220	16/09	40/40	14/9	–	GD	IMS	EP	–	30/50	LPS	P	MR
2. Coinjock Marina & Restaurant ▢ (WiFi) 50	252-453-3271	150	16/68	24/24	12/12	–	GD	GIMS	EP	–	30/100	LS	P	GMR

▢ Internet Access (WiFi) Wireless Internet Access (WG) Waterway Guide Cruising Club Partner ⏺onSpot dockside WiFi facility
See WaterwayGuide.com for current rates, fuel prices, web site addresses, and other up-to-the-minute information. *(Information in the table is provided by the facilities.)*

3 feet MLW at green "111," so favor the red side of the channel. Vessels regularly report obstructions in the vicinity of flashing red "116" at Long Point. The boat ramp on the east side of the North Carolina Cut can be very busy on weekends. At Mile 49.9, just south of the marinas, you pass beneath the **Coinjock (U.S. 158) Bridge**, a high-level fixed span with a 65-foot vertical clearance. Note that Coinjock is a state-posted and enforced No-Wake Zone.

Check the current before tying up at any of the marinas in Coinjock. Although there is no tidal rise and fall here, the current is wind-driven and can be strong. The wind funnels up and down the cut, and the strongest current will be with northerly or southerly winds. If it is calm, consider the most recent period of strong wind in trying to determine the strength and direction of the current. If northbound, check the current flow against the bridge; if southbound, start checking at the first pilings you come to in the cut or at flashing green "123." Also don't to check the current before untying from one of the docks after a stay. It may be different than when you docked and can possibly cause just as much trouble when you leave as it did when you arrived.

Heavy fog can be an occasional problem in the morning, especially in the fall, although it usually burns off by 9:00 a.m. The route from Coinjock through the upper North River follows a winding but well-marked channel. Be sure to stay in the center of the narrow dredged stretch between flashing red "128" and red daybeacon "132," as it is very shallow outside the channel. Groundings occur here frequently. Heading south, the river becomes wider and deeper, finally reaching Camden Point and the approach to Albemarle Sound. Fish stakes extend from Buck Island southward to flashing green "155."

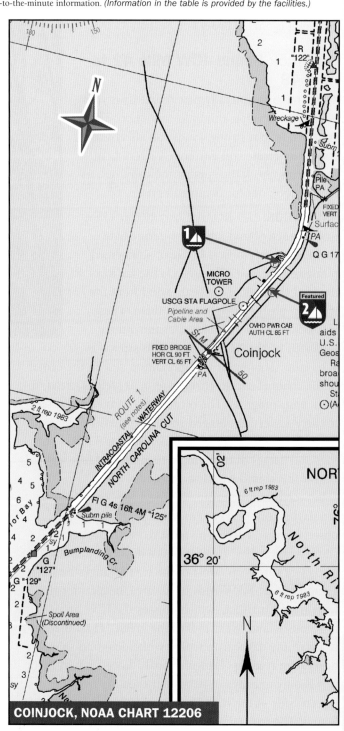

COINJOCK, NOAA CHART 12206

North River

Coinjock

COINJOCK MARINA
& RESTAURANT

There are shoals encroaching the channel between green daybeacon "169" and green daybeacon "171" (Mile 65) at Camden Point on the red side of the channel. Numerous groundings have occurred where the NOAA chart shows 3-foot depths on the outside edge of the dredged channel. Note that green daybeacon "169" is difficult to see when approaching it from the south.

Dockage: Two popular marinas–Midway Marina & Motel and Coinjock Marina & Restaurant–are situated along the cut within a stone's throw across from one another. On the western side of the cut, the Midway Marina & Motel is the first facility encountered on the way south. Portions of the marina were purchased by Coinjock Marina in 2019, which plans to refurbish the docks and implement a ferry service between the two marinas.

Coinjock Marina has a popular restaurant (252-453-3271) on the premises with an outdoor deck where you can dine with waterfront views. The marina's wide 1,000-foot-long dock provides quiet, secure dockage with all the expected amenities, including a modern bathhouse and laundry. Fuel and pump-out service are available and mechanics are on call. They also have a

well-stocked convenience store. Fuel prices here are always competitive.

Because marine facilities and secure berths are scarce along this stretch of the ICW, both marinas fill up rapidly during the fall and spring transient seasons. Be prepared to be tightly packed in bow to stern and during busy times, you may be asked to let a boat tie up alongside. Making an advance call for reservations by phone or on VHF Channel 16 is advised.

Anchorage: Several North River anchorages offer good holding and reasonable protection, depending on wind direction. Immediately north of Buck Island, due east of quick flashing green "153" (around Mile 56.5), there is good shelter during a southerly blow with 7- to 8- foot MLW depths with good holding in mud, although boats drawing more than 5 feet should check the NOAA chart carefully to avoid shallower areas north of the anchorage area. Southeast of Buck Island, there is ample anchorage room in 7- to 9-foot MLW depths with good holding in mud and good protection from the east and northeast.

Due west of quick flashing red "164" (Mile 61), Broad Creek affords excellent protection in virtually all conditions and carries 7-foot MLW depths. Once beyond the mouth of the creek, however, boats drawing more than 5 feet should proceed slowly with an eye on the depth sounder, as there have been reports of an uncharted shallow spot. In westerly winds, it is possible to comfortably anchor off the mouth of Broad Creek if it is crowded, or if you are too deep-drafted or large to go all the way in.

■ DISMAL SWAMP CANAL ROUTE

Back north, the Dismal Swamp route heads off west of the ICW, just south of the I-64 Hwy. Bascule Bridge (65-foot closed vertical clearance) at Mile 7.1. The Deep Creek land cut leads to Deep Creek itself and the Deep Creek Lock, which introduces you to the Great Dismal Swamp Canal. The distance is approximately 51 miles from Norfolk to Elizabeth City, but the distance does not have to be covered in one day.

Birds, reptiles, winged insects and bears inhabit this unique primeval forest. (Use screens and cover up before entering the canal during the summer months.) In 1763, George Washington first proposed draining the swamp, harvesting the timber (cypress for shipbuilding and cedar for shingles) and then farming the land. He and other prominent businessmen purchased 40,000 acres of swampland. Washington first supervised the digging for the ditch from the swamp to Lake Drummond, today known as Washington Ditch. Disenchanted with the business venture, Washington tried to sell his interest in the land to "Lighthorse" Harry Lee, father of Robert E. Lee, 30 years later. However, when it came time to close the deal, Lighthorse Harry was a little light on cash and Washington wound up keeping the land and passing it on to his heirs.

In 1909, a lumbering company purchased the swamp and continued to harvest virgin timber until they cut the last tree down in the 1950s. In 1973, the Union Camp Company donated its swamp holding to create the Great Dismal Swamp National Wildlife Refuge.

Today, recreational boaters cruise past a number of historical sites on the Dismal Swamp Canal. The Dismal Swamp Welcome Center, Dismal Swamp State Park and Dismal Swamp Canal are all recognized with the distinction as being a designated site on the National Park Service National Underground Railroad Network to Freedom.

Boats today follow the same course as James Adams' Floating Theatre, which inspired Edna Ferber to write "Showboat." It is a beautiful, unspoiled waterway and one of the prettiest on the whole ICW, while also offering the considerable benefit of being easier to transit compared to the narrow, busy, and frequently wind-driven Virginia Cut.

Welcome to North Carolina!

You are now in NC waters. Here you will encounter small towns, quiet anchorages and the first of the shoal spots on the ICW. The waters off Cape Hatteras are known as the "Graveyard of the Atlantic" due to the deceptively shallow water offshore here. Cape Lookout and Cape Fear to the south are delightful ports that—like the rest of the Outer Banks—are best visited from the protected inside (ICW) route with its combination of rivers, canals, bays and sounds.

Weather is a critical consideration. The best time to cruise through NC is spring and fall, and you'll have plenty of company. Hurricane season is June 1 through November 30 with a peak from early August through the end of October. Since 1851, a total of 47 hurricanes have made direct hits in the NC coast. As always, be aware of the weather around (and ahead of) you.

Important Note: It is an NC requirement that the owner or operator of a vessel that has a Marine Sanitation Device (MSD) and is in coastal waters that are either designated as a no-discharge zone or are included in a petition to the U.S. EPA to be designated as a no-discharge zone, must maintain a record of each pump-out of the MSD and the location of the pump-out facility. At press time in 2018, the no-discharge zone begins at New River Inlet and extends to the SC border. It includes the ICW and adjacent and offshore waters. See details at deq.nc.gov.

Dismal Swamp Canal

Great Dismal Swamp Canal, VA, NC

DISMAL SWAMP ROUTE		Dockage					Supplies		Services				
	VHF Channel Monitored	Largest Vessel Accommodated	Approach / Dockside Depth (reported)	Transient Berths / Total Berths	Floating Docks	Gas / Diesel	Groceries, Ice, Marine Supplies, Snacks	Repairs: Hull, Engine, Propeller	Lift (tonnage), Crane, Rail	Min/Max Amps	Pump-Out Station	Nearby: Grocery Store, Motel, Restaurant	Laundry, Pool, Showers, Courtesy Car
1. Chesapeake Yachts Inc. 8.3	757-487-9100	200	16	10/10	16/8	F	GD	M	HEP	L70,C	30/30	–	–	GMR
2. Dismal Swamp Canal Welcome Center 🖥 WiFi WG 28 252-771-8333		100	–	–	6/6	–		S						

🖥 Internet Access WiFi Wireless Internet Access WG Waterway Guide Cruising Club Partner ⊂onSpot dockside WiFi facility

See WaterwayGuide.com for current rates, fuel prices, web site addresses, and other up-to-the-minute information. *(Information in the table is provided by the facilities.)*

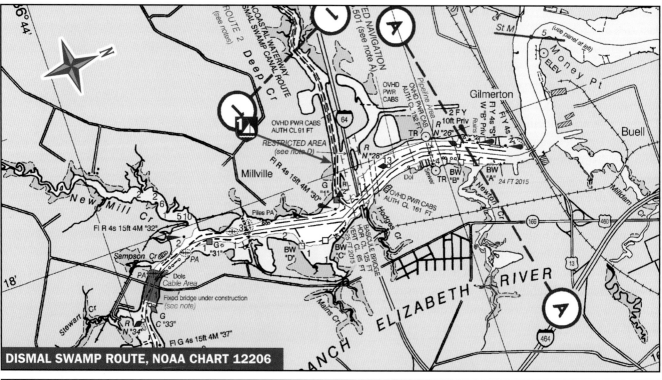

DISMAL SWAMP ROUTE, NOAA CHART 12206

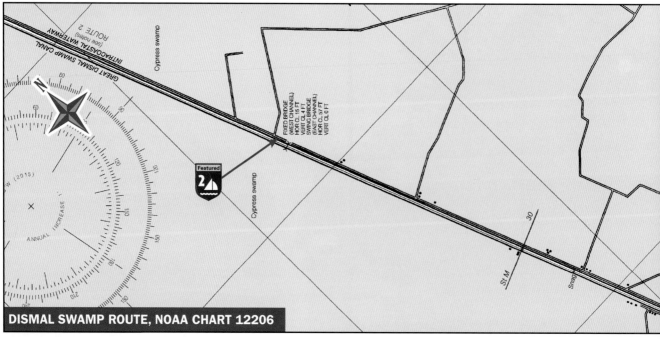

DISMAL SWAMP ROUTE, NOAA CHART 12206

As a rule, skippers using this route are more interested in seeing the magnificent countryside than in making fast time. There is no speed limit here, but you are responsible for your wake. "No Wake" signs are posted in the canal proper in a stepped-up effort to reduce the problem of bank erosion. Regardless of restrictions, common sense dictates slow speed through the canal.

For those who choose to decide their route when already underway, the sign at ICW Mile 7.3–just past the 65-foot vertical clearance I-64 Hwy. Bridge and on the west side at the entrance of the Dismal Swamp Canal–states the lock schedule, the controlling depth and whether the canal is open or closed. Information about the status of the Dismal Swamp Canal is also available from the Army Corps of Engineers at 757-201-7500 (option 3) or from the Dismal Swamp Canal Welcome Center (877-771-8333).

Deep Creek to Turner Cut

The 3-mile stretch of Deep Creek leads to the Dismal Swamp Canal itself. The creek is pretty, with wooded banks and small beaches used by local four- and two-legged inhabitants. The **Deep Creek Lock** (Mile 10.5) raises you 8 feet in elevation, while the **South Mills Lock** (at Mile 32.7) lowers you the same amount. At both locks, boats must furnish and tend their own lines. Be sure to have plenty of line and watch your stern, which may want to swing toward the center during the locking process. The canal is fed primarily by freshwater drainage from Lake Drummond and its feeder system.

When the locks are open, the tenders will ask the draft of each vessel and warn those with drafts of more than 6 feet that they may proceed only at their own risk. Tell the tender where you plan to spend the night, so he will know your expected locking needs. The locks at Deep Creek and South Mills open four times daily (unless low water levels cause restricted openings) at 8:30 a.m., 11:00 a.m., 1:30 p.m. and 3:30 p.m. Boats entering the canal are locked first, meaning at Deep Creek Lock, southbound boats are locked first; at the South Mills Lock, northbound boats are locked first. For boats leaving the canal, the lock openings may be delayed while the entering boats are locked through. Prepare to wait before the bridge, in that case.

The lockmasters do double duty as bridgetenders and open the adjacent bridges so you will have to wait for them to drive to the bridge to open it after opening the lock. Vessels are allowed to moor overnight in the canal. If you plan to stay on the bulkhead between the bridge and the lock on either side, it is courteous to notify the lockmaster on VHF Channel 13.

A plaque at Deep Creek tells of a Civil War battle at the quiet and friendly village of South Mills, about 3 miles from the Dismal Swamp Canal Welcome Center. There, Confederate soldiers prevented the Union from blowing up the locks, and thus were able to keep the canal open. Information about this and other Civil War battles is available at the Dismal Swamp Welcome Center.

To run the Dismal Swamp Canal in a single day, a boat traveling 6 knots can enter the **Deep Creek Lock** at either the 8:30 a.m. or 11:00 a.m. openings. The passage from Deep Creek Lock to South Mills Lock is 22 miles long. Once through South Mills Lock, it is only 18 miles to Elizabeth City.

NAVIGATION: Use NOAA Chart 12206. While narrow and unmarked, Deep Creek presents no unusual problems, unless there is an extremely low tide, in which case there may be a little over 5 feet depth. Travel at a reasonable speed and do not be misled by the nice-looking side waters; they are extremely shallow. Keep to the center of the main stream and give points a good berth, as shoaling is chronic.

The Dismal Swamp Canal has 6-foot depths as long as there is adequate water in Lake Drummond. Stay to the middle, as the edges are shoal. This route no longer carries commercial traffic except from below South Mills (Mile 32) to Elizabeth City (Mile 50), so the stretch north of this is not as carefully maintained as it once was. The Army Corps of Engineers, however, regularly cleans the ICW and clips overhanging tree limbs. In 2019 there were numerous reports of dead heads and large logs in the canal, so proceed through this area with extreme caution. Report dead heads or obstructions to lockmasters or the Visitor Center and the Corps will get out and tend to them. If you encounter a maintenance barge, you may have a wait, as there is not always ample room to pass.

Openings at the **Deep Creek (U.S. 17) Bascule Bridge** at Mile 11.1 (4-foot closed vertical clearance) are coordinated with the lock, which opens at 8:30 a.m., 11:00 a.m., 1:30 p.m., and 3:30 p.m. From Deep Creek, the Dismal Swamp Canal reaches south in two arrow-straight stretches. The feeder ditch from Lake Drummond intersects the canal toward the end of the first of these at Mile 21.5.

We received a report of a farmer's bridge at Mile 20.9, which stopped a boat in its tracks in the summer of 2018. The farmer who owns land on both sides of the canal has permission to slide a portable steel bridge back and forth to get his livestock and farm equipment across the canal. This bridge (3 feet above the waterline) is normally only in place long enough for the farmer to accomplish his task. Be patient if the waterway is blocked when you get there. For help with this bridge call the Visitors Center (252-771-8333).

At Mile 21.5, the Lake Drummond feeder ditch intersects the canal. If your schedule allows, you can travel the 3 miles up to Lake Drummond in a boat 16 feet or less and with a draft that is less than 3 feet. At the head of the feeder ditch, there is a free rail trolley for carrying boats less than 1,000 pounds (including dinghies) over a small peninsula into Lake Drummond.

The Army Corps of Engineers has placed small pipe markers, white with a red top, along every mile of the Dismal Swamp Canal, indicating statute mileage from Norfolk. At about Mile 23, there is a sign marking the beginning of a measured nautical mile.

There is a pontoon bridge south of the visitor's dock at the Welcome Center. The **Dismal Swamp Canal Visitors Center Foot Bridge** allows visitors to access the Dismal Swamp State Park on the opposite side of the canal. It is generally kept in place for pedestrians to cross and opened whenever a boat approaches. (Navigation takes precedence over pedestrians.) Call 252-771-6593 or VHF Channel 13, if you should need an opening. If heading south and planning to stop at the visitor's dock, a courtesy call to the bridgetender will prevent an unnecessary opening.

The fixed **U.S. 17 Hwy. Bridge** crosses the Dismal Swamp Canal at Mile 31.5 (65-foot vertical clearance). The South Mills Lock is at Mile 32.7. It also opens at 8:30 a.m., 11:00 a.m., 1:30 p.m., and 3:30 p.m. and coordinates with the **South Mills Bascule Bridge** at Mile 32.6 (4-foot closed vertical clearance). An average of 2,000 recreational boats pass through the South Mills Lock annually.

Dockage: Chesapeake Yachts Inc. located just off the main ICW channel at the northern entrance to the Dismal Swamp route at Mile 8.3, will accept transient visitors at its long floating face dock, but the facility is not set up for extensive catering to transients. They do, however, sell all fuels and offer repairs.

Inside the canal, on the west side in Deep Creek Lock Pond at Mile 10.7, you will find a long, wooden dock south of the locks and north of the bascule bridge with 8-foot depths (except at the far north end). Known locally as "Elizabeth's Dock," this landing is popular with crews wanting to transit the canal the morning after a late-afternoon locking. Restaurants and shopping are nearby.

Between Miles 18 and 19, the parks department maintains Douglas Road Landing, a fixed wharf running alongside the canal for 70 feet and then another 30 feet after a jog, as a part of a hike and bike trail. There are restrooms available. At Mile 21.5, there is a small dock across from the Lake Drummond feeder ditch, across from Arbuckle Landing, which is available to cruising mariners, compliments of the Army Corps of Engineers. Rafting is permitted here.

The Dismal Swamp Canal Welcome Center (Mile 28) offers an 150-foot wharf running parallel to the canal. There are no slips but there is space for about four cruising boats to tie directly to the dock. Additional boats raft up so be prepared to have neighbors. No power or water is available at the dock, but clean restrooms and a water fountain are available. This is a highway rest stop as well as a State Park. The staff monitors VHF Channel 16 or can be reached by phone at 252-771-8333. You will find a friendly atmosphere here, with charcoal grills and picnic tables, bike trails with rental bikes, and a nature trail. Keep an eye out for bears, bobcats, snakes and other such "locals." If you decide to spend the night here, take time to visit the Dismal Swamp State Park Museum. It is a 3-minute walk from the dock and provides an interesting history and facts on the area (and it's air conditioned).

If you continue on through the South Mills Bridge, you may be able to find an overnight spot along the west bulkhead between the lock and the bridge, with about 6-foot MLW depths reported alongside and cleats along the middle third. There is a convenience store just west of the bridge and a family grocery store about 1 mile further west.

Anchorage: The Deep Creek Basin (also known as "Hole-in-the-Wall" and "The Cove") is private and anchoring is no longer allowed here. South of the South Mills Lock, anchoring is possible in 6- to 8-feet MLW depths, off the channel just before Turner Cut (at about Mile 33.4). Do not anchor directly in Turner Cut.

Turner Cut to Pasquotank River

South Mills is the place to check your time and decide whether to lock through or to stay put for the night. It is 18 miles to Elizabeth City, and the winding, narrow, unmarked headwaters of the Pasquotank River are hazardous to run after dark. In the daytime, the tall

Dismal Swamp Canal Welcome Center

cypress and mistletoe-festooned gum trees give the upper Pasquotank a wild and eerie splendor. Here you will see some of the most undisturbed and natural cruising grounds on the entire ICW.

Give tows all the room you can in the narrow, straight area of Turner Cut and in the twisting upper Pasquotank River. When encountering a tow, slow down or stop, hug the bank and allow the tow as much room as possible. Give points a fair berth, especially where Turner Cut enters the Pasquotank River, and watch out for floating debris.

NAVIGATION: Use NOAA Chart 12206. Follow the straight Turners Cut about 3 miles, where it joins the Pasquotank River. About 4 twisty miles farther the river straightens and gradually widens as markers begin to appear. The first, green daybeacon "19," shows up suddenly around a sharp bend near Mile 41.

⚠️ In spring 2019, we received a report of a 10-inch-diameter pylon embedded in the bottom north of green daybeacon "19." Appoximately 1 foot is visible above the water.

Note that you are now going downstream in a river marked from seaward: Keep green to starboard (markers have yellow triangles). Shoaling is a continuing problem between green daybeacons "17" and "15." (Note that green daybeacon "15" is on or near shore, not at the edge of the shoal.)

Farther on at Mile 47.7, the manually operated **Norfolk Southern Railroad Swing Bridge** (3-foot closed vertical clearance) is usually left in the open position. If the bridge is closed, the drawtender will answer to horn signals. The draw is difficult to see until you are almost on top of it.

Anchorage: There are three anchorage possibilities on the Pasquotank River before reaching Elizabeth City. The first, at Mile 43, is behind Goat Island at green daybeacon "13" with good holding in 6- to 10-feet MLW with and room for several boats. There is a small kayak dock nearby where you can land a dinghy. The second anchorage is located in the beautiful deep water Camden Causeway Cove at Mile 48. Depths here are deeper than the 9 feet MLW shown on the NOAA charts. It is, however, open to wakes. The third is along the eastern shore near Mile 49. This area is often used as an alternative to the Elizabeth City town docks when strong east to south winds make those docks uncomfortable.

Elizabeth City: Harbor of Hospitality

One Sunday after church in 1983, two Elizabeth City boating enthusiasts, Fred Fearing and Joe Kramer, decided to host an impromptu wine and cheese party for 17 boaters visiting the recently completed docks at Mariners' Wharf. While Fearing gathered food and drinks for the boaters, Kramer trimmed roses from his garden for the First Mates, thus beginning the "Rose Buddies" tradition. The idea was to welcome the city's growing number of boaters with a sampling of its famous hospitality. That boaters started an ongoing tradition that survives to this day.

As the story goes, the Rose Buddies attracted national attention, leading NBC weatherman Willard Scott to donate a golf cart to help transport the party supplies to the waterfront. Fearing and Kramer were easy to spot, coasting along the docks in the "official" Rose Buddy golf cart, often stopping to greet and chat with incoming boaters. In those days, if there were less than five boats, the party would be held at Fearing's house.

After Kramer's passing, his rose bush was transplanted at Mariners' Wharf Park. Fearing continued the tradition for several more years, well into his 90s. (He passed away in 2007.) The Rose Buddy golf carts have since been retired but the tradition continues. Today, a group of volunteers greet boaters through a program administered by the Convention & Visitors Bureau.

A marker honoring the original buddies was dedicated on the 25th anniversary of their first party.

In keeping with tradition, parties are held if there are at least five boats docked at the waterfront. If there are less than five, Grouper's host the party on its deck, offering a bit of the city's famous "harbor of hospitality."

Pasquotank River, NC

ELIZABETH CITY		Largest Vessel Accommodated	VHF Channel Monitored	Dockage: Transient Berths / Total Berths	Approach / Dockside Depth (reported)	Floating Docks	Supplies: Gas / Diesel	Groceries, Ice, Marine Supplies, Snacks	Services: Repairs: Hull, Engine, Propeller	Lift (tonnage), Crane, Rail	Min/Max Amps	Laundry, Pool, Showers, Courtesy Car	Pump-Out Station	Nearby: Grocery Store, Motel, Restaurant
1. Lambs Marina 🖥 WiFi 47.2	252-207-7302	65	16	4/60	8/8	–	GD	GIS	–	–	30/50	LSC	–	GR
2. Mariners' Wharf, Elizabeth City 🖥 WiFi 50.9	252-335-5330	80	–	14/14	12/15	–	–	–	–	–	–	S	–	GMR
3. Elizabeth City Shipyard 51.2	252-335-0171	50	–	call/50	12/20	–	–	M	HEP	L60	30/50	–	–	–
4. The Pelican Marina 🖥 WiFi 51.2	**252-335-5108**	70	16/68	9/58	10/7	–	call	IMS	–	–	30/50	LS	P	MR

🖥 Internet Access WiFi Wireless Internet Access WG Waterway Guide Cruising Club Partner ◉onSpot dockside WiFi facility
See WaterwayGuide.com for current rates, fuel prices, web site addresses, and other up-to-the-minute information. *(Information in the table is provided by the facilities.)*

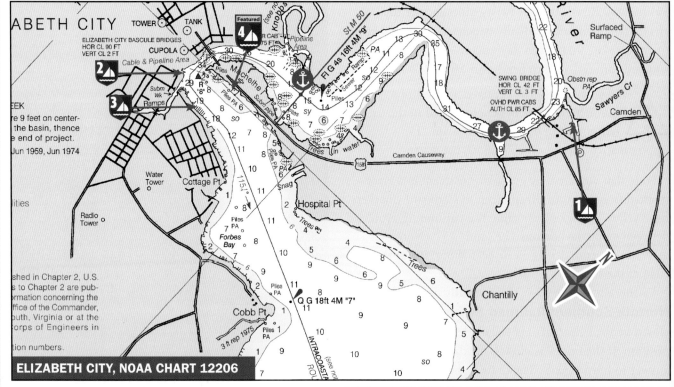

ELIZABETH CITY, NOAA CHART 12206

Elizabeth City, Pasquotank River

From the Dismal Swamp Canal Route, you emerge in Elizabeth City. Here you will find convenient dockage, friendly people and lots to see and do. This is a stop on the Albemarle Loop. (See sidebar.)

NAVIGATION: Use NOAA Chart 12206. The **Elizabeth City (U.S. 158) Bascule Bridge** at Mile 50.7 (2-foot closed vertical clearance) opens on signal, except from 7:00 a.m. to 9:00 a.m. and from 4:00 p.m. to 6:00 p.m., Monday through Friday, when the draw need only open at 7:30 a.m., 8:30 a.m., 4:30 p.m., and 5:30 p.m. if vessels are waiting to pass. Call the bridgetender on VHF Channel 13 once the fast-opening bridge comes into view. The No-Wake Zone along the city is strictly enforced with a 6-mph speed limit.

⚠️ At Elizabeth City you are now going downstream in a river marked from seaward: Keep green to starboard. (River markers have yellow triangles.)

Dockage: Lambs Marina, at Mile 47.2 on the Dismal Swamp Canal north of Elizabeth City, has the only fuel in the area. They also have an on-site convenience store and a café.

Depending on your direction, the town docks in Elizabeth City at Mile 51 mark the beginning or end of your trip through the Dismal Swamp Canal. Elizabeth City is part of the Albemarle Loop and offers 48-hour complimentary dockage at Mariners' Wharf, right in the downtown area. The 14 transient slips are offered

Elizabeth City Waterfront

on a first-come, first-served basis. (See details at albemarleloop.com.) The finger piers between slips are quite short, so backing in provides easier access from a boat. The outer pilings are about 35 feet from the seawall, so larger boats will need to use spring lines to stay off the wall. The slips range from 11 to 18 feet in width, and the clearance for each slip is indicated in white paint on the seawall. You can dispose of your trash ashore, but no water or electrical hookups are available. New comfort facilities, with restrooms and hot showers, as well as free WiFi is available. Bicycles are available on loan from Visit Elizabeth City, located at the nearby Museum of the Albemarle. There is a place to tie dinghies, although there are no attendants. Strong east to south winds can cause an uncomfortable surge at the dock.

If there are more than five boats, you may be treated to a wine and cheese party. (See "Harbor of Hospitality" sidebar.) And if you are lucky, it will be "movie night" and you can catch a classic on the huge outdoor screen from the comfort of your boat slip. Classic American films are shown on at Mariners' Wharf Tuesday evenings in June and July.

West of the city slips and along the Waterfront City Park there is a concrete/steel seawall painted with "No Dockage" signs. East of the city slips there is a short steel seawall dedicated to the U.S. armed services with

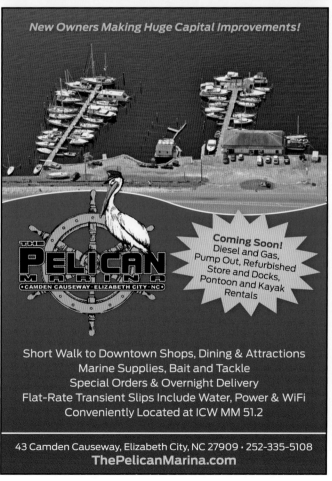

GOIN' ASHORE: **ELIZABETH CITY, NC**

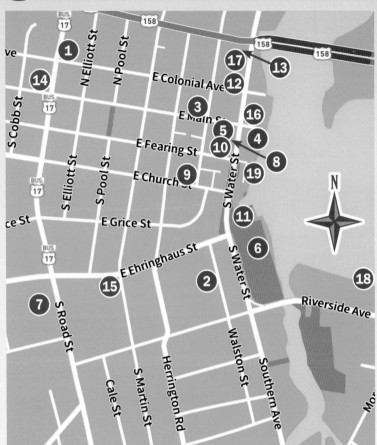

SERVICES	
1	Library
2	Visitor Information
ATTRACTIONS	
2	Museum of the Albemarle
3	Arts of the Albemarle
4	Moth Boat Park
5	Port Discover
6	Waterfront Park
SHOPPING	
7	CVS Pharmacy
8	Page After Page Bookstore
9	Todd's Pharmacy

DINING	
10	Cypress Creek Grill
11	Grouper's Waterfront Restaurant
12	Hoppin' Johnz
13	Island Breeze
14	Muddy Waters
15	Quality Seafood
16	The Flour Girls Café & Bakery
17	Toyoma Japanese Restaurant
MARINA	
18	Elizabeth City Shipyard
19	Mariners' Wharf

Billed the "Harbor of Hospitality," Elizabeth City has long been a favorite stop for sailors going to or coming from the Chesapeake Bay area. Along the docks, you will find roses and impromptu wine parties and new friends. On the docks at the Mariners' Wharf, another participant in the Albemarle Loop, the legacy of the Rose Buddies endures. The harbor here beckons to sailors enjoying life in the slow lane. In fact, you don't even have to leave your boat to enjoy classic American films shown on a large outdoor screen at Mariners' Wharf on Tuesdays during June and July. Shows start at 8:30 p.m.

Attractions: A self-guided walking tour of the waterfront Historic District begins at the Visitors Bureau located in Museum of the Albemarle and includes homes in the Federal, Greek Revival, Neo-Classical Revival and Gothic Revival styles. Grab a map, relax at one of the two waterside parks and plan your tour. There are over 60 historic buildings and sites in the downtown area alone. Near the waterfront you will find a historical marker noting that the Wright Brothers came by rail with their gliders and planes. They hired a local fisherman's sailing vessel to carry them to Kill Devil Hills.

Over 700 artifacts are displayed at the free Museum of the Albemarle (501 S. Water St., 252-335-1453), covering 400 years of local history and telling stories of Native Americans, colonists, farmers and fishermen who settled in the Albemarle region. The Discovery Room features interactive displays. Nearby Port Discover (611 E. Main St., 252-338-6117) is an interactive science center for kids of all ages.

Arts of the Albemarle (516 E. Main St., 252-338-6997) showcases fine art and traditional crafts from both regional and local artists. Performing arts of all kinds are featured in its McGuire Theatre, which has been renovated to rival its original 1895 glory. You can also see local artists offerings every first Friday of the month from 5:00 p.m. to 7:00 p.m. at various locations around downtown.

Moth Boat Park (corner of Water St. and Main St.) pays tribute to the Moth Boat, an 11-foot one-design sailboat that was designed in Elizabeth City. Every September, the Moth Boat Regatta takes over the city's harbor. This boat evolved into the foiling Moth, which is a separate class that sails above the water on hydrofoils. The original Moth dinghy class is still raced here.

On South Water St., Waterfront Pavilion is perfect for a picnic or potluck. The pavilion was built as a memorial to the old Albemarle

Hospital and College of the Albemarle; the dome roof was part of the old entrance and was saved from demolition to come to roost here.

Coast Guard Air Station Elizabeth City is home to one of the largest and most diverse Coast Guard command centers in the nation. You will see the large installation, just south of town on the west bank of the river.

Shopping: Page After Page Bookstore at 111 S. Water St. (252-335-7243) carries a great selection of North Carolina books, including nautical titles, plus art supplies, gifts, toys and stationery.

Todd's Pharmacy at 207 S. Poindexter St. (252-335-2901) is convenient to Mariners' Wharf, but should you need something more, there's a CVS Pharmacy about four blocks from the waterfront at 101 W. Ehringhaus St. (252-338-5077) Close by there at 300 W. Ehringhaus St. is Colonial Cleaners & Laundromat (252-335-2797).

For provisions, there are two grocery stores within a few miles of the waterfront: Soho Organic Market (406 S. Griffin St.) with specialty foods, spices, beer, and wine, and Food Lion (1515 W. Ehringhaus St.). You will need transportation. You may also find what you want, however, at the downtown waterfront market, held on Saturdays from 9:00 a.m. to 1:00 p.m. from May through October.

Dining: Elizabeth City provides a number of outstanding dining opportunities. For breakfast, lunch or dessert, try The Flour Girls Café & Bakery at 102 N. Water St. (252-331-2230). Muddy Waters Coffee House at 100 W. Main St. (252-338-2739) is another great spot for breakfast and coffee or tea. (The Flour Girls also sell ice cream.)

The Cypress Creek Grill at 113 S. Water St. (252-334-9915) is a good choice for lunch or dinner with great water views, as is Hoppin Johnz at 606 E. Colonial Ave. (252-679-7716). Island Breeze at 220 N. Poindexter St. (252-338-0048) offers wonderful Caribbean food with a great lunch buffet. Grouper's Waterfront Restaurant (400 S. Water St., 252-331-2431) is only steps away from Mariners' Wharf and has a deck overlooking the river. Quality Seafood Market (309 E. Ehringhaus St., 252-335-7648) serves the freshest seafood in town. Toyama Japanese Restaurant (218 Poindexter St., 215-338-2437) is known for its Asian fare and sushi.

The Albemarle Loop

The Albemarle Loop provides an opportunity to cruise and explore the protected waters of the historic Albemarle Sound. Each of the participating marinas offers at least 48 hours of free slip rental fees, fresh water and pump-out service (where available), as well as use of all amenities, such as restaurants, tennis courts and swimming pools.

To qualify for these special promotions, present the coupon from the Albemarle Loop website (albemarleloop.com) or printed brochure. (You will need to print the coupons for the slips prior to arrival.) You are invited to visit the participating marinas once per season (or more if approved by the marina dockmaster). Participating facilities are:

- Albemarle Plantation Marina (Hertford)
- Columbia Municipal Marina
- Yacht Doc @ Cypress Cove (Columbia)
- Edenton Harbor
- Elizabeth City Mariners' Wharf
- Hertford Bay Marina
- The 51 House @ Wharf Landing (Edenton)
- The Pelican Marina (Elizabeth City)
- Plymouth Landing Marina

Several marinas support the Albemarle Loop Passport program by allowing boaters to accrue points when visiting. However, unless there is a special program available at the time of your visit, slip fees are at the discretion of the marina. Participating facilities are:

- Alligator River Marina
- Dismal Swamp Visitors Center
- Shallowbag Bay Marina (Manteo)
- Waterside Marina (Norfolk)

Please note that while this list was accurate at press time in summer 2019, participating marinas may change. Visit albemarleloop.com for the most up-to-date list.

the flags of every branch of service flying. Boats docking here will need sufficient fenders for the steel bulkhead. The adjacent Elizabeth City Shipyard offers repairs and has a 60-ton lift.

The Pelican Marina, on the eastern side of the Pasquotank, south of the bascule bridge, is also a participating marina in the Albemarle Loop (albemarleloop.com) and offers transient slips and sells bait and tackle as well as marine supplies. The marina was completely renovated in 2018. It is only a short walk or dinghy ride from the marina to downtown.

■ NEXT STOP

Depending on the route, you will find yourself approaching Albemarle Sound either from Elizabeth City or Coinjock. Once in the Sound, cruisers may choose to venture west for the Albemarle Loop or east to the Outer Banks; consult Chapter 3, "Side Trip: The Albemarle & Roanoke Sounds, NC." Boaters with a schedule to keep can continue south on the ICW; see Chapter 4, "Albemarle Sound to the Neuse River, NC." Fast boats may wish to take the Croatan Sound route south and rejoin the waterway at the Neuse River; for this, refer to Chapter 5, "Side Trip: The Pamlico Sound & Outer Banks, NC." This route will save you 18 miles, but you not only have exposed waters in the Croatan Sound but also very open, exposed waters in the Pamlico Sound. Pick your weather carefully.

The Albemarle and Pamlico Sounds, along with their big rivers, which at times almost become sounds in themselves, are convenient to the ICW and offer isolated side waters and out-of-the-way waterside communities. The major rivers are moderately deep, largely unobstructed, and adequately marked. Some side waters have naturally deep entrances, hold their depths until near the head, and are full of unexpected tranquil anchorages and untouched landscapes. Boating facilities are largely well-priced and welcoming of cruising families.

Side Trip: The Albemarle & Roanoke Sounds, NC

 ICW Mile 50–Mile 80   **(VHF)** NC Bridges: Channel 13

CHARTS NOAA 11548, 11553, 11555, 12204, 12205

The Albemarle Sound covers 50 miles, east to west, from Kitty Hawk on the Outer Banks to Edenton at the mouth of the Chowan River. An east or west wind can stir the relatively shallow waters of Albemarle Sound into a short, nasty chop, making conditions uncomfortable and sometimes dangerous. Many a prudent skipper has holed up on either side of Albemarle Sound for days, waiting for the weather and seas to calm down before making the crossing. Albemarle Sound compensates by offering some picturesque and peaceful cruising waters in the tributaries along its banks. Several of these are deep and easy to enter, with many good anchorages.

Originally an instrumental route for the East Coast's first English settlers, and still a popular destination for water lovers of all varieties, the Roanoke Sound separates the central Outer Banks from Roanoke Island. On the western side of the sound lies the towns of Manteo and Wanchese, which can be accessed by the Washington Baum Bridge, (better known as the Manteo/Nags Head

Causeway or vice versa), which stretches across the Roanoke Sound. Because Roanoke Island is bordered by two sounds–the Croatan Sound, which separates it from the mainland, and the Roanoke Sound, which separates it from the beaches–the little waterfront community is surrounded by water.

■ ALBEMARLE SOUND

Pasquotank River to Little River

About 8 miles west of the Pasquotank River Entrance Light flashing green "1PR" (or 14 miles from flashing green "173" at the North River), off the north side of Albemarle Sound, you will find the entrance to Little River. The abundance of good anchorages makes Little River a natural place where groups of boaters can rendezvous.

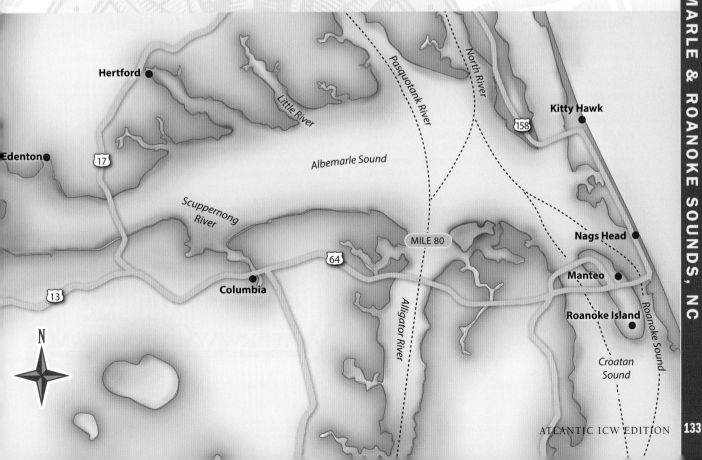

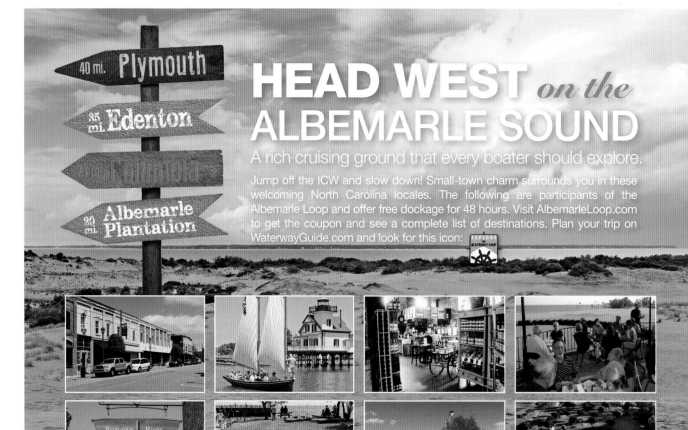

NAVIGATION: Use NOAA Chart 12205. Little River is easy to enter. The entrance is marked by green daybeacon "1L," and there is a platform to its northwest. Use your NOAA chart and depth sounder and, as usual in these waters, watch carefully for fish stakes. Depths in the river run 8 to 10 feet, but be wary of the shoals that extend from Mill and Stevenson Points at the entrance. The remainder of the river is unmarked.

Anchorage: On the way from Elizabeth City to Little River you will pass Wharf Bay on the east shore at Mile 64. This anchorage offers 8 to 11 feet MLW with good holding and some protection from the north and east. The river's mouth is spacious, with fair holding in hard mud, and makes a good stop when winds are from the east or west. You will be accompanied by a lot of crab pots and the friendly crabbers who stop by to check them.

Depths are suitable for anchoring in the coves upriver, and the scenery is lovely for those who don't mind the long trip to the upper reaches. Because of the long fetch, anchorages could be choppy in a strong southeast wind, especially near the mouth of the river. The NOAA chart indicates a hard bottom in some places, so make sure

your anchor is set well. Once firmly set, the boat will be secure in even a strong blow. There may be crab pots in the area, so be careful of your swing.

Hertford, Perquimans River

Four miles to the west of green daybeacon "1L," at the mouth of Little River, lies the Perquimans River. Boats that can clear the **U.S. 17–NC 37 Twin Bridges** (33-foot fixed vertical clearances) at Ferry and Crow Points will find Hertford, a true river town well worth visiting.

A port of entry as early as 1701, Hertford's records go back to a 1685 deed book. You can visit the restored Newbold-White House, said to be one of North Carolina's oldest brick houses. The local Chamber of Commerce sponsors a walking tour of historical sites, including the Jim "Catfish" Hunter museum, named for the famed Major League Baseball player and Herford native. See more at visitperquimans.com or call the Chamber of Commerce at 252-426-5657.

NAVIGATION: Use NOAA Chart 12205. Navigation is fairly straightforward up the well-marked Perquimans River. Start your approach at flashing red "2P," just south of Reed Point, and then head northwest into the river,

Albemarle Sound, NC

Marina	Phone	Dockage — Largest Vessel Accommodated	VHF Channel Monitored	Transient Berths / Total Berths	Approach / Dockside Depth (reported)	Floating Docks	Supplies — Gas / Diesel	Groceries, Ice, Marine Supplies, Snacks	Services — Repairs: Hull, Engine, Propeller	Lift (tonnage), Crane, Rail	Min / Max Amps	Laundry, Pool, Showers, Courtesy Car	Pump-Out Station	Nearby: Grocery Store, Motel, Restaurant
PERQUIMANS RIVER														
1. Hertford Bay Marina	252-426-7805	–	–	9/9	11/11	–	–	S	–	–	30/50	–	P	GR
YEOPIM CREEK														
2. Albemarle Plantation Marina ⌨ WiFi	252-426-4037	60	16/68	25/166	6/7	–	GD	IS	EP	–	30/50	LPS	P	R
EDENTON														
3. Edenton Harbor ⌨ WiFi	252-482-2832	130	16	9/9	6/6	F	–	I	–	–	30/50	SC	P	GMR
4. Edenton Marina	252-482-7421	85		15/107	6/8		GD	–			30/50	LS	–	GMR
ROANOKE RIVER														
5. Plymouth Landing Marina WiFi	252-217-2204	55	19	9/9	12/7.5	–	–	–			30/50	LS	P	GR
SCUPPERNONG RIVER														
6. Columbia Marina	919-495-1028	45	–	1/10	9/						30/50	LS	P	GR
7. Yacht Doc Inc. @ Cypress Cove Marina ⌨ WiFi	252-796-0015	50	16/68	15/55	6/8	–	GD	IMS	HEP	L25	30/50	LSC	P	GMR

⌨ Internet Access WiFi Wireless Internet Access WG Waterway Guide Cruising Club Partner onSpot dockside WiFi facility

See WaterwayGuide.com for current rates, fuel prices, web site addresses, and other up-to-the-minute information. *(Information in the table is provided by the facilities.)*

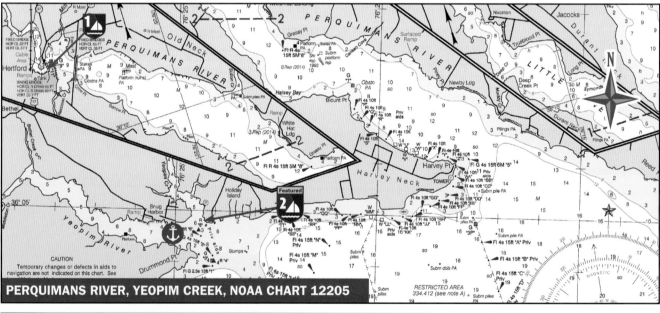

PERQUIMANS RIVER, YEOPIM CREEK, NOAA CHART 12205

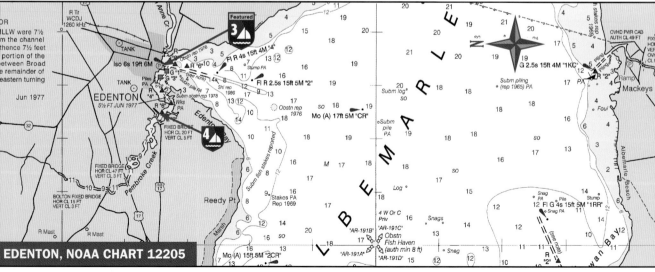

EDENTON, NOAA CHART 12205

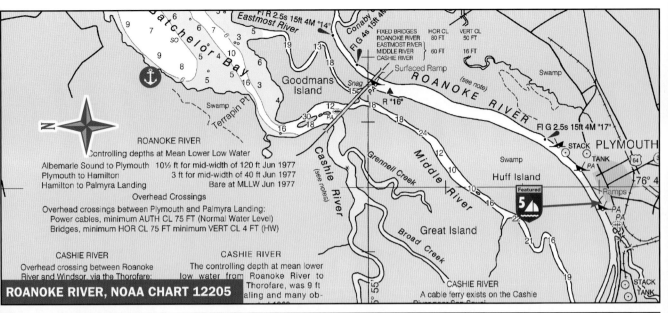

ROANOKE RIVER
Controlling depths at Mean Lower Low Water
Albemarle Sound to Plymouth   10½ ft for mid-width of 120 ft Jun 1977
Plymouth to Hamilton   3 ft for mid-width of 40 ft Jun 1977
Hamilton to Palmyra Landing   Bare at MLLW Jun 1977

Overhead Crossings
Overhead crossings between Plymouth and Palmyra Landing:
    Power cables, minimum AUTH CL 75 FT (Normal Water Level)
    Bridges, minimum HOR CL 75 FT minimum VERT CL 4 FT (HW)

CASHIE RIVER
Overhead crossing between Roanoke
River and Windsor, via the Thorofare:

CASHIE RIVER
The controlling depth at mean lower
low water from Roanoke River to
Thorofare, was 9 ft
aling and many ob-

CASHIE RIVER
A cable ferry exists on the Cashie

FIXED BRIDGES   HOR CL   VERT CL
ROANOKE RIVER   80 FT   50 FT
EASTMOST RIVER   60 FT   16 FT
MIDDLE RIVER
CASHIE RIVER

ROANOKE RIVER, NOAA CHART 12205

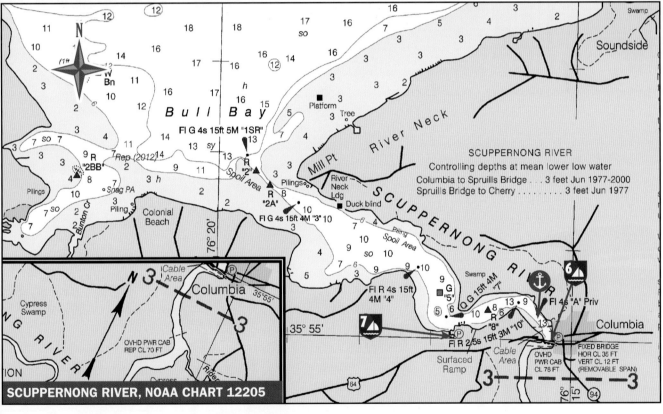

SCUPPERNONG RIVER
Controlling depths at mean lower low water
Columbia to Spruills Bridge . . . 3 feet Jun 1977-2000
Spruills Bridge to Cherry . . . . 3 feet Jun 1977

SCUPPERNONG RIVER, NOAA CHART 12205

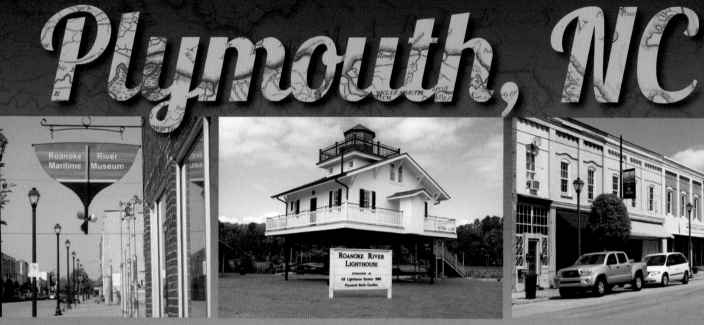

making sure to honor the markers positioned at most of the points. Eight- to 11-foot MLW depths prevail in the river proper. The twin bridges just east of town on the Perquimans River are referred to as the Jim "Catfish" Hunter Bridge. If you can clear the fixed 33-foot vertical clearance bridge, there is also a swing bridge (opens on request) at the entrance to the town harbor. Call on VHF Channel 13 or 252-426-7241 from 8:00 a.m. to midnight (seasonal hours). The town manager suggests that boaters contact the town office prior to arrival at the marina at 252-426-1969.

Dockage: Adjacent to the public boat ramp, the Hertford Bay Marina is part of the Albemarle Loop. With the loop coupon (albemarleloop.com), access complimentary dockage for up to 48 hours at one of its 9 fixed-pier slips, which can accommodate a wide range of transient vessels. Free electric, pump-out service and water are also available with dockage. The marina is located one block from the historic downtown with restaurants, shops, a hardware store and a convenience store with groceries. Should you arrive late, the after-hours number for the marina is 252-426-5751.

Anchorage: There is a good anchorage, except for a southeast exposure and a lot of crab pots, about 1 mile past Mill Point on Little River. The holding ground is good for anchoring in 7 to 9 feet MLW in Halsey Bay, less than halfway between the river entrance and Hertford, and you can dinghy ashore. Here you will find 9 to 11 feet MLW with a soft mud bottom. Blount Point, just to the southeast, provides good protection, but strong winds from the southeast can blow up a stiff chop. It is also possible to anchor above the twin bridges and dinghy into the town dock. There is not much swing room here, as boats are coming and going in this twisted section of the river.

Yeopim River

NAVIGATION: Use NOAA Chart 12205. The Yeopim River is 6 miles west of the mouth of the Perquimans River. Enter the river from flashing green "1," and then follow the private aids northward to Albemarle Plantation. The approach to the dock is easy, but pay attention to the marks. Also, be aware that there are lots of crab pot buoys in the area.

Dockage: Albemarle Plantation, off the entrance channel to the Yeopim River, is part of the Albemarle Loop. They offer complimentary dockage, showers, and WiFi with a 48-hour limit for those doing the loop. (Get the coupon at albemarleloop.com.) This 166-berth

marina sells competitively priced gas and diesel, and amenities include a free laundry, saltwater pool and fitness center. Clubhouse Restaurant offers fine dining and beautiful views. The more casual Dockside Café has a large deck with both screened and open areas and the menu includes wood fired pizza. The award-winning Sound Golf Links are open to visiting boaters. Call 252-426-5555 to arrange a tee time.

Anchorage: Yeopim River offers good anchorage in protected waters (from all directions except east). Tuck in behind Drummond Point for protection from all but east winds. Water depths are 5 to 7 feet MLW once you have cleared the well-marked entrance channel. Mind the depth sounder carefully.

Edenton Bay

Edenton is a delightful side trip from the ICW. Largely unscathed through the Revolutionary and the Civil Wars, Edenton maintains many historic colonial buildings while also being a thriving small town. The welcoming atmosphere and short entrance makes this a good destination while exploring the western reaches of the Albemarle Sound.

NAVIGATION: Use NOAA Chart 12205. Cruising west on Albemarle Sound toward Edenton, you will pass under the fixed high-rise **Albemarle Sound Bridge** (65-feet fixed vertical clearance). Overhead power lines farther upriver have a 94-foot minimum vertical clearance in the marked channel. Once you have passed the power lines, watch for flashing red "2" leading into Edenton. Reedy Point, on the west side of Edenton Bay, hosts submerged fish stakes as well as the taller ones seen throughout the area. The entrance is a broad funnel and the channel here is well marked, with a controlling depth of 5.5 feet past the turning basin.

Dockage: The 9-slip Edenton Harbor is part of the Albemarle Loop. With the loop coupon (albemarleloop. com), access complimentary dockage for up to 48 hours. Reservations are accepted. A breakwater protects the docks from the chop that can develop from a southerly breeze. Enter on the west side of the breakwater. These town docks put you in the heart of the village with restaurants and shops within easy walking distance and offers showers, pump-out service, WiFi and a courtesy car. Kayaks and canoes are available for rent at the marina office. Dockage is also available at Edenton Marina, up Pembroke Creek before the 5-foot fixed vertical clearance W. Queen St. Bridge.

EDENTON HARBOR

The 51 House @ Wharf Landing at the foot of the U.S. 17 Bridge in Edenton is an Albemarle Loop participating facility with all fuels, a pool and an on-site restaurant. A combination of the gorgeous waterfront setting, exceptional food and hospitality make this a destination. (Closed on Mondays.) Call ahead to inquire about hours and dockage at 252-482-2500.

While you may see small boats anchored in or near Edenton Harbor, we cannot recommend it due to shoal water outside the channel and poor protection outside the harbor.

Upriver on the Chowan River

Three miles west of Edenton Bay, the wide mouth of the Chowan River opens up, with the picturesque river swinging northward for many undeveloped miles. The shores, with their high wooded banks, are especially scenic. These inland freshwater rivers offer many miles of delightful cruising.

Located 32 miles upriver from the high rise U.S. 17 Bridge (65-foot fixed vertical clearance) is Winton, the county seat of Hertford County. There is no public dockage but there is a boardwalk that can accommodate dinghies. A short walk will bring you to the courthouse, restaurants, banks and convenience stores. The real attraction is the journey–beautiful scenery, abundant wildlife and quiet anchorages. Look for old ballast piles at creek entrances from the days that the Chowan River was a major trading link.

NAVIGATION: Use NOAA Chart 12205. The high-rise **U.S. 17 Bridge** at Emperor Landing and Edenhouse Point has a 65-foot fixed vertical clearance. The river carries 12-foot depths for 80 miles but is interrupted by a 35-foot fixed vertical clearance **U.S. 13 Bridge** located 32 miles upriver at Winton. Underwater snags, especially in the bend around Holiday Island, dictate caution. Beyond Winton, near the mouth of the Meherrin River, skippers need to exercise caution in the cable ferry area; do not pass any cable ferry until it has reached the other side of the river and its cables have dropped.

Anchorage: There is a well-protected anchorage at Rockyhock Creek with 7 to 14 feet MLW with fair holding in soft mud. It is exposed to the south. Off the north bank of the Chowan, just beyond green flashing daybeacon "13" is Bennett's Creek, which carries 11 feet at MLW and offers all-around protection.

GOIN' ASHORE: **EDENTON, NC**

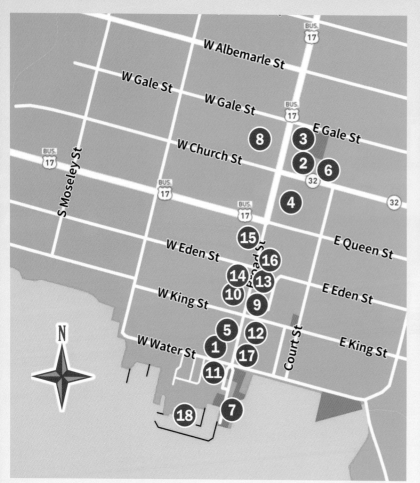

	SERVICES
1	Library
2	Post Office
3	Visitor Information
	ATTRACTIONS
4	Chowan County Courthouse
5	Cupola House
6	James Iredell House
7	Penelope Barker House
8	St. Paul's Episcopal Church
	SHOPPING
9	Blount's Mutual Drugs
10	Byrum Hardware Company
11	Chowan Arts Council and Gallery Shop
12	Garden of Readin'
	DINING
13	309 Bistro & Spirits
14	Edenton Coffee House
15	Emilio's General Store
16	Soda Shoppe
17	Waterman's Grill
	MARINAS
18	Edenton Harbor

Sailing into Edenton Harbor is a voyage back in history. Here, stately mansions built of brick and stone were awe-inspiring to a population of settlers accustomed to one-room cabins and outdoor plumbing. Edenton remains a regal town, steeped in tradition, but richly independent, as evidenced by its early revolt against the British Crown.

At one time, Edenton was the Colonial Capital of North Carolina, serving as the center of cultural and economic commerce. It became a regular port of call as hundreds of ships sailed up the river to trade European goods. Prominent citizens included Samuel Johnson, James Iredell and Joseph Hewes, who were active in signing the Declaration of Independence and the U.S. Constitution.

Today the Courthouse Green remains a gathering place for people talking politics and ports. Standing on the broad-columned porch of the Penelope Barker House, you can look across Edenton Bay at a row of Revolutionary War cannons supplied by France. The Edenton Battery protects stately homes nestled among cypress trees and serves as a reminder that the town on Queen Anne's Creek began a cultural revolution that changed the future of the Colonies. From a bluff overlooking Edenton Bay and the Albemarle Sound, the open windows of shops and homes catch the full effect of the water's breeze.

Edenton was a stop on the Underground Railroad, helping slaves get to the north. Harriet Jacobs, author of *Incidents in the Life of a Slave Girl*, hid here for 7 years and was instrumental in the maritime Underground Railroad, helping slaves move to the north and, later after her emancipation, working to establish programs to educate and train freed slaves.

Attractions: Visitors can begin their walk through history at the Historic Edenton State Historic Site (108 N. Broad St., 252-482-2637) offering exhibits, maps, brochures, a short orientation film on Edenton's history and information on where tours can be coordinated, such as a trip to the Roanoke River Lighthouse. On the waterfront is the Penelope Barker House (505 S. Broad St.), home to the Edenton Historical Commission and the famous Edenton Tea Party. It serves as a Welcome Center and offers exhibits and a gift shop.

Edenton guided walking tours include St. Paul's Episcopal Church, built in 1736 and the state's second oldest surviving church (the oldest is St. Thomas Episcopal Church in Bath). The Chowan County Courthouse, built in 1767, is a National Historic Landmark as the oldest and most intact Colonial courthouse in the country. In 1819, it hosted a gala reception for President James Monroe.

The Cupola House is a National Historic Landmark that was built in 1758 for Francis Corbin, controller of customs, and was restored in 1967 as a museum. The 1800-1827 James Iredell House was the home of James Iredell, an attorney with an impressive career, culminating in his appointment (at age 39) to the first Supreme Court by President George Washington.

The Edenton Trolley Tour (505 S. Broad St.) runs Tuesday through Saturday, allowing travelers an opportunity to see and hear the richness of the town and its history. Tickets can be purchased at the Penelope Barker House. Narrated Edenton Bay Cruises (860-367-5786) are available aboard *Liber-Tea*, a 22-foot all-electric launch. Cruises leave Edenton Harbor Thursday through Monday. Call 860-367-5786 for a schedule and reservations.

Also nearby and worth exploring is the Robert Hendrix Park & Cannon's Ferry Heritage River Walk (315 Cannon's Ferry Rd.). Or visit the Edenton National Fish Hatchery (1102 W. Queen St., 252-482-4118), one of more than 80 federal hatcheries located throughout the country dedicated to the preservation of America's fishing tradition.

Shopping: Chowan Arts Council on the waterfront at 112 W. Water St. (252-482-8005) features unique and affordable works by local and regional artists. Nearby is Byrum Hardware Company (314 S. Broad St., 252-482-2131), offering both the necessary and the frivolous. Garden of Readin' at 103 E. King St. (252-482-7323) is a used book and tea shop. Should you need a pharmacy, Blount's Mutual Drugs is at 323 S. Broad St. (252-482-2127) and a Walgreens is at 717 N. Broad St. There are no grocery stores downtown.

Dining: Located a block off the waterfront, the Waterman's Grill (427 S. Broad St., 252-482-7733) provides a rustic setting to a delightful experience. Inside, you will find brick walls covered with nautical photos and artifacts, a spiral staircase and a paneled bar. 309 Bistro & Spirits (309 S. Broad St., 252-482-0997) serves regional cuisine.

For breakfast pastries, try Edenton Coffee House (302 S. Broad St., 252-482-7465). (They also serve lunch and dinner.) At the other end of the day, hit up the Soda Shoppe (301 S. Broad St., 252-482-8300) for dessert. Emilio's General Store at 206 S. Broad St. (252-482-8240) is a specialty food shop with locally procured, international and organic food items. They offer sandwiches for take away.

Plymouth, Roanoke River

Across from Edenton, around Black Walnut Point, and then through Swan Bay, the Roanoke River leads to the southwest. The lower reaches are marked and the upper reaches are deep. There is still some commercial traffic on the river, which keeps it open.

Plymouth, located 6 miles upriver, is a quaint town perfect for a diversion from the ICW or a day trip.

NAVIGATION: Use NOAA Chart 12205. The Roanoke River is much narrower than the Chowan River but is generally deep (about 10-foot depths) and well marked. Shoaling is reported in the area of red daybeacons "8" to "12" along Rice Island. The fixed **Roanoke River Bridge** (50-foot vertical clearance) crosses the river about 2.5 miles upstream.

Dockage: Plymouth Landing Marina participates in the Albemarle Loop, offering a complimentary 48-hour stay for boaters making the loop. (Get the coupon at albemarleloop.com.) These floating docks have complimentary water, power and showers, while laundry and pump-out service are available for a fee. A Post Office, groceries, shopping and restaurants are nearby along Hwy. 64. Ask the dockmaster at the marina about transportation.

There are restaurants within walking distance of the marina and two fine museums: Port O' Plymouth Museum (252-793-1377), which is housed in a 1923 Atlantic Coast Line train depot, and the Roanoke River

Lighthouse Museum (252-217-2204), a perfect replica of the second Roanoke River Lighthouse. Nearby, the Davenport Homestead (252-797-4336) was built around 1790 and is the oldest surviving homestead open to the public in the region. A short distance from town is the 18,000-acre Pungo Wildlife Refuge.

Anchorage: You can anchor almost anywhere along the cypress shores and marshes of Rice Island. There is a good anchorage before the Roanoke River Bridge with 10-feet MLW depths and all-around protection. On the southwest corner of the Albemarle Sound is Batchelors Bay, at the confluence of the Roanoke and Cashie Rivers. This somewhat open bay has a channel with at least 7 feet MLW all the way to the 16-foot fixed vertical clearance **Cashie River Bridge**. The channel is narrow and there is more swing room near the mouth but less protection. You can anchor closer to the western shore in 7 to 9 feet MLW with protection from all but the northeast through east.

Columbia, Scuppernong River

Broad, open Bull Bay forms the entrance to the scenic Scuppernong River, located along the Albemarle Sound's southern shore between the Alligator River and Laurel Point. About 4 winding, well-marked miles upriver is the town of Columbia, once an important shipping point, now popular as a boating center. Sportsmen use Columbia as a year-round base to fish the waters of Albemarle Sound, and the improved waterfront provides access to downtown shops and restaurants.

Vineyards on the Scuppernong (117 S. Elm St., 252-796-4727) is a local winery with a shop right off the waterfront offering gourmet foods alongside their wines. Within a few blocks of the municipal marina, visitors have an array of restaurant choices, as well as pharmacy, banks (with ATM), a hardware store and a Post Office.

Take the boardwalk under the highway to the large Tyrrell County Visitor Center to get situated. Just to the south is the Walter B. Jones Sr. Center for the Sound exhibits the flora and fauna of the three-county, 110,000-acre Pocosin Lakes National Wildlife Refuge. The Scuppernong River Interpretive Trail starts just outside their door. The raised boardwalk takes you into the pristine bottomland swamp and makes a 0.75-mile loop complete with signage to explain the blackwater ecosystem. The town of fewer than a thousand residents swells to several times its population for the Scuppernong River Festival, held in early October.

NAVIGATION: Use NOAA Chart 12205. The entrance to the Scuppernong River is marked by flashing green "1SR" and is followed by a series of daybeacons past Mill Point. The locals will tell you that the hardest thing about the Scuppernong River is getting into the Scuppernong River. Be sure to hug the two red daybeacons, "2" and "2A," between the two lighted greens, as 2- and 3-foot depths border either side of the channel. After passing flashing green "3," the river widens and deepens to 10 feet. The NOAA chart shows 3 feet at MLW near the town marina, but the river actually deepens on approach to 15 to 25 feet MLW after leaving the two white lighted markers to the east and the collection of fish stakes to the west.

All sailing vessels have reached the extent of their Scuppernong excursion at the town dock as three low bridges cross the Scuppernong River. The first is immediately after Columbia's town dock (12-foot closed vertical clearance, removable span), while the other two are further upriver (one at Cross Landing with a 5-foot fixed vertical clearance and the other at Creswell, a removable span with an overhead cable limiting vertical clearance to 25 feet). To continue upriver past Columbia, make prior arrangements for a bridge opening by calling 252-797-4468. Be aware that the projected depths upstream are just 3 feet MLW.

Dockage: Yacht Doc at Cypress Cove is located on the south shore in the first hard bend of the river. The entrance is marked by red- and green-topped stakes. In addition to transient dockage, Everett Marine offers haul-out, complete repair services and sells gas and diesel fuels, as well as fishing supplies. They also have a loaner car.

The municipal Columbia Marina has transient slips available right downtown. Dockage is available for boats up to 45 feet; the pilings, however, are no more than 25 feet from the seawall. Restrooms, showers, water, shore power and pump-out service are available. Note that an uncomfortable chop can develop in a heavy northwest wind.

Both marinas are part of the Albemarle Loop. Dockage is complimentary on a first-come, first-served basis for boats up to 45 feet. (Coupon available at albemarleloop.com.)

Anchorage: You will find several good anchorages in the Scuppernong with 7 to 10 feet MLW and a mud bottom. Columbia is easily accessible by dinghy. The cypress swamps of the river's upper reaches warrant exploration by dinghy or the town of Columbia's guided boat tours.

■ ROANOKE SOUND

After exploring the western end of Albemarle Sound, it's decision time again. The Alligator River and the ICW proper head south and west, but the distant outline of rising dunes to the east heralds the beginning of the Outer Banks and the shorter route south.

NAVIGATION: Use NOAA Charts 12204 and 12205. From ICW Mile 70, cruise east on Albemarle Sound, setting a course to lighted "MG," at the head of Croatan and Roanoke Sounds.

⚠ Vessels that cannot clear the 44-foot fixed vertical clearance **U.S. 64 Bridge** crossing Croatan Sound can reach Manns Harbor and other Croatan Sound points via Roanoke Sound (crossed by the 64-foot vertical clearance **Washington Baum Bridge**).

Roanoke Sound, NC

		Largest Vessel Accommodated	VHF Channel Monitored	Transient Berths / Total Berths	Approach / Dockside Depth (reported)	Floating Docks	Gas / Diesel	Groceries, Ice, Marine Supplies, Snacks	Repairs: Hull, Engine, Propeller	Lift (tonnage), Crane, Rail	Min/Max Amps	Laundry, Pool, Showers, Courtesy Car	Pump-Out Station	Nearby: Grocery Store, Motel, Restaurant
MANTEO (ROANOKE ISLAND)					**Dockage**			**Supplies**				**Services**		
1. Manteo Waterfront Marina 💻 📶	252-473-3320	150	16/09	25/50	7/7	–	–	IS	–	–	30/100	LS	P	GMR
2. Marshes Light Marina 💻 📶	252-305-4737	60	16	52/60	10/9	–	–	IMS	–	–	30/50	LS	P	GMR
3. Shallowbag Bay Marina 💻 📶	252-305-8726	75	16/69	50/75	7/6	F	GD	GIMS	EP	–	30/50	LPS	P	GMR
ROANOKE ISLAND														
4. Pirate's Cove Yacht Club & Marina 💻 📶	800-367-4728	90	78	125/195	10/13	–	GD	GIMS	HEP	–	30/100	PSC	–	GMR
WANCHESE (ROANOKE ISLAND)														
5. Bayliss Boatworks 📶	252-473-9797	100	16/09	7/7	11/20	F	GD	IM	HEP	L100	30/100	S	P	GMR
6. Gregory Poole Marine-Wanchese	252-473-1501	–	–	–	7/7	–	–	M	HEP	L	–	–	–	GMR
7. Outer Banks Marina	252-473-5344	70	–	call/45	14/14	F	GD	–	HEP	L10	30/30	S	–	GMR
8. Bluewater Outer Banks Yacht Yard 📶	252-475-1420	90	–	6/6	14/14	F	–	IM	HEP	L70	30/100	S	–	GMR
OREGON INLET														
9. Oregon Inlet Fishing Center	252-441-6301	65	69	6/55	6/6	–	GD	GIMS	–	–	50/50	–	–	G

💻 Internet Access 📶 Wireless Internet Access **WG** Waterway Guide Cruising Club Partner 🛰 **onSpot** dockside WiFi facility
See WaterwayGuide.com for current rates, fuel prices, web site addresses, and other up-to-the-minute information. *(Information in the table is provided by the facilities.)*

Atlantic Ocean

Roanoke Sound

BLUEWATER OUTER BANKS YACHT YARD

Wanchese

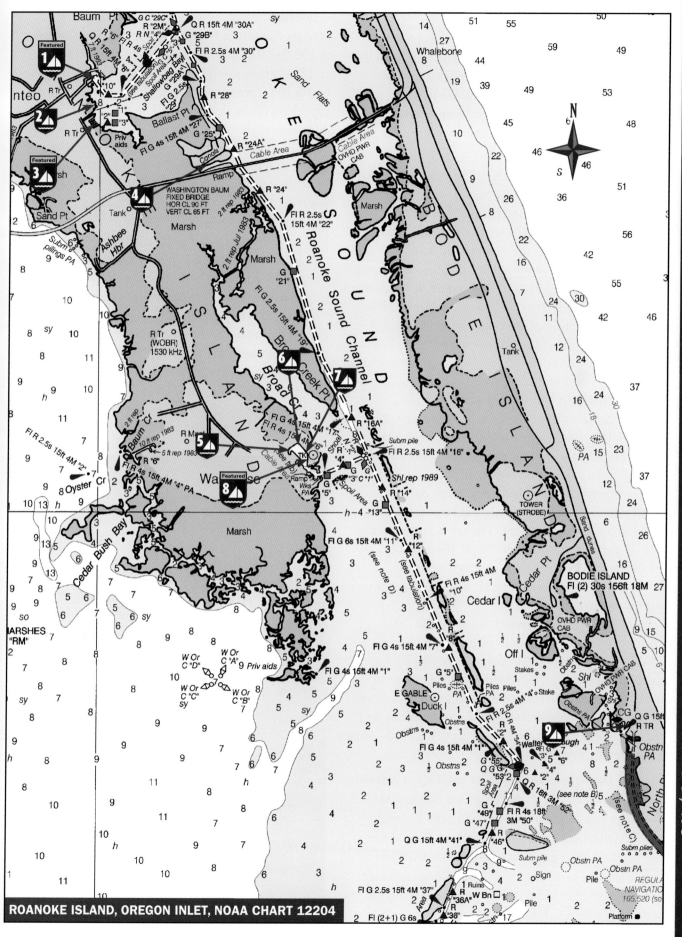

ROANOKE ISLAND, OREGON INLET, NOAA CHART 12204

Manteo, Shallowbag Bay

Manteo (pronounced "man-knee-oh" if you want to sound like a local) is on the northern and western sides of Shallowbag Bay, off Roanoke Sound, and is often overlooked by cruisers moving along the ICW, but it is well worth the side trip. It is just a 5-minute taxi ride to the Outer Banks beaches, and the town itself has a friendly air and much to offer.

NAVIGATION: Use NOAA Charts 12204 and 12205. To proceed to Manteo on Roanoke Sound, head south from light "MG" to Croatan Sound flashing green "3CS," approximately 4 miles to the south-southeast. Continue to flashing red "42" and the well-marked Roanoke Sound channel. Proceeding southward, keep the red lights and daybeacons on your port side. Use caution. It is winding, and aids are not as prevalent south of Shallowbag Bay, which can be confusing, especially farther down at Oregon Inlet. South of the Manteo entrance, the Roanoke Channel is crossed by the 65-foot fixed vertical clearance Washington Baum Bridge.

Approach depths into Manteo are 7 to 12 feet, despite what is noted on the latest NOAA charts. The *Elizabeth II* replica, which draws 8 feet, transits the channel frequently. Shoaling does occur at the entrance to Shallowbag Bay, so slow down, mark the buoys and daybeacons carefully and keep an eye on your depth sounder. Some chartplotters fail to show all the buoys unless zoomed in tight. The key is remembering that all markers with numbers in the 20s and 30s are for the main Roanoke Bay channel, while the markers with numbers starting at "2M" belong to the Shallowbag Bay channel.

From either direction, wait to turn west to the Shallowbag Bay Channel until just north of the red "30A." Give red buoy "2M" lots of room and keep a sharp lookout for additional buoys, added in case of further shoaling. After your turn, hug green daybeacons "5" and "3" for deep water. The channel broadens until red "8," where it turns west to red daybeacon "10." Most directions are figured from this last red daybeacon.

⚠️ Due to the shoaling at the entrance of Manteo Channel, the Coast Guard has changed Manteo channel green daybeacon "5" and flashing red "6" (which are currently marked with emergency buoys) from fixed aids to buoys. The Coast Guard will re-evaluate the possibility of re-establishing fixed aids in the future. Stay tuned to the Waterway Explorer at waterwayguide.com for updates.

Dockage: North of red daybeacon "10," the 50-slip Manteo Waterfront Marina can accommodate vessels to 150 feet. The marina is run by the town of Manteo and has climate-controlled showers and laundry, shore power and a pump-out facility, all available for a fee payable to the dockmaster. Call on VHF Channel 16 for directions to the office, which is only manned between 10:00 a.m. and 2:00 p.m. on weekends (unless you have a reservation). Pull into a slip on the wharf ending in the brown gazebo. The Manteo Waterfront Marina is adjacent to many shops, inns, restaurants and the 1-mile-long town boardwalk. They can arrange repairs, haul-out, rental cars and airport shuttle service.

Marshes Light Marina is part of a waterfront community and offers some transient dockage on protected canals for (mostly power) vessels to 60 feet.

A set of private markers to the south lead from the red daybeacon "10" into Shallowbag Bay Marina, which accommodates vessels up to 75 feet on floating docks and boasts five fueling stations providing "in slip" fueling to most boats. They also have an on-site restaurant, pool, hot tub and laundry facilities. If you have any interest in a day of offshore fishing there are

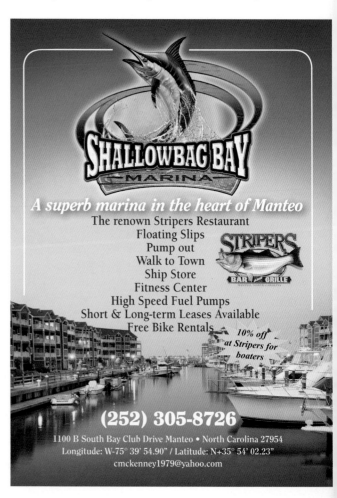

GOIN' ASHORE: **MANTEO, NC**

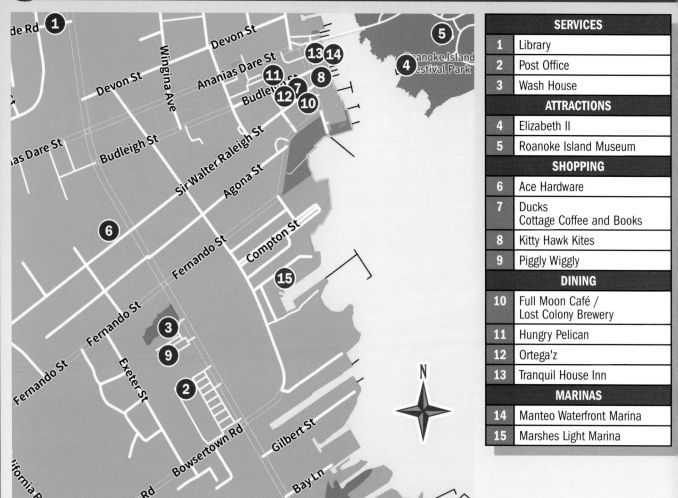

SERVICES	
1	Library
2	Post Office
3	Wash House
ATTRACTIONS	
4	Elizabeth II
5	Roanoke Island Museum
SHOPPING	
6	Ace Hardware
7	Ducks Cottage Coffee and Books
8	Kitty Hawk Kites
9	Piggly Wiggly
DINING	
10	Full Moon Café / Lost Colony Brewery
11	Hungry Pelican
12	Ortega'z
13	Tranquil House Inn
MARINAS	
14	Manteo Waterfront Marina
15	Marshes Light Marina

The Roanoke Marshes Lighthouse, at the entrance to Dough's Creek, is a replica of the 1877 screwpile lighthouse that was once found at Croatan Sound. The Manteo Weather Tower, also on the downtown waterfront, flew flags to warn locals, fishers, and sailors about oncoming weather. Weather messages came in by telegraph, so Manteo's first telegraph operator, Adelphus P. Drinkwater, naturally became the first operator of the weather station and tower as well. Drinkwater took part in history when he telegraphed news to the world of the Wright Brothers' first flight. The Weather Tower is one of only five still used by NOAA to fly weather flags during the day and lights up at night.

Attractions: The Roanoke Island Maritime Museum (104 Fernando St., 252-475-1750 and George Washington Creef Boathouse are located on the waterfront. This is a great nautical museum and a fun way to learn the nautical history of the area, especially about the famous shad boats built by Mr. Creef here over 100 years ago. They also have an eclectic collection of small boats like a New England Beetle Cat, a Hampton Bay One Design and a 50s vintage outboard hydroplane. Admission is free and there are usually volunteers on hand to answer your questions. The museum hosts two noteworthy events: the Annual One-Design Regatta takes place on the last Saturday in July and the Annual Wooden Boat Show is held on the last Saturday in October.

The *Elizabeth II*, anchored across from the Manteo waterfront, is a replica of a 16th-century ship. It is named after one of the seven vessels in Sir Walter Raleigh's fleet. Also at Roanoke Island Festival Park is an American Indian town, a settlement site and an adventure museum. Concerts are held at the outdoor pavilion here as well. The Park allows guests of all ages to experience what life was like for the original settlers here in the 1500s. Costumed interpreters are featured here to show how the colonists lived, worked, and played on Roanoke Island.

In addition to the attractions on Roanoke Island itself, there are a number of other side trips available, though all will require transportation. (Taxi service is readily available.) The North Carolina Aquarium (374 Airport Rd., 252-473-3494), located 3 miles north of Manteo, draws visitors into the undersea world, allowing a sneak peak at life below the waters around the island. If you love drama, the nation's oldest and longest-running outdoor play, "The Lost Colony," plays throughout the summer at the nearby Waterside Theatre, near the site of the colonists' first settlement (1409 National Park Dr., 252-473-2127). Combining dance and song, the production is the forerunner of the modern American musical. Be sure to bring bug spray or cover up completely. If the wind is blowing from the "wrong" direction, the mosquitoes can be brutal in the summertime. Call 252-473-3414 for ticket information.

Further afield, the Wright Brothers National Memorial in Kill Devil Hills (1000 S. Croatan Hwy., 252-473-2111) honors the first powered flight. Here, you will find a full-scale reproduction of the original plane, great exhibits, a walking tour on the history of the Wright Brothers and other flight-related reproductions. The memorial is open year-round. There is also a General Aviation landing strip called First Flight Field. If you are a pilot or an aviation enthusiast, a pilgrimage to Kill Devil Hills should be on your bucket list.

On nearby Jockey's Ridge, you will find a 400-acre state park comprising sand dunes only, providing one of the East Coast's premier hang-gliding locations. Lessons and rentals are available from the main Kitty Hawk Kites, located directly across the street (252-473-2357). (There is also a store in downtown Manteo.) The park is open year-round.

Outer Banks Distillery (510 Budleigh St., 252-473-3011) offers a tour ("From Molasses to Glasses"), Tuesdays through Fridays at 1:00 p.m. (must be 21 years or older).

Shopping: Downtown Manteo offers a compact shopping experience. On Saturday mornings in the summer, you can visit the Farmers' Market in the downtown square. There are several galleries, specialty shops and handcrafted items in the downtown area. You will be sure to find a perfect souvenir or gift here.

For provisioning, there is a Piggly Wiggly (252-473-3727) and Food-A-Rama (252-473-2924) on Hwy. 64. There is also an Ace Hardware nearby (252-473-1444) and a Wash House laundromat (866-825-6052).

Dining: The Full Moon Café and Lost Colony Brewery (208 Queen Elizabeth Ave., 252-473-6666) remains a cruiser and local favorite. Enjoy beer-battered fish and chips before tucking into the cozy tasting room next door for a Buxton Brown Ale or Kitty Hawk Blonde. The Hungry Pelican at 205 Budleigh St. (252-473-9303) offers sandwiches on fresh baked bread, homemade soups and fresh salads, milkshakes and smoothies, plus packaged gourmet foods.

To dine with wine and water views, try the Tranquil House Inn's 1587 Restaurant at 405 Queen Elizabeth St. (800-458-7069). For fine Italian dining, visit La Dolce Vita at 814 Hwy. 64 North (252-473-9919). (They are not close by but will pick you up from the docks at no charge.)

Ortega'z Southwestern Grill and Wine Bar is at 201 Sir Walter Raleigh St. (252-473-5911). They offer "casual dining with elegance." You can enjoy lunch or dinner on the covered outdoor patio or inside. For a quick meal or a cold drink, head to the Wine Bar located in the center of the restaurant.

MANTEO WATERFRONT MARINA

over 20 large charter boats based here that can make the run to the offshore canyons in comfort.

Pirate's Cove Yacht Club & Marina, located just on the north side of the Washington Baum Bridge on Roanoke Island, is part of a large residential development and offers transient slips and sells all fuels. They cater to sportfishing boats.

The town of Manteo also provides free overnight tie-up with no services on a "space available" basis with room for 3 to 4 boats on the docks between the lighthouse and the town gazebo. There is a pump-out service available and a public restroom at the nearby maritime museum.

Anchorage: The dockmaster for Manteo describes the anchorage area as a triangle created by three points: the red daybeacon "10" to the south, the lighthouse to the northwest, and the brown gazebo to the northeast. Anchor in hard mud and sand in 6 to 8 feet MLW with no tide, only wind-driven changes in depth. Protection is excellent from the north and west, but strong south or east winds can kick up a chop. Farther west, the bottom shoals swiftly, and a charted pipe restricts anchoring to the south. You can take the dinghy to the town dock for land access.

Wanchese, Broad Creek

At the south end of Roanoke Island is a real commercial fishing and boat building village that is home base for several fishing companies that receive and ship the catch for the substantial oceangoing fleet that operates from here. Wanchese is the home base for the reality show "Wicked Tuna–Outer Banks," as well as several custom sportfishing boat manufacturers. You will find few amenities for recreational boaters. Silting has been an ongoing problem in the harbor so proceed cautiously.

Dockage: Bluewater Outer Banks Yacht Yard, Outer Banks Marina and Bayliss Boatworks are located here. If you need your boat fixed, this is the place. There are several yards with large travel lifts, prop shops, canvas shops, metal fabricators, and engine shops, including Gregory Poole Marine-Wanchese and Bluewater Outer Banks Yacht Yard. Bluewater's extensive facilities maintain full capabilities, including engine repair, welding, machinist, metal work, wood and composite work, mechanical, electrical, electronic and complete rigging up to and including total custom construction.

Herbert C. Bonner Bridge

Side Trip: Oregon Inlet

A well-defined channel, with 9- to 10-foot minimum depths, is used by the trawler fleet and leads south from Wanchese, 6 miles down to Oregon Inlet. It is also used by one of the East Coast's largest sportfishing fleets. Be aware that aids to navigation are not charted here because they change so frequently at the Oregon Inlet intersection. This inlet regularly experiences severe shoaling and is NOT a recommended inlet. Proceed with an abundance of caution and local knowledge. Construction of the new **Herbert C. Bonner Bridge** that crosses Oregon Inlet was completed in 2019. Use caution transiting this area. Shoaling has been reported to 2 feet in the inlet near the bridge.

NAVIGATION: Use NOAA Chart 12205. Oregon Inlet is considered the most changeable of all the East Coast inlets. Always obtain accurate local information before attempting this inlet, as it can be quite dangerous, even in calm conditions. Check with Coast Guard Station Oregon Inlet at 252-441-6260 for information regarding the marking system at Oregon Inlet. Surveys of this inlet are made frequently.

⚠️ Shoaling has been reported in Oregon Inlet across the entire channel between red buoys "4" and "6." Shoaling has been observed to a depth of 4 feet MLW. Shoaling was also extended across the channel between green buoys "19" and "21."

The east-west channel inside the inlet is subject to shifting from the inlet to its intersection with the north–south channel. Seek local knowledge or follow one of the local charter or fishing boats in or out of the inlet if you are in doubt. Do not try to run the inlet in foul weather.

Dockage: Oregon Inlet Fishing Center sits north of the inlet, offering fuel and transient berths and is a good resource on the Oregon Inlet channel.

■ CROATAN SOUND

NAVIGATION: Use NOAA Charts 12204, 12205, 11548, 11553 and 11555. Boats that can clear the 44-foot fixed **U.S. 64 Bridge** can run 4 miles down Croatan Sound (western side of Roanoke Island) from flashing green Croatan Light "3CS" to Manns Harbor (no transient facilities), on the mainland side just before the 66-foot fixed **Virginia Dare Memorial Bridge**. Check water levels carefully if your mast approaches this height. (Local knowledge says that the U.S. 64 Bridge actually has a vertical clearance of between 42 and 44 feet.) After clearing both bridges in Croatan Sound heading south, your next waypoint will be Roanoke Marshes, flashing white 20-foot "RM."

Vessels that cannot clear the fixed bridge crossing Croatan Sound can reach Manns Harbor and other Croatan Sound points via Roanoke Sound. From Oregon Inlet, Old House Channel carries at least 7-foot depths west into Pamlico Sound. The channel is well marked. Carry the red lights and daybeacons on the starboard side from this point south to Pamlico Sound. The buoys change here and they can be confusing. Slow down here and sort it out before proceeding or you may find yourself aground. They can run the dredged channel east of Roanoke Island, round the island via Old House Channel in Pamlico Sound, then head north up Croatan Sound. Note that aids to navigation reverse between flashing red "4" and flashing green "OH" in Old House Channel.

■ NEXT STOP

Many power vessels use the Croatan Sound Route to the Pamlico Sound to circumvent the ICW and slower vessels. This open water route starts at Mile 66 after entering the Albemarle Sound from the North River and ends at Mile 169 in the Neuse River. The well-marked channel carries 7- to 8-foot depths. Red aids are to the west (starboard when heading south). Your subsequent waypoints from the southern end of Croatan Sound, through Pamlico Sound and ending with the Neuse River, are as follows: Stumpy Point (27-foot flashing white "N"), Long Shoal (15-foot flashing red "LS2"), Bluff Shoal (40-foot isophase "BL"), Brant I Shoal (40-foot flashing white "BI") then Neuse River (24-foot flashing white "NR"). A licensed boat captain and long-time user of this route reported to us that it shaves 18 miles off the trip north or south.

Whether you choose to take the Roanoke Sound or Croatan Sound route, both converge in Pamlico Sound, leaving you poised to continue north to the Chesapeake Bay or south on the ICW.

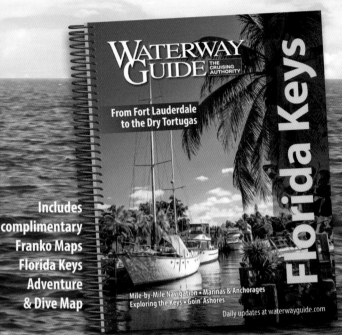
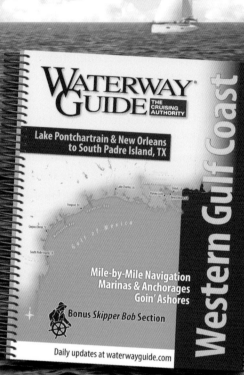

Albemarle Sound to the Neuse River, NC

 ICW Mile 80–Mile 185   NC Bridges: Channel 13

CHARTS NOAA 11541, 11548, 11552, 11553, 11554, 12206

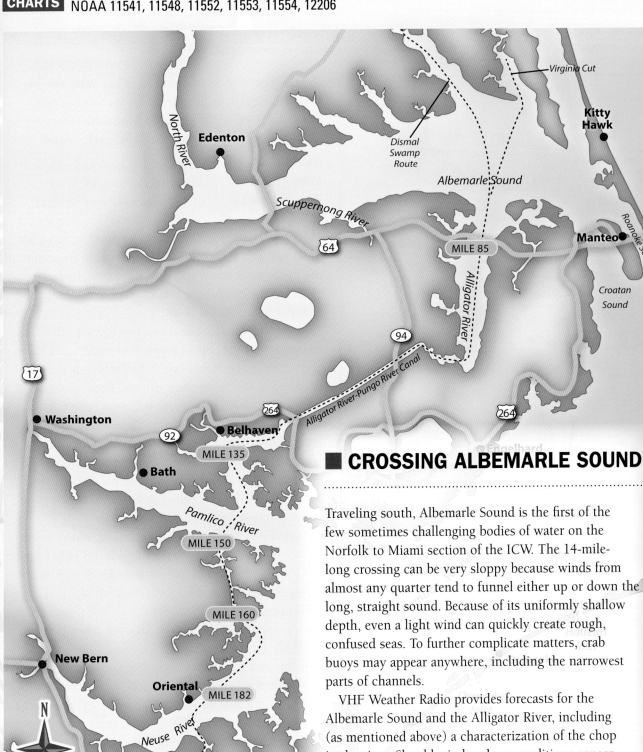

■ CROSSING ALBEMARLE SOUND

Traveling south, Albemarle Sound is the first of the few sometimes challenging bodies of water on the Norfolk to Miami section of the ICW. The 14-mile-long crossing can be very sloppy because winds from almost any quarter tend to funnel either up or down the long, straight sound. Because of its uniformly shallow depth, even a light wind can quickly create rough, confused seas. To further complicate matters, crab buoys may appear anywhere, including the narrowest parts of channels.

VHF Weather Radio provides forecasts for the Albemarle Sound and the Alligator River, including (as mentioned above) a characterization of the chop in the river. Should wind and sea conditions appear unfavorable for an Albemarle crossing, prudent boaters

Alligator River, NC

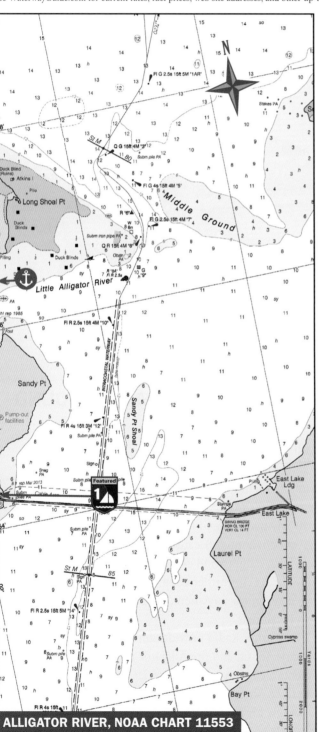

ALLIGATOR RIVER	Dockage					Supplies			Services			
1. Alligator River Marina ⬚ 📶 1.5 W of 84	252-796-0333	160	16/69	20/32	6.5/10	–	GD	GIS	EP	–	30/100	LS	P	GR

Column headers (diagonal): Largest Vessel Accommodated · VHF Channel Monitored · Approach / Dockside Depth (reported) · Transient Berths / Total Berths · Groceries, Ice, Marine Supplies, Snacks · Floating Docks · Gas / Diesel · Repairs: Hull, Engine, Propeller · Lift (tonnage), Crane, Rail · Min/Max Amps · Laundry, Pool, Showers, Courtesy Car · Pump-Out Station · Nearby: Grocery Store, Motel, Restaurant

⬚ Internet Access 📶 Wireless Internet Access **WG** Waterway Guide Cruising Club Partner ⬤onSpot dockside WiFi facility

See WaterwayGuide.com for current rates, fuel prices, web site addresses, and other up-to-the-minute information. *(Information in the table is provided by the facilities.)*

ALLIGATOR RIVER, NOAA CHART 11553

should remain in or return to their last port, whether that be Coinjock or Elizabeth City for those coming down the ICW, or Columbia or Albemarle Plantation for those who opted to see more of Albemarle Sound.

NAVIGATION: Use NOAA Charts 12206 and 11553. From Elizabeth City along the Pasquotank River, Camden Point is about 19 miles southeast. When crossing Albemarle Sound, you can save a couple of miles by deserting the chart's ICW course to make for flashing green "1PR" east of Wade Point in the mouth of the Pasquotank River, and then directly to flashing green "1AR" at the entrance to the Alligator River. Watch for crab pot buoys off the point.

Along the Virginia Cut route, two lighted aids to navigation set the course across Albemarle Sound from the mouth of the North River: the flashing 6-second white isophase "N" to the north and flashing 4-second white "S" to the south (about 6.5 miles apart). As the course from the Dismal Swamp Canal Route from the Pasquotank River across Albemarle Sound converges with the Virginia Cut Route, the second marker, flashing 4-second white "S," will lie close to the course. It is another 3.5 miles to flashing green "1AR" at the mouth of the Alligator River.

Should you decide to cross Albemarle Sound when the wind is up, it is a good idea to call (on VHF Channel 13) the bridgetender of the Alligator River (U.S. 64) Swing Bridge at Mile 84.2 for a situation report. The bridge opens on signal, except during unsafe conditions (in wind speeds of 34 mph or greater), when the bridgetender need not open. You should be aware of this potential obstacle before beginning your crossing. If the wind comes up en route and the bridge is closed, you have the option of ducking into Alligator River Marina just before the bridge for protection or anchoring as described in the next section. If the wind is as little as 15 mph out of a westerly direction the resulting waves can make for a very unpleasant crossing of the sound.

◼ ALLIGATOR RIVER

Long Shoal Point, at the mouth of the Alligator River, is popular with the local hunting crowd and can be thick with duck blinds, boats and shotguns during duck season. In late fall, migrating whistling swans settle onto the shallows in large flocks, a sight that is beautiful to behold.

NAVIGATION: Use NOAA Chart 11553. This heavily marked channel is confusing, even to veteran ICW travelers, so be sure to slow down and take time to sort out the markers. Just before Mile 80 is the entrance marker for the Alligator River, flashing green "1AR." A wreck has been marked with a small green can buoy numbered "1A WR." Next in line to the south is quick flashing green "3," which is difficult to see approaching from either direction, but is the location of the Mile Marker 80 sign.

⚠️ There have been numerous groundings by vessels missing flashing green "3" and heading straight to flashing green "5." The board for flashing green "5" is visible only when approached from the correct direction.

Red daybeacon "6" is just north of Long Shoal Point, and quick flashing red "8" marks the shoal southeast of Long Shoal Point. Long Shoal seems to get longer with each passing year. Flashing green "7" is just east of quick flashing red "8" and marks the eastern boundary of the ICW channel here. Make sure you honor both marks, favoring the green side. The pole from the charted former white "Danger" beacon is still on the shoal but has no boards. Favor the east side of the channel between flashing green "7" and green daybeacon "9." As you approach buoy "8A" that is located between daybeacons "9" and "10," stay near the red side of the channel. From here, set your course for the opening span of the Alligator River Swing Bridge at Mile 84.2.

⚠️ Always follow the markers, especially in this area, as the markers are moved frequently. Up-to-date NOAA charts are a necessity for accurate navigation, but are still updated less frequently than the markers are moved. Any departure from the main channel carries the risk of prop damage or worse. Do not shortcut points, do not hug the banks too closely, and approach anchorages cautiously.

The **Alligator River Swing Bridge** at Mile 84.2 (14-foot closed vertical clearance) normally opens on signal, but it cannot open in winds stronger than 34 knots and, at the discretion of the bridgetender, may remain closed in winds of lesser velocities. In either case, look for a good spot to hole up in, should it become necessary. Southbound boats might want to check weather conditions at the bridge and call the bridgetender on VHF Channel 13 before crossing the Albemarle. You certainly don't want to make this crossing only to find the bridge closed due to high winds. As of the summer of 2019 a new fixed bridge to replace the swing bridge remained in final review. Check Waterway Explorer (waterwayguide.com) for updates.

Drought conditions and prolonged strong winds can lower the water level throughout the Alligator River. A north or south blow can kick up 6-foot waves and make this transit very uncomfortable. While the Alligator River continues wide and deep almost to its head, snags are frequent outside the channel, and boaters should follow the markers carefully. The most snags have been observed between red daybeacon "24" and green "37." An extra pair of eyes is always helpful in this area.

Snags and obstructions are often partially submerged and difficult to see, and you may hear other skippers reporting them to the Coast Guard on VHF Channel 16 and making Sécurité calls.

⚠ At press time in summer 2019, the following hazards to navigation have been observed: (1) An obstruction has been reported in the channel north of daybeacon "24". (2) Across the channel from flashing green daybeacon "37" is a submerged pile. Do not cut this corner when headed southbound. (3) Alligator River daybeacon "52" is destroyed and is a hazard to navigation.

South of the Alligator River Swing Bridge, the east bank of the Alligator River is primitive, with side streams worth exploring only by dinghy. Milltail Creek, east of the bend in the channel at quick flashing red "18" (about Mile 88), is pristine but hard to locate. Five miles upstream are the turning basin and the decaying town wharf of Buffalo City. The creek is narrow, and fallen trees may lie across the creek in areas.

Dockage: At the northwestern end of the Alligator River Swing Bridge (Mile 84.2) is Alligator River Marina, with a well-protected harbor and the only fuel available along the 86 miles on the Virginia Cut Route between Coinjock (Mile 50) and Belhaven (Mile 136). This friendly marina accepts transients of all sizes and offers all the usual amenities plus early morning breakfast as well as other short-order favorites at the on-site restaurant, along with a convenience store. It is easily recognizable by its candy cane-striped lighthouse. Alligator River Marina participates in the Albemarle Loop. See more at albemarleloop.com for offers and discounts.

Anchorage: Little Alligator River offers limited protection on the east side of the river, north of the bridge, especially in any northerly or easterly wind. There is 6 feet MLW and fair holding behind Mill Point near the mouth of the Little Alligator. It is not a spot to wait out a cold front passage, nor is it a comfortable refuge if the Alligator River Swing Bridge cannot open because of strong winds when southbound.

If planning to stay north of the bridge for weather reasons, it is better to head further off the track to the west and anchor to the southwest side of Durant Island, the common entrance to East and South Lakes. Here you will find good shelter from northeast winds among the numerous crab pots.

Just past Briery Hall Point at the mouth of Broad Creek on South Lake offers some protection. Venture carefully into East or South Lakes if you draw more than 5 feet; the channel is unmarked and narrow. Although both carry 8- to 10-feet MLW depths, they shallow to 3 to 5 feet just outside of the channel. Both anchorages have good holding and wind protection.

If you are northbound and there is a bridge closure, you will need to find a spot close to the southwestern end of the bridge to drop the hook and wait it out. This is not a good anchorage in a north or northeast wind, so when in doubt, contact the bridge. A better bet is Catfish Point at Mile 94.3, which is an excellent all-around anchorage in clay with 6- to 14-foot MLW depths.

The Alligator River in the proximity of Mile 100 is big so choose a location that provides wind protection. In season there may be plenty of bugs and fisherman traffic early morning. It is recommended that a trip line be used when anchoring in the Alligator River, due to the many snags on the bottom. Anchoring options include Newport News Point at Mile 101 with good holding in 7 to 8 feet MLW (exposed to the north), Deep Point at Mile 102, with good holding in 7- to 8-foot MLW depths in mud (exposed to the east) and Bear Point at Mile 103 (exposed to the east). When anchoring here, position yourself as far out of the channel as possible to stay away from maneuvering tugs and barges in this vicinity.

Tuckahoe Point (Mile 104), just before the entrance to the 20-mile-long Alligator River-Pungo River Canal, offers the best all-around protection in 6- to 10-feet MLW depths. Turn to the north off the ICW between green daybeacon "49" and red daybeacon "52" (which has been reported to be destroyed and may be missing) and then proceed slowly to Tuckahoe Point. Do not get too close to the point; the area is foul with tree stumps. Holding, swing room and protection are good. Position yourself as far out of the channel as possible to stay away from maneuvering tugs and barges in this vicinity and show anchor lights at night.

Alligator River-Pungo River Canal– ICW Mile 105 to Mile 126

The 21-mile-long Alligator River-Pungo River Canal runs northeast to southwest. It is scenic and heavily wooded at its upper end. Do not be in a hurry or you might miss deer snacking near the shore or a black bear swimming across the channel. The occasional alligator has been spotted here as well. Farther on are areas that have burned in the past but now have their second growth.

Wilkerson Bridge

The canal is relatively narrow, and boats dragging huge wakes have a tendency to damage the banks. Each year, more and more trees topple into the water. Please proceed slowly.

The Fairfield Canal at Mile 113.8 leads to Lake Mattamuskeet, part of the Mattamuskeet Wildlife Refuge. The refuge is popular with hunters and naturalists from November through May, when huge flocks of water birds gather in the lake and marshes. Arrangements to visit the refuge can be made in Belhaven.

NAVIGATION: Use NOAA Chart 11553. While enjoying the scenery and wildlife, keep a lookout for stumps and snags outside of the channel. This is another area where deadheads have been spotted in the channel. Keep a watchful eye on the water when transiting this canal. It is a good idea to stick to the center of the channel and maintain a radio watch; tugs and recreational boats will frequently point out possible hazards with Sécurité calls on VHF Channel 16. Channel markers in the vicinity of the Fairfield Bridge at Mile 113.9 and farther west will help you maintain your mid-channel position in those areas.

At Mile 113.6, just before the fixed **Fairfield (NC 94) Bridge** at Mile 113.9, Fairfield Canal crosses the ICW. The bridge has a charted 65-foot vertical clearance, but we have received reports of closer to 64 feet being observed. Tree stumps line both sides of the channel, and there can be considerable current present here. Boats

have been observed anchoring here with lines tied to shore and anchors astern. Note that this is not a recommended anchorage, except possibly in an emergency situation.

The Alligator River-Pungo River Canal's controlling depth is 12 feet; however, keep a close eye on the depth sounder, stick to the center of the channel and squeeze to the side carefully if you must pass another boat.

⚠️ Just east of Mile 120 there is an obstruction on the green side of the center of the channel; favor the red side.

Flashing green "59AR," east of the Wilkerson Bridge, is the last ICW marker before the Pungo River marking system takes over. At Mile 125.9, you pass under the high-level **Wilkerson (U.S. 264) Bridge** (also known as the Walter B. Jones Bridge), which has a charted 64-foot fixed vertical clearance, which is 1 foot less than the Army Corps of Engineers' authorized fixed vertical clearance of 65 feet at mean high water. (See photo.)

⚠️ Sailboats with masts over 60 feet should know their exact mast height with antennas and exercise extreme caution when passing under the Wilkerson Bridge. The slight tidal range here may or may not provide the extra clearance required for safe passage. If the tide boards are missing from this bridge, check locally for information.

■ BELHAVEN AREA

Pungo River

NAVIGATION: Use NOAA Charts 11553 and 11554. Green daybeacon "27PR" is the first Pungo River marker, with red daybeacon "28" just to its south. The river is easy to follow, although floating logs and submerged obstacles require caution. During periods of extreme low water, the tips of several submerged pilings are sometimes visible along the channel between the

RIVER FOREST MANOR & MARINA

Pantego Creek

Wilkerson Bridge and flashing green "23" on the north edge of the channel. Heading southwest on the Pungo River, stay in the channel and give flashing green "21" a wide berth to avoid the chronic shoaling extending from the western bank. The channel is well marked up to Belhaven's entrance channel, which is reached by heading northwest from quick flashing red "10" in the Pungo River.

Dockage: After exiting the Alligator River-Pungo River Canal, the well-regarded Dowry Creek Marina is just north of the channel at green daybeacon "15" (Mile 131.6). The marked entrance channel has a minimum depth of 8 feet MLW. Experienced deckhands will help you dock. The marina sell all fuels and offers transient slips with amenities such as WiFi, a laundry, a swimming pool, tennis courts and a courtesy car. Major upgrades to the docks and power was completed in 2019.

Anchorage: When the wind is up, the best protection in the area can be found in the headwaters of the Pungo River, just north of the lower end of the Alligator River-Pungo River Canal in 7 to 10 feet MLW among crab pots. Enter Back Landing Bay at flashing green "23" (Mile 127.3) proceeding north to select a spot with desired protection, well off the ICW. Minding the depth sounder, you can pick your way for some distance into the river. The bottom is uneven, soft and given to hump-like shoals, even in what is ostensibly the center channel. It may be difficult at first to get the anchor to set, but it will usually dig in tightly by backing down. This anchorage gets high marks for its protection and there is a sandy beach for shore access for the dog. This is a large anchorage area, with space for many boats, so spread out upriver if the first cove is crowded.

Scranton Creek, on the south side of the Pungo River at Mile 129.5, has good holding in mud in 8 to 10 feet MLW. It is exposed to the west. Local knowledge advises that you stay in the middle of the creek due to sunken pilings beneath the surface along both sides.

Another anchorage is available across the river in the center of Upper Dowry Creek (Mile 131.6), north of Dowry Creek Marina. The creek carries 5- to 6-foot MLW depths for about a 0.25 mile north of the mouth. Secure holding in clay and a short fetch make this location a favorite retreat for local skippers when even the most severe storms approach. Cruisers also frequent this anchorage on a regular basis, arranging for facilities use with Dowry Creek Marina for a modest daily fee. Several smaller side creeks along the Pungo River have adequate depths for anchoring shallow-drafted boats.

Belhaven

Belhaven (which translates as "beautiful harbor") is a popular rest stop for ICW travelers. The town sits among old forests and wide creeks, good anchorages and dark water. It offers the charm of an historic small town life with pastoral views and many opportunities to observe wildlife. Drop anchor or tie up at the town dock or one of the marinas and take a short walk into town where you will find shops, restaurants and the museum. You will pass beautiful Victorian homes along Belhaven's tree-lined streets, many with their windows open to catch the river breeze.

NAVIGATION: Use NOAA Chart 11553. The approach to the full-service marinas and boatyards of Belhaven is easy and well marked. On approach, reduce your

Pungo River, NC

		Dockage					Supplies		Services					
Marina	Phone	Largest Vessel Accommodated	VHF Channel Monitored	Transient Berths / Total Berths	Approach / Dockside Depth (reported)	Floating Docks	Gas / Diesel	Groceries, Ice, Marine Supplies, Snacks	Repairs: Hull, Engine, Propeller	Lift (tonnage), Crane, Rail	Min/Max Amps	Laundry, Pool, Showers, Courtesy Car	Pump-Out Station	Nearby: Grocery Store, Motel, Restaurant
UPPER DOWRY CREEK														
1. Dowry Creek Marina 💻 WiFi 132	252-943-2728	130	16/71	53/73	9/9	–	GD	IS	HEP	–	20/200+	LPSC	P	–
BELHAVEN AREA														
2. River Forest Boatyard/Shipyard 💻 WiFi WG	252-943-2151	65	16/68	–	8/8	–	–	IM	HEP	L40	15/50	LSC	P	GMR
3. River Forest Manor and Marina 💻 WiFi WG	252-943-0030	140	16/68	13/31	9/9	–	GD	I	HEP	–	30/100	LS	P	GMR
4. Belhaven Marina 💻 WiFi 2 W of 136	252-944-0066	150	16/09	23/23	9/9	–	–	I	HEP	R75	30/50	LS	–	GR
5. Belhaven Town Docks At Wyne's Gut 💻 WiFi	252-944-0066	–	16	5/5	7/6.5	–	–	I	–	–	30/30	–	P	GMR
6. Belhaven Cooperage Town Docks	252-943-3055	50	–	8/8	7/6	–	–	–	–	–	–	–	–	GR
PUNGO CREEK														
7. Pungo Creek Marina 💻 WiFi 135	252-964-3777	110	16/17	10/48	10/10	–	GD	IS	–	–	30/50	LS	–	–

💻 Internet Access WiFi Wireless Internet Access WG Waterway Guide Cruising Club Partner onSpot dockside WiFi facility

See WaterwayGuide.com for current rates, fuel prices, web site addresses, and other up-to-the-minute information. *(Information in the table is provided by the facilities.)*

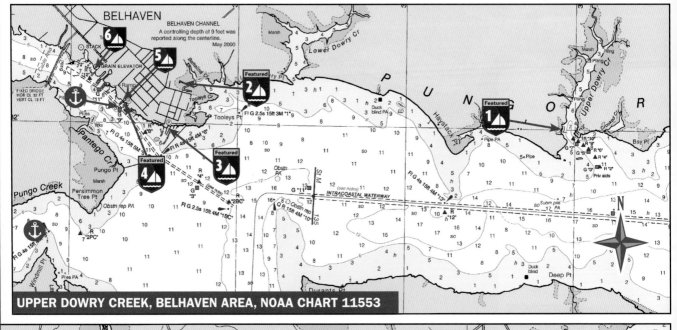

UPPER DOWRY CREEK, BELHAVEN AREA, NOAA CHART 11553

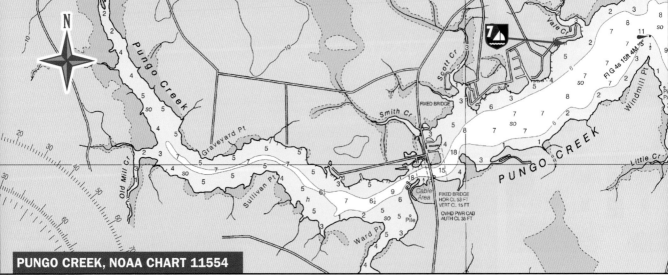

PUNGO CREEK, NOAA CHART 11554

GOIN' ASHORE: **BELHAVEN, NC**

	SERVICES
1	Library
	ATTRACTIONS
2	Belhaven Main Street Landing
3	Belhaven Memorial Museum
	LODGING
4	Between Water & Main
5	Belhaven Water Street B&B
6	Bellport Inn B&B

	SHOPPING
7	Riddick & Windley Hardware/ Hand Picked Sister
8	Winbrandt Creations
	DINING
9	Farm Boy's Restaurant
10	Fish Hooks Cafe
11	Georgie's Sport & Oyster Bar
12	Gingerbread Bakery and O'Neals Snack Bar

13	Rack Time
14	Spoon River Artworks & Market
15	Tavern at Jack's Neck
	MARINAS
16	Belhaven Marina
17	Belhaven Town Docks
18	River Forest Boatyard/Shipyard
19	River Forest Manor and Marina

When Daniel Latham built a hunting and fishing camp in 1868 on what is now the River Forest Manor, Jack's Neck was little more than a small settlement inhabited by a few farmers and fishermen. In time, the town changed its name to Belhaven, and several lumber companies began supplying wood products produced from the local mills. With the addition of a rail spur from the Norfolk and Southern Railroad, and the port's location near the Pamlico Sound, the town became a vital transportation artery for the distribution of goods throughout eastern North Carolina. Today, the town's businesses mainly serve the surrounding farming communities, the local residents, and tourists. Many of the grand homes built in the late 1800s and early 1900s remain standing today. The largest

of all is River Forest Manor, completed in 1904, which has undergone a recent renovation. (See sidebar.)

Attractions: The town offers a number of local historical sites, including the Belhaven Memorial Museum (211 E. Main St., 252-943-6817), located on the second floor of the old Belhaven Town Hall. Here, you will find antiques from Eva Blount Way's collection. Gathered in the early 1900s as a means of raising money for the American Red Cross, the collection includes an eight-legged pig, a wedding party of dressed fleas and more than 30,000 buttons of varying colors and shapes.

There are plenty of ways to immerse yourself in Belhaven's unique culture. There are bluegrass jams every Tuesday night (open to the public) at 6:30 p.m. at Belhaven Mainstreet Landing (226 Main St.) Belhaven's famous 4th of July Celebration and Parade has been held continuously for over 70 years and is in old-time style, complete with fireworks, concerts, contests, games, street dancing and more. Belhaven holds an annual ICW celebration in the fall of each year featuring artists, antique boats and cars, a roaring 20s fashion show and the now-famous Downeast Chowder Cook Off featuring over 15 different types of chowder.

Shopping: If you are looking for pipes and fittings or a little red wagon, you will probably find it at Riddick & Windley (235 Pamlico St., 252-943-2205). This Ace Hardware affiliate is located within walking distance of most marinas and the Town Dock. It is an old-fashioned hardware store, and they have just about everything, including a great wine selection and ice. They also have a nice selection of stainless fasteners for marine use. Located within Riddick & Windley is Handpicked Sister (235 Pamlico St., 252-943-2205), which has an eclectic and artistic array of gifts, home décor and design ideas meshing old and new.

Just across from the Town Docks is Winbrandt Creations (273 E. Water St., 252-943-8360), home to local one-of-a-kind arts and crafts made by local artisans. Market 32 (292 E. Main St., 252-943-9101) is a collection of shops with everything from flowers and antiques, mermaids to homemade jam, and clothing for big girls to little tots. Attic Life (288 Pamlico St., 252-943-0550) is eye candy for the picker. Whether it's an old pull-toy, a vintage vanity set, or an antique truck filled with hand stitched linen, you'll find something sure to bring back memories of a special time or a special someone in your life.

To fill prescriptions, call O'Neal's Drug Store (820 W. Main St., 252-943-2643); they deliver to the Town Dock. This is also the location of Coastal Family Practice (252-943-0056), which accepts walk-ins.

For outboard engine service contact Radcliffe Marine (252-943-3923), a dealer for Honda, Mercury, and Yamaha outboards. They are located out by the Food Lion but are willing to pick up small engines for service. For cruisers with bicycles, a Food Lion grocery store, pharmacy and liquor store are a short ride from the marina. You can also call Diana at the Belhaven Community Chamber (252-943-3770) and she'll be happy to provide transportation.

If you want a break from the bunk, spend a few nights at one of the three bed and breakfast inns in town. Belhaven Water Street Bed and Breakfast Ltd. (567 E. Water St., 252-943-2825) is a beautifully decorated and furnished 100-year-old home with three guest rooms, each with views of the Belhaven Harbor. Call ahead for pick up. The Bellport Inn (723 E. Main St., 252-943-9910) is a lovely B&B with four rooms decorated with international themes. Between Water & Main located at 367 E. Water St. (252-943-0367) offers spacious rooms, some with water views and all with en suite baths. The innkeeper is a registered yoga instructor and has a yoga studio on site. Classes are open to guests.

The River Forest Manor and Marina (738 E. Main St., 252-943-0030) has detached bungalows, three mini-suites and a large room with two queen sized beds over the marina office for rent. The Manor House is open for weddings and special events.

Dining: Get the kids off the boat and spend the afternoon at Rack Time. This lively location is part bar, part family entertainment venue (333 Pamlico St., 252-944-0212). Gingerbread Bakery and O'Neal's Snack Bar (278 E. Main St., 252-944-0099) is a favorite among locals who enjoy the delicious daily breakfast and lunch specials. The baked goods and pastries are homemade. Fish Hooks Café (231 E. Main St., 252-943-9948) is known for fresh local seafood entrées, daily lunch buffets, Sunday brunches and great service. You might also enjoy the beef sandwich at Farm Boy's Restaurant (216 Pamlico St., 252-943-3295), which is crowded with locals at lunchtime. On Friday and Saturday nights you can dine on the Front Porch (seasonal), where there is frequently live music.

If you are in town Thursday through Saturday night, make sure you try Georgie's Sport & Oyster Bar (458 Pamlico St., 252-943-2102) for tasty NC grilled, broiled or steamed seafood, steaks or cheeseburgers. The Tavern at Jack's Neck (238 Pamlico St., 252-943-6100) serves anything from a 12-oz flame grilled rib eye steak to made-from-scratch pizzas, which people say are the best they've ever had. They are open for dinner Wednesday through Sunday starting at 5:00 p.m. and feature a full bar and numerous televisions.

For a very special dining experience, stop in at the farm-to-fork Spoon River Market & Artworks (263 Pamlico St., 252-945-3899), just a short stroll from the Town Dock. You can browse their wine room with over 300 selections and the prices are modest. Reservations are highly recommended on weekends as this restaurant draws from a regional clientele.

In this unique waterfront town you will find fine dining at great prices, and you will be more than welcomed in your shorts and flip flops.

Explore *Belhaven,*

Belhaven Marina

Located in downtown Belhaven, North Carolina, ICW# 136. All restaurants, shops, and attractions are within steps of the marina. Over 1000' of dockage accommodating boats up to 150'. Amenities include: Private bathrooms (towels, soap & shampoo provided), free laundry, high speed internet, stocked bar, lounge, ship's store, outdoor grills, kayaks, large gazebo, and putting green. Best customer service on the ICW with over 500 online 5 star reviews!
belhavenmarina.com | 252-944-0066 | 332 E. Water St.

Spoon River

Farm-to-fork style restaurant located just steps from the waterfront! Artful, creative food and drinks in a uniquely elegant environment. We source locally as much as possible and believe in supporting NC agriculture. Menus change seasonally, weekly, and even daily based upon what is available. Visit our website for hours. **SpoonRiverNC.com | 252-945-3899 | 263 Pamlico St.**

Rack Time

Get off your boat and have some fun! Rack Time is the perfect blend of lively bar and family entertainment venue. We have 3 pool tables, numerous arcade games, juke boxes and live music. Come enjoy the "coldest beverages in town!"
RackTimeBelhaven.com | 252-944-0212 | 333 Pamlico St.

Fish Hooks Cafe

Family owned and operated for 14 years, Fish Hooks Cafe is well known for fresh seafood, prime cuts of beef and delicious entrees. They offer daily specials, a fresh buffet featuring southern food and a bountiful salad bar, plus a lighter-fare-menu for those looking for smaller portions. Enjoy their full-service bar and extra spacious room for private parties or festive occasions.
Check them out on Facebook! | 252-943-9948 | 231 East Main St.

Georgie's Sport & Oyster Bar

Family restaurant specializing in fresh local seafood and steaks! We are popular with locals and also have a great kids menu. Open for dinner Thursday through Saturday from 5:30 – until.
Visit us on Facebook! | 252-943-2102 | 458 Pamlico St.

Farm Boys Restaurant

Located in the heart of Belhaven just steps from the Town Dock, Farm Boys serves breakfast, lunch and dinner from 7am to 7pm Mon-Sat. "Home of the Beef sandwich" their menu also includes burgers, BBQ, seafood plates, corn nuggets, milkshakes & more. A local hometown favorite since 1969, Farm Boys also boasts "the best sweet tea in town". Get it to go or cozy up to one of our waterview picnic tables and watch the boats sail by!
www.facebook.com/FarmBoysRestaurant | 252-943-3295 | 216 Pamlico St.

SHOPPING • DINING • ENTERTAINMENT

Belhaven Water Street B&B

Innkeepers Andrew & Karen Fisher cruised to Belhaven on their 32' Nordic Tug in 2002 and loved the town so much they never left! All bedrooms have private baths, fireplaces, waterfront views, and high-speed WiFi. They will gladly pick you up at the Town Dock or local marina, just call ahead!

BelhavenWaterStreetBandB.com | 252-943-2825 | 567 East Water St.

Low Tide Realty

Our mission for Low Tide Realty is simple, we want to build strong, lifelong relationships. Our clients become friends and when their friends and family have real estate needs, they strongly recommend us. Specializing in Beaufort County waterfront real estate, our office is located directly across from the town dock

lowtiderealty.com/belhaven | 252-923-9310 or 252-402-8103

That's Sew Marti LLC

Welcome to That's Sew Marti where you can enjoy monograms and embroidery without having to leave Belhaven! Digitized logos for boats to business logos are available with quick turn-around! Enjoy your logo or monogram on shirts, hats, cozies and even BOOTS!!!

etsy.com.shop/ThatsSewMarti | 252-943-8766 | 293 East Water St., Ste. 253

Radcliffe Marine

We are a full-service marine dealership specializing in Mercury, Yamaha, Honda, and Suzuki outboards, and also have the largest selection of boating parts and accessories in Belhaven! With over 40 years of experience, we know that top service is key to maintaining client relationships. Delivery to area marinas is available upon request. **RadcliffeMarine.com | 252-943-3923 | 865 U.S. 264 Bypass**

Southern Tuck

Southern charm "tucked" right in the heart of Belhaven! Southern Tuck offers boutique style shopping at affordable prices. We carry men and women's apparel, jewelry, shoes, home decor, and gifts for any occasion!

Visit them on Facebook and Instagram! | 252-943-8138 | 292B East Main St.

Tavern at Jack's Neck

The Tavern's diverse menu includes "the best Shrimp & Grits ever," Certified Angus Beef steaks and burgers, world-class pizzas, pasta dishes, fresh salads and Chef Specials most every night. Relax and enjoy the atmosphere of our incredible Teak & Walnut bar. Visit our website for hours.

TavernAtJacks.com | 252-943-6100 | 238 Pamlico St.

SHOPPING • DINING • ENTERTAINMENT

Explore Belhaven, NC —Birthplace of the ICW

Belhaven Main Street Landing

Free live music every Tuesday evening from 6:30-8:30pm! Experience Bluegrass, Country, Gospel, and a little Rock & Roll. Bring your instruments and join the jam session, or just come and enjoy the music. Located a short walk from Town Dock, or dinghy under the bridge and tie up at their dock. Visit them on Facebook for photos & videos.
www.facebook.com/BelhavenMainstreetLanding | 252-945-7028 | 226 East Main St.

Riddick & Windley

This Ace Hardware store, family owned & operated since 1938 has everything you expect from a local hardware store & much more. Their motto is "If we don't have it, you don't need it!" Inside the Handpicked Sister boutique offers an uncommon mix of home furnishings, gifts & apparel. This store is an adventure you don't want to miss! A must see one-stop-shop for travelers & locals alike! **www.facebook.com/rwhardwarenc www.facebook.com/handpickedsister | 252.943.2205 | 235 Pamlico St.**

SHOPPING • DINING • ENTERTAINMENT

Pantego Creek

Belhaven, NC: Birthplace of the ICW

Poised on the estuary of the Pamlico Sound up the Pungo River at the mouth of Pantego Creek, Belhaven is an ideal side trip for cruisers who appreciate the rich history of U.S. maritime commerce and recreation.

In September 1928 the Alligator River–Pungo River Canal was completed and opened. This was the last remaining link to complete the 1,090-mile Atlantic Intracoastal Waterway from Norfolk to Miami and when it was officially opened and dedicated 20,000 people descended on the tiny town of Belhaven for the ceremonies. The Navy sent two seaplanes, the Coast Guard sent several cutters and the Army sent a blimp. Many high-ranking politicians from Washington, DC, were present for the festivities. Belhaven was designated as "The Birthplace of the ICW" by the Atlantic Intracoastal Waterway Association in a special ceremony in 2013. This is a distinction its townsfolk hold in the highest regard. It's so important, in fact, that the town recognizes the waterway's completion with an annual ICW Celebration that includes a chowder tasting, street festival, flotilla with antique boats and traditional Blessing of the Boats ceremony.

Among its appeal as an important mariner's destination, Belhaven's restaurants and businesses have garnered great reviews from cruisers who travel the world. Of those with the greatest acclaim is the River Forest Manor & Marina. Commissioned over a century ago in 1899 by John Aaron Wilkinson, president of the J.L. Roper Lumber Company and vice president of Norfolk and Southern Railroad, the River Forest Manor & Marina has undergone an extensive restoration to showcase the original beauty and splendor of the historical landmark.

Once a must-visit destination for celebrities, politicos and wealthy stakeholders including American actor and dancer James Cagney, businessman Harvey Firestone and British model Twiggy, the River Forest Manor & Marina fell into disrepair and closed in 2011. It was purchased in October 2014 by a group of visionary Belhaven residents and investors focused on transforming the grand property to meet Mr. Wilkinson's original vision of an impressive place to entertain, host lavish parties and welcome cruisers from all over the world.

Renovations to the well-known marina came first, including an updated main pier and new secondary pier with deep-water transient and long-term docking slips. The group then turned its attention to the manor seeking to preserve much of the original construction, especially the detailed finishes and ornately carved plasterwork ceilings sculpted by many of the same Italian craftsman who contributed to the intricate designs at the Biltmore Estate in Asheville, NC. Today, the restored mansion serves as a boutique hotel and wedding and events venue.

Consider a stop in Belhaven. The beautiful harbor town and the River Forest Manor & Marina are truly worth a visit.

speed and wake just beyond green daybeacon "3" and red daybeacon "4" when entering Pantego Creek. The channel carries 9-foot depths along the centerline.

At Belhaven, the Pungo River makes a 90-degree turn to the south for the 10-mile run to the Pamlico River. Heading south into the Pungo River the buoys suddenly reverse, with green aids to starboard, but still with the familiar ICW yellow triangles and squares marking the boards to signify they are ICW markers. This is because you are going downstream here on the Pungo River, which is marked from seaward.

Dockage: Just north on Pantego Creek is River Forest Boatyard/Shipyard, a full-service shipyard specializing in prop and shaft repair, hull painting, electrical repairs and all types of marine overhauls. They have a full-time mechanic and diver, plus a 40-ton lift. Do-it-yourself boaters are welcome. Rental cars are available and they have complimentary golf carts for getting around town.

Immediately inside the charted Belhaven storm barrier to the right (via a marked channel) is River Forest Manor and Marina. The recently renovated manor is open (see sidebar) and the new detached bungalows can accommodate those looking for a land vacation or a location for meeting friends and family. The marina has transient slips with water and power, plus complimentary laundry, a tennis court and electric golf carts. They also sell all fuels.

Belhaven Marina is to the north with slips and offers some repairs. They are known for their clean heads and showers with soap and towels. They also offer a free laundry.

Immediately to the north are the Belhaven Town Docks at Wynne's Gut with power (30 amp) and water. A nice boater lounge, restrooms and showers are only available when the Chamber of Commerce is open (closed Saturday, Sunday and Monday). Payment for the town docks can be made by calling the dockmaster at Belhaven Marina (252-944-0066). He will come to you or you can go to him. There is a maximum 3-night stay.

Also owned by the town is Belhaven Cooperage Town Docks just past red daybeacon "12" on Pantego Creek. The fixed docks (no water or electrical service) are available on a first-come, first-served basis with a maximum stay of 72 hours.

Anchorage: Once inside the storm barrier at Belhaven, you can anchor northwest of the channel in 7- to 9-foot MLW depths with fair holding. This is a popular spot despite considerable wave action when the wind picks up, as it often does in the afternoon. This is not a good anchorage in wind from any southerly quadrant. Care should be taken to avoid a shoal in front of the (closed) hospital.

To access the dinghy landing, follow Wynn's Gut past the town docks and under the **Water Street Bridge** (7-foot fixed vertical clearance, depending on tide). The Belhaven Mainstreet Landing is to starboard with 130 feet of dockage suited for dinghies or small powerboats visiting downtown sites. This is the site of the popular free jam held every Tuesday and featuring bluegrass, country, gospel and a little bit of rock and roll. All are welcome.

Pungo Creek–ICW Mile 135

NAVIGATION: Use NOAA Chart 11554. Steer between red daybeacon "2PC" and flashing green "3" and then run southwest of Windmill Point. Crab pot buoys are scattered throughout the creek; work your way in carefully.

Dockage: Pungo Creek Marina at Mile 135 sells all fuels and offers transient slips. This quiet marina offers canoes for rent, great fishing, picnic tables and a BBQ for you to use.

Anchorage: There is an anchorage to port past Windmill Point. This is a great location to sit out strong winds excellent holding in 7 to 10 feet MLW and good wind protection.

Jordan Creek–ICW Mile 140

Jordan Creek is 5 miles south of Pungo Creek and to the south and east of the flashing red "4" at Mile 140. The entrance is marked but has a bar and should not be attempted without local knowledge if you draw more than 5 feet. (You will see large sailboats inside.) Favor the green side of the channel.

Dockage: Limited transient dockage may be available at the friendly River Rat Yacht Club for members of reciprocating clubs. There is not a full-time harbormaster, but there are usually "Rats" around willing to help.

Anchorage: Jordan Creek offers protection from all but strong easterly winds. Good holding can be found in main bowl or to north at the fork. Directly across the river across from Jordan Creek is unmarked Slade Creek. This harbor is difficult to enter without local knowledge due to shoaling on both sides of the twisty entrance and very shallow depths outside the channel. Once inside, Slade Creek is deep (7 to 9 feet MLW) and wide with good holding and wind protection.

◼ SIDE TRIP: PAMLICO RIVER

Sixty-five miles (via the ICW) south of Albemarle Sound lays the northwestern prong of Pamlico Sound, which reaches up to meet the Pamlico River. The Pamlico River is wide and easily navigable to Washington, NC, where the Pamlico River becomes the Tar River. This wide, beautiful river is lined with wooded banks and one industrial site–a phosphate mine on the south side of the river, a little more than 10 miles from the ICW.

NAVIGATION: Use NOAA Charts 11553 and 11554. If you are southbound, the entrance to the Pamlico River from the ICW is around the junction flashing red (2+1) "PR" (Mile 146), marking the shoal off Wades Point at the mouth of the Pungo River. Do not attempt to cut inside the marker unless you are very familiar with the area. Take care not to hit the unmarked, unlighted Mile 145 marker on the east side of the Pungo River prior to Wades Point.

⚠️ The Pamlico River ferry runs between Aurora and Bayview (year-round) at 6:30 a.m., 8:00 a.m., 10:15 a.m., 11:45 a.m., 2:45 p.m., 5:00 p.m., 6:15 p.m. Keep your eyes open and stay out of its way.

South Creek

South Creek lies just west of the small charted Indian Island on the south shore of the Pamlico River. Deep and well marked all the way to the town of Aurora, this is an excellent creek for exploration or anchorage, but be aware that there are no facilities for transient boaters. Dinghies can tie to the former town docks, which are now leased by North Carolina Fish and Wildlife.

Downtown Aurora is about three blocks from the waterfront. The Aurora Fossil Museum (400 Main St., 252-322-4238), located near the head of South Creek off the Pamlico River, is well worth a visit. It houses a collection of shark teeth, whalebones and other fossils. Visitors can sift through fossil bed soil (compliments of the nearby phosphate mine) and find their own souvenir shark teeth, free of charge.

NAVIGATION: Use NOAA Chart 11554. When approaching Aurora, the channel narrows and depths shoal to 5 to 7 feet. Follow the daybeacons carefully and save any shallow-water exploration for your dinghy.

Anchorage: South Creek offers numerous anchorage possibilities off of the well-marked channel, but has no protection from the east or west. Nearby Bond Creek to the south (at the town of South Creek) has good holding in soft mud with 7 to 9 feet MLW.

North Creek

North Creek lies directly across the Pamlico River on the north shore. Flashing green "1" marks the entrance to the channel. The channel has about 4 feet of water and is very tricky, especially where it narrows dramatically at red daybeacon "2."

Dockage/Anchorage: There is fuel and ice available at North Creek Marina, which caters to small fishing boats. Anchoring is possible, but be aware of a very soft, muddy bottom, which may cause anchors to drag. Ski-boats are common here in the summer months, creating a lot of traffic and uncomfortable wakes.

Pamlico River, NC

		Largest Vessel Accommodated	VHF Channel Monitored	Approach / Dockside Depth (reported)	Transient Berths / Total Berths	Floating Docks	Groceries, Ice, Marine Supplies, Snacks	Gas / Diesel	Repairs: Hull, Engine, Propeller	Lift (tonnage), Crane, Rail	Min/Max Amps	Laundry, Pool, Showers, Courtesy Car	Pump-Out Station	Nearby: Grocery Store, Motel, Restaurant
BATH AREA					**Dockage**			**Supplies**				**Services**		
1. Bath Harbor Marina 💻 📶	252-923-5711	60	16	2/43	6/8	–	–	M	–	–	30/50	LSC	–	GMR
2. Harding's Landing Marina, Bath State Dock	252-923-3971	40	–	7/7	6/6	–	–	–	–	–	30/30	–	–	GMR
BROAD CREEK														
3. Broad Creek Marina	252-946-4924	38	–	20/100	4/4	–	–	–	–	–	30/30	S	P	GR
4. McCotters Marina & Boatyard 💻 📶	**252-975-2174**	**65**	**16**	**15/180**	**6/6**	–	–	IMS	HEP	L36	30/50	LSC	P	–
5. Washington Yacht & Country Club 💻 📶	252-402-5153	55	–	4/177	6/6	GD	IS	–	–	–	30/50	LPS	P	R

💻 Internet Access 📶 Wireless Internet Access 🅆🅖 Waterway Guide Cruising Club Partner 📶onSpot dockside WiFi facility
See WaterwayGuide.com for current rates, fuel prices, web site addresses, and other up-to-the-minute information. *(Information in the table is provided by the facilities.)*

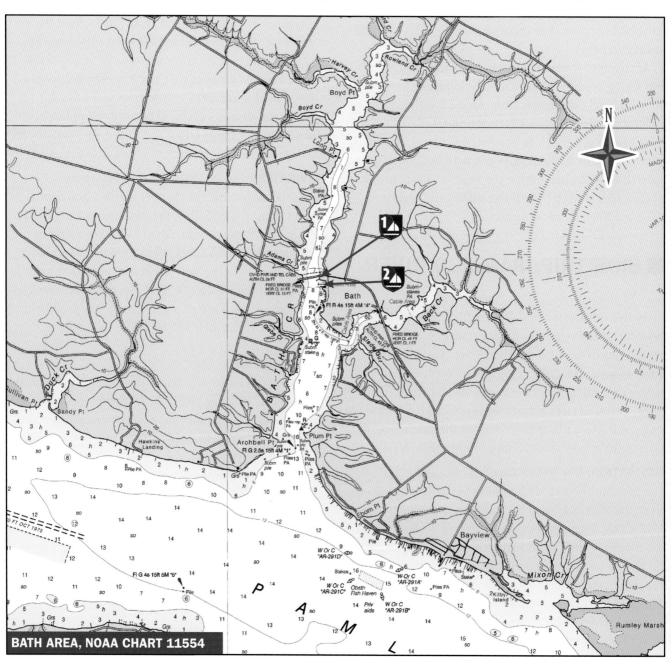

BATH AREA, NOAA CHART 11554

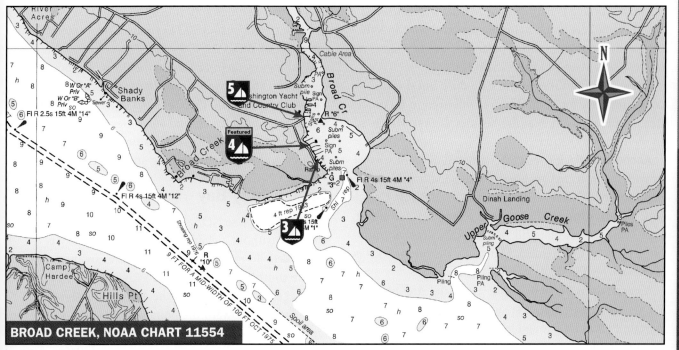

BROAD CREEK, NOAA CHART 11554

Bath Creek

The waterfront at the little historic town of Bath on the north shore of the Pamlico River is well worth a visit, especially if you are a history buff. Founded in 1696 and established in 1705, it is listed as the oldest town in North Carolina. Bath's most notorious citizen was Edward Teach, also known as Blackbeard (the pirate). Standing in front of the historic Bonner House and looking south across the bay, it is easy to see why Blackbeard selected Bath and Plum Point as his base of operation: privacy. That much has not changed. You can find information about Blackbeard and Bath at the Visitor Center (252-923-3971) between Main St. and Harding St. just one block from the water.

NAVIGATION: Use NOAA Chart 11554. Beyond the ferry crossing, 3 miles northwest of flashing red "4" off Gum Point, set a northerly course into Bath Creek. Upon entry, avoid the fish stakes and be wary of any possible submerged pilings after clearing flashing green "1" at the entrance. The harbor is easy to enter if you mind the NOAA chart and watch out for the crab pots around flashing green "1" and red daybeacon "2" (Plum and Archbell Points).

Dockage: Pass green daybeacon "3" and flashing red "4" to reach dockage at the Bath Harbor Marina or Harding's Landing Marina (Bath State Dock). Both facilities are just to the south of the **Bath Creek Bridge** (13-foot fixed vertical clearance) and have at least 6-foot MLW approach depths. To starboard just

before the bridge is Bath Harbor Marina with slips for vessels to 60 feet and hotel rooms to rent. It is directly across the street from the popular Blackbeard's Slices and Ices (101 N. Main St., 252-923-9444).

There are no utilities at the state dock but dockage is complimentary for 72 hours. You will need to fill out a free permit application at the Visitors' Center, which is in the Historic District.

Anchorage: Back Creek (to starboard off Bath Creek) provides a protected anchorage with good holding and depths of 6 to 7 feet MLW up to the fixed **Back Creek (NC 92) Bridge** (7-foot vertical clearance). Ice cream, cold beer and a casual grill (burgers, hot dogs, shrimp burger) are at Quarterdeck Marina by the bridge. Gas is also available for shallow-draft boats.

You can drop the hook inside Plum and Archbell Points on the east and west sides of the creek at the mouth. Pull in far enough to be out of the way of any passing traffic.

Broad Creek

Broad Creek is seven miles to the west of Bath. Several hundred sail and powerboats make Broad Creek their home port, and it is the main boating center for Washington, 7 miles farther to the north-northwest.

NAVIGATION: Use NOAA Chart 11554. Broad Creek's entrance is well marked and easy to negotiate from the east. Steer in a northwesterly direction from flashing green "7" (in the main Pamlico River channel off Maules Point) until flashing green "1" is visible north of the main channel and then follow the channel to green daybeacon "3" and flashing red "4." Have a current version of NOAA Chart 11554 handy, and note the spoil areas south of the entrance. If coming from the west, steer east past the red daybeacon "8" before turning north, then turn northwest once on a line between flashing green "7" in the main channel and flashing green "1" in the Broad Creek channel. There is no room for anchoring in this small harbor.

Dockage: To starboard you will see the Pamlico Plantation private docks (no transient dockage). To port are Broad Creek Marina and McCotters Marina & Boatyard. Broad Creek is a small-boat marina with 4-foot approach and dockside depths and can accommodate boats to 38 feet.

Locally-owned and operated McCotters Marina & Boatyard has haul-out facilities and can handle repairs and upgrades, storage and boat sales. Their canvas department can fabricate custom dodgers, biminis,

enclosures, awnings and sail covers, plus restore upholstery and cushions. They may have a transient slip for you; call ahead.

Washington Yacht & Country Club is beyond red daybeacon "6." (Give the marker good clearance.) The over 50-year-old club sells gas and diesel fuel and offers transient dockage and amenities to members of reciprocating clubs. The club features a championship 18-hole golf course, fine dining and tennis courts.

Chocowinity Bay

NAVIGATION: Use NOAA Chart 11554. This is a tricky entrance without a chartplotter because the bay is unmarked. To reach the marina on Chocowinity Bay, stay on the south side of the Pamlico River, south of Fork Point. Leave the channel at the 4-second flashing red "12" and head toward the point at Cals Creek until even with the main channel's 2.5-second flashing red "14." Favor the south shore slightly, giving Fork Point plenty of clearance for shoals, submerged pilings and a hard bottom. Once inside Fork Point, the middle of the bay carries 6-foot depths almost all the way to Sidney Creek. Proceed up the bay until even with Cypress Landing Marina to avoid tree stumps to the east of the marina on the southwest side of the bay. Chocowinity Bay is shallow in places, so call ahead for local advice if you have a deep draft.

Dockage: Cypress Landing Marina is part of the Cypress Landing development and is private. They may be able to accommodate you but call ahead.

Washington

This small community of just under 10,000 residents has a maritime culture all its own, with dozens of colorful crab statues lining the downtown streets, hundreds of boats—both big and small—lining the waterfront, and miles of open Tar and Pamlico River views, extending in virtually every direction. Here you will find a sprawling waterfront with stores, businesses and the historic haunts of pirates. (See "Blackbeard the Pirate" sidebar.)

NAVIGATION: Use NOAA Chart 11554. The NOAA chart shows plenty of water in the Pamlico River even outside the channel until flashing red "14." From there, markers "16," "17," "18" and "19" lead to the **Norfolk Southern Railroad Swing Bridge**. The bridge has 7-foot closed vertical clearance and is usually open; however, the bridge may be closed between 7:30 a.m. and 10:30 a.m. on weekdays and Saturday. Past the railroad swing bridge is the Washington riverfront, located to starboard before the **U.S. Hwy. 17 Swing Bridge** (6-foot closed vertical clearance), which will open with 24-hour notice. This bridge marks the confluence of the Pamlico River and the Tar River and actually changes names at this point. When approaching the town, keep Castle Island to port, and stay within the 9-foot-deep MLW channel.

Dockage: Moss Landing Marina is part of an upscale condo complex. They offer deeded slips in a gated facility but may be able to accommodate you; call ahead. Free dockage is available at no charge for up to 48 hours along four 80-foot bulkheads on the east end of the waterfront. Water and electricity are not available. A fee is charged for stays longer than 48 hours. Transient slips with electricity, water and WiFi are available for a per-foot fee. Reservations are accepted. The lighthouse building has climate-controlled heads and showers and a laundry (fee charged). Short-term docking also is available for $10.00 for up to six hours.

Anchorage: Boats anchor off the free dock when its full but there is no protection here; it is completely open to wind and wakes. Be sure to stay out of the channel.

A floating dinghy dock is located at the west end of the waterfront, near the lighthouse building. Boats anchored in the harbor may use the dinghy dock and the heads and showers once registered with the dock attendant.

Washington Waterfront

Blackbeard the Pirate

You will find many references to Edward Teach (also known as Blackbeard) in this guide. The Pamlico Sound and River were his home waters and the scene of much of his pirating on his flagship, the *Queen Anne's Revenge*.

Supposedly born in Bristol, England, Teach had friends in high places, was quite the lady's man (with as many as seven wives) and had great successes as a pirate. He became a renowned pirate, known for his thick black beard and fearsome appearance; it was reported that he tied lit fuses under his hat and into his beard to frighten his enemies.

Blackbeard's pirate forces terrorized the Caribbean and the southern coast of North America and were notorious for their cruelty. Sometime in June 1718, Blackbeard and at least 20 members of his crew passed through Ocracoke Inlet, NC, entered Pamlico Sound and headed for the town of Bath on the Pamlico River. There he met with Governor Charles Eden who agreed to pardon Blackbeard on behalf of England in exchange for a share of his sizable booty and a promise that he would stop pirating.

When Teach began pirating again, Governor Alexander Spotswood of Virginia dispatched a British naval force under Lieutenant Robert Maynard to North Carolina to deal with Blackbeard. On November 22, Blackbeard's forces were defeated, and he was killed in a bloody battle of Ocracoke Island. Rumor has it that his treasure is buried at Springers Point on Ocracoke. This is now a National Park Service Preserve, so you need not bring your metal detector or shovel.

GOIN' ASHORE: WASHINGTON, NC

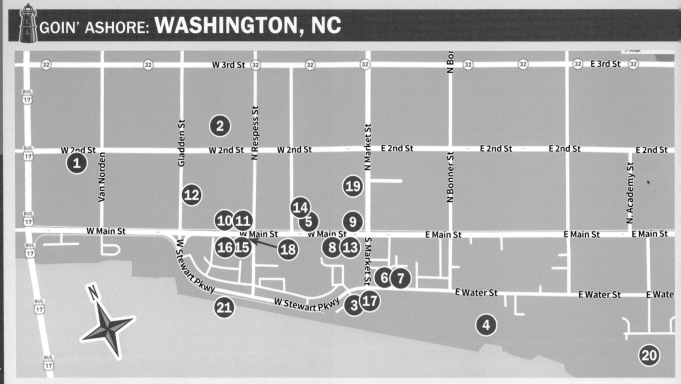

SERVICES	
1	Library
2	Post Office
3	Visitor Information
ATTRACTIONS	
4	Estuarium
5	Turnage Theater
6	Tyndall Studio
7	Wine & Design

SHOPPING	
8	Little Shoppes of Washington
9	Nauti Life
10	Wine & Words
DINING	
11	Bank Bistro & Bar
12	Bill's Hot Dogs
13	Down on Mainstreet
14	Grub Brothers Eatery

15	Main Street Scoops
16	Meeting Place Café
17	On the Waterfront
18	Patty Cakes Cupcake Boutique
19	Rachel K's Bakery
MARINAS	
20	Moss Landing Marina
21	Washington Waterfront Docks

First called Forks of the Tar, the city name was changed in 1776 in honor of Gen. George Washington. Because it was America's first city to be named for Gen. Washington, it is sometimes referred to as "The Original Washington" or "Little Washington" to avoid confusion. The entire waterfront of Washington is listed in the National Register of Historic Places. West of the Highway 17 bridge lays one of the scars from the Civil War. In the spring of 1864, Union forces set fire to Haven's Wharf in an effort to keep naval stores and cotton from falling into the hands of the Confederates. Chimneys were all that remained. There are two homes that withstood the fires and barrages of the war; cannonballs are still lodged in their walls. The Union ship *S.S.V. Picket* can still be seen in the water.

Attractions: Town maps are available at the Visitor Center/Chamber of Commerce at 102 Stewart Pkwy. (252-946-9168). The self-guided Historic Washington Walking Tour starts at 102 Stewart Parkway and takes you through the historic district. Don't miss the Estuarium at 223 E. Water St. (252-948-0000). This is an aquarium with unique exhibits about the Pamlico–Tar River System and features over 200 exhibits with unique environmental artworks, living aquariums and the Crab Pot gift shop. Special programs are offered throughout the year. River Roving Educational Tours of the estuary are seasonal and require reservations.

Inner Banks Outfitters (252-975-3006) at 1950 E. Main St. is located on Runyon Creek at the Haven's Garden public boat ramp. Rent a bike there and pedal over to the Pacific Seacraft factory at 1481 W. 2nd St. (252-948-1421) for a tour where they produce several models of these high quality, blue water sailing yachts. Or visit nearby Goose Creek State Park (2190 Camp Leach Rd., 252-923-2191) is a 1,669 acre National Natural Landmark. If you are in town for the monthly Art Walk (4th Friday, April through October), do take the time to participate. If not, Tyndall Studio (110 E. Water St., 252-943-8573) is a great place to select a painting of North Carolina to take home (or have shipped). There are numerous other galleries along Main St., or unleash your own inner artist at Wine & Design (132 Water St., 252-362-0413).

The Turnage Theatre at 150 W. Main St. (252-946-2504) is an old renovated Vaudeville showhouse that brings an array of musical and theatrical performances to the community. On Saturdays during the spring and summer you will find a Farmers' Market adjacent to the Washington Waterfront.

There is some sort of special event here every month (or more). The Summer Festival is a street fair held in June and the town has a huge 4th of July fireworks display. Pickin' on the Pamlico, held in August, is a crab feast with crabs harvested fresh from the Pamlico River. Smoke on the Water (in October) is an annual chili cook-off with some of the best cooks in the state, plus live music. There is often live music on the waterfront such as the annual BoCo Music Fest and Music in the Streets (held every 3rd Friday, April through October).

Shopping: With the exception of groceries (a 2-mile trek to the Food Lion), most of what you will need is a short walk from the docks. The Little Shoppes of Washington (127 W. Main St., 252-940-1954) features over 25 original boutique shops selling home décor, clothing, jewelry, and accessories. For home and boat décor, visit Nauti Life (112 W. Main St., 252-940-1986). After all that shopping, you may need a glass of wine from Wine & Words (220 W. Main St., 252-974-2870), offering wine, beer and wine accessories, specialty foods, and books.

Dining: Wake up with a treat from Rachel K's Bakery (126 N. Market St., 252-946-2253). Later, wander down to the original Bill's Hot Dogs (109 Gladden St.) for an easy, no-frills lunch. They are renowned for their white chili dogs. This location is strictly for take-out, although

they have a second, newer location with seating that requires transportation.

Meeting Place Café at 225 W. Main St. (252-975-6370) offers a varied menu with patio, waterview dining or indoor seating (daily lunch only and Sunday Brunch), while Down on Mainstreet (107 W. Main St., 252-940-1988) is a family restaurant featuring American cuisine with a Down East flair and outdoor seating with views of the Pamlico River.

For seafood, check out Washington Crab & Seafood Shack (1212 John Small Ave., 252-974-2722). It's a bit off the beaten path but worth it.

For dinner, there are several good choices. Grub Brothers Eatery (156 W. Main St., 252-940-4782) specializes in southern and Cajun cuisine. On the Waterfront (1 Harding Square, 252-946-3463) has patio dining, plus oyster and martini bars. The Bank Bistro & Bar (216 W. Main St., 252-948-9000) serves southern-inspired cuisine in a renovated bank building. Top it all off with something sweet from Patty Cakes Cupcake Boutique at 141 S. Market St. (570-460-7388) or Main Street Scoops at 217 W. Main St. (252-974-1114).

Market Street Pub (143 N. Market St., 252-833-4517) has live entertainment Wednesday through Saturday.

Pamlico River, NC

		Largest Vessel Accommodated	VHF Channel Monitored	Transient Berths / Total Berths	Approach / Dockside Depth (reported)	Floating Docks	Gas / Diesel	Groceries, Ice, Marine Supplies, Snacks	Repairs: Hull, Engine, Propeller	Lift (tonnage), Crane, Rail	Min/Max Amps	Laundry, Pool, Showers, Courtesy Car	Pump-Out Station	Nearby: Grocery Store, Motel, Restaurant
				Dockage			**Supplies**		**Services**					
CHOCOWINITY BAY														
1. Cypress Landing Marina - PRIVATE (WiFi)	252-975-3955	42	16	0/222	7/6	F	–	IS	–	–	30/50	PS	P	–
WASHINGTON														
2. Moss Landing Marina (Internet)(WiFi)	252-623-1314	60	16/09	4/52	10/15	F	–	IMS	–	–	30/50	LS	P	GMR
3. Washington Waterfront Docks (WiFi)	252-940-1231	80	16/17	8/36	14/18	–	–	I	–	–	30/50	LSC	P	GMR

(Internet) Internet Access   (WiFi) Wireless Internet Access   **WG** Waterway Guide Cruising Club Partner   ☁onSpot dockside WiFi facility

See WaterwayGuide.com for current rates, fuel prices, web site addresses, and other up-to-the-minute information. *(Information in the table is provided by the facilities.)*

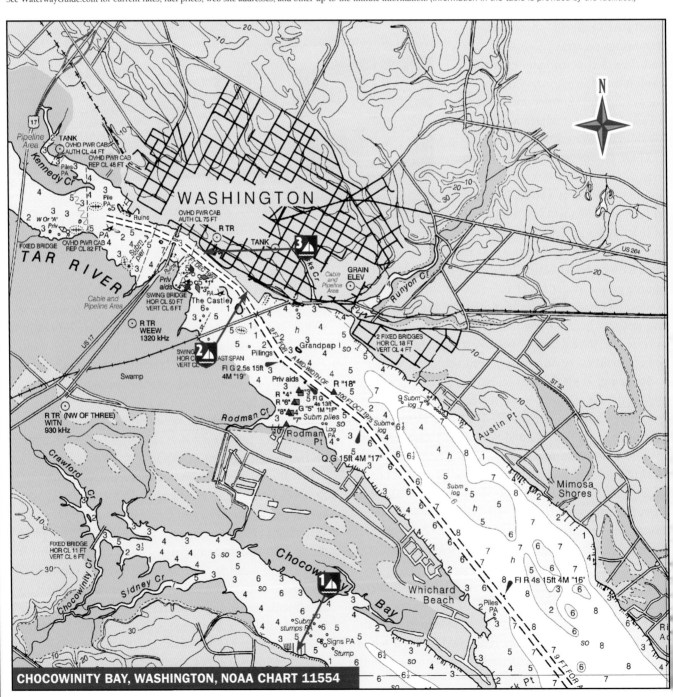

CHOCOWINITY BAY, WASHINGTON, NOAA CHART 11554

■ PAMLICO RIVER TO ORIENTAL

Pamlico River Crossing to Goose Creek– ICW Mile 145 to Mile 155

The ICW follows the broad lower reach of the Pungo River to the junction of the Pamlico River. (Markers are still reversed, green to starboard going south; continue running the yellow squares and triangles.) The markers in the lower Pungo River are spaced far apart and sometimes difficult to locate, but the river is wide and adequately deep.

NAVIGATION: Use NOAA Charts 11553, 11554 and 11548. The Pamlico River crossing is straight and is usually an easy run; however, conflicting currents meet at the junction of the Pungo and Pamlico Rivers. When easterly or westerly winds are strong and gusty, the crossing of the Pamlico River can be rough and wet. Confused seas are common, especially within a mile or so of Wades Point flashing red "PR," which is located around Mile 145.7. Watch for flashing red (2+1) 18-foot light, with red over green triangular boards (on three sides, all reading "PR") on a multi-pile structure. It can be difficult to locate, especially if northbound from Goose Creek.

    Anchorage: On the west side of Goose Creek on the shore of the Pamlico River at Mile 153, Snode Creek offers some protection for all but the northeast in 5- to 6-foot MLW depths with good holding. Turning east at Mile 153.5 (at green daybeacon "13"), you will find 5- to 6-foot MLW depths with good holding in Eastham Creek, with some protection for all but the west, just northeast of the creek's red daybeacon "4" (a private aid). Directly across Goose Creek on the west side is Campbell Creek with good holding in 6 to 7 feet MLW. It is exposed to the east.

ICW Cut to Bay River–ICW Mile 155 to Mile 160

NAVIGATION: Use NOAA Chart 11548.

⚠️ After crossing the Pamlico River to Goose Creek, aids to navigation return to the ICW configuration of red-to-starboard running south. This is especially important when entering Goose Creek, where red daybeacon "4" marks the southeastern edge of a 3-foot shoal and submerged piles. There is shoaling between green daybeacons "5" and "7" so be sure to stay in the middle of the channel.

At Mile 157.2, the area surrounding the **Hobucken (NC 33/304) Bridge** and the Coast Guard Station is a No-Wake Zone. The Hobucken Bridge is concrete, and the underside arches slightly towards the center. There are no bridge boards. The bridge is charted at 65-foot fixed vertical clearance but closer to 64 feet has been observed at mean high water. At about Mile 159, the land cut (canal) ends at Gale Creek, an arm of the Bay River. Use caution in transiting Gale Creek, which is naturally winding though the channel is charted as arrow-straight.

⚠️ Shoaling is encroaching on the channel on the red (west) side of the channel between flashing red "22" and green daybeacon "23" at Hobucken. Boats have reported grounding hard here. It is also a good idea to keep clear of Gale Creek Point, as it is continually building out and encroaching on the channel. Depths outside the markers are a scant 0.5 foot MLW in places.

Be on the lookout for crab pot floats that may be present in the channel between green "25" and green

Jones Bay, NC

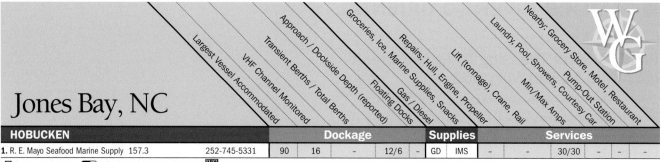

HOBUCKEN				Dockage				Supplies			Services			
	Largest Vessel Accommodated	VHF Channel Monitored	Approach / Dockside Depth (reported)	Transient Berths / Total Berths	Floating Docks	Gas / Diesel	Groceries, Ice, Marine Supplies, Snacks	Repairs: Hull, Engine, Propeller	Lift (tonnage), Crane, Rail	Min/Max Amps	Laundry, Pool, Showers, Courtesy Car	Pump-Out Station	Nearby: Grocery Store, Motel, Restaurant	
1. R. E. Mayo Seafood Marine Supply 157.3	252-745-5331	90	16	–	12/6	–	GD	IMS	–	–	30/30	–	–	–

🖥 Internet Access 📶 Wireless Internet Access **WG** Waterway Guide Cruising Club Partner 🔵onSpot dockside WiFi facility
See WaterwayGuide.com for current rates, fuel prices, web site addresses, and other up-to-the-minute information. *(Information in the table is provided by the facilities.)*

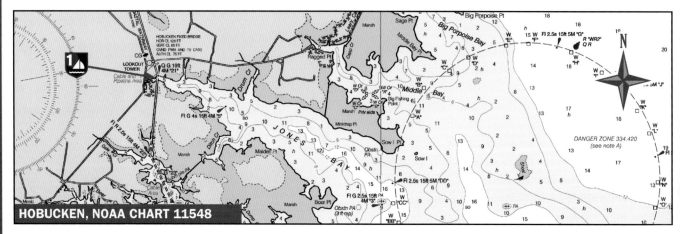

HOBUCKEN, NOAA CHART 11548

"27." When leaving Gale Creek do not mistake the Bay River markers that lead west to Vandemere for those leading southeast to the Neuse River. The colors of the markers on the Bay River are reversed with green on starboard going south, until the Neuse River Junction.

From Gale Creek, the ICW cuts 5 miles down Bay River to Maw Point and Maw Point Shoal (near Mile 165), which continues to build out into the Neuse River. The Hobucken Coast Guard station can give you information on conditions around Maw Point (252-745-3131). When strong winds blow down the Bay River, wave action can be almost as bad as on the much larger Neuse River.

Dockage: The commercial facilities at R. E. Mayo Seafood Marina Supply are on the south side of the Hobucken Bridge (Mile 157.2). Dockage and fuel are available, but this is a working shrimp dock and is usually full of commercial vessels. There can be a considerable wind-driven current at this bridge.

Anchorage: You can anchor along Gale Creek (approximately Mile 159), west of flashing red "22" in 4- to 6-foot MLW depths. An underwater electric cable runs from the mainland to the Jones Island Club, a private lodge on the island shore just east of green daybeacon "23." A sign in the bay warns "Danger High Voltage" so do not anchor here. Another convenient nearby anchorage is in the Bay River at Bear Creek (Mile 160.8) in 7 to 10 feet MLW with a mud bottom and exposure from the east to the south.

Bay River–ICW Mile 160 to Mile 165

NAVIGATION: Use NOAA Chart 11548. Southeast along the Bay River, Pine Tree Point is marked by flashing green "3" to starboard (Mile 162.2), and then by flashing green "1," which marks the shoaling off Deep Point. Do not pass too close to flashing green "1," as shoaling has been reported to extend slightly into the channel from the marker. Like the Pungo River, the marking system for the Bay River is numbered from seaward.

Maw Point and the Neuse River are often an easier run in the morning just after dawn when surface winds may be lighter, so anchoring in Bay River the night before is a good idea. Adequate depths run well upriver to the quaint and quiet towns of Vandemere ("village by the sea") and Bayboro.

To reach Bayboro, proceed past Vandemere, continuing to follow the markers carefully, especially green daybeacon "11" and red daybeacon "12." Do not mistake red daybeacon "14" for red daybeacon "12," or you will find yourself in 4-foot depths along the southwest shore.

Dockage: Vandemere is still a nice place to stretch your legs or wait out bad weather. The 60-slip Up The

Creek Marina@Vandemere may have dockage on their floating docks but call ahead. Hurricane Boatyard in Bayboro has a great do-it-yourself boatyard. They can also provide full or partial service if needed. Transients have access to clean showers and a small but well-stocked chandlery.

Anchorage: To the south, there is a good anchorage in Bonner Bay. To reach Bonner Bay, exit the ICW at quick flashing green "27" (Mile 161) and head southwest. Feel your way in via the unmarked channel with the depth sounder and go up Long Creek (the left fork) to anchor in 9 to 11 feet MLW with good holding in mud. It is a beautiful secluded anchorage, with no structures in sight, but it can be buggy in the summer months.

Although there are no amenities, you can anchor off Vandermere's village dock on Bay River, with exposure from the southeast to the southwest. Stay clear of the channel because shrimp boats use it. Steer toward the village docks from flashing green "5," and drop the anchor in 9 to 10 feet MLW. An east to southeast wind can create rough conditions. Show an anchor light at night and always ask permission to tie up the dinghy if you go ashore.

■ THE NEUSE RIVER

The Neuse is a large river that is open to the Pamlico Sound and can get rough. Check the weather and proceed with respect. First-timers should run compass courses and use radar or GPS whenever possible. A southwest wind can make the 18-mile run to Oriental at Mile 182 a very wet ride. A fall northwester, however, will leave the river calm with the wind coming from the shore. At those times, the wide, lovely Neuse River can be a pleasant change from the narrow land cuts of the ICW, especially for sailors who want to shake out the sails.

NAVIGATION: Use NOAA Chart 11548. Maw Point Shoal introduces you to the Neuse River. Follow the magenta line carefully as you make the 90-degree turn around the Neuse River Junction Light, a 15-foot flashing red light (6-sec intervals). Use special caution here. The three red flashing lights (uncharted) in the prohibited area of Rattan Bay can be confused with the entrance light. More importantly, there are 30 miles of open water between Maw Point and the Outer Banks. Winds out of the east

make it rough and, if you are not careful, you could be set onto the shoal.

If on station, flashing green "1" (off Deep Point) and flashing red "2" (off Maw Point Shoal) make a shortcut inside the Neuse River junction light, but do not use it if brisk winds make Maw Point Shoal a lee shore. Even though depths are at least 8 feet along this shortcut route, crab traps are scattered throughout the area and require attention. From Bay River flashing green "1" off Deep Point, run a course that will put you at least 0.25 mile off flashing red "2" and then head for flashing red "4," off the tip of the shoal extending from Piney Point (at Mile 172.3) on a south-southwesterly course.

If heading west to the Neuse River from Pamlico Sound through the Brant Island Slue be aware that shoaling to 3 feet MLW has been reported in the area off the southeast tip of the charted shoal across from daybeacon "1." Also, at press time in summer 2019 there was discussion of extending the existing Marine Corps bombing range to include Brant Island Shoals. This would effectively prevent all vessels from crossing Brant Island Shoal through the Brant Island Slough, forcing them to go all the way around the end of Brant Island Shoal.

Broad Creek–ICW Mile 173

Northbound boats will appreciate the anchorages in Broad Creek off the Neuse River's western shore. This is also home to the amenity-rich Grace Harbor at River Dunes, a destination in itself.

NAVIGATION: Use NOAA Chart 11548. The white danger marker "BW" guides skippers bound for Broad Creek around the extending shoal south of Piney Point. Shoals at Piney Point and Gum Thicket Shoal continually build out. The danger beacon marks the tip of the shoal between flashing red "4" and the warning daybeacon platform. Do not mistake the more slightly dilapidated white warning daybeacon for flashing red "4" off Piney Point. Depths inshore of the platform are less than 2 feet in spots. All markers off Piney Point should be left well to the north.

Boats bound for Broad Creek should exit the ICW halfway between red daybeacon "4" and red "6" on the Neuse River and follow the markers into Broad Creek. Give green daybeacon "3" a wide berth. Be on the lookout as there may be numerous crab pot floats in the creek.

Neuse River, NC

The following table lists the column groupings: **Dockage** covers Transient/Total Berths, Approach/Dockside Depth and Floating Docks; **Supplies** covers Groceries/Ice/Marine Supplies/Snacks and Gas/Diesel; **Services** covers the remaining columns.

Marina	Phone	Largest Vessel Accommodated	VHF Channel Monitored	Transient Berths / Total Berths	Approach / Dockside Depth (reported)	Floating Docks	Groceries, Ice, Marine Supplies, Snacks	Gas / Diesel	Repairs: Hull, Engine, Propeller	Lift (tonnage), Crane, Rail	Min / Max Amps	Laundry, Pool, Showers, Courtesy Car	Pump-Out Station	Nearby: Grocery Store, Motel, Restaurant
BAYBORO, VANDEMERE														
1. Up The Creek Marina @ Vandemere	252-676-8703	60	–	call/47	9/9	F	–	–	–	–	50/50	–	P	G
2. Hurricane Boatyard 💻 WiFi	252-745-3369	60	–	17/17	8/6.5	F	MS	–	HEP	L50	30/30	LS	–	R
BROAD CREEK														
3. Grace Harbor at River Dunes 💻 onSpot 173	252-249-4908	125	16/72	20/400	7/9	F	IMS	GD	–	–	30/200+	LPS	P	MR
ORIENTAL														
4. Whittaker Pointe Marina 💻 WiFi 181	252-249-1750	100	16/11	8/53	8/6	–	I	–	–	–	30/50	LPSC	–	–
5. Whittaker Creek Yacht Harbor 💻 WiFi 181	252-670-3759	140	16	10/140	7/8	–	M	G	E		30/50	S	–	GMR
6. Sailcraft Marina 💻 WiFi 181	252-249-1754	50	–	2/39	7/6	–	–	–	HEP		30/50	LPS	–	GMR
7. Sailcraft Service 💻 WiFi 181	**252-249-0522**	65	16	12/12	8/7	–	M	–	HEP	L35,C2	30/50	LPS	–	GMR
8. Deaton Yacht Service 💻 WiFi 181	**252-249-1180**	65	16/10	4/29	7/7	–	MS	–	HEP	L35	30/50	LSC	P	GMR
9. Oriental Marina & Inn 💻 WiFi 181.5	**252-249-1818**	100	16/71	27/27	8/6.5	–	IS	GD	–	–	30/50	LPS	–	GMR
10. Oriental Harbor Marina WiFi 181.5	252-671-9692	50	16	25/110	8/6	–	GIMS	–	–	–	30/50	LS	P	GMR
11. Blackwell Point Marina WiFi	252-725-7868	50	16/78	2/10	6/6	F	–	–	–		20/20	S	–	GMR

💻 Internet Access WiFi Wireless Internet Access WG Waterway Guide Cruising Club Partner onSpot dockside WiFi facility
See WaterwayGuide.com for current rates, fuel prices, web site addresses, and other up-to-the-minute information. *(Information in the table is provided by the facilities.)*

Dockage: Grace Harbor at River Dunes is reached by heading northwest from the ICW halfway between flashing reds "4" and "6," and then following the marked channel into Broad Creek. Give the markers at least 50 yards as you pass. The marina is on the port side of the creek at red daybeacon "4." Entry is through a private, well-maintained and marked, bulkheaded channel with charted 8-foot depths. Unless you have the latest updates on your electronic charts, you will not see the channel marked, so follow the private markers. The floating docks at River Dunes have full-length finger piers and 8 feet MLW. They offer resort-type amenities, including croquet on the green, tennis and billiards. A courtesy car is available for the 10-mile trip into Oriental and its many services and amenities.

Anchorage: Anchor beyond red daybeacon "4" in 7 to 8 feet. (Note: This can be buggy!) Another favorite is Burton Creek on Broad Creek's north side, where depths are 5 to 6 feet MLW and protection is excellent except from the east.

Oriental–ICW Mile 182

Oriental has become widely known as the "Sailing Capital of North Carolina," and locals claim sailboats outnumber people three to one, although boating facilities in the area also attract visiting power boaters. The sheltered creeks provide immediate access to the country's second largest estuary and sailing, cruising and gunkholing areas. Local marinas welcome transients and offer supply and repair capabilities to handle virtually any requirement. This is a popular place and space is limited, so reservations are recommended.

NAVIGATION: Use NOAA Chart 11541. Marine facilities begin at Mile 181, where a marked entrance leads to Whittaker Creek. There are more markers here than shown on the NOAA chart, and they make it easy to stay on the range (not charted), which can be picked up on entry. Be sure to give flashing green "5" a wide berth before turning left into the facility-lined creek. Depths of 8 feet are reported for the channel; nevertheless, southwesterly winds can lower this depth, and some shoaling persists in the area around and south of flashing green "5."

In this entire area, it is best to call ahead to the marina of your choice to check for current depths and steering directions at time of entry. Mind the crab traps and do not be surprised to see them in mid-channel. Oriental has no tide to contend with, only the wind-driven ups and downs of eastern and western storms.

Just to the southwest of the entrance to Whittaker Creek on the Neuse River, a well-marked channel carrying 8.5 feet leads to the basin confluence of Smith Creek and Greens Creek, immediately beyond the fixed **Oriental Rd. (NC 1308) Bridge** spanning the junction.

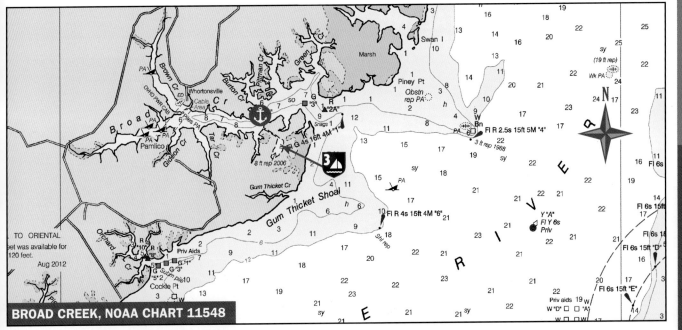

BROAD CREEK, NOAA CHART 11548

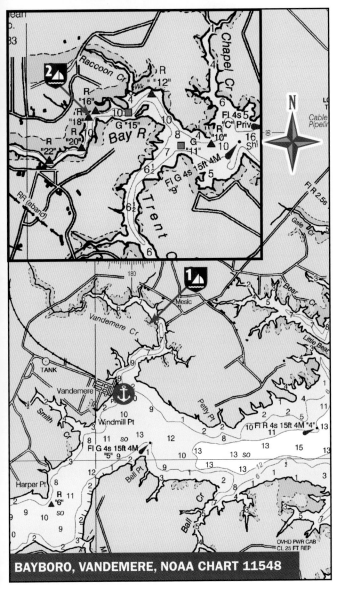

BAYBORO, VANDEMERE, NOAA CHART 11548

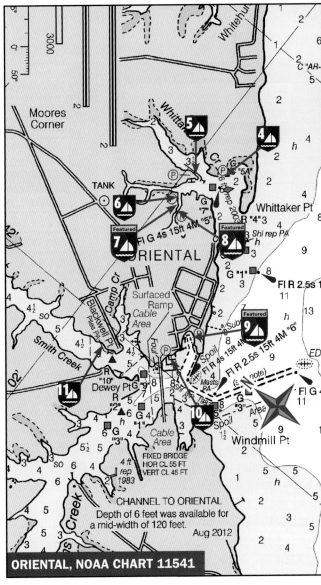

ORIENTAL, NOAA CHART 11541

GOIN' ASHORE: **ORIENTAL, NC**

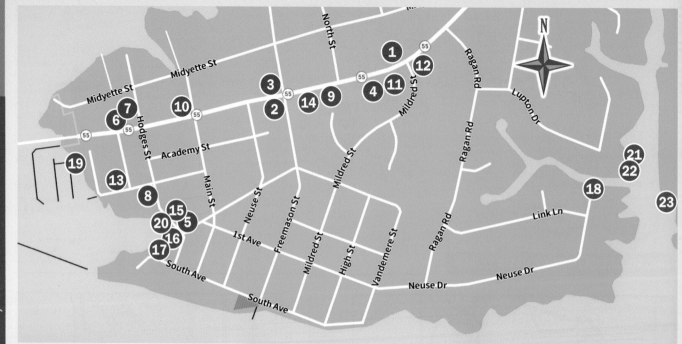

Life moves slowly in this welcoming village. Boats and bikes rest against dock pilings and porch railings. The aroma of shrimp nets drying on trawl doors fills the inner harbor, where sailboats and skiffs thump the town dock. Across the street at The Bean, local politics are discussed over strong coffee and visitors enjoy an ice cream cone on the porch. Talking and walking may not be considered official recreational activities in most towns, but in Oriental, they fit with the feel of a quaint waterfront town where biking, sailing, kayaking, fishing, and boating are popular pastimes. Long known as the "Sailing Capital of North Carolina," Oriental is blessed with wide waters, steady winds and easy access to dozen of creeks and estuaries. Today, there are almost 3,000 vessels berthed in the lower Neuse River area.

Oriental got its proper name in the 1870s when Lou Midyette became postmaster. His wife thought the village needed a better name than Smith's Creek. When Rebecca saw the nameplate from the shipwrecked *Steamship Oriental* while visiting the Outer Banks, she suggested that as a name for the town. In a nod to its namesake, the town is home to dozens of Asian-style dragons…lingering, lounging, hiding and peeking out from the most unusual places.

Attractions: Oriental's History Museum (802 Broad St., 252-249-3340) displays model skiffs, oyster scoops, the bronze porthole from the *S.S. Oriental*, a Wurlitzer juke box and much more documenting Oriental's history. Pick up a Historic Walking Tour brochure and follow the route past over 70 historical buildings and sites. If you prefer to explore on two wheels, The Inland Waterway Provision Company on the harbor (252-249-7245) has bikes for rent (as well as kayaks and paddleboards).

While "casual and relaxed" defines the ambiance of Oriental, the village does offer a bit of cultural fare. The Village Gallery (300 Hodges St., 252-249-0300) features works in oil, pastels, acrylic, photography, jewelry, watercolor, pottery, glass and more, which you can buy directly from the juried artists. Friday movies with free popcorn screen in The Old Theater (609 Broad St., 252-249-0477) and the Pamlico Music Society (pamlicomusic.org) brings renowned national and international performers to town throughout the year to perform there.

Sailing regattas are held throughout the year from the "Instead of Football Regatta" on New Year's Day to the Croaker Fest, Dragon's Breath, Summer Solstice and Oriental Cup in the summer and fall. The annual Oriental In-Water Boat Show in April is the largest in-water boat show between Annapolis and Savannah. See details at orientalboatshow.com.

The annual Croaker Festival, held during Fourth of July weekend, is the town's largest event, attracting 10,000 visitors. This old-fashioned celebration features a festive parade, live music, coronation of the Croaker Queen, food and crafts vendors and unforgettable fireworks over the harbor.

In October, enjoy the Old Front Porch Music Festival with musicians playing on porches throughout town and a street dance at the history museum.

Each December, boats compete for the best Christmas light decorations, luminaries line the streets, and Santa rings in the season riding on a boat in the Christmas parade. New Year's Eve in Oriental celebrates the "heritage of the Orient," with the Running of the Dragon (during which a magnificent Chinese dragon takes to the streets) and the dropping of the croaker (modeled on a local fish) from a sailboat mast in the harbor.

For free street maps and information about events and attractions, visit Town Hall at 507 Church St. (252-249-0555) or go to townoforiental.com or visitoriental.com.

Shopping: A town called the "Sailing Capital of North Carolina" has to have marine supplies. Inland Waterway Provision Company sells marine supplies that you can order in advance and have waiting for you upon you're arrival. They sell some groceries (including beer and wine) and personal care products. They also offer a Cruisers Corner, where visitors can chill out or warm up with free WiFi and a swap bookcase.

Nautical Wheelers, with locations in Oriental and New Bern, is a cruiser favorite, offering nautical gift items, clothing, shoes and jewelry. They also sell wine and frequently host wine tastings on the porch at 411 Broad St. (252-249-0359).

Other shops in the area include Village Hardware & Marine Supply (804 Broad St., 252-249-1211), West Marine Express (1104 Broad St. Ext., 252-249-3200) and Marine Consignment of Oriental (708 Broad St., 252-249-3222) with rooms crammed full of new and used nautical products and treasures.

For sail and canvas repair, Hodges Street Sail Repair (603 Hodges St., 252-249-0739) and Down East Canvas & Gallery (301 Broad St., 252-249-1004) are located in the village. Inner Banks Sails & Canvas is farther afield (112 Straight Rd., 252-249-3001), but worth the effort. They can build almost any product sewn for a boat, from complete frame structures and enclosures, interior or exteriors cushions and covers to fast, durable sails.

A welcome addition to the town is the Piggly Wiggly grocery store at 1400 Broad St. (252-249-3100). It not only has provisions, but provides a convenient "Piglet" shuttle that will pick you up at the dock and return you to your vessel with your purchases.

Dining: Toucan Grill & Fresh Bar (101 Wall St., 252-249-2204) offers outdoor seating and a great view of the inner harbor. They serve burgers and seafood and live music in the summer. The Tiki Bar between the Toucan and Oriental Marina Inn opens every evening with a great mix of locals and visiting boaters. M&M's Café (205 S. Water St., 252-249-2000) is another harborside favorite with great food, screened outdoor seating and a breakfast buffet on Sundays.

The Silos Restaurant (1111 Broad St., 252-249-1050) is a local and boater favorite located in a couple of reclaimed silos. It's about a 15-minute walk from the Town Dock and offers a specialty pizza and pasta menu. Everyone is invited to bring an instrument on "Open Mike Night" every Wednesday. Around back, the Red Rooster outdoor bar and stage offers a casual outdoor venue with frequent live concerts.

Brantley's Village Restaurant (900 Broad St., 252-249-3509) is great for home-cooked "comfort" food. Grab a morning or after dinner cup of coffee or an afternoon ice cream at The Bean (304 Hodges St., 252-249-4918).

After dinner, check out the New Village Brewery & Taproom (702 Broad St., 252-249-6132), which provides craft beer samples, along with board games, foos ball and arcade games.

⚠ The Oriental Road Bridge is not on the ICW and only has a vertical clearance of 45 feet. Do not attempt to navigate up Greens Creek to the anchorage or marina if your vessel's air draft exceeds 40 feet. Also, note that charted depths in these creeks can be misleading. Wind and weather can raise (as well as lower) the water level appreciably in this area. If winds have been out of the west or southwest for any length of time, a drop in water levels of as much as 3 feet is possible. Sound your way in.

Entering Oriental's collection of creeks from the north, only deep-draft boats will need to line up with all the green markers. Others can head for the 15-foot-high flashing red "6" and join the channel there. Oriental's harbor (known locally as Raccoon Creek) lies immediately to starboard after passing flashing red "8" at the end of the rock jetty. This harbor is tight, with the distance between the north and south shores being not much more than a generous fairway.

Dockage: Whittaker Pointe Marina is located at the mouth of Whittaker Creek on the east side of the entrance. The marina welcomes transients in a quiet, park-like setting. They will loan you a courtesy van to provision after helping you settle in. Nearby Whittaker Creek Yacht Harbor is immediately visible just inside the point. The 140-slip marina reserves 10 transient slips and sells gas (no diesel).

Upstream to port on an arm of Whittaker Creek, Sailcraft Marina has limited transient dockage and is a convenient walk to a grocery store and West Marine. Adjacent to the marina is Sailcraft Service, a well-respected boatyard with a 35-ton lift and a 2-ton crane. They also have a 65-foot bucket lift and offer complete repair services including woodwork, welding and metal fabrication, plumbing and HVAC, painting, mechanical service and cleaning and detailing. Do-it-yourself boaters are welcome.

Deaton Yacht Service is a full-capacity boatyard located across the canal. They have on-site mechanics and 24-hour towing service, plus they allow owners to work on their own boats. The family-owned business was founded in 1979 and is capable of handling any boat project.

To the south in Oriental Harbor, the Oriental Marina & Inn manages the Oriental Harbor Marina dockage; however, the protected berths are privately owned and the only transient dockage is on a 700-foot face dock that is exposed to winds with a southerly component.

The breakwater only minimally protects it from bouncy and uncomfortable chop when the winds blow over 10 knots across the 5-mile fetch of the Neuse River.

A better bet is to follow the dredged channel past the Oriental Yacht Club to the north, which is usually packed with boats (but no transient slips) and proceed straight ahead is Oriental Marina & Inn. This is actually a complex of facilities: docks, an inn and lounge, a swimming pool with a tiki bar, a fuel dock for gas and diesel and the on-site Toucan Grill & Fresh Bar, famous for fresh seafood meals (open for lunch and dinner).

There are two town docks in Oriental Harbor, on either side of Oriental Marina & Inn. The first has approximately 80 feet of dockage and is complimentary for up to 48 hours. There is no shore power or water but there are clean restrooms next to the dock and you may pay for use of the showers at Oriental Marina & Inn. Directly at the end of the harbor channel is a second public pier with room for just two boats. It sits directly across the street from The Bean, a popular coffee shop.

These docks are immediately adjacent to the channel under the bridge going upriver, which gets considerable traffic, especially on weekends. Unfortunately, this is NOT in a "No Wake" area, resulting in bumpy conditions on the face dock.

Blackwell Point Marina may be an option for those who can fit under the fixed 45-foot vertical clearance Oriental Road Bridge to access Smith Creek. This is very well protected. Call ahead for slip availability.

Anchorage: There is no room to anchor in Whittaker Creek but just south of the Oriental Yacht Club in the harbor, there is a popular anchorage spot in soft mud with 5- to 8-foot MLW depths. This is exposed to the south. Several boats are usually at anchor, but there is generally room for more as long as you are careful to stay out of the resident shrimp boat's channel. With soft mud, holding is poor without good scope. Check with other anchored boats to be sure you don't anchor within their swing circle.

The long seawall for Oriental Harbor Marina is reserved for transient moorage, so leave space for boats coming and going from the seawall while also staying outside the route under the bridge. Across the channel, a two-anchor system can keep a boat in place along the breakwater, safe from both the breakwater itself and edging into the shrimp boat's channel.

Anchorage is possible in Smith and Greens Creeks, if your boat can handle both the 45-foot vertical clearance of the fixed Oriental Road Bridge and controlling depths

TOUCAN GRILL & FRESH BAR

ORIENTAL MARINA & INN

INLAND WATERWAY PROVISION COMPANY

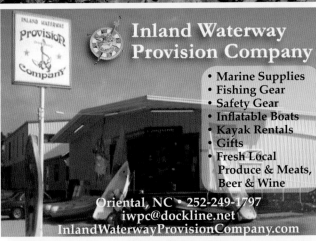
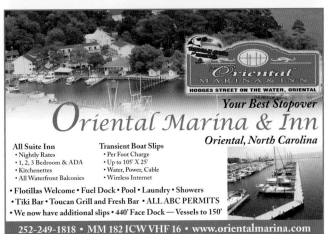

Neuse River, NC

		Largest Vessel Accommodated	VHF Channel Monitored	Transient Berths / Total Berths	Approach / Dockside Depth (reported)	Floating Docks	Gas / Diesel	Groceries, Ice, Marine Supplies, Snacks	Repairs: Hull, Engine, Propeller	Lift (tonnage), Crane, Rail	Min/Max Amps	Laundry, Pool, Showers, Courtesy Car	Pump-Out Station	Nearby: Grocery Store, Motel, Restaurant
MINNESOTT BEACH				**Dockage**				**Supplies**			**Services**			
1. Arlington Place & Marina Club 6 SW of 185	800-967-7639	–	–	call/10	–	–	G	–	–	–	30/30	P	–	R
2. Wayfarers Cove Marina & Boatyard 🖥 📶 185	252-249-0200	55	–	call/150	6.5/7	–	–	–	HEP	L60	30/50	LS	P	
MITCHELL CREEK														
3. Matthews Point Marina 🖥 📶 6 SW of 185	252-444-1805	46	16	6/110	6.5/6.5	–	GD	I	E	–	30/50	LS	P	–

🖥 Internet Access 📶 Wireless Internet Access 🅆🅖 Waterway Guide Cruising Club Partner 🔵onSpot dockside WiFi facility

See WaterwayGuide.com for current rates, fuel prices, web site addresses, and other up-to-the-minute information. *(Information in the table is provided by the facilities.)*

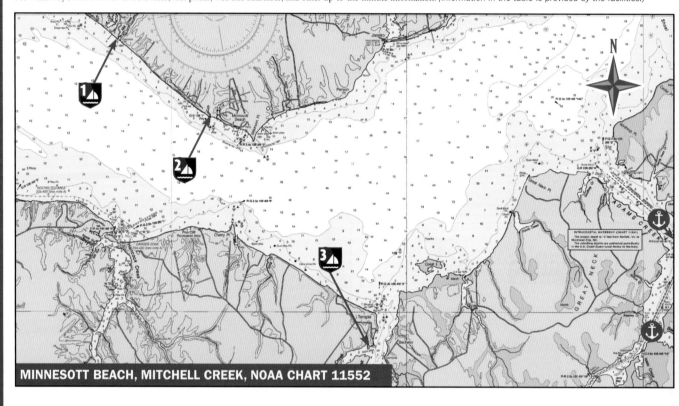

MINNESOTT BEACH, MITCHELL CREEK, NOAA CHART 11552

Minnesott Creek

of 4.5 to 5 feet MLW. The length of the creek is open to southerly winds.

If you do not mind a remote setting off the beaten path, the South River, located across the Neuse River from Oriental, is well marked with depths at 9 to 12 feet MLW. The holding is secure in firm mud with sand or shells, and the high banks provide good wind protection with some exposure from the north. It is undeveloped, pretty and mercifully clear of crab traps.

Side Trip: To New Bern

The Neuse River provides a delightful side trip for anyone with the time and inclination. The southwestern prong of Pamlico Sound leads 31 miles up the Neuse River to New Bern, where the Trent River comes in. A trip up river can be a great time or a real challenge, depending on wind direction.

The wind's direction and strength, not the moon, cause the tide fluctuations in the upper Neuse. No tables or regular schedules can be established, but water depths change by a foot or two in each direction. Overall, the depth is adequate for all drafts, but pay attention to your charts. The Cherry Point Marine Corps Air Station occupies the Hancock Creek and Slocum Creek areas on the south side of the river.

New Bern is 21 miles from flashing green "1AC," which is near ICW Mile 185 at the mouth of Adams Creek. The town offers visitors hospitality and Southern charm with the best of modern conveniences. New Bern's greatest assets are its natural resources: abundant water, steady winds and a vibrant waterfront. This is a river town, not a coastal city. In New Bern, you will find park benches and city sidewalks, restaurants and brick storefronts adorned with polished brass. This is the home of Pepsi-Cola and best-selling author Nicholas Sparks. It is the state's first capital and the final port of call for those seeking small-town living without the big-box feel.

NAVIGATION: Use NOAA Chart 11552. The channel up the Neuse River to New Bern is well marked and easy to navigate. The lighted clock tower on City Hall is an excellent landmark. The 65-foot fixed vertical clearance **Neuse River (U.S. 17/NC 55) Hwy. Bridge,** immediately south of New Bern, is visible for about 10 miles. Be aware that strong northeasterly winds

Neuse River, NC

		Dockage						Supplies		Services				
		Largest Vessel Accommodated	VHF Channel Monitored	Transient Berths / Total Berths	Approach / Dockside Depth (reported)	Floating Docks	Gas / Diesel	Groceries, Ice, Marine Supplies, Snacks	Repairs: Hull, Engine, Propeller	Lift (tonnage), Crane, Rail	Min/Max Amps	Laundry, Pool, Showers, Courtesy Car	Pump-Out Station	Nearby: Grocery Store, Motel, Restaurant
NEW BERN														
1. Northwest Creek Marina ⌨ WiFi	252-638-4133	60	16/68	12/274	8/12	–	GD	I	–	–	30/50	LPS	P	–
2. Duck Creek Marina & Boatyard	252-638-1702	45	–	2/60	7/6	–	–	–	–	L35, C	30/30	S	P	GR
3. BridgePointe Hotel and Marina ⌨ WiFi	252-637-7372	150	16	10/125	16/10	F	–	IS	–	–	30/30	LPS	P	MR
4. **New Bern Grand Marina Yacht Club ⌨ WiFi**	**252-638-0318**	**200**	**16/71**	**35/225**	**12/12**	**F**	**–**	**IS**	**–**	**–**	**30/100**	**LPS**	**P**	**GMR**
5. Galley Stores Marina WiFi	252-633-4648	100	16	25/25	–	F	GD	GIS	–	–	30/50	S	P	GR
BRIDGETON														
6. Bridgeton Harbor Marina WiFi	252-349-1194	150	–	call/135	7/10	F	–	IM	HEP	L	30/50	LS	P	–

⌨ Internet Access   WiFi Wireless Internet Access   WG Waterway Guide Cruising Club Partner   onSpot dockside WiFi facility

See WaterwayGuide.com for current rates, fuel prices, web site addresses, and other up-to-the-minute information. *(Information in the table is provided by the facilities.)*

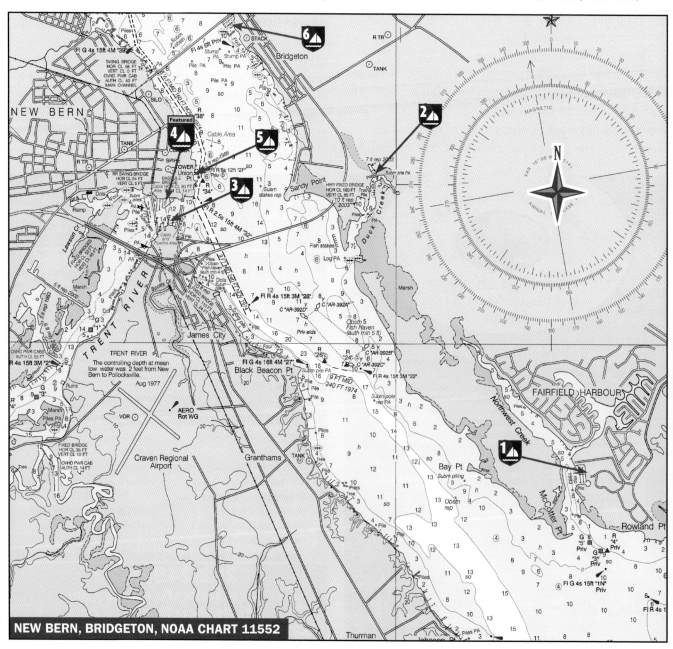

NEW BERN, BRIDGETON, NOAA CHART 11552

New Bern Grand Marina Yacht Club · Nautical Wheelers · Neuse River

can raise the water level, resulting in reduced bridge clearance.

The **Alfred Cunningham (U.S. 70) Bascule Bridge** at Mile 0 in the Trent River has 14-foot closed vertical clearance and opens on signal, Monday through Friday, except from 6:30 a.m. to 8:30 a.m. and from 4:00 p.m. to 6:00 p.m., when the draw need not open. It will open, however, at 7:30 a.m. and at 5:00 p.m. if vessels are waiting. The bridge also need not open between 2:00 p.m. and 7:00 p.m. on Sundays and federal holidays from May 24 through September 8, but will open at 4:00 p.m. and 6:00 p.m. if vessels are waiting.

The **Norfolk and Southern Railroad Swing Bridge** (5-foot closed vertical clearance) also crosses the Trent River. This bridge is usually open except for during the infrequent train crossings. Two thousand feet upstream are the twin fixed **U.S. 17/U.S. 70 Hwy. Bridges** (45-foot vertical clearances). Note that winds may affect water levels, and there may be less than the charted 45-foot clearances.

Dockage: About 7 miles up the Neuse River from Oriental at Minnesott Beach is Wayfarers Cove Marina & Boatyard, offering a well-protected alternative to a stopover in Oriental. They can accommodate vessels to 50 feet and offer repairs (60-ton lift). Call ahead for

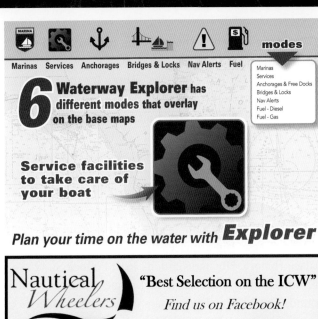

GOIN' ASHORE: **NEW BERN, NC**

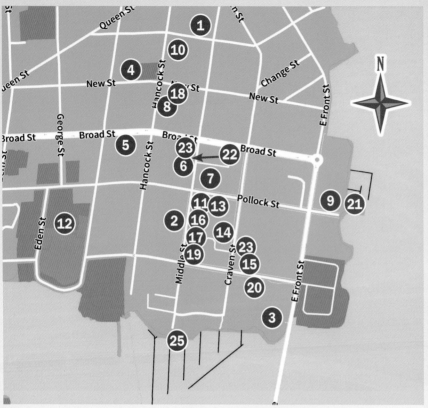

	SERVICES
1	Library
2	Post Office
3	Visitor Information
	ATTRACTIONS
4	Academy Museum
5	Attmore-Oliver House
6	Bank of the Arts
7	Christ Church Parish
8	Fireman's Museum
9	Galley Stores and Marina
10	Masonic Theater
11	Pepsi Store
12	Tryon Palace Historic Site and Gardens
	SHOPPING
11	The Four C's
13	Carolina Creations
14	Mitchell Hardware
15	Nautical Wheelers
16	Surf, Wind, and Fire
17	The Boathouse
	DINING
2	Baker's Kitchen Restaurant & Bakery
18	Brewery 99
19	Captain Ratty's
20	Circa 1810 at Harvey Mansion
21	Persimmons Waterfront Restaurant
22	Sweet Pea's Café
23	The Chelsea
24	Trent River Coffee Company
	MARINAS
9	Galley Stores and Marina
25	New Bern Grand Marina Yacht Club

From the downtown marinas you can walk and explore all of the historic downtown of New Bern. For greater trips afield, Enterprise will pick you up at the marinas. (Hint: Try their location on M.L. King Blvd. for an economy car at low daily rates.) New Bern is a town of firsts. It was North Carolina's first capital, and the home of the state's first printing press, as well as its first publicly chartered school, its first motion picture theater, and was also the first town to hang electric Christmas lights above city streets. Be aware that New Bern residents are quick to point out that Caleb Bradham's soda pop (Pepsi-Cola) has a better kick than the "other" brand. Stop in the Pepsi Store at 256 Middle St. (252-636-5898) for a free sample and judge for yourself!

Attractions: The primary attractions in New Bern are the Tryon Palace Historic Site and Gardens (610 Pollock St., 252-639-3500) and the surrounding Historic District homes, many of which are open year-round. The 13-acre Tryon estate includes the palace (a mansion), the George W. Dixon House, the John Wright Stanly House, stables, a series of landscaped gardens and the Academy Museum. Demonstrations of the period include cooking, blacksmithing and weaving. Tryon Palace was originally built between 1767 and 1770, as the first permanent capitol of the Colony of North Carolina and a home for the Royal Governor and his family. Adjacent to Tryon Palace is the North Carolina History Center. This is a large and impressive museum with many interactive exhibits. One price gets you into the museum (a must-see) and the Tryon Palace.

The Attmore–Oliver House (512 Pollock St., 252-638-8558) is home to the New Bern Historical Society and serves as a Civil War Museum. Four miles south of town is the Battle of New Bern site from 1862. This was a coordinated Union attack between their 13 gunboats on the Neuse River and their 12,000 land forces ashore. The site is open for self-guided walking tours. New Bern Tours & Convention (333 Middle St.) offers 1.5-hour historic trolley tours of the area.

The Masonic Theater (514 Hancock St., 252-633-3318) is the oldest theater in America to be used continuously. The first schoolhouse in North Carolina is also worth a visit. The Academy Building, on the corner of New and Hancock streets, once served as a schoolhouse for boys and girls, and later as a hospital during the Civil War. In 1881, it became part of the New Bern Graded School System.

Christ Church Parish (320 Pollock St.) was established in 1715. In 1752, King George II gave the church a silver communion service, a prayer book and a Bible, all of which are still in use today. The church, built from plans by Sir Christopher Wren who designed St. Paul's Cathedral in London, served as a hospital during the Civil War. The belfry still shows carved names and initials of Union soldiers.

At Skipjack Landing's Galley Stores and Marina, you will find a real skipjack, the *Ada Mae*, built here in 1915. She is the last surviving boat of many built here to harvest oysters under sail. While skipjacks are most often associated with the Chesapeake Bay, they were also used here on the Pamlico and Albemarle Sounds and the rivers of North Carolina.

At the Fireman's Museum (408 Hancock St., 252-636-4087), you will find early steam pumpers, a brass sliding pole, and an extensive collection of early fire-fighting equipment. For more historical perspective, take a 90-minute trolley ride through Historic New Bern, narrated by knowledgeable local residents. Call New Bern Tours at 800-849-7316.

The Bank of the Arts (at the Craven Arts Council and Gallery, 317 Middle St., 252-638-2577) features monthly exhibits of painting, sculpture, photography, and pottery.

The Farmers' Market (421 S. Front St.) is a great place to go for fresh vegetables and fruits, seafood, flowers, and crafts on Saturdays year-round and on Tuesdays in season.

Shopping: Galley Stores, a gourmet provisioning establishment on the waterfront, offers everything you need to provision the boat, along with a wide selection of wine, beer and gifts (300 E. Front St., 252-633-4648).

Mitchell Hardware (215 Craven St., 252-638-4261) is an authentic turn-of-the-century hardware store with a little bit of everything, including books and gifts. The

Boathouse (220 Middle St., 252-633-5501) also carries a selection of nautical books and gifts.

Nautical Wheelers, which also has a store in Oriental, is centrally located down the street from Mitchell's Hardware. Stop in for nautical gift items, clothing, shoes and jewelry. They also sell specialty wines at 202A Craven St. (252-514-2553).

Surf, Wind, and Fire (230 Middle St., 252-637-6695) is a surf-inspired, outdoor lifestyle store offering both expertise and merchandise for an active lifestyle, and The Four C's (250 Middle St., 252-636-3285) offers camping gear and travel accessories. At Carolina Creations (317-A Pollock St., 252-633-4369), you will find art, crafts and gift gallery items.

Dining: Start your morning at Sweet Pea's Café (3515 Trent Rd., 252-637-6695) for coffee and homemade breakfast (also open for lunch). Baker's Kitchen Restaurant & Bakery (227 Middle St., 252-637-0304) offers fried chicken with all the trimmings, as well as homemade breads, desserts, and their famous Dutch potatoes. The Chelsea (335 Middle St., 252-637-5469) is located in Caleb Bradham's old drug store and offers a 1920s atmosphere. It's a bit of a walk but worth it. After lunch or dinner, head over to nearby Brewery 99 in the parking lot of Artisan Square for a craft beer (252-259-6393). It's only open on Friday and Saturday from 2:00 p.m. to 10:00 p.m. Don't let the appearance of this small shack deceive you; it's quite a happening brewery and bar for those who know where to look for it.

A cruiser favorite, Captain Ratty's (202 Middle St., 252-633-2088) features an upstairs wine bar with Wednesday tastings. Check out their rooftop bar with river views. Persimmons Waterfront Restaurant (100 Pollock St., 252-514-0333) is located at Skipjack Landing with deck dining and sweeping views.

For upscale dining, Circa 1810 at Harvey Mansion (221 S. Front St., 252-635-3232) offers a wonderful atmosphere and fine dining in this 17th-century mansion.

For an early-morning jolt or late-night snack, try Trent River Coffee Company (208 Craven St., 252-514-2030), where you can hear live nightly music on weekends.

slip availability. Also on the way north to New Bern is the 10-slip Arlington Place & Marina Club, offering some transient slips and gas (call ahead). Across the river, 6 miles southwest of Mile 185, Matthews Point Marina at Mitchell Creek sells fuel and has six reserved transient slips.

Closer to New Bern (4 miles southeast) is the well-protected Northwest Creek Marina. The marina has 274 slips and can accommodate yachts up to 60 feet with the usual amenities. Beyond the marina is Fairfield Harbour, a private community on a deepwater canal.

Farther up the Neuse River, but before and east of the fixed, 65-foot vertical clearance Neuse River (U.S. 17/NC 55 Hwy.) Bridge, is Duck Creek. The Duck Creek Marina & Boatyard has a 35-ton lift and a crane but only two reserved transient slips. Call ahead.

Marine facilities on the Trent River are convenient to all the amenities of New Bern. Between the Cunningham Bridge and the Railroad Bridge on the south side of the Trent River is the BridgePointe Hotel and Marina with 125 slips on floating docks with a wave attenuator. The marina was closed at press time in summer 2019 due to damage sustained during Hurricane Florence. Call ahead for current status.

Directly across the Trent River, the New Bern Grand Marina Yacht Club has a 1,000-foot face dock with 12-foot depths inside a protected breakwater. The marina is located in front of the waterfront DoubleTree Hotel by Hilton and all the hotel amenities are available to marina guests, including the fitness center and pool. This is a convenient location for crew changes or for accommodating visiting family and friends. They also offer free day dockage to visit historic New Bern.

Galley Stores Marina is located directly on the channel on the Neuse River, north of the Trent-Neuse intersection. This facility offers full-service transient dockage, sells all fuels and has an on-site gourmet store, featuring wine, beers and specialty items, including daily "gourmet to go" meals.

While there is a no wake zone here, locals appear to ignore it and law enforcement seems to be nonexistent. On weekends, you will rock and roll due to wakes; however, extensive shopping, restaurant and bars and an excellent market are nearby to keep you off the boat. Across Front Street from Union Point is a convention center, which hosts the Visitor Center.

Across the Neuse River from New Bern is Bridgeton. Before the **Neuse River Railroad Swing Bridge**

"Bern" is the old Germanic word for bear, which is the symbol of New Bern. Founded by Swiss and German settlers in the 1700s, New Bern is home to over 50 bear statues dressed in every imaginable costume. They are colorful, entertaining, and photogenic.

(usually open) is Bridgeton Harbor Marina with slips on floating docks for vessels to 150 feet and all the usual amenities. Call ahead.

Anchorage: There are places along the Neuse River to tuck in and several good creeks on both side. Sound your way in and anchor according to wind direction.

■ NEXT STOP

Back on the ICW, we follow Adams Creek to the historic seaport of Beaufort and then on to Morehead City, where you could spend weeks exploring or just relaxing on the beaches of the "Crystal Coast." But first, we take a side trip to explore the expansive waters of the Pamlico Sound and Outer (and Lower) Banks of North Carolina.

NAUTICAL WHEELERS

NEW BERN GRAND MARINA YACHT CLUB

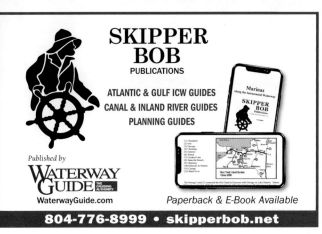

Side Trip: The Pamlico Sound & Outer Banks, NC

VHF NC Bridges: Channel 13 **CHARTS** NOAA 11545, 11555

Pamlico Sound, which is the second largest ICW estuary after the Chesapeake Bay, is 65 miles (via the ICW) south of Albemarle Sound and deserves the same amount of respect. The afternoon sea breeze, combined with prevailing southwesterlies, can often produce winds in excess of 20 knots and a short, steep chop that can fairly be called "vicious."

In November, migratory waterfowl transiting the Atlantic Flyway visit the refuge area halfway between Englehard and Swan Quarter (also written as Swanquarter at times, including on NOAA charts). Swan Quarter, the seat of Hyde County, is the trading center for this area and an embarkation point for ferries crossing Pamlico Sound to Ocracoke Island.

NAVIGATION: Use NOAA Chart 11555. Pamlico Sound markers are generally 5 to 15 miles apart, so we strongly recommend that you run compass courses or GPS routes between them. Currents, often set up by the wind, can cause you to drift 10 to 15° magnetic off course. Where

these currents begin and end is impossible to predict, but they are indeed there, so you should check your position continually. Pamlico Sound, along with the other sounds, is a good area in which to use the GPS. An alternative route to the ICW, via the Croatan and Roanoke Sounds, is covered in Chapter 3 of this guide, "Side Trips: The Albemarle & Roanoke Sounds, NC."

Dockage: On the western shore of Pamlico Sound (north of the intersection with Pamlico River) is the well-marked Far Creek leading to Big Trout Marina. A small "southern comfort food" café is on site with pork chops, butter beans, mac and cheese...(You get the idea.) Open for lunch only. The marina reports 5-foot dockside depths and can accommodate boats to 60 feet. Groceries, a hardware store and a hotel are nearby in the town of Englehard. Farther west, Bayside Marina & Campground is tucked up Germantown Bay with 4-foot MLW approach and dockside depths and slips for vessels to 40 feet.

Anchorage: The Long Shoal River to the north of Big Trout Marina offers anchorage in 6 to 8 feet MLW in hard mud with a bit of wave break due to the encroaching shoals at the south entrance but no protection from the north.

Wysocking Bay to the south beyond Far Creek has a hard mud bottom and marshy borders with protection from chop except from the south to southeast. From July to April, this harbor is likely to be busy with commercial fishing boats. Juniper Bay, the next bay to the west, can be followed upriver to good protection and 6-foot MLW depths in soft mud. This location can be buggy on still summer nights.

The many bays west of Swan Quarter Bay look good on the NOAA chart, but they are low marsh, have soft bottoms and offer little protection. Large trawlers use this entrance so be especially diligent here.

Pamlico Sound, NC

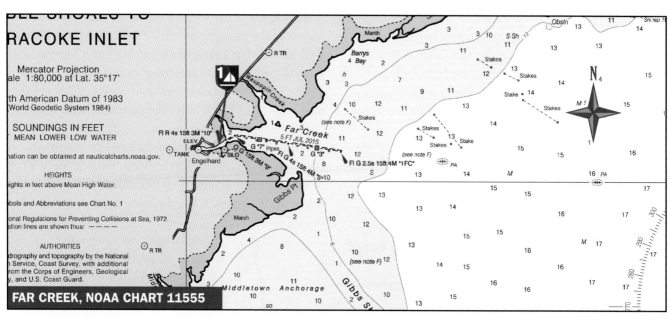

FAR CREEK		Dockage					Supplies		Services				
		Largest Vessel Accommodated	VHF Channel Monitored	Transient Berths / Total Berths	Approach / Dockside Depth (reported)	Floating Docks	Gas / Diesel	Repairs: Hull, Engine, Propeller	Groceries, Ice, Marine Supplies, Snacks	Lift (tonnage), Crane, Rail	Min/Max Amps	Laundry, Pool, Showers, Courtesy Car	Pump-Out Station	Nearby: Grocery Store, Motel, Restaurant
1. Big Trout Marina	252-925-6651	60	18	call/25	6/5	–	–	IS		–	30/30	S	–	GMR
GERMANTOWN BAY														
2. Bayside Marina & Campground	252-926-6621	40	16/01	6/15	4/4		G	IMS		E	30/30	S	–	M

⌨ Internet Access 📶 Wireless Internet Access 🅦🅖 Waterway Guide Cruising Club Partner 🔵 onSpot dockside WiFi facility
See WaterwayGuide.com for current rates, fuel prices, web site addresses, and other up-to-the-minute information. *(Information in the table is provided by the facilities.)*

FAR CREEK, NOAA CHART 11555

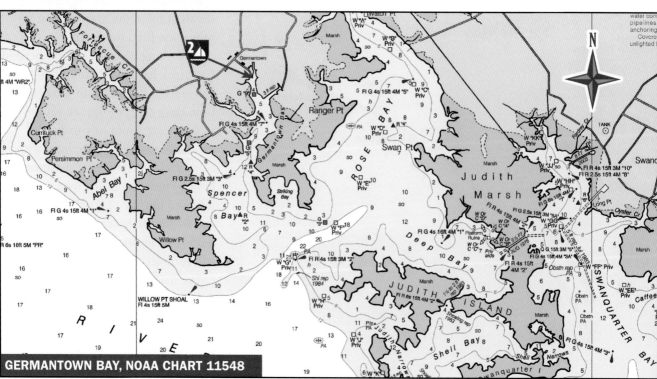

GERMANTOWN BAY, NOAA CHART 11548

THE OUTER BANKS

North Carolina's Outer Banks, a long strip of barrier islands, are unlike any other islands along the Mid-Atlantic coast. Vulnerable to wind and wave, they extend in a crescent from the Virginia state line, bending farther and farther out to sea until Cape Hatteras and the abrupt sweep back west, leaving an exposed and dangerous cape. They finally meet with the mainland at Cape Lookout, near Morehead City and Beaufort.

The Outer Banks enclose Currituck, Albemarle, Roanoke, Croatan, Pamlico and Core Sounds, in that order. As an alternative to the better-protected ICW route that cuts across Albemarle and Pamlico Sounds, this route offers higher speeds, more opportunity to sail and some of the most pristine and wild scenery on the East Coast, should you choose to go ashore. Currituck and Core Sounds, at the two extremes, are narrow, shoal and suitable only for small or shoal-draft craft with local knowledge.

The northern end of the Outer Banks has been a popular summer resort for generations, with many cottages, condominiums and commercial services. Below Nags Head, the Cape Hatteras National Seashore stretches the length of the barrier islands to meet Cape Lookout National Seashore at Core Sound beyond Ocracoke. The wild beaches, dunes, marshes and woodlands, preserved as National Seashores, are interrupted in only a few places by villages and private property holdings. The Outer Banks are truly one of our nation's natural treasures and well worth your time to explore and enjoy.

The best way to see the Outer Banks is from the inside (not from the Atlantic) and the best time is summer, when the sounds are relatively placid. The waters in the sound is often shoal, and channels near inlets shift rapidly. Although channels are marked, they may not be entirely reliable after a storm. Off-channel waters are sprinkled with crab floats and fishnet stakes, which warrant a wide berth.

For those who would like to avoid the wide-open waters of Pamlico Sound but also wish to see more of North Carolina's treasures, the Pamlico and Neuse Rivers

---

Note that **Roanoke and Croatan Sounds**, including the town of Manteo, are described in Chapter 3 of this guide: "Side Trip: The Albemarle & Roanoke Sounds, NC."

Graveyard of the Atlantic

The treacherous waters off the NC Outer Banks have earned the nickname "Graveyard of the Atlantic" due to the over 600 shipwrecks scattered across the ocean floor here. So many shipwrecks occurred that the government eventually required that lifesaving stations be built every 7 miles along the coast of the Outer Banks. These stations and their personnel would later become the U.S. Coast Guard.

From the Outer Banks north to the southern entrance of Chesapeake Bay off the Virginia coastline, two forces collide to create stormy, dangerous seas on a regular basis. One of those forces is the Labrador Current, which is an arctic stream of icy water that originates off the coast of Greenland. The other is the Gulf Stream, which contains warm waters from the Caribbean. When these two forces collide, rough seas and dense fog are usually the result.

In addition to severe weather, these areas have strong currents that can cause sandbars to shift, making it hard to navigate. It is believed that Blackbeard the Pirate used these factors to his advantage to keep from being captured. There is no doubt that this section of the Atlantic Ocean is extremely dangerous.

The first recorded shipwreck in the area occurred in 1526 at the mouth of the Cape Fear River. Explorers were attracted to the area because it was wild and new. It quickly became known as a dangerous spot for mariners, though, as ships began to encounter the deadly conditions often present in the area. Legend has it that the wild Spanish mustangs of the Outer Banks got there by swimming ashore from sinking colonial ships.

The Graveyard of the Atlantic Museum, located in Hatteras Village at 59200 Museum Dr. (252-986-0726), focuses on the history of this area and features many artifacts recovered from area shipwrecks. Blackbeard's ship, *Queen Anne's Revenge*, was discovered here in 1996. Parts of the ship are on display at the North Carolina Maritime Museum in Beaufort, NC.

Pamlico Sound, NC

HATTERAS ISLAND		Largest Vessel Accommodated	VHF Channel Monitored	Dockage					Supplies			Services				
				Approach / Dockside Depth (reported)	Transient Berths / Total Berths	Floating Docks	Gas / Diesel	Groceries, Ice, Marine Supplies, Snacks	Repairs: Hull, Engine, Propeller	Lift (tonnage), Crane, Rail	Laundry, Pool, Showers, Courtesy Car	Min/Max Amps	Pump-Out Station	Nearby: Grocery Store, Motel, Restaurant		
1. Hatteras Boatyard	252-995-4331	55	07	3/9	6/6	–	–	M	HEP	L30	30/30	–	–	GMR		
2. Oden's Dock 🖥	252-986-2555	75	01	19/25	6/10	–	GD	GIM	–	–	30/50	S	–	GMR		
3. Village Marina Hatteras 🖥 WiFi	252-986-2522	70	01	call/23	7/6	–	G	IMS	–	–	30/100	LS	–	GMR		
4. Hatteras Harbor Marina 🖥 WiFi	800-676-4939	60	01	25/44	7/6	–	D	I	–	–	30/100	LS	–	GMR		
5. Teach's Lair Marina Inc. WiFi	252-986-2460	70	–	75/85	6/6	–	GD	GIMS	–	–	30/50	S	–	GMR		
6. Hatteras Landing Marina 🖥 WiFi	252-986-2077	90	–	20/37	9/9	–	GD	GIMS	–	–	30/50	LS	P	GMR		

🖥 Internet Access WiFi Wireless Internet Access WG Waterway Guide Cruising Club Partner ⏺ onSpot dockside WiFi facility
See WaterwayGuide.com for current rates, fuel prices, web site addresses, and other up-to-the-minute information. *(Information in the table is provided by the facilities.)*

both offer excellent waters, anchorages and historic towns for exploration. These waterways are described in Chapter 4 of this guide, "Albemarle Sound to the Neuse River, NC."

Hatteras Island

Hatteras Island is the longest of the barrier islands, stretching from Oregon Inlet south and around the elbow of Cape Hatteras to Hatteras Inlet. Occupied since the 1700s by European settlers, the community has always lived off the sea. In 1846, a hurricane opened Hatteras Inlet to the ocean and the community began to thrive. Damage from various storms has at times separated Hatteras Village from the remainder of Hatteras Island.

While there is still a commercial fishing industry here, charter sport fishing is the lifeblood of the community. It is a short run from the island out to the deep waters of the Gulf Stream where the marlin, swordfish and sailfish wait to be caught.

Start your visit at the north end of town in the old Weather Station, which has been restored and now serves as the visitor center. This was an active weather station from 1901 until 1946 and issued the first hurricane warnings ever in the U.S. Its radio operator happened to pick up the SOS from the *Titanic* the night she sank. A guided tour of Hatteras Village includes 20 historic sites and markers.

Since the 1500s, more than 600 ships have wrecked along the treacherous coastline surrounding Cape Hatteras. The Graveyard of the Atlantic Museum at Hatteras Village features displays on shipwrecks and North Carolina's maritime history. (See sidebar in this chapter for details.)

Do not fail to visit the Cape Hatteras Lighthouse (10 miles from Hatteras Village). To protect it from beach erosion, it was moved 2,900 feet inland in 1999. It is the largest structure of its kind ever moved. The moving company built short railroad tracks and moved it along at about an inch an hour. After it reached the end, the tracks were taken up, moved ahead and re-laid. A new foundation was built, and 6 months later the 1870 lighthouse was in its new home. The view from its top toward famous Diamond Shoals is an unforgettable sight. It is 268 steps to the top but definitely worth the effort. Climbing hours are 9:00 a.m. to 4:30 p.m. daily. Tickets (purchased on site) are required.

NAVIGATION: Use NOAA Chart 11555. The Pamlico Sound side of the island is shoal for a considerable distance out from the shore. Approach Hatteras Village from Pamlico Sound (flashing red "42 RC") via long, well-marked Rollinson Channel. The channel was charted at 4 feet in a May 2015 survey but slightly deeper mid-channel depths have been recently observed. Leave red markers to port.

 Shoaling has been observed between flashing red "36" and "34" in Rollinson Channel. An easterly wind will reduce all depths.

The Pamlico Sound is big, open water and can get rough. If you are going to venture to the Outer Banks and visit Hatteras and Ocracoke, check your weather window carefully. This is one of those places you can get stuck for many days if bad weather blows in. (In our opinion, there are much worse places to get stuck.) Be sure to call ahead and check the status of transient dockage before making your way to Hatteras Village.

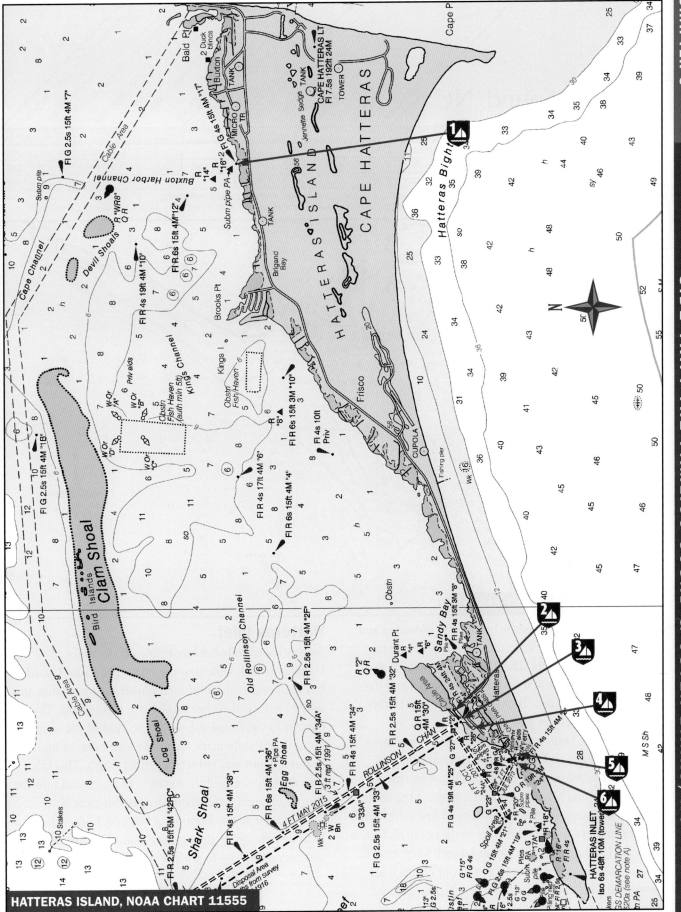

HATTERAS ISLAND, NOAA CHART 11555

Pamlico Sound, NC

OCRACOKE		Dockage					Supplies		Services					
		Largest Vessel Accommodated	VHF Channel Monitored	Transient Berths / Total Berths	Approach / Dockside Depth (reported)	Floating Docks	Groceries, Ice, Marine Supplies, Snacks	Gas / Diesel	Repairs: Hull, Engine, Propeller	Lift (tonnage), Crane, Rail	Min/Max Amps	Laundry, Pool, Showers, Courtesy Car	Pump-Out Station	Nearby: Grocery Store, Motel, Restaurant
1. Ocracoke National Park Service Docks	252-928-5111	60	–	call/15	7/5	F	–				30/50	–	–	GMR
2. Anchorage Inn & Marina	252-928-6661	100	16	25/35	10/9		GD	IMS			30/50	PS	P	GMR
3. Down Creek Marina ⌨	901-491-0111			3/10	12/8						30/50	S	–	GMR

⌨ Internet Access   WiFi Wireless Internet Access   WG Waterway Guide Cruising Club Partner   onSpot dockside WiFi facility

See WaterwayGuide.com for current rates, fuel prices, web site addresses, and other up-to-the-minute information. *(Information in the table is provided by the facilities.)*

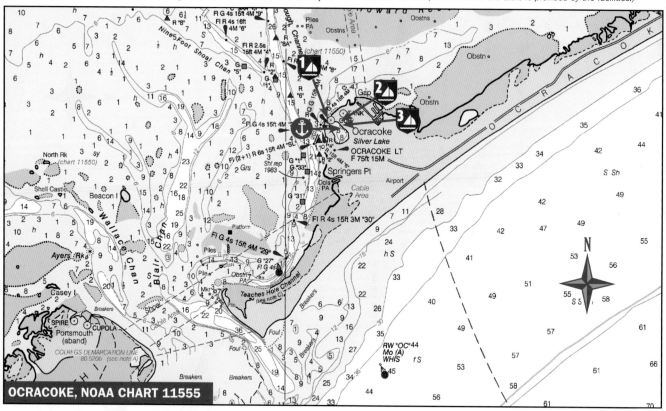

OCRACOKE, NOAA CHART 11555

Dockage: Hatteras Basin is breakwater protected and the facilities here cater to serious sportfishermen and accept transient boaters. The 25-slip Oden's Dock also sells all fuels; Village Marina Hatteras sells gas and has a waterfront restaurant (Dinky's); and Hatteras Harbor Marina sells diesel (no gas).

In a separate basin to the south, Teach's Lair Marina Inc. sells all fuels and is the base of several fishing charters. It is managed by the same folks who run Hatteras Landing Marina in the next basin to the south, which is surrounded by a community of fine stores and eateries and extensive boardwalks to the ocean and sound. Hatteras Landing also sells gas and diesel. Keep an eye out for the car ferries that run in and out of this basin from 5:00 a.m. until midnight. The schedule changes seasonally. View a schedule at ferry.ncdot.gov.

Hatteras Inlet

Storms have eroded about 1 mile off the point of Hatteras Island, widening the inlet. The Coast Guard has temporarily discontinued numerous navigation aids in the vicinity of Hatteras Inlet due to shoaling. The current navigational aids in this section of the waterway do not accurately mark navigable water due to limited channel depth and reduced channel width. This inlet is frequently dredged; however, seas push sand into the shorter channel faster than dredges can clear it.

We do not advise attempting Hatteras Inlet without local knowledge, as the twisting channel shifts regularly and may shoal to 4-foot MLW depths or less.

Ocracoke Island

Ocracoke Island is the last link in the Cape Hatteras National Seashore and is about as close as you can get to out-island cruising in North Carolina. The anchorage is well protected, bordered by beautiful beaches with a marine forest and an ancient lighthouse. Although motels, cottages, shops and restaurants cater to a large number of tourists, most of the island's longtime residents strive to preserve the small-town atmosphere and staunchly defend its merits. The road wasn't paved until 1957 when regular ferry service began. Geography is also a contributing factor: Ocracoke has a road but no bridge so access is by boat or aircraft only; motorists must take a ferry from Swan Quarter, Cedar Island or Hatteras Island.

The car ferry runs generally from 5:00 a.m. until midnight between Hatteras and Ocracoke. At press time in summer 2019, a passenger-only ferry between Hatteras and Ocracoke islands was planned for the 2019 season. The schedule changes seasonally. View a schedule at ferry.ncdot.gov.

NAVIGATION: Use NOAA Chart 11555. Use the Cape Hatteras Tide Table. For high tide, add 9 minutes; for low tide, add 11 minutes. Big Foot Slough Channel, routinely used by the large car ferries coming from the mainland, carries minimum depths of 10 feet. It is the obvious choice for deep-draft vessels and those lacking current local knowledge. The channel shoals constantly and portions are frequently dredged. Shoaling has been reported between red daybeacon "10" and green buoy "11." Temporary buoys mark where shoals encroach on the channel so keep a lookout for red nuns and green cans with a letter suffix (although those are sometimes missing or off station).

⚠️ Dangers are not restricted to shoaling. Dredges work just outside the temporary buoys and ferry traffic is a regular and serious hazard. Time your trip, if possible, to enter the channel after any exiting ferry traffic or to follow incoming ferries.

Two steel pipes, protruding far above the water near flashing green "13" at the channel entrance, will be visible from the sound well before the channel becomes evident. These pipes are part of a sunken dredge boat that appears (both on the NOAA chart and on first sighting) to be a partial obstruction. In fact, the wreck is located off to the east side of the channel. There is also a charted 6-foot spot in that vicinity, as shown on NOAA Chart 11550 (by flashing red "NB").

GOIN' ASHORE: OCRACOKE ISLAND, NC

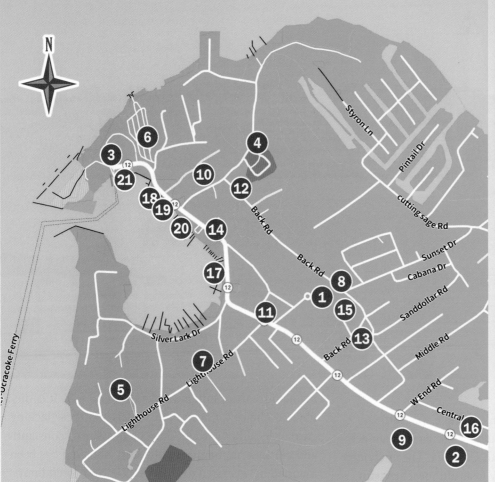

SERVICES	
1	Library
2	Post Office
3	Visitor Information
ATTRACTIONS	
4	British Cemetary
5	Ocracoke Lighhouse
6	Ocracoke Museum
SHOPPING	
7	Albert Styron's Store
8	Java Books
9	Ocracoke Variety
10	Over the Moon
11	Village Craftsmen
12	Zillie's Island Pantry
DINING	
9	Ocracoke Coffee Company
13	Back Porch Restaurant
14	Dajio
15	Flying Melon
16	Howard's Pub & Marina
17	Jolly Roger Pub & Marina
18	SMacNally's Raw Bar and Grill
MARINAS	
19	Anchorage Inn & Marina
20	Down Creek Marina
21	Ocracoke National Park Service Docks

Exuding a Cape Cod ambiance, Ocracoke Island is peppered with pirate legends and a rich nautical heritage. You will hear Ocracokers speaking with an old English "brogue," a unique dialect passed down from the early settlers of the Outer Banks. (Remember that to the locals, you are the one speaking with an accent!)

Attractions: The dominant physical feature of the village is the Ocracoke Lighthouse, which overlooks Silver Lake and the Pamlico Sound. The first light station was built on the island in 1803, but 15 years later was destroyed by lightning and replaced with the current lighthouse. The original lens was destroyed during the Civil War, but a new lens was installed in 1864 and remains today.

The British cemetery is another popular attraction. Four British sailors who perished in the sinking of the *HMS Bedfordshire* are buried here. Tradition dictated that they be buried on British soil, so the small graveyard was leased to Great Britain in perpetuity. It is cared for by the U.S. Coast Guard.

The Ocracoke Preservation Society operates a museum (252-928-7375) at 49 Water Plant Rd. (on the National Park Service property) that displays photographs, artifacts and exhibits pertaining to island life and culture. A small gift shop exhibits works from local artists. Upstairs is a small research library. The Teach's Hole Blackbeard Exhibit & Pirate Shop at 935 Irvine Garrish Hwy. (252-928-1718) is a good place to learn all about the infamous pirate and buy some booty to take home.

Ocracoke Island has almost 15 miles of unspoiled beaches and was recently voted the number-one beach in America. The wide swath of shoreline is clean and free of development, which means on many days you will have the beach all to yourself (except for the occasional pony).

About 7 miles north of the village, just off the main highway, are the Ocracoke Pony Pens built to protect the pony herd from traffic. Many of the ponies were sold off the island and today around 24 ponies graze on a 180-acre pasture. It is free to visit, but donations are welcomed to help pay for the food and veterinary care of the ponies. The ponies are not tame, so do not try to feed or touch them.

For more natural encounters, the Hammock Hills Nature Trail is a 0.75-mile trail through the island's maritime forest and salt marsh. It is a great stroll for nature lovers and bird watchers. You will find informative signposts along the way. The hike takes about 30 minutes.

Springer's Point near South Point is believed to be the site of the earliest settlements on the island. According to legend, Blackbeard met here with some fellow pirates shortly before his death and spent several days drinking rum and playing music. The deep hole just off the point is a popular fishing spot and still called Teach's Hole.

You can easily see most of Ocracoke by foot, but bicycles are available for rental from the Anchorage Marina, Slushie Stand, Pony Island Motel, Ocracoke Harbor Inn and Ocracoke Island Realty. Golf carts are also available for rent, but are confined to the village area. For a very complete map of the village, visit ocracokevillage.com.

The annual Ocrafolk Festival is held each June. Local musicians perform sea ditties, traditional island ballads and classical music. Those who like to wander will find island jewelers, potters, woodworkers and artists joined by other regional craftspeople. Auctions draw day crowds that stay through the big fish fry, but even the evenings hold special events like a dock party, square dancing, and storytelling.

The local Fire and Rescue squad has a Memorial Day weekend BBQ and dance. It is extremely popular with local sailing clubs (e.g., Neuse River Sailing Club, River Rat Yacht Club) who make this an annual cruise event. Halloween often draws many boaters and visitors making the last trip of the season.

Shopping: If you are looking for provisions for the next leg of your passage, visit the Ocracoke Variety Store (950 Irvin Garrish Hwy., 252-928-4911) about 1 mile from the harbor. They sell groceries, clothes, souvenirs and beach toys in one area; hardware and marine supplies in another; and wine, beer and liquor in a store at the end of the building. If they don't have it, you probably don't need it.

Zillie's Island Pantry (538 Back Rd., 252-928-9036) features an incredible selection of wines, microbrews and beers from around the world, along with gourmet provisions, cheeses and premium cigars. It may not be the place to do your major provisioning, but it's an excellent place to have a glass of beer or wine on their popular "Wine and WiFi" deck.

Albert Styron's Store at the corner of Creek and Lighthouse Rd. (252-921-0100) first opened in 1920. The merchandise has changed from dry goods and fishing equipment to souvenirs and snacks, but they still have a Coca-Cola cooler with Nehi, Cheerwine and Sun-Drop sodas.

The Village Craftsmen (170 Howard St., 252-928-5541) is a venerable institution headed toward 40 years of American crafts. Java Books (226 Back Rd., 252-928-7473) is located in the back of Ocracoke Coffee Company. There are many artists in residence here and a number of galleries showcasing their fine art and crafts. Over the Moon (64 British Cemetary Rd., 252-921-0411) features unique gifts made by local artists.

Dining: The Jolly Roger Pub & Marina (252-928-3703) overlooks Silver Lake and has a large outdoor dining area. This is a great place to grab a burger and beverage and watch your vessel swing on the hook. Howard's Pub and Raw Bar (252-928-4441) is 1 mile from the harbor (at 1175 Irvin Garrish Hwy., 252-928-4441) but is well worth the walk. Of course, a stop in Ocracoke would not be complete without dining at the Back Porch Restaurant & Wine Bar (110 Back Rd., 252-928-6401) where you will find local seafood, beef and poultry, plus a cookbook so you can make these extraordinary dishes for yourself.

The Flying Melon (181 Back Rd., 252-928-2533) is said by some locals to be the best eatery on the island, offering Creole and Southern specialties. Dajio (305 Irvin Garrish Hwy., 252-928-7119) is open for breakfast (seasonal), lunch and dinner serving fresh seafood and also specializing in flatbread pizza. They have a full bar and live music. Check their website for a schedule (dajiorestaurant.com) or call (252-928-7119).

Dining on the docks at SMacNally's Raw Bar and Grill (180 Irvin Garrish Hwy., 252-928-9999) is a great way to see who is in port and is very popular with the local boaters. Ocracoke Coffee Company at 22 Back Rd. (252-928-7473) is a popular place after dinner.

These are just a few of the dining options, so your best bet is to ask the locals for a recommendation. Many businesses close in the winter; call ahead.

Back Sound, NC

	Largest Vessel Accommodated	VHF Channel Monitored	Approach / Dockside Depth	Transient Berths / Total Berths	Groceries, Ice, Marine Supplies, Snacks	Floating Docks	Repairs: Hull, Engine, Propeller	Gas / Diesel	Lift (tonnage), Crane, Rail	Laundry, Pool, Showers, Courtesy Car	Min/Max Amps	Nearby: Grocery Store, Motel, Restaurant	Pump-Out Station
HARKERS ISLAND					**Dockage**			**Supplies**			**Services**		
1. Harkers Island Fishing Center Motel & Marina (WiFi) 252-728-3907	48	69	call/70	4/6	–		GD	IS	E	L	–	S	– GMR

🖳 Internet Access (WiFi) Wireless Internet Access **WG** Waterway Guide Cruising Club Partner 💧onSpot dockside WiFi facility
See WaterwayGuide.com for current rates, fuel prices, web site addresses, and other up-to-the-minute information. *(Information in the table is provided by the facilities.).*

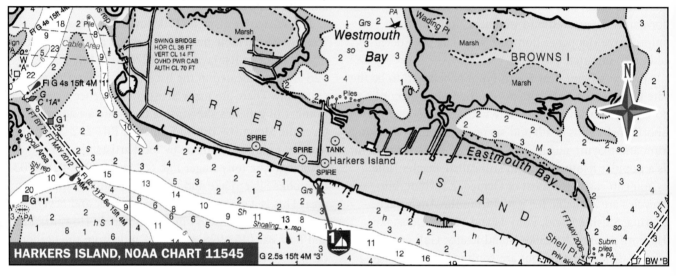

HARKERS ISLAND, NOAA CHART 11545

⚠ Be careful not to confuse the Nine Foot Shoal Channel markings for the Big Foot Slough Channel. The most confusing spot is where the Big Foot 6-second flashing red "8" marking the channel into Ocracoke appears close by the Nine Foot 2.5-second flashing red "4." Heading toward the "4" may put you hard aground. Binoculars will be handy for checking the number to ensure you don't head toward the wrong red.

Ocracoke's harbor, known as Silver Lake (or Cockle Creek by locals), is entered using a secondary channel that heads north from a junction marker. The marker has a 6-second flashing red light and a red-over-green "SL" board. Once south of the junction marker, head north along the entrance channel, which is well marked and straightforward, keeping reds on the starboard side. Stay in the middle of the channel, but watch for ferries. Prop thrust from the ferries can cause a considerable current inside Silver Lake.

Dockage: The National Park Service (NPS) offers dockage near its offices, on the port side of the Silver Lake entrance between two working ferry docks (to port when approaching) and one (to starboard) that is no longer in service. Rates are reasonable, with discounts for senior citizens possessing a Park Service "Golden Age Passport." Enter these transient docks between two clusters of huge pilings, and tie up alongside sturdy piers faced with large, widely spaced bollards. (These were originally built for PT boats during World War II.) In the summer, the maximum allowable stay here is two weeks. There is room for about a dozen transients on a first-come, first-served basis. Expect some surge here as the ferry enters and departs.

The 35-slip Anchorage Inn & Marina has space for transients and sells all fuel. This can be a busy place during in-season weekends; it is best to call ahead for reservations. The Anchorage Inn can sometimes work with slipholders in the area and place you in a private slip for a night or weekend. Nearby Down Creek Marina has transient space as well. Note that there is a no laundry service on the island.

Anchorage: Silver Lake is a perfectly protected harbor, with anchoring depths of 7 to 13 feet MLW, except in the shallow cove to the southwest. Holding is good, but watch for a weedy bottom, which can give a false sense of security. There are also reports of debris on the bottom. Make certain you set your anchor well. There is ample room for those who want to drop a hook, even on summer weekends. Be sure to anchor away from the ferry channel and dock.

There are two dinghy docks—the NPS dock and one by the Community Docks. These provides easy access to groceries, restaurants and shops. Many restaurants and coffee shops offer outdoor seating and are pet friendly. Note that many of the restaurants and stores are closed between November and March.

Ocracoke Inlet

NAVIGATION: Use NOAA Chart 11555. Ocracoke Inlet can be an alternative to the long diversion to Beaufort when heading north or south around Cape Hatteras, but this is not an inlet to be attempted under anything but the most benign conditions and only with local knowledge. Although protected from the north, shoaling is constant and breakers on both sides are evident in nearly all conditions. Check with Coast Guard Sector North Carolina via VHF Channel 16 for current conditions before using the inlet at or near low tide.

■ THE LOWER BANKS

To the south, 27-mile-long Core Sound runs behind the narrow ocean barrier of Core Banks. Once part of the ICW route, it was abandoned when the land cuts that link the present ICW were dredged. Cruising boats now usually bypass the sound due to the very shallow water: 3.5-foot draft is the limiting factor when transiting Core Sound. Drum Inlet is closed to navigation.

⚠️ The channels in Core Sound call for local knowledge and there are only a few wide-spaced markers. Shallow-draft boats less than 25 feet long can reasonably consider cruising here. Shoaling to 3-feet MLW has been reported across the channel between Core Sound flashing red "5" and red daybeacon "5A."

Harkers Island

When locals talk about the Harkers Island area, they usually include the adjacent mainland villages fronted by The Straits, which separates the island from the mainland. This marshy region is known as "Down East" and has a total of only 3.8-square miles.

The Harkers Island Visitor Center at the east end of the island also serves as home to the National Park

Administrative Offices and Headquarters (1800 Island Rd., 252-728-2250). They have an interactive map of the Cape Lookout National Seashore Park, exhibits and seasonal programs. It is open daily April through October from 9:00 a.m. to 5:00 p.m. (252-728-2250).

The Core Sound Waterfowl Museum & Heritage Center at 1785 Island Rd. (252-728-1500) was closed at press time in summer 2019 due to damage from Hurricane Florence. See updates at coresound.com.

NAVIGATION: Use NOAA Chart 11545. The **Harkers Island Swing Bridge** with a 14-foot closed vertical clearance crosses The Straits. (Opens on signal.) An offshoot channel before the bridge, which is marked and has 6-foot depths, leads to Marshallberg after flashing green "42A" (a private aid). This is strictly small-boat territory; otherwise, rent a car in Morehead City and take the "long way around" to visit this area.

Dockage: Harkers Island Fishing Center Motel & Marina sells all fuels and may have a slip for vessels to 48 feet. This is accessed from the south side of the island via a channel with 2- to 3-foot MLW depths. Seek local knowledge and plan to enter with a rising tide.

Lookout Bight

One of the most beautiful anchorages of the Carolinas, Lookout Bight offers a secure place to set the hook in all but the most inclement weather, within the protective arm and elbow of the cape. Miles of unspoiled, dune-backed beaches of the Cape Lookout National Seashore provide the perfect setting to search for shells of the giant whelk or watch the antics of laughing gulls, a variety of terns, willets, dunlins, cavorting oystercatchers and the inimitable working patterns flown by resident black skimmers. Look for the wild horses on nearby Shackleford Banks, where they have roamed since the 1500s when a failed colony released the horses. They have fended for themselves and prospered ever since. Cape Lookout Lighthouse has been a landmark for the coast since 1812.

While arriving in Cape Lookout Bight on your own vessel is the better way to see the bight, you can also go by passenger ferry from Beaufort or Harkers Island. The ferry runs daily (year round). The schedule is seasonal. See islandexpressferryservices.com for details.

NAVIGATION: Use NOAA Chart 11545. Cape Lookout is best accessed from the ocean from Beaufort Inlet, although it can be accessed in a shoal-draft vessel via Back Sound, which leads between Shackleford Banks (part of Rachel Carson Reserve) and Middle Marsh. This is strictly small-boat territory.

⚠️ Note that the Coast Guard has temporarily discontinued eight lateral aids to navigation in Barden Inlet due to extensive shoaling that is causing navigational safety issues. Heavy shoaling from Barden Inlet from flashing red "26" to flashing green "35" has progressed making the waterway inaccessible. Significant shoaling also exists in Barden Inlet between red nun "8" and green nun "15" (may not be shown on all charts) to an average channel depth of less than 3 feet MLW. In the past, buoys have been frequently moved to mark the deepest water; however, under current conditions, the aids to navigation system can no longer be configured to safely mark a passable channel. Mariners are advised to use extreme caution while navigating this area.

At the eastern end of Cape Lookout, a dredged channel leads to Lookout Bight and Cape Lookout. Coming from the ocean, the entrance buoy to the Bight (flashing red "4") is located 6.2 miles from flashing red "6" on the Beaufort Inlet Channel on an east-southeasterly course coming from the inlet. (Beaufort Inlet is discussed in more detail in the next chapter of this guide and in the Inlet section at the front of this guide.)

Anchorage: During summer months, most skippers anchor just east of Power Squadron Spit (depths in the 20-foot range), taking advantage of prevailing southwesterly breezes with a short fetch. Holding is excellent in thick mud at depths ranging from 8 to 26 feet MLW. Anchor for up to 14 days within the boundaries of Cape Lookout National Seashore. For a grand view, climb to the top of the Cape Lookout Lighthouse (open through late September).

Did you know? The distinctive black-and-white diamond pattern on the Cape Lookout lighthouse helps you locate your position. Black diamonds indicate you are north or south of the light, while white diamonds indicate you are east or west.

■ NEXT STOP

The next section gets you back on your way south on the ICW bound for Morehead City and beyond to Charleston, SC. This succession of dredged channels and shallow sounds doesn't allow for much sailing but the scenery makes up for it. You will begin to feel the pull of the tides, which become progressively greater as you head towards Georgia, where they peak at 9 feet.

Cape Lookout Lighthouse

Beaufort, NC to Isle of Palms, SC

■ BEAUFORT TO SOUTHPORT, NC   ■ LOCKWOODS FOLLY, NC TO ISLE OF PALMS, SC

Cape Lookout
Bardens Inlet
MILE 205
Beaufort
Beaufort Inlet
Bogue Inlet
MILE 229
Morehead City
New River Inlet
Swansboro
New Topsail Inlet
Jacksonville
Mason Inlet
Sneads Ferry
Wrightsville Beach
Masonboro Inlet
MILE 309
Southport
MILE 283
Cape Fear River Inlet
Wilmington
Cape Fear River
Lockwoods Folly Inlet
Shallote Inlet
Little River Inlet
Murrells Inlet
MILE 365
Myrtle Beach
MILE 403
Waccamaw River
Georgetown
Bull Bay
Charleston Harbor Entrance
MILE 469
Charleston

Neuse River

ATLANTIC OCEAN

NORTH CAROLINA
SOUTH CAROLINA

Visit Waterway Explorer at waterwayguide.com

Beaufort, NC to Isle of Palms, SC

Roughly 265 miles along the ICW from Bogue Sound in North Carolina to Charleston, SC, this passage will slowly reveal different kinds of waterways and scenery. The wide, deep waters of the North Carolina sounds are behind you, and the route now follows a succession of dredged channels through small sounds, shallow sloughs and salt marshes, all connected by a series of land cuts. Halfway along the passage, North Carolina gives way to South Carolina and you begin to enter the aptly named "Lowcountry."

Cruising Conditions

This section of the ICW has more than its fair share of bridges, particularly in the stretch between Swansboro and Georgetown (South Carolina). Seventeen of these are fixed high-level bridges. Some bridges open only once an hour and your trip may be delayed by their schedules. Boats with masts taller than 65 feet must run outside from Beaufort Inlet, NC, to Georgetown or Charleston, SC, both of which have safe big-ship entrances. (See Inlet section at the front of this guide for more detailed information.)

Bald Head Island, historically Smith Island, is the southernmost barrier island in NC. It is located where the mouth of the Cape Fear River meets the Atlantic Ocean. The eastern tip of the island forms Cape Fear Point.

Shoaling continues to be an issue in some sections of this stretch of the ICW. While we cover these areas in detail in this section, certain areas require your utmost attention and are noted in the guide by "navigation alerts." Several of the problem areas were dredged in the 2017 and again in 2019, including the channel near Browns Inlet, Mason Inlet, Carolina Beach Inlet, Lockwoods Folly Inlet and Shallotte Inlet. Other areas have not been dredged since 2010, including the entire Bogue Sound from the Atlantic Beach Bridge (Mile 206.7) to the Cedar Point Highway Bridge (Mile 226)

north of Swansboro. When shoaling becomes a problem, the Army Corps of Engineers does its best to survey these areas and frequently gives specific GPS waypoints that you can use to avoid the shoals. Be aware that conditions may change between the survey date and the time you pass through.

While the mile marker figures do not change, aids to navigation are frequently relocated and additional aids added to reflect the current deep part of navigable channels especially near inlets. If a marker or two on your chart appears to be on the wrong side of the magenta line, don't be alarmed. In most cases, the marker has been moved as conditions have changed and is in the correct position on the chart, but the magenta line has not been changed in 35 years. It is our recommendation that you always follow the markers and not the magenta line unless you have extremely reliable local information.

Rather than constantly changing the magenta line, it has been removed on some charts in areas where there is frequent shoaling and markers are changed often. The Waterway Explorer at waterwayguide.com tracks changes and also receives frequent postings from cruisers transiting the area. Also check the *Local Notice to Mariners* (Fifth District) for possible changes in the markers.

Bridge Openings

ICW bridges will not delay openings if boats are already waiting, so you must know your speed and calculate your transit carefully; slow boats may not be able to synchronize their passages with the openings. Bridges

Bridges/Distances
(Approximate Statute Miles from Mile Zero, Norfolk, VA)

LOCATION	MILE	CLEARANCE
Atlantic Beach Bridge	206.7	65'
Cedar Point (Emerald Isle) Bridge	226.0	65'
Onslow Beach Swing Bridge	**240.7**	**12'**
U.S. 210 Hwy. Bridge	252.3	64'
Surf City Bridge	**260.7**	**65'**
Figure Eight Island Swing Bridge	**278.1**	**20'**
Wrightsville Beach Bascule Bridge	**283.1**	**20'**
Snows Cut (U.S. 421) Hwy. Bridge	295.7	65'
Oak Island Bridge	311.8	65'
Middleton St. Bridge	316.8	65'
Holden Beach Bridge	323.6	65'
Ocean Isle (SR 1904) Bridge	333.7	65'
Mannon C. Gore (Sunset Beach) Bridge	337.9	65'
Nixons Crossroads Hwy. Bridge	347.2	65'
Little River Swing Bridge	**347.3**	**7'**
Robert Edge Pkwy. Bridge	349.1	65'
Barefoot Landing Swing Bridge	**353.3**	**31'**
Conway Bypass (U.S. 17) Bridges	355.5	65'
Grande Dunes Bridge	357.5	65'
Grissom Parkway Bridge	360.5	65'
SCL Railroad Bascule Bridge	**365.4**	**16'**
U.S. 501 Hwy. Bridge	365.4	65'
Fantasy Harbor Bridge	366.4	65'
Socastee Swing Bridge	**371.0**	**6.5'**
Socastee (SR 544) Hwy. Bridge	371.3	65'
Lafayette (U.S. 17) Hwy. Bridge	402.1	65'
Estherville-Minim Creek Bridge	**411.5**	**0'**
Isle of Palms Connector Bridge	458.9	65'
Ben Sawyer Memorial Swing Bridge	**462.2**	**31'**
James Island Expressway Bridge	469.9	67'
Wappoo Creek Bridge (SR 171)	**470.8**	**33'**

in VA and NC respond on VHF Channel 13, while SC and GA bridgetenders monitor VHF Channel 09. It is a good idea to monitor both. See more on bridges and schedules in the *Skippers Handbook* in the front of this guide.

Tidal Currents

Keeping an eye on tidal currents is important in this area; beginning at Morehead City, you suddenly encounter tide and tidal current conditions quite different from those on the run down from Norfolk. The 3-foot tidal fluctuation becomes progressively greater and peaks at 9 feet in Georgia. It is important to have accurate tide and current information available when traveling this portion of the ICW. This information is available at tidesonline.nos.noaa.gov.

Tidal currents, growing stronger as you head south, are strongest around inlets, bridges and converging waterways, which have a side-sweeping effect. Try to visualize beforehand which way the current might push (or pull) your boat and consider how an ebb or flood tide might affect the situation. Learn to check your course astern from the relative position of the markers and steer to compensate. Places where the side-setting effect of the current can be serious are detailed in the text.

When approaching a bridge with the current, have your boat under control and do not move in too close while waiting for the bridge to open. There is no regulation on these waters as to which boat has the right-of-way passing through bridges, but it is generally accepted that a boat going against the current should yield to one going with the current. It is foolish and dangerous to contest the channel with another boat under any circumstance.

Be careful to follow the marked channel, particularly on a falling tide, as going aground then can be serious. Your boat might wind up high and dry, allowing for the possibility of a swamping when the tide begins to rise.

Navigation & Weather Briefings

Informative navigation and weather briefings are held nightly at Southport Marina (ICW Mile 309) at 6:00 p.m. and are sponsored by Southport Marina and Zimmerman Marine. There is no charge to attend. The schedule is seasonal so call ahead (910-457-9900). See more details in the Southport section of Chapter 6 in this guide.

Beaufort to Southport, NC

 Mile 185–Mile 320   (VHF) NC Bridges: Channel 13

CHARTS NOAA 11534, 11537, 11541, 11542, 11545

Beaufort and its sister city, Morehead City, are two of the most popular stopovers between Norfolk and Florida. Beaufort is well-known as a transient stop with numerous marinas and service facilities that can handle the needs of cruisers, both power and sail. Morehead City is a renown commercial and sportfishing center with a large fishing charter fleet year-round. Note that tides and currents now begin to be a major consideration as you proceed south on the ICW in close proximity to the coast.

■ ADAMS CREEK–ICW MILE 185 TO MILE 200

The ICW route leaves the Neuse River at Mile 185 and enters Adams Creek. Farther south, Adams Creek is connected to Core Creek via the Adams Creek Canal, a 5-mile-long land cut that ends at the headwaters of Core Creek below the Core Creek (NC 101) Bridge. Adams Creek Canal is mostly undeveloped. Keep an eye out for deer, eagles and other wildlife along the way. Adams and Core Creeks, as well as the canal, may have floating debris, so keep a close eye on the course ahead. The area of Core Creek below the bridge was holding its charted depth (12 feet MLW) at press time (summer 2019).

NAVIGATION: Use NOAA Chart 11541. Do not be tempted to cut inside Garbacon Shoal flashing green "7" in the Neuse River (Mile 180.6) when approaching Adams Creek. The fishermen's markers off Winthrop Point indicate nets just below the surface. Follow the magenta line on the NOAA chart around flashing green "1AC" (Mile 183.8), which marks the entry to Adams Creek, and make a dogleg approach. You will then be on a range for 1.5 miles.

The aids to navigation along Adams and Core Creeks are located 30 to 35 feet outside the channel limits. Although the chart shows 8-foot depths in Adams Creek opposite marker "9," cutting this corner puts you in 6-foot MLW depths. In general, the marks are widely spaced here. Flashing red "8A" helps with this. Where you have a green on one side and a red a long way farther along, go almost to the green before changing course for the red. Unlike the common practice of marking the inside edges of turns and shoals, the channel markers are usually set on the outside edge. This makes it tempting to cut the corners but it is safer to follow the legs to their full natural extensions before making your turns.

Adams Creek, NC

ADAMS CREEK CANAL		Largest Vessel Accommodated	VHF Channel Monitored	Approach / Dockside Depth (reported)	Transient Berths / Total Berths	Floating Docks	Groceries, Ice, Marine Supplies, Snacks	Gas / Diesel	Repairs: Hull, Engine, Propeller	Lift (tonnage), Crane, Rail	Laundry, Pool, Showers, Courtesy Car	Min/Max Amps	Nearby: Grocery Store, Motel, Restaurant	Pump-Out Station
1. Sea Gate Marina 💻 📶 193.3	252-728-4126	60	16	2/70	6/6	–	GD	GIMS	–	–	30/50	LS	P	G
2. Bock Marine 💻 📶 196	252-728-6855	75	16/13	7/7	8/8	–	–	MS	HEP	L70,C	15/50	LSC	–	–
3. Jarrett Bay Boatworks 💻 📶 198	252-728-2690	125	16/17	9/15	12/9	F	GD	IMS	HEP	L300,C15	30/100	S	P	–
4. Western Branch Diesel-Beaufort 198	252-504-2185	–	–	– REPAIR FACILITY –			–	M	HEP	–	–	–	–	–
5. Gregory Poole Marine Power 198	252-504-2640	350	16	–	–	–	–	M	E	–	30/30	–	–	–
6. Moores Marine Yacht Center 💻 📶 198	252-504-7060	150	69	–	12/9	–	–	MS	HEP	L220,C50	30/100	SC	P	–
7. Bluewater Yacht Sales-Beaufort	252-728-2645	–	–	call/8		–	–	–	EP	L	–	–	–	–
8. Beaufort Marine Center 💻 📶	252-728-7358	–	–	–	–	–	–	M	HEP	L200,C25	30/100	SC	P	–
9. True World Marine 📶 198.5	252-728-2541	100	16	4/4	7/5	F	–	M	HEP	L75	15/50	S	–	–

💻 Internet Access 📶 Wireless Internet Access WG Waterway Guide Cruising Club Partner 🔵 onSpot dockside WiFi facility
See WaterwayGuide.com for current rates, fuel prices, web site addresses, and other up-to-the-minute information. *(Information in the table is provided by the facilities.)*

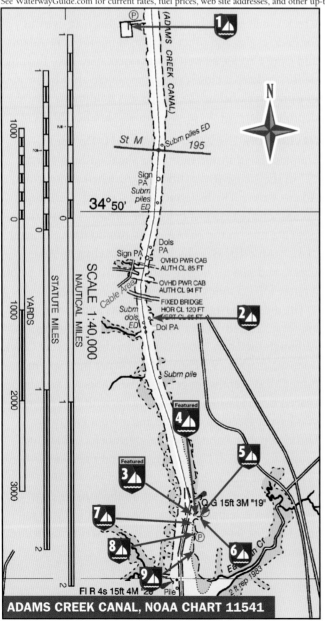

ADAMS CREEK CANAL, NOAA CHART 11541

Flashing red "18" is the last marker before the canal, which is unmarked but holds good 12-foot MLW depths. Keep to the center of the channel except when passing other boats or being passed. There is a huge residential development on the Adams Creek Canal, north of the fixed **Core Creek (NC 101) Bridge** (65-foot vertical clearance) at Mile 195.8, with numerous docks extending toward the ICW channel. Tidal currents from the Beaufort Inlet begin to appear in the vicinity of the Core Creek Bridge. Currents are particularly strong around the bridge, at Bock Marine just below the bridge and at the outside docking area at Jarrett Bay Boatworks. Strong wind-driven currents can be felt as well in the Adams Creek Canal and into lower Adams Creek in certain conditions. From Core Creek Bridge to the Morehead City/Beaufort area at Mile 205, ebb current provides strong assistance to southbound craft.

At Mile 199.3, the ICW route turns to the southeast, after flashing red "24." From there, follow the Newport River as it makes several dogleg turns.

⚠ The split between the ICW and the channel to Beaufort causes much confusion. Heading south pass red daybeacon "28" and red nun buoy "30" to starboard, then pass flashing green (2+1) junction marker "RS" to port and red nun buoy "30A" starboard, as you approach the 65-foot fixed vertical clearance **Beaufort Channel (U.S. 70) Bridge** at Mile 203.8 and adjacent **Beaufort Channel Railroad Bascule Bridge** (4-foot closed vertical clearance, usually open). Between flashing green "29" and green daybeacon "31" there may be additional uncharted buoys.

Even tugboat captains can get confused in this area. In 2019 our Waterway Guide cruising editor observed a tug pushing a barge south on the ICW entering the Russell Slough Channel that leads directly to Beaufort. The captain, realizing his mistake, stopped the barge, backed up, then turned to starboard reentering the ICW heading south.

Dockage: At Mile 193.3, Sea Gate Marina is located on the west side of the Adams Creek Canal with all fuels and slips. The marina is part of a neighborhood association. Just beyond the Core Creek Bridge (Mile 195.8), the family-run Bock Marine has repair and service capabilities and welcomes DIY boaters. The tidal flow can make docking demanding but you will find plenty of helping hands.

Jarrett Bay Boatworks, a Down East Carolina custom builder and full-service boatyard, operates a large facility in the Jarrett Bay Marine Industrial Park at Mile 198 on Core Creek. With a 175-acre yard, a 200-ton lift and a 12-foot-deep basin, Jarrett Bay's service department can handle virtually any project on vessels up to 130 feet in length or a draft of up to 10 feet. Transient dockage is available for vessels up to 125 feet, including nine

22-foot-wide slips fronting the ICW. Fuel (gas and diesel) and a well-stocked ship store are on site.

Adjacent to Jarrett Bay is Western Branch Diesel-Beaufort, one of the largest power dealers on the East Coast. They have a fully stocked parts department and respond to after-hour emergencies. In the same marine industrial park are Gregory Poole Marine Power (offering engine repair) and Bluewater Yacht Sales-Beaufort (boat brokerage).

Beaufort Marine Center offers storage, repairs, refits and paint services. They welcome all kinds of vessels and are committed to getting you in and, just as importantly, back out on the water. Nearby Moores Marine Yacht Center is a sister facility to Beaufort Marine Center. These folks lovingly restore classic powerboats from the 1920s through the 1960s. True World Marine is also in the Jarrett Bay Marine Industrial Park with repairs and may have space for you. Call ahead.

Anchorage: Just beyond the straight stretch of the first range in Adams Creek and behind quick flashing green "9" is the mouth of Cedar Creek (Mile 187.6), a good anchorage for vessels with drafts of 6 feet or less, with

WESTERN BRANCH DIESEL-BEAUFORT

JARRETT BAY BOATWORKS

Adams Creek (ICW)

more room than you might think from the chart. The secret is to go farther in where you get good protection from a south wind. Anchor towards the south shore and east of the 5-foot line as shown on the charts. There is about 7 feet MLW as you snug up behind the point of land to protect you from a south wind. There is a strip of sand on the south shore for pet relief. Be sure to pick up when done. Shrimp boats leave this harbor at all hours (day and night) in season. Many years ago, a sailboat sunk in this anchorage. The wreck of a sailboat is approximately 150 to 200 yards to the east-northeast of flashing green "9A"and is marked by white PVC poles.

Although the chart shows only 5 feet MLW, 6-foot depths or better are available in the much more protected Jonaquin Creek farther back to port off Cedar Creek. It provides all-around protection with excellent holding.

Back Creek (Mile 189)–1.5 miles south of Cedar Creek–can provide excellent protection from southwest and northeast winds and wakes from the ICW for boats drawing 4.5 feet or less.

There are no other protected anchorages until you reach Beaufort and Morehead City.

■ BEAUFORT AREA–ICW MILE 200 TO MILE 204

Founded in 1709, the charming city of Beaufort, NC (pronounced "BO-fort" not "BEW-fort" as in the SC town), preserves traces of its nautical history as a backdrop to a thriving modern boating center. Year-round, Beaufort is home to yachts of all descriptions, either moored out or tied up along the town side of the waterfront channel. During the fall, passage-making sailboats dominate the scene with preparations for ocean voyages from this major jumping-off point for trips to the Caribbean.

Long hailed as the "Gateway to the Caribbean," Beaufort is often cooled by a brisk sea breeze. Then, in the fall, as the western edge of the Gulf Stream veers to within 40 miles of the inlet, fresh northwest winds carry eager sailors into the Atlantic. It is a 4-day sail to the Bahamas, and one day more to Bermuda. This close proximity to the Atlantic trade routes was not lost on the early settlers, and to this day Beaufort is still receiving cargo and sailors from afar. It is a great walking town with eclectic shops, good restaurants and a waterfront full commercial fishing vessels, shrimpboats, kayaks and paddleboards as well as pleasure boats of all sizes.

ICW– Beaufort, NC

BEAUFORT AREA		Largest Vessel Accommodated	VHF Channel Monitored	Transient Berths / Total Berths	Approach / Dockside Depth (reported)	Floating Docks	Gas / Diesel	Groceries, Ice, Marine Supplies, Snacks	Repairs: Hull, Engine, Propeller	Lift (tonnage), Crane, Rail	Min/Max Amps	Laundry, Pool, Showers, Courtesy Car	Pump-Out Station	Nearby: Grocery Store, Motel, Restaurant
				Dockage			**Supplies**		**Services**					
1. Gallants Channel	252-728-2762	100	–	10/20	12/12	F	–	–	–	–	30/50	–	–	GMR
2. Town Creek Marina ⌨ WiFi 1.3 S of 202	252-728-6111	180	16/08	24/88	10/12	F	GD	IMS	HEP	L50	30/100	LSC	P	GMR
3. Beaufort Yacht Basin ⌨ WiFi	252-504-3625	100	16/67	call/74	7/5.5	F	–	IS	–	–	30/50	LSC	P	GR
4. Homer Smith Docks and Marina onSpot	252-728-2944	150	16/06	10/95	10/8	F	GD	I	–	–	30/100	LSC	P	GR
5. Beaufort Inn WiFi 1.7 E of 202.3	252-728-2600	45	–	6/12	12/5	–	–	–	–	–	30/30	–	–	M
6. Beaufort Docks Marina ⌨ WiFi 202	252-728-2503	250	16/09	98/98	16/16	F	GD	IS	HEP	–	30/100	LSC	P	GMR
7. BoatHouse at Front Street Village ⌨ WiFi 202	252-838-1524	100	16/68	19/30	15/12	F	GD	IMS	HEP	L18	30/200+	LPSC	P	MR
RADIO ISLAND														
8. Radio Island Marina 203.9	252-726-3773	35	16	call/8	5/4	F	G	IMS	HEP	L	30/30	–	–	GMR

⌨ Internet Access   WiFi Wireless Internet Access   WG Waterway Guide Cruising Club Partner   onSpot dockside WiFi facility
See WaterwayGuide.com for current rates, fuel prices, web site addresses, and other up-to-the-minute information. (Information in the table is provided by the facilities.)

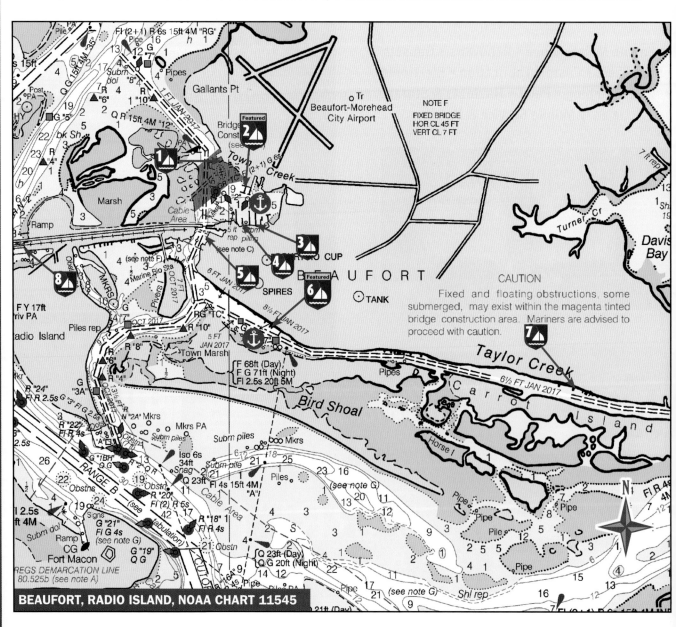

BEAUFORT, RADIO ISLAND, NOAA CHART 11545

TOWN CREEK MARINA

The North Carolina Maritime Museum Conservation Lab, located northwest of the marina repair yard on Russell Slough Channel (referred to locally as the Gallants Channel) is a receiving and conservation area for the artifacts brought up from the nearby wreck of Blackbeard's *Queen Anne's Revenge.* (See sidebar in previous chapter.) It is not open to the public although there are occasional guided tours of the premises. This facility has a new bulkhead on the creek, and there has been considerable expansion ashore. The museum sponsors a junior sailing program and a rowing club based here.

Beaufort–Town Creek

NAVIGATION: Use NOAA Chart 11545. Use the Cape Hatteras Tide Table. For high tide, add 7 minutes; for low tide, add 11 minutes. Southbound vessels heading for Town Creek should depart the ICW by passing daybeacon "28," red daybeacon "30" (shown on the latest NOAA chart as a nun buoy), flashing green (2+1) junction marker "RS" and red daybeacon "2" to starboard (Mile 200.8), then follow the Russell Slough Channel east of the ICW and west of Russell Creek.

Favor the green side of the channel at red daybeacon "4," and after making the turn to starboard at flashing green "5," plot a course to green daybeacon "7." Red nun buoy "6A," beyond red daybeacon "6," assists you in reaching green daybeacon "7." Where "8" used to be, there is now a lighted junction marker, flashing "RG"

with red at the top and green at the bottom of its board. Once past green daybeacon "7," turn immediately to port toward red daybeacon "10," and continue southeast on to quick flashing red "12."

Dockage: There are several great marinas in the Town Creek area. Gallants Channel is an annex of the North Carolina Maritime Museum. Although it is a bit removed from the facilities of Beaufort (1 mile from the waterfront), it does have attractive transient pricing. It offers floating docks with water and power but no heads, showers or other facilities.

The full-service Town Creek Marina is located on Town Creek Basin at Mile 202 (turn to port at green daybeacon "1"), where you can find transient dockage, take on gas or diesel at the marina's floating fuel dock, pick up a complimentary town map and catch the latest report on the Weather Channel. This is a major repair facility with a 50-ton lift. Between 2017 and 2018 the marina installed new 40-, 45-, 50- and 55-foot docks with plans to install 65-foot docks prior to the 2020 boating season. The popular City Kitchen is above the marina office and is a great spot for catching a sunset. The marina provides a courtesy car for trips to the nearby supermarket or the Beaufort waterfront.

Beaufort Yacht Basin may have space for you on their floating docks. They cater to sportfishers, powerboats and sailboats in an attractive and comfortable environment.

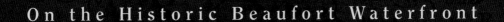

GOIN' ASHORE: **BEAUFORT, NC**

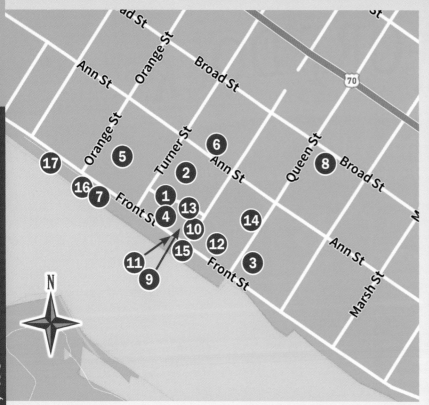

ATTRACTIONS	
1	Beaufort Ghost Walk
2	Beaufort Historic Site
3	Inlet Inn
4	Kitty Hawk Kites
5	North Carolina Maritime Museum and Watercraft Center
6	Old Burying Ground
SHOPPING	
4	Kitty Hawk Surf Co.
7	Beaufort Olive Oil Company
8	Coastal Community Market
9	Harbor Specialties
10	Scuttlebutt Nautical Books
11	Island Traders Beaufort
12	The General Store
DINING	
13	Aqua Restaurant
14	Beaufort Grocery Company
15	Dock House
16	Front Street Grill at Stillwater
17	The Spouter Inn
MARINAS	
15	Beaufort Docks Marina

In Beaufort, the town is the culture and its seascape the canvas. A flourishing arts community of painters, photographers, sculptors and writers reside here, as evidenced by the numerous galleries, all within walking distance of the docks.

Attractions: The North Carolina Maritime Museum and Watercraft Center (315 Front St., 252-504-7740) is the highlight of any visit to Beaufort and the area's major draw. The museum has an active boatbuilding program and offers environmental education programs, including the Cape Lookout Studies Program. In their maritime store, you will find nautical and coastal books, gifts, prints and souvenirs. At their annex facility on Gallants Channel, next to Town Creek Marina, there is an exhibit on North Carolina shipwrecks. Photographs and artifacts include the wreck of *Queen Anne's Revenge*, Blackbeard's flagship. For more information, call 252-728-7317.

On the 400 block of Ann St., beneath the shade of live oak trees, you will find the Old Burying Ground (252-728-5225). Listed on the National Register of Historic Places, the cemetery was deeded to the town in 1731 by Nathaniel Taylor. The weathered tombstones chronicle the heritage of Beaufort and the surrounding coast. Union soldiers, Confederate soldiers, freed African-Americans and slaves all rest together in the Old Burying Ground.

The Beaufort Historic Site (100 block of Turner St.) consists of ten buildings, six of which have been authentically restored. The Leffers Cottage was the home of Samuel Leffers, a schoolmaster, merchant and clerk of the court. Inside are artifacts relating to the daily chores of cooking, spinning, sewing, candlemaking and weaving. From here you can catch a double-decker bus tour of the historic area (April through October). The Carteret County Courthouse is the oldest wood-framed courthouse in North Carolina. The John C. Manson House, with its Bahamian architecture, still stands on its original site. The Josiah Bell House served as the residence of the influential Bell family. The Old Jail has 28-inch-thick walls and boasts legends of ghosts and a single hanging in 1874. Built in 1859, the Apothecary Shop houses a unique collection of medicinal and pharmaceutical artifacts, most of which are original to the shop. For more information, call the Beaufort Historical Association at 252-728-5225.

NC Maritime Museum

To see the town from a different point of view, the popular Beaufort Ghost Walk covers approximately nine blocks and lasts around one hour. You will be entertained by pirate guides, who will regale you with an enjoyable assortment of chilling stories about ghost ships and haunted houses. Tours start at 108 Middle Ln. (252-772-9925).

Beyond the Front Street docks and across Taylors Creek, you will see the Rachel Carson Reserve (252-838-0890), part of the North Carolina National Estuarine Research Reserve. Wild ponies are frequently seen grazing near the anchorage along the shores of Carrot Island. Rent a kayak and paddle over or land in your tender. There are several ferries that can shuttle you to Shackleford Island and to Cape Lookout. Call Island Ferry Adventures (610 Front St., 252-728-4129) or Island Express Ferry Service (600 Front St., 252-728-7433) to book your tour of these unspoiled barrier islands. Kitty Hawk Kites at 412 Front St. offers kayak and paddleboarding tours of Taylor Creek and the Rachel Carson Reserve (year round). They also offer hang gliding flights (seasonal). Call 252-504-2039.

For those who prefer to be under the water, check out Discovery Diving Co. at 414 Orange St. (252-728-2265). They specialize in wreck dives and are a full-service dive operation offering training, gear sales and rentals and equipment repair.

There are several special events planned throughout the year in Beaufort. In April, guests enjoy the Beaufort Food and Wine Weekend, which includes wine tastings, an auction, seminars, dinners, art exhibits and two

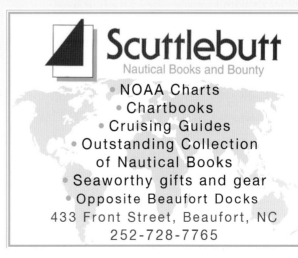

days of delicious dining. Call 252-728-5225 for more information. In May, catch the Beaufort Music Festival and the Wooden Boat Show. Also in May or June, you'll find the Old Homes and Gardens Tour, which draws people from far and wide. If you are passing through the area, it is worthwhile to stop and enjoy these events.

Family visiting or need a crew change? The Inlet Inn at 601 Front St. offers the privacy of a hotel but with the amenities of a bed and breakfast. They offer cozy rooms (all with private porches and some with views), continental breakfast and the newspaper delivered to your room. Call 800-554-5466 or 252-728-3600 for details.

Shopping: Immediately across Front St. from the docks, there are banks, a laundry (the only one in town) and a pharmacy. The Post Office is located out of town by the Food Lion on Highway 70. Some provisioning may be done at Coastal Community Market, a health-food store a few blocks from the waterfront at 606 Broad St. (272-728-2844). Beaufort Olive Oil Company (300 Front St., 252-504-2474) offers a wide variety of oils and vinegars with samples. They have four locations: Morehead City, Beaufort, Swansboro and Emerald Isle.

For many, strolling through the shops and boutiques along Beaufort's waterfront and side streets is a just reward for the offshore passages and long hours on the ICW. Perhaps no store captures the flavor of Beaufort better than Harbor Specialties at 437 Front St. (252-838-0059). They sell dock and foredeck apparel including Tilley, Sperry and Henri Lloyd. For women, you will find handbags from Vera Bradley and flip-flops from Douglas Paquette. They also offer monogramming and embroidery.

Island Traders Beaufort at 431 Front St. (252-838-1576) sells Costa, O'Neil and Reef, while the Beaufort Trading Company (252-504-3209), located on the second floor of the Somerset Square, is where you can find hats and outdoor wear by Colombia, Teva and Sea Dog. Kitty Hawk Surf Co. (419 Front St., 252-728-6670) also has popular brands of clothes, shoes and accessories.

The General Store (515 Front St., 252-728-7707) is just what the name implies: You can enjoy ice cream, fudge (32 flavors) and other treats while you shop for Guy Harvey, Simply Southern and Columbia Sportswear, as well as toys and souvenirs. They also have a coin-operated laundry.

Since 1993 Scuttlebutt Nautical Books has been a legendary fixture on the Beaufort waterfront at 433 Front St. (252-728-7765). Scuttlebutt specializes in "nautical books and bounty" such as NOAA charts, guidebooks and nautical gifts and gear. They ship, offer gift certificates and accommodate special orders.

Dining: You will not need to stroll far to find a great meal in Beaufort. There are more restaurants than we can count within a 5-minute walk of the docks. Right at the Beaufort Docks is the Dock House Restaurant (500 Front St., 252-728-4506) offering a casual seafood menu and live entertainment, either directly on the boardwalk and in the upstairs lounge. They have been around for 30 years, so you can rest assured the food is very, very good.

At 117 Queen St. you will find the popular Beaufort Grocery Company (252-728-3899), where you can eat inside or out. Open six days a week (closed on Tuesdays) for lunch and dinner. They also offer take out service, including prepared picnic baskets, and serve brunch on Sundays.

For more upscale fare, Aqua Restaurant at 114 Middle Ln. (252-728-7777) offers exceptional dining in an urban-chic decor setting. The martinis are special, as is the crème brûlée.

On Front St., The Spouter Inn (218 Front St., 252-728-5190) is a favorite with boaters, as is Front Street Grill at Stillwater (300 Front St., 252-728-4956), serving lunch, dinner and Sunday brunch from a menu featuring regional cuisine with an emphasis on seafood.

Homer Smith Docks and Marina is nearby with some transient space and all fuels, and even though it is a working dock, they have many attractive cruiser amenities. Beaufort Inn, on the south side of the Gallants Channel Bridge, has 6 reserved transient slips (with 5-foot dockside depths).

Anchorage: Boats sometimes anchor to the northwest of Town Creek Marina in 6 to 12 feet MLW. Anchorage space is minimal, however, due to the remains of sunken boats in the anchorage and a few private moorings. The holding is poor and the anchorage is exposed to the northwest. Anchoring space here is further limited by the docks and shoreside activities at the Maritime Museum. You can, however, land your dinghy on the small sandy beach to the southwest.

Beaufort–Taylor Creek

NAVIGATION: Use NOAA Chart 11545. Use the Cape Hatteras Tide Table. For high tide, add 7 minutes; for low tide, add 11 minutes. Southbound vessels on the ICW can bear south and follow the Russell Slough Channel markers to Taylor Creek and the Beaufort waterfront. (Note that Russell Slough Channel is known locally as "Gallants Channel" where it passes Gallants Point and leads towards the bridge.) The new 65-foot fixed vertical clearance **Gallants Channel (Hwy. 70) Bridge** replaced the Grayden Paul (Beaufort) Bascule Bridge to the south. Note that the overhead power lines remain in place. They are charted with an 87-foot vertical clearance but have been observed to be closer to 85 feet.

If northbound on the ICW and bound for Beaufort, turn southeast from the turning basin into the Morehead City Channel. Heading toward the inlet, round the southern tip of Radio Island and pick up quick flashing red buoy "2," the entrance marker to Beaufort. (This is the same approach if traveling north from Beaufort Inlet.)

⚠️ Note that shoaling has been reported between flashing red "2" and red nun "2A" (on the red side of the channel) and in the vicinity of flashing green "3" at the southern tip of Radio Island (which appears to be off-station on some electronic charts) to depths as low as 6 feet MLW.

Remember that the numerous range markers for the entrance from the Beaufort Inlet are different from the red or green ICW lateral system or the lateral markers for the inlet. Some boats have mistaken these range markers (especially at night) for other navigation aids in this area, realizing their errors only once they have run aground.

Dockage: The largest and most convenient marina to town is the Beaufort Docks Marina, where the marina slips along Front St. are adjacent to the sights, sounds and activities of downtown Beaufort and convenient to all the waterfront attractions, businesses and services. Beaufort Docks Marina has 98 slips with floating piers maintained solely for transients. There are 25 restaurants and ample shopping within a short walk, and the marina offers free WiFi and an adjacent laundry. Beaufort Docks Marina has diesel fuel available in-slip and multiple courtesy cars for trips around town.

The BoatHouse at Front Street Village bills itself as "part boat storage facility, part yacht club." They offer a variety of amenities, a complete ship store and sell all fuels. The on-site 34° North Restaurant (252-838-7250) is open to the public and offers a weekend brunch menu on Saturday and Sunday (reservations recommended). There is also a boutique hotel on site. Trolley service into Beaufort is available.

Anchorage: This is a harbor where we recommend that you take a slip. The anchorage in Taylor Creek is very limited; you may not be able to find space to drop the hook. Keep this in mind as you plan ahead.

The swift tidal current and the close quarters dictate that you use caution when anchoring. Anchor only on the southern side of the channel and consider using a Bahamian moor. Be mindful of the precipitous shoaling along the southern side of the anchorage. Large excursion vessels use the channel at all hours to get to their docks upstream and The Coast Guard frowns on anchored boats that encroach upon the channel.

The town dock, across the street from the Post Office, has a convenient floating dinghy dock; look for the gazebo at the shore end. The bathhouse at the western end of the Beaufort Docks is available for a modest charge. There is a second dinghy dock two blocks away, at the foot of Orange Street.

Beaufort Inlet

Beaufort Inlet is a big ship inlet that is wide, deep and very well marked. From the Beaufort Inlet area, you can take the dinghy and do some real exploring. The long dinghy trip east through Taylor Creek out into Back Sound past Harkers Island and down to Cape Lookout provides a glimpse of North Carolina that transients do

Bogue Sound, NC

	Dockage					Supplies		Services					
MOREHEAD CITY	Largest Vessel Accommodated	VHF Channel Monitored	Transient Berths / Total Berths	Approach / Dockside Depth (reported)	Floating Docks	Gas / Diesel	Groceries, Ice, Marine Supplies, Snacks	Repairs: Hull, Engine, Propeller	Lift (tonnage), Crane, Rail	Min/Max Amps	Laundry, Pool, Showers, Courtesy Car	Pump-Out Station	Nearby: Grocery Store, Motel, Restaurant
1. Morehead City Yacht Basin 🖵 📶 **WG** .7 W/203.5 252-726-6862	200	16/71	40/88	12/8	F	GD	I	–	–	30/100	LSC	P	R
2. Portside Marina 🖵 📶 205 844-486-7724	150	16/10	10/25	35/10	F	GD	I	HEP	L8	30/100	LS	P	GMR
3. Dockside Yacht Club–PRIVATE 📶 203.9 252-247-4890	80	16/09	0/75	14/14	F	–	GIS	–	–	30/50	LS	P	GMR
4. Sanitary Fish Market & Restaurant 204.9 252-247-3111	55	–	4/15	12/12	–	–	IS	–	–	–	–	–	GMR
5. Morehead Gulf Docks .7 W of 204.9 252-726-5461	120	16	3/9	14/14	–	GD	GIMS	–	–	50/50	–	–	G
6. Morehead City Transient Docks 📶 252-725-5025	50	16/71	10/10	8/8	F	–	–	–	–	20/50	S	–	GMR
7. Russell Yachts .7 W of 205 252-240-2826	100	–	5/5	12/12	–	–	GM	HP	L35	30/30	–	–	GMR
BOGUE BANKS													
8. Anchorage Marina 🖵 📶 1 S of 205.7 252-726-4423	60	16/68	5/130	6/6	F	GD	GIMS	EP	–	30/50	S	–	GMR
9. Fort Macon Marina 🖵 1 S of 205.7 252-726-2055	35	16	–	6/4	–	G	IMS	HEP	L	–	–	–	GMR

🖵 Internet Access 📶 Wireless Internet Access **WG** Waterway Guide Cruising Club Partner onSpot dockside WiFi facility

See WaterwayGuide.com for current rates, fuel prices, web site addresses, and other up-to-the-minute information. *(Information in the table is provided by the facilities.)*

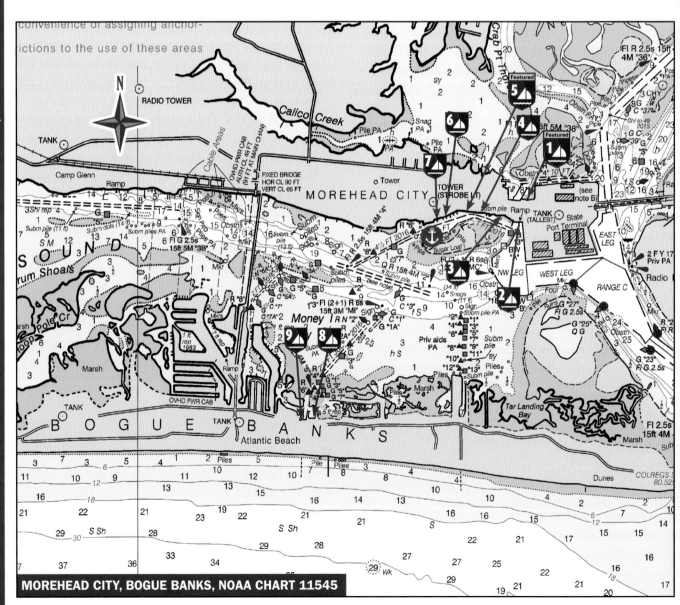

MOREHEAD CITY, BOGUE BANKS, NOAA CHART 11545

Morehead City Moorings

not often witness. This trip is for anyone with a large, sturdy, fast and reliable dinghy or shoal-draft cruiser and time on their schedule to play. On the return trip, follow Shackleford Banks on the inside from Middle Marsh to the inlet. There is some beautiful, clear water with many deserted sandy islands, quaint shoreline and plentiful wildlife, including birds, fish and turtles. Be sure to leave time to explore Cape Lookout. (See more on Harkers Island and Cape Lookout in Chapter 5.)

NAVIGATION: Use NOAA Chart 11541. To reach the Beaufort Inlet from Taylor Creek, head west out of the creek, following the marked channel that swings to port past Radio Island and then joins the Morehead City and inlet channels. The inlet channel leads south past Shackleford Banks, then south-southwest out to sea.

Lights on the Shackleford Range markers at night are bright green, and skippers should identify them when making a night entry through the inlet. The range markers are much brighter than channel markers and have different characteristics. An offshore jaunt to the south from Beaufort Inlet to Masonboro Inlet at Wrightsville Beach is approximately 73 miles, while the inside route is about 70 miles. (See Inlet section at the front of this guide for more information about Beaufort Inlet.)

Dockage: Radio Island Marina and Olde Towne Yacht Club are both located on Radio Island south of the Beaufort Channel Bridge (65-foot fixed vertical

clearance) and adjacent Beaufort Channel Railroad Bascule Bridge (4-foot closed vertical clearance, usually open) between Beaufort and Morehead City (Mile 203.8). The 8-slip Radio Island Marina reports 4-foot MLW dockside depths and can accommodate vessels to 35 feet. They also sell gas. Island Marina offers repairs only. (No transient slips or fuel.)

■ MOREHEAD CITY–ICW MILE 204 TO 206

Like its sister city, Beaufort, Morehead City is a strategic spot on the southeast coast, and it has become a favorite for offshore skippers heading north to avoid the rigors of Cape Hatteras and with ICW boaters heading south and looking forward to some free travel along the open Atlantic. Thus, a large marine community serving both commercial and recreational boats flourishes here. All repairs, from electronics and propellers to diesel engines, are available at Morehead City and the waterfront is packed with restaurants to feed the crew.

NAVIGATION: Use NOAA Charts 11545 and 11541. Use the Cape Hatteras Tide Table. For high tide, add 26 minutes; for low tide, add 27 minutes. The ICW channel that leads down the Newport River to the bridges at Mile 203.8 is holding its depths (12-feet MLW), but has

Adams Creek Canal

MOREHEAD CITY
YACHT BASIN

ICW

MOREHEAD GULF DOCKS

Morehead City

Sugarloaf Island

a very strong crosscurrent (1 to 2 knots). Southbound vessels heading for Morehead City should stay on the ICW by passing daybeacon "28," red daybeacon "30," flashing green (2+1) junction marker "RS" and continuing on the well-marked Newport River channel.

 Note that the most recent NOAA chart, from May 2018, shows marker "30" (at Mile 201) as a red nun, but it is actually a daybeacon.

The shoal to the west is bare at low tide (rather than 2 feet deep as indicated on the NOAA chart) and extends slightly into the ICW channel at the marker. There may be additional uncharted buoys in this area.

Proceed under the **Beaufort Channel Bridge** (65-foot fixed vertical clearance) and adjacent **Beaufort Channel Railroad Bascule Bridge** (4-foot closed vertical clearance, usually open) between Beaufort and Morehead City (Mile 203.8). The horizontal opening at the Beaufort Channel Bridge is very narrow with strong current and is made more difficult by the narrow opening of the railroad bridge on the other side. This is a "one boat at a time" passage.

As a peninsula, Morehead City has two waterfronts. Morehead City Yacht Basin is the only facility for recreational vessels on the back (north) side of the Morehead City waterfront. From the north, leave the ICW about 0.25 mile north of the Beaufort Channel Bridge and adjacent Beaufort Channel Railroad Bridge at Mile 203.8, turning west into Calico Creek at red nun "2," the next red marker south of the flashing red "38." Do not confuse this buoy with the red nun buoy on Chimney Island Channel farther north and east of the bridges. Leave red markers to starboard on the way in.

The Morehead City waterfront proper (on the south side of the peninsula) is approached from the ICW by taking a sharp turn to the west around the Port Terminal Turning Basin (at Mile 204.2) before reaching the junction light "MC" at Mile 205 (where the marker numbers start over). Stay well off the bulkhead and be alert for ship and tug traffic around the terminal.

The channel between Sugar Loaf Island and Morehead City carries at least 7 feet MLW to the west end, where it shallows dramatically. A channel is shown on some charts leading back to the ICW to the west, but depths reach as low as 5 feet MLW in spots. At low tide or in a deep-draft vessel, returning to the ICW via the channel east of Sugar Loaf Island is the safer, if slower, option.

Local authorities and the Coast Guard enforce a No-Wake Zone here 24 hours a day. Since currents run swiftly at 1 to 2 knots through the harbor cut, skippers of underpowered or slow-turning craft should pick a slack tide for docking duties.

High-speed reversing tidal currents rip through this area. Ebb tide begins at the Beaufort Channel Highway and the adjacent railroad bridge (Mile 203.8) 11 minutes after the times given for Charleston Harbor. If you leave Morehead City southbound at low water slack, you can carry the flood tide south to around Mile 220. This is especially advantageous for smaller and slower boats.

Dockage: The "back way" into Morehead City's north side (above the Beaufort Channel Highway Bridge) has a well-marked canal, Calico Creek, which holds 9.5-foot MLW depths and leads directly to the well-protected Morehead City Yacht Basin. The facility has been around since 1947 and has played host to Ernest Hemingway, along with legions of other renowned sportsmen, and is the original home of the Big Rock Blue Marlin Tournament. Transient dockage on well-maintained floating docks and all fuels are available here. Amenities include an on-site laundry facility, clean restrooms and spacious showers, plus a comfortable lounge/office area overlooking the harbor. You can walk to the fun Floyd's 1921 restaurant and bar from here, which offers creative food options and live music on weekends.

Proceeding under the bridge, and then entering Morehead City's waterfront from the Turning Basin, you will encounter a large number of establishments, including marinas, commercial docks and seafood restaurants; the uninhabited Sugar Loaf Island and marshland to port strike a natural counterpoint.

Traveling west from the Turning Basin (on the south side), the full-service Portside Marina is the first facility to starboard behind a protective breakwater. They offer slips and repairs and sell all fuels. Dockside Yacht Club in the next basin is private. Sanitary Fish Market & Restaurant, a large retail seafood market and popular restaurant, offers face-dock moorage (without service or dockside amenities). Do take the time to stop and eat here; the portions are huge and the food (mostly seafood) is fresh. They are most well-known for their hush puppies. Sugarloaf Island Deli and Yellowfin Pub are located next door.

The Morehead Gulf Docks are next, in the heart of Morehead City, and can accommodate large (up to 130 feet), deep-draft (up to 12 feet) vessels. They have high-speed pumps for gas and diesel and a well-stocked

GOIN' ASHORE: **MOREHEAD CITY, NC**

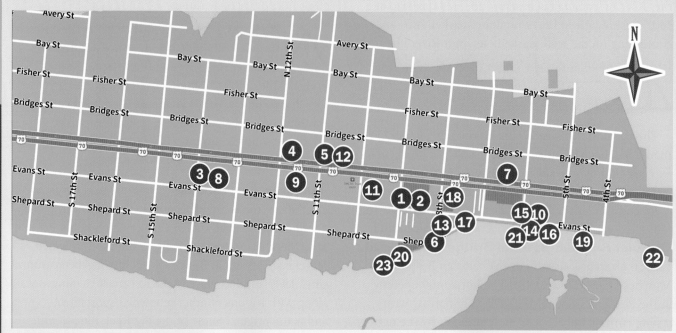

SERVICES		
1	Library	

ATTRACTIONS		
2	Carolina Artists Gallery	
3	Carteret Community Theater	
4	Carteret Contemporary Art	
5	History Museum of Carteret County	
6	Olympus Dive Center	

SHOPPING		
7	Ace Marine Rigging & Supply	

8	Carteret County Curb Market
9	Crystal Coast Cordage
10	Dee Gee's Gifts & Books
11	Promise Land Market
12	Sugarloaf Island Bakery

DINING	
13	Red Fish Grill
14	Ruddy Duck Tavern
15	Sammy's Seafood
16	Sanitary Fish Market

17	Southern Salt Seafood Co.
18	Tightlines Pub & Brewing Company

MARINAS	
16	Sanitary Fish Market & Restaurant
19	Dockside Yacht Club
20	Morehead City Docks
21	Morehead Gulf Docks
22	Portside Marina
23	Russell Yachts

Morehead City was originally called Shepherd's Point and marked the confluence of Newport River, Bogue Sound and Beaufort Inlet. Governor John Motley Morehead envisioned a great commercial hub, so he designed a town built around city blocks with a system of alleys between each block in the form of an "H." In this way, all houses and businesses could be serviced from the alleys. Each block contained 16 lots, and much of that "Philadelphia plan" remains today.

Attractions: A good place to begin your tour of Morehead City is at the History Museum of Carteret County at 1008 Arendell St. (252-247-7533), which houses a collection of local artifacts and an excellent research library with one of the best collections of Civil War materials in eastern North Carolina. The Jack Spencer Goodwin Library also has more than 6,000 publications related to the Civil War. A gift shop offers books on a wide variety of subjects, and unique gifts for children and adults. The History Museum hosts special events year-round, as does the Carteret Community Theatre (1311 Arendell St., 252-726-1501), a 550-seat theater featuring live music. You will also find live music at Alive at Five on the first and third Friday evenings and all Saturday evenings at Jaycee Park throughout the summer.

For an up close look at history, the Olympus Dive Center at 713 Shepard St. (252-726-9432) offers deep sea diving. Depending on conditions, you may be able to dive on an 18th-century schooner, cargo ship, British fishing trawler, World War I gunboat or German submarine.

Fort Macon

In calm conditions, you can dinghy to Fort Macon State Park in Atlantic Beach, although it may be more convenient to rent a car. The pentagon-shaped fortress, built between 1826 and 1834, is the centerpiece of a 398-acre state park that offers swimming, fishing, nature programs and trails, and guided tours of the fort. If you rent a car, make sure you visit the North Carolina Aquarium in Pine Knoll Shores (1 Roosevelt Blvd., 252-247-4003). The Precious Waters exhibit features a 2,000-gallon salt marsh aquarium and a riverbank display with live alligators.

In June, the Morehead City waterfront is bustling with activity during the Big Rock Blue Marlin tournament. Fish are weighed in daily during the tournament at Big Rock Landing near the marlin fountain.

In October, the Morehead City waterfront hosts the North Carolina Seafood Festival (ncseafoodfestival.org), where you can sample fresh seafood while listening to live entertainment.

Shopping: The Carteret County Curb Market, located at the corner of 13th and Evans Streets, runs the oldest continuously operating curb market in North Carolina. Stalls open each Saturday through Labor Day at 7:30 a.m. Come and pick from fresh vegetables, local seafood, cut flowers and baked goods. Promise Land Market has a nice array of fine wine, craft beer and artisan coffee. They also offer sandwiches, salads and snacks (909-B Arendell St., 252-222-0422). Coffee, tea and sweets are available at Sugarloaf Island Bakery (1002 Arendell St., 252-222-0433). You will need transportation to reach the Lowe's Food, Rite Aid and Walgreens located on Highway 70. There is also a West Marine nearby (252-240-2909) at 5160 Hwy. 70 West.

You will have choices, however, for boat and hardware supplies. Ace Marine Rigging & Supply is at 600 Arendell St. (252-726-6620) and Crystal Coast Cordage is at 1103 Evans St. (252-795-9293) with twine and rope for all types of uses.

Dee Gee's Gifts & Books (508 Evans St., 252-726-3314) carries a great selection of nautical books, fiction, non-fiction and works by local authors. For art, pottery and sculpture, visit Carteret Contemporary Art (1106 Arendell St., 252-726-4071). Carolina Artist's Studio Gallery (801 Arendell St., 252-726-7550) is a non-profit cooperative offering a diverse selection of original two-and-three dimensional art and a limited number of prints. There are several other galleries and studios within walking distance of the marinas.

Dining: For years the two staples on the Morehead City waterfront were Sanitary Fish Market (501 Evans St., 252-247-3111) and Captain Bill's. Sanitary opened in 1938 as a 12-stool restaurant with a small 2-kerosene burner stove and is as popular today as it was then. (Expect to wait for a table in "high season.") They offer daily specials (usually whatever has just come in off the fishing boats) and specialize in broiled and fried seafood.

Capt. Bill's also opened in 1938 and was recently refurbished and renamed Southern Salt Seafood Co. & Waterfront Restaurant (701 Evans St., 252-499-9528), specializing in "sea-to-table" dining that includes a raw bar, steaks, pasta dishes and more. They have a huge bar, an enormous waterfront deck and live music. Call 252-499-9528 for a schedule.

Sammy's Seafood, nearby at 109 S. 6th St. (252-648-8399), is another good choice for classic seafood and a raw bar. Red Fish Grill at 711 Shepard St. (252-648-8269) does not accept reservations but comes highly recommended. Ruddy Duck Tavern at 509 Evans St. (252-726-7500) offers burgers and thin-crust pizza in addition to seafood. With such an abundance of fine dining options, you might want to stroll the downtown waterfront before making your final choice.

Just a short walk from the waterfront is Tightlines Pub & Brewing Company (709 Arendell St., 252-773-0631) has 30 craft beers on tap and serves lunch and dinner. The third Saturday of every month they have live music in the outdoor beer garden (April through October).

Visit downtownmoreheadcity.com for complete information and a schedule of events.

chandlery, where in addition to tackle and clothing, they also sell coffee, ice cream, snacks and some groceries. Transients are welcome.

Morehead City Transient Docks and Russell Yachts are to the west. The municipal dock are managed by Morehead City Parks and Recreation Department. They have 10 slips for vessels to 50 feet with 8- to 10-foot MLW dockside depths. Complimentary dockage is available for up to 4 hours. (No free overnight dockage.) Russell Yachts has repair capabilities but only five total slips so call ahead.

Keep in mind the high-speed reversing tidal currents that rip through this area. All of these facilities can pose a docking challenge when the tidal current is running at 3 to 4 knots. Check with the dockmaster before you approach.

Anchorage: Swing room is limited but anchoring is possible in the lee of Sugar Loaf Island with good holding in 7 to 8 feet MLW (despite the 3.5 feet MLW designated on the NOAA chart). Several vessels appear to be permanently anchored fore-and-aft, decreasing the amount of space available and requiring some careful consideration of placement in order to remain distant from the non-swinging boats.

■ BOGUE SOUND–ICW MILE 207 TO MILE 229

Below Morehead City, the ICW follows Bogue Sound almost 25 miles to Swansboro (Mile 229), the port for Bogue Inlet. The ICW channel to Swansboro is marked with daybeacons and lights; green and red are staggered, with few exceptions.

The Bogue Sound route is by no means monotonous. Covered with tall pines and windswept oaks, the high mainland side is dotted with beautiful homes, many with private docks along the sound. Dolphins often frequent the sound's lower portion, and goats sometimes appear on the spoil islands. You can also expect to see people digging for clams (although clamming is banned in some places so check before you join them).

Opposite the mainland, Bogue Banks stands in stark contrast. From the ICW, this long barrier island no longer appears as a dense growth of scrub pine and myrtle. More and more, vacation homes, condominiums and resorts are covering the sand dunes.

Farther down Bogue Sound, waters alongside the channel turn shoal, with the bottom just inches below the surface. Commercial watermen sometimes wade rather than work from their boats, and often the workboats are deliberately grounded on tiny islets.

NAVIGATION: Use NOAA Charts 11541 and 11534. If your vessel draws 4 feet or more and you want to continue southbound down the ICW from Morehead, go back east around Sugar Loaf Island to the Morehead City Harbor's entrance, then follow the buoys carefully to rejoin the ICW channel. The western exit of the Morehead basin, which is adequately marked, has been sounded at depths from 12 to 4.5 feet MLW in different portions of the channel and carries a raging current.

Currents and tides are something to contend with here. Be aware of tides and the timing of their occurrences; you can use them to your advantage with proper planning. However, where there are ocean inlets, the currents will change at and between each one. Fast boats will see many floods and ebbs on any given day; slower boats may be able to use a flood to find the turnaround point, then take the ebb to the next inlet.

The channel through Bogue Sound is narrow so it is a good idea to set your depth sounder alarm at 8 feet; if it sounds and the depth continues to decrease, slow down. This method helps you stay in the channel and spot shoal areas. With its sometimes scattered shoaling and shallow water outside the channel, Bogue Sound is a good place to use this technique.

The aids to navigation in Bogue Sound on to New River and then to the Cape Fear River are located 30 to 35 feet outside the channel limits; this is yet another good reason never to cut marks too closely. Many areas between Morehead City and Swansboro are subject to shoaling, despite frequent dredging. Encroaching shoals are frequently marked with temporary floating aids to navigation until dredging can correct problems. If you see a stationary beacon and a temporary floating marker of the same identification (sometimes the temporary marker will be designated with an "A" or a "B"), honor the temporary marker. Additionally, if the original marker was lighted, it will be extinguished and the light on the temporary marker should be honored. Of course, it is always advised to travel in the safety of daylight whenever possible and use the most recent (print-on-demand) NOAA charts.

Another hazard of Bogue Sound is that a strong wind on your beam can set you on the often-hard edge of

the dredged channel. Watch behind you and be sure to steer toward the windward side of the channel so if you go aground, the wind will help push you off. Keep current with the *Local Notice to Mariners* regarding shoaling in this stretch and check Waterway Explorer at waterwayguide.com for additional navigational alerts and notices.

Side Trip: Bogue Banks

The north end of Bogue Banks (the long barrier strip running south from Beaufort Inlet, protecting Morehead City and nearby communities from Atlantic swells) is a resort area. Money Island and Atlantic Beach are set on grassy sand dunes that are among the highest and most scenic on the East Coast.

Atlantic Beach, like Long Island, NY, runs east to west and faces south. Restaurants, motels and condominiums are here. Some of the approach channels were reportedly shoaling, so check locally for depths. The Atlantic Beach Causeway Marina can provide information and assistance on VHF Channel 16, as can local towboat operators.

At the east end of Atlantic Beach is Fort Macon, built between 1826 and 1834. The pentagon-shaped fortress is part of a 400-acre state park. In 1862, the fort came under attack for 30 days. Union troops eventually captured the fort, which gave them control of North Carolina's coastline. The fort is an interesting place to experience guided tours, audiovisual displays and other various historical exhibits. Swimming, fishing, nature trails and picnic tables are also available at the state park. If time permits, another interesting stop is the North Carolina Aquarium at Pine Knoll Shores. The Coast Guard Station for the area is also at Fort Macon.

NAVIGATION: Use NOAA Chart 11541. At Mile 206, the markers to the side channels in Atlantic Beach become very confusing. Be sure to sort them out before proceeding along the ICW or up one of the side channels. To reach the westernmost of Morehead City's services from Bogue Banks, follow the marked ICW channel through the **Atlantic Beach Bridge** at Mile 206.7 (65-foot fixed vertical clearance). (Note that the tide boards and cruisers consistently report 2 to 3 feet less than the charted 65-foot fixed vertical clearance at this bridge.)

⚠️ Do not mistake the "Resume Speed" sign just before (east of) the bridge for green daybeacon "3A." The sign is in shallow water, and boats have gone aground here by making that mistake.

Bogue Sound, NC

PELETIER CREEK		Largest Vessel Accommodated	VHF Channel Monitored	Transient Berths / Total Berths	Approach / Dockside Depth	Floating Docks (reported)	Gas / Diesel	Groceries, Ice, Marine Supplies, Snacks	Repairs: Hull, Engine, Propeller	Lift (tonnage), Crane, Rail	Min/Max Amps	Laundry, Pool, Showers, Courtesy Car	Pump-Out Station	Nearby: Grocery Store, Motel, Restaurant
				Dockage				**Supplies**		**Services**				
1. 70 West Marina 209.2	252-726-5171	55	16	call/70	5/5	–	GD	GIMS	HEP	L20	30/50	–	–	GMR
2. The Harbor Master Inc. 209.2	252-726-2541	50	16	2/30	8/5	F	–	M	HEP	L35,C	30/30	S	–	GMR
3. Taylor Boat Works 209.2	252-726-6374	55	–	3/8	4.6/6	–	–	M	HEP	R50	30/50	–	–	GMR
4. Coral Bay Marina 209.2	252-247-4231	45	–	call/12	5/5	F	G	I	E	–	30/30	–	–	GMR
SPOONER CREEK														
5. Spooners Creek Marina ⌨ 📶 210	252-726-2060	100	–	10/85	6/8	F	GD	I	–	–	30/100	PS	P	GMR

⌨ Internet Access 📶 Wireless Internet Access **WG** Waterway Guide Cruising Club Partner ⬤onSpot dockside WiFi facility
See WaterwayGuide.com for current rates, fuel prices, web site addresses, and other up-to-the-minute information. *(Information in the table is provided by the facilities.)*

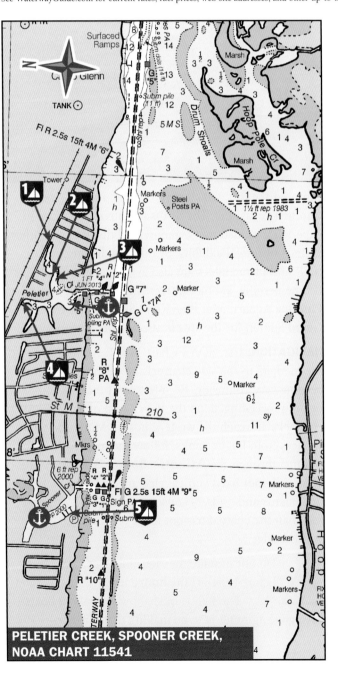

PELETIER CREEK, SPOONER CREEK, NOAA CHART 11541

You may see small powerboats taking the marked side channel through Money Bay (south of ICW green daybeacon "3") but it carries just 1.5-foot MLW depths (last surveyed in 2018). This is strictly small-boat territory.

Dockage: Anchorage Marina (with transient slips, all fuels and repairs) and Fort Macon Marina (with repairs and gas) are located at the end of the shoal (charted 1.5-foot MLW) channel in Money Island Bay.

Peletier Creek–ICW Mile 209

Peletier Creek is a couple of miles west of Morehead City and considered part of the city. The Peletier Creek marinas and anchorage are popular with locals and transients who can handle the 3-foot MLW approach depths. Once inside, the depths increase some, making the creek accessible to deeper boats that can time their arrival and departure for higher tides.

NAVIGATION: Use NOAA Chart 11541. Leave the ICW just east of green daybeacon "7." Severe shoaling has been reported in Peletier Creek to a depth of 3 feet MLW. Multiple aids to navigation have been removed from Peletier Creek and Peletier Creek daybeacons "1" and "5" have been converted into non-lateral warning aids. Inside the creek, 5-foot MLW depths (or better) continue to the complex of yards and marine installations up the right-hand prong.

Dockage: Peletier Creek has several marinas as well as a shopping center with a grocery store, liquor store and deli. There are several fast food restaurants to the east within walking distance. Services and repairs are available at 70 West Marina, Taylor Boat Works, The Harbor Master and Coral Bay Marina (engine repair). 70 West Marina specializes in dry storage and sells all fuels.

Coral Bay Marina is a yacht brokerage and sells gas. There are not many transient slips here; see the adjacent marina table for details.

Anchorage: It is possible to drop the hook in 4 to 8 feet MLW depths (once past the 3-foot MLW entrance).

Spooner Creek–ICW Mile 210.7

NAVIGATION: Use NOAA Chart 11541. One mile west of Peletier Creek on the ICW, nice homes and docks surround the large basin at Spooner Creek (or "Spooners Creek" as it is referred to by locals). A marked entrance channel off the ICW at flashing green "9" leads to the marked entrance channel, which is reported to be 7 feet MLW but is prone to shoaling. Watch for crosscurrents when entering channel. High tide is approximately 2.5 hours later here than at Beaufort.

Dockage: Spooners Creek Marina has transient dockage on floating docks and competitive fuel prices (for both gas and diesel). There is a 24-hour Walmart within walking distance, as well as other shopping and restaurants.

Anchorage: Boats sometimes anchor in the middle of the widest part of the creek, but the area offers poor holding in soft mud. Go past the condominium development and anchor in the basin. You will see a boat ramp and small floating dock; these are private and should not be used to go ashore. Numerous private docks on Spooner Creek reduce anchorage space.

ICW Mile 211 to Mile 228

NAVIGATION: Use NOAA Chart 11541.

⚠️ At Mile 211 shoaling has been reported between red daybeacon "10" and red daybeacon "14," 30 feet into the channel along the red side to depths of 1 to 2 feet MLW. At flashing red "6" and red daybeacon "10," favor the red side of the channel. At red nun "10A," favor the green side (passing 90 feet off) through red daybeacon "12" for 7.3 MLW depths. Then favor the green side when passing red daybeacon "14."

Another spot of concern is at Mile 224.4. Favor the red side at red daybeacon "40" then gradually cross the channel to the green side at daybeacon "41" for about 8 feet MLW. Watch your depth and feel your way between the two charted shoals.

Currents in Bogue Sound occasionally run swiftly at velocities up to 1 to 2 knots. Be especially careful at the **Cedar Point Hwy. Bridge** (65-foot fixed

vertical clearance) at Mile 226, which is known locally as the Emerald Island Bridge. From here to Mile 290, current reversals at the various inlets work to cancel each other out.

Slow boats leaving Morehead City during the last part of the flood tide usually catch the first of the ebb tide at about Mile 220. Then, a fair tide carries to the point where Bogue Inlet meets at Swansboro, a few miles below the Cedar Point Bridge.

Favor the mainland side when crossing Bogue Inlet, since the area is subject to shifting bars and shoaling. In 2018 the Coast Guard reopened Bogue Inlet after closing it in 2017; however, the inlet is subject to severe shoaling and should not be attempted by cruising boats without local knowledge.

■ SWANSBORO TO TOPSAIL

Swansboro–Mile 228

Popular with inland anglers, Swansboro also has a sizable charter fishing fleet of considerable commercial importance because of its inlet. Swansboro is a friendly little town with a few good dining spots, convenient provisioning and numerous small antiques shops, all making it increasingly popular as a tourist destination.

NAVIGATION: Use NOAA Chart 11541. In approaching Swansboro, be wary of crosscurrents and their side-setting effect, particularly on the ebb. Here, and at other places like it, the flow out of the river accelerates the current. Stay to mid-channel, favoring the mainland side between green can "45A" and red daybeacon "46B" and keep an eye on the depth sounder. This area is regularly dredged but is a persistent shoaling problem. In the summer of 2019 our Cruising Editor observed 9-foot MLW depths at green can "45A."

Local boaters traditionally considered the area from red daybeacon "44" to flashing red "48" (Mile 227 to Mile 229) a No-Wake Zone; however, the signs have been removed, and there are no speed/wake restrictions. There are two marinas in the area, however, and (as always) you should control your wake.

Directly off the ICW at the mouth of the White Oak River is Swansboro. The ICW turns abruptly west and the turn is marked on its outside corner by flashing red "46C." If bypassing Swansboro while heading south, pass green daybeacon "47" and continue toward flashing

Bogue Inlet, NC

SWANSBORO AREA		Largest Vessel Accommodated	VHF Channel Monitored	Approach / Dockside Depth (reported)	Transient Berths / Total Berths	Floating Docks	Gas / Diesel	Groceries, Ice, Marine Supplies, Snacks	Repairs: Hull, Engine, Propeller	Lift (tonnage), Crane, Rail	Min/Max Amps	Laundry, Pool, Showers, Courtesy Car	Pump-Out Station	Nearby: Grocery Store, Motel, Restaurant
		Dockage					**Supplies**		**Services**					
1. Dudley's Marina 🖳 (WiFi) 228.7	252-393-2204	75	16	8/26	6/5	–	GD	IMS	HEP	R60	30/50	SC	–	GMR
2. Church St. Town Dock (WiFi)	910-326-2600	100	–	10/10	8/8	F	–	–	–	–	30/100	–	P	GMR
3. Casper's Marina 🖳 229.3	910-326-4462	180	16/09	10/20	10/9	–	GD	IMS	–	L	30/50	S	–	GMR
4. US Boatworks	910-708-1295	–	–	call/8	15/9	F	–	M	HEP	L75	–	–	–	–

🖳 Internet Access (WiFi) Wireless Internet Access **WG** Waterway Guide Cruising Club Partner ☁onSpot dockside WiFi facility
See WaterwayGuide.com for current rates, fuel prices, web site addresses, and other up-to-the-minute information. *(Information in the table is provided by the facilities.)*

red "46C" until green can buoys "47A" and "47B" are lined up, then turn west.

⚠ If a visit to Swansboro is on the itinerary, the secondary channel's entrance is marked by red nun buoy "2," which should be left to starboard on entry. Do not miss the nun buoy and head straight for red daybeacon "4." Although clearly charted, these marks seem to confuse newcomers. Periodically, a boat will try to go between them, with little success. An immediate grounding awaits those who attempt to go between these markers.

There continues to be considerable shoaling in the 70-mile stretch between Swansboro and Carolina Beach. Many areas along this stretch are 8 to 10 feet at MLW. Cruisers should exercise caution in transiting these areas and seek local knowledge. Note that the dredging referred to here is in the ICW proper where the inlets cross or meet the waterway, not in the inlets to the ocean.

Dockage: Approaching Swansboro, cruising boaters can tie up comfortably or have most hull and engine repairs handled at Dudley's Marina, which has a large-boat marine railway at Mile 228.7. They offer dockside fueling, a well-stocked bait and tackle store and a courtesy car. They are family-owned and -operated and have been in business since 1938. (You can't miss the large facility with their name on the front.) Call ahead for exact depths and directions.

Church St. Town Dock has been rebuilt since Hurricane Florence pounded this area in 2018. This facility is run off-site by Swansboro Parks & Recreation and one of their 10 slips can be reserved online. There is a maximum 5-night stay. The docks host eco-tours and cruises in season. Dockage and fuel are available at the 20-slip Casper's Marina, located adjacent to Swansboro's Historic District. A short-term tie-up for breakfast or lunch is available for a small fee.

To the south of Swansboro at Mile 223 is US Boatworks (formerly Armstrong Marine Inc. East). This facility offers all types of boat repairs (with a 75-ton lift) and may have space for you. Call ahead.

Anchorage: There is a tight anchorage if needed between Casper's Marina and the **NC 24 Hwy Bridge** (fixed vertical clearance 12 feet). Holding is fair and the current is swift. We recommend backing down hard on your anchor so you don't end up dragging into the bridge. It may be difficult to get the anchor initially set. Exposure from the northeast and southwest may make for a bumpy stay and wakes can be common. There is a free dinghy dock at the end of Main St.

Swansboro to New River Inlet– ICW Mile 229 to Mile 246

NAVIGATION: Use NOAA Chart 11541. Departing from Swansboro, the ICW zigzags its way southwest with two noteworthy bends–one at quick flashing red "48" and another at flashing green "49" at Mile 230. Neither marker is on the exact edge of the turn, so exercise care not to cut or overshoot the channel.

Around Mile 232, a narrow marked channel leads southeast to Hammocks Beach State Park at Bear Island. (See sidebar.) Watch for shoaling on the northwest side of flashing green "55" off Sanders Creek at Mile 231; there is less than 7 feet at MLW.

From Mile 235 to the New River at Mile 246, the ICW cuts through the U.S. Marine Corps' Camp Lejeune military reservation, where signs along the way prohibit landing. Camp Lejeune extends about 18 miles upstream on the New River, almost to Jacksonville.

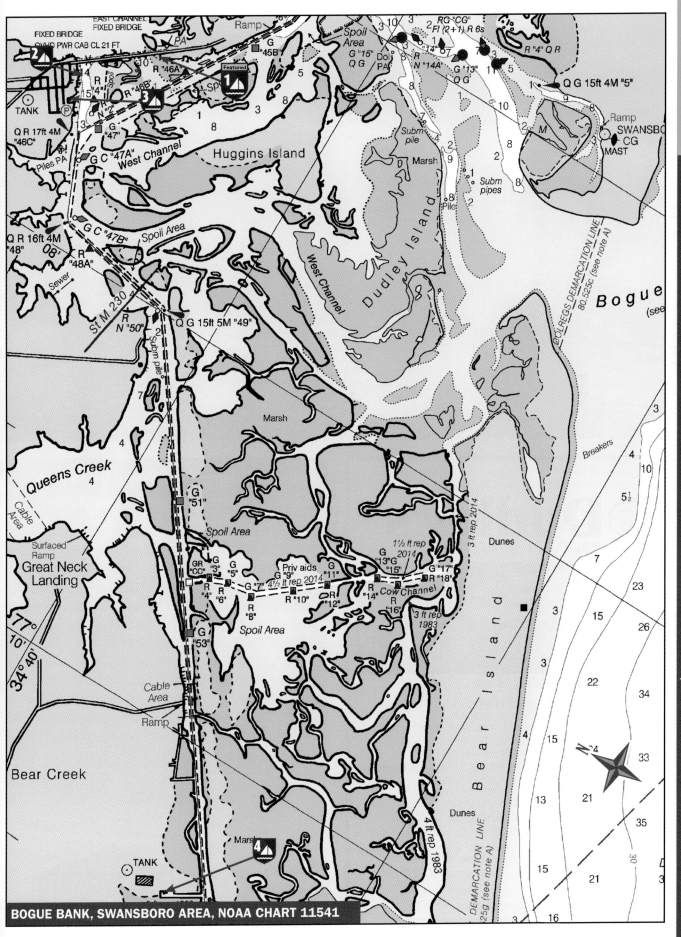

BOGUE BANK, SWANSBORO AREA, NOAA CHART 11541

DUDLEY'S MARINA

ICW

Side Trip: Hammocks Beach State Park

Around Mile 232, a narrow marked channel leads southeast to Hammocks Beach State Park at Bear Island. This 3-mile-long undeveloped barrier island is for small boats only (canoes or kayaks). The dunes at Hammocks Beach State Park are impressive, and you can visit them via the park service's pontoon ferryboats if you make prior arrangements (ncparks. gov/hammocks-beach-state-park).

Note that at press time (summer 2019) Hammocks Beach was still recovering from the effects of Hurricane Florence. Several park facilities remained closed, including camping and ferry service due to damage sustained from the hurricane. (Ferry service was expected to resume by the end of 2019.)

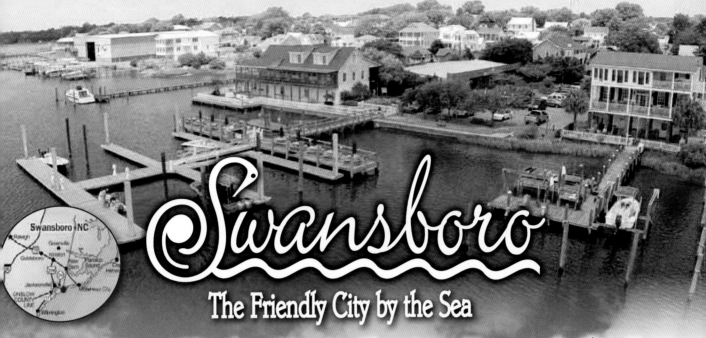

Swansboro

The Friendly City by the Sea

Accommodations   Waterfront Dining   Shopping   History   Outdoor Fun

Annual Events

APRIL - Swansboro Historic Homes Tour

APRIL - Pirate Fest

MAY - Derby Day

MAY - Rotary Blue Water Tournament

JUNE - Military Appreciation

JUNE - Arts by the Sea Festival

JUNE - Pogies PaddlePalooza

JULY - Fourth of July Fireworks

OCTOBER - Rotary King Mackerel Tournament

OCTOBER - Annual Swansboro Mullet Festival of NC

NOVEMBER - Swansboro by Candlelight

NOVEMBER - Christmas Flotilla

NOVEMBER - Friendly City Speckled Trout Tournament

DECEMBER - Santa Fest / Reindeer 5K Run

MAY thru SEPTEMBER - SwanFest Outdoor Summer Concert Series

VisitSwansboro.org   910.326.1174

⚠ The ICW through Camp Lejeune is occasionally closed for artillery, small-weapons firing and beach-landing exercises. The affected area is from just south of red daybeacon "58" (Mile 235.2) to Mile 240, north of the Onslow Beach Swing Bridge. Prominent lighted signs stand at both ends of the range area. Further, all navigable waters between the south bank of Bear Creek and the north bank of Browns Inlet are strictly off-limits due to highly sensitive unexploded ordnance in the area. Boaters may proceed through the inlet (without stopping) during periods of non-military use.

⚠ Persistent shoaling has been observed in the vicinity of Browns Inlet Crossing (Mile 238), where temporary markers may be placed. The area was last dredged in February 2019. This area is prone to constant shoaling due to the strong currents flowing in and out of the small inlets to the ocean. The prudent mariner will check the Waterway Explorer at waterwayguide.com for navigational updates.

At the southern end of the Camp Lejeune range at Onslow Beach, Mile 240.7, is the **Onslow Beach Swing Bridge** (12-foot closed vertical clearance),

which is owned and operated by the Marine Corps. The bridge opens on signal except between 7:00 a.m. to 7:00 p.m., when it need only open on the hour and half-hour. The drawtender will only open for vessels actually at the bridge at the appointed times and only if you contact them on VHF Channel 13 to request an opening. This bridge is very slow to open (openings usually take about 8 to 10 minutes). Use the northwest side, which swings away from boats heading south. Note that sails must be furled during a bridge opening.

Even though you have passed the danger area when through the bridge, there can be heavy military activity along the sides of the ICW to the south, where the Marines practice amphibious landings. Watch for shallow water near the edge of the channel in the long straight stretch below the Onslow Beach Swing Bridge.

Anchorage: About 2 miles north of the three-way junction where the ICW, New River and New River Inlet channel meet, a large dredged basin in Mile Hammock Bay (Mile 244.5) offers a very good and popular anchorage. The entrance channel has adequate depths for deep-draft vessels to enter the channel (10 to 12 feet MLW) and to anchor inside. Do not go too far east of the eastern wharf, where depths are only 1 or 2 feet

GOIN' ASHORE: **SWANSBORO, NC**

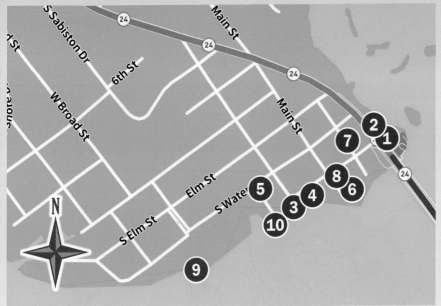

ATTRACTIONS	
1	Bicentennial Park
2	Swansboro Paddle Boarding
SHOPPING	
3	Bake Bottle & Brew
4	Poor Man's Hole
DINING	
5	Church Street Irish Pub & Deli
6	Icehouse Waterfront Restaurant
7	Swansboro Food & Beverage Co.
8	Yana's Ye Olde Drugstore Restaurant
MARINAS	
9	Casper's Marina
10	Church St. Town Dock

Located along the shoreline where the White Oak River joins the ICW, this "Friendly City by the Sea" is a quaint waterfront community with a rich, maritime history dating back to the 1700s. Recent years have also brought tourism to this quaint town but its maritime history and quiet waterfront remain the same. While there is a relaxed pace to this small, seaside town, finding something fun to do in the warm coastal sun is as easy to do as finding the perfect seafood dinner with a view.

That view includes barrier islands that are part of Hammocks Beach State Park (1572 Hammock Beach Rd., 910-326-4881), nationally recognized as a coastal wildlife nature preserve and a nesting area for the beloved loggerhead sea turtles. The park's largest island, Bear Island, is known for its expansive beach but access is by boat only. Take your own or board the park's ferry for the relaxing ride. And don't forget a bag for seashells. Shelling, camping, swimming, kayaking, and picnicking are all enjoyed here.

Attractions: The best way to see Swansboro's historic downtown, the Croatan National Forest and other historic landmarks is to bike along the 25-mile Bicentennial Bicycle Trail. Didn't pack your bike? Bike and kayak rentals are available in downtown Swansboro at Second Wind Eco Tours at 208 W. Main St. (910-325-3600). Additional kayaks rentals are available at Swansboro Paddle Boarding at 108-5 W. Corbett Ave. (910-389-1471) and Paddle NC located at Hammocks Beach State Park (910-612-3297).

Shopping: Swansboro's historic downtown features a variety of quaint shops, many housed in historic buildings. Shopping opportunities abound. One noteworthy shop is Poor Man's Hole at 131 N. Front St. (252-671-0020), offering antiques mixed in with collectibles and nautical items and an impressive small used book section.

For basic needs, the Piggly Wiggly grocery store (715 W. Corbett Ave., 910-326-8500) and Walgreens (702 W. Corbett Ave., 910-325-0038) are within walking distance of the downtown waterfront area. Waters Ace Hardware (778 W. Corbett Ave.) is also located close by. Bake Bottle & Brew sells wine, beer, coffee and ice cream at 147 N. Front St. (910-325-7550).

Dining: Yana's Ye Olde Drugstore Restaurant (119 Front St., 910-326-5501) is a 1950s-style diner famous for its breakfasts, fruit fritters, burgers and lunch specials. Seafood lovers will enjoy the Icehouse Waterfront Restaurant (103 Moore St., 910-325-0501) and Saltwater Grill (99 Church St., 910-326-7300). Swansboro Food & Beverage Co. serves coastal cuisine with a southern influence (106 Front St., 910-708-1305), while Church Street Irish Pub & Deli (105 Church St., 910-326-7572) offers a variety of sandwiches, soups, and coffees. Olea Mediterranean Kitchen (674 W. Corbett Ave., 910-325-8332) is known for its exceptional Mediterranean dishes and will also deliver.

New River, NC

SWAN POINT			Approach / Dockside Depth (reported)	Transient Berths / Total Berths	VHF Channel Monitored	Largest Vessel Accommodated	Dockage	Gas / Diesel	Floating Docks	Groceries, Ice, Marine Supplies, Snacks	Supplies	Repairs: Hull, Engine, Propeller	Lift (tonnage), Crane, Rail	Services	Min/Max Amps	Laundry, Pool, Showers, Courtesy Car	Pump-Out Station	Nearby: Grocery Store, Motel, Restaurant

SWAN POINT			Dockage				Supplies		Services			
1. Swan Point Marina (WiFi) 247	910-327-1081	100	16/12	10/40	8/5	–	–	–	HEP	L40	30/50	LSC – –
2. New River Marina (☐) (WiFi) 247	910-327-2106	90	16/09	2/13	6/9	–	GD	GIMS	E	–	–	S – G

☐ Internet Access (WiFi) Wireless Internet Access [WG] Waterway Guide Cruising Club Partner 🌐 onSpot dockside WiFi facility
See WaterwayGuide.com for current rates, fuel prices, web site addresses, and other up-to-the-minute information. *(Information in the table is provided by the facilities.)*

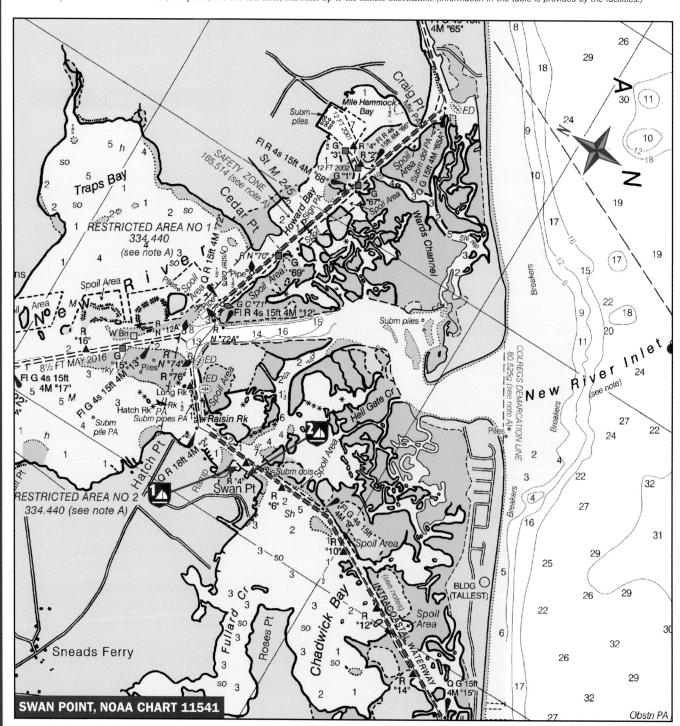

SWAN POINT, NOAA CHART 11541

MLW. Except for a few soft spots, holding is very good in the area. Stay clear of the docks; an Army Corps of Engineers dredge often ties there.

This is Marine Corps property, and civilians are prohibited from going ashore. Frequent military activity and exercises in this basin can sometimes be interesting to observe. Note that a helicopter, Osprey aircraft or inflatables full of well-armed marines may buzz you.

New River Inlet to Swan Point–ICW Mile 246 to Mile 247

NAVIGATION: Use NOAA Charts 11541 and 11542. At the junction of the New River Inlet and the ICW at Mile 246, be prepared for strong side currents and favor the ocean side. Be aware of changing depths in the area. Take time beforehand to sort out markers, as the upriver channel buoys can be confusing. Note that at the junction of the ICW and inlet channels, red buoys are used to mark inshore shoals. These are moved as required to show deep water limits. At this point, New River, with a well-marked channel, heads off sharply to starboard.

After closing the inlet in 2017, the Coast Guard reopened it in 2018; however, shoaling has again been reported to a depth of 2 feet MLW in the channel. The Coast Guard moves temporary markers to show best water but has discontinued some of the permanent ones. (See Inlet section at the front of this guide for more information about New River Inlet.)

⚠️ There has been considerable shoaling of the ICW channel at the New River Crossing. Going south, split flashing red buoy "72" and green daymarker "71" and proceed 150 feet, then turn to port and pass red nun buoy "72A" to starboard. Stay 150 to 200 feet off the southern shore, but no more than that. Stay 100 feet off red nun buoy "72A" then aim for red nun buoy "74." Pass red nun buoy "74" to starboard by 100 feet and then return to the center of the channel. Check the *Local Notice to Mariners* for updates on dredging. Also refer to the Waterway Explorer at waterwayguide.com for additional navigational updates.

It is possible to journey up the New River to the Marine Corps training base, Camp Lejeune and on to the City of Jacksonville. Some areas of the New River above its intersection with the ICW are shoal. Seek local

knowledge before heading up this river. Below New River, the ICW doglegs and the marina facilities at Mile 247 become visible. Just north of red daybeacon "4" you will find a mix of local recreational boats, small-scale commercial fishermen and cruisers.

Dockage: South on the ICW at Swan Point, you may find transient dockage at Swan Point Marina or New River Marina. There is a small store with a few staples and fishing tackle at Swan Point Marina. The marina was still recovering from Hurricane Florence at press time (summer 2019). Immediately south of red daybeacon "4," the New River Marina's fuel dock faces the ICW. Deep-draft vessels should call ahead for docking information; there may be space for larger vessels when the fuel pumps have closed for the evening. They also offer some repairs.

Sneads Ferry is just a few miles away (transportation needed), where you can find a grocery store, Post Office, bank, liquor store and drugstore. The Riverview Café is a family-owned and -operated seafood restaurant (119 Hall Point Rd., 910-327-2011) that will pick you up from the marina. Open 11:00 a.m. to 9:00 p.m. daily.

Topsail Island, NC

TOPSAIL BEACH		Largest Vessel Accommodated	VHF Channel Monitored	Dockage				Supplies				Services			
				Transient Berths / Total Berths	Approach / Dockside Depth (reported)	Floating Docks	Gas / Diesel	Groceries, Ice, Marine Supplies, Snacks	Repairs: Hull, Engine, Propeller	Lift (tonnage), Crane, Rail	Min/Max Amps	Nearby: Grocery Store, Motel, Restaurant	Pump-Out Station	Laundry, Pool, Showers, Courtesy Car	
1. Topsail Island Marina **WiFi**	980-241-5912	70	16/11	call/15	6/6	F	GD	M	–	–	30/100	LS	P	GMR	
2. Anchors Away Boatyard 264	910-270-4741	70	–	2/2	6.5/6.5	–	–	M	HEP	L68	15/50	–	–	–	
3. Harbour Village Marina Inc. 🖳 **WiFi** 267	910-270-4017	100	–	10/200	8/8	F	GD	IS	EP	–	30/50	S	P	–	

🖳 Internet Access **WiFi** Wireless Internet Access **WG** Waterway Guide Cruising Club Partner 🔵 onSpot dockside WiFi facility
See WaterwayGuide.com for current rates, fuel prices, web site addresses, and other up-to-the-minute information. *(Information in the table is provided by the facilities.)*

TOPSAIL BEACH, NOAA CHART 11541

Swan Point to New Topsail Inlet– ICW Mile 247 to Mile 270

In this stretch to Topsail Beach and beyond, a wide expanse of channel and slough-threaded marsh separates the ICW from barrier beaches. Most of these small waterways dead end inside the barrier beach dunes. (Watch for side-setting currents and shoaling where these meet the ICW.) Others provide access to small inlets, and some are even deep enough for anchoring, if you feel adventurous.

A Coast Guard patrol boat may check on you if you anchor near the channel. The bottom is very sandy here, and currents can run swiftly. Because of increased hurricane activity over the past decade, last year's good anchorage may be too shallow this year, or a formerly shoaled entrance channel may have been scoured deep. The ICW channel tends to shoal near small inlets. Deep-draft boats should proceed cautiously in such areas.

The countryside begins to change in this section. Inlets appear with more frequency, and the high wooded shores gradually become lined with year-round houses and vacation cottages. Because this is popular fishing and boating territory, most homes have their own boats at docks snuggled up side creeks or in dredged private channels. Some of these small communities have landings, but they are not set up to handle transients.

NAVIGATION: Use NOAA Chart 11541. The route from Swan Point runs southwest along a mostly straight dredged path for about 10 miles. Before the **U.S. 210 Hwy. Bridge** (64-foot fixed vertical clearance) at Mile 252.3, shoaling has been noted between flashing green "23" and green daybeacon "25" along Alligator Bay (marked as "spoil area" on the NOAA chart). Favor the green side of the channel. There are several areas along this area that deserve your undivided attention, including between green daybeacon "31" and green daybeacon "37" (Mile 254.4). Stay 50 feet off the green side for 12 feet MLW. At Mile 257, shoaling to a depth of 1 foot MLW has been reported near daybeacon "47." Favor the red side of the channel. Farther southwest at Mile 257.6, shoaling is continually a problem between green daybeacons "51" and "53" in the charted spoil area with depths of 7 to 8 feet MLW reported.

The fixed 65-foot **Surf City (NC 50) Bridge** at Mile 260.7 was completed in 2019 and replaces the Surf City Swing Bridge. All the remains of the old bridge have been removed and the area has been dredged.

At junction flashing green "BC" at about Mile 263.5, a marked channel makes off to the southeast and meanders along the backside of the barrier island, past Topsail Beach to New Topsail Inlet. Used extensively by locals, this scenic side trip is suitable only for shallow-draft boats (despite depths shown on the NOAA chart).

Howards Creek Crossing at Mile 270 on the ICW was dredged in December 2016 and the channel has remained stable. Favor the red side of the channel by green can "99" for 11 feet MLW. Five temporary aids to navigation have been removed, but green can "99A" remains at the mouth of the channel.

New Topsail Inlet is primarily used by local fishermen. In 2019 the Coast Guard has reported significant shoaling throughout the inlet. Several aids to navigation have been discontinued and any remaining are unreliable. Mariners should use extreme caution while navigating this area.

Dockage: The 15-slip Topsail Island Marina at Mile 261 (before the Surf City Swing Bridge) is convenient to Surf City and offers all fuels and dockage. (Call ahead.) Within two blocks you will find a groceries, marine supplies, shopping, restaurants and beach access. Anchors Away Boatyard at Mile 264 is a do-it-yourself and full-service boat yard that also offers boat storage and has limited space for transients.

A channel at Mile 267 on the mainland side leads into Harbour Village Marina, which is private but will rent a slip to you if one is available. You must call ahead (at least one day in advance). They will provide a drone video of the approach and marina, written directions for tie up and a picture of the marina layout.

Anchorage: On the way south, you will pass several loading basins used by pulpwood barges, many of which are abandoned and shoaled, so we do not recommend anchoring there. For a proper anchorage, leave flashing green "BC" to starboard to head for the anchorage off Sloop Point. Follow the channel markers, favoring the

red (east) side of the channel around the curve, and anchor in sand between red daybeacon "14" and green daybeacon "15" in 6 feet MLW. At the foot of Humphrey Ave. is a small public beach. You can land a dinghy and walk across the peninsula to the ocean beach.

■ NEW TOPSAIL INLET TO MASONBORO INLET

New Topsail Inlet to Wrightsville Beach–ICW Mile 270 to Mile 283

NAVIGATION: Use NOAA Chart 11541. Continuing from New Topsail Inlet at Mile 270 to Wrightsville Beach at Mile 283, the ICW channel is straight, well marked and easy to run.

⚠ When approaching green "105" from either the north or south, favor the red side to avoid the developing shoal on the green side of the channel.

The **Figure Eight Island Swing Bridge** at Mile 278 (20-foot closed vertical clearance) opens on the hour and the half-hour, 24 hours a day. The bridge will not open when the sustained wind is stronger than 30 miles per hour and can remain closed at the discretion of the bridgetender in bad weather.

In the 5 miles between Figure Eight Island Swing Bridge and the Wrightsville Beach Bascule Bridge at Mile 283, the route is straightforward, although aids to navigation are fewer and farther apart. When the marshes flood at high tide, it is hard to make out the channel. At such times, monitor your chart plotter closely and run compass courses between marks.

Going through Middle Sound after mid-afternoon, watch for commercial mullet fishermen with their nets stretched across the channel. (It is hard to identify even on the most up-to-date NOAA charts, but it extends from around Mile 278 to Mile 283.) Ordinarily, fishermen tend to the nets and promptly lower them so that approaching boats can pass over them. To be on the safe side, boaters should travel at a reasonable speed and allow ample time for the nets to reach the bottom. The Coast Guard at Wrightsville Beach has stated that the nets are to be at least 6 feet below the surface and always tended.

GOIN' ASHORE: SURF CITY (TOPSAIL BEACH), NC

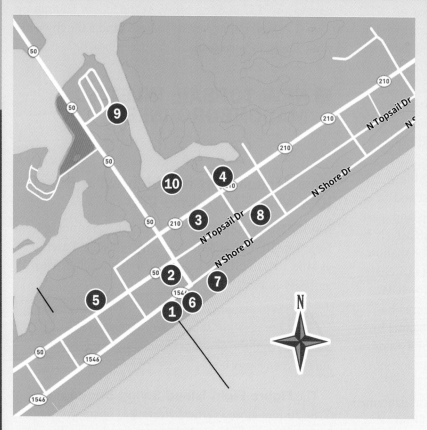

	ATTRACTIONS
1	Surf City Pier
	SHOPPING
2	Surf City Shopping Cente
3	Swingbridge Beer & Win
4	Topsail Island Trading Company
	DINING
5	Beauchaines 211
6	Buddy's Crab House & Oyster Bar
7	Daddy Mac's Beach Grille
8	New York Corner Deli
9	The Bistro at Topsail
	MARINAS
10	Topsail Island Marina

There was a time, not too long ago, when you could camp beneath the concrete launch pad of a space rocket on Topsail Island. A tent was still necessary for privacy, but the launch pad kept out the rain better than the canvas. Cars and pickup trucks carved narrow tracks in soft sand, and some nights you would spend as much time pulling vehicles off the beach as you would be reeling in bluefish. Fishing off the Jolly Roger pier was the reward for a hard week's work, and fish in the cooler provided dinner for days to come. But the tides of change are sweeping over the dunes of Topsail.

Topsail Island almost became Cape Canaveral or, at least, a base for space exploration. In 1946, Topsail was a barrier island that the military called "the sand spit." Following World War II, the U.S. government took over the island and used it to develop a long-range defense missile for the Navy. During the next two years, the military launched more than 200 experimental rockets. The test launchings resulted in the ramjet rocket, which was the foundation of the U.S. guided missile program. Due to the success of the rockets, the project was divided and transferred to other test sites, one of which would become Cape Canaveral. Today, you can still find several observation towers strategically placed on the island. These silos, and the concrete slab that serves as the Jolly Roger Motel's patio, are all that remain of the island's contribution to space exploration.

Much has been made about the name Topsail Island, which has to do with a different type of exploration. Folklore became fact and now many historians attribute the name to pirate ships anchored in the lee of the dunes. When a vessel laden with gold or goats strayed too close to shore, the pirates would hoist the topsail to give them steerage as they raced for the inlet to begin the chase.

Attractions: The beach is the number one attraction here. A stroll down the Surf City Pier (originally built in 1948) will cost you a well-spent dollar. Like any popular beach, Topsail has surf and skate shops, charter fishing tours, sightseeing cruises, outdoor sporting goods and rentals and a mini-golf course.

The Missiles and More Museum (720 Channel Blvd., 910-328-8663) celebrates the contributions of the WASP (Women's Air Force Service Pilots) during World War II. This select group of young, daring, female pilots served domestically, ferrying and testing, towing targets and training men to fly. Other exhibits at the museum include Pirates of the Carolinas, Operation Bumblebee, Camp Davis, The Towns of Topsail Island, Topsail's Natural Beauty and Fragility, Traces of Native Americans on the Island and an International Shell Exhibit. See missilesandmoremuseum.com for more information.

Located on the mainland side just west of the Surf City Bridge (302 Tortuga Ln.), the Karen Beasley Sea Turtle Rescue Rehabilitation Center is a nonprofit organization whose mission is the rescue, rehabilitation and release of sick and injured sea turtles (910-329-0222).

Shopping: Shopping on the island is a compact experience. At the intersection of Roland Avenue and Topsail Dr., you will find the Surf City Shopping Center (106 S. Topsail Dr., 910-328-0835), home of the Surf City IGA (910-328-3961). For a different type of provisioning, Swingbridge Beer & Wine has several hundred beers on their shelves and eight wines in tap (yes, wine). After sampling, shop by the glass or buy a bottle to enjoy on the patio.

Topsail Island Trading Company (201 N. New River Dr., 910-328-1905) carries a good selection of jewelry, gifts and fudge. They also have a selection of tide and weather clocks and instruments.

Dining: New York Corner Deli (206 N. Topsail Dr., 910-328-2808) serves deli-style food and offers a good breakfast. Buddy's Crab House & Oyster Bar (101 Roland Ave., 910-328-1515) has a great neighborhood feel and serves steamed seafood on open air dining porches or indoors. Nearby Daddy Mac's Beach Grille at 108 N. Shore Dr. (910-328-5577) has an outdoor deck overlooking the ocean.

Beauchaines 211 is a waterfront location with fine dining and great views (211 S. Topsail Dr., 910-328-1888). The Bistro at Topsail is located on the causeway (602 Roland Ave., 910-328-2580) and features a cozy, wood-paneled dining room overlooking Topsail Sound.

Off the waterfront area but worth the trip is Surf City Barbecue (13500 NC Hwy. 50, Suite 112, 914-328-4227), which specializes in local Carolina cuisine.

Check visitpender.com for more options. Be prepared to wait for a table at any of these options in season; like all beach towns, there seem to be more people than restaurants.

Wrightsville Beach, NC

WG

WRIGHTSVILLE AREA		Dockage					Supplies		Services					
		Largest Vessel Accommodated	VHF Channel Monitored	Transient Berths / Total Berths	Approach / Dockside Depth (reported)	Floating Docks	Gas / Diesel	Groceries, Ice, Marine Supplies, Snacks	Repairs: Hull, Engine, Propeller	Lift (tonnage), Crane, Rail	Min/Max Amps	Laundry, Pool, Showers Courtesy Car	Pump-Out Station	Nearby: Grocery Store, Motel, Restaurant
1. Wrightsville Beach Marina 🖥 WiFi 283.3	910-256-6666	250	16/09	8/100	15/15	F	GD	IMS	–	–	30/100	LPS	P	GMR
2. Bridge Tender Marina 🖥 WiFi 283.3	910-256-6550	200	16/10	15/65	18/18	F	GD	IMS	–	–	30/100	–	P	GMR
3. MarineMax Wrightsville Beach 284	910-256-8100	100	16	–	–	F	–	M	HEP	L50	–	–	–	MR
4. Atlantic Marine 284	910-256-9911	26	16/09	–	8/5	F	G	IMS	HEP	L	30/30	–	–	GMR
5. Seapath Yacht Club & Transient Dock 🖥 WiFi 284	910-256-3747	150	16	10/190	8/10	F	GD	IMS	–	–	30/100	LSC	P	GMR

🖥 Internet Access   WiFi Wireless Internet Access   WG Waterway Guide Cruising Club Partner   🛜 onSpot dockside WiFi facility

See WaterwayGuide.com for current rates, fuel prices, web site addresses, and other up-to-the-minute information. *(Information in the table is provided by the facilities.)*

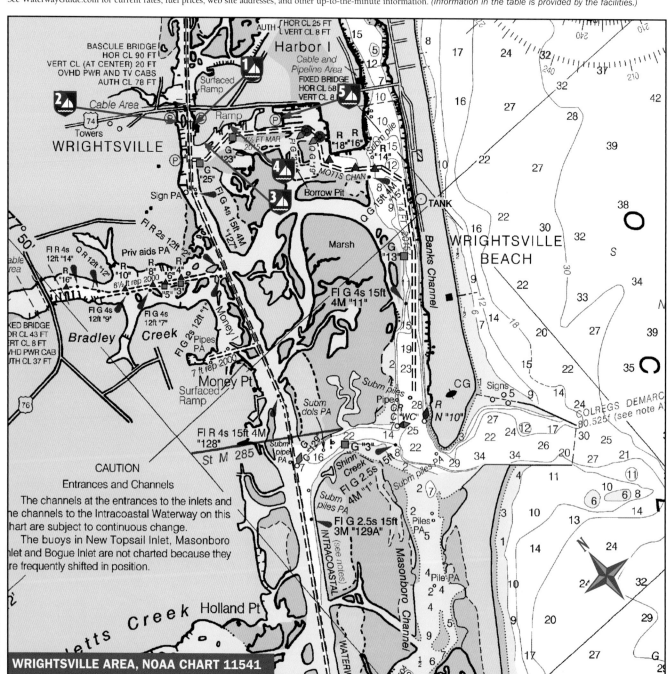

WRIGHTSVILLE AREA, NOAA CHART 11541

Mason Inlet at Mile 280.2 was dredged in the spring of 2019. It's a straight path through; just follow the aids to navigation. It is mostly used by local fisherman as it is prone to shoaling.

Wrightsville Beach–ICW Mile 283

Wrightsville Beach is a burgeoning water-oriented community and for the ICW traveler, it is well worth a visit. The ICW itself is only part of what Wrightsville Beach has to offer. Motts Channel has more marinas and Banks Channel offers secure, if busy, anchorages as well as a public (during daylight only) group of floating docks.

NAVIGATION: Use NOAA Chart 11541. Several marinas are right on the ICW after the bridge and navigation is straightforward. At Mile 283.1, the **Wrightsville Beach (NC 74) Bascule Bridge** has a charted 20-foot closed vertical clearance but it has been observed to be closer to 14 feet MLW. The bridge opens on signal except between 7:00 a.m. and 7:00 p.m., when it need only open on the hour. (This does not hold true if there is a race or other special event so call ahead at 910-256-2886.)

The current picks up as you approach the Wrightsville Beach Bridge, and then reverses just north of the bridge, making it difficult for slower vessels to correctly time arrivals at the bridge. Sailboats and slower trawlers have a difficult time making the 5 miles between this and the Figure Eight Island Swing Bridge to the south. Currents are particularly strong directly at the bridge and at the marinas adjacent to the ICW below the bridge. Exercise care in holding for this bridge on either side. You may receive instructions to bunch with other boats during the unrestricted hours. Traffic from a busy launching ramp just north of the bridge adds to the congestion. Boats waiting on the south side of the bridge will also see congestion from marina traffic and Motts Channel.

⚠ Shoaling to 6 feet MLW has been observed 300 feet north of green can "129" in the middle of the channel. You can avoid this spot by favoring either the red or green side, just not the middle.

Just south of Mile 285 strong crosscurrents can make it difficult to maintain a mid-channel course. Favor the ocean side of the main channel on the flood tide and the mainland side on the ebb. Tidal range is from 3 to 4 feet.

Dockage: Just south of the Wrightsville Beach Bascule Bridge on the mainland side, the Bridge Tender Marina has face dock space available for transients (limited amenities) and sells all fuels. The on-site Bridge Tender Restaurant offers fine dining (reservations recommended). To the south, Dockside Marina and Restaurant offers limited transient dockage (no showers or dedicated restrooms) for diners.

Across the waterway is the full-service Wrightsville Beach Marina on Harbor Island. Be sure to follow marina docking instructions here regarding the current. There are always plenty of hands to help as you approach. The Bluewater Waterfront Grill (910-256-8500) is beside the marina and several others are within one block.

When docking at face docks at any of these marinas, exercise caution and dock against the current.

Motts Channel

NAVIGATION: Use NOAA Chart 11541. Motts Channel is south of the Wrightsville Beach Bridge and runs east from the ICW at green daybeacon "25" (not an ICW number) to Banks Channel, which extends southwest to Masonboro Inlet.

⚠ There are two areas of persistent shoaling in Motts Channel. In the vicinity of green daybeacon "25" where it joins the ICW, 4.5-feet MLW depth has been observed, with more water closer to the daybeacon rather than the marina, as one might expect. Even with frequent dredging, this is an area to watch because it fills in quickly.

The second area of concern is between green buoys "21" and "19." These were formerly daybeacons and are now moved regularly to more accurately mark the shoaling. This is not reflected on NOAA charts, which show "19" as either in the middle of the channel or marking the eastern boundary of the channel. This is incorrect. Green "19" is left to port when westbound and to starboard when eastbound or you will be in 3 feet at MLW.

Dockage: MarineMax Wrightsville Beach and Atlantic Marine are on the turn into Motts Channel. Atlantic Marine sells gas and both facilities offer repairs. (MarineMax has a 50-ton lift.) Call ahead for slip availability. Seapath Yacht Club & Transient Dock is located farther east on the northern side of the channel and offers 600 feet of floating face docks for transients. This is a large, clean and well-maintained marina. Gas and diesel fuel are available on their outer dock.

GOIN' ASHORE: **WRIGHTSVILLE BEACH, NC**

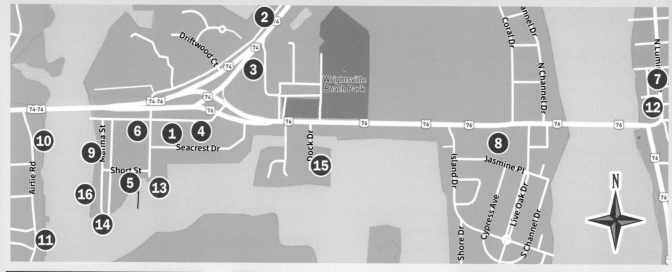

SERVICES	
1	Post Office
ATTRACTIONS	
2	Wrightsville Beach Museum of History
SHOPPING	
3	Farmers Market
4	Lighthouse Beer & Wine
5	Motts Channel Seafood

6	Redix
7	Roberts Market
DINING	
8	Banks Channel Pub & Grille
9	Bluewater Grill
10	Bridge Tender Restaurant
11	Dockside Restaurant
12	King Neptune

MARINAS	
10	Bridge Tender Marina
11	Dockside Marina & Restaurant
13	Atlantic Marine
14	MarineMax Wrightsville Beach
15	Seapath Yacht Club & Transient Dock
16	Wrightsville Beach Marina

For cruisers, Wilmington (west side of the ICW) and Wrightsville Beach (east side of the ICW) offer a convenient stopover for replenishing, dining or sightseeing. Marinas line both sides of the ICW beginning immediately south of the Wrightsville Beach Bascule Bridge and just off the ICW on Motts Channel, but a word of caution: This is a popular stopover so make a reservation in advance.

The tourist area of Wrightsville Beach along the ocean side is an old school, family-style beach that has matured in a manner that makes it the envy of other seaside communities. Here, you will find parking meters and public rinse stations, fishing piers and municipal parks, soccer fields and surfing and a whole lot of sunning. Guests have discovered that it is a great place to retreat, relax and rinse away the stress of mainland living. Locals recognize this as the "eastern suburb" and beach community for the City of Wilmington, only 6 miles away.

The first structures on Wrightsville Beach were temporary ones for hunters, fishermen and sailors. The earliest permanent building was the Carolina Yacht Club built in 1854. The original building is long gone but the Carolina Yacht Club remains the third oldest yacht club residing in its original location (401 S. Lumina Ave., 910-256-3396). Before 1900 the area between the mainland and the beach was known as The Hammocks and it held a large hotel and pavilion. During the initial dredging of the ICW in the 1920s, sand and clay were deposited here to increase its footprint. This is currently known as Harbor Island. In 1887, the railroad was extended across the marsh from the mainland, but it stopped at the eastern tip of Harbor Island, leaving visitors to unload their towels and blankets and hike across a foot bridge to the beach. In 1889, the railroad was extended to Wrightsville Beach and down to the southern part of the island, fueling development there. A decade later the railroad was converted to a reliable, electric-powered trolley system.

Traveling on these "beach cars," visitors made Wrightsville Beach a popular summer destination. In 1905, the pavilion known as Lumina was opened at the last trolley stop. The 12,500-square-foot complex, outlined in hundreds of light, was famous for hosting live music for 60 years. The pavilion included an outdoor movie screen aimed towards the ocean so viewers could sit in the sand or view it from the pavilion's extensive Oceanside upstairs porch. In the 1930s, a new road system was developed to connect the island to the mainland, and within a few years the "beach cars" ceased to run, replaced by automobiles and buses.

Attractions: Framed by the two inlets and shadowed by both old and new cottages, the sand and surf remain the highlight of the town. Masonboro Island, just south of Masonboro Inlet, is a protected wildlife preserve and makes a pleasant dinghy trip. Wrightsville Beach Park is a great place to shoot hoops, walk pets or toss a Frisbee.

And speaking of pets and frisbees...if you are around in October, you don't want to miss the Bark in the Park Skyhoundz Hyperflite Canine Disc Championships. Mutts and purebreds compete to catch flying discs. The event takes place at Wrightsville Beach Park from 11:00 a.m. until about 1:00 p.m. Call the Parks and Recreation Department (910-256-7925) for more information.

If you seek adventure, visit one of the surf shops to rent a long or short board and paddle out into the surf. (Lessons are available from several shops.) In April, the three-day Carolina Cup attracts stand up paddleboard (SUP) competitors for races and fun activities. In August, drop by the Crystal Pier at the Oceanic for the annual Wrightsville Beach Wahine Classic (for female surfers only). Competition includes surfing in the categories of shortboard, longboard, pro longboard, advanced shortboard, bodyboard and novice divisions.

If history is more your style, the Wrightsville Beach Museum of History (910-256-2569) is located in the Myers Cottage at 303 W. Salisbury St. and preserves and shares the history of Wrightsville Beach. Exhibits include a scale model of Wrightsville Beach circa 1910.

If you have time and transportation (5 miles away), Arlie Gardens (300 Airlie Rd., 910-798-7700) is a combination of formal gardens, wildlife, historic structures, walking trails, sculptures, 10-acres of freshwater lakes, more than 100,000 azaleas and the grandeur of the 467-year-old Airlie Oak.

Shopping: The small but complete Roberts Market is at 32 N. Lumina (910-256-2641) for provisioning. They also offer sandwiches and have a beer cave. The Farmers Market provides an opportunity to purchase fresh, locally grown produce. It is held from May 15 to October 30 from 8:00 a.m. to 1:00 p.m. on Mondays.

Motts Channel Seafood (120 Short St., 910-256-3474) will be happy to put together a seafood sampler of fresh shrimp, fish steaks and scallops. You are likely to find locally grown produce out front to accompany your meal. Lighthouse Beer & Wine (220 Causeway Dr., 910-256-8622) carries over 400 different types of beers plus a wide variety of wine. They also sell cigars, cheese, gourmet snacks and gift baskets.

Adjacent to the Post Office is Redix (120 Causeway Dr., 910-256-2201), a good bet for basic fishing supplies, beachware and beverages. They also carry over-the-counter medicines. There are also numerous surf and beachwear shops along the beach road.

Just a short half-mile walk to the west of the ICW and within easy reach of all the marinas, you will find an open shopping center with a large Harris Teeter grocery, West Marine, bank, restaurants, fast food and numerous specialty shops. Craft American Hardware (7002 Wrightsville Ave., 910-256-4782) is located just south of the Harris Teeter, refills propane tanks, and is known for locating hard-to-find specialty items.

Dining: Directly on the ICW on Harbor Island, try Bluewater Waterfront Grill (4 Marina St., 910-256-8500) for dinner. This sprawling two-story restaurant overlooks the ICW and serves a great meal. Banks Channel Pub & Grille (530 Causeway Dr., 910-256-2269), open until 2:00 a.m., is a favorite with the late night crowd.

On the mainland side of the ICW, Bridge Tender Restaurant (1414 Airlie Rd., 910-256-4519) serves steaks and seafood with a spectacular panoramic view of the ICW. They have been in business since 1976 and are a favorite for both lunch and dinner. Located nearby is the Dockside Restaurant (1308 Airlie Rd., 910-256-2752). The menu boasts fresh seafood, either broiled or fried, snow crab legs, shrimp Creole and Baja tuna.

Over on the beach (a short taxi ride away from the marinas or a short walk from the anchorage), you will find several good dining options. Our managing editor favors Oceanic Restaurant (703 S. Lumina Ave., 910-256-5551), where you can enjoy indoor dining directly on a large pier overlooking the beach and ocean. King Neptune at 11 N. Lumina Ave. (910-333-6688) is also highly recommended by our staff. This restaurant has been around for over 70 years and has remained a family-owned, iconic eatery and neighborhood bar.

This is another locale where there are more restaurants than we can list here. Go to visitwrightsvillebeachnc.com for more options.

Masonboro Sound, NC

MASONBORO	Largest Vessel Accommodated	VHF Channel Monitored	Approach / Dockside Depth (reported)	Transient Berths / Total Berths	Floating Docks	Gas / Diesel	Groceries, Ice, Marine Supplies, Snacks	Repairs: Hull, Engine, Propeller	Lift (tonnage), Crane, Rail	Min/Max Amps	Laundry, Pool, Showers, Courtesy Car	Pump-Out Station	Nearby: Grocery Store, Motel, Restaurant
			Dockage					**Supplies**			**Services**		
1. Masonboro Yacht Club and Marina 🖵 📶 288.2 910-791-1893	60	16	20/103	7/7	F	–	IS	–	L	30/50	LS	–	GR

🖵 Internet Access 📶 Wireless Internet Access 🆆🅶 Waterway Guide Cruising Club Partner 🌐onSpot dockside WiFi facility
See WaterwayGuide.com for current rates, fuel prices, web site addresses, and other up-to-the-minute information. *(Information in the table is provided by the facilities.)*

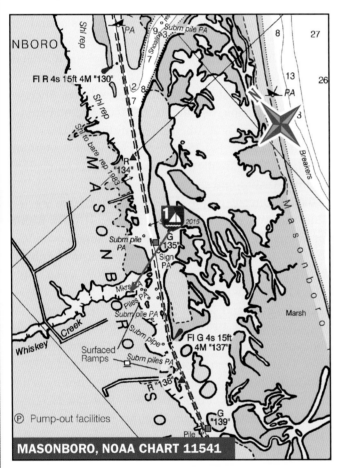

MASONBORO, NOAA CHART 11541

Anchorage: A favorite (but busy) anchorage is in the bight just southwest of the Motts Channel junction with Banks Channel (south flashing red "15"), inside the protective arm of Wrightsville Beach. There are 12- to 15-foot MLW depths with a fine sand ("mucky") bottom, which will require you to back down hard on your anchor for a good set. This is exposed to wakes and wind from the southwest. Expect lots of traffic, even at night so leave the lights on–both anchor and navigational, if possible.

An equally good anchorage (better protected from the wakes of large boats but busy with smaller vessels) lies northeast of Motts Channel and south of the **Causeway Drive Bridge** (8-foot fixed vertical clearance) between Harbor Island and Wrightsville Beach. This anchorage has a varied type of bottom in 10-foot MLW depths. The shallower parts have a very hard bottom with poor holding, while the deeper areas have a softer bottom and usually will hold with some extra work in backing down. In both anchorages, boats will swing, sometimes rather wildly, with the current rather than the wind, unless the wind is quite strong. Those dropping the hook here should plan accordingly. There is wind exposure from the southwest. Expect lots of boat traffic and even some water skiers.

Dinghy to the municipal docks located just south of the bridge on the beach side. The municipal docks have 4 feet MLW alongside. There is a grocery store and other amenities nearby.

Masonboro Inlet Area–ICW Mile 285

NAVIGATION: Use NOAA Chart 11541. Masonboro Inlet is the first major inlet south of Beaufort and is popular with sportfishers. It is an uncomplicated entrance protected by jetties on both sides and has good depths within. Depths are maintained at 12 feet in the 400-foot-wide channel running midway between the jetties. The uncharted buoys in Masonboro Inlet are frequently relocated. Once inside, if you are heading to Wrightsville Beach bear to starboard at green and red daybeacon "WC" into Banks channel and then turn to port at Motts Channel bit farther up. If Masonboro is your destination, continue straight ahead.

Deep-draft boats can enter the Banks Channel anchorage area via Masonboro Inlet to Shinn Creek (10- to 15-foot MLW depths) at Mile 285.1. The Coast Guard maintains dockage on Banks Channel, just north of Masonboro Inlet and responds quickly to emergency calls. The channel from the inlet to Shinn Creek is marked and readily passable. On summer weekends, however, this area resembles Fort Lauderdale and is packed with boats of all types.

Note that when you use these channels, you are off the ICW and away from its marking system. Refer to the NOAA chart for buoy information before leaving the ICW. The area is wide with good water depths.

When turning off the ICW into Shinn Creek, watch for current set, and treat ICW green can "129" (Mile 285.1) as a green marker for the ICW as well as for Shinn Creek, which is marked with red on the right coming from the sea. Cut halfway between green can "129" and the sandy north shore of Shinn Creek for 8 feet MLW. Check the most recent Army Corps of Engineers survey for Shinn Creek Crossing.

Dockage: Five miles south of Wrightsville Beach at Whiskey Creek (Mile 288.2), the Masonboro Yacht Club and Marina is visible to starboard. The marina has floating docks with transient dockage. Its two-story clubhouse has a fantastic view, along with showers and laundry facilities. This is home to an exceptional community of active sailors and recreational boaters.

■ MASONBORO INLET TO CAROLINA BEACH

Below Wrightsville Beach, the route follows a dredged channel through a succession of marshy sloughs for about 12 miles to Snows Cut, at Mile 295, the connecting link with the Cape Fear River. Continuing straight in Myrtle Grove Sound at Mile 295 will take you to Carolina Beach. This is one of the state's busiest (and oldest) summer resorts, but its grocery stores and restaurants stay open off-season as well.

Masonboro Inlet to Snows Cut– ICW Mile 289 to Mile 298

NAVIGATION: Use NOAA Charts 11541 and 11534. Through Masonboro Sound and Myrtle Grove Sound, the route runs straight and narrow. Shoaling frequently occurs here, especially at the many junctions where side creeks cross the ICW, and temporary buoys are placed to mark the shallow areas. The Carolina Beach Inlet Crossing of the ICW at Mile 293.5 and parts of Snows Cut were last dredged in spring 2017.

Conditions can change quickly and this area is prone to shoaling, so caution and seeking local knowledge are advised in transiting. Areas of particular concern include:

- Mile 287.5–Move to the red edge of the channel for 0.10 miles north and south of green daybeacon "135." You may still see 7 feet MLW just north of the shoaling area. The major shoaling is on the green side.
- Mile 288.4–Favor the red side 450 feet north of flashing green "137" to avoid shoaling to 5 feet MLW on the green side.
- Mile 293.7–Stay off red nun "154" by 150 feet between it and red daybeacon "156." Otherwise, favor the green side of the channel here.
- Mile 295–There is a shoal coming in from the red side to 3 MLW. Favor the green side around the bend, turning by flashing green "161."

Carolina Beach Inlet (Mile 293.5) is closed due to shoaling. The Coast Guard has pulled all the navigational aids until further notice. This is a local knowledge, small-boat inlet in the best of conditions and should be avoided until the buoys are reset after dredging (date undetermined). Mariners should use extreme caution while navigating this area.

At Mile 295, immediately before the ICW turns to enter Snows Cut, a deep, well-marked channel leads to Carolina Beach and the marinas.

The fixed **Snows Cut (U.S. 421) Hwy. Bridge** (65-foot vertical clearance) and the overhead power cables (68-foot vertical clearance) just west of the bridge at Mile 295.7 should provide enough room for most. Exercise care here, as the current runs strong at the bridge, and eddies can make boat handling difficult. Stay in the channel as parts of this area tend to shoal and the current runs swiftly. With the frequent dredging in this area, tugs towing long runs of dredging pipe can be expected. These can be as long as 0.25 mile and can completely block Snows Cut to navigation. Listen to "Sécurité" broadcasts from tows before entering Snows Cut.

Carolina Beach–ICW Mile 295

Like many NC coastal towns, Carolina Beach was "wiped off the map" by the Category 4 Hurricane Hazel in 1954. The town took the opportunity to rebuild from the ground up. This is a boater friendly location, both on the water and in town.

Dockage: At the north entrance to Snows Cut (Mile 295), you will find transient facilities to port at Carolina Beach Yacht Club & Marina. Be aware that its fuel and transient dock is just off the ICW beyond flashing green

Cape Fear River, NC

CAROLINA BEACH AREA		Dockage						Supplies		Services					
		Largest Vessel Accommodated	VHF Channel Monitored	Transient Berths / Total Berths	Approach / Dockside Depth (reported)	Floating Docks	Gas / Diesel	Groceries, Ice, Marine Supplies, Snacks	Repairs: Hull, Engine, Propeller	Lift (tonnage), Crane, Rail	Min/Max Amps	Laundry, Pool, Showers, Courtesy Car	Pump-Out Station	Nearby: Grocery Store, Motel, Restaurant
1. Carolina Beach Yacht Club & Marina 🖥 📶 295	910-458-5053	100	16/11	15/69	6/6	F	GD	IMS	–	–	30/50	LS	P	GMR
2. Carolina Beach NC Mooring Field	919-215-4593	55	–	moorings	30/14	F	–	–	–	–	–	–	–	GR
3. Mona Black Marina 🖥 📶	910-232-0211	60	–	4/24	20/20	F	–	IM	–	–	30/50	LS	P	GMR
4. Carolina Beach Boatyard & Marina 📶	910-707-1007	60	16	–	20/10	F	–	–	HEP	L35	30/50	–	–	GMR
5. Federal Point Yacht Club Marina 🖥 📶	910-458-4201	140	–	10/110	15/25	F	–	I	–	–	30/50	LPS	P	GMR
6. Carolina Beach Municipal Marina	910-458-2540	25	–	call/7	–	F	–	–	–	–	–	–	P	GMR
7. Carolina Beach State Park 297.1	910-458-7770	48	16	call/54	5/4	F	GD	IMS	–	–	30/50	LS	–	GR

🖥 Internet Access 📶 Wireless Internet Access WG Waterway Guide Cruising Club Partner ⊕onSpot dockside WiFi facility
See WaterwayGuide.com for current rates, fuel prices, web site addresses, and other up-to-the-minute information. *(Information in the table is provided by the facilities.)*

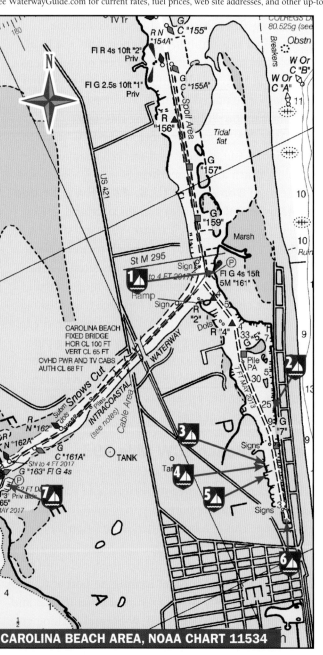

CAROLINA BEACH AREA, NOAA CHART 11534

"161" and should be passed without a wake. Although this is a 2-mile dinghy ride from the "business end" of the island, there are good bus service connections into Wilmington (6 miles away).

The 24-slip Mona Black Marina to the south has some reserved transient space but is mostly a liveaboard facility. Carolina Beach Boatyard & Marina is a working boatyard offering all types of repairs (35-ton lift); call ahead. The 110-slip Federal Point Yacht Club Marina gets high marks for its clean facilities. It is walking distance to restaurants and shopping and has bikes on site for rental. At the south end of the channel, Carolina Beach Municipal Marina may have short-term space available on their floating docks. Call ahead.

The marina at Carolina Beach State Park, in a basin at the southeast end of Snows Cut, has shower facilities, restrooms and fuel (gas and diesel). The largest boat accommodated is 48 feet. It has been reported that there is 5.5 MLW at the entrance. The draw here are miles of hiking trails that traverse a variety of distinct habitats, including that of the storied Venus flytrap.

Moorings: The City of Carolina Beach mooring field is a welcome addition for those who prefer not to anchor. Located beyond green daybeacon "5" and the small grassy island beyond, the 10 moorings accommodate boats between 26 and 55 feet. There is a beach across the street with public restrooms and outside showers. A dinghy dock is located to the south of the mooring field (near mooring number 1). Pick up a mooring, then call 910-667-0004. Moorings are available on a first-come, first-served basis.

Anchorage: The entire bight at Carolina Beach (south of Snows Cut and behind the beach) has more than adequate water off the marked channel, except where specifically noted on the NOAA chart. Be aware of sharp shoaling and submerged pilings in the harbor near red daybeacon "4." North of green daybeacon "5" and the grassy island it marks, a deep, 30-foot hole provided long-scope anchorage for boats with plenty of rode.

South of green daybeacon "5" and north of the large moorage area sign, there is room for several boats in 14 feet MLW. Boat traffic, particularly on summer weekends, is intense. Holding is fair here but be prepared for an eddy effect under certain wind and tide conditions.

From here, it is easy to get an early morning start through Snows Cut and down the Cape Fear River.

Side Trip: Wilmington, Cape Fear River

While you could use a rental car to drive from Wrightsville Beach to Wilmington, the 15-nm trip upriver on the deep, well-marked shipping channel provides an easy passage with interesting features. Renting a car from Wrightsville Beach might still be your best bet if you want to see the surrounding area.

NAVIGATION: Use NOAA Chart 11537. Use Wilmington Tide Tables. The easiest way to make this upriver run is to go with the flood tide but be prepared for a rough chop if the wind is against the current. Conditions will improve in the upper reaches where the river narrows, but currents will be strong during the ebb tide.

From Snows Cut, set a course southwest to join the main Cape Fear River shipping channel at green daybeacon "33," then turn north toward Wilmington. The main shipping channel is wide and well marked with several charted ranges. Note, however, that numerous ranges have been changed recently and may not correspond with those on your NOAA chart.

Do not be tempted by the channel shown on the NOAA chart that runs northwest from Snows Cut (just after red nun "162A") and joins the shipping channel farther north. Local commercial fisherman and towing companies indicate this has silted in to less than 2 feet MLW.

Cape Fear Memorial Lift Bridge crosses the river south of the marinas. It has 65-foot closed vertical clearance and opens on signal (except during special events) for large ships. The bridgetender monitors VHF Channel 18.

Dockage: Upriver at flashing green buoy "59" (approximately 7 nm north of ICW Mile 297), a well-marked channel leads off to starboard to the Wilmington Marine Center (Marina & Service). The facility maintains 6-foot MLW depths (at extreme low tide) in its entrance channel and well-protected basin. Even with a tidal range of about 4 feet, deep-draft vessels find good water depths. The facility can also accommodate multihulls. This marina has full transient facilities, floating docks, pump-out service and sells all fuels. Yard capabilities at the Marine Service Center include a 75-ton mobile lift and a 400-ton marine railway used for commercial vessels. Also on site are a chandler (for

Wilmington Riverwalk

GOIN' ASHORE: **WILMINGTON, NC**

SERVICES	
1	Library
2	Post Office
3	Visitor Information
ATTRACTIONS	
4	Bellamy Mansion Museum
5	Burgwin-Wright House

6	Cape Fear Museum
7	Riverwalk
8	Thalian Hall
9	USS North Carolina
10	Wilmington Children's Museum
11	Wilmington Railroad Museum

SHOPPING/DINING	
12	Cotton Exchange
13	Manifest Design
14	Old Wilmington City Market
MARINAS	
15	Wilmington City Docks

The heart of downtown Wilmington is its riverfront. Once a bustling wharf of warehouses, boatsheds, docks and stables, today, a cluster of shops and restaurants span several city blocks along the Cape Fear River. Stroll along cobblestone streets, and listen to the river breeze blowing through branches gray-bearded with Spanish moss. You can also hear the clip-clopping of hooves as carriage tours pass antebellum homes wrapped in picket fences, jasmine and magnolias.

For more than a century, the Chandler's Wharf (225 S. Water St.) was the center of commerce with warehouses brimming with naval supplies, tools, cotton and turpentine. A fire destroyed much of the wharf, but the flavor of the 1870s has been restored, giving Wilmington the feel of the Old South without the heat and humidity of Charleston, SC. This may be why the Wilmington waterfront has been featured in numerous movies, including *Iron Man 3* and *Safe Haven*, as well as several television shows and series.

Attractions: The 1-mile-long Riverwalk follows the borders of the Cape Fear River and provides beautiful view with shops and restaurants to visit along the way. The wooden walkway passes a number of famed landmarks, including the *USS North Carolina* Battleship, the Cape Fear Memorial Bridge, and the heart of the waterfront downtown itself.

USS North Carolina (1 Battleship Rd., 910-399-9100) is one of Wilmington's best-known attractions. Visitors can tour the main deck, interior rooms and 16-inch gun turrets. There is a Roll of Honor in the wardroom listing the names of North Carolinians who died in the line of duty during World War II. The site also features a gift shop, visitor's center and picnic area.

If it's too hot to walk, Cinematique of Wilmington shows foreign and classic films several nights a week. It is located at Thalian Hall (310 Chestnut St., 910-632-2285), which is the home of the country's oldest community theater and currently hosts national touring companies as well as numerous local theater companies.

The Bellamy Mansion Museum (503 Market St., 910-251-3700) is a great example of antebellum architecture. After the fall of Fort Fisher in 1865, Federal troops used the home as their headquarters. Inside, you will find historical exhibits, arts and exhibitions. Carriage and walking tours begin out front.

One of the best ways to see the waterfront area is by buggy. Call Horsedrawn Carriage & Trolley Tours (910-251-8889) to reserve your ride. Another stop on your tour should be the Burgwin-Wright House (224 Market St., 910-762-0570), which is distinguished by its wrap-around, two-story porches and tiered gardens. The massive ballast-stone foundation is the remains of an abandoned town jail.

The Cape Fear Museum (814 Market St., 910-798-4370) is the oldest history museum in North Carolina. Inside, there is a 20-foot-tall giant ground sloth skeleton, a miniature recreation of the second battle of Fort Fisher and a room dedicated to native son and basketball great Michael Jordan. The Discovery Gallery includes a giant, crawl-through beaver lodge, dinosaur fossils and an entertaining Venus flytrap model.

Wilmington Railroad Museum (505 Nutt St., 910-763-2634) has an extensive library of railroading history. It is conveniently located on the waterfront and is open year-round.

The Azalea Festival comes to town every April, drawing big stars and big crowds. The street fair, parade and garden tours attract many; make sure to book your reservations early. Call 910-794-4650 for more information. At the end of Market St. on the waterfront, you will find free live concerts on Friday nights during the summer months and a farmers market on Saturday mornings from April through December.

Shopping/Dining: At the turn of the century, cotton was still king and one of the largest and busiest cotton export companies in the world was located in Wilmington. Today, eight restored buildings, connected by brick walkways and open-air courtyards, house 30 unique specialty shops and restaurants, each a charming reflection of the style and feel of Wilmington's 19th-century working port days. If you are looking for a gift, book, art or home décor item, spend time strolling through the Cotton Exchange (321 N. Front St., 910-343-9896). Also, don't miss the Old Wilmington City Market (120 Front St.), established in 1880. It is a collection of eclectic and unique merchandise offered by numerous independent vendors. If you get thirsty, there are no less than five breweries within walking distance.

Prefer wine? Noni Bacca Winery (420 Eastwood Rd., Ste. 108, 910-397-7617) offers tastings of their award-winning wines that have won them 179 international medals (transportation required).

This is a wonderful town for strolling and exploring and there are way too many dining and shopping opportunites to list them all here. Visit wilmingtondowntown.com for more options, or download the Wilmington Chamber mobile app from the iTunes store.

Cape Fear River, NC

WILMINGTON AREA		Largest Vessel Accommodated	VHF Channel Monitored	Transient Berths / Total Berths	Approach / Dockside Depth (reported)	Floating Docks	Gas / Diesel	Groceries, Ice, Marine Supplies, Snacks	Repairs: Hull, Engine, Propeller	Lift (tonnage), Crane, Rail	Min/Max Amps	Laundry, Pool, Showers, Courtesy Car	Pump-Out Station	Nearby: Grocery Store, Motel, Restaurant
				Dockage			Supplies		Services					
1. Wilmington Marine Center (Marina & Service) 💻 WIFI	910-395-5055	120	16/09	12/106	5.5/5	F	GD	IMS	HEP	L75,R400	30/50	S	P	R
2. Wilmington City Docks WIFI 13.6 N of 297	910-520-6875	100	16/68	30/30	38/16	F	-	-	-	-	30/50	-	P	GMR
3. Port City Marina WIFI	910-251-6151	250	16/72	call/204	25/10	F	GD	IM	-	-	30/100	S	P	GMR
4. Cape Fear Marina 💻 WIFI 14.4 N of 297	910-772-9277	175	16	25/75	40/20	F	-	IS	HEP	L70	30/100	LS	P	GMR
5. Bennett Brothers Yachts 💻 WIFI 14.4 N of 297	910-772-9277	175	16	25/75	28/18	F	-	IMS	HEP	L70	30/100	LS	P	GMR

💻 Internet Access   WIFI Wireless Internet Access   WG Waterway Guide Cruising Club Partner   ◉onSpot dockside WiFi facility
See WaterwayGuide.com for current rates, fuel prices, web site addresses, and other up-to-the-minute information. *(Information in the table is provided by the facilities.)*

charts), marine fabrication and welding, a marine power (service and sales) company and a custom yacht builder.

The Wilmington City Docks (just across from flashing green "63" or approximately 14 nm from ICW Mile 297) offers transient dockage with public restrooms and a laundry nearby. The docks are located downtown in the center of the Historic District with museums, shops, restaurants and nightlife all within walking distance.

Port City Marina to the north can accommodate boats up to 250 feet with a 10-foot dockside depth on concrete floating slips. The call themselves "the marina in the middle of it all." A short distance upriver, beyond the **I-117 Bascule Bridge** (20-foot closed vertical clearance), Cape Fear Marina has transient slips on floating docks and a fully equipped dock house with shower and laundry facilities. It is adjacent to Bennett Bros. Yachts offers repairs a full range of yacht restorative and repair services (with a 70-ton lift). There is also an on-site brokerage.

◼ SOUTHPORT AREA

Back on the ICW, the route to Southport leads through Snows Cut and down the Cape Fear River. A good procedure along this 12-mile-long downstream run to Southport is to run compass courses for each leg to assist in identifying the navigational aids that mark the course. The color of the marks changes from side to side, and also the numbering changes as you continue down the Cape Fear River. Studying your charts before departure is, as always, a very wise decision.

NAVIGATION: Use NOAA Chart 11534. South of Snows Cut, additional buoys have been added in the Cape Fear River, increasing the ease of maintaining a visual ICW channel course from the helm. The numerous ranges used by the large ships in the Cape Fear River have been changed recently and may not correspond with those on your NOAA chart.

⚠ Note that the buoys are reversed from the normal ICW system when you reach the Cape Fear River at Mile 299: The yellow squares and triangles are what count for the ICW skipper. Keep the yellow triangles on your starboard side, even if the aid is painted green, and leave the yellow squares to port when traveling south.

Between Mile 299 and 302 on the west side of the Cape Fear River, you will pass the Army's Military Ocean Terminal at Sunny Point with its three large piers. This is a restricted area protected by a security barrier marked by 45 mooring dolphins connected to each other with cables with three openings for ships to pass. Each dolphin pile shows a white light and white and orange sign worded "Danger Restricted Area." This is the largest ammunitions port in the U.S. and is patrolled by smaller vessels. Steer clear of this area.

Also of note in navigating the Cape Fear River is the Fishers Island Ferry, which makes regular runs across the river between Federal Point (Mile 303.5) and the Ferry Terminal just north of Price Creek (Mile 306.5). You may also encounter large ships going to and from the port of Wilmington.

Southport is another spot where you can't go wrong if you arrive at or before low-water slack, going either north or south. Currents can run in excess of 2 knots during flood tide. Low-water slack, before flood tides, occurs in the river off Southport 1 hour and 16 minutes after the time listed in the tide tables for Charleston

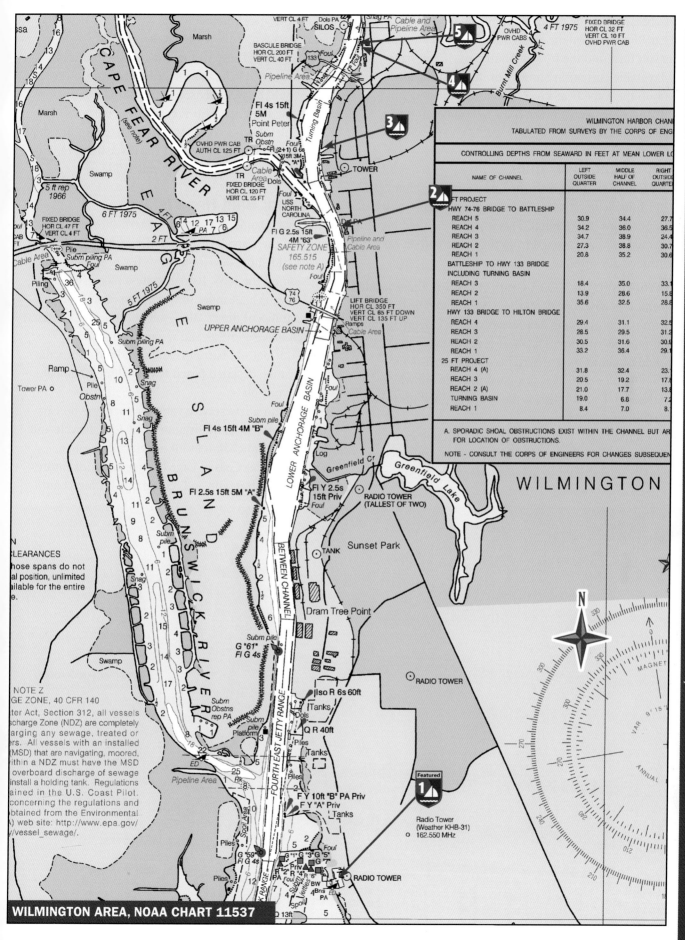

WILMINGTON HARBOR CHANN[...]
TABULATED FROM SURVEYS BY THE CORPS OF ENG[...]

CONTROLLING DEPTHS FROM SEAWARD IN FEET AT MEAN LOWER LO[...]

NAME OF CHANNEL	LEFT OUTSIDE QUARTER	MIDDLE HALF OF CHANNEL	RIGHT OUTSIDE QUARTER
[...] FT PROJECT			
HWY 74-76 BRIDGE TO BATTLESHIP			
REACH 5	30.9	34.4	27.7
REACH 4	34.2	36.0	36.5
REACH 3	34.7	38.9	24.4
REACH 2	27.3	38.8	30.7
REACH 1	20.8	35.2	30.6
BATTLESHIP TO HWY 133 BRIDGE			
INCLUDING TURNING BASIN			
REACH 3	18.4	35.0	33.1
REACH 2	13.9	28.6	15.8
REACH 1	35.6	32.5	28.8
HWY 133 BRIDGE TO HILTON BRIDGE			
REACH 4	29.4	31.1	32.5
REACH 3	28.5	29.5	31.2
REACH 2	30.5	31.6	30.9
REACH 1	33.2	36.4	29.1
25 FT PROJECT			
REACH 4 (A)	31.8	32.4	23.7
REACH 3	20.5	19.2	17.8
REACH 2 (A)	21.0	17.7	13.8
TURNING BASIN	19.0	6.8	7.2
REACH 1	8.4	7.0	8.[...]

A. SPORADIC SHOAL OBSTRUCTIONS EXIST WITHIN THE CHANNEL BUT AR[...]
FOR LOCATION OF OBSTRUCTIONS.

NOTE - CONSULT THE CORPS OF ENGINEERS FOR CHANGES SUBSEQUEN[...]

WILMINGTON

Harbor. If you ride the maximum ebb down the Cape Fear River, you will be facing into a wicked current as you turn into the ICW at Southport. If you have a favorable current in Snows Cut, it will be against you in the Cape Fear River. When the tide and wind are opposing, batten down for a wet, uncomfortable ride to Southport.

Cape Fear River Inlet

The Cape Fear Inlet is the first port south of Morehead City suitable for all sizes of oceangoing vessels via a major deepwater channel. This is a well-marked big ship channel that is protected from the north and an easy entrance day or night.

NAVIGATION: Use NOAA Chart 11534. For those headed north, it is wise to stay on the ICW to avoid a significant detour around Frying Pan Shoals, which extend 30 nm out into the Atlantic. The most prudent tactic is to use Masonboro Inlet at Wrightsville Beach as your jumping-off point. This is a good inlet for snowbirds with several good inlets to the south to duck into should conditions deteriorate.

Because of Jay Bird Shoals, buoys on Cape Fear's main shipping channel should be observed, and the Western Bar Channel should be avoided. Many charts still show the old entrance channel to the west of the new channel that replaced it. Follow the markers.

The current is very strong; time your entrance to take advantage of the tides. Northbound in slower boats would be well-advised to check the tides before attempting the Cape Fear Rivers strong currents. This is a busy inlet, keep a constant watch posted for big ships. For more details on the Cape Fear River Inlet, refer to the Inlet section in the front of this guide.

Side Trip: Bald Head Island

Bald Head Island, on the northeastern shore at the mouth of the Cape Fear River, offers a destination marina and shore development well worth the 2-mile diversion off the ICW. Its remoteness (accessible only by water), 14 miles of wide, unspoiled beaches and magnificent dunes, alongside meandering creeks through diverse forests and waving marsh grass makes this natural barrier island stand out. If a walk on a pristine, deserted beach is your thing, then Bald Head is your place.

Except for a few service vehicles, there are no cars on the island, so transportation is by foot, bicycle and electric cart. You can rent bikes and carts near the marina office at Coastal Urge or Riverside Adventure Co. to reach shopping and restaurants (at Merchant's

Old Baldy Lighthouse

WILMINGTON MARINE CENTER

BALD HEAD ISLAND MARINA

Row) and 14 miles of beaches. All Bald Head beaches are public with access via paths from the road. You will pass several trail heads along the way marking trails that wind through the forest and marsh.

While you are exploring, be sure to stop by "Old Baldy," the original Cape Fear Lighthouse and the Keeper's House and one of the oldest standing lighthouses (built in 1817). You can climb the 108 steps and the ladder to the lantern room for a wonderful view of the entire area.

NAVIGATION: Use NOAA Chart 11534. Bald Head Island is easily reached either from the ICW, which turns to the west at Southport, or from the ocean. It is an excellent jumping-off or landing point to or from a voyage south. Bald Head Island's deep-dredged and well-marked channel lies southeast of flashing green "13A" on the Smith Island Range of the Cape Fear River (east of Jay Bird Shoals). The ebb and flood currents range from 2 to 3 knots and run perpendicular to the island's entrance channel. The entrance channel is narrow and care must be exercised to maintain control of your vessel in the current. Do not try to enter if another boat is exiting the channel fairway.

Dockage: Bald Head Island Marina is located in a 10-acre, protected harbor with neatly lined floating docks and surrounded by an adorable village. Along with dockside conveniences such as showers, laundry facilities, casual dining and boating supplies, marina guests may purchase temporary memberships at the Bald Head Island Club for superb golf, tennis, pool and croquet facilities and elegant dining, and at the private Shoals Club for fine and casual dining, swimming in the crystal clear salt water pool and direct beach access with chairs and umbrellas provided. The marina can accommodate vessels to 115 feet and 8-foot drafts. Call ahead for availability, docking instructions and assistance (monitoring VHF Channel 16). There is no room for anchoring in the enclosed basin.

The Maritime Market grocery store on Bald Head Island has an excellent selection of fine food and wine as well as staples, a café and deli. It is located 1.5 miles inland and not difficult to find, considering the main road is basically one large circle. There is plentiful shopping and dining on the island. Visit baldheadisland. com for a complete listing.

Southport Channel, NC

	Largest Vessel Accommodated	VHF Channel Monitored	Transient Berths / Total Berths	Approach / Dockside Depth (reported)	Floating Docks	Gas / Diesel	Groceries, Ice, Marine Supplies, Snacks	Repairs: Hull, Engine, Propeller	Lift (tonnage), Crane, Rail	Min/Max Amps	Laundry, Pool, Showers, Courtesy Car	Pump-Out Station	Nearby: Grocery Store, Motel, Restaurant
BALD HEAD ISLAND			**Dockage**				**Supplies**			**Services**			
1. Bald Head Island Marina ⌨ 📶 WG 2.8 S of 309 910-457-7380	115	16/10	25/155	8/7	F	GD	IMS	–	–	30/100	LPS	P	GMR
SOUTHPORT													
2. Deep Point Marina 📶 307 910-269-2380	100	16/10	20/82	8/8	F	GD	IMS	–	–	30/100	LPS	P	R
3. Southport Marina ⌨ 📶 309.3 910-457-9900	200	16/09	15/200	8/8	F	GD	IMS	HEP	L75	30/100	LS	P	GMR
4. Zimmerman Marine-Southport Yard 📶 309.3 910-477-9044	-	-	-	8/6	F	-	IMS	HEP	L75	30/100	LS	P	GMR
5. Indigo Plantation & Marina 📶 310 910-269-2380	80	16	1/65	10/8	F	-	-	-	-	30/50	LS	P	R
6. South Harbour Village Marina ⌨ 📶 WG 311.4 910-454-7486	200	16/68	35/153	15/12	F	GD	IS	HEP	-	30/100	LS	P	MR
OAK ISLAND													
7. American Fish Shop & American Marine Const. 312 910-457-5488	-	-	-	-	-	-	M	HEP	L50	-	-	-	-
8. St. James Marina ⌨ ⊙onSpot 315 910-253-0463	120	16	50/155	7/7	F	GD	GIMS	HEP	L	30/50	LS	P	GMR

⌨ Internet Access   📶 Wireless Internet Access   WG Waterway Guide Cruising Club Partner   ⊙onSpot dockside WiFi facility
See WaterwayGuide.com for current rates, fuel prices, web site addresses, and other up-to-the-minute information. *(Information in the table is provided by the facilities.)*

Southport–ICW Mile 309

About 2 miles north of the Cape Fear River Inlet (to the Atlantic), the ICW leaves the river, takes a hard turn to the west, enters a dredged land cut and arrives in the peaceful little village of Southport. Southport's numerous restaurants and much of its business district are within easy walking distance of the waterfront. The downtown combines all the charm of a laid-back coastal village with historic southern architecture and style. A "drive on" (car) ferry terminal is 2 miles north of Southport and runs to the tip of Fort Fisher at the mouth of the Cape Fear River. The enjoyable 45-minute one-way trip is filled with unique, beautiful views and is a bargain at $5 per carload.

NAVIGATION: Use NOAA Chart 11534. Shoaling has been observed along Southport's waterfront and the nameless island just southwest of the village. When entering the ICW channel from the Cape Fear River, there is no shortcut. The two rectangular condo buildings on the point at Southport make a prominent landmark.

⚠️ Shoaling to 6-foot MLW has been observed at flashing green "1." Pass 100 feet off the marker before proceeding to red nun "2."

Dockage: At Mile 307, the modern Deep Point Marina offers comfortable dockage, along with easy ocean, ICW and river access. They sell all fuels and have clean showers, a pool (seasonal) and laundry facilities in an impressive Harbor Master facility, which also houses

OAK ISLAND, NOAA CHART 11534

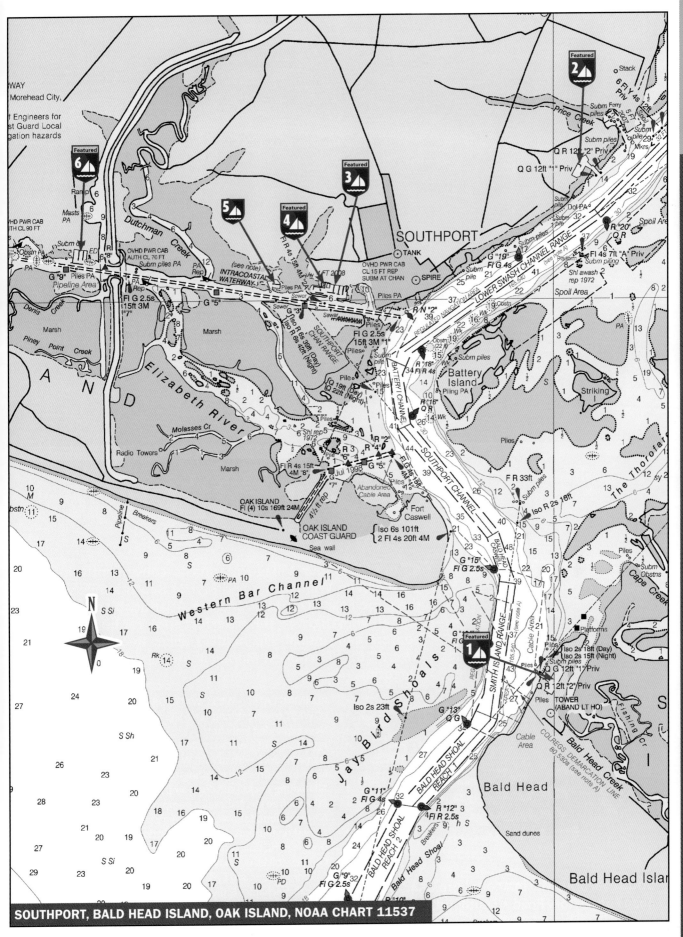

SOUTHPORT, BALD HEAD ISLAND, OAK ISLAND, NOAA CHART 11537

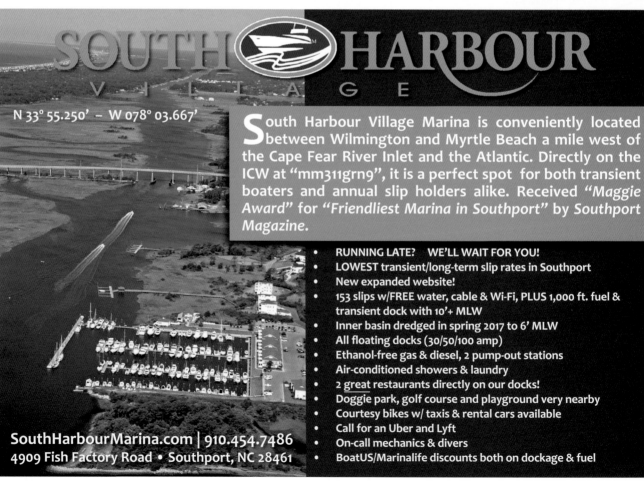

an on-site store (open to the public) sells snacks and ice. The marina is adjacent to the Bald Head Island Mainland Ferry Terminal.

A short distance into the southbound ICW land cut, a channel opens to the right at flashing red marker "2A" into Southport Marina. This one of the largest and most amenity-laden marinas in North Carolina. The full-service marina has over 200 in-water protected slips with deep water access, a well-appointed ship store and a fuel dock. They also have a 220 unit dry-storage facility and a 75-ton travel lift. Zimmerman Marine's Southport yard is located here offering full boat repair services, from rigging to mechanical and electrical and including carpentry and fiberglass. (They have four other yards: Deltaville, VA; Mobjack Bay, VA; Herrington Harbour, MD; and Charleston, SC.) A public boardwalk surrounds the marina along the bulkhead as part of Southport's Riverwalk. It is a five-minute walk into downtown.

The floating docks at the entrance to the basin are private and associated with the condos on the point. Dockage is sometimes available at a few of the private slips in the town basin (check the posted signs). Past these docks and in front of The Provision Company restaurant, there are four slips for dining patrons. If you eat there you can stay overnight at the dock. There is no water or power and it may be noisy when the restaurant is full. Nearby Fishy Fishy (910-457-1881) may also have dockage for diners.

Note that the Southport Town Dock was damaged in Hurricane Mathew and as of summer 2019 repairs to the dock had not begun. You can check the status with the local police station (910-457-7913) or on the Waterway Explorer (waterwayguide.com).

Immediately south on the ICW, Indigo Plantation & Marina has limited transient space. This is home to the Indigo Plantation Yacht Club. The road to town from here is not direct, making a taxi ride necessary for shopping or dining out.

At Mile 311 (day beacon green "9"), South Harbour Village Marina offers a spacious 500-foot facing dock parallel to the ICW plus two on-site restaurants. The face dock has 12-foot depths and can handle vessels as large as 200 feet. They offer all fuels, pump-out stations, ice and oil on the face dock. Both restaurants offer great water views of the marina, the marshes, bird life and the ICW. Rusty Hooks Dockside Grill has great food (try the signature fish tacos), a bar and live music, while Joseph's Italian Bistro offers fine dining with European decor. South Harbour Village Marina is

Navigation & Weather Briefings for ICW Boaters

If you are transiting the Atlantic Intracoastal Waterway (AICW) in the spring or fall you should plan your schedule to be near Southport Marina to attend one of Hank Pomeranz's nightly navigation and weather briefings. For over 5 years Hank has developed and presented navigation and weather briefs geared toward vessels on the AICW.

Retired U.S. Navy meteorologist, cruising sailor and owner of Carolina Yacht Care, Hank hosts the daily discussions complete with graphics, handouts and insight into what to expect on the next leg of your journey.

The briefings include the latest U.S. Army Corps of Engineers surveys, *Local Notice to Mariners*, recent fellow cruiser postings, direct cruiser feedback and local knowledge to help you safely navigate the ICW problem areas from Southport to Norfolk, VA (Mile 0) for northbound vessels beginning April 15 through Memorial Day 2019.

On the weather side, Hank reviews current advisories, watches and warnings, analyses and forecast charts and discusses the forecasts for winds and seas, precipitation, temperatures, fog and severe weather potential for the Carolina coast, and the Pamlico and Albemarle Sounds.

Fall briefs are scheduled from October 15 through December 15 and focus on the stretch of the AICW from Southport to Savannah, GA.

The briefings are held nightly at Southport Marina (ICW Mile 309) at 6:00 p.m. and are sponsored by Southport Marina and Zimmerman Marine. There is no charge to attend. Call ahead to verify schedule (910-457-9900).

known for being cruiser- and pet-friendly. Because of this reservations are recommended.

Anchorage: The Old Southport Basin at the beginning of the land cut is shallow (3- to 7-foot MLW depths) with poor holding. It is open to the south and ICW wakes. You would be better served to take a slip at one of the nearby dock and dine restaurants (which are all very good, by the way).

The entrance to Dutchman Creek anchorage at Mile 310.2 has shoaled, and we can no longer recommend it. Unfortunately, this is also true of the anchorage on the west side of Pipeline Canal (north of red "8" at Mile 311). This anchorage is just 3 feet MLW in some spots.

In short, this is a good area to plan on taking a slip.

Oak Island–ICW Mile 310 to Mile 320

From Oak Island through Long Beach, you will pass through several small towns and a series of beach developments. You will likely encounter numerous small fishing boats testing the waters for red fish and flounder. These are also some of the most beautiful sections of the ICW.

The Oak Island Nature Center at 5202 E. Yacht Dr. has trails, plus displays on fossils and native animals (910-201-1392). The Nature Center is nestled between

tall native pines, oak trees and a beautiful salt marsh eco-system. A tree trail, butterfly garden, floating dock and fishing pier are open seasonally, April through August, Thursdays through Saturdays from 11:00 a.m. to 2:00 p.m. Hours are subject to change.

To the east, Oak Island Lighthouse has sweeping views over Caswell Beach and Bald Head Island. Tours to the second level (12 steps up to a solid concrete floor) are offered during the summer months on Wednesdays and Saturdays from 10:00 a.m. until 2:00 p.m. Reservations are not required. To take a tour to the top (up 131 steps to an outside balcony), call well in advance (4 weeks in summer). During the summer, top tours are only conducted on Tuesday and Thursday mornings and some Sundays. All tours are free.

NAVIGATION: Use NOAA Chart 11534. The **Oak Island (NC 33) Bridge** (65-foot fixed vertical clearance) at Mile 311.8 is the first bridge encountered after Snows Cut. There is another high-level bridge–**Middleton St. Bridge** with 67-foot fixed vertical clearance–between Oak Island and the mainland at Mile 316.8 (at Swains Cut). From Mile 310 to Mile 396 below Myrtle Beach, the National Ocean Service (NOS) tables do not provide information on currents.

SOUTHPORT MARINA

Visit with us today!

See for yourself why Southport Marina is always ready to meet your needs!

- State-of-the-art docks
- Live oak park and events venue
- Indoor storage facility
- Professional dock staff
- Wireless internet
- Full service boat yard
- Service by Zimmerman Marine
  – Yamaha Authorized Sales and Service

606 W. West Street | Southport, NC 28461 | (910) 457-9900 | www.southport-marina.com

ICW Marker 2A at mouth of the Cape Fear River

GOIN' ASHORE: **SOUTHPORT, NC**

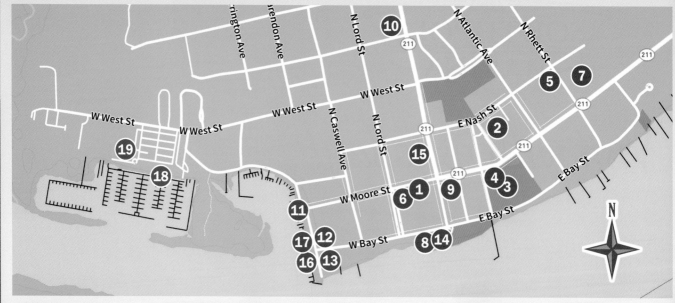

SERVICES	
1	Library
2	Post Office
3	Visitor Information
ATTRACTIONS	
3	Fort Johnston-Southport Museum
4	North Carolina Maritime Museum
5	Old Brunswick County Jail
6	Old Indian Trail Tree

7	Old Smithville Burying Ground
8	River Pilot's Tower
SHOPPING	
9	Silver Coast Winery Tasting Room
10	Wine Rack
DINING	
11	Fishy Fishy Café
12	Flava's Ice Cream Shop
13	Frying Pan

14	Oliver's on the Cape Fear
15	Port City Java
16	Provision Company
17	Yacht Basin Eatery
MARINAS	
18	Southport Marina
19	Zimmerman Marine-Southport

Southport was originally named Smithville after Benjamin Smith who served under Gen. George Washington in the Revolutionary War. What began as a small fishing and military town has blossomed into a community for retirees and commuters working in Wilmington. The first Spanish explorers arrived in 1521 and settled up the Cape Fear River in what became known as Brunswick Town. In the early 1700 Southport was a harbor for pirates. Stede Bonnet, the "Gentleman Pirate," was a frequent visitor. Between 1745 and 1754, Fort Johnson was built as a quarantine service for incoming seamen and to protect settlements farther up the river. Located at the mouth of the Cape Fear, Fort Johnson attracted a small community of river pilots and fishermen, and the area began to thrive. At the close of the Civil War, local businessmen sought to create a major port by combining the city's river transportation with the new railroad system. The town's name was changed from Smithville to Southport, but the project failed to attract commercial shipping. The mild temperatures and the deep waters of the Cape Fear River attracted vacationers and soon the town blossomed. River steamers served it until 1925 and rail from 1911 until World War II.

Attractions: Southport is a great walking town. Maps are available at the Fort Johnston–Southport Museum & Visitor's Center located at 203 E. Bay St. and at most area marinas. You can also pick up information on a variety of tours available to explore the town in greater depth and learn about its unique place in the lore of the Lower Cape Fear region. The North Carolina Maritime Museum at 204 E. Moore St. is dedicated to the history of the Lower Cape Fear Region (910-457-0003). The museum contains a detailed and fascinating collection that covers shipwrecks, piracy, the Civil War, commercial fishing, hurricanes and a number of other natural and manmade events that have left a permanent mark on the North Carolina coast.

Southport, NC

ICW

Other sites for history buffs are the Old Smithville Burying Ground, the Old Brunswick County Jail Museum (318 E. Nash St., 910-457-7927), the Model 1922 Fire Truck Museum and River Pilot's Tower. The Old Indian trail tree is an ancient gnarled oak has been estimated to be more than 800 years old. Indians may have bent the young tree to mark the trail to their fishing grounds. The tree took root a second time, thus developing the unusual formation; you can't miss it.

This picturesque city has served as the backdrop for a number of movies and TV series. Locals are accustomed to having studio equipment, crew and actors in and around town. (You can even take a golf cart tour of movie locations.)

Start at the Fort Johnson-Southport Visitor's Center (203 E. Bay St., 910-457-7927) or check the website (cityofsouthport.com) for up-to-date information on special events like outdoor movies, concerts and festivals. Summer is an especially vibrant time of year. On Wednesdays (May through September, 8:00 a.m. to 1:00 p.m.) the lawn at Fort Johnston is home to the Waterfront Market, where you will find a variety of vendors selling everything from vegetables to crafts. Local musicians entertain the shoppers and create a festive scene.

For over 200 years, Southport has celebrated America's independence, making this one of the state's largest and the official North Carolina state Fourth of July celebration. Each year, between 40,000 and 50,000 people set up chairs along the main roads and enjoy an old-fashioned Independence Day celebration. You will find over 100 handmade arts and crafts on display, beach music on the waterfront, a naturalization ceremony, veterans' recognition ritual, flag retirement observance, freedom run and walk and, of course, a huge fireworks display that lights up the sky over the Cape Fear River.

In September, the Southport Wooden Boat Show (10th anniversary in 2019) is a popular event where you can view boat displays, arts and crafts, maritime demonstrations, kids' events, and help rank chowder in the annual cook-off. October brings the Stede Bonnet Regatta, requiring all participants to arrive in buccaneer costumes and act like pirates during the race.

Shopping: Three supermarkets are available for provisioning: Walmart, Food Lion and Lowes Foods within three miles. None are accessible by foot or bike (due to distance and lack of bike paths) but can be easily reached by a short shuttle ride from area marinas. You can take a complimentary shuttle (with your pet) to Carolina Yacht Care, offering concierge and provisioning services. They will deliver food, beer and wine, sundries and even tackle and bait supplies directly to you. They also offer mail packaging and shipping, boat monitoring (long- and short-term) and storm preparation. Call 910-742-0083 for details.

NAPA Auto and Marine (721 N. Howe St., 910-457-5022) is your best bet for finding boating supplies. Directly across the street from NAPA you'll find the liquor store. Beer and wine are available at the supermarkets and local wine and beer shops, including Uncorked by the Sea (602 N. Howe St., 910-454-0633), the Wine Rack (102 W. Brown St., 910-457-5147) and Silver Coast Winery Tasting Room (105 S. Howe St.). Silver Coast wines are modeled after traditional European styles. The winery offers full tours of the production facility along with daily wine tastings. Call 910-777-5151 for more information.

Visit downtownsouthport.org for more shopping options, including galleries, jewelers, crafts and apparel.

Dining: From casual to fine dining, Southport boasts many excellent restaurants. Several informal eateries line the Yacht Basin downtown, several with slips for diners. Restaurants typically offer the fresh catch of the day and include Frying Pan (910-363-4382), Provision Company (910-457-0654), Yacht Basin Eatery (910-363-4108) and Fishy Fishy Café (910-457-1881), all of which are worth a visit.

Convenient to South Harbour Village Marina is Joseph's Italian Bistro & Chop House (5003 O'Quinn Blvd. SE, 910-454-4440), which opens at 5:00 p.m. daily (except closed on Sunday), and offers inside and outside dining. The popular Rusty Hooks Dockside Grill is also on site at South Harbour Village with great food and a fun atmosphere (910-477-6616). They specialize in dishes made with fresh, local seafood.

Waterfront dining is also available at the more upscale Oliver's on the Cape Fear at W. Bay St. (910-477-9299). The site of Oliver's was originally a ship's chandler dating back to the 1700s where sailing ships could obtain supplies and served as such for the menhaden boats up until the 1930s.

Start your day at Port City Java at 113 N. Howe St. (910-454-0321).Your lunch and dinner choices continue a short walk up Howe Street from the river. Finish off the day with a scoop of cookies and cream at the riverfront at Flava's Ice Cream Shop at 318 W. Bay St (910-457-5150).

Note: Some restaurants close Sunday or Monday year round and some close or reduce hours during winter, so call ahead.

In general, the flood runs south in this area, but expect current reversals as you pass inlets. This area is relatively straightforward cruising, except for a couple of shoal areas:

- Mile 315–A shoal is shown on some charts ("Shl rep") just 200 yards west of the entrance to St. James Plantation Marina on the south side of the channel. Proceed with caution.
- Mile 317.4–At flashing red "18" on the north side, an unmarked shoal extends some 50 feet into the channel. This is likely silt from the unnamed creek near the marker. At dead low tide, the shoal is just 1 foot above water.
- Mile 318.9–At flashing green daybeacon "29" the channel makes a sharp turn to starboard. Stay close to the marker. An uncharted shoal, partly visible at low water, extends toward the channel from the mainland side.
- Mile 321–Take a wide turn between red nun "46A" and red nun "46B" and favor red nun "48A" in the channel.

Dockage: American Fish Shop & Marine Construction occupies the docks on the west side of the ICW north of the Oak Island Bridge (65-foot vertical clearance) at Mile 311.8. This is a full-service boat yard with competitive pricing. St. James Marina at Mile 315 in Oak Island has transient slips on floating docks and sells all fuels. This is part of a large residential development, including three golf courses, a small general store, a gift shop and an on-site restaurant.

■ NEXT STOP

Looking ahead, boaters will find some true "ditch" cruising, punctuated by side-setting inlets. When you reach Myrtle Beach at Mile 346, you may want to spend a few days enjoying the many amenities and public beaches. Then it's on to the beautiful Waccamaw River as you move toward the Lowcountry and Charleston.

Lockwoods Folly, NC to Isle of Palms, SC

ICW Mile 321–Mile 456

VHF NC Bridges: Channel 13/SC Bridges: Channel 09

CHARTS NOAA 11518, 11534

Approaching Lockwoods Folly Inlet, the shoreline shifts to low marshland extending back to scrub trees. Along the banks at Holden Beach, just below the inlet, an increasing number of houses have appeared on the ocean side of the ICW. This section carries heavy commercial and recreational boat traffic, particularly on weekends, and there are long stretches of No-Wake Zones. If you make the passage in late June when North Carolina rivers are open for fishing, you will find a lot of boat traffic. Boats vary from outboard-powered skiffs and center consoles with families aboard to miniature shrimp boats. Although the traffic is chaotic and some skippers are uncooperative, one reward is that a fresh shrimp or fish meal is readily available at almost any tie-up.

ICW Bridges will not delay openings if boats are already waiting, so you must know your speed and calculate your transit carefully; slow boats may not be able to synchronize their passages with the openings.

■ LOCKWOODS FOLLY INLET TO LITTLE RIVER, SC

Lockwoods Folly Inlet Area–ICW Mile 321 to Mile 325

NAVIGATION: Use NOAA Chart 11534. Just past Mile 321, the ICW crosses the junction of Lockwoods Folly Inlet and Lockwoods Folly River. The proximity of the ICW to the ocean in this area makes conditions extremely changeable at both Lockwoods Folly Inlet crossing and Shallotte Inlet crossing a few miles farther south. Strong ebb and flow currents alone continually move the sand, while storms off the ocean can reshape the bottom in hours. Be aware of crosscurrents and adjust your heading as required. The channel past Lockwoods Folly Inlet usually has extra floating markers (which can be readily moved) that are not shown on the NOAA chart, plus other charted markers may be

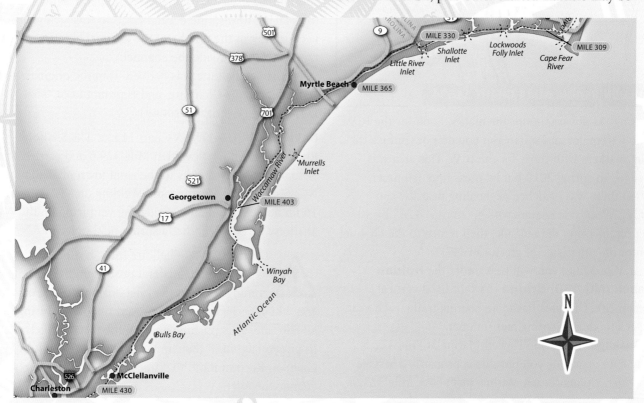

Lockwoods Folly Inlet, NC

HOLDEN BEACH		Largest Vessel Accommodated	VHF Channel Monitored	Transient Berths / Total Berths	Approach / Dockside Depth (reported)	Floating Docks	Gas / Diesel	Groceries, Ice, Marine Supplies, Snacks	Repairs: Hull, Engine, Propeller	Lift (tonnage), Crane, Rail	Min/Max Amps	Laundry, Pool, Showers, Courtesy Car	Pump-Out Station	Nearby: Grocery Store, Motel, Restaurant
				Dockage			**Supplies**		**Services**					
1. Hewett Marina 322.5	910-842-9104	72	–	8/8	–	–	–	–	H	L60	30/30	–	–	–
2. Holden Beach Marina 324	910-842-5447	50	16	4/15	6/6	F	GD	IMS	HEP	L	30/50	S	–	GR
3. Holden Beach Transient Dock (WiFi) 324	910-842-6488	–	–	3/3	–	F	–	–	–	–	20/50	LS	P	R

💻 Internet Access (WiFi) Wireless Internet Access (WG) Waterway Guide Cruising Club Partner ⌖ onSpot dockside WiFi facility

See WaterwayGuide.com for current rates, fuel prices, web site addresses, and other up-to-the-minute information. *(Information in the table is provided by the facilities.)*

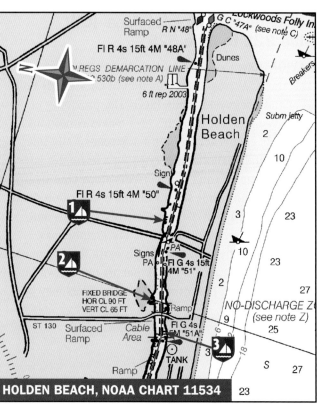

HOLDEN BEACH, NOAA CHART 11534

missing. As always, honor the marks. Look for the ICW yellow triangles and squares so you do not confuse the inlet markers with those for the ICW. This area was dredged in spring 2019 but by press time (summer 2019) there was evidence of shoaling near the can buoys. We advise boaters pass green can "47A" by 40 feet off, favoring the red side, then return to the channel center on either side of green can "47."

At Mile 323.6, you will pass under the **Holden Beach (NC 130) Bridge** (65-foot fixed vertical clearance). This area has more boating traffic each year, especially during spring and summer.

Dockage: The 8-slip Hewett Marine at Mile 322.5 may have space for you but this is primarily a service provider. Holden Beach Marina, just above Mile 323, is

primarily a dry-stack marina but they do reserve some a few of their 15 slips for transients. Gas and diesel fuel are available. You can walk to a grocery store and several restaurants. The nearby Provision Company (910-842-7205) has good seafood, a casual atmosphere, dockage and live music on weekends. The municipal Holden Beach Transient Docks is at Mile 324 with just three slips; call ahead.

Shallotte Inlet to Little River Inlet–ICW Mile 325 to Mile 341

At both Holden Beach and Ocean Isle Beach, long colonies of oceanfront houses (many on stilts) are on dredged canals (Florida-style) from the ICW to the ocean. Houses on the mainland side are more substantial, spaced farther apart and appear among the trees facing toward the ocean beach. In this area you need to stay in the middle of the channel because of rapid shoaling outside the channel.

The name Shallotte was derived from the original settlement name Charlotte, and is pronounced "sha-LOTE" (with a long "o" sound).

NAVIGATION: Use NOAA Chart 11534. The Shallotte River makes off northward at Mile 329.6 and carries 3- to 5-foot MLW depths to the rural town of Shallotte, NC. Call Coastal Machine and Welding on VHF Channel 16 for advice if you are considering venturing up the Shallotte River, which has a spring tidal range of 6 feet.

⚠️ On the ICW at Shallotte Inlet, boaters can expect a sudden lateral push from the current coming through the inlet during a rising tide. You will experience a "pull" toward the ocean during an ebb tide. This pushing and pulling is more likely to put you aground than any shoaling along the ICW channel. Keep in mind that one storm can completely change the inlet.

Shallotte Inlet was dredged in the spring of 2019 and was holding its depths at press time in summer 2019 (unlike Follys Inlet to the south). Stay in the middle of the channel, do not hug any buoys. Despite the recent dredging, we do not advise use of Shallotte Inlet, even with local knowledge. This inlet is used primarily by local small fishing boats.

The next 8 miles are straightforward. The **Ocean Isle (NC 904) Bridge** at Mile 333.7 is a fixed 65-foot span. Between the **Mannon C. Gore (Sunset Beach) Bridge** at Mile 337.9 and Little River (Mile 343) intersection with the ICW, stay in mid-channel to avoid the frequent shoals, which often crop up where various creeks cross to the ocean. Flashing green daybeacons "117" and "119" are out of the water, about 20 feet up on the bank at very low tide, so give both a wide berth. Furthermore, there is a shoal at flashing green daybeacon "117" on the opposite (mainland) side of the channel.

Dockage: Ocean Isle Marina & Yacht Club is located at Mile 335.5. This facility mostly caters to sportfishing boats and offers repairs, storage, rentals and fishing charters. They also sell gas and diesel fuel. There are no viable anchorage areas along this stretch.

Little River Inlet–ICW Mile 341

Just inside the South Carolina State Line, the ICW crosses Little River, which offers relatively easy and well-marked access to the ocean through the well-maintained channel between jetties. This inlet is deep, wide and busy, with a steady flow of tourist and fishing boats.

NAVIGATION: Use NOAA Chart 11534. Little River Inlet has jetties and is relatively stable. This inlet is used regularly by casino boats and head boats docked at Little River (SC). Casino boats are not required to have AIS transponders and many do not. There is a 5-foot shoal just off the east jetty that is awash at low tide. Note that the aids to navigation are frequently moved here to mark shifting shoals. Seek local knowledge before traversing the inlet. See the Inlet section at the front of this guide for more information about Little River Inlet.

Tip: Many cruisers rely heavily on their **autopilots**. When you are hit by one of the push or pull cross currents at an inlet, most autopilots will have trouble reacting to the quick heading change. Our Cruising Editors have found that disengaging the autopilot and hand steering through these inlet crossings makes it much easier to control course and stay within the marks.

Welcome to South Carolina!

The canals and dredged cuts of NC give way to the wide river mouths, large sounds and coastal inlets of SC. The natural waterways are deep to the banks of low, marshy grasslands that are backed by hummocks of trees, including stately moss-covered oaks. At low tide, the vast salt marshes will teem with bird life.

Beyond Charleston, there is a noticeable increase in tidal currents and heights. The tidal range runs about 8 feet and depths can change quickly. Shoaling is an issue in some areas, and strong tidal currents throughout the region can change depths overnight. This section of the ICW also has many bridges, including many fixed high-level (65-foot vertical clearance) bridges. All SC bridges monitor VHF Channel 09. Be aware of the South Carolina Department of Transportation (SC DOT) Hurricane Evacuation Rule (posted on most opening bridges): Draw and swing bridges will not open when wind reaches a sustained 25 knots or if mandatory evacuation is ordered. During periods of strong winds, these bridges may be closed. (Swing bridges are especially vulnerable to damage from high winds.) Boats with taller masts must run outside from Beaufort, NC, to Georgetown or Charleston, SC, both of which are safe, big ship inlets. Be sure to refer to the Waterway Explorer at waterwayguide.com for navigational alerts, tidal information and bridge restrictions and schedules.

Little River, SC

			Approach / Dockside Depth (reported)	VHF Channel Monitored	Transient Berths / Total Berths	Largest Vessel Accommodated		Groceries, Ice, Marine Supplies, Snacks	Repairs: Hull, Engine, Propeller	Gas / Diesel	Floating Docks		Lift (tonnage), Crane, Rail	Laundry, Pool, Showers, Courtesy Car	Min/Max Amps	Nearby: Grocery Store, Motel, Restaurant	Pump-Out Station

OCEAN ISLE						**Dockage**				**Supplies**		**Services**				
1. Ocean Isle Marina & Yacht Club 🖥 WiFi WG 335.5 910-579-6440	75	16	6/28	12/6	F	GD	IM		HEP	L15	30/100	LS	P	GR

🖥 Internet Access WiFi Wireless Internet Access WG Waterway Guide Cruising Club Partner ●onSpot dockside WiFi facility
See WaterwayGuide.com for current rates, fuel prices, web site addresses, and other up-to-the-minute information. *(Information in the table is provided by the facilities.)*

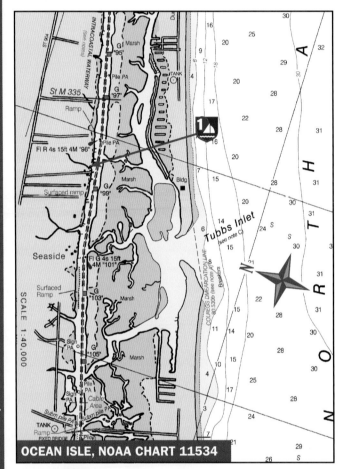

OCEAN ISLE, NOAA CHART 11534

Little River to Pine Island Cut–ICW Mile 341 to Mile 346

The village of Little River is a good stopping point for boats coming from the north or south. About a one-day run from Wrightsville Beach to the north and just before the long stretch of the ICW behind Myrtle Beach, it is the northern gateway to popular vacation resorts, which line the ocean beach for more than 20 miles as you head south. The mild climate has attracted permanent residents as well as vacationers. It also attracts anglers who come to patronize its charter fishing boats as well as golfers, who come to take on the 100-plus golf courses.

This area is very busy with small boats, especially on weekends and holidays.

NAVIGATION: Use NOAA Chart 11534. Use Myrtle Beach tide tables. About 1 mile above the junction of the ICW and the channel from the Little River Inlet, the route crosses the border from North Carolina into South Carolina (Mile 340.9). You can assume that you are in South Carolina when you make the turn below flashing red daybeacon "116."

Nixon Crossroads has two bridges: the **Nixon Crossroads Hwy. Bridge** at Mile 347.2 (fixed vertical clearance 65 feet) and the **Captain Archie Neil "Poo" McLauchlin Swing Bridge** (formerly Little River Swing Bridge) at Mile 347.3 with a closed vertical clearance of 7 feet. (The Little River Swing Bridge was renamed in 2018 after a lifelong resident.) The bridge opens on request. The Captain Poo Swing Bridge is old and frequently in need of repair. These two bridges denote the dividing line between fresh and saltwater. Southwest of the bridges, where the water becomes fresh, you need a freshwater fishing license to do any angling.

⚠ Keep an eye out for a "Danger Submerged Rock" sign just northeast of the Nixon Crossroads Hwy. Bridge, about one-third of the way out into the channel from the east (or ocean) side. Below the Captain Poo Swing Bridge, be careful of shoals along both sides of the waterway and submerged obstructions (likely pilings) on the ocean side for the next 0.25 mile.

Dockage: Cricket Cove Marina at Mile 345 sells fuel (both gas and diesel) and has one of the largest indoor dry storage facilities in the Myrtle Beach area. They are known for their excellent floating docks and the nearby Snooky's restaurant (843-249-5252).

Coquina Harbor, a large deepwater basin on the west side of the ICW at Mile 346 (green daybeacon "13") is home to three marinas serving transients and selling fuel: Coquina Yacht Club, Myrtle Beach Yacht Club and Lightkeepers Marina. Southbound boaters need to go slightly south of this entrance and come back to the north and enter at an angle. Do not try to cut the corner on this well-marked channel; it is shallow outside the entrance markers. Deep-draft vessels should call ahead for entrance information. A black and white lighthouse replica marks the harbor entrance. The entire harbor is surrounded by a three-mile boardwalk.

Transients are welcome at the popular Myrtle Beach Yacht Club at Coquina Harbor. They have a large pool, covered grilling area, laundry room and well-appointed restrooms and showers, plus a restaurant (the Officers Club), which you can visit as a guest of the marina manager. Other restaurants are close by. The marina also offers pump-out service at your slip as well as WiFi and the only fuel dock in Coquina Harbor selling both gas and diesel. Coquina Yacht Club and Lightkeepers Marina also have ample reserved transient space but it's a good idea to call ahead. By the way, don't be surprised if someone on a floating tiki bar motors over to offer you a drink after you dock!

Anchor Marina is located just before the Nixon Crossroads Bridge (Mile 347.2) on the south side of the ICW, with a 35-ton lift and complete repair capabilities plus a few transient slips. Harbourgate Resort & Marina is directly on the ICW at Mile 347.7 (between the bridges) with transient slips on floating docks, repairs

and gas and diesel fuel. A large shopping plaza with groceries and a West Marine is within walking distance.

Just south of the two bridges is North Myrtle Beach RV Resort and Marina with covered dry storage and 38 wet slips that can accommodate boats to 35 feet. Restrooms and showers, a pool and a fuel dock (with both gas and diesel) are available.

Anchorage: You can anchor in Calabash Creek on the mainland side of the junction between the ICW and Little River Inlet at Mile 342. At extreme low tides, the entrance bar carries around 5 feet. You will be subject to wakes from the ICW if you anchor toward the mouth of the creek. This is a pleasant spot otherwise, with a golf course on the wooded northern shore.

Give Calabash Creek red daybeacon "2A" (not the ICW red daybeacon "2," which features the distinctive ICW yellow triangle) a wide berth to avoid the shoal mentioned above. Then, turn toward the row of charted dolphins and drop the hook near the north side of the center of the river. The opposite shore, just upstream of the dolphins, has increased shoaling. Do not anchor near the entrance, as other vessels may arrive after you. Use two anchors in bad weather or if the anchorage is too crowded for normal swinging room. As always, show an anchor light. Shrimp boats and sightseeing vessels, whose wakes may disturb you, use the channel at night.

The NOAA chart shows a deceivingly inviting spot on the north side of the ICW channel at about Mile 342.5, near red daybeacon "6." Do not attempt to enter. It has shoaled badly and most of it is bare at low tide.

Captain Archie "Poo" McLauchlin (Little River) Swing Bridge

Little River, SC

LITTLE RIVER AREA		Largest Vessel Accommodated		VHF Channel Monitored	Transient Berths / Total Berths	Approach / Dockside Depth (reported)	Floating Docks	Gas / Diesel	Groceries, Ice, Marine Supplies, Snacks	Repairs: Hull, Engine, Propeller	Lift (tonnage), Crane, Rail	Min/Max Amps	Laundry, Pool, Showers, Courtesy Car	Pump-Out Station	Nearby: Grocery Store, Motel, Restaurant
				Dockage					**Supplies**			**Services**			
1. Cricket Cove Marina ▢ WiFi 345	843-249-7169	50	16/12	10/73	10/7	F	GD	IMS	–	–	30/100	LS	P	GMR
2. Coquina Yacht Club ▢ WiFi WG 346	843-249-9333	102	16/08	12/87	8/8	F	–	GI	–	–	30/50	LS	P	GMR
3. Myrtle Beach Yacht Club ▢ WiFi 346	**843-249-5376**	**85**	**16/14**	**10/153**	**7/10**	**F**	**GD**	**IMS**	**–**	**–**	**30/100**	**LPS**	**P**	**GMR**
4. Lightkeepers Marina ▢ onSpot 346	843-249-8660	120	16	10/125	6/6	F	–	IS	–	–	30/50	LPSC	P	R
5. Grande Harbour Marina	843-427-7934	48	16/14	–	9/6	F	G	IMS	HEP	L58	–	–	–	R
6. Anchor Marina WiFi 347	843-249-7899	48	16	3/100	7/6	F	–	I	HEP	L35	30/30	S	P	GMR
7. Harbourgate Resort & Marina ▢ WiFi 347.7	843-249-8888	150	16/12	15/100	8/6	F	GD	IMS	HEP	–	30/50	LPS	P	GMR
8. North Myrtle Beach RV Resort and Marina WiFi	843-390-4386	35	–	call/36	8/	–	GD	GIS	–	L	50/50	LPS	P	GR

▢ Internet Access WiFi Wireless Internet Access WG Waterway Guide Cruising Club Partner onSpot dockside WiFi facility
See WaterwayGuide.com for current rates, fuel prices, web site addresses, and other up-to-the-minute information. *(Information in the table is provided by the facilities.)*

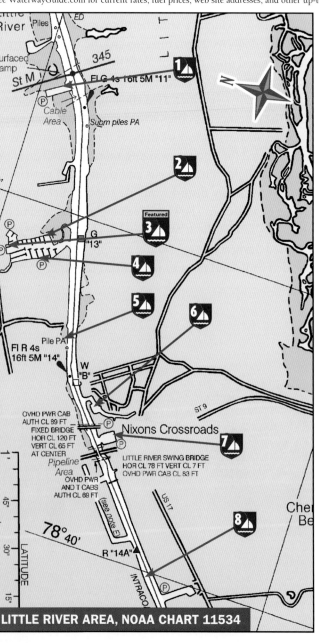

LITTLE RIVER AREA, NOAA CHART 11534

■ PINE ISLAND CUT TO WACCAMAW RIVER

Pine Island Cut to Myrtle Beach– ICW Mile 347 to Mile 354

Below Little River the ICW route enters a 26-mile-long high-banked land cut known as Pine Island Cut. For some unexplained reason, its name is not on the NOAA chart, labeled only as "Intracoastal Waterway."

Barefoot Landing at Mile 354 (North Myrtle Beach) is a large complex featuring two theaters, plus over a dozen restaurants and 100 plus specialty shops. This open air "mall" has ponds, bridges, turtles, alligators and birds in addition to shopping and dining.

NAVIGATION: Use NOAA Chart 11534. There is a tall white sign ("Danger Rocks") that marks the start and the ending of this stretch of the waterway. New development and clearing along this once-heavily wooded area give the illusion that the channel is wider than it really is. Be extremely careful to remain in the center of the channel.

⚠️ This stretch is known as the "Rock Pile" due to the rock ledges along both sides of the channel from ICW Mile 3352 to around Mile 349. A number of charted daybeacons mark the most worrisome of the rock ledges, many of which are visible only at low tide. Not all of them are marked, so keep a sharp watch.

Green daybeacon "19" is in the correct place at Mile 351.8, even though it appears to be too close to the middle of the cut due to clearing of the

MYRTLE BEACH YACHT CLUB

surrounding shoreline. Boaters should exercise extreme caution in this area.

Check on VHF Channels 13 or 16 to see if any tug or barge traffic is passing through the area. Stay in the center of the channel and follow the markers. It is wise to make a "Sécurité" call on VHF Channels 13 or 16. Keep to mid-channel and watch for shoaling at bends and places where drainage ditches enter the waterway. When passing or being passed by another boat, do not crowd too close to the edge of the channel. Keep an eye out for flotsam and snags. Numerous trees have toppled into the cut, and many woodpiles on the banks appear ready to follow. There is heavy development along much of this stretch.

The North Myrtle Beach Connector Bridge (officially the **Robert Edge Parkway Bridge**), with 65-foot fixed vertical clearance, crosses the ICW at Mile 349.1, while the **Barefoot Landing Swing Bridge** (31-foot closed vertical clearance) crosses at Mile 353.3. The bridgetender at the swing bridge monitors VHF Channel 09, and the bridge opens on signal. Two dolphins are on the edges of the channel on the east side of the bridge between the bridge and the docks. At approximately Mile 354 (upon reaching the No-Wake Zone), you can visit the Barefoot Landing shopping and entertainment

Little River, SC

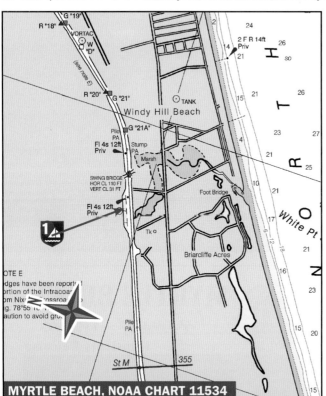

						MYRTLE BEACH		Dockage					Supplies				Services		

Column headers (diagonal): Largest Vessel Accommodated / VHF Channel Monitored / Transient Berths / Total Berths / Approach / Dockside Depth (reported) / Floating Docks / Groceries, Ice, Marine Supplies, Snacks / Gas / Diesel / Repairs: Hull, Engine, Propeller / Lift (tonnage), Crane, Rail / Laundry, Pool, Showers, Courtesy Car / Min/Max Amps / Pump-Out Station / Nearby: Grocery Store, Motel, Restaurant

MYRTLE BEACH			Dockage				Supplies				Services		
1. Barefoot Marina 🖥 📶 354	843-390-2011	150	16	32/142	8/12	F	GD	IS	–	–	30/50	LPS	P	GMR

🖥 Internet Access 📶 Wireless Internet Access **WG** Waterway Guide Cruising Club Partner *onSpot* dockside WiFi facility
See WaterwayGuide.com for current rates, fuel prices, web site addresses, and other up-to-the-minute information. *(Information in the table is provided by the facilities.)*

MYRTLE BEACH, NOAA CHART 11534

Mile 350.5 Rock Pile

complex. The development has expanded to both sides of the ICW above and below the swing bridge.

Dockage: Free daytime dockage is available at the dock at Barefoot Landing. Absolutely no overnight docking is allowed. This is a great place to stop for lunch or shopping. There is some current, and you will be docking with the current on the beam. There is dock in front of Greg Norman Australian Grille (843-361-0000).

Barefoot Marina is across the ICW from the shopping area. Access to a huge pool, private showers and well-priced laundry are among the perks here. The marina provides free transportation (by golf cart) to Barefoot Landing (1 mile walk across bridge), or you can dinghy across the river and tie up for even easier access.

Myrtle Beach Area–ICW Mile 354 to Mile 374

There has been almost continuous new shoreside development between Barefoot Landing at Mile 354 and about Mile 362, on both sides of the ICW. Golf is very popular here, with over 100 courses in the greater Myrtle Beach area. Single-family homes, docks and huge condominium developments surrounding golf courses line much of the ICW.

Supermarkets, marine supplies and restaurants are within walking distance of most marinas and are too numerous to list here, which is why there is no **Goin' Ashore** for Myrtle Beach. They do a better job than we can at visitmyrtlebeach.com.

NAVIGATION: Use NOAA Chart 11534. Just beyond Barefoot Landing, you will pass under the **Conway Bypass (U.S. 17) Twin Bridges** (65-foot fixed vertical clearance) at Mile 355.5. Several new markers have been placed in shoaling areas north of the Conway Bypass Bridge. Shoaling has been observed near the drainage ditches between the Conway Bypass Bridge and the U.S. 501 Hwy. Bridge and the SCL Railroad Bascule Bridge at Mile 365.4.

At Mile 356, cables for an overhead gondola giving access to a now defunct golf course across the ICW may look too low for comfort, but the clearance is at least 67 feet, as clearly charted. At Mile 357.5 is the **Grande Dunes Bridge** (65-foot fixed vertical clearance) spanning both sides of the ICW. Be careful not to confuse the small floating markers at the two entrances to the Marina at Grande Dunes just south of the bridge with ICW markers. Should you need it, Grand Strand Medical Center is located adjacent to the Grand Dunes development (843-692-1000).

Another fixed 65-foot high-rise bridge, the **Grissom Pkwy. Bridge**, is at Mile 360.5. At Mile 361.5 favor the green side and pass the dock by 30 feet for 7 feet MLW. At Mile 362.5, between green daybeacons "23" and "25," there is a very conspicuous shoal at another drainage ditch on the north side of the ICW. Additional markers are near Mile 363 to mark shoaling.

The fixed 65-foot **U.S. 501 Hwy. Bridge** crosses the ICW at Mile 365.4, along with a **SCL Railroad Bascule Bridge** (16-foot vertical clearance), which is usually open. ICW veterans and commercial skippers refer to these two bridges as the "Combination Bridges."

At Mile 366, numerous cypress stumps and a lone tree encroach into the north side of the ICW from the extensive stone riprap meant to prevent soil erosion around a new condominium development (one of many along this stretch). The 65-foot **Fantasy Harbor Bridge** at Mile 366.4 is the connector to access the defunct Freestyle Music Park.

⚠️ At Mile 369, there is shoaling to 4 feet MLW on the red side of the channel by the creek. Just stay in the middle of the channel for 11.5 feet MLW.

The **Socastee (SC 544) Swing Bridge** (which opens on request) at Mile 371.0 has an official closed vertical clearance of 11 feet, although its tide board shows less. It opens on request; use the southeast draw. The Socastee (pronounced "sock-a-stee") Swing Bridge is old and frequently in need of repair. Call the drawtender on VHF Channel 09 or by phone (843-302-8640) for up-to-date status. The No-Wake Zone on both sides of the swing bridge is locally enforced. If there is swift current flowing between the fixed bridge and the swing bridge, holding your position may be difficult.

Clearance as low as 60 feet has been observed at the **Socastee Hwy. Bridge** (Mile 371.3), despite the charted 65 feet of clearance. Sailboats with tall masts should check conditions carefully here.

⚠️ Expect ongoing construction at Mile 372, where the **Carolina Bays Pkwy. (SC 31) Bridge** is being erected. The anticipated completion date was summer 2019 but construction was ongoing at press time (summer 2019). Construction will necessitate some waterway restrictions/closures. These will be announced in the *Local Notice to Mariners*. Use caution when transiting this area, as various floating equipment will be in the vicinity throughout the project.

Dockage: The Marina at Grande Dunes is at Mile 357 with transient slips, gas and diesel and the on-site Anchor Café. Several dining options are within walking distance, as is a grocery store and other shopping.

At around Mile 368, a No-Wake Zone protects the two entrances to Hague Marina in a protected basin off the ICW. This is a well-kept boat yard (35-ton lift) that can locate hard-to-find parts and has a skillful service staff.

The family-oriented Osprey Marina, located at red daybeacon "26" (Mile 373), has fuel (both gas and diesel), floating transient slips, pump-out service and a dockmaster's building with showers, laundry and a well-stocked ship store. The entrance to the protected basin is well marked and has 10-foot MLW depths. This marina is an ICW favorite with consistently low fuel prices.

Once in a slip here, expect a welcome from dozens of turtles looking for a handout. This may be your first experience with "southern" turtles and yes, they do know how to beg. If you don't happen to have turtle food aboard, they are glad to accept hush puppies, crackers, pet food or anything else you throw their way.

Anchorage: The upper Waccamaw River is laden with great anchorages. This is one of the most rewarding areas to anchor south of the Chesapeake Bay, but bass-boat fishermen may sometimes come full-bore around the bends, so bear that in mind when picking your spot. Always use your anchor light. Also be aware the bugs can be troublesome in this area of the river. Screens are a must all the time.

Waccamaw River Area, SC

			Approach / Dockside Depth (reported)	Transient Berths / Total Berths	VHF Channel Monitored	Largest Vessel Accommodated	Groceries, Ice, Marine Supplies, Snacks	Gas / Diesel	Floating Docks	Repairs: Hull, Engine, Propeller	Lift (tonnage), Crane, Rail	Min/Max Amps	Laundry, Pool, Showers, Courtesy Car	Pump-Out Station	Nearby: Grocery Store, Motel, Restaurant

MYRTLE BEACH AREA			**Dockage**				**Supplies**			**Services**					
1. Marina at Grande Dunes 🖥 📶 357	843-315-7777	120	16/12	18/126	12/8	F	GD	GIMS	–	–	30/100	LPSC	P	GMR
2. Hague Marina 🖥 📶 368.2	843-293-2141	100	16/68	6/20	6/6	–	–	IM	HEP	L35	30/50	C	–	MR
3. Osprey Marina 🖥 📶 373	**843-215-5353**	**300**	**16**	**13/119**	**10/9**	**F**	**GD**	**GIMS**	**–**	**L10**	**30/50**	**LS**	**P**	**G**
WACHESAW LANDING														
4. Wacca Wache Marina 🖥 📶 383	843-651-2994	150	16/10	10/100	25/8	F	GD	IM	–	L10	30/100	S	P	R
BUCKSPORT RIVER														
5. Bucksport Plantation Marina & RV Resort 📶	843-397-5566	200	16/68	22/50	20/8	F	GD	IMS	E	–	30/50	LSC	P	–

🖥 Internet Access 📶 Wireless Internet Access 🆆🅶 Waterway Guide Cruising Club Partner ⬭onSpot dockside WiFi facility
See WaterwayGuide.com for current rates, fuel prices, web site addresses, and other up-to-the-minute information. *(Information in the table is provided by the facilities.)*

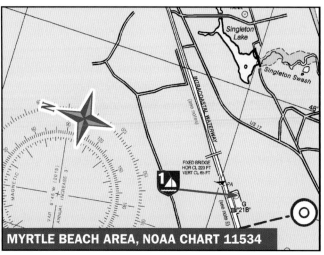

MYRTLE BEACH AREA, NOAA CHART 11534

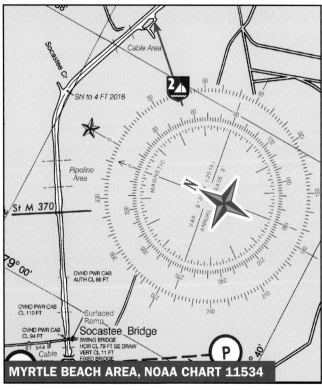

MYRTLE BEACH AREA, NOAA CHART 11534

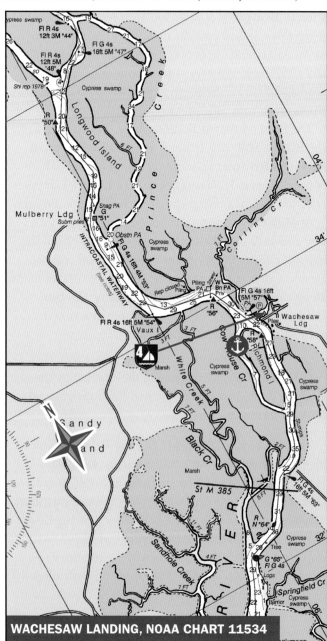

WACHESAW LANDING, NOAA CHART 11534

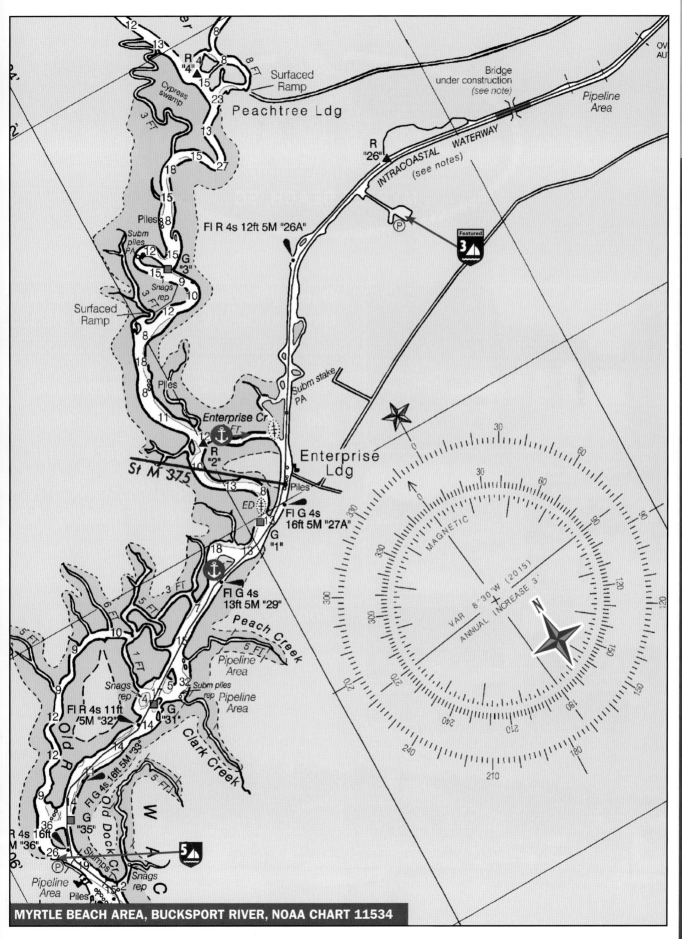

MYRTLE BEACH AREA, BUCKSPORT RIVER, NOAA CHART 11534

■ WACCAMAW RIVER–ICW MILE 374 TO MILE 444

When you talk to cruisers about their favorite rivers, there seem to be several that are always mentioned for their beauty: the Hudson, Tennessee, St. Johns and Waccamaw seem to be on everyone's list. The Waccamaw River, deep to its wooded banks, is the most scenic part of the ICW. Moss-draped cypresses line its side streams, and turtles sometimes sun themselves along the shore. Wildflowers of all descriptions grow in cypress stumps, and the water looks like tea. Your boat's bow will get a brown mustache, but it is easy to remove with lemon juice or a commercial cleaner. Ospreys abound and there are some eagles. Peaceful anchorages are plentiful.

Side Trip: Upriver to Conway

Conway is a beautiful and interesting side trip off 15 miles north of the ICW. The upper Waccamaw River, while not completely charted, is well marked. Stay to the outside of the bends and be prepared to face a speeding bass boat or two as you round the curves. Set your depth sounder alarm and hold down your speed. The **U.S. 501 Bypass Bridge** has a 65-foot fixed vertical clearance. The upriver bridge (**Main St. Bridge**) has no clearance gauge but charts show a charted 35 feet of vertical clearance. You'll find some eclectic shops and good cafés in this quaint southern town. Read more at cityofconway.com.

NAVIGATION: Use NOAA Chart 11534. At Enterprise Landing, Mile 375, the ICW enters the upriver waters of Waccamaw River. Note that at Mile 375.2, charted green daybeacon "1" appears on the red-marker side of the channel. Its location can be confusing until you realize that it is not an ICW marker, but actually the first in a series of aids that mark the upper Waccamaw River leading off to the north and to Conway. Although the ICW route continues downriver on the Waccamaw, the upriver 15-mile-long stretch to Conway carries 4.5-foot MLW depths. This section of the Waccamaw is highly trafficked by local boats.

Watch for flotsam along the entire length of the Waccamaw. It can vary from harmless bundles of reeds to a whole tree or a water-soaked log (or deadhead) with only the top exposed. Tugs with tows frequently announce their presence in the narrow and winding upper Waccamaw River with a "Sécurité" call on VHF Channel 16, or occasionally on VHF Channel 13.

Dockage: Conway has a city marina that mostly caters to local boats, usually in the 30-feet-or-less category. Call 843-248-1713 for details.

Anchorage: You can anchor upriver between the high-level U.S. 501 Bypass Bridge and the Main St. Bridge (35-foot fixed vertical clearance) in 5 to 6 feet MLW with good holding in mud. Make sure you stay out of the channel. From here you can dinghy to shore and the town of Conway.

Bucksport Area–ICW Mile 375

Enterprise Landing (Mile 375) was once the departure point for huge shipments of yellow pine and cypress. This was the domain of Capt. Henry Buck, who brought over 100 shipwrights from Bucksport, ME, to Bucksport, SC, where they built the 210-foot sailing ship *Henrietta*, which carried cargoes worldwide for over 30 years. Bucksport lies on a sharp bend where the Waccamaw River begins to widen, making navigation easier.

NAVIGATION: Use NOAA Chart 11534. There is a large, busy public boat ramp on the southeast side of the ICW at Enterprise Landing, north of green daybeacon "27A" (around Mile 375), so watch for small-boat traffic. There is also a series of private docks here extending toward the ICW channel. Slower boats will carry a fair current all the way to Georgetown (Mile 403) when leaving Enterprise Landing about 1.5 hours after high tide.

Dockage: The Bucksport Plantation Marina & RV Resort, located on the west side at the bend in the river at Mile 377 is easy to access and typically has good prices on gas and diesel. The on-site restaurant (Captain Buck) is open daily with an outdoor tiki bar and live music (seasonal). The marina also offers kayak rentals for exploring the more shallow waters in the area.

Anchorage: There is a good anchorage in mud at the oxbow just north of Enterprise Landing (Mile 374.8) at with at least 6 feet MLW and all-around protection. A better anchorage option is at Mile 375.5, in the deeper loop south of Enterprise Landing on the north side of the river, across from flashing green daybeacon "29." The holding is fair in 13 feet MLW near the southern part of the oxbow. This spot will hold 3 or 4 boats and may be full on a weekend. We recommend the use of an anchor trip line in case you snare a submerged stump or log and make sure your anchor is set. It is a short run up the river to the county launching ramp where you can dinghy your pet ashore.

One of the prettiest, most secluded anchorages anywhere is at Prince Creek, east of the ICW across from flashing red "44" at Mile 380.4. The north and south entrances both have approximately 15-foot MLW depths, but neither end offers protection from ICW wash. The lower end is wide enough to warrant only one anchor, but you may need two at the upper end or narrower parts. If you give the points of Prince Creek a wide berth, you can run the length of Longwood Island and rejoin the ICW south of Mulberry Landing at flashing green "53" (at Mile 381.7).

Just south of the northern entrance to Prince Creek (Mile 381.2), you may turn west off the ICW at flashing red "48" marking the entrance to Bull Creek. Give this marker a very wide berth.) This has better holding and more swing room than other anchorages on the Waccamaw River. Anchor in at least 15 feet MLW with a mud bottom. Go up past the first bend to avoid the wake of ICW traffic and anchor where depths suit. Hunters frequent this area in season, so prepare to awaken early to the sound of shooting.

Wachesaw Landing–ICW Mile 384

It is interesting to note that the address here is actually Murrells Inlet, SC, although the inlet is several miles away and not connected by water to the ICW. The village of Murrells Inlet is a popular fishing resort with many seafood restaurants and good shopping opportunities.

NAVIGATION: Use NOAA Chart 11534. South of Mile 385, the Waccamaw River becomes wider and straighter, making navigation easier, but it is important for slow boats to note that tidal currents here can have an impressive effect on your progress. Coming north during a wet spring, boats should respect the ebb tide, which is accelerated by spring rain runoff. Conversely, there may be no advantage on flood tide when offset by this runoff.

Dockage: Wacca Wache Marina at Wachesaw Landing, located 6 miles below Bucksport, provides a convenient fuel dock with both gas and diesel and transient berthing. The marina also has an on-site restaurant, Deck 383. Eat inside or outside on the deck. Closed on Monday.

Anchorage: A secluded anchorage is available at Mile 383.5 in Cow House Creek. This is somewhat exposed to the north and south but has excellent holding (7 to 12 feet MLW) and is very scenic. It is a great spot to watch the alligators and other wildlife. (We wouldn't recommend swimming.)

Pawleys Island to Butler Island– ICW Mile 388 to Mile 396

Pawleys Island at Mile 388 on the ICW is known for its beaches, sand dunes and hammocks. The original Pawleys Island Hammocks has been in the business of producing rope hammocks since 1889 and that's still their mainstay, along with fabric hammocks and hammock-inspired swings. See more at pawleysislandhammocks.com. At the opposite end of this stretch is Butler Island (near Mile 396), a scenic natural area.

NAVIGATION: Use NOAA Chart 11534. There are no special alerts along this route, other than two long private community docks that extend into the channel in the Butler Island area where the river narrows and the ICW channel turns around the east side of the island. The ends of both docks are marked with flashing white lights.

Dockage: At flashing green daybeacon "71" (Mile 388) is the entrance to Reserve Harbor Yacht Club (Morningstar Marina), which is part of an upscale development near Pawleys Island. The location gives you access to the beach, river and pool all in the same day as well as resort amenities. A full-service restaurant and courtesy car round out the offerings.

To the south at Mile 394, Heritage Plantation Marina is directly on the ICW at Pawleys Island. This friendly marina is part of an upscale gated community. They may have space for you; call ahead.

Anchorage: A good spot to drop the hook is at Mile 389 in Thoroughfare Creek, which carries 14-foot minimum depths. Turn up Thoroughfare Creek at flashing green daybeacon "73" and anchor in 10 to 13 feet MLW with a sandy bottom. Be aware that Thoroughfare Creek is heavily used by locals on the weekends and it may not be the same tranquil spot it is during the week.

Schooner Creek at Mile 393.1 has depths of at least 8 feet MLW with protection in all directions. Enter in mid-channel, proceeding up to where the creek widens slightly just before the sharp bend to starboard.

At Mile 395 you can anchor in at least 9 feet MLW in Jericho Creek, with good holding in mud. (The creek has 8-foot charted MLW depths at the entrance but deepens as you proceed.) Turn into Jericho Creek at Mile 394.9 before flashing green daybeacon "83."

Cruisers have reported a quiet night at anchor within 100 yards of shore at Butlers Island while northwest winds are gusting up to 30 knots. To reach this spot, pass green can 1 to port, and then proceed into the unnamed cove between Contentment Island and Butlers Island. There is good holding in 15- to 30-feet MLW depths but use an anchor trip-line near the island. If you anchor on the channel side north of Butler Island, you will be jostled by wakes from fast-moving boats.

On the north end of Butler Island, there is an underwater high voltage cable crossing. It is indicated on the chart as a cable area, and there are signs ashore, but they are difficult to read. Avoid this area when choosing your anchorage.

◼ GEORGETOWN AREA

This stretch of the Waccamaw River, which includes Georgetown, has become increasingly popular. There has been a proliferation of tour boats of many types–even amphibious craft–along the river and around the inlet at Winyah Bay. There are island tours, plantation tours and wilderness tours. Even vessels that create minimum wake should give these tour boats a slow pass.

NAVIGATION: Use NOAA Chart 11534.

⚠ At press time (summer 2019), the Charleston District U.S. Army Corps of Engineers was dredging parts the ICW between Georgetown and Charleston with an estimated completion date of the end of 2019. Areas to be dredged include Breach Inlet, Capers Inlet, Graham Creek, Awendaw Creek, Matthews Cut, South Santee, Fourmile Creek, North Santee, Little Crow Island, Minim Creek and South Island Ferry. Keep in mind that the information presented in this guide was compiled prior to the anticipated dredging. For up-to-date depths and conditions, check the *Local Notice to Mariners* and Waterway Explorer (waterwayguide.com).

Georgetown Harbor–Mile 403

NAVIGATION: Use NOAA Chart 11534. Use the Charleston Tide Table. For high tide, add 1 hour and 25 minutes; for low tide, add 2 hours and 9 minutes. The high-level **Lafayette (U.S. 17) Bridge** (65-foot fixed vertical clearance) at Mile 402.1 is a short distance above Georgetown on the Waccamaw River.

After passing under the bridge, take the time to sort out the markers leading to the Georgetown Harbor entrance channel. Four bodies of water converge here, below the big shoal extending south from Waccamaw Point: Waccamaw River, Winyah Bay, Great Pee Dee River and Georgetown's Sampit River. The buoys can be confusing. Near the junction of the four bodies of water is flashing red daybeacon "W." Read your chart carefully and do not cut behind this daybeacon; rather, leave it to starboard, as it sits in 5 feet MLW.

The channel into Georgetown Harbor is wide and deep with at least 9-foot MLW depths. Once off the ICW and heading toward the harbor, the channel for yachts and small commercial craft bears off to starboard just before flashing red "S." The Sampit River turns abruptly to port, and the Factory Basin is straight ahead. If your intention is to visit Georgetown, take the channel to starboard. Exercise some care and do not cut too close to the starboard shore, as it is infested with broken and submerged pilings. Once abeam of the first docking area, the harbor is relatively clear of obstacles.

The upper reaches of the small, but attractive Sampit River are readily open to exploration. Beyond the twin-span 65-foot fixed bridge (**U.S. Hwy. 17 Bridge**), the river is unmarked and uncharted.

Waccamaw River, Winyah Bay, SC

		Dockage					Supplies			Services				
		Largest Vessel Accommodated	VHF Channel Monitored	Approach / Dockside Depth (reported)	Transient Berths / Total Berths	Floating Docks	Gas / Diesel	Groceries, Ice, Marine Supplies, Snacks	Repairs: Hull, Engine, Propeller	Lift (tonnage), Crane, Rail	Min/Max Amps	Laundry, Pool, Showers, Courtesy Car	Pump-Out Station	Nearby: Grocery Store, Motel, Restaurant
PAWLEYS ISLAND														
1. Reserve Harbor Yacht Club ▢ WiFi 388.2	843-235-8262	60	16/68	10/50	6/6	F	GD	IS	–	L5	30/50	PS	P	GMR
2. Heritage Plantation Marina ▢ WiFi 394	843-237-3650	200	16/16	call/40	30/30	F	–	–	–	–	15/50	LS	P	GR
GEORGETOWN AREA														
3. Georgetown Landing Marina ▢ WiFi 402	843-546-1776	200	16/10	25/171	19/17	F	GD	IMS	–	–	30/100	LS	–	MR
4. Hazzard Marine ▢ onSpot .9 N of 403	843-527-3625	200	16	5/37	10/9	F	GD	IMS	HEP	L50	30/50		P	GMR
5. Georgetown Dry Stack Marina ▢ WiFi 1 N of 403	843-546-1700	80	16/05	call/15	10/9	F	GD	IMS	–	L	30/50	S	–	GMR
6. Harborwalk Marina, Georgetown SC ▢ onSpot	843-546-4250	200	16/68	30/40	12/10	F	GD	IM	–	–	30/100	LS	P	GMR
WINYAH BAY														
7. Belle Isle Marina – Georgetown, SC/Winyah Bay WiFi	843-546-8491	55	16/09	10/80	5/7	F	GD	IMS	–	–	30/50	LPSC	P	R

▢ Internet Access WiFi Wireless Internet Access WG Waterway Guide Cruising Club Partner onSpot dockside WiFi facility
See WaterwayGuide.com for current rates, fuel prices, web site addresses, and other up-to-the-minute information. *(Information in the table is provided by the facilities.)*

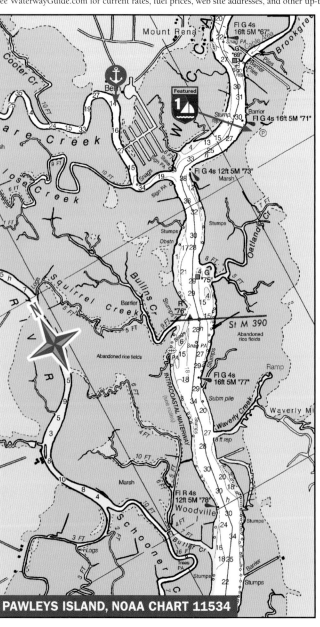

PAWLEYS ISLAND, NOAA CHART 11534

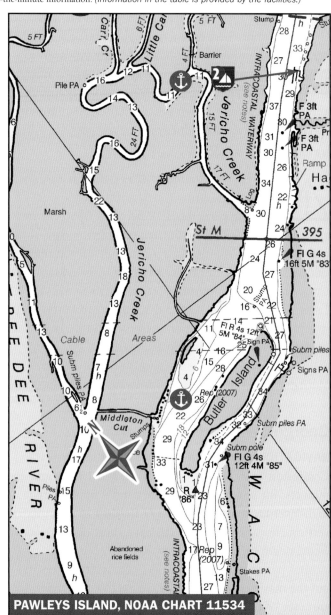

PAWLEYS ISLAND, NOAA CHART 11534

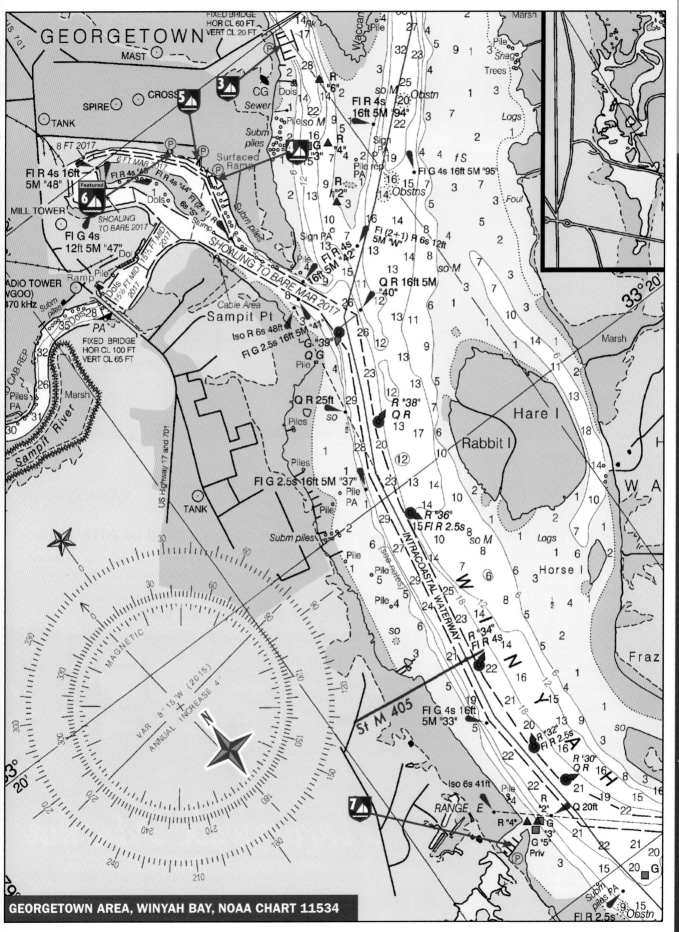

GEORGETOWN AREA, WINYAH BAY, NOAA CHART 11534

Harborwalk Marina

The Great Pee Dee River channel is marked with red and green daybeacons leading upriver toward Georgetown Landing Marina, just before the **Lafayette (U.S. 17) Hwy. Bridge** with 20-foot fixed vertical clearance at Mile 402. The Coast Guard station at Georgetown is next to the marina.

Dockage: The 171-slip Georgetown Landing Marina on the Great Pee Dee River is a good option when the Georgetown Harbor is full. Note that it is somewhat exposed, which can make the long face dock uncomfortable in a south wind. The walk into town is almost a mile but the marina does have loaner bicycles.

All the facilities in this area sell gas and diesel, but Hazzard Marine in Georgetown Harbor is the only haul-out facility (50-ton lift) between the Myrtle Beach area, 40 miles to the north, and Charleston, 65 miles to the south. The marina can accommodate vessels to 200 feet. The Georgetown Dry Stack Marina next door accepts transients if space is available with showers, a tackle shop/ship store and free WiFi.

The well-regarded Harborwalk Marina is directly adjacent to Georgetown's business district. Floating docks with shore power and WiFi are available as well as climate-controlled restrooms/showers and laundry facilities. They can accommodate vessels up to 200 feet. The marina is just a short walk from the restaurants, museums and shopping. The knowledgeable and helpful staff can help you decide what to explore. Independent Seafood Market will likely be at the top of the list for fresh shrimp and/or fish to take home (1 Cannon St., 843-546-6642).

Anchorage: There are several local boats anchored here, but there is still room for transients to anchor. The bottom is deep mud in this location; however, if you set your anchor well in 10 feet MLW, it can be delightful. Shore access is easy thanks to the two public docks along the Harborwalk. The docks will accommodate anything from a dinghy to a 60-footer, but both have signs indicating for daytime use only, which is strictly enforced. One is at the south end of the walk behind the clock tower at Lafayette Park, and the other is in the middle of the walk at Francis Marion Park (next to the SC Maritime Museum).

Winyah Bay Area–ICW Mile 403 to Mile 410

NAVIGATION: Use NOAA Chart 11534. For boats making the ocean run along the coast, Winyah Bay is the first shipping inlet south of the Cape Fear River and Southport, NC. If you bypass Georgetown to go down Winyah Bay, note that the aids to navigation at the junction of Georgetown's harbor channel and the ICW are colored and numbered as from seaward. Three miles below Georgetown at Mile 406, the ICW route leaves the Winyah Bay ship channel, bears off to the south and continues down the well-marked Western Channel to just past Mile 410. The ICW marking system resumes at the Western Channel. Currents in the Western Channel are strong–up to 3 knots on the ebb. Don't be tempted to anchor here.

It pays to watch the tide here and enter or leave with the current. Low-powered boats headed north should leave Georgetown 1 hour after slack tide, before flood at Charleston, to carry a fair current up the Waccamaw River. The Western Channel to the inlet, although unmarked beyond the ICW turn into the Estherville-Minim Creek Canal, is true to its charted depths.

If the Winyah Bay Entrance is your goal, follow the main shipping channel beginning at Frazier Point. If you should end up in the wrong channel, note the shoal between the two channels and be cautious. There are swift currents and whirlpools on the ebb tide. The tremendous volume of water that passes through the jetties at this entrance should not be underestimated. Use caution, especially on the ebb tide with opposing winds. To make matters worse, much of the south jetty is visible only at low water. Use extreme caution. See the Inlet section in the front of this guide for more information about Winyah Bay Entrance.

Dockage: The marked entry channel to Belle Isle Marina is just to the west of the ICW at Mile 406. This marina, however, was closed at press time (summer 2019) for redevelopment. The marina reported an anticipated completion date of the end of 2019.

Anchorage: You can drop the hook in Western Channel behind the unnamed marshy island at the north end of the Estherville-Minim Canal in 10 feet MLW with good holding. There is a strong current, but if you drag it would be in the current direction, not toward the shore. Expect traffic in the morning in season.

GOIN' ASHORE: **GEORGETOWN, SC**

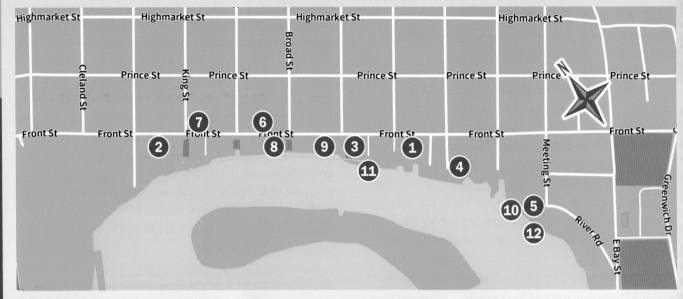

SERVICES		
1	Visitor Information	
ATTRACTIONS		
2	Kaminski House Museum	
3	Rice Museum	

SHOPPING		
4	Independent Seafood Market	
5	Stormy Seas Seafood	
DINING		
6	Alfresco Georgetown Bistro	
7	Aunny's Restaurant	

8	The River Room
9	Thomas Café
MARINAS	
10	Georgetown Dry Stack Marina
11	Harborwalk Marina
12	Hazzard Marina

Georgetown's entire downtown is a National Historic District, where visitors can stroll along the live oak-shaded streets and adjacent neighborhoods, admiring the city homes of former plantation owners. There are 63 downtown homes on the National Historic Register. The town and its residents welcome transients with a wealth of services, including good restaurants and interesting shopping.

The beauty of the town is largely due to W.D. Morgan, a New Yorker whose family moved to Georgetown before the Civil War. Among his many accomplishments as mayor was the planting of the live oaks along the city streets a century ago. He continually advanced ideas to improve Georgetown, including keeping the harbor dredged, digging a deep water channel from the inlet and building rock jetties at the entrance to Winyah Bay to keep a sandbar from blocking the inlet. The jetty construction was completed in 1904.

Attractions: The Visitors Center and Chamber of Commerce are at 531 Front St. (843-546-8436), next to Harborwalk Marina. They have everything you need on information about the area. A Trolley Tour leaves from

814 Front St. to tour the revitalized downtown. The narrator provides a good story of the town's history. The marinas can supply the packets of information when you register for dockage.

Aside from strolling along the tree-lined streets enjoying the pre-Revolutionary and antebellum homes, a visit to the Kaminski House Museum should be part of your itinerary. Built in 1769 by a local merchant, it is now used as a teaching tool for the area's history. Another must-stop is the Rice Museum (originally the Old Market built in 1842) at the opposite end of Front St., which includes a 45-minute guided tour about the local rice culture, featuring the 1842 Clock Tower and the Kaminski Hardware Building. The third floor of the Rice Museum houses the skeleton of America's oldest known vessel, *Brown's Ferry,* an 18th-century all-purpose freighter. The whole history of this area is linked to rice, and there is no better and more enjoyable way to find out all about that than to tour the Rice Museum.

Your next stop should be the South Carolina Maritime Museum at 729 Front St. (843-520-0111), which features photographs, documents, artifacts and

interactive exhibits related to South Carolina's rich and remarkable maritime history. Exhibits include the prized Fresnel lens of the old North Island lighthouse, a photographic representation of the chronology of the Port of Georgetown and (coming soon) a model of the *Henrietta,* the largest wooden ship ever built in South Carolina. The ship was 201 feet long and the top of her mainmast was 147 feet above the deck.

The third weekend in October is a great time to be in Georgetown for the Georgetown Wooden Boat Show, hosted by the Georgetown Harbor Historical Association (woodenboatshow.com). Proceeds go toward adding exhibits to the maritime museum.

Shopping: For groceries, the Piggly Wiggly is at 1620 Highmarket St. A Food Lion is a little north of town at 1045 N. Fraser St. About one-mile from the waterfront is a Circle K convenience store (315 Church St., 843-527-1161) where you can find a limited selection of basic grocery items.

Stroll along Front St. to shop antiques and gift shops, or to find a hairdresser like Palmetto Trendz at 602 Front St. (843-527-7888), or a barber at Cuttin' Edge Barber Shop (835 Front St., 843-546-9939). Georgetown has its own shrimp dock and fishing fleet, so freshly caught seafood is available at both Independent Seafood Market (1 Cannon St., 843-546-6642) and Stormy Seas Seafood (130 S. Meeting St., 843-545-8430). They are located along the waterfront between the marinas.

Dining: The River Room (801 Front St., 843-527-4110) offers casual southern coastal dining at its finest. For the best down-home cooking in town, try Aunny's Restaurant (926 Front St., 843-461-4750). Thomas Café (703 Front St., 843-546-7776) is great for either breakfast or lunch.

Another favorite is Alfresco Georgetown Bistro (812 Front St., 843-344-3869), which specializes in Italian cuisine and seafood.

Visit historicgeorgetownsc.com for more shopping and dining options.

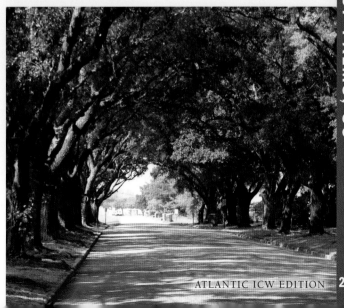

■ TO ISLE OF PALMS

Estherville-Minim Canal to McClellanville–ICW Mile 410 to Mile 430

NAVIGATION: Use NOAA Chart 11534. The ICW makes a sharp departure southward from the Western Channel at flashing red daybeacon "2" into the Estherville-Minim Creek Canal. Careful navigation is necessary to ensure that you take the desired route.

⚠️ Shoaling was observed in summer 2019 at the entrance to the Estherville-Minim Creek Canal (Mile 410). Split flashing red "2" and the shore for 17-foot MLW depths. After the entrance, it shoals to 7.5 MLW for the next 0.5 mile. Stay centered in the channel when entering the canal. This area was scheduled to be dredged by year end 2019.

At Mile 411.5, the **Estherville-Minim Canal Swing Bridge** is open to vessel traffic except when a vehicle needs to cross (infrequent). Watch for flashing yellow lights on sign. In the open position, the floating bridge rests against the east bank of the river. Continuing south on the ICW, the channel turns to starboard just past Mile 415 and immediately crosses Minim Creek, where it enters a long cut with shoal edges.

⚠️ Several shoal areas have been observed in the ICW between flashing red "4" (Mile 415) and flashing red "22" (Mile 420 at Fourmile Creek Canal). This area was scheduled to be dredged by year end 2019.

Areas of particular concern on this stretch at press time (summer 2019) included the following.

- Mile 415–The charted shoal just north of flashing red daybeacon "12" has been observed to be bare at low tide and very close to the channel. In general, stay off all marks 50 to 100 feet and stay in the channel.
- Mile 418–Expect 7-feet MLW at the intersection of Fourmile Creek Canal and the North Santee River, especially between red daybeacon "16" and flashing red "18," where there is a shoal on the red side. You will find an additional 2 feet in depth by favoring the green side rather than the middle of channel when as little as 20 feet off the centerline. Take this section with at least 2 feet of tide.

- Mile 420–The currents are strong across the opening of Fourmile Creek Canal at the South Santee River. It is easy to get set to one side or the other and into shallows. Note your course on your chartplotter for a direct path to the opposite entrance to the ICW so you can crab along if needed to maintain your course. Expect 7 to 8 feet MLW. Generally, the flood tidal current runs north.

Anchorage: Although it has a good deal of tidal current, Minim Creek is the best anchorage for many miles to come. Either side of the creek has good holding, but the west side just below Mile 415 offers excellent protection with 8- to 20-foot MLW depths and all-around protection. You will have to dodge the crab pots and bugs will come visit at dusk but your reward will be a beautiful sunset and sunrise. The east side has 8- to 11-foot depths with excellent holding in mud and protection from all but north and southeast.

The anchorage on the west side of the South Santee River at Mile 420.1 (behind Brown Island) has 10- to 12-foot depths, a sand and mud bottom and excellent holding. Crab pots usually line both sides of the river. Several channels lead off the ICW just past Mile 425, but don't be tempted; depths are suspect for anchoring.

McClellanville to Andersonville–ICW Mile 430 to Mile 444

This area between Charleston and Georgetown was one of the primary territories for Francis Marion (also known as "the Swamp Fox") during the American Revolution. He earned a great reputation for harrying the British and then disappearing into the swamps. Several forays by the British to capture him ended in failure.

If time permits, do visit the small community of McClellanville. There is a nice museum right by the fire tower, a few shops and a cruiser favorite, TW Graham & Co. (810 Pinckney St., 843-887-4342) for grilled and fried seafood. The town also boasts an old Forest Service building designed by Frank Lloyd Wright and some amazing live oak trees draped with Spanish moss. Near the marina is the Deerhead live oak tree, which is over 150 feet tall and 36 feet in circumference and estimated to be over 1,000 years old.

NAVIGATION: Use NOAA Chart 11518. From Mile 436, the ICW follows another land cut for about 10 miles. On the mainland side Francis Marion National Forest Recreation Area offers picnic areas, campsites and a boat ramp, but no facilities for transient boaters.

McClellanville Waterfront

Shrimp boats have been observed using a surprisingly well-marked channel across from Jeremy Creek to access Five Fathom Creek (Mile 430). If you want to explore the Cape Romain area, it is an easy run to the ocean on this route.

⚠️ There are several shallow stretches of water on the ICW from Mile 429.5 to Mile 439. In May 2019, the shallowest depths observed was 4.2 MLW by flashing red "40" (Mile 433).

In general, stay off all marks by 100 feet, go slow and test the depths side to side. Use your chartplotter to maintain that 100-foot line off marks when between marks. A deviation of 30 feet can result in a change in depth of up to 2 feet. The bottom is soft mud. With a strong east wind, the water can be a foot higher, with a west wind, a foot lower. Keep in mind that Mathews Cut was scheduled to be dredged by year end 2019. Areas of particular concern on this stretch at press time (summer 2019) included the following.

- Mile 430–Shoaling has been reported near flashing green "35." There is another spot of severe shoaling just to the south at green daybeacon "37," where 2 feet MLW was observed on the red side opposite the entrance to Town Creek. The deeper water is on the green side.
- Mile 431.6–A depth of 4 feet MLW has been reported between flashing red "38" and red daybeacon "42."

- Mile 435.7–Pass 120 feet off flashing red "48" and green daybeacon "47" for 7 feet MLW. Do not hug either marker, as there is shoaling by each side; stay in the middle.
- Mile 439–Shoaling is coming from both sides where Graham Creek intersects the ICW. Favor the red side north of red daybeacon "64" and the green side to the south for 8 feet MLW.

Dockage: The 8-slip Leland Oil Company in McClellanville provides dockage and sells gas and diesel. Many boats emulate the shrimpers by rafting up, particularly during the annual shrimp festival each spring. Note that major shoaling has been observed across channel just south of this location. Proceed with caution.

Anchorage: There are many uncharted side creeks, but these are of questionable depths for the tidal range. Five Fathom Creek near McClellanville is pristine. Leave the ICW at green daybeacon "25" and proceed south about 0.50 mile on Town Creek. When you get to Five Fathom Creek turn to port (north) and go up Five Fathom a hundred yards or more to anchor in 15 feet MLW. This gets you out of the main channel and is a wonderful anchorage. (Do have your bug screens ready.) Like all creeks in this area, this creek is deep with strong currents. Be prepared for a rather eerie experience as the shrimpers come and go; you can only see the marsh grass and not the creeks they are in so they appear to be moving through the grass.

McClellanville, SC

MCCLELLANVILLE			Dockage				Supplies		Services			
	Largest Vessel Accommodated	VHF Channel Monitored	Transient Berths / Total Berths	Approach / Dockside Depth (reported)	Floating Docks	Gas / Diesel	Groceries, Ice, Marine Supplies, Snacks	Repairs: Hull, Engine, Propeller	Lift (tonnage), Crane, Rail	Min/Max Amps	Laundry, Pool, Showers, Courtesy Car	Pump-Out Station	Nearby: Grocery Store, Motel, Restaurant
1. Leland Oil Company WiFi .5 N of 430	843-887-3641	75	16/68	6/8	10/6	F	GD	I	–	–	30/50	LS	–	GR

🖥 Internet Access WiFi Wireless Internet Access WG Waterway Guide Cruising Club Partner ●onSpot dockside WiFi facility

See WaterwayGuide.com for current rates, fuel prices, web site addresses, and other up-to-the-minute information. *(Information in the table is provided by the facilities.)*

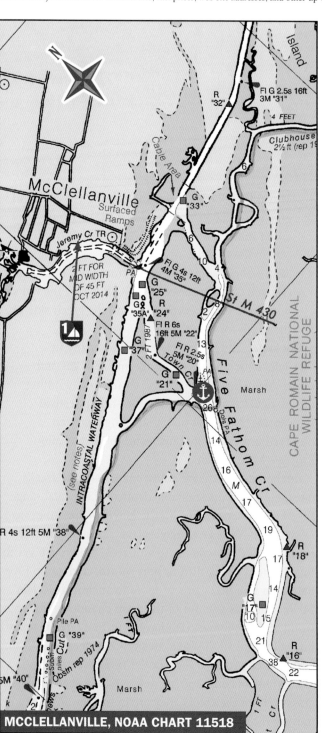

MCCLELLANVILLE, NOAA CHART 11518

Proceeding 2 miles south on Five Fathom Creek will afford another anchorage spot at its intersection with Bull River. Depths vary, so sound your way in.

> There are many "lost" crab pots and lines on the bottom in **Five Fathom Creek.** Use an anchor retrieving line and have a wire cutter ready as some lines are steel.

You can anchor east of the ICW at Mile 435.6 in Awendaw Creek, opposite flashing red daybeacon "48." Go around the bend heading east and anchor in the 12-foot MLW spot shown on the NOAA chart. The bottom is sand, and the anchorage is protected from waves but not wind. There is space for several boats. Your boat position will reverse in a good current. This is convenient for staging for the two shallow areas: Isle of Palms (to the south) and McClellanville (to the north) since it's hard to get through both areas the same day on a high tide. There is shore access for pets at an oyster pile at the eastern end of the anchorage at any time other than high tide.

At Mile 439 (Graham Creek), there is good holding in sand with protection from waves and slightly higher elevation on the west-southwest bank for reasonable wind protection. Approach the creek near red daybeacon "64" and proceed south down Graham Creek. Anchor midstream in 10-foot MLW depths or better up to the bend.

Andersonville to Isle of Palms– ICW Mile 444 to Mile 456

NAVIGATION: Use NOAA Chart 11518. At about Mile 444, the area of Andersonville appears with a development on the mainland side. For the next mile or more, a wake is undesirable, so use caution. This stretch of the ICW is also subject to shoaling at the edges, so it is prudent to stay to mid-channel. Use caution in the area of the ferry docks at Mile 445.5; there is a lot of activity around them. The area between Miles 448 and 455 is subject to shoaling; however this part of the waterway was dredged in 2019.

⚠ At Mile 454.9, a 10-inch piling remnant was observed barely above the water at mid-tide inside the channel and before flashing red "108." Proceed with caution.

Anchorage: You will find several lovely spots to drop the hook along the way to Charleston Harbor. Price Creek, at Mile 448, is a local favorite for weekend and holiday outings. Feel your way in near flashing red daybeacon "86," below the islet blocking the entrance (submerged at high tide), then proceed a short distance to a suitable spot in 15- to 20-foot MLW depths with a sandy bottom. Proceeding seaward, this winding creek widens into Price Inlet.

Because of its proximity to Capers Island State Park, Whiteside Creek at Mile 451.1 is a favorite overnight anchorage for skippers who are ready for an ocean swim or a hike along the beach. Whiteside Creek can get extremely congested during the spring and fall. It is too deep for anchoring at the bend, and shoals unpredictably upriver of the bend. Depths are generally shallower before the bend than shown on the NOAA chart. Take the dinghy to the park dock at the western tip of Capers Island to visit the state park. A trail from the dock leads to an ocean beach after passing an impounded lake, which is home to numerous alligators.

Dewees Creek (Mile 455) is wide and deep, but the current flows swiftly, and a commuter boat from the mainland serves the island residents, so bear these things in mind when dropping the hook.

On the opposite side of the ICW at Mile 455 is an anchorage behind Big Hill Marsh with deep (12 to 17 feet) water and protection from wind and wakes from all but the east. To reach this anchorage, you must navigate around the east side of Big Hill Marsh by turning to port at green daybeacon "109" and following the deep-water channel around. Dewees Island is privately owned, so cruising boaters should not venture above the high-water line while walking on the beach.

If you take the unnamed branch to the north 0.25 mile in and go around the bend to the west, you'll find a nice anchoring spot in 20 to 30 feet MLW with good holding in mud. Or, you can proceed up Dewees Creek to Hamlin Sound (north of Eagle Island) and anchor in 15 to 25 feet MLW with a mud bottom.

■ NEXT STOP

Charleston is another 35 miles south along a straight dredged cut with vast marshlands to the east. Watch for persistent shoaling, especially where natural creeks cross the ICW. Plan to stop and enjoy this historic and beautiful city with its burgeoning yachting facilities.

We Always Travel Together

SEA*iq* Pilot

Charleston, SC to St. Marys, GA

■ CHARLESTON AREA ■ STONO RIVER TO OSSABAW SOUND, SC ■ ST. CATHERINES SOUND TO ST. MARYS, GA

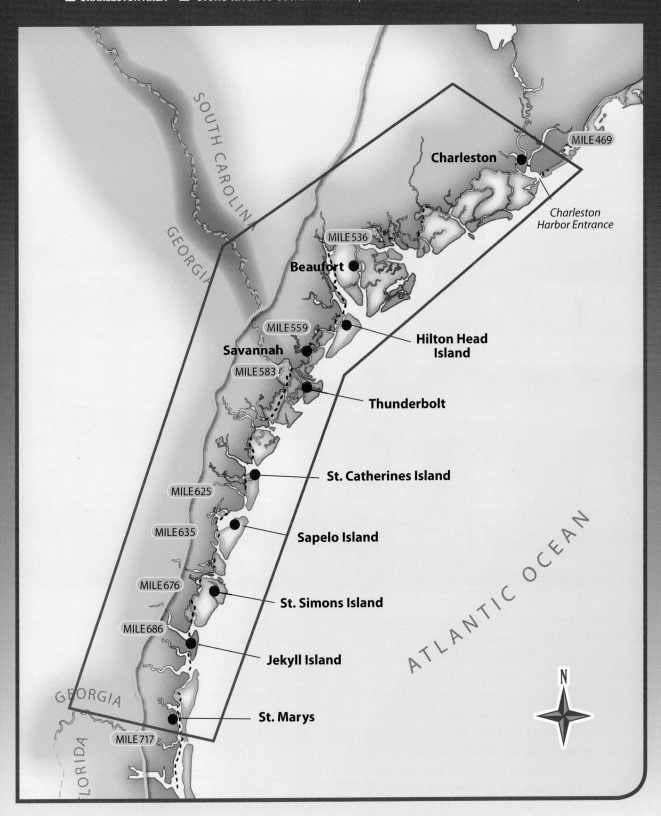

SOUTH CAROLINA

GEORGIA

Charleston

MILE 469

Charleston Harbor Entrance

MILE 536

Beaufort

MILE 559

Hilton Head Island

Savannah

MILE 583

Thunderbolt

St. Catherines Island

MILE 625

MILE 635

Sapelo Island

MILE 676

St. Simons Island

MILE 686

Jekyll Island

GEORGIA

St. Marys

MILE 717

FLORIDA

ATLANTIC OCEAN

N

Visit Waterway Explorer at waterwayguide.com

Charleston, SC to St. Marys, GA

A long the 244 miles of the ICW from Charleston, SC (Mile 469) to Florida's state line (just south of St. Marys, GA, at Mile 714), the route departs from the canals and dredged cuts common in North Carolina. Instead, expect to wend your way across wide river mouths, through sounds and past coastal inlets.

The low, marshy grassland appears almost pristine in this area: You can cruise for 10 miles without seeing any signs of human habitation. The landscape's predominant feature is marshland, backed by woods or hummocks of trees. In some places, the marsh gives way to wooded banks, some with stately moss-covered oaks. You will also pass some big sand dunes and even catch occasional glimpses of the Atlantic Ocean.

Be prepared for a rather eerie experience as the shrimpers come and go; you can only see the marsh grass and not the creeks they are in so they appear to be moving through the grass.

At low tide, the vast salt marshes and exposed fringes of mud teem with bird life. You might see dolphins playing alongside your boat or cruising along with your bow wake. You also might catch glimpses of the majestic great blue herons that patrol the water's edge, hunting for fish.

Historic District waterfront of Savannah at twilight. Each year, the Historic District attracts millions of visitors, who enjoy its eighteenth- and nineteenth-century architecture and green spaces.

Cruising Conditions

This portion of the ICW is made up of natural waterways, which are usually deep to the banks. This results in straightforward piloting. It is a good idea to keep in mind that the broader waters can make it easier to lose your way. Keep track of the markers and run approximate compass courses at a minimum. Shoals still exist here; and strong tidal currents throughout the region can change depths almost overnight, creating shoals in previously dredged spots. You may hear about people going offshore to avoid Georgia and others talking about the shallow water. While this section requires your attention, it need not be avoided or cause undue anxiety. Make sure you follow this guide closely and heed the warnings of shallow water along the way. These are noted in the guide as "navigation alerts."

With careful navigation and patience with the tide in a few areas, even deeper-draft boats can pass through this entire area of South Carolina's and Georgia's beautiful coastal waters with no problems.

Weather plays an important role as you cruise these waters. The ICW route is designed for maximum protection from the elements, but crossing large sounds and rivers can still call for caution. When a stiff wind

runs contrary to the strong currents, or a sudden thunderstorm kicks up, the going can get uncomfortably rough. You should consider tidal conditions (i.e., rising, falling or slack) and currents when running, docking or selecting an anchorage.

For safety's sake, you should run navigational ranges whenever they are present. However, do not be surprised if ranges on your charts are no longer there. Aids to navigation are frequently moved or relocated to reflect the current deep part of navigable channels.

The Waterway Explorer at waterwayguide.com tracks changes and also receives frequent postings from cruisers transiting the area. Also check the *Local Notice to Mariners* (Fifth District) for possible changes in the markers.

Marinas and Anchorages

Marinas, docks and marine repair facilities are not as numerous along this stretch, particularly when compared to the high concentrations of marinas on the Chesapeake Bay and in Florida waters. As a plus, marina owners along the ICW between Charleston and Florida are generally top-drawer and knowledgeable.

Remember that there is a 6- to 9-foot tidal range along this stretch. When approaching any marina, exercise caution, especially if your boat draws more than 4 feet, and dock into the current if at all possible. Before you tie up, tell the attendant what your draft is so they can assign you an appropriate berth. Waterway Guide's marina listings in this guide are updated annually with approach and dockside depths for each marina; use these as a guide and, if in doubt, call ahead.

Your other choice, of course, is to anchor out. Anchorages are plentiful along the ICW for those who like to take a break from the marina lifestyle. Be mindful of the silted conditions you will often encounter when dropping the hook along this stretch. Don't forget about the 8-foot tides when selecting your anchorage. Make sure you'll have enough water at low tide and enough anchor rode scope at high tide. (With 8 feet of tide, you might need between 25 and 60 feet of additional rode at high tide.) Also, when anchoring in areas with large tidal ranges, be aware that the anchorage may be subject to strong currents.

When you encounter a working dredge, contact them via VHF (Channels 9 or 13) and wait for clearance before passing.

Charleston Area

 ICW Mile 456–Mile 475   **VHF** SC Bridges: Channel 09

CHARTS NOAA 11518, 11521, 11523, 11524, 11525

The ICW north of Charleston offers wide scenic marsh views to the east and alternating marsh and forest on the west. Here, the dredged ICW channel cuts through low marshy islets, across several small rivers and finally through a long land cut before reaching Charleston Harbor.

Numerous marsh streams and small rivers cross the ICW channel from all directions in this area. All of these can affect the tidal current flow and the side currents crossing the ICW channel. Slow boats need to pay more attention than fast ones, but both should be aware that shoal areas can and do creep out near these crossings. The charted depths are somewhat optimistic along this stretch, so be more precise in keeping to the channel at low tide. Our advice is that keeping in the center of the channel is always the best. If the water gets too "skinny," then start slightly moving from side to side in an attempt to find good water.

From Mile 415 to about Mile 450, the National Ocean Service does not provide tidal current information. Generally, the flood tidal current runs north. From Mile 450 to Mile 460, the current reversals cancel each other out.

◼ TO CHARLESTON–ICW MILE 456 TO MILE 469

The ICW channel between Mile 437 and Mile 456 is among the straightest stretches along the entire ICW. Be sure to mind the markers. At Mile 456.7, you pass through a land cut between Isle of Palms on the ocean side and Goat Island on the mainland side. The two islands are quite different. The Isle of Palms is well developed with golf courses, resort hotels and restaurants, while Goat Island was formerly inhabited by only a few hearty souls who commuted to their jobs by boat. Now, although the island remains relatively isolated, more and more weekend getaway cottages have appeared on Goat Island.

NAVIGATION: Use NOAA Charts 11521, 11523 and 11523. An "Idle Speed, No-Wake" zone starts near Mile 456 and green daybeacon "115" and ends at flashing red "116." The Isle of Palms was dredged in summer 2019. It will undoubtedly shoal in again but it's good for a while. For up-to-date depths and conditions, check the Waterway Explorer (waterwayguide.com).

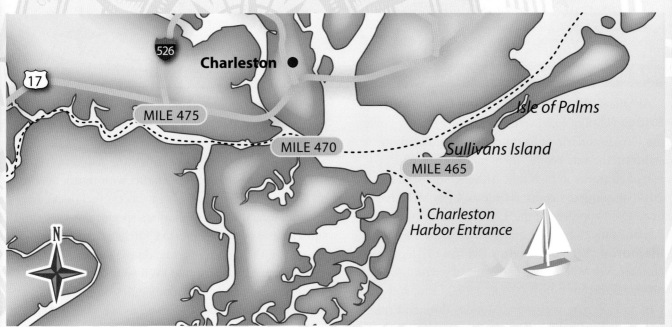

Charleston Harbor, SC

ISLE OF PALMS			Dockage				Supplies				Services			
	Largest Vessel Accommodated	VHF Channel Monitored	Transient Berths / Total Berths	Approach / Dockside Depth (reported)	Floating Docks	Gas / Diesel	Groceries, Ice, Marine Supplies, Snacks	Repairs: Hull, Engine, Propeller	Lift (tonnage), Crane, Rail	Min/Max Amps	Laundry, Pool, Showers, Courtesy Car	Pump-Out Station	Nearby: Grocery Store, Motel, Restaurant
1. Isle of Palms Marina 🖥 📶 456.5	843-886-0209	220	16/71	14/55	12/12	F	GD	GIMS	–	–	30/50	LS	P	GR
2. Toler's Cove Marina 🖥 📶 462.3	843-881-0325	110	16/71	20/140	8/8	F	GD	IMS	–	–	30/50	–	P	GMR

🖥 Internet Access 📶 Wireless Internet Access WG Waterway Guide Cruising Club Partner onSpot dockside WiFi facility
See WaterwayGuide.com for current rates, fuel prices, web site addresses, and other up-to-the-minute information. *(Information in the table is provided by the facilities.)*

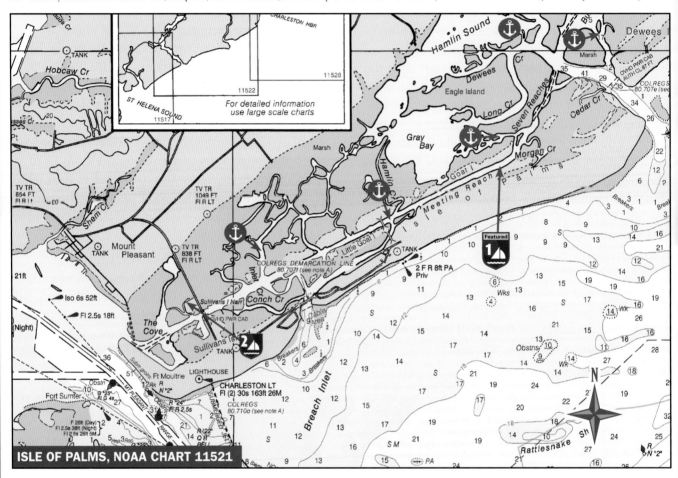

ISLE OF PALMS, NOAA CHART 11521

At Mile 458.9, the **Isle of Palms Connector Bridge** (65-foot fixed vertical clearance) crosses over the ICW to the Isle of Palms community. Based on stains on the tide boards, there may only be 63 to 64 feet of clearance at high tide. Although dredged in 2017, shoaling to depths as little as 4 feet MLW have once again appeared in the 3.3-mile stretch from the Isle of Palms Connector Bridge to the **Ben Sawyer Memorial (SR 703) Swing Bridge** (31-foot vertical clearance) at Mile 462.2. The Ben Sawyer Bridge opens on signal, except from 7:00 a.m. to 9:00 a.m. and 4:00 p.m. to 6:00 p.m. year-round Monday through Friday (except federal holidays), when the draw need not open.

The bridge need only open on the hour from 9:00 a.m. to 7:00 p.m. on weekends and holidays. Be sure to use the western span.

Dockage: At Mile 456, near flashing red "116," is the municipal Isle of Palms Marina with transient slips on floating docks and an easy to access fuel dock. The on-site Morgan Creek Grill offers spectacular views and sunsets, as well as two creative kitchens and menus, giving you the choice of a fine dining experience or a casual open experience that even your dog will love. There are few provisions or amenities on the island but the well-stocked Marina Market has everything you

Isle of Palms

Isle of Palms Marina

might need. This is a pleasant stop close to but out of the hustle and bustle of Charleston.

Just through the Ben Sawyer Memorial Swing Bridge (Mile 462.5) on the mainland side is Toler's Cove Marina. This is part of a private condominium development, but transients are welcome if space is available. It is best to call ahead on VHF Channel 16 for slip availability.

Anchorage: At Mile 456, north of Isle of Palms Marina, Seven Reaches Creek offers 7-foot MLW depths with good holding in mud. To the south, Hamlin Creek at Mile 458 offers a protected anchorage off the south side of the ICW near green daybeacon "117." Anchor before the 28-foot fixed vertical clearance **Isle of Palms Connector Bridge.** There is 7 to 10 feet MLW here and good holding in sand. It is exposed to the northeast.

Inlet Creek at Mile 461 is a regular stop for cruisers heading north or south. It offers fair holding in at least 11 feet MLW and is exposed to the south. This is the last good anchorage before the large and busy Charleston Harbor, which you will want to enter in daylight if possible.

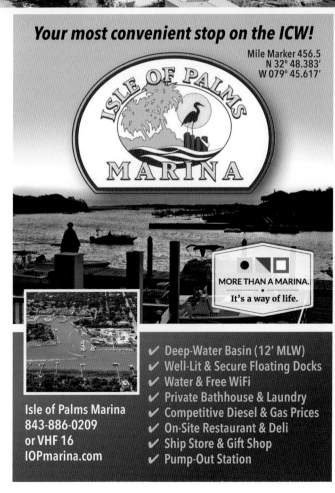

Side Trip: Mount Pleasant

The original village of Mount Pleasant is a picture-perfect community of tree-lined streets with large, handsome and lovingly maintained homes. This is home of the Patriots Point Links (843-881-0042), well known for its spectacular views of the city, Fort Sumter, and ships arriving from all over the world.

NAVIGATION: Use NOAA Chart 11524. South along the ICW, just before Charleston Harbor, a well-marked channel arcs northward inside Crab Bank, leading to Mount Pleasant and Shem Creek. Depths in the Mount Pleasant Channel are at least 8 feet. The closest marina is Charleston Harbor Resort & Marina (described in the next section).

■ CHARLESTON–ICW MILE 469

Charleston Harbor Entrance

It is difficult to enter the Charleston Harbor Entrance from the ocean and not take note of Fort Sumter on the northeastern tip of James Island. On April 12, 1861, Capt. Abner Doubleday fired the first Union shot of the Civil War defending the fort. It fell to the Confederates 34 hours later and remained in their hands for the duration of the war. The Union placed it under siege for over 550 days and conducted 5 major bombardments, which effectively flattened the fort, but never retook it. Private boats should not attempt to tie up at the fort. According to the National Park Service, all ladders, cleats and lines are for the use of ferries and tour boats. You can either beach or anchor your boat on the western side of the fort.

Once in the harbor, you can follow the well-marked channel to reach the facilities of Mount Pleasant or those on Town Creek off the Cooper River. Alternatively, boaters can head for the Charleston Harbor Resort & Marina at Patriots Point or the Charleston Maritime Center. Be alert for commercial traffic when crossing the harbor and give these big vessels plenty of room.

There are two **private islands** in Charleston harbor. Crab Bank is a major bird nesting sanctuary and at Shutes Folly there are concerns about unexploded ordnance from the old fort. This island is also a major bird nesting sanctuary. Do not land at either of these!

NAVIGATION: Use NOAA Chart 11525 (Charleston Harbor Entrance and Approach), which was released in July of 2014, replacing NOAA Chart 11523 (Charleston Harbor Entrance). It expands chart coverage further east, covering an additional 345 square nautical miles that wasn't on the old chart. This is a heavily used ship channel and there is a great deal of commercial traffic here day and night. Smaller vessels are advised to stay to the edge of the channel until reaching the inlet jetties. When entering Charleston Harbor from the ICW–anytime after low-water slack tide to about 2 hours before high-water slack for Charleston Harbor–the current will give slower boats a healthy boost up to the marinas on the Ashley River. When leaving Charleston to head north, slow boats should leave a couple of hours before low-water slack tide for an easier run.

The sea buoy is 10 nm farther out than necessary for recreational craft. A waypoint at N 32° 42.860/ W 79° 47.550 between green buoy "15" and red buoy "16" saves considerable time, although southbound vessels need to be aware of the shoaling to the north and guide their course appropriately, coming in on a southwesterly heading.

Follow the markers in and if continuing south on the ICW, bear to the west on the South Channel Range. Those northbound or heading for the Cooper River continue using the Mount Pleasant Range and follow it out of the channel, watching for flashing green "1" about 0.25 mile to the east marking the entrance to the northbound ICW. (See the Inlet section at the front of this guide or the Waterway Explorer at waterwayguide. com for more information about Charleston Harbor Entrance.)

During daylight, the entrance markers and the forest of harbor buoys leading to Charleston Harbor are easy to sort out. If yours is a first-time passage, however, it is best to run rough compass courses without shortcutting any of the buoys.

Starting at flashing red daybeacon "130," set a course for flashing yellow buoy "L" (Mile 465) to the South Channel Range. There is plenty of water depth in the area, which is frequently dredged. Follow your chart's ICW magenta line to the Ashley River and allow for the stiff current (about 3 knots at flood). If the current is flowing contrary to a wind of any strength, prepare yourself for a rough crossing.

If Charleston Harbor is busy (which it normally is), you may want to leave the ICW and take a shortcut. Skirt the southern edge of the charted Middle Ground

Cooper River

to pick up the ICW again at flashing red buoy "BP" south of Potts Shoal, using flashing yellow buoy "L" as a mid-way point.

Cooper River

On the east side of Charleston's peninsula, the Cooper River enters from the north to meet the harbor at Shutes Folly Island, where historic Castle Pinckney stands. On the east side of the Cooper River at Hog Island is Patriots Point, where the aircraft carrier *USS. Yorktown*, the submarine *USS Clamagore*, and the destroyer *USS Laffey DD-736* are permanently berthed and open for tours. (See Goin' Ashore for more information.)

NAVIGATION: Use NOAA Chart 11524. Above Drum Island, the Wando River feeds into the Cooper from the northeast. The **Arthur Ravenel Jr. Bridge** over the Cooper River at Drum Island has a vertical clearance of 186 feet, and where the same highway crosses Town Creek, on the west side of Drum Island, the vertical bridge clearance is 65 feet.

Dockage: Charleston Harbor Resort & Marina at Patriots Point is a destination in itself but it is also a convenient place to dock for easy access to the adjoining Patriots Point Naval & Maritime Museum. Turn in at quick flashing red buoy "34" for the a slip on the floating docks or to take on gas and diesel at the 24-hour fuel dock near the entrance. Amenities include a water taxi to Charleston and a free shuttle to a well-stocked gourmet grocery store nearby in Mount Pleasant. The on-site restaurant, The Charleston Harbor Fish House (843-284-7070), has a rooftop bar with a great view. This is the site of the famous Charleston Race Week sailing regatta, which draws hundreds of boats.

Zimmerman Marine's Charleston yard is located here offering full boat repair services, from rigging to mechanical and electrical and including carpentry and fiberglass. (They have four other yards: Deltaville, VA; Mobjack Bay, VA; Herrington Harbour, MD; and Southport, NC.)

Farther north, at the entrance to Shipyard Creek, is Cooper River Marina, with 200 slips (35 reserved for

Ashley River, SC

		Dockage					Supplies		Services					
		Largest Vessel Accommodated	VHF Channel Monitored	Transient Berths / Total Berths	Approach / Dockside Depth (reported)	Floating Docks	Gas / Diesel	Groceries, Ice, Marine Supplies, Snacks	Repairs: Hull, Engine, Propeller	Lift (tonnage), Crane, Rail	Min / Max Amps	Laundry, Pool, Showers, Courtesy Car	Pump-Out Station	Nearby: Grocery Store, Motel, Restaurant
COOPER RIVER														
1. Charleston Harbor Resort & Marina ⌨ onSpot	843-284-7062	200	16/72	35/459	12/12	F	GD	IS	-	-	30/100	LPS	P	GMR
2. Zimmerman Marine - Charleston	843-849-2458	Mobile Repair Service							HE					GMR
3. Cooper River Marina ⌨ WiFi	843-406-6966	150	16/11	35/200	45/25	F	-	GIMS	-	-	30/100	LS	P	G
4. Cooper River Boatyard ⌨ WiFi	843-554-7775	90	16	-	48/10	F	D	MS	HEP	L70,C99	30/50	S	-	R
5. Charleston Maritime Center ⌨ 0.5 N of 467	843-853-3625	180	16	24/30	30/20	F	GD	I	-	-	30/50	LS	P	GMR
WANDO														
6. Safe Harbor City Boatyard ⌨ WiFi	843-884-3000	125	16/72	-	15/10	F	-	M	HEP	L75,C14	30/50	SC	-	R
ASHLEY RIVER														
7. Safe Harbor Charleston City ⌨ WiFi 469.5	843-723-5098	300	16/68	125/415	20/25	F	D	GIMS	-	-	30/200+	LS	P	GMR
8. Charleston Yacht Club - PRIVATE 469.5	843-722-4968	-	-	-	/8	-	-	IS	-	-	30/30	S	-	R
9. Ripley Light Yacht Club WiFi	843-766-0908	100	-	5/83	5/6	F	-	IS	-	-	30/100	PS	P-	MR
10. The Harborage at Ashley Marina ⌨ onSpot 469.5	843-722-1996	120	16/71	50/230	15/22	F	GD	I	-	-	30/100	LS	P	GMR
11. Safe Harbor Bristol	843-723-6600	70	16	call/145	15/22	F	-	-	-	-	30/50	S	P	GMR
12. Dolphin Cove Marina WiFi	843-744-2562	60	16	10/70	28/6	F	G	IMS	HEP	L25	30/30	LS	P	GMR
NORTH CHARLESTON														
13. RiversEdge Marina ⌨ WiFi	843-554-8901	45	16/68	20/60	5/5	F	G	IMS	-	L10	30/50	LS	P	GMR

⌨ Internet Access WiFi Wireless Internet Access WG Waterway Guide Cruising Club Partner onSpot dockside WiFi facility
See WaterwayGuide.com for current rates, fuel prices, web site addresses, and other up-to-the-minute information. *(Information in the table is provided by the facilities.)*

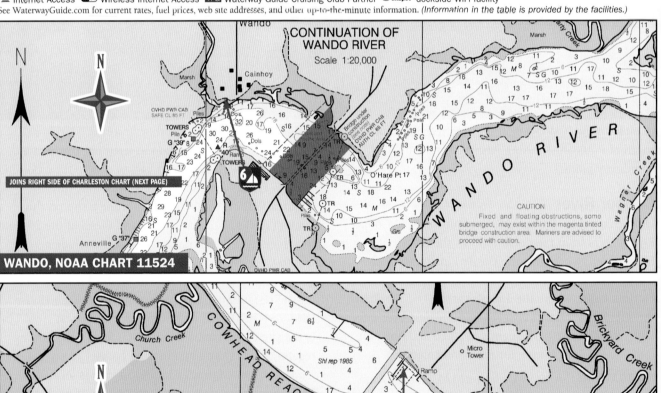

WANDO, NOAA CHART 11524

NORTH CHARLESTON, NOAA CHART 11524

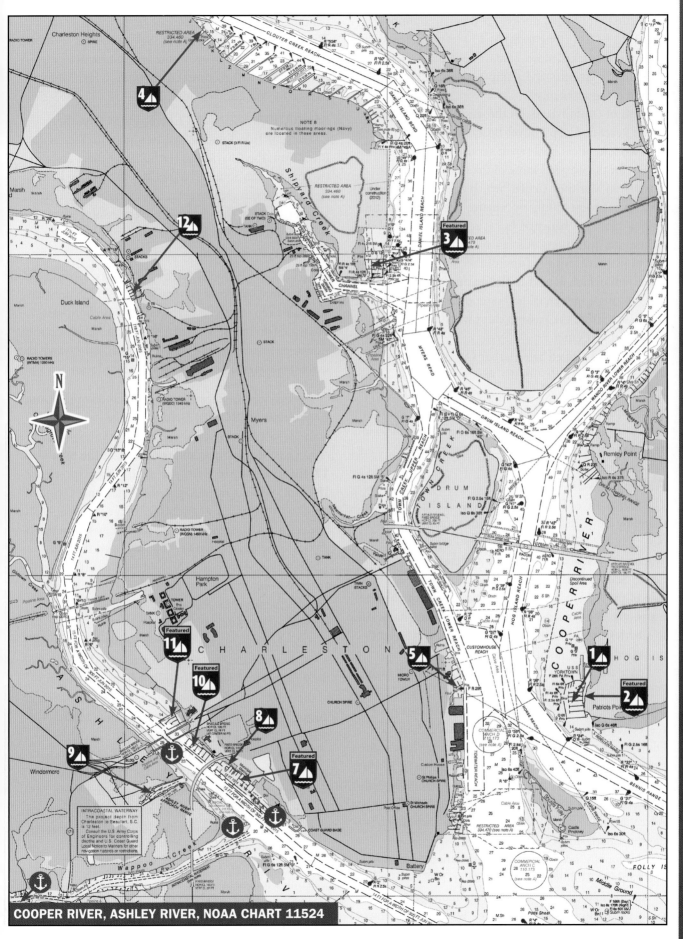

COOPER RIVER, ASHLEY RIVER, NOAA CHART 11524

transients) on floating docks. They can accommodate vessels to 42 feet (long term) or 150 feet (transients) and have a well-stocked store, climate-controlled showers and laundry facilities and pump-out service. They also offer docking assistance.

North of Drum Island, on the west side of Clouter Creek Reach is Cooper River Boatyard, which sells diesel (no gas) and offers boat repair services. South of Drum Island, on the western shore of the Cooper River, is Charleston Maritime Center, which offers some transient dockage adjacent to Liberty Square. The current at this marina can be a challenge, but it is close to most of the sightseeing attractions. A free trolley that serves the downtown area stops in front of the South Carolina Aquarium, which is next to the marina. Charleston is a working commercial harbor and you can expect some surge from the passing ships when docked at the Maritime Center.

The well-protected Safe Harbor City Boatyard is located about 20 miles up the Wando River from Drum Island. The full-service boatyard offers complete yacht repair and service. While this facility may be a bit off the beaten path, they offer mobile service at any Charleston area marina, even emergency after-hours service.

Ashley River

The Ashley River forms the west fork of the two rivers that flow along the peninsula of downtown Charleston. Note that the ICW leaves the Ashley River and enters Wappoo Creek across from, and just past, the Coast Guard Station in Charleston. The shoreline along the city side of the Ashley River, marked by the row of colonial mansions, is known as The Battery. The name dates back to Charleston's earliest days, when gun emplacements protected the city here.

Above the James Island Expressway (SR 30) Bridge (56-foot vertical clearance) and two U.S. Hwy. 17 Bascule Bridges (18- and 14-foot closed vertical clearances, respectively) on the west side of the Ashley River at Old Town Creek is Charles Towne Landing. This is the site of the first permanent English settlement in South Carolina. This historic site recreates the colonists' daily lives and includes a full-scale replica of the trading vessel *Adventure* and is worth a visit, if you are spending a few days in Charleston.

Additionally, several beautiful plantation homes and gardens–Middleton Place, Drayton Hall, Magnolia Plantation and Gardens and the Audubon Swamp Gardens–are upriver on the Ashley. Both Charles Towne

Landing and the plantations are best visited by car. The historic downtown lends itself to the horse-drawn carriage tours, but many of the areas attractions are outlying and will require transportation. (See Goin' Ashore for more information.)

NAVIGATION: Use NOAA Charts 11524. Use the Charleston Tide Table. When heading into the Ashley River from the Charleston Harbor Inlet there are two ranges–the South Channel and the Ashley River Approach (both clearly charted)–to assist you. The southern part of the channel into the Ashley River shows 15 feet from a June 2015 survey. This area is frequently dredged.

⚠️ Near the breakwater by the Coast Guard Station in Charleston Harbor strings of crab pots have been observed in the channel on both sides. They are barely visible, green on top and black on their side at or just below the water. The "tell-tale" wake they leave in strong currents will reveal their location.

The marinas are located south of the **James River Expressway (SC 30) Bridge** on the Ashley River with 56-foot fixed vertical clearance. If you wish to cruise past the marinas and cannot clear the twin **U.S. 17 Hwy. Bascule Bridges**, with their respective 18- and 14-foot controlling vertical clearances, you will need to call ahead to request the bridges openings. The bridges open on signal daily, except from 4:00 p.m. to 9:00 a.m., when the draws will only open if at least 12-hour notice is given. The bridges are 0.10 of a mile apart. Beyond the turning basin, the Ashley River's minimal depths prohibit all but small shallow-draft boats from proceeding.

Note that the current can be extremely swift, from 1 to 2 knots, with tides ranging 4 to 6 feet in this area. Check the currents and winds carefully before entering any of the marinas and call for assistance if needed. Space during the traveling seasons can be at a premium, so reservations are highly recommended.

Dockage: The Coast Guard base is to starboard about 1 mile up the river beyond The Battery, followed by the Safe Harbor Charleston Marina, Charleston Yacht Club (private), and then The Harborage at Ashley Marina. A convenient walkway under the James Island Expressway connects the marinas.

The Safe Harbor Charleston Marina, at Mile 469.5, welcomes transients of all sizes. It offers 3,000 feet of floating docks, with high-speed fueling (diesel) stations, deep-draft slips with no height limitations and

THE HARBORAGE AT ASHLEY MARINA

SAFE HARBOR BRISTOL

Ashley River

an impressive floating bathhouse with laundry. The Mega Dock (the main floating dock of the marina) is almost 0.25 mile long, and as the name suggests, you can expect to find megayachts tied there. Safe Harbor Charleston Marina also has a full-service convenience store, an internet café and a marina courtesy van that makes hourly trips to the downtown area and daily trips to West Marine. The marina is also home to the popular Marina Variety Store Restaurant (843-723-6325).

The Charleston Yacht Club is private and does not accommodate transients, but members of reciprocal clubs are welcome in their clubhouse.

Moxy Marine Services is located between Safe Harbor Charleston Marina and Charleston Yacht Club, offering diagnostics, repairs and new installs. Their service technicians are available seven days a week, plus nights and holidays.

The full-service Harborage at Ashley Marina is above the 56-foot fixed vertical clearance James Island Expressway Bridge and is capable of accommodating vessels up to 150 feet. The marina has high-speed fuel pumps, WiFi, pump-out service and a laundry, as well as a courtesy shuttle to take transients to and from many of downtown Charleston's most popular attractions.

There are plenty of restaurants within walking distance and groceries within 2 miles. The marina is adjacent to two hotels, making it a great location for hosting visitors or crew changes.

Across the Ashley River (on the west side) is the 83-slip Ripley Light Yacht Club. They report 5-foot approach depths; call ahead for transient space.

Safe Harbor Bristol, located past the U.S. Hwy. 17 Bascule Bridges and adjacent to the Citadel, was designed and engineered for easy docking, with 128 wet slips for boats less than 70 feet (14-foot maximum vessel height/air draft) and 63 drive-on docks for boats from 12 to 20 feet. They have a mobile pump-out station, cable and water at every slip and welcome transients.

Farther up the Ashley River, across from Duck Island, is Dolphin Cove Marina, which sells gas, offers some boat repairs and may have transient space. This marina primarily caters to liveaboards and is one of the most economical in the area (but with less amenities).

A little farther north on the Ashley River, past the **Cosgrove Ave. (SC 7) Bridge** (with a fixed vertical clearance of 50 feet) and before the **Gen. William C. Westmoreland (I-526) Bridge** (with a fixed vertical clearance of 35 feet), you will find RiversEdge Marina.

SAFE HARBOR CHARLESTON CITY

THE HARBORAGE AT ASHLEY MARINA

SAFE HARBOR BRISTOL

Ashley River

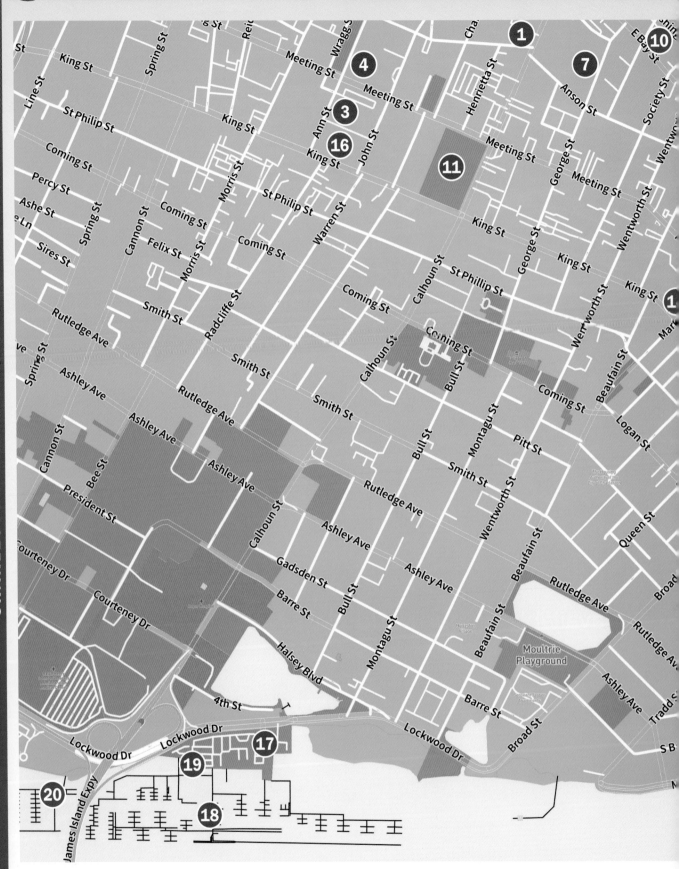

SERVICES	
1	Library
2	Post Office
3	Visitor Information
ATTRACTIONS	
4	Charleston Museum
5	City Hall
6	Dock Street Theatre
7	Gaillard Auditorium
8	Old Exchange Building
9	Old Market
SHOPPING	
10	East Bay True Value Hardware
11	Farmers' Market
12	Harris Teeter
DINING	
13	Belgium Gelato
14	Charleston Grill
15	Fleet Landing
16	Hall's Chophouse
MARINAS	
17	Marina Variety Store Restaurant
18	Safe Harbor Charleston Marina
19	Charleston Yacht Club
20	Harborage at Ashley Marina

Charleston is a favorite destination for cruisers, offering superb protection in bad weather, and with its numerous marinas and boatyards, an excellent stopover point to attend to you and your boat's needs. Have the boat serviced, replenish the larder and take a break from the galley with gourmet restaurants onshore. Tours of plantations, battlefield sites and monuments, concerts, art walks, museums, garden tours and a myriad of festivals provide welcome diversions. One of the more popular events is Charleston Harborfest held in mid-June and coinciding with the start of the Charleston to Bermuda Race in odd-numbered years.

Charleston has also been called the "Holy City," due to its number of churches (12 in the historic district alone). The culture is a mélange of influences. The British founded Charleston in 1670 and the original English influences later blended with those of the French Huguenots fleeing religious persecution. Many came by way of Barbados and added a Caribbean flair to the city's lifestyle. The Spanish were here, and slaves certainly had a huge impact on the population from food to the arts and language. Gullah, a patois of all the languages, is still spoken on the Sea Islands today.

Attractions: Start your visit downtown with a trip to the Charleston Visitors Center at Meeting and John Streets. A short film will acquaint you with the history and layout of the city, and brochures are available for the many adventures available in the Charleston area. The Charleston Museum is across the way on Meeting Street. The museum, founded in 1773 by the Charleston Library Society, is regarded as "America's First Museum." The changing exhibits include a replica of the Confederate States of America submarine *Hunley*, as well as tours of the *Hunley* restoration project, which is currently housed at the former Navy base in North Charleston.

Starting here and going south is Charleston's "Museum Mile" boasting six museums, five nationally historic homes, four scenic parks, numerous historic churches, the Old Market and City Hall. Frequent tours by the Historic Charleston Foundation and the Preservation Society offer a peek inside the old homes and their glorious gardens. Historic Charleston Foundation's annual Festival of Homes and Gardens runs from mid-March to mid-April. Tickets are limited and normally sell out by the end of January. Do take one of the ghost tours if you have time. Even if it does not make your hair stand on end, you will have a new insight into the city's past. (Example: The cobblestone streets in the historic district were built from the rocks used as ship's ballast.)

Be sure to visit the Old Exchange Building (122 E. Bay St., 843-727-2165) that used to house a prison and the Old Market (188 Meeting St.) that was actually a market for food items, not slaves, as commonly thought. (The Slave Market is a few blocks away.) The Old Market may now be the best spot to see the sweet grass basket weavers at work. There are many and the variety of their work is impressive.

If you are like most cruisers, you almost always need a new flag of one sort or another. There is a flag seller booth in the Old Market, and if he doesn't have what you want right there, he can get it for you. (A good tip we picked up here to extend the life of a flag: Spray it with silicone tent waterproofing available at Walmart. You will get at least twice the life out of your flags and maybe more.)

Dock Street Theatre (135 Church St., 843-577-7183) is an experience, if only to see its stunning interior. Reopened in 1937, the theater is the first building in the U.S. designed specifically for theatrical performances. The Charleston Symphony Orchestra and the Charleston Ballet perform frequently at the Gaillard Auditorium, and the Charleston Coliseum and Performing Arts Theater book top performers and Broadway acts. Of course, many movies and television shows are filmed here and the Spoleto Festival, held in May, is world renowned for its symphonies, operas, plays, music festivals and the many gala events that accompany it.

Don't miss the architecture of the unique Charleston single houses. Built one room wide, they are entered through a door onto a piazza, giving the occupants privacy in town. Several of the large mansions are open for tours including the Edmondston-Alston House (521 E. Battery), The Calhoun Mansion (the largest at 24,000 sq. ft.) at 16 Meeting St., the Nathaniel Russell House (51 Meeting St.) and the Aiken-Rhett House at 48 Elizabeth St. The most "desirable" area is South of Broad, on the tip of the Peninsula.

Liberty Square houses the South Carolina Aquarium (on the west side of the river in the city of Charleston), extending 200 feet over the Cooper River. Residents include an albino alligator, playful river otters, bright green moray eels and stingrays. There are numerous exhibits (of both aquatic and wildlife), a touch tank and a stingray tank and the two-story, 385,000-gallon Great Ocean tank, which houses a 220-pound loggerhead sea turtle and several tiger sharks. A majestic bald eagle (with a partial wing) is rehabbing at the aquarium as well as several turtles. The best times to visit are weekdays before 11:00 a.m. or after 2:00 p.m. For information, call 843-577-3474 or visit the website at scaquarium.org.

From the aquarium you can take a ferry for the tour of Fort Sumter; another ferry (run by Spirit Line Cruises), leaves from Patriots Point. The Harbor Tours leave from the Charleston Maritime Center. A water taxi travels between the docks here and the Charleston Harbor Resort and Marina, next to Patriots Point. A boat tour along The Battery on the Cooper River gives visitors a unique view of the antebellum mansions built by merchants for easy access to arriving ships.

Up the river, cruise underneath a magnificent engineering marvel, the impressive Ravenel Bridge, North America's longest cable-stayed bridge, which connects Mt. Pleasant and downtown. Across the Cooper River, Patriots Point Naval Museum offers a hands-on history lesson and houses a wealth of naval history (843-884-2727, patriotspoint.org). Or head out to Fort Sumter, which Citadel (the Military College of South Carolina) cadets shelled to begin the Civil War. (At least that's the local lore. The U.S. Park Service rangers who maintain the site have a slightly different interpretation.) By the way, The Citadel is in the northwest part of the city, and you can tour the campus and archives (843-953-6846).

Besides the marina shuttles, bus service is also available. The CARTA trolleys leave on a regular schedule from the Visitors Center (375 Meeting St., 800-774-0006) and circle most of the downtown area, arriving near the Variety Store Restaurant. To visit Mt. Pleasant and the outlying plantations (Boone Hall, Middleton Plantation, Drayton Hall), you will need to rent a car.

For less history and more local immersion, the Charleston River Dogs, a Class A minor league baseball team affiliated with the New York Yankees, play at Joe Riley Park on the banks of the Ashley River.

Shopping: Provisioning is easy here. Most marinas have shuttles that will take you to the Harris Teeter grocery store (290 E. Bay St., 843-722-6821), or you can pop into the Farmers' Market at Marion Square, every Saturday from mid-March until Christmas. The East Bay True Value Hardware (18 Society St., 843-577-9196) has a complete line of hardware and isn't too far away from the Harris Teeter market. Both are walking distance to the marina at the Charleston Maritime Center. At the Historic City Market (188 Meeting St.) you will find artists, music and food. It is open daily. Visit thecharlestoncitymarket.com for details. King Street is one of the best shopping streets in the country. If you have transportation, all of the big-name U.S. retailers are here, along with many foreign brand stores.

Dining: Restaurants in every price range and to suit every taste abound in Charleston. Even locals find it difficult to name a favorite. One way to try several at once is at the Charleston Wine and Food Festival in early March, which showcases the talents of local and nationally known chefs with lectures, classes and tastings.

Our on-the-water Cruising Editors have a few favorites, including Charleston Grill at 224 King St., which offers upscale dining with French and southern dishes (843-577-4522), and Hall's Chophouse (434 King St., 843-727-0090), serving cuts of beef and seafood in elegant environs.

For more casual dining, a long-standing favorite is Marina Variety Store Restaurant (843-723-6325) at Safe Harbor Charleston City. The Altine family has been feeding visiting sailors and local business folk for years, with good, down-home cooking and a view of the harbor and marina. Pick the homemade chips to go with sandwiches and burgers.

Fleet Landing (186 Concord St., 843-722-8100), a unique spot with terrace dining over the Cooper River, has great grouper dishes and a fantastic view of the Ravenel Bridge. Back in the day when naval ships anchored in the Cooper River, they used their small boats to ferry sailors ashore for "liberty." Fleet Landing was where the sailors came ashore and returned to their ships. There is a bit of naval memorabilia here to enjoy. Tip: If there is a line out front, bypass it for the outside bar seats, which are first-come, first-served. Afterwards, take a walk over to Belgian Gelato at 6 Venue Range (843-743-5043), across from Waterfront Park, for dessert. Toss a coin in the Pineapple Fountain before claiming a waterfront swing on the covered pier to finish your gelato.

Visit charleston.com for more options.

The marina has transient slips on floating docks but reports 5-foot approach and dockside depths; call ahead. They also sell gas.

Anchorage: Boats swing differently in the current here, so pay careful attention to how the boats around you are swinging (some on a single anchor, some on two; some on rode, some on chain) when you set the hook. There are three popular anchorages directly on the Ashley River. One anchorage is just north of the channel entrance to Ripley Light Marina, between the high rise and the bascule bridges. There is 12 to 25 feet of water with good holding in mud. It is exposed to the northwest and southeast, however. The anchorage is also home to a lot of local boats and is usually congested.

Another anchorage is in the small area adjacent to the Coast Guard Station, before Safe Harbor Charleston Marina, in 10 feet with a mud bottom. It is exposed to the northwest through the southeast. There are a handful of long-term-anchored boats here taking up most of the useful space. Watch for crab pots.

There is a large designated anchorage on NOAA Chart 11524, across from Safe Harbor Charleston Marina (near Wappo Creek entrance). It has good holding in mud (12 to 20 feet of water) and is exposed to the northwest and southeast. You should also be aware that there are a lot of snags on the bottom.

Anchored vessels may dock a dinghy at Safe Harbor Charleston Marina for a fee, at the nearby boat ramp or possibly at the Charleston Yacht Club. With the strong current, do factor the current into your trip ashore.

Charleston Waterkeeper offers a mobile pump-out service in the lower Charleston Harbor. They will come to your slip or location at anchorage and pump out your holding tank for free. The service was on a temporary hiatus at press time in summer 2019. Call 843-608-9287 for a current schedule.

■ TO STONO RIVER

Wappoo Creek–ICW Mile 469 to Mile 472

From Mile 472 at Elliott Cut to Mile 535 at Beaufort, SC, the South Carolina Lowcountry scenery is lush and beautiful with water birds and marsh grass creating picture-postcard sights everywhere you look. Beaufort is a beautiful stopping place and the next community of any size past Charleston.

Cooper River

NAVIGATION: Use NOAA Charts 11518. Continuing down the ICW on the Ashley River opposite the Safe Harbor Charleston Marina, you enter Wappoo Creek, which then leads into narrow Elliott Cut. Immediately inside Wappoo Creek's northern entrance, at Mile 469.9, is the **James Island Expressway Bridge** (official fixed vertical clearance of 67 feet, but there are no tide boards), followed by the **Wappoo Creek (SR 171) Bascule Bridge** (33-foot closed vertical clearance) at Mile 470.8. The draw here will open on signal, except from 6:00 a.m. to 9:29 a.m. and 3:31 p.m. to 7:00 p.m., Monday through Friday (except federal holidays), when the draw need not open. Between 9:30 a.m. and 3:30 p.m., Monday through Friday (except federal holidays), the draw need only open on the hour or the half-hour.

Just before the bascule bridge on Wappoo Creek, if you are southbound on the ICW (your heading will be west at this point), a boat ramp is on the north (starboard) side. This entire section, through Elliott Cut, is a patrolled No-Wake Zone. Almost every pier has a sign saying, "Slow, you are responsible for your wake." Go as slowly as you can, even though it may be difficult when the strong current is dead against you.

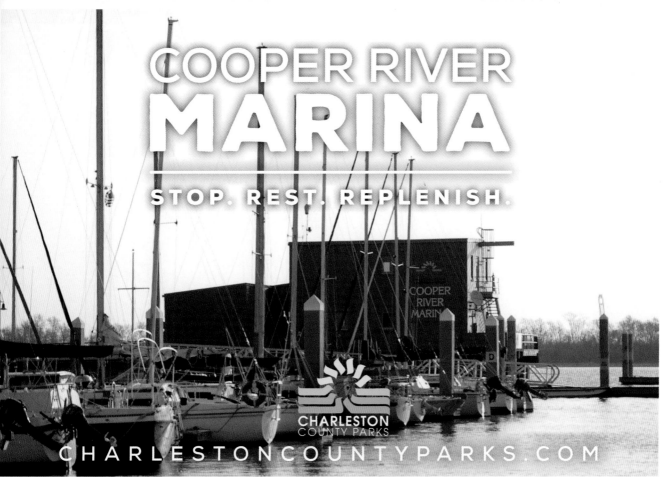

COOPER RIVER MARINA

STOP. REST. REPLENISH.

CHARLESTON COUNTY PARKS

CHARLESTONCOUNTYPARKS.COM

Stono River, SC

STONO RIVER AREA			Largest Vessel Accommodated	VHF Channel Monitored	Transient Berths / Total Berths	Approach / Dockside Depth (reported)	Floating Docks	Groceries, Ice, Marine Supplies, Snacks	Gas / Diesel	Repairs: Hull, Engine, Propeller	Lift (tonnage) Crane, Rail	Min/Max Amps	Pump-Out Station	Nearby: Grocery Store, Motel, Restaurant Laundry, Pool, Showers, Courtesy Car
			Dockage					**Supplies**			**Services**			
1. St. Johns Yacht Harbor 🖥 WiFi 1S of 472.5	843-557-1027		120	16/71	20/224	25/8	F	GD	GIMS	–	–	30/50	LPSC	P	GR
2. Ross Marine 476	843-559-0379		150	16/79	0/40	12/12	F	GD	IM	HEP	L75,C	30/50	–	–	–

🖥 Internet Access WiFi Wireless Internet Access WG Waterway Guide Cruising Club Partner 💬onSpot dockside WiFi facility
See WaterwayGuide.com for current rates, fuel prices, web site addresses, and other up-to-the-minute information. *(Information in the table is provided by the facilities.)*

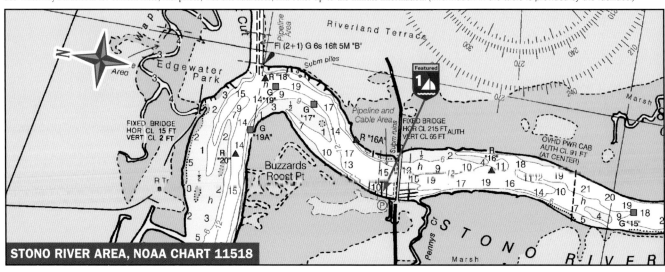

STONO RIVER AREA, NOAA CHART 11518

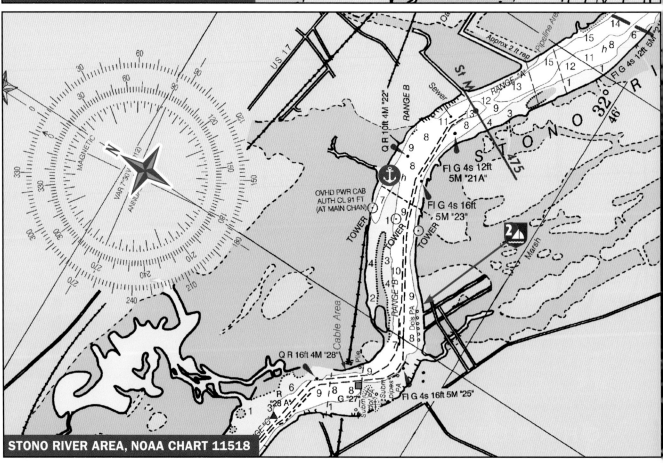

STONO RIVER AREA, NOAA CHART 11518

ST. JOHNS
YACHT HARBOR

⚠ You must be able to maintain steerage when the current is with you. Slow boats might do better by waiting until the current moderates. The flood tide runs west in the cut toward the Stono River; ebb tides run east toward Charleston Harbor.

The passage through Wappoo Creek and Elliott Cut between green daybeacon "9" and the charted overhead power cables at the northern entrance to Elliott Cut has shoaling to a depth of 9 feet MLW on the red side of the channel, adjacent to green daybeacon "9." At Mile 472, favor the red side for 20 feet MLW to avoid shoaling to less than 7 MLW on the green side. Don't cut the corner! The rest of the stretch has 12- to 20-foot depths. For slower, southbound boats, the best time to leave Charleston for Beaufort is toward the end of a flood tide. You can save 2 to 3 hours on this 65-mile-long stretch. Moreover, a passage through Elliott Cut's narrow channel against a 2- to 4-knot current can guarantee an all-too-memorable experience.

Ebb tide begins at the Wappoo Creek entrance 43 minutes before it begins at Charleston Harbor. Leaving at other times, slower auxiliary-powered craft may prefer to make the trip to Beaufort in 2 days and take advantage of the many excellent anchorages en route.

Anchorage: The most protected overnight anchorage in the Charleston area at Mile 471 is just beyond the Wappoo Creek Bascule Bridge (33-foot closed vertical clearance, restricted schedule), in 11 to 15 feet at MLW behind the unnamed small island. This anchorage is very narrow and not very large (with space for only a few small to mid-size cruising boats) and subject to strong current. It is a long dinghy ride to downtown, but it is a quiet, secluded spot for those who get there early. It is in a residential area, and there are docks on the south side.

Stono River–ICW Mile 472

NAVIGATION: Use NOAA Chart 11518. From Elliott Cut, the ICW enters the Stono River just beyond Mile 472. Shoaling has been reported at the confluence of Elliott Cut and the Stono River near red daybeacon "18."

Note that red daybeacon "18" and green daybeacon "19" are not ICW markers but mark the Stono River channel leading in from its inlet to intersect the ICW at this point. The ICW channel up the Stono River begins with green daybeacon "19A."

If you are using older charts, you need to be aware that there have been markers changed in this area. There is now a new red daybeacon "28A" and red daybeacon "34" is missing. Red daybeacon "40" has been replaced with a red nun buoy. All these changes are present on the most current print-on-demand and electronic charts.

Farther downstream, the Stono River leads to the Folly and Kiawah Rivers, frequented by local recreational boaters. Folly and Kiawah Islands are home to several ocean resorts with beaches, shopping, restaurants and several golf courses.

Dockage: A short side trip to port from Elliott Cut, down the Stono River, brings you to the St. Johns Yacht Harbor. They offer "yacht club amenities in a family-friendly environment." The facility sells non-ethanol gas and diesel and has laundry facilities, a ship and sundries store, free in-slip pump-out services and a saltwater pool. They also offer a courtesy car. This is just before the 65-foot fixed vertical clearance **Paul J. Gelegotis (Stono) Bridge.**

As you turn slightly to starboard coming out of Elliott Cut to continue along the ICW, Ross Marine, a full-service yacht repair yard located about 3 miles ahead near flashing green daybeacon "25" to port (Mile 476), is equipped to handle major repairs on any size boat with their crane and 75-ton lift. They also sell diesel fuel.

Anchorage: The best anchorage in this area is across the Stono from red daybeacon "16A" (at Mile 472.6 behind Buzzards Roost Point) in the 10-foot MLW charted area near St. Johns Yacht Harbor. There can be considerable current in the river; however, there is excellent holding here in clay. Anchorage is also available up the Stono River at Mile 475.5 (before Ross Marine) with 8-foot MLW depths with good holding in mud.

■ NEXT STOP

Ahead on your southbound journey down the ICW lies the lush and lovely Lowcountry. The following chapters offer trips off the ICW via the North Edisto River or South Edisto River to Seabrook and Edisto islands, respectively. Different in character and amenities, each has something to offer. Back on the ICW, Beaufort and Hilton Head, SC, await your arrival.

Stono River to Ossabaw Sound, SC

 Mile 475–Mile 615 ((VHF)) SC Bridges: Channel 09/GA Bridges: Channel 09

CHARTS NOAA 11507, 11511, 11512, 11514, 11516, 11518, 11521, 11522

From Elliott Cut, which leads from Charleston, SC, south to the Stono River, the ICW route continues along the Stono River for about 12 miles. This stretch of lush and lovely South Carolina marsh is teeming with wildlife. The delicate colors of the grasses and the unique scents wafting off the marsh make cruising through these parts a unique experience. You are now in open country. At about Mile 475, the first of a series of navigational ranges makes the going a lot easier in this area of swift tidal currents. Be aware that the range markers are becoming less and less frequent with the advent of electronic navigation. Plus, with shifting shoals range markers don't always mark the best course to take. Check Waterway Explorer at waterwayguide.com (updated daily) for advice.

■ TO BEAUFORT AREA

ICW Mile 475 TO Mile 535

NAVIGATION: Use NOAA Chart 11518. A short distance beyond the **John F. Limehouse Highway Bridge** at Mile 479.3 (65-foot fixed vertical clearance), the Stono River narrows and the ICW channel follows a winding path past Johns Island. When heading north through the starboard side of the channel at the Limehouse Bridge, be aware of small-boat traffic coming from the busy boat ramp north of the bridge. Just beyond Mile 480, red daybeacon "40" marks a shoal off the creek to the north. This marker appears to be in the wrong place,

North & South Edisto River, SC

				Dockage					Supplies		Services					
		Largest Vessel Accommodated	VHF Channel Monitored	Approach / Dockside Depth	Transient Berths / Total Berths	Floating Docks	Gas / Diesel	Groceries, Ice, Marine Supplies, Snacks	Repairs: Hull, Engine, Propeller	Lift (tonnage), Crane, Rail	Pump-Out Station	Nearby: Grocery Store, Motel, Restaurant	Laundry, Pool, Showers, Courtesy Car	Min/Max Amps		
BOHICKET CREEK																
1. Bohicket Marina & Market ⌨ 📶 7.2 S of 497	843-768-1280	150	16/68	50/200	14/14	F	GD	GIMS	–	–	30/100	LS	P	GMR
2. Marine Propulsion, Inc. ⌨ 📶	843-559-1025	100	16/68	call/17	8/16	F	–	MS	HEP	L60,C15	30/50	C	–	–
EDISTO ISLAND																
3. The Marina at Edisto Beach ⌨ 📶 4.5 S of 511	843-631-5055	55	16/68	5/72	17/12	F	GD	GIMS	–	–	30/50	LS	–	GR

⌨ Internet Access 📶 Wireless Internet Access 🅦🅖 Waterway Guide Cruising Club Partner ⬤onSpot dockside WiFi facility
See WaterwayGuide.com for current rates, fuel prices, web site addresses, and other up-to-the-minute information. *(Information in the table is provided by the facilities.)*

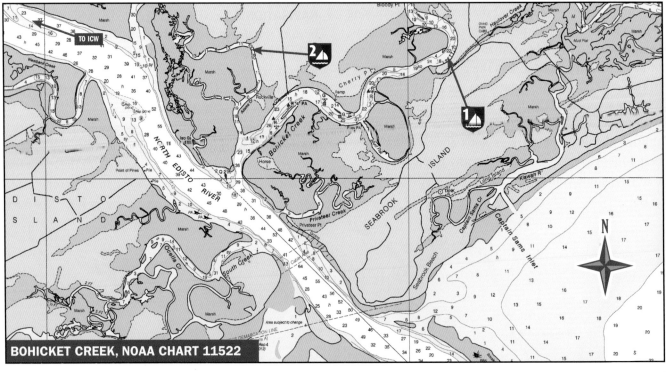

BOHICKET CREEK, NOAA CHART 11522

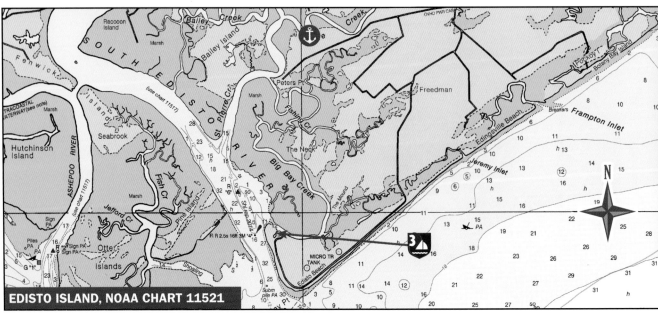

EDISTO ISLAND, NOAA CHART 11521

North Edisto Inlet

but it is not. Give it space, as a shoal extends slightly farther into the channel from the creek. The current usually reverses at this point.

At Mile 485, the ICW leaves the Stono River and enters a short land cut leading to the headwaters of the Wadmalaw River. At Church Flats (Mile 485), the tides meet. (The name "Church Flats" is derived from the practice of going to church on the flood tide and coming home on the ebb.) Near red daybeacon "78" there are submerged rocks on both sides of the channel.

In the Wadmalaw River, run the long stretch between red daybeacon "92" and flashing red daybeacon "94" on a compass course. If transiting at mid to high tide, check your position with respect to the current along the way to avoid the mud flats to the north and in deep water. Swing wide toward flashing red daybeacon "94" and avoid the shortcut to green daybeacon "95."

Several aids to navigation mark the shoals on the Wadmalaw River between flashing red daybeacon "82" and green daybeacon "101." Swing wide to the outside on curves and follow the magenta line through this area for the best water. Red daybeacons "98" and "100" indicate a shoal area that is visible at low tide but can be difficult to spot at high tide. These two markers need to be given a wide berth. Between green daybeacon "89" and red daybeacon "92" you will see the large commercial hauling and repair facility. Note that green daybeacon "109" is not shown on some charts.

The ICW follows the North Edisto River to flashing red daybeacon "110." Stay in the center of the river, slightly favoring the southern bank.

Anchorage: There is an anchorage on the north side of the waterway at Mile 475.5, with good holding but with minimum wake and wind protection. At Mile 479.8 at Johns Island there is another somewhat protected spot on the north shore for more shoal-draft vessels with 4 to 6 feet MLW.

There is another at Mile 487 at Church Creek, which is especially popular during the spring and fall. The holding here is good in about 15 feet MLW, and the anchorage is fairly well protected. To reach this anchorage, turn off the ICW at green "77" and proceed east into Church Creek for less than 0.50 mile, taking care to stay an equal distance from the shores. Low tide will reveal the hidden oyster beds on the north side and shallow mud flats on the south side. However, dropping anchor in the middle of the creek will give you plenty of swing room and depth to handle the tide change. This anchorage offers a lovely panoramic view of the sunset and sunrise.

Side Trip: North Edisto Inlet

NAVIGATION: Use NOAA Chart 11522. About 6 miles down the North Edisto River from the ICW, you can head up swift-running Bohicket Creek to the village of Rockville and Seabrook Island, both popular weekend destinations with Charleston-based boaters.

A side trip, with access to the ocean, can be made by continuing down the North Edisto River, which is well charted (NOAA Chart 11522) and easy to run, except for shoaling along both riverbanks. (See the Inlet section at the front of this guide for more information about North Edisto River Inlet.)

Dockage: Up Bohicket Creek off the North Edisto River is Bohicket Marina & Market, which lies just north of the village of Rockville. Maximum ebb and flood currents call for both advance planning and dockside help to assure a smooth docking and departure. The marina has dockage and fuel (both gas and diesel), and there are some amenities on site, including several restaurants, a spa and a gift shop. Adams Creek, located off the north side near the mouth of Bohicket Creek is the home of Marine Propulsion, Inc., which offers boat repairs and marine supplies but no transient dockage.

Anchorage: At Mile 495, leave the ICW and turn to starboard to enter Toogoodoo Creek. Use great caution when entering Toogoodoo Creek, as there are large areas of mud banks on both sides at its entrance. You will find good holding in 10- to 15-foot MLW depths in packed mud. You will also be subjected to some wakes from passing fisherman, but that settles down in the early evening.

If you continue on the ICW for another 0.50 mile, you will find Tom Point Creek, with 8 to 20 feet MLW and good holding. Note that there is an uncharted shoal on the outside bend with less than 3 feet MLW. Stay in the center of the channel.

Steamboat Creek, to the south on the west side of the North Edisto River, has an excellent anchorage in 17-plus feet MLW with a clay bottom, but you might encounter some snags on the bottom. There is limited protection from the wind until you are well into the creek. There is also a boat ramp in this creek that has a small dock where you can land dinghies to exercise your pets.

Dawho River–ICW Mile 497

NAVIGATION: Use NOAA Chart 11521. Beyond the North Edisto River at flashing red buoy "110," the ICW channel enters the Dawho River at White Point (Mile 496.7). (Green "109" is not shown on some charts.) Remember that at low tide floating aids in areas of extreme tidal range will pull in the direction of the current, away from their anchored position.

The entrance to the Dawho River has a very narrow (90-foot-wide) channel with current depths of 9.3 feet MLW, despite dredging in 2018.

⚠ As of press time (summer 2019) green marker "109" had not yet been moved to mark the recently dredged channel, meaning by following the dredged channel, you will pass on the "incorrect" side of the marker, but it's the correct path. See the detailed route at Waterway Explorer at waterwayguide.com.

At Mile 501, you will notice a pair of sloughs coming into the Dawho River from the north. These little slivers of water actually connect behind marshland to form an oxbow. Do not be tempted to try to anchor in either slough, as shoals become bare at low tide.

The ICW enters a land cut at Mile 501.3, just before the **McKinley Washington Jr. Bridge** (with a published fixed vertical clearance of 65 feet, but it is closer to 63- to 64-foot according to the tide boards). A portion of the old swing bridge is used as a fishing pier. Beyond the bridge, the ICW passes through narrow North Creek and Watts Cut before emptying into the broad and swiftly flowing South Edisto River.

Watts Cut is another area that was dredged in 2018 but has already shoaled some. Lowest depths observed in the channel were 6.7 feet MLW in summer 2019.

Anchorage: Just south of the McKinley Washington Jr. Bridge, it is possible to anchor in the approach to Fishing Creek. Be aware that the charted depth at its entrance is 4 feet MLW and that there are charted submerged piles outside the ICW channel here. If you decide to enter Fishing Creek, favor the red daybeacon "132" side when entering. You will find at least 9-foot MLW depths and good holding, despite some current. There is some highway noise and it can be buggy; nevertheless, this is one of the best anchorages along this section of the ICW. As in all anchorages, be sure to use your anchor light at night.

South Edisto River–ICW Mile 504

The main destination along the South Edisto River is Edisto Island, overlooking the Atlantic Ocean. Edisto Island is home of the community of Edisto Beach and offers deep-sea fishing opportunities. The town has beautiful, well-preserved Colonial homes, a popular residential resort with golf course, an oceanfront state park and good stores and boutiques. You will find a slower pace that harks back to the 1950s; there are no high-rise motels or typical carnival-type boardwalk activities here.

NAVIGATION: Use NOAA Charts 11521. The South Edisto River is easy to follow. Remember, however, that you are in a strong tidal zone, so do not cut too close to the markers or the bends in the channels.

At Mile 510, Range "C" marks the ICW course along the South Edisto River between Watts Cut and Fenwick Cut. These ranges keep boaters off the river's wide shoals and projecting points. Note that green daybeacon

"161A" at Mile 510.7 in the South Edisto River is not shown on older charts. Also, green daybeacon "161B," shown on some older charts, no longer exists.

At Fenwick Cut, Mile 511, the ICW heads southwest along the Ashepoo River, while the South Edisto River meanders in a southeasterly direction toward the Atlantic Ocean. Despite recent dredging, shoals continually build at both the north and south entrances to Fenwick Cut and along its entire length.

> ⚠️ Shoaling has been observed to 7.0 MLW at the northern entrance of the Fenwick Cut. Follow the aids to navigation for a safe passage. See the detailed route at Waterway Explorer at waterwayguide.com.

Dockage: The Marina at Edisto Beach is located behind Edisto Island on Big Bay Creek, 4.5 miles south from the ICW. This sportfishing-oriented facility has transient slips and sells fuel (both gas and diesel). Nature and fishing charters leave from here daily. Be sure to call the marina well in advance.

Anchorage: The South Edisto River provides a good fair-weather anchorage at Mile 504.2. When southbound out of Watts Cut, bear off to starboard into the South Edisto River. Anchor in the middle about 1 mile from Watts Cut where the chart shows 10- and 11-foot MLW depths with a soft, mud bottom. This is a wide open, relatively quiet spot with good holding, although we advise against anchoring here in any strong wind. There is considerable current (1 to 2 knots), just as with all the rivers in this area of the ICW, and conditions can become uncomfortable with opposing wind and current. Continuing around the next bend is an option. This is a good spot to wait if you are going north and want to time the tide through Dawho River.

Just past the lower end of Alligator Creek at Mile 509.4 and opposite green daybeacon "157" is an anchorage for settled weather with good protection from the northwest. Be cautious when entering this creek as it has been reported to have a shallow entrance. Once you are in, sound your way toward the shore to avoid trap markers, and anchor in 8 to 11 feet MLW, well off the channel. The current may reach 1.5 knots, so vessels may lay to the current, rather than the wind.

There is an anchorage up the St. Pierre Creek south of the ICW (east side) with good holding in mud and 9- to 17-foot MLW depths.

Ashepoo River and Ashepoo Coosaw Cutoff–ICW Mile 511

The ICW route continues to the southwest, leading from the South Edisto River through Fenwick Cut and into a short section of the Ashepoo River.

NAVIGATION: Use NOAA Chart 11518. Do not get too close to the Ashepoo River's north shore between flashing green daybeacon "165" and quick flashing red daybeacon "166," due to increased shoaling along the north bank. Follow the curve of the channel, as shown by the magenta line on the chart. If heading up the Ashepoo River toward B&B Seafood House Marina, be aware that there is less water just beyond quick flashing red daybeacon "166" than indicated on the chart.

Once you have transited this section of the Ashepoo River, the ICW enters the first part of the Ashepoo Coosaw Cutoff. The Ashepoo Coosaw Cutoff soon jags in a northwesterly direction, entering Rock Creek at Mile 515, before it continues as a narrow land cut toward the wide Coosaw River.

> The Ashepoo Coosaw Cutoff was dredged in fall 2018; however, in spring 2019 shoaling was observed in the southern part of the cutoff to 6.0 feet MLW at the southern end. Stay in the center of the channel (when possible). See the detailed route at Waterway Explorer at waterwayguide.com.

Crab pot floats are normally placed in the shallow water on the northeast side of the channel.

Dockage: B&B Seafood House Marina is 1.8 miles off the Ashepoo River on Mosquito Creek. They have fuel and can accommodate two vessels up to 50 feet on floating docks. Power is available (30 amp), but you'll need a long cord to reach it. There are restrooms but no showers. This is a seafood wholesale/retail outlet and in season the oysters and shrimp are fresh off the boat and very economical (sold by the bushel).

Anchorage: Just past B&B Seafood is an anchorage on Mosquito Creek with at least 7 feet MLW with a mud bottom. Most anchorages along the Ashepoo River are open but pleasant, with good holding. There are two anchoring possibilities at Fenwick Island. The one north of the cut on the ICW (Fenwick Island North) is at Mile 511.6 and is fairly open with a strong current, making anchoring challenging. At Fenwick Island South, which is south of the ICW, there is an anchorage with at least 11 feet MLW. The headwaters of Rock Creek at Mile 516 provide a narrow but well-protected anchorage

Ashepoo River, SC

					VHF Channel Monitored	Transient Berths / Total Berths	Approach / Dockside Depth (reported)	Floating Docks	Gas / Diesel	Groceries, Ice, Marine Supplies, Snacks	Repairs: Hull, Engine, Propeller	Lift (tonnage), Crane, Rail	Largest Vessel Accommodated	Laundry, Pool, Showers, Courtesy Car	Min/Max Amps	Pump-Out Station	Nearby: Grocery Store, Motel, Restaurant

MOSQUITO CREEK						Dockage					Supplies			Services			
1. B & B Seafood House Marina 1.8 N of 513.5			843-844-2322		50	68	2/2	10/10	F	GD	GIMS	–	–	30/30	–	–	GR

⌨ Internet Access 📶 Wireless Internet Access **WG** Waterway Guide Cruising Club Partner ☁ **onSpot** dockside WiFi facility
See WaterwayGuide.com for current rates, fuel prices, web site addresses, and other up-to-the-minute information. *(Information in the table is provided by the facilities.)*

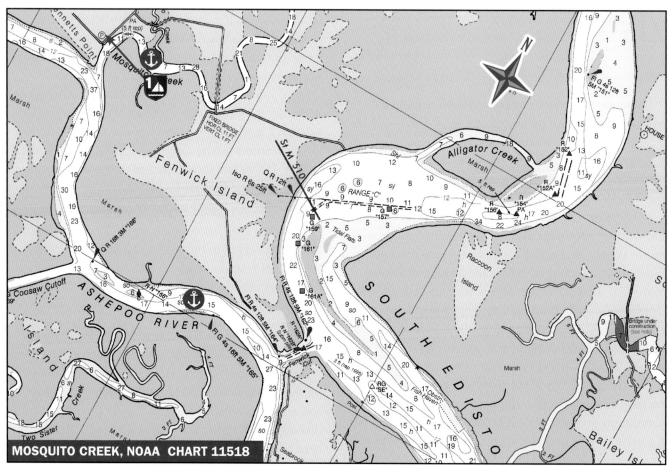

MOSQUITO CREEK, NOAA CHART 11518

with minimum 8-foot MLW depths to the second bend. Use the depth sounder to avoid the shoals on the inside of the turns in the creek; however, deep-drafted boats swinging on the current have also frequently grounded in this anchorage.

> Given the proximity of Port Royal Sound, Charleston and North Edisto Inlets, **St. Helena Inlet** should be skipped. See the Inlet section in the front of this guide for details on the closest big ship inlets.

Coosaw River–ICW Mile 518

While the Coosaw River is wide and unobstructed, it is always best to keep to the channel and run at least a rough compass course to help you spot the markers, which are spaced fairly far apart.

NAVIGATION: Use NOAA Chart 11518. The Bull River at Mile 521.5 and the Combahee River at Mile 518.5 flow off the north side of the Coosaw River. Approximately 2 miles south of red daybeacon "186," Parrot Creek leads south off the Coosaw River to a marina at Morgan River and an anchorage at Lucy Point Creek. Depths exceed 10-foot MLW depths for the entire approach to Parrot Creek from the ICW.

Dockage: You can access Dataw Island Marina, which is 3 miles south of ICW Mile 521, by following Parrot Creek and rounding the south side of Coosaw Island on the Morgan River. The marina is owned by a community owner's association and offers dry stack storage and has a full-service boat yard on site (Ace Basin Boatworks) with maintenance and repair services. Sweetgrass Restaurant is a local favorite for fun fare in a casual atmosphere. This facility was under renovation at press time (summer 2019), so call ahead to confirm if fuel and slips are available (843-838-8410).

Anchorage: Many spots in this area are suitable for anchoring. At Mile 521.5, you can anchor inside Wimbee Creek, off the Bull River, just off the ICW to the north. Watch for the shoal below Summerhouse Point and leave the island to starboard. Holding is good here in 11 to 18 feet MLW, although the bottom also is hard with shells in some areas.

South of the ICW (Mile 521.5) there are anchoring possibilities east and south of Coosaw Island accessed by Parrot Creek. Bass Creek (directly off Parrot Creek)) has 13 to 16 feet MLW and wave (but not wind) protection. Continuing south, you can anchor past Dataw Island Marina at Lucy Point Creek. Even though there is an entrance to Lucy Point Creek directly off the ICW, a fixed 14-foot vertical clearance **SC 802 Bridge** at the mouth necessitates the "back door" approach.

Brickyard Creek–ICW Mile 529

The ICW leaves the Coosaw River at Mile 529, where you will find a well-marked entrance range heading into Brickyard Creek. As you travel south on Brickyard Creek, military aircraft might buzz you. While the noise from the military aircraft in this area can disrupt a peaceful anchoring experience, the U.S. Marine Corps Air Station here–along with the nearby famous Parris Island Recruit Depot–is a major contributor to the local economy.

NAVIGATION: Use NOAA Chart 11518. Stay to mid-channel where the ICW begins its 4-mile run along Brickyard Creek (the headwaters of the Beaufort River). There are flats along both sides of the channel, particularly where the Coosaw River enters Brickyard Creek.

⚠️ Flashing red "210" is adjacent to a 1-foot MLW shoal. Between "210" and flashing red "214," go outside the channel on the green side by 50 feet for 8.9 feet MLW.

Slow boats should note that the current between Brickyard Creek and Beaufort changes at about flashing red daybeacon "224" (Mile 532). If you catch the end of the flood or the slack, you can usually ride the current to Beaufort.

Dockage: At Mile 533, just north of green daybeacon "233," a marked channel leads into Marsh Harbor Boat Works on Ladys Island. Marsh Harbor is a working boat yard with a 50-ton lift. They generally do not take transients.

Anchorage: Mile 530.4 at Brickyard Creek has 5 to 9 feet MLW with a mud bottom and all-around protection. The deep-water channel is very narrow and residential docks extend far out from the shore, limiting space, so we recommend exercising caution when anchoring here.

■ BEAUFORT AREA–ICW MILE 536 TO MILE 553

The City of Beaufort appears to starboard at about the point where Brickyard Creek becomes the Beaufort River. Beaufort's attractions include an entire downtown on the National Register of Historic Places, a multi-purpose park along the waterfront, an amphitheater, markets and a bandstand, all within sight of bed and breakfasts, attractive shops and meticulously restored historic houses. The homes in Beaufort are typically West Indies-style in a T-shaped floor plan, with a raised first floor, high ceilings and double porches. Over time, Beaufort has spread gently southward along the western bank of the river toward Port Royal.

By the way, Beaufort is pronounced "Bew'-fort" not "Boe'-fort" as when referring to Beaufort, NC. If you are new to cruising the ICW in the Carolinas, do take an extra moment to get the pronunciation of the two straight, as it will save you the embarrassment of being corrected by the locals.

Beaufort to Port Royal–ICW Mile 536 to Mile 540

NAVIGATION: Use NOAA Chart 11518. Use the Savannah River Entrance Tide Table. For high tide, add 1 hour and 9 minutes; for low tide, add 51 minutes. Heading south along the ICW, Brickyard Creek reaches Beaufort and the **Ladies Island Swing Bridge** at Mile 536 (closed vertical clearance of 30 feet). To port (south), just above the Ladies Island Swing Bridge

Discover life with the Lowcountry tides.

From convenient marinas and stunning natural beauty to authentic culture and cuisine, refuel in more ways than one in historic Beaufort, SC. Experience the transformative beauty of a place that has turned countless overnight anchorages into week-long retreats—and lifelong cruisers into locals.

inner coastal

VISIT
BEAUFORT
PORT ROYAL ◆ SEA ISLANDS

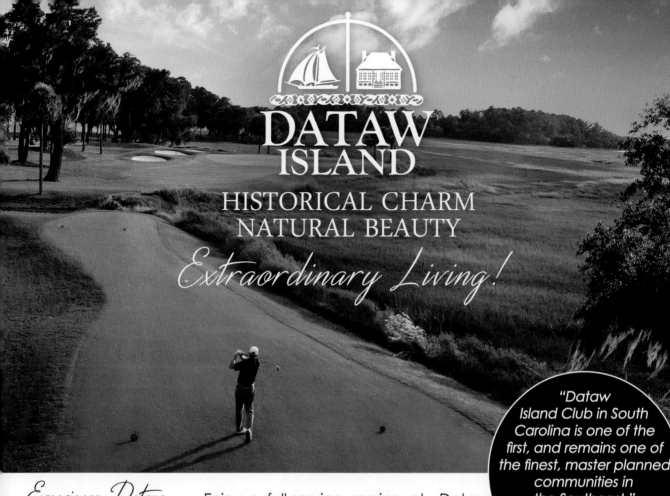

DATAW ISLAND

HISTORICAL CHARM
NATURAL BEAUTY

Extraordinary Living!

"Dataw Island Club in South Carolina is one of the first, and remains one of the finest, master planned communities in the Southeast."

~ Tom Fazio
Golf Course Designer

Experience Dataw ~ Enjoy a full-service marina at Dataw Island, a gated golf, tennis & boating community located six miles east of the historic Lowcountry town of Beaufort, SC. Conveniently situated between Hilton Head, Savannah, and Charleston and close to the beach, shopping, history, and fine & performing arts, Dataw is away from it all but close to everything. At this active lifestyle community, you'll enjoy indoor & outdoor pools, fishing, crabbing, walking & cycling trails, bird watching, bocce, croquet, and a growing list of 100+ of on-site clubs & organizations, ranging from philanthropic to sports, arts to yachting, and everything in between. Visit Dataw Island to see for yourself why it's been called the hidden gem of South Carolina!

"Bliss Award: Best South Carolina Community" (Real Estate Scorecard)

"#1 Best Community in South Carolina" (Best Retirement Destinations)

"Outstanding Facility Award" (USTA - Tennis Association)

"Best Golf" "Best Kayaking," "Best Island Community" (ideal-LIVING)

"2018 Club of the Year" (SC Golf Association)

Six miles from historic Beaufort, SC

(843) 838-3838
Dataw.com

Morgan River, Beaufort River, SC

		Largest Vessel Accommodated	VHF Channel Monitored	Approach / Dockside Depth	Transient Berths / Total Berths	Floating Docks	Gas / Diesel	Groceries, Ice, Marine Supplies, Snacks	Repairs: Hull, Engine, Propeller	Lift (tonnage), Crane, Rail	Min/Max Amps	Laundry, Pool, Showers, Courtesy Car	Pump-Out Station	Nearby: Grocery Store, Motel, Restaurant
DATAW ISLAND			**Dockage**				**Supplies**		**Services**					
1. Dataw Island Marina	843-838-8410	–	16/68	–	–	–	GD	–	–	L50	–	LS	–	R
BEAUFORT AREA														
2. Marsh Harbor Boat Works 🖥 WiFi 534.4	843-521-1500	70	16	call/16	6/6	F	–	M	HEP	L50	30/50	S	–	GMR
3. Lady's Island Marina 🖥 WiFi .8 S of 536	843-522-0430	210	16/17	10/75	7/14	F	–	IS	–	–	30/50	LSC	P	GMR
4. Safe Harbor Beaufort WiFi 536.2	843-524-4422	150	16/68	25/100	20/15	F	GD	IMS	HEP	–	30/50	LSC	P	GMR
5. Port Royal Landing Marina, Inc. 🖥 WiFi 539	843-525-6664	120	16/12	10/140	20/15	F	GD	IMS	–	–	30/50	LSC	P	GMR

🖥 Internet Access WiFi Wireless Internet Access WG Waterway Guide Cruising Club Partner 💧onSpot dockside WiFi facility
See WaterwayGuide.com for current rates, fuel prices, web site addresses, and other up-to-the-minute information. *(Information in the table is provided by the facilities.)*

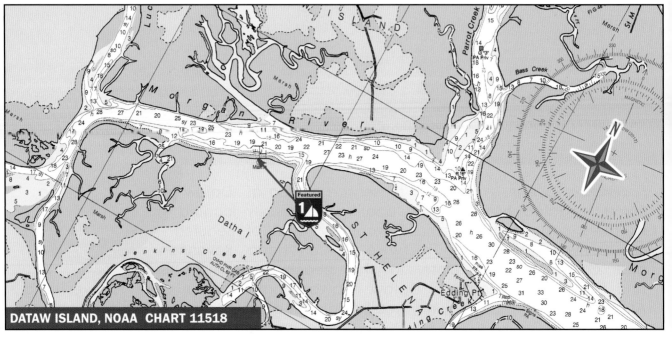

DATAW ISLAND, NOAA CHART 11518

(officially named the **Richard V. Woods Memorial Bridge**), is Factory Creek, with ample water depth and Lady's Island Marina.

South of Beaufort, note the charted shoaling between Spanish Point (flashing red "242') and the Port Royal Landing Marina, on the west side of the channel.

While there is ample maneuvering room both above and below the Ladies Island Swing Bridge, the strong side-current is tricky; adequate power and careful boat handling are required. The Ladies Island Swing Bridge has a restricted schedule. The bridge opens on signal, except Monday through Friday, from 6:30 a.m. to 9:00 a.m. and 3:00 p.m. to 6:00 p.m., when the draw need not open to navigation; and between 9:00 a.m. and 3:00 p.m., when the draw need open only on the hour.

During the months of April, May, October and November from Monday through Friday (except federal holidays), from 7:00 a.m. to 9:00 a.m. and 4:00 p.m. to 6:00 p.m., the draw need not open to navigation; and between 9:00 a.m. and 4:00 p.m., the draw need open only on the hour and half-hour. The Ladies Island Bridge is slow and cumbersome to open and is frequently under repair. There may be lengthy delays, so check ahead to see if there are any problems.

You may have noticed that the spelling of "ladies" when referring to the **Ladies Island Swing Bridge** differs from the proper spelling of Ladys Island. To further complicate matters, the official bridge name has nothing to do with ladies or ladys; it's the **Richard V. Woods Memorial Bridge**.

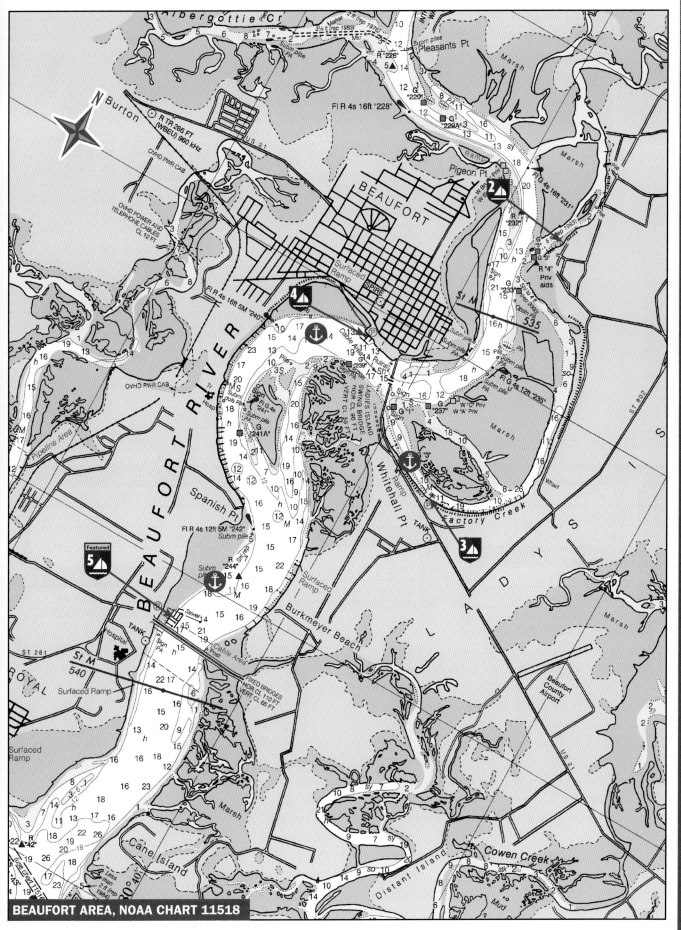

BEAUFORT AREA, NOAA CHART 11518

GOIN' ASHORE: **BEAUFORT, SC**

SERVICES	
1	Library
2	Post Office
3	Visitor Information
ATTRACTIONS	
3	Beaufort History Museum
4	George Elliott House
5	Harry C. Chambers Park

6	John Mark Verdier House
7	Petit Point
8	St. Helena's Episcopal Church
SHOPPING	
9	Lowcountry Produce Market and Café
10	Old Bay Market Place

DINING	
11	Blackstone's Deli & Café
12	Plum's
13	Saltus River Grill
14	Breakwater
MARINAS	
15	Downtown Marina of Beaufort

Beaufort is a thriving city surrounded by rivers and waterways with cool breezes and lush gardens under oak tree canopies that enchant the most seasoned visitor. It is a gracious place that is true to its Southern heritage. Lazy summer days are spent casting a shrimp net, walking on an undeveloped island beach or kayaking down the river. People come for the Lowcountry seafood, tomato stands and the Sea Islands.

Attractions: The Beaufort Visitor Center is located in the heart of Historic Beaufort in the Arsenal at 713 Craven St. (843-525-8500). The Arsenal was built in 1798 to house the Beaufort Volunteer Artillery after it fought with the Continental Army during the Revolutionary War. The Beaufort History Museum is located in the same building with a collection of artifacts,

documents and photos, which tell in a compelling manner the fascinating stories of the area. Open daily except Sunday from 10:00 a.m. to 4:00 p.m.

Take time to enjoy the wealth of local knowledge that the Visitor Center staff will share with you, along with maps, brochures, regional books and guides to enhance the Beaufort experience. Information and tickets for tours are available seven days a week. Choose from walking, boat, carriage, small van or charter fishing tours. (There are even year-round ghost and vampire tours as well as movie and TV tours). Festival and special events tickets are sold seasonally. The two most popular festivals (for which you may need to book dockage up to a year ahead) are the annual Water Festival in July and the Beaufort Shrimp Festival in early

October. All the festivals are held in Waterfront Park and along Bay Street.

This is one of those towns that is ideal for horse drawn carriage tours. There are 36 homes, churches and other sites of historical importance within the downtown area and you can see them all in an hour tour. It is great way to get to know Beaufort at the start of your visit.

Be sure to visit Petit Point (503 Washington St.), a smaller house with extensive gardens overlooking the Beaufort River. The John Mark Verdier House (801 Bay St.), now a museum, was built around 1790 and was headquarters for the Union forces in the area during the Civil War. It also hosted the aged Marquis de Lafayette upon his return to the country after the Revolutionary War. The George Elliott House (1001 Bay St.) was built around 1840 and still has its original slate mantels, crown molding, chandeliers and authentic furnishings, which survived its use as a Union hospital during the Civil War. It is privately owned but can occasionally be toured during one of Beaufort's House Tours.

St. Helena's Episcopal Church (507 Newcastle St.), erected in 1724, is surrounded by a wall built of bricks arriving from England as ships' ballast. The church has an ancient graveyard where tombstones served as operating tables for wounded soldiers during the Civil War.

Historic forts in the area include Fort Beauregard at Bay Point, and Fort San Felipe and Fort San Marcos at Parris Island. Be sure to visit the Parris Island Museum in the War Memorial Building (111 Panama St.) while there (mcrdpimuseum.com).

The Annual Spring Tour of Homes in March and the Fall Festival of Houses & Gardens in late October will allow you a peek inside a selection of private homes and gardens normally not open to the public. This includes some of the 18th- and 19th-century houses in the area and their remarkable architectural variety.

If all that is just too exhausting, grab one of the 20 bench swings at Harry C. Chambers Park and enjoy the water views, people watch or read a good book.

Should you decide to stay awhile, check out the gated waterfront community of Dataw Island, just 6 miles east of Beaufort. This tennis and golf community offers several dining options, a Community Center, resort-style pool and a community garden. Membership options range from Dining Membership to full Sports and everything in between. They offer an Experience Dataw package that includes a discovery tour. See details at dataw.com. The nearest major airports are in Charleston (1.5-hour drive) and Savannah (45-minute drive).

Shopping: Provisions are abundant in downtown Beaufort. Lowcountry Produce Market and Café (302 Carteret St., 843-322-1900) is just a few blocks from the marina and has been discovered by the yachting crowd. The Old Bay Market Place (917 Bay St.) has a number of individual shops and the Southern Sweets Ice Cream Parlor. Beaufort's grocery stores are within easy reach. A grocery store is downtown and one is on Lady's Island, as is Bill's Liquors & Fine Wine (132 Sea Island Pkwy., 843-522-2022). On the Beaufort side of the river, restaurants and unique shops abound on Bay and adjacent streets, including banks, a pharmacy and the library.

Dining: A local favorite is Blackstone's Deli & Café (205 Scott St., 843-524-4330), serving breakfast and lunch. Its Lowcountry shrimp and grits is the real deal, made with stone-ground grits. The Saltus River Grill (802 Bay St., 843-379-3474) offers dinners of fresh-caught seafood as well as a sushi bar. Breakwater (203 Carteret St., 843-379-0052) has a tapas menu that includes intriguing items such as soy ginger-glazed ribs. A more economical choice is Plum's (904 Bay St., 843-525-1946).

These are just a few of our Cruising Editor's favorites. For more options, visit beaufortsc.org.

A strictly enforced No-Wake Zone extends nearly all the way from the Ladies Island Swing Bridge to the fixed **J.E. McTeer Memorial Hwy. Twin Bridges** (65-foot fixed vertical clearance) over the Beaufort River at Port Royal (also called the **Ladys Island Dr. Bridges**). Signs on both bridges warn that violators of the No-Wake Zone will pay a fine of $1,025 or spend 30 days in a South Carolina jail cell.

Dockage/Moorings: Immediately across the Ladies Island Bridge from Beaufort, on protected Factory Creek, is Lady's Island Marina, with transient space at floating docks. They have all the usual amenities plus a yoga studio, canvas shop, massage therapist and restaurant, Lady's Island Dockside (843-379-3288), with a great menu of seafood and steaks. (We recommend the shrimp and grits.) Historic downtown Beaufort is one mile away, a scenic 15-minute walk across the swing bridge.

The Beaufort River and ICW lead to safe harbor at the Safe Harbor Beaufort, which overlooks the lush Henry C. Chambers Waterfront Park. Restaurants, inns and charming shops open to the waterfront and the historic business district. The marina offers ample dockage, all fuels and marine services. Currents are very strong here, with 7- to 9-foot tides, so use considerable caution in docking. Call ahead to the marina for dockage availability and assistance. Floating docks on the T-head accommodate transient cruisers; even so, set ample fenders on approach. The marina also manages moorings located downstream. The fee includes the use of showers and the dinghy dock.

Smaller boats may tie up along the seawall at the Waterfront Park, managed by Safe Harbor Beaufort. These docks are only useful for short tie-ups during periods of high or slack tide due to the strong currents, large tidal range (7 feet) and plethora of oyster shells on the seawall. Dock dinghies on the inside of this dock.

The courtesy "day dock" (the 140-foot-long floating dock south of the marina) is owned by the city, which does not allow overnight docking. Depths at the courtesy dock are 8 feet at the west end and 5 feet at the east end.

Anchorage: A protected anchorage is available in Factory Creek, which opens just north of and parallel to the Ladies Island Swing Bridge (at Mile 536). This anchorage is somewhat narrow for larger vessels. Enter as if heading to the Lady's Island Marina, favoring the red side of the channel, as there is only 6 feet MLW near green daybeacon "1." Then anchor in a minimum of 7-foot MLW depths past the marina. Anchored boats can pay a fee to dock dinghies at the Lady's Island Marina,

or you can anchor closer to the public boat ramp before the marina and dinghy ashore there. The current is less intense here than on the ICW, and you will not be rolled by nighttime traffic.

It is possible to anchor west of Safe Harbor Beaufort if you keep well clear of ICW traffic and anticipate the effects of strong southerlies, substantial tidal-current swings and lots of boat traffic. The 30 moorings here are closely spaced (with more to come), making it difficult to anchor. It is best to anchor near the turn in the river. The depths are generally 10 to 20 feet MLW with a mud bottom with good holding. The staff at the Safe Harbor Beaufort asks that vessels anchor at least 200 feet away from their facility. This is part of a city ordinance of which even some locals are not aware. And, of course, use a light when anchored. You can dock your dinghy behind Beaufort's courtesy dock, next to Safe Harbor Beaufort

Another anchorage is located in the eastern fork of the Beaufort River, just south of the city, at Mile 537.5, before the J.E. McTeer Memorial Highway Bridge. Enter from the south near flashing red "242" (at Mile 538.6) off Spanish Point. Proceed east, and then turn north between the marsh island to the west and the marshes to the east. Set your hook in 15 to 20 feet MLW over a sandy bottom. Do not try to re-enter the Beaufort River proper (to the north) due to severe shoaling.

Port Royal–ICW Mile 540

The Beaufort River runs broad and deep, and its well-marked main channel is easy to follow past Port Royal, Parris Island (the Marine Corps Recruit Depot) to the Port Royal Sound Entrance. There is plenty of commercial fishing traffic in the channel and much to see ashore, as the river arcs along between Parris Island and St. Helena Island.

NAVIGATION: Use NOAA Charts 11507, 11516 and 11518. Battery Creek joins the Beaufort River from the west. On Battery Creek's north shore is Port Royal, the deepwater commercial shipping center for the Beaufort area. If headed up Battery Creek, keep red daybeacon "42" to starboard and follow the channel to Port Royal. Farther upstream is the fixed **U.S. 21 Hwy. Bridge** (45-foot vertical clearance). The creek carries 12-foot MLW depths or more for 4 miles upstream and is charted (NOAA Chart 11516), but no markers are present.

If northbound on the ICW, be sure to make the turn to the north on the Beaufort River between red nun "40"

Beaufort, SC

PORT ROYAL LANDING MARINA

and quick flashing green "41," beyond which you will pick up the ICW markers again, rather than continuing straight westerly into Battery Creek and Port Royal. Both routes have bridges visible ahead and this mistake has been known to dismast sailboats.

⚠ At the junction of Battery Creek and the Beaufort River, the familiar ICW marker system reverses: Keep red to port for the next 6.5 miles.

The ICW returns near Parris Island Spit as you make the turn to cross Port Royal Sound towards Hilton Head Island. Stay clear of the Spit and the shoaling in that area. To do so, when leaving the Beaufort River channel, lay a course from ICW flashing red daybeacon "246" off Parris Island Spit to red nun buoy "2," and then to flashing green daybeacon "3" just past Dolphin Head as you make the 5-mile-long crossing of Port Royal Sound. It can be bumpy if wind and tide oppose. At Mile 553, you enter Skull Creek between Hilton Head Island and Pinckney Island (a wildlife refuge).

Dockage: Three miles south of downtown Beaufort, immediately north of the high-rise J.E. McTeer Twin Bridges, family-owned Port Royal Landing Marina, Inc. offers pump-out service, clean restrooms and showers, laundry facilities, good WiFi and cable TV. The easy-access floating face dock has gas and diesel fuel, the ship store is fully stocked and the marina's courtesy car puts you downtown in just a few minutes. It is less than a 1-mile drive or walk from Port Royal Landing Marina to a supermarket, liquor store, drug store, ATM and West Marine. Be sure to phone ahead for reservations or hail the marina on VHF Channel 16 before you approach to check for dockage availability and directions to a berth on its floating docks.

Anchorage: There is an anchorage at Port Royal on Battery Creek with 8 to 20 feet MLW and a sand bottom. It is protected from all directions except southeast. There have been reports of debris on the bottom so make sure your anchor is well set.

If you really want to get off the beaten path, explore the upper reaches of Cowen Creek, off the ICW at Mile 544.5. You will find deep water throughout the creek. On Distant Island Creek, tuck into the deep water slot behind the unnamed island between Distant Island and the marsh for complete solitude in at least 12 feet MLW.

Port Royal Sound Entrance–ICW Mile 550

NAVIGATION: Use NOAA Chart 11518. Port Royal Sound is a big ship inlet and is wide, deep and very long. If you are headed south offshore, this is not the best option as a point of entry, as you will backtrack some distance to re-enter the ocean. However, it is a great exit to use to make an overnight run south to St. Marys. When a cold front passes through the area, expect breaking ocean swells throughout the channel until rounding Bay Point. Under these conditions, the going will be tedious but still negotiable for well-found vessels. More difficult is the combination of a stiff onshore breeze against an ebb tide (driven here by local tides of 9 feet); this is a situation best avoided.

See the Inlet section in the front of this guide and Waterway Explorer (waterwayguide.com) for details on the Port Royal Sound Entrance.

■ HILTON HEAD ISLAND

A bustling but beautiful year-round resort, Hilton Head Island, named after 17th-century explorer William Hilton, is probably the best known of South Carolina's Sea Islands. As one of the largest barrier islands on the Atlantic Coast, it is amply endowed by nature and history, and offers something nearly year-round for everyone, including a choice of excellent marina resorts. The ICW amenities offered on Hilton Head range from the ultra-luxurious to comfortable casual. As you progress through Skull Creek, you will notice many commercial and private docks along the way.

Note the No-Wake Zones around Hilton Head Island; proceed at slow speed in these areas, especially in Broad Creek and Skull Creek. These signs are sometimes small and hard to spot. As on any waterway, be courteous and do not let your wake roll into the docks. The numerous ferry boats plying the waters of Calibogue Sound between Hilton Head and Daufuskie Island can leave large wakes. The ferries usually slow down to "no-wake speed" when passing recreational boats.

The **J. Wilton Graves (U.S. 278) Twin Hwy. Bridges** (65-foot fixed vertical clearance) at Mile 557.6 provides the only automobile access to and from Hilton Head Island.

Skull Creek Area–ICW Mile 553 to Mile 564

NAVIGATION: Use NOAA Chart 11507. Use the Savannah River Entrance Tide Table. For Skull Creek high tide, add 22 minutes; for low tide, add 26 minutes. Markers lead past oyster beds until Mile 555, where the first of Hilton Head Island's several marinas, Skull Creek Marina, shows to port. (Note that several markers were reported missing at press time in summer 2019.) At Skull Creek Marina, slack tide is 2 hours after slack tide at the south end of Skull Creek. Watch for the shoal just in front of the marina to the north. The No-Wake Zone around Skull Creek Marina is strictly enforced. If you throw a wake, the marina will call you out on the radio in no uncertain terms. Local marine patrols are frequently in this area and will stop boaters throwing a wake into the marinas.

Dockage: Skull Creek Marina offers slips on modern concrete floating docks and can accommodate vessels to 200 feet. They also offer repairs and sell both gas and diesel. There is a restaurant a short walk from the docks. Other services will require transportation. At Mile 555.6 is Hilton Head Boathouse, which does not have transient dockage but sells gas (no diesel) and offers repairs.

At Mile 557, Hilton Head Harbor Marina has an easily accessed fuel dock with both gas and diesel right on the ICW. The independently owned marina offers dockage in an enclosed basin and is also a luxury RV resort with two pools, saunas, Jacuzzi, tennis court, laundry, WiFi, two bath houses, a five-star restaurant (reservations only for dinner), exercise room, playground and beer and wine sales. They are also pet friendly. Car rentals and shuttle service are available upon request. Note the direction and velocity of the current carefully as you approach the marina. When approaching from the north, favor flashing green daybeacon "19" and give red daybeacon "20," just below the entrance channel, a fair berth. A bar extends well up from the daybeacon.

In Calibogue Sound on the port side (to the east) before Jarvis Creek, a pier marks the entrance to the lock leading into Windmill Harbour Marina, which lies in one of two secure, tide-free, lock-controlled harbors along the ICW. (The other is at the Wexford Plantation, also on Hilton Head.) The harbormaster monitors the lock and stands by on VHF Channels 14 and 16. This harbor is home to the South Carolina Yacht Club and is surrounded by the well-maintained grounds of a gated residential community. A pool, restaurant and bar

GOIN' ASHORE: **HILTON HEAD, SC**

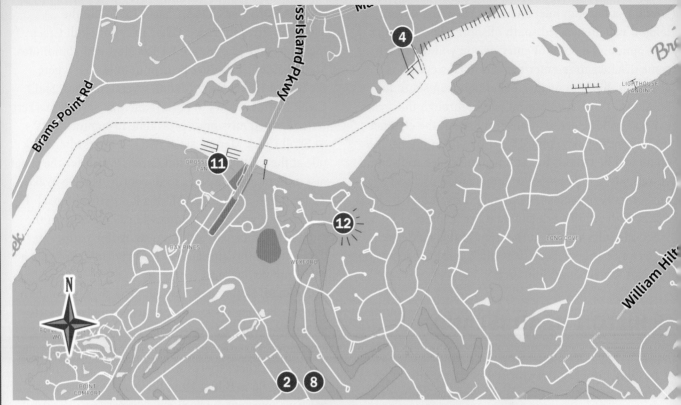

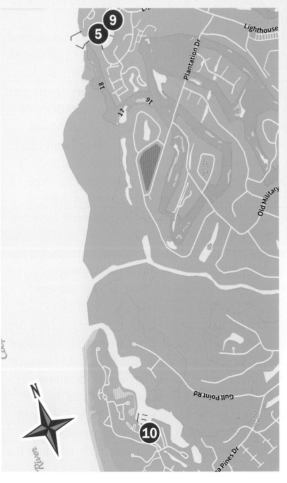

SERVICES	
	SERVICES
1	Library
2	Post Office
3	Visitor Information
	ATTRACTIONS
4	Aerial Adventure Hilton Head
	SHOPPING
5	Harbour Town Yacht Basin
	DINING
4	Up the Creek Pub & Grill
6	Santa Fe Café

7	Shelter Cove Harbour (with 9 restaurants)
8	Signe's Heaven Bound Bakery & Café
9	The Crazy Crab
10	The Salty Dog Café
	MARINAS
4	Broad Creek Marina
5	Harbour Town Yacht Basin
7	Shelter Cove Harbour & Marina
11	Palmetto Bay Yacht Center
12	Wexford Plantation

Most people know Hilton Head Island for its red and white striped lighthouse and fine golf courses, but it is also a great family getaway with long beaches, and walking and bicycling trails through its well-preserved natural areas. Dozens of restaurants cater to every taste. The island has more than its share of celebrities in residence, so you never know when you will be sharing the dining room with a well-known author, musician or athlete.

Attractions: Fortunately, when Hilton Head incorporated as a town in 1983, strict zoning laws were passed that limit signage and building materials so the non-commercial feeling of the island

has been preserved. Even the Walmart is tastefully hidden behind lush foliage and a discreet sign, as are the fast-food chains that have begun to proliferate. The 12-mile stretch of ocean beach is still beautiful, with houses set well back behind the dunes. Wildlife sanctuaries ensure that forest and marshland with abundant wildlife are untouched. Access is carefully controlled, but winding nature paths and catwalks for walking and biking allow you to explore. You can also take museum-sponsored beach walks, and the local Audubon Society at Newhall Nature Preserve (88 Palmetto Bay Rd., 843-842-9246) organizes and leads regular bird walks. Lawton Stables at The Sea Pines Resort offers trail rides and pony rides and has a small animal farm. Call 843-671-2586 for hours and directions.

The Coastal Discovery Museum at Honey Horn (70 Honey Horn Dr.) offers a wide range of activities including guided tours (walking and by boat or kayak) of the local area, led by museum curators and trained volunteers who teach about the ecology and history of the region. For more information, call 843-689-6767, or visit coastaldiscovery.org. The Sandbox, an interactive children's museum, has hands-on exhibits.

If you feel adventurous, Aerial Adventure Hilton Head, a playground in the sky, is located at Broad Creek Marina Adventures (843-682-6000). The canopy tour shows you the world from heights of up to 75 feet in the salty air. The two-hour tour on eight interconnected ziplines takes you from a tree platform to a suspended bridge to an aerial staircase ("don't look down") to a 75-foot tower tour. Kayaking, sailing, boating and fishing charters are offered here as well.

For those who prefer a slower pace, there are over 20 premier courses including the famous Harbour Town Golf Links at The Sea Pines Resort, the Palmetto Dunes Robert Trent Jones, Arthur Hills and George Fazio courses and The Heritage Golf Collections' seven courses. The RBC Heritage PGA Tournament is played here every April the week after The Masters. During that week, don't expect to find space at Harbour Town without reservations well in advance.

Shopping: Shopping centers, more than 250 restaurants and golf courses have proliferated on the island. Perhaps the most well known area is Harbour Town Yacht Basin, with its signature red and white striped lighthouse. (You can climb to the top for a small fee.) The marina has a shopping center with specialty shops (book shops, clothing, gift and nautical shops), including a grocery and deli. A larger supermarket is nearby. Coligny Plaza at Forest Beach, Shelter Cove Harbour at Palmetto Dunes, and The Village at Wexford are other options. Bigger shopping areas are located along William Hilton Parkway (Hwy. 278), the main drag on the island, where you can find all the "big-box" stores, nautical supplies and just about anything you even think you might need.

Dining: Have a Creek burger or smoked wings at the friendly Up the Creek Pub & Grill (843-681-3625) before or after your zipline flight at Broad Creek Marina. Eat in or on the deck.

A favorite spot in Harbour Town for dining is The Crazy Crab (843-363-2722), which has everything from fabulous burgers to good fried shrimp. The Crazy Crab at Jarvis Creek is now open as well and is pet friendly (843-681-5021). Santa Fe Café, located mid-island at 807 William Hilton Pkwy. (843-785-3838), is great for southwestern food. An unexpected find is the Sunset Grille (843-689-6744) at the Hilton Head Harbor RV Resort & Marina.

Located in South Beach Marina Village, The Salty Dog Café offers waterfront dining for lunch and dinner (843-671-2233). Be sure to stop by Signe's Heaven Bound Bakery & Café, serving meals and sweets for visitors and residents of Hilton Head for over 40 years (93 Arrow Rd., 843-785-9118). (Closed on Sundays.)

Shelter Cove Harbour at Palmetto Dunes offers a variety of dining establishments, including Ela's Blu Water Grille (843-785-3030), Bistro 17 (843-785-5517), San Miguel's Restaurant (843-842-4555), Scott's Fish Restaurant (843-785-7575), Bucci & Murray's Pub on the Harbor (843-785-3300) and the Mediterranean Harbour Bar & Grill (843-842-9991).

COME ASHORE TO THE BEST OF HILTON HEAD ISLAND
Enjoy Harbour Town Yacht Basin and the unparalleled amenities of The Sea Pines Resort

Be surprised and captivated by The Sea Pines Resort and a luxury experience unmatched by any coastal resort destination. Experience miles of beautiful beaches, world-class dining, tennis and golf, including Harbour Town Golf Links, host to the PGA TOUR's RBC Heritage Presented by Boeing. For accommodations off the boat, stay at the stunning Inn & Club at Harbour Town, Hilton Head Island's only AAA Four-Diamond, Forbes Four-Star hotel, just steps from the Harbour Town Yacht Basin.

Harbour Town Yacht Basin features:

- LOA up to 150-foot vessels
- MLW 8.5 feet
- Daily/weekly/monthly dockage rates
- Electric: 30/50/100A, some 3-phase 100A
- VHF 16/68
- Fuel: High-speed gas and diesel; ValvTect fuels
- Complimentary pump-out
- Restrooms/showers/private laundry

- Complimentary Wi-Fi internet
- Complimentary access to The Sea Pines Resort Fitness Center equipment
- Complimentary access to the Harbour Town Pool
- Beach access
- Complimentary access to the Harbour Town Clubhouse, Sea Pines Beach Club and Plantation Golf Club
- Resort Guest Amenity Card for valuable benefits and room-charging privileges

Inn & Club Guest Room   Harbour Town Golf Links   Links, an American Grill   Sea Pines Beach Club

ValvTect Marine Fuels' Marina of the Year
Marina Dock Age magazine's Marina of the Year
Marinalife's Second Best Small Marina

EXPERIENCE HARBOUR TOWN
Shopping, dining, watersports and much more

Enjoy unique boutique shopping, a variety of premier dining options featuring views of the harbour and Calibogue Sound, and exciting watersports and recreation, including the famous Harbour Town Lighthouse. It all combines to create a Hilton Head Island vacation experience you'll never forget.

» *Over 20 unique shops*
» *A total of 10 fabulous dining options*
» *Live entertainment*
» *Kayaks, WaveRunners, parasailing, stand-up paddleboards and more*
» *Fishing charters and kids' adventures*

Shopping

Dining

Watersports

Request dockage at
harbourtownyachtbasin.com
or call (843) 363-8335.

THE SEA PINES RESORT

HARBOUR TOWN
YACHT BASIN

32° 08' 20" N / 80° 48' 40" W - St. Mile 564 | HILTON HEAD ISLAND, SC | (843) 363-8335 | harbourtownyachtbasin.com

Hilton Head Area, SC

	Phone	Largest Vessel Accommodated	VHF Channel Monitored	Transient Berths / Total Berths	Approach / Dockside Depth (reported)	Floating Docks	Gas / Diesel	Groceries, Ice, Marine Supplies, Snacks	Repairs: Hull, Engine, Propeller	Lift (tonnage), Crane, Rail	Min/Max Amps	Laundry, Pool, Showers, Courtesy Car	Pump-Out Station	Nearby: Grocery Store, Motel, Restaurant
SKULL CREEK				**Dockage**				**Supplies**				**Services**		
1. Skull Creek Marina WiFi 555	843-681-8436	200	16/10	25/179	12/10	F	GD	I	-	L30	30/100	LSC	P	R
2. Hilton Head Boathouse 555.6	843-681-2628	35	69		6/6	F	GD	IMS	HEP	L20	-	S	-	GMR
3. Hilton Head Harbor Marina ▢ WiFi 557	843-681-3256	100	16/12	15/100	50/35	F	GD	IS	-		30/50	LPS	-	MR
4. Windmill Harbour Marina ▢ onSpot 558.3	843-681-9235	70	14/14	70/258	8/8	-	GD	IMS	EP		30/50	LPS	P	MR
COOPER RIVER														
5. Freeport Marina WiFi	843-342-8687	100	-	20/50	20/12	F	GD	GIS	-	L	-	S	-	GMR
BROAD CREEK														
6. Harbour Town Yacht Basin onSpot 565	843-363-8335	160	16/68	25/85	8/8	F	GD	GIMS	-	-	15/100	LPS	P	GMR
7. Palmetto Bay Yacht Center ▢ WiFi 3.5 E of 563.8	843-686-5989	70	-	-	20/20	F	GD	IMS	HEP	L75,C	30/50	LS	P	GMR
8. Wexford Plantation – PRIVATE WiFi	843-686-8813	70	16/14	23/280	7/7	F	-	IS	-	-	30/50	S	P	-
9. Broad Creek Marina WiFi 4.5 E of 563.8	843-681-3625	100	16/68	45/55	23/16	F	GD	IMS	HEP	L20	30/50	LS	P	R
SHELTER COVE														
10. Shelter Cove Harbour & Marina ▢ onSpot	844-238-3237	160	16/71	20/178	9/9	F	GD	IMS	HEP	-	30/100	LS	P	GMR

▢ Internet Access   WiFi Wireless Internet Access   WG Waterway Guide Cruising Club Partner   onSpot dockside WiFi facility

See WaterwayGuide.com for current rates, fuel prices, web site addresses, and other up-to-the-minute information. *(Information in the table is provided by the facilities.)*

are among the amenities. Be aware that this is a sizable harbor and depending on where you are docked, it may be a hike to the bathhouse or to the club's dining room.

Anchorage: To reach the northernmost anchorage in the Hilton Head area, bear east off the ICW at Seabrook Landing, Mile 553.5 into Skull Creek. Anchor along the east or south shore of the unnamed island shown on the chart in 10- to 15-foot MLW depths (east side).

Broad Creek–ICW Mile 565

Just opposite the spot where the ICW leaves Calibogue Sound for the Cooper River (Mile 565) is beautiful Broad Creek. To the north, handsome houses, many with their own docks, line the creek at Shelter Cove. Oyster beds line the banks, crab pot markers dot the marsh flats and fishing drops are at the entrance to tidal streams along the way.

NAVIGATION: Use NOAA Charts 11507 and 11516. The break between Brams Point and Buck Island at green daybeacon "29A" is too tricky for strangers. Do not attempt to use this secondary entrance to Broad Creek without local knowledge. Instead, run down to green daybeacon "1" at the proper entrance to Broad Creek. Give the marker a rather wide berth at low tide and enter between it and red daybeacon "2" on the opposite side. The shoal extends northeast of green daybeacon "1," so use caution. Once you are inside, Broad Creek runs deep to its banks all the way to the marinas well upstream.

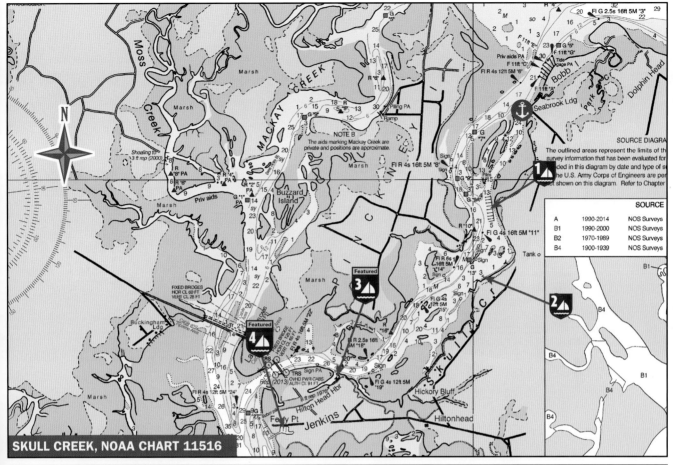

SKULL CREEK, NOAA CHART 11516

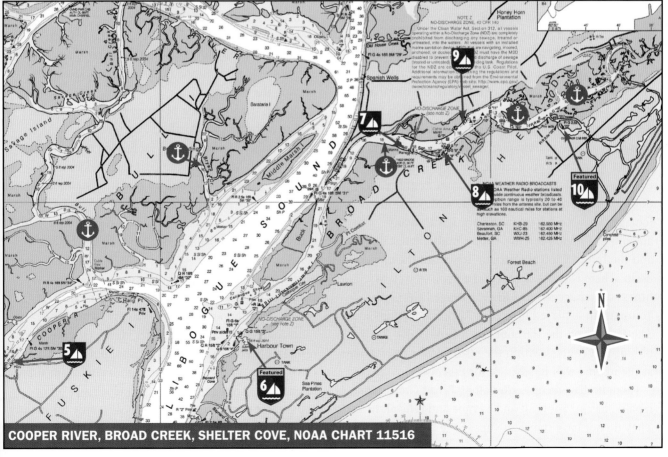

COOPER RIVER, BROAD CREEK, SHELTER COVE, NOAA CHART 11516

HARBOUR TOWN YACHT BASIN

Calibogue Sound

Dockage: Perhaps one of the best-known features along this stretch of the ICW is the red and white striped 90-foot-tall lighthouse, east of Mile 564 and south of the entrance to Broad Creek. This marks Harbour Town Yacht Basin, entrance to the original residential development on Hilton Head Island, Sea Pines Plantation. Enter between two jetties (the one to port is an observation pier) into Harbour Town's circular basin, with its floating concrete docks. A 270-foot-long floating face dock across from the fuel dock at the marina's entrance offers additional linear footage. This is a full-service marina with many amenities. Condominiums, shops, multiple restaurants and the Inn & Club at Harbour Town rim the circular basin. There is beach access and a pool, as well as fitness center access. The RBC Heritage PGA Golf Tournament is played here each April the week after The Masters on the Harbour Town Golf Links, the best of four golf courses within the resort. Make reservations at the marina well in advance for this event.

Palmetto Bay Yacht Center along Broad Creek offers repairs, has a 75-ton lift and a crane and sells all fuels. They do not have transient slips. Note that the **Cross**

Island Expressway Bridge (65-foot fixed vertical clearance) crosses Broad Creek after the Palmetto Bay facility. Vessels with mast heights greater than 65 feet will not be able to continue up Broad Creek except by playing the tides.

On the starboard side of Broad Creek beyond the bridge is the private Wexford Plantation. You must be a member of a reciprocal yacht club to stay here. Broad Creek Marina on the port side welcomes transients and has fuel and an on-site restaurant (Up the Creek Pub & Grill). This is the location of the Broad Creek Marina Land & Water Adventures (with a zipline and parasailing) described in the Hilton Head "Goin' Ashore."

Shelter Cove Harbour & Marina, across from Palmetto Dunes Oceanfront Resort, is an oasis for waterfront shopping, dining, water activities and tours, and has spectacular water views. Offering seven restaurants and a variety of fine shopping, Shelter Cove Harbour & Marina is the place to unwind from a day of championship golf, tennis, pickleball and other activities. Be sure to bring the whole family for nightly entertainment during the summer with special activities

WINDMILL HARBOUR MARINA

just for kids. Featured events continue during the fall, holiday season and spring. Along with private fishing charters and kayak and paddleboard rentals, Shelter Cove Harbour & Marina also offers a full-service marina store with boating gear, the latest coastal merchandise, snacks, convenience items, bait, tackle and more.

Anchorage: It is possible to anchor outside the channel in Broad Creek, just off Buck Island in at least 19 feet MLW. You may want to set two anchors because the area outside the channel is narrow and the current reverses strongly.

Three miles up Broad Creek is Opposum Point, just before Palmetto Point Yacht Center. Anchor near the south shore for good protection. The holding in Broad Creek is excellent in thick mud. There is a public landing and boat ramp under the Cross Island Bridge. Be aware that ferries to Daufuskie and other destinations use this creek.

At the head of Broad Creek, you can anchor in the channel near green daybeacon "19." Holding in clay is good here, with 10-foot depths in the middle of the creek. There is also an anchorage at green daybeacon "13" in at least 15 feet MLW. Access to Hilton Head is easy from either of these.

Side Trip: Bluffton, May River

NAVIGATION: Use NOAA Chart 11516. The May River, which comes into the ICW at Mile 560, offers an interesting side trip to the small town of Bluffton. Flood tide at Mile 560, at the head of Calibogue Sound, begins 1 hour and 23 minutes before the flood tide at the Savannah River entrance and ebbs 54 minutes before. The May River offers good anchorage almost anywhere past the bar at the mouth of its tributary stream, Bass Creek. The anchorage at Bluffton offers all-around protection in 10 to 20 feet MLW with a mud bottom.

Calibogue Sound Entrance

NAVIGATION: Use NOAA Chart 11516. Many boats use the ocean entrance to Calibogue (pronounced "Cal-eh-BOE-gie") Sound in fair weather and seas. It is a shortcut to reach the ICW from the ocean and is much shorter than the Savannah River approach. The markers, however, are widely spaced and sometimes difficult to locate. It is approached from the Jones Island Range area of Tybee Roads. Note that if using this route to the Tybee Roads channel, the shoal to the east of quick flashing green buoy "3" has built to the west to within about 200 feet of that buoy. See the Inlet section in the front of this guide for more information about Calibogue Sound Entrance.

Anchorage: Across Calibogue Sound and the ICW at Mile 563 is well-protected Bryan Creek. When entering, take care to clear the 2-foot MLW bar extending from the north. Once inside, favor the west shore. Anchor in 8- to 11-foot MLW depths with a sandy bottom. This anchorage is pretty tight and can get buggy in warmer weather.

■ TO SAVANNAH RIVER

Daufuskie Island–ICW Mile 565 to Mile 571

Heading south on the ICW, Daufuskie Island awaits at the confluence of Calibogue Sound and the Cooper River. (The ICW continues to run past Daufuskie Island as the channel goes south along the Cooper River, Ramshorn Creek and the New River.) With no bridge linking Daufuskie Island to the mainland, the small native population (direct descendants of slaves brought from Africa) once lived an isolated life, having little

contact with the outside world. Nowadays, inspired by Hilton Head Island's development, Daufuskie Island continues to undergo extensive development of its own, with resorts and residential areas springing up each year. There is still, however, no vehicular access to the island.

NAVIGATION: Use NOAA Chart 11507. The old lighthouse on Daufuskie Island at Haig Point serves as a landmark for spotting the lighted buoy at the entrance to the Cooper River. When passing Daufuskie Landing on the Cooper River, follow the dredged channel of narrow Ramshorn Creek into the New River, and split the channel between flashing green daybeacon "39" and red flashing buoy "40" for 9.3 feet MLW.

Over the years, the wakes of passing vessels have damaged locally berthed craft at the floating dock and boat ramp at Daufuskie Landing. Along this stretch, the tidal current reverses every 2 or 3 miles.

Dockage: Near red daybeacon "36" on the Cooper River is Freeport Marina, which offers slips and fuel. Cottages and the Old Daufuskie Crab Co. Restaurant (843-785-6652) are nearby. During the day, dockage at the marina is free when you dine at the restaurant. This is a popular restaurant for boats in transit to stop for a quick lunch.

You can tie up at Daufuskie Landing at green daybeacon "39" during the day. Be sure to stop in at the "not so general" General Store located just off the ferry docks for groceries and gifts, or at the tiny and historic Silver Dew Winery, located in an unassuming building that dates all the way back to 1883. Call 843-785-8242 for details on both.

Anchorage: Bull Creek, just past Mile 565, is a favorite anchorage and rafting site for local boats and ICW travelers alike. Just inside the entrance is good holding with sufficient depths, but the currents are strong, and there is no place to go ashore. The best spot to anchor on Bull Creek is past the little creek to the west because shrimp boats use the lower part of Bull Creek.

You can anchor in 8 to 15 feet MLW with excellent holding in mud on the northern branch of the Cooper River, which leaves the ICW before green daybeacon "37." South of flashing green "39" at Mile 570, the New River offers a good anchorage in 8- to 20-feet MLW depths with excellent holding in mud. Enter from the south side of the river, watch your depth gauge and avoid the shallow water to the northwest

Savannah River, GA

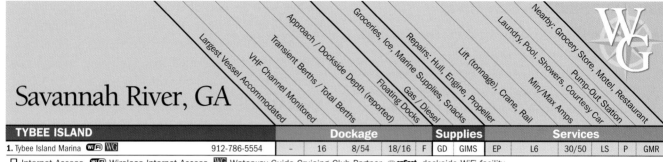

TYBEE ISLAND				Dockage				Supplies		Services				
1. Tybee Island Marina WiFi WG	912-786-5554	–	16	8/54	18/16	F	GD	GIMS	EP	L6	30/50	LS	P	GMR

🖥 Internet Access   WiFi Wireless Internet Access   WG Waterway Guide Cruising Club Partner   🛜 onSpot dockside WiFi facility
See WaterwayGuide.com for current rates, fuel prices, web site addresses, and other up-to-the-minute information. *(Information in the table is provided by the facilities.)*

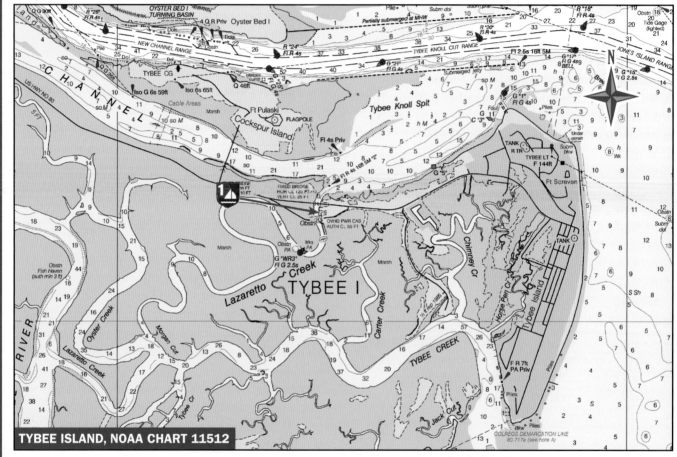

TYBEE ISLAND, NOAA CHART 11512

Fields Cut/Walls Cuts–ICW Mile 571 to Mile 576

Leaving South Carolina, you pass through several shallow land cuts before reaching the Savannah River at the end of Fields Cut. This has typically been an area of concern due to constant shoaling. Fields Cut and Walls Cut were dredged in summer 2019 and depths are holding except for the spots indicated below. The tidal range here is 8 to 9 feet, so most boats will have no trouble at mid to high tide.

NAVIGATION: Use NOAA Chart 11507. Heading south through Walls Cut follow the deep water path as indicated on your chartplotter, which will result in favoring the red side of this passage for 9 feet MLW. Red nun buoy "48A" at the north entrance of Fields Cut was missing at press time in summer 2019.

Be advised that when approaching red daybeacon "50" you will be entering the Savannah River. This river carries very heavy large shipping traffic that can create large swells. Keep your radio on and lookout for these large ships. They are visible above the marsh grass. You might have to wait to cross the river, and it is definitely advisable to do so.

Anchorage: In calm weather, cruisers will sometimes anchor south of the ICW and Walls Cut in the Wright

River at Mile 572.2 (Turtle Island). There is 10 to 15 feet MLW here and a mud bottom. This is a convenient spot to stop north of the Georgia border with good holding and wave/wake protection. It is pretty anchorage but has little wind protection and no amenities.

■ SAVANNAH RIVER

You have to make a decision when you reach the Savannah River: (1) You can turn east to head to the Savannah River Entrance (Tybee Roads) and out to sea; (2) head west up the river to the beautiful city of Savannah; or (3) continue on the ICW through the Elba Island Cut to the Wilmington River.

In this area, it is important to stay in the channel, use the charted magenta ICW line as a guide (except where noted in the text), make use of the numerous navigational ranges and give markers–especially those at turns in natural rivers–a wide berth. Plan ahead in timing your arrival at the known trouble spots. If it is low tide when you arrive, drop the hook for a while to wait for higher water; it doesn't take long for the tide to come up a foot or two. "Mid-tide and rising" is always preferable in these areas. Remember that strong winds and the lunar cycle affect tidal range. Conditions change, so check the latest *Local Notice to Mariners* before you go or check for updated information on Waterway Explorer at waterwayguide.com.

Option 1: To Tybee Roads Inlet

NAVIGATION: Use NOAA Chart 11507. Sixteen miles down the Savannah River from Savannah is the Savannah River Entrance (also called Tybee Roads Inlet). This is a big ship entrance, offering entry to Savannah via the ICW and Savannah River. Slower boats bound for the Savannah River on this route should try to enter Tybee Roads with a favorable current, if possible, as the effects of the current start many miles offshore in the Atlantic. See the Inlet section at the front of this guide for more information about the Tybee Roads Inlet.

Dockage: The entrance to the Savannah River near Tybee Island, Savannah's primary beach area, makes a good fuel stop for powerboaters going south on the outside run down the Atlantic. Tybee Island Marina offers fuel (both gas and diesel) and some transient dockage. The marina is on the south side of the Savannah River's mouth but the 35-foot fixed vertical

Welcome to Georgia!

After passing through Fields Cut, you will encounter the Savannah River and the State of Georgia. Islands, estuaries, creeks and bars dominate the Georgia coast. If South Carolina is the Lowcountry then Georgia is the Backcountry, with miles of salt marsh, rushing tides, plentiful anchorages and mosquitoes (bring bug spray).

The channels are narrow here with wind-driven tides and sizable mud banks. It is best to travel on a high tide, especially through the challenging Hells Gate channel south of Savannah, the Sapelo River (ICW Mile 635) and Cumberland Dividings into Cumberland Sound. The charts may not represent the most recent placement of navigation aids, which are frequently moved by the Army Corps of Engineers to mark the shifting channels. (As always, listen on VHF Channel 13 for dredging operations and give them a wide berth.) Refer to the Waterway Explorer at waterwayguide.com for navigational alerts and updates.

You often hear about skippers choosing to run offshore to avoid Georgia but with good planning and prudent navigation, this isn't necessary. While you can easily jump outside at Tybee Roads or St. Simons Sound, you would miss the natural beauty of these pristine waters and endless sky.

Savannah River, GA

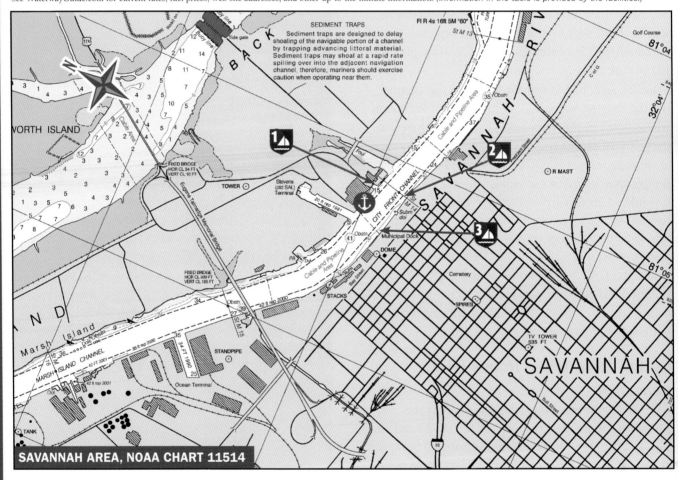

SAVANNAH AREA		Largest Vessel Accommodated	VHF Channel Monitored	Transient Berths / Total Berths	Approach / Dockside Depth (reported)	Floating Docks	Groceries, Ice, Marine Supplies, Snacks	Gas / Diesel	Repairs: Hull, Engine, Propeller	Lift (tonnage), Crane, Rail	Min/Max Amps	Pump-Out Station	Laundry, Pool, Showers, Courtesy Car	Nearby: Grocery Store, Motel, Restaurant
		Dockage					Supplies			Services				
1. The Westin Savannah Harbor Golf Resort & Spa 🖥 📶	912-201-2021	300	–	25/25	27/16	F	–	IS	–	–	30/200+	LPS	–	GMR
2. River Street Market Place Dock 🖥 📶	912-398-6038	250	–	–	24/18	F	–	IS	–	–	30/100	–	–	GMR
3. River Street LLC	912-232-4252	150	–	–	27/14	F	–	–	–	–	30/100	–	–	GMR

🖥 Internet Access 📶 Wireless Internet Access WG Waterway Guide Cruising Club Partner onSpot dockside WiFi facility
See WaterwayGuide.com for current rates, fuel prices, web site addresses, and other up-to-the-minute information. *(Information in the table is provided by the facilities.)*

clearance **U.S. 80-GA 26 Hwy. Bridge** over the marina's access channel restricts usage by sailboats.

Option 2: Upriver to Savannah

NAVIGATION: Use NOAA Chart 11507. Savannah is about 8 miles up the Savannah River from ICW Mile 576. Expect strong currents, a 9-foot tide and heavy commercial traffic on the way. Those with low-powered boats should check the tide tables and plan arrivals and departures accordingly. Following the Savannah River another 170 miles will bring you to Augusta,

home of the Professional Golf Association's annual Masters Championship.

When returning to the ICW, you can do so via the south channel (below Elba Island), assuming you can navigate under the 35-foot-fixed vertical clearance **Elba Island Road Bridge**.

Dockage: The Westin Savannah Harbor Golf Resort & Spa on Hutchinson Island is directly across from River Street with slips on floating docks. They can accommodate vessels to 300 feet with 16-foot dockside depths. Be sure to call well in advance for reservations.

Water ferry service is available to reach the other side of the harbor.

Across the channel, River Street Market Place Dock offers concrete floating dockage with direct access to downtown. They can accommodate vessels up to 250 feet with 18-foot dockside depths and full amenities. The River Street Market features recreations of the sheds that stood on River Street in the mid 1800s. Today the open-air market has more than 50 shops representing countries from all over the world. River Street LLC is nearby on the city side of the river and may offer transient dockage for vessels to 150 feet; call ahead.

The Savannah River Docks are limited to 3-hour tie-ups and offer no water or electrical services.

Option 3: ICW to Thunderbolt

Study your charts before beginning this passage since the next 140 miles down the ICW are visually interesting and also physically demanding. You will use your GPS, compass, depth sounder and binoculars as you wind along serpentine rivers and cross open sounds that can be choppy and downright nasty when the wind kicks up. The route winds past Georgia's barrier islands and then becomes an entirely different kind of ICW when you cross into Florida.

As you cross the Savannah River, going from Fields Cut to Elba Island Cut, traveling south along the ICW, you leave South Carolina and enter Georgia. From here until the sheltered waters of Florida, pay close attention to currents and depths, as well as markers and ranges.

The Bonaventure Cemetery, made famous in the book "Midnight in the Garden of Good and Evil," is visible from the ICW along the Wilmington River between flashing red daybeacon "30" and flashing green daybeacon "31" (past Mile 580) on the west side of the route.

NAVIGATION: Use NOAA Chart 11507. Use the Savannah River Entrance Tide Table. For high tide, add 32 minutes; for low tide, add 12 minutes. Heading south on the ICW, you can pick up the beginning of the flood current and carry a fair (flood) current all the way through Walls Cut (Mile 572) and Fields Cut to just south of Thunderbolt (Mile 585). (An ebb current gives the same advantage to northbound vessels.)

The ICW passage is not straight across the Savannah River, but diagonal. When you cross the Savannah River, allow for the strong river current. Slow boats may have to correct course several times. Watch for big ships that will have announced their presence on VHF Channels 13 and 16. They approach fast from both directions, and port pilots have had many close encounters with pleasure boats in the river where the ships have no room to maneuver in the narrow, swiftly running channel.

⚠️ A rock jetty at Elba Island Cut's confluence with the Savannah River (on the southeast side of the river) is submerged at high tide but marked with a white danger beacon. Because of the shoal on the west side in Elba Cut, flashing red daybeacon "2" and flashing red daybeacon "4" have been moved eastward and appear to be in the middle of the channel. Pass 50 feet off red daybeacon "2" and 130 feet off red daybeacon "4" for 8.7-feet MLW. The channel passes close to the eastern quarter for 10-foot MLW depths. Favor the green side.

Depths are well maintained here, but since the tidal range is between 8 and 9 feet MLW, be sure to stay in the channel. From Elba Island Cut, the ICW heads briefly westward along St. Augustine Creek. It then enters the winding upper reaches of the Wilmington River, which is not nearly as intricate as it appears on the chart, and then approaches the town of Thunderbolt. Multiple sets of ranges guide you through this area.

From flashing green daybeacon "19" (at Mile 578.7) to flashing red daybeacon "36" (at Mile 583.5), stay in the center of the channel and use the magenta line only as a guide to avoid shoals along the banks in this area.

The **Causton Bluff (Sam Varnedoe) Bascule Bridge** at Mile 579.9 has a closed vertical clearance of 21 feet and is the only opening bridge in Georgia for southbound vessels. Georgia bridges monitor VHF Channel 09, as they do in South Carolina and Florida. The bridgetender will often request that boats bunch together for openings. Note that the approaches are No-Wake Zones on both sides. The Causton Bluff Bascule Bridge is restricted year-round: It opens on signal, Monday through Friday (except federal holidays), except from 6:30 a.m. to 9:00 a.m., and from 4:30 p.m. to 6:30 p.m., when the draw will only open for waiting traffic at 7:00 a.m., 8:00 a.m. and 5:30 p.m.

The tidal current reverses between the Causton Bluff Bascule Bridge and the high-rise **State of Georgia Memorial (U.S. 80) Bridge** (65-foot fixed vertical clearance) at Mile 582.8. (The bridge is known locally as the **Thunderbolt Bridge**.) Run along the green edge of the channel around red daybeacon "30" to avoid a charted shoal.

GOIN' ASHORE: **SAVANNAH, GA**

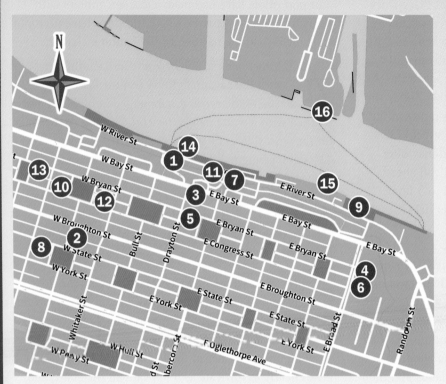

	SERVICES
1	Library
2	Post Office
3	Vistor Information
	ATTRACTIONS
4	Herb House
5	Olde Pink House Restaurant
6	Pirate House 1789
7	Savannah Cotton Exchange
8	The Telfair Academy of Arts and Sciences/Bird Girl Statue
9	The Waving Girl
	SHOPPING
10	City Market
	DINING
7	Savannah Cotton Exchange Tavern
11	Huey's on the River
12	Lady & Sons Restaurant
13	Vinnie Van Go-Go's
	MARINAS
14	River Street LLC
15	River Street Market Place Dock
16	The Westin Savannah Harbor Golf Resort & Spa

Savannah sits serenely on a bluff 40 feet above the banks of the Savannah River, where General James Oglethorpe and 120 passengers landed in 1733 to found Britain's last American colony. General Oglethorpe laid out the city in a series of 24 squares, 22 of which remain as lovely parks surrounded by a mix of architectural styles, including Federal, Georgian, Victorian and Italianate. The town's colonial heritage is well preserved, and synchronizes nicely with Savannah's youthful vibe. Southern hospitality manifests itself in a desire to entertain, welcoming visitors to dine and drink, enjoy carriage or riverboat tours and explore spooky cemeteries.

Attractions: In the 1950s, a group of women founded the Historic Savannah Foundation, which has worked to restore many of the old buildings. At 2.5 square miles, the Historic District is the largest urban National Landmark, with more than 1,000 architecturally or historically significant structures restored and in use. Cotton was the major source of income in the area, especially after the cotton gin was invented on a plantation outside the city. The Savannah Cotton Exchange (100 E. Bay St.), which still exists, is said to have set the world's cotton prices, and Savannah rivaled Charleston as a commercial port. Today, tourism plays a major role in the economy, although the port is still a vital part.

Walking and driving tours, carriage tours, audio tours and guided bus tours highlighting the historic homes built around Savannah's squares are all available. The easiest way to move around downtown Savannah is aboard the Express Shuttle with 24 stops around the Historic District. It operates daily. If you wander on your own, be sure to visit the Pirate House built in 1754 and mentioned in "Treasure Island," which is now a restaurant (20 E. Broad St., 912-233-5757); the site of Georgia's first bank, built in 1789, which is now the Olde Pink House Restaurant (23 Abercorn St., 800-554-1187); and the oldest building in Georgia, the Herb House, built in 1734 (20 E. Broad St., 912-233-5757). One of the south's first public museums, The Telfair Academy of Arts and Sciences, was built as a mansion in 1812 (121 Barnard St.) and was then established in 1886 as the oldest public art museum in the South. The 1938 bronze Bird Girl statue, made famous on the cover of John Berendt's novel "Midnight in the Garden of Good and Evil," is on display at the Telfair Museum. (She originally resided at the

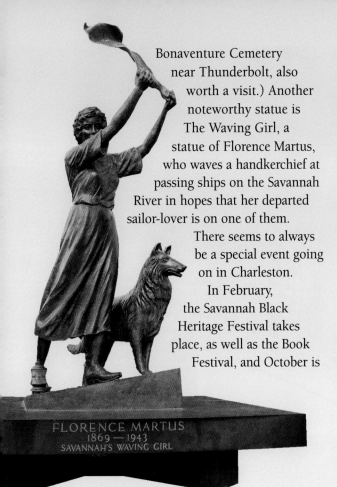

FLORENCE MARTUS
1869 — 1943
SAVANNAH'S WAVING GIRL

Bonaventure Cemetery near Thunderbolt, also worth a visit.) Another noteworthy statue is The Waving Girl, a statue of Florence Martus, who waves a handkerchief at passing ships on the Savannah River in hopes that her departed sailor-lover is on one of them. There seems to always be a special event going on in Charleston. In February, the Savannah Black Heritage Festival takes place, as well as the Book Festival, and October is active with the Savannah Jazz Festival and the Savannah Film Festival, but there is some sort of festival every month. Savannah's more well-known party is the St. Patrick's Day Celebration, said to be the second largest in the country. Throngs of revelers gather on historic River Street to sample fresh seafood, drink green beer and watch the parade.

Photo op alert: You must join all the other tourist who have their photo taken in front of the fountain at Forsyth Park at Drayton St. and E. Park Ave. Try to visit at twilight when tall lanterns around the fountain begin to illuminate the impressive fountain.

Shopping: Factors Row is located on a bluff just above the River Walk. A series of iron and concrete walkways, known as Factors Walk, connected the buildings to the bluff. The buildings on Bay St./River St. have been renovated into antique shops, historic inns and offices. The old cotton warehouses on the River Street level have been converted into pubs, restaurants and specialty shops. Street musicians play along the river walkway. On a foggy evening, you can just picture drunken sailors on shore leave spilling out of tavern doors.

The City Market (Jefferson and W. St. Julian) has gone through several renditions, the first in 1755, when it was a hub of commercial and social activity, with fishermen and farmers selling fresh fish and produce, farriers shoeing horses and barbers trimming hair. The first two market buildings burned down, and two were torn down, the last in 1954. Today, it is a revitalized area with a series of courtyards featuring art, entertainment, shopping and dining. Private art galleries abound, or one can visit the Art Center at City Market. Various entertainers hold forth in the courtyards, while the surrounding shops offer everything from handmade cigars to gourmet gifts and souvenirs.

Provisioning and marine supplies (including a West Marine) are farther from the waterfront and require a taxi or rental car. Bus service, called Catch A Cat, is provided by the Chatham Area Transit and includes a line to the Savannah/Hilton Head International Airport (912-233-5767, catchacat.org).

Dining: According to locals "the best pizza in Savannah" is served at Vinnie Van Go-Go's at 317 W. Bryan St. (912-233-6394). If you want casual dining try Savannah Cotton Exchange Tavern (201 E. River St., 912-232-7088) for tasty southern dishes. For Cajun cuisine and mouth-watering fresh beignets, try Huey's on the River (115 E. River St., 912-234-7385). They serve lunch and dinner and is one of the only places for breakfast on the waterfront.

Another stalwart on the dining scene is Paula Deen's Lady & Sons Restaurant (102 W. Congress St., 912-233-2600) for southern-style fried chicken, lump crab cakes, shrimp and grits, or go "whole hog" with the Southern buffet. Make reservations weeks or months in advance. Otherwise, just hope you're really lucky. While she does visit from time to time, don't be disappointed if Paula is not there.

Another iconic restaurant is Mrs. Wilkes Dining Room at 107 W. Jones St. (912-232-5997). Here you'll eat family style and your Cruising Editor counted 27 dishes offered at lunch (Monday through Friday only). Expect to wait in line; reservations and credit cards are not accepted. Folks cue up early (10:00 a.m.) for this Savannah tradition, and it is well worth the wait. This is southern cooking served with southern hospitality like you've read about and dreamed of.

Because restaurants frequently change names and ownership, we suggest you check with savannahvisit.com or savannah.com for more options.

Thunderbolt Waterfront

At Thunderbolt, and farther down the ICW at Isle of Hope (Mile 590), the current and direction of flow must be considered when docking. Marina personnel are generally knowledgeable and when assigning berths, they try to put the less maneuverable, single-screw boats in slips that are easy to enter and leave in this area of high tides and swift currents. If no attendant is around, it is best to put in at the fuel dock to size up the situation and then locate someone who can give directions or lend a hand. All marinas at Thunderbolt have floating docks.

Dockage: Hinckley Yacht Services Savannah, located to starboard just northwest of the Thunderbolt Bridge, is a service facility with a 50-ton lift and all types of engine repair. They have just eight transient slips on their floating docks, so call ahead. Across the ICW, at Mile 582, is Savannah Bend Marina with four reserved transient slips and all fuels.

At Mile 582, Morningstar Marinas Bahia Bleu, on the south side of the Thunderbolt Bridge, sells fuel (both gas and diesel) and is convenient to the ICW and to Thunderbolt's restaurants and shops. They also offer boat repairs and can accommodate vessels up to 200 feet at their deep-water docks. They have a well-stocked ship store and offer boat detailing and storage.

Thunderbolt Marine is at Mile 583 with transient dockage close to town and full-service repairs. Their lifts are capable of hauling the smallest to the largest of yachts. They also have fuel (gas and diesel), a ship store, WiFi, 24-hour security, spacious laundry facilities, restrooms/showers and pump-out facilities. As a bonus, fresh warm Krispy Kreme donuts are delivered to your boat daily. Restaurants and a bus stop are within walking distance.

The private Savannah Yacht Club is about 2 miles past Thunderbolt to port. The yacht club has limited space and its reciprocation policy varies, so be sure to contact the club before you arrive.

Anchorage: A mile or so below Thunderbolt, the Wilmington River widens, and the channel begins to straighten out. The popular Herb River anchorage is located at Mile 584.5. Most skippers anchor along the east bank before the first turn. The river bottom is a bit irregular and very deep at the bend, but holding is better than in the lower stretch of the river, where there is an oyster bank. Local boat traffic is minimal and the tidal currents moderate. Depths are good, at 13 to 15 feet MLW with a mud bottom, but be sure to set the anchor well and, as always, show an anchor light. This anchorage is well protected.

Side Trip: South on the Wilmington River

NAVIGATION: Use NOAA Chart 11512. Southeast of Mile 585, you will find additional dockage and anchorage opportunities on Turner Creek, off the Wilmington River. Beware of the charted 4-foot MLW area soon after the first bend.

Dockage: There are two options on Turner Creek: Sail Harbor Marina & Boatyard and Hogans' Marina. Both offer some repairs and Hogan's sells gas (no diesel). Farther south on the Wilmington River is Landings Harbor Marina, with all fuels and just two reserved transient slips; call ahead.

Anchorage: It is possible to anchor before or after the fixed **Spence Grayson Bridge** (35-foot vertical clearance) on Turner Creek and dinghy into Hogans' Marina. Remember to get permission to leave the dinghy should you decide to shop. Several boats on private mooring balls leave room for only one or two boats to anchor.

Wassaw Sound Entrance

NAVIGATION: Use NOAA Chart 11512. Wassaw Sound, the next Atlantic inlet south of Tybee Roads, provides quick access to the Savannah area from the Atlantic Ocean. A fair amount of local traffic regularly uses this inlet, but we do not recommend it except with up-to-date local knowledge, excellent visibility, calm seas and at mid-tide. This is not an inlet for dark and stormy arrivals, as it is poorly marked and surrounded by shoals nearly 5 nm out from the entrance. This is the Atlantic inlet sometimes used by vessels bound for Thunderbolt Marina and unable to clear the 65-foot Thunderbolt Bridge over the Wilmington River at Mile 582.8. Local boats anchor off a beautiful sandy beach at a spit on the northeast corner of Wassaw Island for day outings. See the Inlet section at the front of this guide for more information about the Wassaw Sound Entrance.

Wassaw Sound and the Wilmington River carry about 25-foot MLW depths between flashing red buoy "10" in the Atlantic Ocean to flashing green daybeacon "29" at Skidaway River (Mile 585.5). In 2019 all the charted buoys between sea buoy flashing red "2W" and flashing red buoy "10" were missing.

Dockage: Bull River Marina is accessible from Wassaw Sound, with no bridges or other height restrictions but with a shallow bar (6- to 7-foot MLW spots charted) across its entrance channel. It is located 4 miles from ICW Mile 586 on the Bull River before the 20-foot fixed vertical clearance **Bull River (U.S. 80) Bridge**. The marina can accommodate vessels up to 110 feet and sells all fuels.

■ TO OSSABAW ISLAND–ICW MILE 590 TO MILE 615

Isle of Hope–ICW Mile 590

Isle of Hope at Mile 590 is a charming village of winding roads and old houses scattered among the tall pines and oaks located on the shore of the Skidaway River. It is 7 miles by water down the twisting ICW from Thunderbolt, but only half that by road. The town stands on a bend high above the river and is listed on the National Register of Historic Places. Signs politely request that you slow down as you pass and keep your wake to a minimum; better yet, tie up here to enjoy a walk among the antebellum homes.

About 1 mile from the Isle of Hope Marina is the Wormsloe Historic Site (7601 Skidaway Rd.) with a museum, ruins of a fortified house and a nature walk. Wild deer and pigs leave their tracks and sometimes appear on the grounds. The on-site Wormsloe Mansion is not open to the public because it is a private residence still occupied by the descendants of Noble Jones, one of the earliest Georgia settlers and the original owner of the property. You can visit Wormsloe Historic Site on foot, bike or by tour bus from Savannah.

NAVIGATION: Use NOAA Chart 11507. When heading south from Thunderbolt, take flashing green daybeacon "37" a little wide, and then favor flashing green daybeacon "37A," avoiding the shoal near red daybeacon "38." Turn into the Skidaway River for a meandering 5-mile cruise to Isle of Hope.

Dockage: Located in one of the most beautiful settings on the entire ICW, the convenient Isle of Hope Marina provides large slips at concrete floating docks, with full amenities including laundry facilities and a pool. This is the logical jumping-off point for the long run south, and the first landing near Savannah when you are headed north, with bus service to the city. The marina also offers a courtesy car and bicycles. Note

Wilmington River South, Savannah, GA

		Largest Vessel Accommodated	VHF Channel Monitored	Transient Berths / Total Berths	Approach / Dockside Depth (reported)	Floating Docks	Gas / Diesel	Groceries, Ice, Marine Supplies, Snacks	Repairs: Hull, Engine, Propeller	Lift (tonnage), Crane, Rail	Min/Max Amps	Laundry, Pool, Showers, Courtesy Car	Pump-Out Station	Nearby: Grocery Store, Motel, Restaurant
THUNDERBOLT AREA				**Dockage**				**Supplies**				**Services**		
1. Hinckley Yacht Services Savannah ▭ onSpot 582.4	912-629-2400	65	16/68	8/30	12/12	F	–	IM	HEP	L50	30/50	SC	P	GR
2. Savannah Bend Marina ▭ WiFi 582.3	912-897-3625	100	16/68	4/28	12/10	F	GD	GIMS	HEP	L	30/50	LS	–	GR
3. Morningstar Marinas Bahia Bleu ▭ onSpot 582.6	912-354-2283	200	16/71	20/45	26/20	F	GD	IMS	HEP	L9	30/50	LS	P	GMR
4. Thunderbolt Marine ▭ WiFi 583	912-356-3875	200	16/11	15/45	20/20	F	GD	IS	HEP	L1200,C	30/100	LS	P	GR
5. Savannah Yacht Club-PRIVATE	912-644-4100	45	–	0/60	20/20	F	GD	IS	–	–	30/30	PS	–	R
TURNER CREEK														
6. Sail Harbor Marina & Boatyard ▭ WiFi SE of 585.4	912-897-2896	50	16/71	5/45	7/10	F	–	IMS	HEP	L50	30/50	LSC	P	GR
7. Hogans' Marina 585.4	912-897-3474	–	–	–	8/8	F	G	IMS	HEP	L12	30/30	S	P	GR
WILMINGTON RIVER														
8. Landings Harbor Marina ▭ WiFi	912-598-1901	40	16	2/29	20/8	F	GD	GIMS	HE	L9	30/50	S	P	GR
BULL RIVER														
9. Bull River Marina ▭ WiFi 4 NE of 586	912-897-7300	110	16/67	10/70	25/18	F	GD	IMS	E	–	30/100	S	P	GR
ISLE OF HOPE														
10. Isle of Hope Marina WiFi 590	912-354-8187	220	16/68	15/125	12/15	F	GD	IS	–	L	30/100	LSC	P	GR

▭ Internet Access   WiFi Wireless Internet Access   **WG** Waterway Guide Cruising Club Partner   onSpot dockside WiFi facility
See WaterwayGuide.com for current rates, fuel prices, web site addresses, and other up-to-the-minute information. *(Information in the table is provided by the facilities.)*

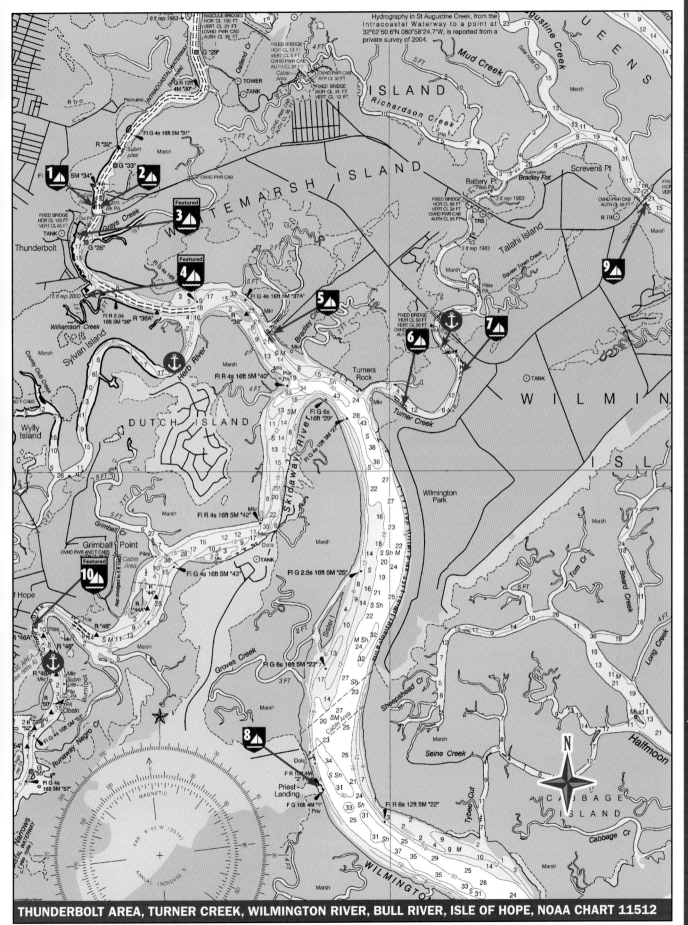

THUNDERBOLT AREA, TURNER CREEK, WILMINGTON RIVER, BULL RIVER, ISLE OF HOPE, NOAA CHART 11512

that this is the last fuel stop on the ICW (southbound) for 90 miles. There are food markets, a West Marine, Walmart and restaurants within courtesy car range.

Skidaway Narrows–ICW Mile 590 to Mile 600

Skidaway Narrows, immediately below Isle of Hope, is a twisting stretch of the ICW, weaving erratically back and forth around curves and bends. Take your time, cut your speed as necessary, watch your course, and enjoy this winding creek with its fringes of salt marsh extending back to distant woods. Skidaway Narrows is the preferred swimming hole of the local river otter population.

NAVIGATION: Use NOAA Chart 11507. Slow boats should note that high slack water at Mile 592 (Skidaway Narrows) occurs 49 minutes before the Savannah River Entrance. This is good to keep in mind, as arriving at Skidaway Narrows at slack water provides the most favorable currents from Mile 585 to Mile 603. Tidal currents reverse in the vicinity of the fixed

ISLE OF HOPE MARINA

ICW

Skidaway River

65-foot vertical clearance **Diamond Causeway (Skidaway) Bridge**.

The channel narrows from red daybeacon "46A" (Mile 592.9) to the bridge. Favor the eastern bank until red daybeacon "50." A boat ramp just below the bridge creates considerable small-boat traffic, so keep alert. There is also a buoyed-off swimming area. Note the Slow-Speed signs here.

The pretty Vernon View (Mile 596), another Savannah suburb overlooking the Burnside River portion of the ICW, begins at Skidaway Narrows' southern end, about 6 miles below Isle of Hope. Private docks line the shore (and are well charted), but there is no public marina. Remember, you are responsible for your wake here.

On the Burnside River, favor the north side of the channel between red daybeacon "76" and flashing green daybeacon "79," which marks the turn into the Vernon River. A shoal is building out along the southeast side of the Burnside River, so don't cut flashing green daybeacon "79" too closely, despite the charted path of the magenta line. Shoaling exists between flashing green daybeacon "79" and flashing green daybeacon "81."

Anchorage: Anchor just north of the Skidaway Bridge on the eastern shore, just before slight bend. This area shoals up quickly (depth of 15 feet MLW and tide of 7

GOIN' ASHORE: **THUNDERBOLT, GA**

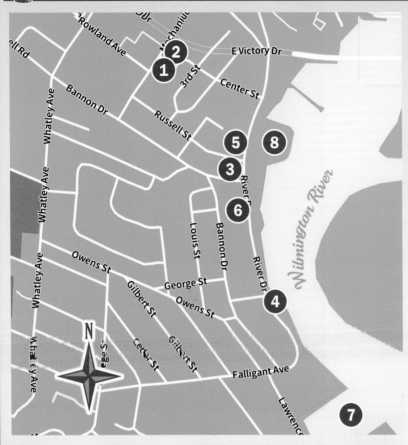

SERVICES		
1	Library	
ATTRACTIONS		
2	Thunderbolt Museum Society	
SHOPPING		
3	River Supply	
4	Thunderbolt Fisherman's Seafood	
DINING		
5	Tortugas Island Grille	
6	Tubby's Tank House	
MARINAS		
7	Thunderbolt Marine	
8	Morningstar Marina	

Thunderbolt, close to Savannah and located on the ICW, is an important seafood-packing center with good marinas and restaurants. The shore is lined with shrimp boats, often rafted two abreast. Bus service is available, with stops about three-tenths of a mile from Thunderbolt's marinas. (A taxi is better for the trip to Savannah.)

First settled by American Indians, legend has it that lightning struck Wilmington Bluff, creating a freshwater spring and spawning the name Thunderbolt. English settlers also came to the area, enjoying the access to the Wilmington River that created a shipping point for the local plantations. By 1856, Thunderbolt had incorporated into the town of Warsaw. Not long after that, the Thunderbolt Battery was constructed to ward off Union attacks from Wassaw Sound. Although Union gunboats anchored near Thunderbolt, the Battery never fell.

Looking at Thunderbolt's waterfront today, it is hard to believe the town used to be Savannah's weekend playground. With the advent of the streetcar and electricity, people flocked to the casino, horse racing track and bandstand and dance pavilion, finishing with dinner at the world-famous Bannon Lodge. Thunderbolt's era as a river resort lasted from the late 19th century into the early 20th century. The casino was actually built by the Savannah Electric Company, owner of the streetcar company, to increase ridership and to promote the use of electricity.

Attractions: The Thunderbolt Museum Society at 2702 Mechanics Ave. (912-351-0836) was established in the old town hall to recapture the town's history with exhibits and a staff of informative volunteers. Call the Museum in advance for the days/hours that it is open. Honey Park and Thompson Park are located near the marinas for leisurely strolls along the river.

Bonaventure Cemetery was featured in John Berendt's novel "Midnight in the Garden of Good and Evil." The 1938 bronze Bird Girl statue on the cover of the novel is now on display at the Telfair Museum in Savannah. Bonaventure Historical Society (3300 Bonaventure Rd.) offers free guided tours on the second weekend of the month. Call 912-412-4687 or visit bonaventurehistorical.org/tours for a schedule.

Shopping: Fresh seafood is available at Thunderbolt Fisherman's Seafood (3110 River Dr., 912-354-0417). There is a Kroger (1900 E. Victory Dr., 912-236-9321) and a Whole Foods Market (1815 E. Victory Dr., 912-358-5829) less than 1 mile away for groceries, produce, fresh meats and seafood.

There is a Home Depot at 1901 E. Victory Dr. (912-352-3562). River Supply on the waterfront at 2827 River Dr. has competitive pricing on marine supplies (800-673-9391).

Dining: The attractive waterfront is lined with seafood restaurants and shrimp boats. A favorite dining spot is Tubby's Tank House at 2909 River Dr. (912-354-9040), serving lunch and dinner as well as weekend brunch and featuring fresh seafood in a casual atmosphere. They also have a full-service bar and live entertainment. See their calendar of events at tubbysthunderbolt.com/events. A little farther down the street is Tortugas Island Grille (2815 River Dr., 912-201-3630) for Caribbean and American cuisine.

Three miles out of town (across the river) on Hwy. 80 East is Wiley's Championship BBQ (4700 U.S. 80 East, 912-201-3259). They have won national championships for their pork, brisket, beans and ribs. Open for lunch and dinner or until the BBQ runs out! If you have transportation, it is well worth the drive. (Closed on Sundays.) It is some of the best BBQ you will ever find. (The sign is hard to spot, but it is next to Five Guys, which has a large sign.)

feet), but it is protected and offers small beaches for dog walking. Beware of your swing and don't anchor in the middle of the channel.

Moon River, made famous by songwriter Johnny Mercer, is just short of Mile 595. Boaters have reported shoaling to around 4-foot MLW depths at the entrance, although depths are still charted at 8 feet MLW with shoaling indicated. Anchor behind Marsh Island and remember that in periods of strong and prolonged westerly wind and during the new and full moon phases, tides can be much lower than normal charted depths. Stay clear of flashing red daybeacon "74" and the shoaling before heading northwest up the river.

If you give the long shoal off Possum Point a wide berth, you can turn northward up the Vernon River, well off the ICW, to drop the hook south of the village of Montgomery. Currents can be strong here, and you should allow for an 8-foot tidal range. You will probably share this anchorage with a shrimp boat or two during the season. They usually anchor on one long stretchy nylon rode and keep their arms down, so give them plenty of space to swing. This is a pleasant anchorage in more than 14-foot MLW depths. Anchor before the charted 1-foot MLW bar, which extends out to the middle of the river.

Hell Gate and Florida Passage– ICW Mile 600 to Mile 615

The Vernon River runs wide and deep until you reach Hell Gate, a land cut leading from the Vernon River to the Okeechobee River. If strong northeast winds kick up, you might see swells breaking up the long fetch of the Vernon and Ogeechee Rivers. The Georgia coast's second largest river, the Ogeechee, has a particularly strong ebb current.

From the Ogeechee River, the ICW channel leads south through the Florida Passage, which flows into the Bear River, running the length of Ossabaw Island. One of Georgia's eight major Sea Islands, Ossabaw Island is pierced by a number of narrow, but deep creeks fanning out from the Bear River.

The Ossabaw Inlet to the ocean is used by small local craft but is not really suitable for use by cruising vessels, other than in very calm weather and with a lot of local knowledge. In summer 2019, green daybeacon "5" and red "6" were missing in the inlet.

NAVIGATION: Use NOAA Charts 11507 and 11509. Hell Gate is one of the most notorious sections of the ICW for shoaling, but it was dredged in summer 2019 so

Ossabaw Sound, GA

		Largest Vessel Accommodated	VHF Channel Monitored	Transient Berths / Total Berths	Approach / Dockside Depth (reported)	Floating Docks	Gas / Diesel	Groceries, Ice, Marine Supplies, Snacks	Repairs: Hull, Engine, Propeller	Lift (tonnage), Crane, Rail	Min/Max Amps	Laundry, Pool, Showers, Courtesy Car	Pump-Out Station	Nearby: Grocery Store, Motel, Restaurant
DELEGAL CREEK					**Dockage**		**Supplies**		**Services**					
1. Delegal Creek Marina 🖳 (WiFi)	912-224-3885	150	16/68	15/58	3/15	F	GD	IMS	–	–	30/50	LS	P	–
OGEECHEE RIVER AREA														
2. Ft. McAllister Marina 🖳 (WiFi) 6 W of 605.5	912-727-2632	80	16/68	15/60	15/20	F	GD	IMS	–	C15	30/50	LSC	P	R
3. Coffee Bluff Marina 🖳	912-231-3628	200	–	10/20	25/	F	GD	IMS	–	L10	30/50	LS	P	–

🖳 Internet Access   (WiFi) Wireless Internet Access   **WG** Waterway Guide Cruising Club Partner   ⬤**onSpot** dockside WiFi facility
See WaterwayGuide.com for current rates, fuel prices, web site addresses, and other up-to-the-minute information. *(Information in the table is provided by the facilities.)*

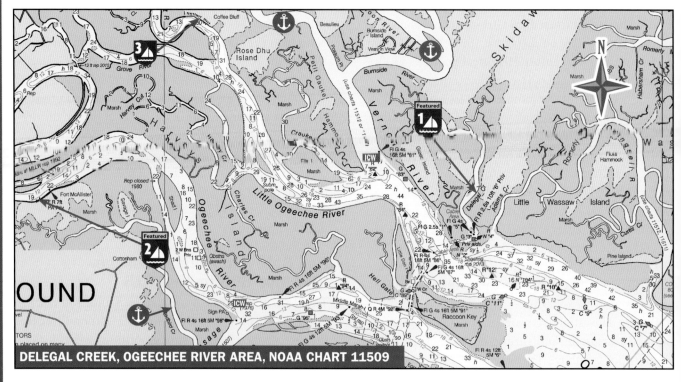

DELEGAL CREEK, OGEECHEE RIVER AREA, NOAA CHART 11509

it should be stable for awhile. Go slow and watch the depthsounder. Mid-tide and rising is the safest time to go through these questionable areas of the ICW and stay in the center of the channel.

There are strong side-sweeping currents at Hell Gate, especially on the ebb when entering from the north (Vernon River), so keep track of your progress by looking both ahead and astern.

Leaving Hell Gate, run beyond flashing green daybeacon "91" and round quick flashing red daybeacon "92" to make the turn for the 3-mile run up the Ogeechee River. Pay particular attention to the markers at the passage through Middle Marsh. Carefully follow the markers, changing course as indicated to pass safely between Middle Marsh to the south (which is obscured at high tide) and

the shoal north of red daybeacon "94" off Charles Creek's entrance.

Dockage: At Mile 601, just above Hell Gate across the Vernon River, Delegal Creek makes off to the north. The marked channel leads to Delegal Creek Marina, a 70-slip marina in a beautiful setting. The marina is part of The Landings on Skidaway Island, a luxury community with six golf courses. Complimentary golf carts are available for runs to the grocery store and restaurants, and kayak rentals are available. We recommend you call the dockmaster's office on VHF Channels 16 or 68 to check depths and get directions for entering the marked channel prior to docking.

Five miles up the Ogeechee River from flashing red daybeacon "98" (Florida Passage intersection) is the Ft. McAllister Marina. This river requires you to cross from the north to the south side after Shad Island. The dockmaster can see vessels approaching up river and may contact you to offer guidance. If not, you should call the marina for directions on your approach. It is easy to fetch up on the sand bar without proper directions. There are signs here which some have found to be confusing. The channel in this rapidly flowing estuary is constantly shifting and even current charts may not be wholly accurate. Study NOAA Charts 11507, 11509 and 11511 before heading upriver and absolutely call for local knowledge before attempting passage.

Ft. McAllister is a friendly marina with a well-trained and very courteous staff. They sell all fuels and offer repairs in addition to slips on floating docks. Loaner vehicles may be available and services are a short drive. The on-site Fish Tales Restaurant (912-727-3473) is a lively waterfront eatery with a Caribbean flair at reasonable prices. They have live music most weekends.

North on the Little Ogeechee River is Coffee Bluff Marina, which may have space for you, sells gas and diesel and offers pump-out service and repairs.

Anchorage: There is a fine selection of anchorages with 10-foot-plus depths and good holding in Redbird Creek, north off the Florida Passage at Mile 606.8. Here you will find 6- to 18-foot MLW depths and good holding in mud. The current is very strong here so be sure to set your anchor well.

On the south side of the Florida Passage at Mile 606.5, there is an anchorage in Queen Bess Creek, with at least 4 feet MLW.

At Mile 608.5, stay on the range until you are well past red daybeacon "102," then turn eastward up the Bear River to Cane Patch Creek or Buckhead Creek, then pick a spot with suitable depths and set the anchor well. Depths vary from 10 to 30 feet here, and the current is exceptionally strong.

At Mile 612, you can turn north into Birthday Creek and anchor in 9- to 14-foot MLW depths with good holding in mud. Nearby Big Tom Creek, at Mile 612.5, is a popular overnight anchorage. Anchor either near its entrance or around the first bend in 9-foot MLW depths.

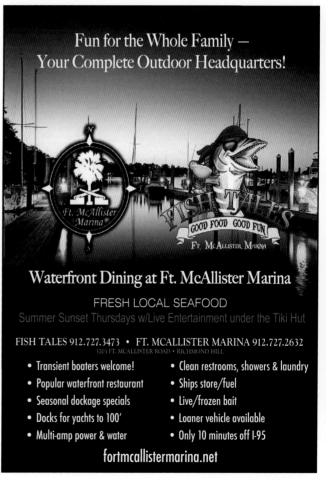

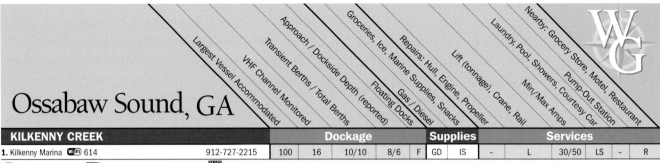

Ossabaw Sound, GA

KILKENNY CREEK		Largest Vessel Accommodated	VHF Channel Monitored	Transient Berths / Total Berths	Approach / Dockside Depth (reported)	Floating Docks	Gas / Diesel	Groceries, Ice, Marine Supplies, Snacks	Repairs: Hull, Engine, Propeller	Lift (tonnage), Crane, Rail	Min/Max Amps	Laundry, Pool, Showers, Courtesy Car	Pump-Out Station	Nearby: Grocery Store, Motel, Restaurant
				Dockage				**Supplies**			**Services**			
1. Kilkenny Marina (WiFi) 614	912-727-2215	100	16	10/10	8/6	F	GD	IS	–		L	30/50	LS	– R

□ Internet Access (WiFi) Wireless Internet Access (WG) Waterway Guide Cruising Club Partner ◉ onSpot dockside WiFi facility
See WaterwayGuide.com for current rates, fuel prices, web site addresses, and other up-to-the-minute information. *(Information in the table is provided by the facilities.)*

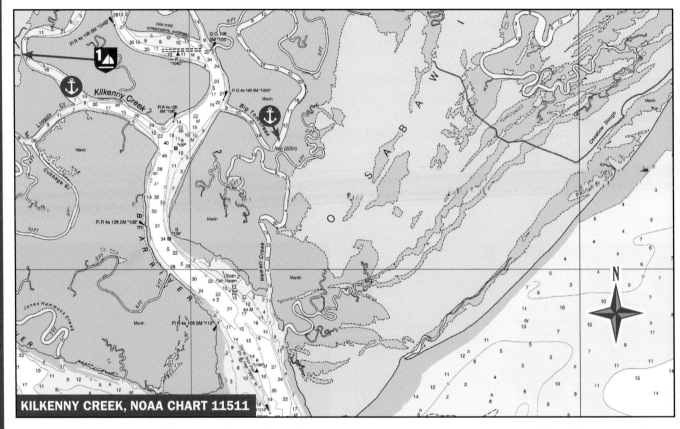

KILKENNY CREEK, NOAA CHART 11511

Side Trip: Kilkenny Creek–ICW Mile 614

NAVIGATION: Use NOAA Charts 11507 and 11511. At Mile 614 on the Bear River, at ICW green daybeacon "107," you can turn westward into Kilkenny Creek. The Texaco sign at its entrance is a good landmark.

Dockage: About 1.5 miles up from flashing green daybeacon "107" is rural Kilkenny Marina, which welcomes transients. The marina reports that its entrance channel carries 10 feet if you stay 30 feet north of the center of the creek. They have an on-site restaurant, Marker 107 (912-727-5999) that is open Wednesday through Saturday for dinner only.

Anchorage: Kilkenny Creek provides a popular but peaceful spot to drop the hook, with 15-foot MLW depths and a mud bottom. This anchorage borders the marsh, making insect screens and repellent essential. There is considerable nighttime traffic from shrimp boats in Kilkenny Creek during the harvesting season, so be sure your anchor light is working properly.

■ NEXT STOP

The next chapter takes you to the first of many sounds. You will pass through St. Catherines Sound on the way to St. Marys, GA, passing the stop-worthy St. Simons Island, Brunswick and Jekyll Island on the way. The open sounds will be a welcome change from the twisty rivers and straight land cuts to the north.

St. Catherines Sound to St. Marys, GA

 ICW Mile 619–Mile 716   **(VHF)** SC/GA Bridges: Channel 09

CHARTS NOAA 11489, 11502, 11503, 11504, 11506, 11507, 11508, 11509, 11510, 11511

The ICW follows the Bear River as it empties into St. Catherines Sound at Mile 618. This is the first in a series of sounds, connected by rivers, that you will pass through as you transit the Georgia portion of the ICW. Other sounds along this stretch include Sapelo Sound, Doboy Sound, Altamaha Sound, Buttermilk Sound, St. Simons Sound, Jekyll Sound and St. Andrews Sound. Some of these sounds are large and exposed enough to get rough, but they also provide a nice change of pace from the rivers and land cuts to the north. It is always advisable to keep a close eye on the weather. You do not want opposing wind and tide anywhere on these sounds.

When the sounds are open for shrimping, keep an eye on all shrimp boats in your vicinity. They move fast when heading to and from their shrimping grounds. When they are working their movements will be erratic, and they will be occupied with their trailing nets, so you will be the one to take evasive action. They often travel with their long "arms" extended so even if you are under sail, do not expect shrimp boats to alter course or raise their booms. They have been known to go under bridges with their "arms" partially or fully down, leaving no room for other boats. Stand well clear of them, keep your horn handy; five blasts is the danger signal.

■ ST. CATHERINES SOUND TO SAPELO SOUND

St. Catherines Sound Entrance–Mile 615

NAVIGATION: Use NOAA Chart 11507. Expect low slack water at Mile 618 to be 39 minutes earlier than at the Savannah River Entrance. For slow-moving north or southbound boats, the best time to arrive at St. Catherines Sound is at low slack water, when the sea is calmest and the currents are most favorable. Tidal range is 7 to 8 feet. Watch your course between Miles 615 and 617 and take care that wind and current do not set your vessel too far to the west. The shoal reported on

the charts does indeed exist near red daybeacon "110A." Give flashing red "112," "114" and "114A" a wide berth and keep to the charted ICW magenta line. Green can buoy "7," which marks the end of the shoal at Middle Ground in St. Catherines Sound off Walburg Creek,

Medway River, Newport River, GA

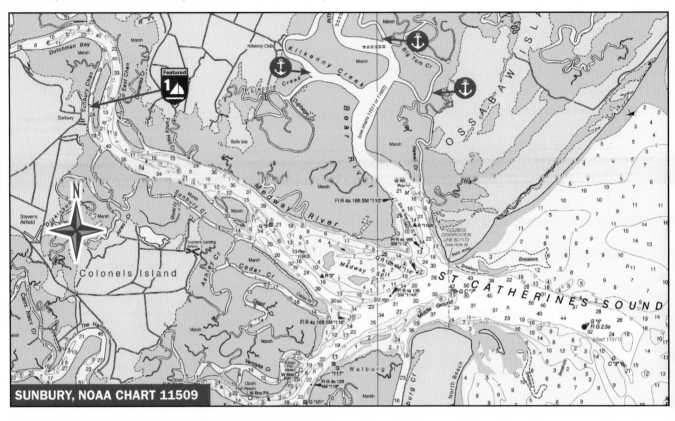

			Approach / Dockside Depth (reported)	VHF Channel Monitored	Transient Berths / Total Berths	Largest Vessel Accommodated		Groceries, Ice, Marine Supplies, Snacks	Floating Docks	Gas / Diesel	Repairs: Hull, Engine, Propeller	Lift (tonnage), Crane, Rail	Min/Max Amps	Pump-Out Station	Laundry, Pool, Showers, Courtesy Car	Nearby: Grocery Store, Motel, Restaurant

			Dockage					**Supplies**				**Services**				
SUNBURY																
1. Sunbury Crab Co. Restaurant & Marina WIFI 618	912-884-8640	125	–	10/28	/23	F	GD	I	–	–	30/100	SC	–	R		
THE HALFMOON																
2. Halfmoon Marina 6 W of 622.5	912-884-5819	100	16/68	4/10	15/30	F	GD	GIMS	E	–	30/50	S	P	GR		

⌨ Internet Access **WIFI** Wireless Internet Access **WG** Waterway Guide Cruising Club Partner **onSpot** dockside WiFi facility

See WaterwayGuide.com for current rates, fuel prices, web site addresses, and other up-to-the-minute information. *(Information in the table is provided by the facilities.)*

SUNBURY, NOAA CHART 11509

needs to be honored if you intend to enter and anchor in Walburg Creek.

St. Catherines Sound Entrance has a wide, uncomplicated entrance with good depths within. As with other smaller inlets in Georgia, channel markers are widely placed and it can be difficult to visually pick them out, even though the offshore sea buoys are in their charted position and easy to locate with GPS. Some of the smaller markers are frequently moved to locate better water. See the Inlet section in the front of this guide for more information.

Heading south, once you transit the 2 miles of the ICW route across St. Catherines Sound, you will enter the North Newport River at Mile 620.

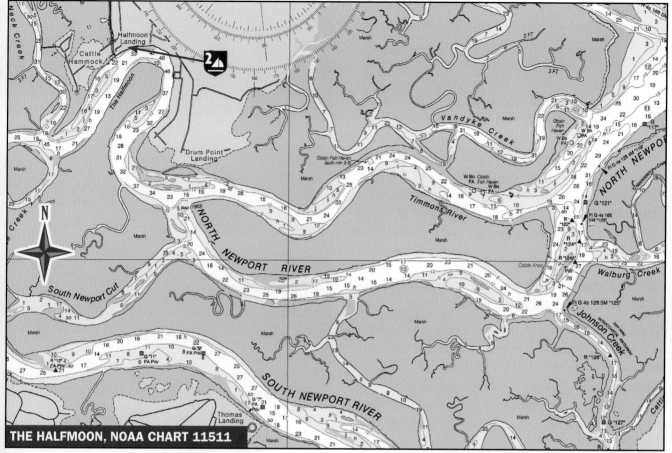

THE HALFMOON, NOAA CHART 11511

Side Trip: Sunbury–ICW Mile 618

NAVIGATION: Use NOAA Chart 11509. About 6 miles northwest of St. Catherines Sound (from ICW Mile 618) on the Medway River is the popular Sunbury Crab Co. Restaurant & Marina. To reach Sunbury, pass between red flashing "114A" and "116" upriver, leaving red daybeacon "2" to starboard, then pass green daybeacon "3" to port. Cross to the west side of the river at Fancy Hall Creek (to starboard). There are no markers, just watch your depth sounder. As you approach Sunbury, hug the western shore and enter the Sunbury channel between the unnamed island and the shore. Sunbury Crab Co. will be the next to last docks on your left. (Look for signs.)

Dockage: Sunbury Crab Co. Restaurant & Marina offers transient facilities with showers and all fuels. This is one of those fun, off-the-beaten-path places that is worth the few extra miles to go visit. The staff is friendly, the docks are in good shape and the restaurant offers large portions at reasonable prices in a relaxed, laid-back atmosphere. If you are there on a Sunday, take in the live music on the outdoor stage (seasonal). This place is funky, eclectic and fun.

Side Trip: Walburg Creek–ICW Mile 620

Walburg Creek flows past the western shore of St. Catherines Island to join with the ICW route at Mile 622.5. The St. Catherines Island Foundation owns the island and limits visitation. From 1974 to 2007, the Wildlife Conservation Society operated a breeding facility here for rare and endangered species. As a result, several thousand mammals, birds and reptiles of 54 different species have lived on the island in their facilities. The breeding facilities are located in the southern section of the main compound, although few are in use today.

NAVIGATION: Use NOAA Chart 11507. A protected, but seldom-used alternate to the ICW route along the exposed North Newport River is the charted Walburg Creeks channel. Green can buoy "7," marking the end of the Middle Ground shoal off Walburg Creek, is in place and should be honored because the shoal it marks extends farther south toward St. Catherines Island than note on the chart. Although the northern entrance to Walburg Creek (from St. Catherines Sound) is straightforward, the southern passage back into the North Newport River is tricky, with depths of 4 to 5 feet MLW.

Anchorage: Walburg Creek's waters provide splendid anchorages. Go northwest 1.2 miles from Mile 630 and anchor by the stand of trees on the north shore. If you go as far as the 90-degree bend to the west, be careful of the shoal on the north side as it is encroaching farther into the channel. You can drop the hook in 15- to 20-foot MLW depths with good sand holding. Shrimp boats often use this anchorage too, so be sure that your anchor light is working properly. Avoid anchoring in the bend of the creek off the southern tip of Walburg Island, where the water is deep and currents run swiftly. A dinghy ride to the north end of St. Catherines Island reveals a desolate, but beautiful sandy barrier island beach.

North Newport River and Johnson Creek–ICW Mile 620 to Mile 630

NAVIGATION: Use NOAA Chart 11511. Beyond Mile 620, the ICW enters the mouth of the North Newport River and follows along that river to about Mile 623, where the North Newport River bears off to the west. The ICW channel continues south along Johnson Creek.

There are a few areas of concern on this stretch, as described below.

- Mile 620–At the entrance to the North Newport River, there is a shoal on the west (at flashing red "116") so be sure to favor the green side as you follow the ICW channel.
- Mile 622.5–There is an area of shoaling on the red side of the North Newport River marked by red daybeacons "122," "124" and "124A" off the southern end of Walburg Creek. (In 2019 an additional buoy was added between "124" and "124A" marking the shoal.) Continue to favor the green side here.
- Mile 623–Don't cut the corner before flashing green daybeacon "125." Round it as the charted magenta line indicates and continue into Johnson Creek.
- Mile 624–Water depths between flashing green daybeacons "125" and "127" range from 10 to 12 feet, which is 3 to 5 feet less than charted. When passing red daybeacon "126" favor the red side, since a shoal is building on the green side of the channel.
- Mile 627–At the lower bend of Johnson Creek, green daybeacons "131" and "131A" mark an extensive shoal building out from the east. Favor the red side of the channel. Be sure not to cut the corner as you will find very shallow water.

Dockage: From flashing green daybeacons "119" and "121" (Mile 623.7) turn to the west, and cruise 7 miles up the North Newport River to the small Halfmoon Marina, which offers space for transients. You can also get there via the Timmons River a couple miles further down the ICW. Be advised that there are no markers on either side of these rivers in this area. Call the marina for directions and follow your chart plotter and depth sounder very carefully. The marina sells all fuels and has room for 4 or 5 cruising boats. Transient prices are very competitive. There are no restaurants or stores in the area, although you might be able to borrow a car for the 13-mile ride to the town of Midway. The Halfmoon Marina is the last marina near the ICW southbound for the next 40 miles.

Anchorage: Cattle Pen Creek, off Johnson Creek, south of Mile 625.5, provides a fine overnight anchorage for boats up to about 40 feet in length, but may be too narrow for larger boats that need more swinging room. While the charted depths inside Cattle Pen Creek are good, expect entrance depths to be only 7 feet MLW, rather than the 14 feet MLW shown on the NOAA chart. The marsh does not provide much protection from wind, but the water is narrow enough that it does not get rough in the anchorage. It provides good holding in mud. The current can be strong, but if you set your anchor well there should not be a problem.

Southbound out of Johnson Creek, the Wahoo River makes off the South Newport River portion of the ICW at Mile 630. The Wahoo River is a fine overnight anchorage if you are willing to backtrack about 2 miles. When entering the Wahoo River, be wary of the shoal that is located between the mouth of the Wahoo and the Newport River. Go slightly past the mouth of the Wahoo and turn back to avoid the shallow, well-marked shoal. Go northwest 1.2 miles and anchor by the stand of trees on the north shore. If you go as far as the 90-degree bend to the west, be careful of the shoal on the north side as it is encroaching farther into the channel. The depth range throughout this area is 10- to 15-foot MLW depths in mud.

SAPELO SOUND TO DOBOY SOUND

Sapelo Sound Entrance–ICW 634

Sapelo Sound is a favorite of area fishermen and shrimpers, not to mention legendary pirate Edward Teach (Blackbeard). You will pass just north of Blackbeard Island and Blackbeard Creek while transiting this inlet. Southbound cruisers hoping to avoid the Georgia ICW rarely use the inlet, preferring to jump offshore through the big ship channels at Charleston or Port Royal, SC, or Savannah. This is not the best inlet in rougher weather, due to extensive shoals to the north and south of the inlet. See the Inlet section in the front of this guide for more information about Sapelo Sound Entrance Inlet.

NAVIGATION: Use NOAA Chart 11501. Note that low slack water on Sapelo Sound (at Mile 632) occurs 30 minutes before it occurs at the Savannah River Entrance. As you cruise along Sapelo Sound, red daybeacon "136," red daybeacon "136A" and flashing red daybeacon "138" need an especially wide berth (our Cruising Editor suggests giving it 200 yards), as shoaling seems to extend farther out every year. (Daybeacon "137" is no longer present; it originally marked a 5-foot-deep bank to the east.) There is less than 12 feet of water between red daybeacon "136" and flashing red daybeacon "138" at mid-tide. Keep in mind that the markers are placed for a reason, and you should honor them, not the magenta line when in conflict.

Heading south along the ICW, you will exit Johnson Creek for a short run along the South Newport River to its mouth. The ICW route heads up Sapelo Sound to the Sapelo River, running past Sapelo Island. On Sapelo Sound, as well as other large sounds, give both lighted aids and daybeacons a wider berth than usual, especially around low tide. Keep track of your markers, running a compass course between distant ones. Many boats have erroneously run for an outlying sea buoy instead of a marker leading into a nearby tributary.

Sapelo River–ICW Mile 635 to Mile 640

NAVIGATION: Use NOAA Chart 11510. Mind the markers at the western end of Sapelo Sound, where the ICW route enters the Sapelo River. At low tide, approach the whole stretch with caution. Specific areas of concern are detailed below.

- Mile 635–There is a shoal building into the channel by green daybeacon "143" so stay at least 100 feet off the mark.
- Mile 637.8–Depths of 10 to 12 feet MLW (less than charted) exist between red daybeacons "150" and "150A." Give "150" a wide berth (at least 600 feet) for 16 feet MLW.

Dockage: If headed upriver to Pine Harbor Marina, located 3 miles west of the ICW on the Sapelo River, mind the constant shoaling (4-foot MLW depths observed between green can "5B" and red nun "6"). Pine Harbor Marina is strictly a small boat marina and can only accommodate vessels to 23 feet. They also sell gas.

Front River to Doboy Sound–ICW Mile 640 to Mile 650

Heading south, the ICW route leaves the Sapelo River and enters the Front River. The Front River is narrow but deep in mid-channel. Many of the hammocks of land west of the channel show piles of ballast stone, which is all that remains of a once-prosperous riverside community.

NAVIGATION: Use NOAA Chart 11507. Note that low slack water in Doboy Sound at Mile 649 occurs 32 minutes before it does at the Savannah River Entrance. The ICW route continues south along the Front River, before heading into Creighton Narrows at Mile 642. Along the stretch through Creighton Narrows a succession of daybeacons and lights mark the channel; observe them all carefully. At Mile 640, red daybeacon "154" marks shoaling along the west bank.

Sapelo River, Altamaha River, GA

		Largest Vessel Accommodated	VHF Channel Monitored	Approach / Dockside Depth (reported)	Transient Berths / Total Berths	Gas / Diesel	Groceries, Ice, Marine Supplies, Snacks	Repairs: Hull, Engine, Propeller	Lift (tonnage), Crane, Rail	Laundry, Pool, Showers, Courtesy Car	Min/Max Amps	Nearby: Grocery Store, Motel, Restaurant	Pump-Out Station
PINE HARBOR				**Dockage**			**Supplies**			**Services**			
1. Pine Harbor Marina 3 W of MM 638	912-832-5999	23	16	call/2	15/15	F	G	–	–	–	–	–	–
DARIEN RIVER													
2. Darien River Waterfront Parks & Docks 🖳	912-437-6659	–	11/16	call/12	25/25	–	–	IS	–	–	30/50	L	–	GMR

🖳 Internet Access 📶 Wireless Internet Access **WG** Waterway Guide Cruising Club Partner 🔵onSpot dockside WiFi facility

See WaterwayGuide.com for current rates, fuel prices, web site addresses, and other up-to-the-minute information. *(Information in the table is provided by the facilities.)*

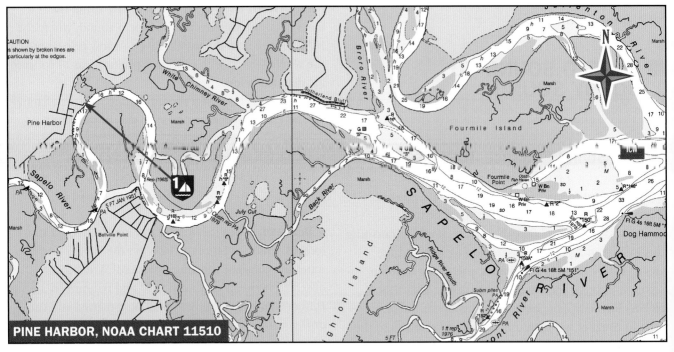

PINE HARBOR, NOAA CHART 11510

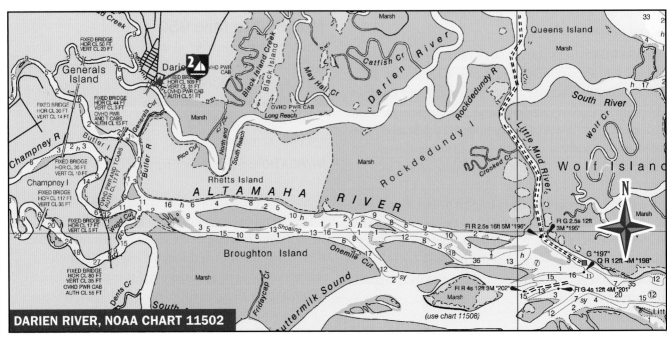

DARIEN RIVER, NOAA CHART 11502

When leaving Creighton Narrows and entering the Crescent River, run straight past red daybeacon "156" until passing flashing green daybeacon "157" to avoid shallow depths to the west. No floating markers are present to denote a mud shoal and the remains of a wrecked shrimp boat that extend far outside the marked channel. Red daybeacon "160" was missing completely at press time (summer 2019). Red daybeacon "158A" is in the middle of the shoal and if you follow the channel as charted here you WILL run aground. (If you go aground here, try powering off toward the eastern bank for deeper water.) Run along the extreme green side for 28 feet MLW.

The marked channel leads you into Old Teakettle Creek, which widens as it reaches Doboy Sound at Mile 649. Arriving at Doboy Sound at low slack water will speed up your run from Mile 644 to Mile 654. (Trying to hit low slack water at either Sapelo Sound or Buttermilk Sound is not quite as critical, as both of these sounds provide more open waters and easier currents to navigate.)

Anchorage: Some boats anchor to the west of where Creighton Narrows empties into the Crescent River in 12 to 15 feet MLW but a large shrimping fleet goes through the anchorage area at all hours, often with their outriggers down, increasing their beam up to 120 feet or more, which consumes the narrow channel. Another nearby anchorage is in Cedar Creek, with 10- to 12-foot MLW depths in mud.

Off Old Teakettle Creek on Shellbluff Creek is an anchorage with 8 to 10 feet MLW and a mud bottom. It provides good protection from the west. Do not go into this creek very far as there is a shoal that crosses the creek about 0.25 mile up from the ICW. This is another anchorage in which shrimp boats come and go at all hours, often with their outriggers down so exercise caution.

The most popular anchorage between Sapelo Sound and Doboy Sound is New Teakettle Creek at Mile 646.5. The charted depths are good (15 to 20 feet MLW), and the best protection lies around the first bend to starboard. Be careful to avoid the charted 2-foot MLW lump in New Teakettle Creek just past Mary Creek.

Another attractive anchorage is up the Duplin River at Mile 649. Go past the very busy ferry dock at Marsh Landing 1 mile or so to the high ground of Little Sapelo Island and anchor in 15 to 16 feet MLW. Note the overhead power cable upstream on the Duplin River with

a 38-foot vertical clearance. The holding here is very good, and you will have plenty of swinging room as it is wide and deep to its banks. The current is swift, but this is a good spot to spend the night. A lot of boats anchor here in order to stage for a favorable tide to transit the Little Mud River.

Doboy Sound Entrance, with 7-foot controlling depths, is not our first choice in bad weather. On the other hand, if you have to get in, it is uncomplicated and the breakwaters may give you some protection from south-setting waves once behind them. The big ship channel of St. Simons Sound is 18 nm to the south. See the Inlet section in the front of this guide for more information about Doboy Sound Entrance.

■ TO ST. SIMONS ISLAND AREA

Doboy Sound to the Altamaha Sound– ICW Mile 650 to Mile 656

NAVIGATION: Use NOAA Chart 11502. Caution: Low slack water at Mile 655 occurs 38 minutes before it occurs at the Savannah River Entrance. At Mile 660, only 5 miles away, low slack water occurs two hours and 6 minutes before it does at Savannah. The ICW continues down Doboy Sound to flashing red daybeacon "178" at the mouth of the North River. There is a shoal building near red daybeacon "178." Favor the green side and stay 300 feet off the mark for 10.8 feet MLW. Follow the channel carefully here and in the dredged areas past the Darien, Rockdedundy and South Rivers. The range markers for this area that are shown on older NOAA charts have been removed. Mariners are advised to use extreme caution while transiting the area.

There is shoaling on the red side between red daybeacon "188" and green daybeacon "189." Favor the green side. Farther south, run along the green edge of the channel by flashing red "190" for 7.7 MLW.

The ICW follows a dredged channel down Little Mud River to the Altamaha Sound and into Buttermilk Sound. Although the Little Mud River is one of the shallowest areas on the entire ICW, this area is not on the list of areas to be dredged due to environmental restrictions. There is no deep water path, you will need mid to high tide to transit comfortably. It is most shallow between green daybeacon "193" and red daybeacon "194." In 2019 shoaling was observed to 3 feet MLW.

Darien River

See route suggestions and details at Waterway Explorer (waterwayguide.com).

Southeast of green daybeacon "197" there is shoaling in mid channel as you make the turn to/from Little Mud River where it enters Altamaha Sound. Depths as low as 4.4 MLW have been observed (spring 2019). Favor the green side and stay 50 to 100 feet from flashing red "196" for deeper water.

Boaters consistently report shallower depths than the NOAA charts/surveys show in this area. It is best to plan this transit for a rising two-thirds tide. Crosscurrents can quickly push slow vessels out of the channel when exiting narrow stretches like the Little Mud River to enter open water like Altamaha Sound.

Anchorage: If you know that the tide will be too low when you reach one of the well-known shallow areas, like the Little Mud River, anchor for a while and let the tide rise before you enter. There is an anchorage on the Back River, at Mile 651.3 in 8 to 11 feet MLW with good holding in sand. It provides protection from all except westerly winds. The North River, at red daybeacon "182," is also a great anchorage. There is plenty of swing room and you can drop your anchor in 12 to 18 feet MLW with good holding. The current is moderate in this entire area. Local fishing boats will come by, but that usually dies down around dinner time.

At Mile 653.7, the South River carries 10 to 14 feet MLW with excellent holding in mud. Across the sound, you can anchor behind Dolbow Island to the south at Mile 659, where there is 13 to 20 feet MLW and fair holding in soft mud.

Side Trip: Darien River–ICW Mile 651.6

NAVIGATION: Use NOAA Chart 11510. The Coast Guard has placed channel markers all the way to Darien, located 7 miles up the Darien River, which shrimp boats use heavily. Plan your passage for mid-tide and rising going off the ICW up the river.

⚠ Shoaling to 3-foot MLW depth has been reported between red daybeacon "12" and "14" at the intersection with Rockdedundy River, and further shoaling on the west side between green daybeacons "27" and "29" of the Darien River.

Some southbound cruisers have been tempted to return to the ICW from Darien via the slightly shorter route on the Rockdedundy River. *We do not recommend this route.* There are no markers of any kind on the Rockdedundy River and 3-foot MLW shoaling has been observed at the bends in the river, as shown on the most recent NOAA chart.

Dockage: Cruising boats making the trip up the Darien River can find transient dockage at the Darien River Waterfront Park & Docks. Be aware that there is an 8- to 9-foot tide and a ripping current. Dockage is strictly first-come, first-served and is not free but is cheap. There is a dockmaster available for most times of the day.

On the north side of the fixed **Walton St. (Hwy. 17) Bridge** (31-foot vertical clearance) is the free dock with a 6-hour limit of use. This dock is unattended and does not offer water or electricity. The town is very welcoming to cruisers, and there are amenities and restaurants within walking distance. Nearby Skipper's Fish Camp Restaurant may have transient dockage (no shore power). This dock is also on a "first-come, first-served" basis. Call 912-437-3474. There is a 48-hour time limit here.

Anchorage: Overnight anchorage for boats up to about 40 feet in length can be found near green daybeacon "1" at Mile 651.6 in 12 feet MLW, but it may be too narrow for larger boats that need more swinging room.

Altamaha Sound–ICW Mile 656

NAVIGATION: Use NOAA Chart 11508. The Coast Guard has removed all markers from the Altamaha Sound entrance channel to and from the Atlantic Ocean (not part of the ICW) due to shoaling. Do not attempt to use this inlet to or from the ocean. Watch for bare-land areas near the ICW channel in Altamaha Sound during extreme low tides, particularly in areas where the NOAA chart shows less than 3 feet MLW. Specific areas of concerns include the following.

- Miles 658-659–There is shallow water between flashing red daybeacon "202" and red daybeacon "208" as you leave Altamaha Sound, so do not hug the channel markers (four red markers) too closely. Our Cruising Editor seldom passes by here without seeing a boat aground. Favor the green side of the channel and stay 200 feet off red daybeacon "204" and "208" for best water. Don't go too close to green daybeacon "209" as shoaling has been observed there as well.
- Mile 659.4–Move to the red edge of the channel as shown on your chartplotter and pass green daybeacon "211" by 300 feet off. Following the range markers here will lead you into shallow water. There is at least 8.2 MLW outside the channel on the green side.

Strong currents and encroaching shoals warrant the use of ranges to well south of Buttermilk Sound. Strong winds and spring tides can lower the water 1 to 2 foot below MLW.

Buttermilk Sound–ICW Mile 660

NAVIGATION: Use NOAA Chart 11508. Heading south from Buttermilk Sound, several sets of ranges guide you over the flats to the headwaters of the southward-flowing Mackay River. Dredging took place in summer 2019 between from green daybeacon "217" to flashing green "223" in Buttermilk Sound and the Mackay River.

In this area of the ICW you may encounter high-speed, outboard-powered boats manned by uniformed personnel. You will find almost a dozen of these docked at Two Way Fish Camp. They are operated by the nearby Federal Law Enforcement Training Center. This is where Customs and Border Patrol, marine patrols and other federal agents receive their boat training.

Dockage: The full-service Two Way Fish Camp, located 5 miles west of the ICW at Mile 664, on the South Althama River, usually has transient space in this a natural setting with friendly people. Bait, tackle and sundries are available in the ship store. Mudcat Charlie's Restaurant (912-261-0055) is on site offering good food at reasonable prices. The current here can be fierce. If approaching the fuel dock during times of maximum current flow, stand by until the current slackens before you approach the dock. Contact the fuel dock for instructions.

Anchorage: You can anchor up the South Altamaha River, off the ICW. The river is deep and well marked with a 7-foot MLW bar at the entrance near red daybeacon "218." Holding is good in 7 to 20 feet MLW with a mud bottom, protected from all but the southeast. The anchorage is large but the current tears through it so we recommend using two anchors. A sandy beach and pine tree-covered bank is accessible by tender where the river enters the waterway.

Side Trip: Hampton River–ICW Mile 664

NAVIGATION: Use NOAA Charts 11507. About 3 miles up the marked channel of the Hampton River, you will find the Hampton River Marina set amidst the naturally beautiful marsh. To reach the marina, follow the Hampton River abruptly back to port at Mile 664, between flashing green "223" and "223A." Shoaling extends into the channel from both riverbanks up

Buttermilk Sound, Mackay River, GA

W G

		Largest Vessel Accommodated	VHF Channel Monitored	Approach / Dockside Depth (reported)	Transient Berths / Total Berths	Floating Docks	Gas / Diesel	Groceries, Ice, Marine Supplies, Snacks	Repairs: Hull, Engine, Propeller	Lift (tonnage), Crane, Rail	Min/Max Amps	Laundry, Pool, Showers Courtesy Car	Pump-Out Station	Nearby: Grocery Store, Motel, Restaurant
SOUTH ALTAMAHA RIVER				**Dockage**			**Supplies**		**Services**					
1. Two Way Fish Camp ⌨ WiFi 5 W of MM 664	912-265-0410	70	16	10/110	10/15	F	GD	GIMS	HEP	L35	30/50	LS	–	GR
HAMPTON RIVER														
2. Hampton River Marina ⌨ WiFi 3.5 E of 664	912-638-1210	–	16/68	call/14	12/14	F	GD	IMS	E	–	30/50	S	P	
TROUP CREEK														
3. Hidden Harbor Yacht Club ⌨ WiFi	912-261-1049	100	16	call/20	15/15	F	–	IMS	EP	–	20/50	LS	P	GMR
ST. SIMONS														
4. Morningstar Marinas Golden Isles ⌨ onSpot	912-434-4751	200	16/68	50/137	10/18	F	GD	IMS	EP	L10	30/100	LPSC	P	R

⌨ Internet Access WiFi Wireless Internet Access WG Waterway Guide Cruising Club Partner onSpot dockside WiFi facility
See WaterwayGuide.com for current rates, fuel prices, web site addresses, and other up-to-the-minute information. *(Information in the table is provided by the facilities.)*

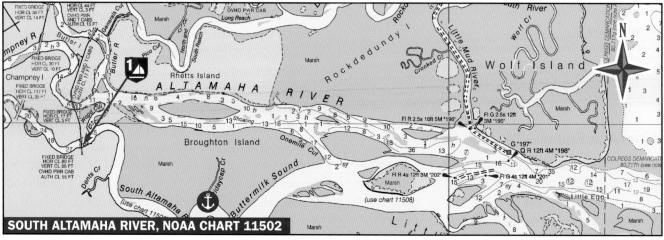

SOUTH ALTAMAHA RIVER, NOAA CHART 11502

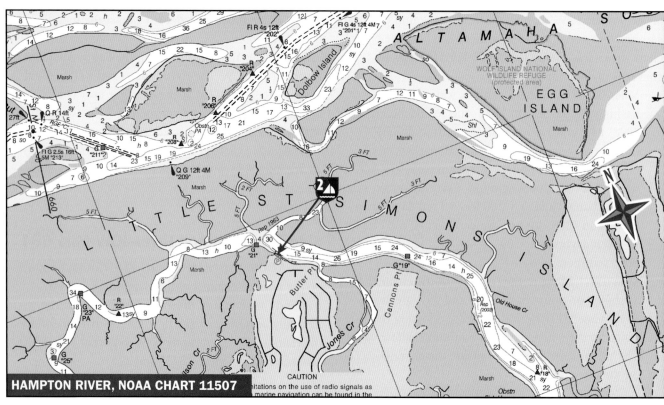

HAMPTON RIVER, NOAA CHART 11507

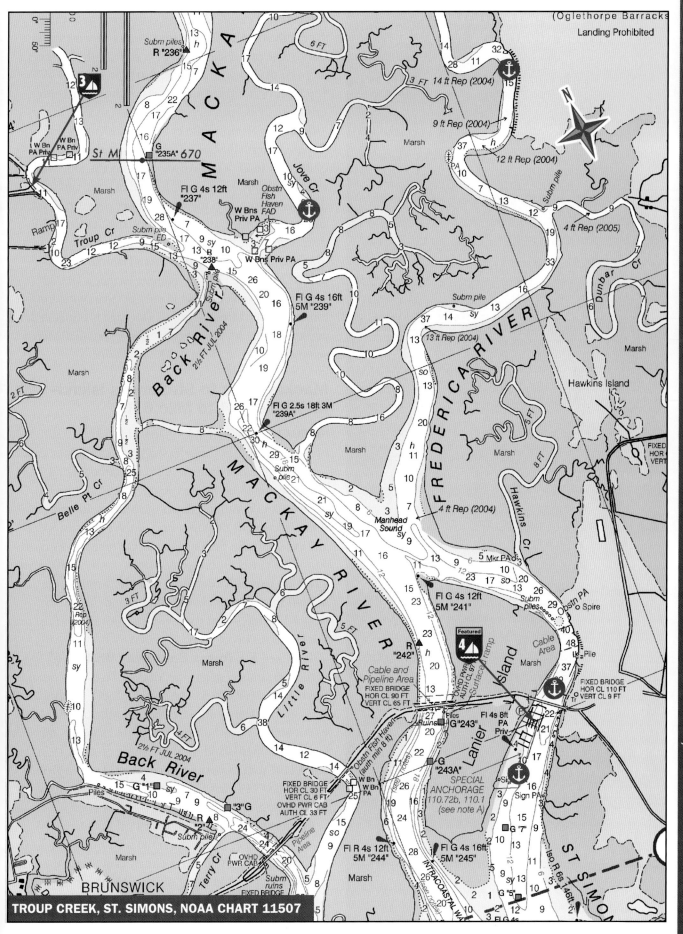

TROUP CREEK, ST. SIMONS, NOAA CHART 11507

Alternate Route:
Frederica River–ICW Mile 666

At Mile 666 and flashing green "229," the Frederica River heads off the ICW to the east. This makes for a fun side trip as you wend your way north or south along the ICW. Slightly more scenic than the ICW in this area, the Frederica River flows past Fort Frederica National Monument on St. Simons Island, rejoins the ICW farther down the Mackay River at approximately Mile 674 and then continues under the 9-foot fixed bridge east of the ICW.

Fort Frederica National Monument preserves the archaeological remnants of a fort and town built by James Oglethorpe between 1736 and 1748 to protect the southern boundary of the British colony of Georgia from Spanish raids. About 630 British troops were stationed at the fort. A Visitor Center (with a bookstore and restrooms), a 23-minute informational movie and ranger programs make this worth a visit (912-638-3630).

NAVIGATION: Use NOAA Chart 11506. Take care if you are entering the Frederica River with the current. A bar protrudes from below flashing green daybeacon "229" and the current seems to split here. Keep well to the north side at the entrance and don't hesitate. Do not confuse flashing green "229" (flashing every 2.5 seconds) with flashing green daybeacon "231" (flashing every 4 seconds) at the entrance to Wallys Leg. Though winding and unmarked, this slightly longer side route runs deep to the shore, except at the mouth of the lower end at Manhead Sound, where the water depth is 5 feet MLW midway between the two banks.

Anchorage: Many cruisers like to anchor in the Frederica River off the Fort Frederica National Monument in 9 to 20 feet of water. Visits ashore are possible at some states of the tide, but be mindful that the tide can sometimes rise and fall 2 feet in an hour during the middle of the cycle. Dinghies can be left high and dry, making re-entry into the water difficult, if not impossible.

to green daybeacon "27." Proceed slowly and watch the depth sounder. Daybeacons farther downstream mark some of the shoals, so pass wide of the markers. At green daybeacon "21," the chart shows a slot of 4 foot MLW but there are reports of the water being substantially deeper.

Dockage: Hampton River Marina welcomes transients if space is available but caters mainly to local boaters (with slips to 25 feet). We are told there is only well water available and it is not for use in your tanks. What this 6-acre operation includes are wet slips, dry stack and trailer storage, all fuels, boat maintenance, a ship store and bait. Call before making plans to stop here.

Across the Hampton River from Hampton River Marina is private Little St. Simons Island, a 10,000-acre barrier island accessible only by boat, with a resort limited to 24 overnight guests. Dockage is available for guests arriving by private boat. The resort's daily ferry service operates at Hampton River Marina.

Mackay River to St. Simons Island–
ICW Mile 664 to Mile 676

NAVIGATION: Use NOAA Charts 11506 and 11507. Flashing green "237" marks shallow water on the east bank. Keep red daybeacon "238" to starboard and continue along the Mackay River. The ICW turns to the west and continues down the Mackay River until it intersects with the lower end of the Frederica River and enters the St. Simons Sound. Current NOAA charts show this correctly, but some skippers who aren't paying attention may still attempt to take the wrong route around the eastern side of Lanier Island, only to be stopped by the 9-foot fixed vertical clearance bridge over the Frederica River.

The fixed **F.J. Torras Causeway Bridge** (65-foot vertical clearance) spans the Mackay River portion of the ICW at Mile 674.5. The current under this bridge is very strong. The 5-mile stretch from Mile 673 to Mile 678 is straightforward; the only problem area is the shoal south of Lanier Island. Leave flashing green "245," "247" and "249" well to port when passing. Flashing green daybeacon "249" has been moved and appears to be far to the east of the ICW channel.

Anchorage: At Mile 666.5, west off the main ICW route, Wallys Leg opens up to the west into a good anchorage but only in fair weather. Wind from the east can be annoying but if out of the west, it will blow your socks off! Enter mid-stream opposite flashing green

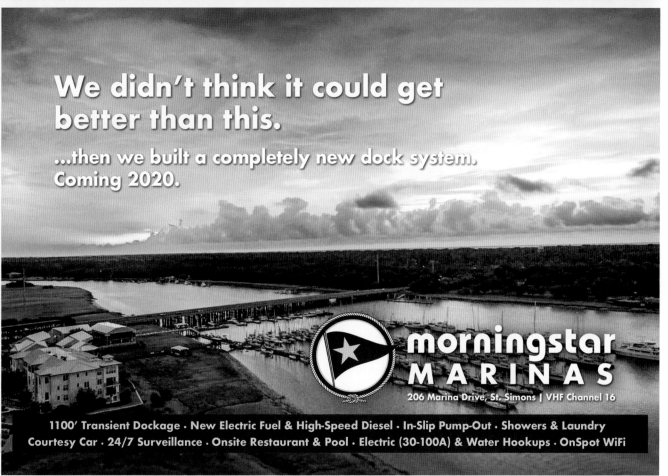

GOIN' ASHORE: ST. SIMONS ISLAND, GA

SERVICES	
1	Library
2	Post Office
3	Visitor Information

ATTRACTIONS	
3	Lighthouse and Museum
SHOPPING	
4	CVS
5	Pier Village District
6	Redfern Village District

7	Retreat Village
8	Winn-Dixie
DINING	
9	Mullet Bay Seafood
10	Sandcastle Café

The "Golden Isles" area includes St. Simon Island, Sea Island, Jekyll Island, Little St. Simon Island and Brunswick. One of Georgia's Golden Isles and largest of its sea islands, St. Simons Island is a draw for history buffs, golf and tennis players, nature lovers and, of course, boaters.

Attractions: Gen. James Oglethorpe brought colonists and soldiers to St. Simon's in 1736, building Fort Frederica as Georgia's first military outpost on the banks of the Frederica River. Today, it is a national monument where visitors can still see the tabby powder magazine, cannons and the foundations of many of the original town buildings.

In the 1740s, the reverends John and Charles Wesley, Anglican priests, accompanied Gen. Oglethorpe to St. Simons Island where John Wesley, the father of Methodism, preached a sermon at a site south of the fort (the eventual site of Christ Church). Near Christ Church you can find the historical marker and the Wesley Oak tree under which he

preached. The original church, the third oldest Episcopal Church in the country, was built in 1820. It was destroyed by Union troops during the Civil War but was rebuilt in 1886 by Anson Phelps Dodge as a memorial to his wife. The church and adjoining graveyard are open for tours.

During the 19th century, many antebellum plantations were established on the island to grow cotton and indigo. Hampton Plantation, on the northern coast, served as the hiding place for Vice President Aaron Burr after he shot Alexander Hamilton to death in an 1804 duel. The ruins of many of the plantations can still be seen, particularly Retreat Plantation, which is now part of the Sea Island Golf Club. The slave burial ground and ruins of the slave hospital and plantation house still exist. The golf courses, however, are only open to members of the club or guests staying at the Lodge or the Cloisters. Visitors can drive along the Avenue of Oaks, the entrance to the club, to view some of the ruins.

St. Simons Island Visitors Center at Neptune Park (912-265-0620) is located across the street from the St. Simons Island Casino Building, and the landmark lighthouse with the original keeper's dwelling and the A.W. Jones Heritage Center. Do make the strenuous climb up the narrow, winding staircase of the 1872 lighthouse for a great view of the island and St. Simons Sound. The keeper's cottage has a museum with the history of the lighthouse. The original, built in 1807, was destroyed by Confederate troops in 1862 to prevent the Union forces from using it. The Heritage Center has exhibits about island history.

Farther along at East Beach, the old Coast Guard Station houses the Maritime Center and the Honey Creek Coastal Encounters Nature Center. For other environmental education experiences, there are beach and marsh explorations, maritime forest ecology walks, kayaking and paddleboat rentals.

There are many festivals in the area throughout the year including the Turtle Crawl Triathlon in May, Kingfish Classic in June, Shrimp & Grits in September, Coastfest in October and McGladrey Classic PGA Tour event in November.

Shopping: The southern tip of the island is a hub of activity centered around the Pier Village District (along Mallery St.). Here, you will find a concentration of tourist-oriented shops and restaurants. Redfern Village District and Retreat Village also offer shopping opportunities. See more at explorestsimonsisland.com.

For provisioning, banks, drugstores and a number of shopping centers populate Frederica and Demere Roads. Also, there is a Winn-Dixie (220 Retreat Village, 912-638-4805) and a Harris Teeter farther north at 600 Sea Island Rd. (912-638-8100). There is a CVS nearby at 1605 Frederica Rd. (912-638-7732) and another at 30 Market St. (912-63-0357). The Brunswick Golden Isles Airport is serviced by Delta Airlines and is less than 30 minutes away.

Dining: Eateries are widely available, from ice cream and sandwich spots to full-service restaurants. The Coastal Kitchen & Raw Bar at Morningstar Marinas at Golden Isles (102 Marina Dr., 912-638-7790) offers lunch, dinner plus brunch (weekends), as well as outstanding views. Another casual spot is Mullet Bay Seafood (512 Ocean Blvd., 912-634-9977), with a wide porch and fresh local seafood and pasta selections. For a tasty breakfast or lunch try the Sandcastle Café (117 Mallery St., 912-638-8883). See saintsimons.com or visitcoastalgeorgia.com for more options.

St. Simons Sound, GA

BRUNSWICK		Approach / Dockside Depth	Transient Berths / Total Berths	VHF Channel Monitored	Largest Vessel Accommodated	Dockage	Groceries, Ice, Marine Supplies, Snacks	Repairs: Hull, Engine, Propeller	Gas / Diesel	Floating Docks	Supplies	Lift (tonnage), Crane, Rail	Min/Max Amps	Services	Laundry, Pool, Showers, Courtesy Car	Pump-Out Station	Nearby: Grocery Store, Motel, Restaurant

BRUNSWICK				Dockage		Supplies		Services			
1. Brunswick Landing Marina ☐ ⬭onSpot	5.5NW of 680	912-265-9264	250	16/71	15/337	36/12	F	GD	IM	HEP	L50,C	30/50	LS	P	GR

☐ Internet Access   (WIFI) Wireless Internet Access   WG Waterway Guide Cruising Club Partner   ⬭onSpot dockside WiFi facility
See WaterwayGuide.com for current rates, fuel prices, web site addresses, and other up-to-the-minute information. *(Information in the table is provided by the facilities.)*

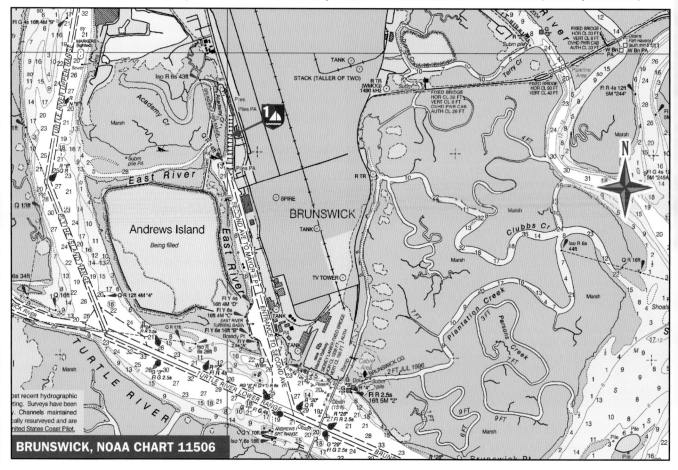

BRUNSWICK, NOAA CHART 11506

"231" and then favor the north shore; go in slowly and use the depth sounder. Anchor in 10- to 12-foot MLW depths off the clump of trees to the north. Holding is good, but the current is strong, so know the state of the tide and set your anchor well. This anchorage can get crowded in season, but there is room for several boats. Some boats anchor in Jove Creek, off the Mackay River at Mile 671, in 9 to 12 feet MLW and good holding in mud. Note that the bottom gets harder deeper into creek and around the bend. Retreat back towards the mouth for softer mud.

■ ST. SIMONS ISLAND

At the southern tip of St. Simons Island, an old village serves as a permanent resort colony. On the island's ocean side, exclusive Sea Island is home to the fashionable 5-star Cloister Hotel and beautifully landscaped residences. Golf courses are plentiful on the islands and one near the Cloister hosts a yearly PGA tournament.

NAVIGATION: Use NOAA Chart 11506. Use the Savannah River Entrance Tide Table. For St. Simon's Sound Bar high tide, subtract one minute; for low tide,

St. Simon Lighthouse

subtract two minutes. St. Simons is the big ship entrance to Brunswick and is an all-weather inlet; nevertheless, St. Simons Sound can be rough when the wind and current are opposed. Extra care should be taken and be sure to study the weather before venturing into the sound. Heading north, you can arrive at Mile 678 at low slack water, and ride the flood current up the Mackay River. See the Inlet section in the front of this guide for more information about St. Simon's Sound Entrance.

Dockage: The Morningstar Marinas at Golden Isles is 2 miles north of Mile 676, on the east side of Lanier Island. This facility is south of the bridge (9-foot vertical clearance) across the Frederica River connecting Lanier Island with St. Simons Island, so it must be approached from the south. When entering and exiting the marked channel to Morningstar Marinas at Golden Isles, follow the chart carefully and do not confuse these channel markers with the ICW markers nearby. The markers have recently been reconfigured and may differ from what is shown on your NOAA chart.

The marina offers ample amenities, including a courtesy car, a pool, laundry facilities, a fully-stocked ship store and concierge service. They also offer complimentary breakfast pastries and newspapers. On site are charter fishing, a dive shop, boat brokers and the excellent Coastal Kitchen restaurant (912-638-7790). The marina provides immediate access to historic St. Simons Island, just over the bridge. The configuration of the docks eases current issues, although there is still a strong current running parallel to the docks, so be sure you have fenders rigged before you come alongside.

Anchorage: There is an anchorage on the northeast side of Lanier Island with at least 17 feet of water and a sandy bottom. To get to this anchorage, turn east just prior to green daybeacon "241" and enter the lower portion of the Frederica River. You can only go a short distance before encountering the 9-foot fixed bridge that crosses from Lanier Island to St. Simons Island. We have received reports that a conflicting current and wind can cause your boat to assume an awkward presentation to both, in which case, you might wish to relocate.

Just slightly below Morningstar Marinas, south of the 9-foot fixed vertical clearance bridge, the Coast Guard has established a special anchorage area here in 10 to 14 feet MLW. Yachts measuring 65 feet or less are not required to show anchor lights in the area, but it is a good idea to do so anyway. The bottom is hard in some places, and it is difficult to get the anchor set. Pick a spot clear of the few (private) moorings and be mindful of the current. Wakes can be a problem at the outer end of the anchorage, near green daybeacon "7." Morningstar Marina provides dinghy dockage for a modest fee.

Side Trip: Brunswick

The downtown district in Brunswick features a growing mix of antique shops, specialty shops, art galleries, theaters and restaurants. With daily shrimping excursions heading in and out of Brunswick's harbor, there is plenty of fresh, local seafood to be had at Brunswick restaurants. See the Brunswick: Goin' Ashore in this chapter for details.

NAVIGATION: Use NOAA Chart 11506. Use the Savannah River Entrance Tide Table. For Brunswick, East River high tide, add 59 minutes; for low tide, add 51 minutes. Quick flashing red "20" in the St. Simons entrance channel should be left to starboard southbound on the ICW heading towards Jekyll Creek or the main shipping channel, which branches off the ICW at flashing red "22" on the Brunswick River.

Heading up the Brunswick River in the vicinity of red flashing "20A" and "22," note that the charted sandbar to the north is a spoils island created with dredge material from a deepening of the entrance to St. Simons Sound. A rock bulkhead surrounds the island, which is

GOIN' ASHORE: **BRUNSWICK, GA**

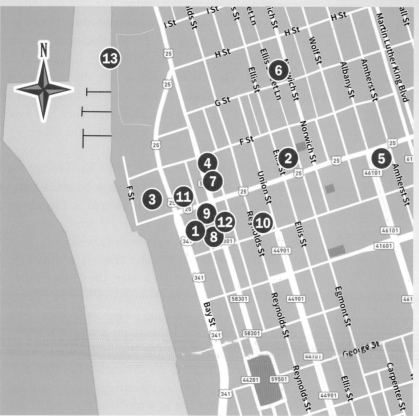

SERVICES	
1	Library
2	Post Office
ATTRACTIONS	
3	Mary Ross Waterfront Park.
4	Ritz Theatre
SHOPPING	
5	Downtown Grocery
6	Grog Shoppe
DINING	
7	Arte Pizza
8	Basil Thai & Sushi
9	Fox's Pizza Den
10	Indigo Coastal Shanty
11	Maggie Mae's
12	Tipsy McSways
MARINAS	
13	Brunswick Landing Marina

Known as the "Gateway to the Golden Isles," the "Land of Five Flags" and the birthplace of the original Brunswick stew, Brunswick now boasts a revitalized commercial and residential historic district. The British gave the town its name from Braunsweig, Germany, the ancestral home of King George III; however, five nations have claimed this area of Georgia as their own. First, explorer Hernando de Soto raised the Spanish flag in 1540; followed by Frenchman Jean Ribault in 1562; then the Spanish expelled the French in 1565 and ruled again until 1736, when the British flag flew until the Revolutionary War. The American flag was lowered during the Civil War, replaced by the stars and bars of the Confederate flag until 1865, when the United States flag was raised once again. All these flags can be found flying at the marina.

Attractions: Brunswick has been a port city since the 1700s and continues its commercial heritage. Besides the cargo and shrimp traffic, the J.A. Jones Company built 99 Liberty Ships in three years during World War II. The shipyard set an unbroken record in December 1944 by constructing seven ships in one month with only six under-construction berths available. There is a memorial to the Liberty Ships at the waterfront park.

What draws visitors to Brunswick is Old Town, a National Historic District, originally laid out in a series of squares, much like a mini Savannah. H Street, Bay Street, First Avenue and Martin Luther King, Jr. delineate the area, with most of the streets retaining their original names honoring English royalty and military officers. The district is known for its turn-of-the-century architecture and eclectic mix of styles encompassing Victorian, Gothic Revival, Italianate, Queen Anne, Tudor and Craftsman, among others.

Built in 1899 as the Grand Opera House, the three-story Historic Ritz Theatre at 1530 Newcastle St. (912-262-6934) is a year-round cultural center that features films (including summer classics), live theater, concerts, and more. There's not a bad seat in the house. The theatre (1530 Newcastle St.) originally opened as the Grand Opera House. The three-story ornate Victorian building also housed the offices of the Brunswick & Birmingham Railroad as well as retail establishments. It turned into a vaudeville stage, and in the 1930s became a movie theater. In the process, the brickwork was covered, and a marquee and the present sign were added, turning it into the art deco Ritz Theatre. The city purchased it in 1980 and altered it again but left the sign. It is slowly being restored to the original brickwork, and live performances once again are seen on its stage. Visit goldenislesarts.org for a schedule of events.

The Brunswick Farmers' Market is held every Saturday from 8:00 a.m. to dark at Mary Ross Waterfront Park. The Brunswick Stewbilee is held annually. Amateur and professional chefs, some with "secret" recipes, face off to compete for the coveted title of "Brunswick Stewmaster." Visit stewbilee.com for details.

Shopping: City Market offers a varied selection of fresh seafood (1508 Gloucester St., 912-265-4430). For your wine and spirits needs be sure to visit the Grog Shoppe (1701 Norwich St., 912-265-8878). For larger supermarkets, the West Marine and the mall, you will need a car to head east. Some provisioning can be done at Downtown Grocery at 1300 Gloucester St. (912-262-6445) and Adams Market at 1700 Norwich St. (912-280-0080).

Dining: The Old Town district has a number of dining options. For pizza, try Fox's Pizza Den (1429 Newcastle St., 912-265-4490), closed on Sundays or Arte Pizza (1518 Newcastle St., 912-265-7878). Tipsy McSways (1414 Newcastle St., 912-267-9991), Basil Thai & Sushi (1401 Newcastle St., 912-342-7625) and Indigo Coastal Shanty (1402 Reynolds St., 912-265-2007) are all in the historic district. For breakfast try Maggie Mae's (205 Gloucester St., 912-264-1543) at the foot of Gloucester St.(closed on Saturday and Sunday) or Daddy Cates Coffee at 302 Gloucester St. (912-264-9363).

Brunswick

highly visible in daylight; however, if you are traveling at night or in other conditions of poor visibility, be sure to stay in the marked channel, as the warning beacons around this island are not lit or currently charted.

This route leads in a westerly direction before turning north at flashing green "1" and heading to downtown Brunswick. Crossing the shipping channel is the **Sidney Lanier Bridge**, which carries SR 17. The suspension bridge has more than 185 feet of clearance and is visible for several miles and is one of the more scenic bridges on the ICW. The town of Brunswick is located just north of the Sidney Lanier Bridge.

Dockage: At flashing green "1," head north, following the Brunswick Harbor range markers to the marina just beyond the shrimp boat docks. This 20-acre marina is in the center of Brunswick's Historic District, is protected from all directions and has little current, making maneuvering easy. The marina's boatyard and lift are north of the transient facilities and has both gas and diesel available.

◼ JEKYLL ISLAND

Heading south from St. Simons Island, the ICW crosses St. Simons Sound and runs 3 miles up the Brunswick River to the mouth of Jekyll Creek (Mile 681), which flows between Jekyll Island and marshland. From there, the ICW proper continues south down Jekyll Creek, which eventually hooks up with Jekyll Sound, farther south.

Jekyll Creek–ICW Mile 681 to Mile 685

NAVIGATION: Use NOAA Charts 11504 and 11506. Jekyll Creek completed much-needed dredging in summer 2019. The tidal range is 7 to 9 feet. Jekyll Creek is greatly affected by wind tides. An east wind of 15 knots or greater will add 1 foot to the depths, while a west wind will lessen the depths by 1 foot. The channel is also affected by the tugs that pass through. Conditions are going to be variable, so plan to traverse the area near high tide or at least on a rising tide.

The charted Jekyll Island Range used to approach Jekyll Creek has unusual characteristics. The dayboard for green daybeacon "1," located on the front structure of this set of range markers, is difficult to see northbound and confusing to line up with when southbound. A range (labeled "Jetty Range" on the chart) leads past a single stone jetty on the red side between the red daybeacons at the entrance to the creek, which is submerged at high tide. Be aware that this jetty extends from the shore all the way out to flashing red "4." Because the current sets strongly to the side, be sure to follow the range until past this jetty.

Jekyll Creek was dredged in summer 2019 from green daybeacon "3" through red flashing "20." For now passage through Jekyll Creek should not be a problem; however, this is a constantly changing area, so go to Waterway Explorer at waterwayguide.com for the latest information.

When approaching flashing green "25" at the mouth of the creek, be aware that it is a short daybeacon (about 10 feet) and is difficult to see at high tide.

Dockage: Jekyll Harbor Marina is on the south side of the high-rise Jekyll Island Bridge. This is the last marina before St. Marys, nearly on the Florida border, so be sure to fuel up and provision if necessary. Fuel will not be available again until Fernandina Beach at about Mile 716. The service-oriented Jekyll Harbor Marina has slips for vessels to 120 feet and offers loaner bikes and golf carts. A grocery, package store, bank, Post Office and such are a 20-minute bike ride. The historic district is 10 minutes away.

Anchorage: At Mile 684.5, southwest of Jekyll Harbor Marina, is an anchorage with 10- to 15-foot MLW depths with a sand bottom. It is exposed to the west and ICW wakes. There are shoal areas here, so set your anchor carefully. The bottom is soft mud and not the best holding, so set your anchor hard and make sure you're not dragging before going ashore. You can land the dinghy at the marina for a daily fee and have access to their many amenities.

Alternate Route: Umbrella, Dover and Floyd Creeks–ICW Mile 685

NAVIGATION: Use NOAA Chart 11489. If you want to avoid St. Andrew Sound and the Cumberland River, a 15-mile-long alternate, foul-weather route avoids the direct crossing. This route, via Umbrella, Dover and Floyd Creeks, is charted and reasonably easy to run. It will add approximately 5 miles to the ICW route, and there are some very shallow spots. Daybeacons were renumbered and additional daybeacons installed in recent years so use recent, print-on-demand charts.

A set of markers leads across Jekyll Sound at Mile 685 and into the Little Satilla River, where you can enter

Jekyll Island

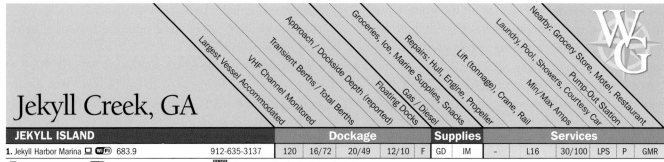

Jekyll Creek, GA

JEKYLL ISLAND		Largest Vessel Accommodated	VHF Channel Monitored	Transient Berths / Total Berths	Approach / Dockside Depth	Floating Docks	Gas / Diesel	Groceries, Ice, Marine Supplies, Snacks	Repairs: Hull, Engine, Propeller	Lift (tonnage), Crane, Rail	Min/Max Amps	Pump-Out Station	Laundry, Pool, Showers, Courtesy Car	Nearby: Grocery Store, Motel, Restaurant
			Dockage				**Supplies**				**Services**			
1. Jekyll Harbor Marina 🖥 📶 683.9	912-635-3137	120	16/72	20/49	12/10	F	GD	IM	–		L16	30/100	LPS	P GMR

🖥 Internet Access 📶 Wireless Internet Access WG Waterway Guide Cruising Club Partner ☁onSpot dockside WiFi facility
See WaterwayGuide.com for current rates, fuel prices, web site addresses, and other up-to-the-minute information. *(Information in the table is provided by the facilities.)*

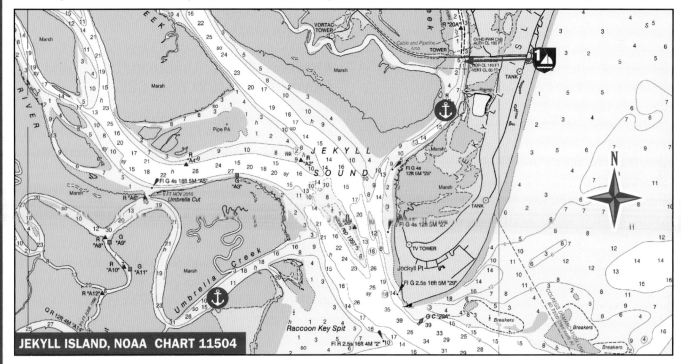

JEKYLL ISLAND, NOAA CHART 11504

Umbrella Creek via the land cut at flashing green "A5." Shallow-draft vessels may attempt this route, but only on a rising tide. Enter Umbrella Cut dead on its centerline instead of trying to line up with the two markers. During strong northeast winds, high water makes it more difficult to navigate by obscuring much of the marsh grass along the shores of Umbrella Creek.

> ⚠ Depths of less than 1 foot MLW have been reported in Umbrella Creek between red daybeacon "A6" and flashing red "A14" to Dover Cut. The tidal range here is 8 feet MLW or better. Run this route on a rising tide or high tide.

A second area that deserves extra attention is Dover Cut, connecting Umbrella Creek with Dover Creek. The cut is narrow and winding with 8-foot charted depths. Continuing along this alternate route, a straight land cut connects Dover Creek to the Satilla River, easily followed for 1.75 miles to the entrance of Floyd Creek, the next section of the alternate route.

The next shoal area to watch for is at the junction of Floyd Creek and Floyd Basin, from green daybeacon "A21" to just past green daybeacon "A31," with a charted controlling depth of 8.5 feet MLW. (Note that red daybeacon "A24" at the intersection with Todd Creek was reported to be missing in spring 2019.)

From here on, it is smooth sailing out to red daybeacon "40," in the center of the Cumberland River and back on the ICW at Mile 696.

Anchorage: Umbrella Creek offers 10 to 15 feet MLW and protection from all but northeast winds. Floyd Creek to the south is deep (17-plus feet MLW) but nighttime commercial shrimp boat traffic makes it a less desirable anchorage.

Jekyll Island

St. Andrew Sound Entrance–ICW Mile 685

The ICW route at the mouth of St. Andrew Sound, just north of Cumberland Island, marks the closest spot to the ocean on the ICW south of Norfolk, VA. Look to the northwest, and you will be looking back at the ocean side of Jekyll Island. A stiff onshore wind running against the current can make the short passage across St. Andrew Sound very wet and uncomfortable. As always, the seas will be calmest when the wind and current are in the same direction.

NAVIGATION: Use NOAA Chart 11504. Low slack water at Mile 690 occurs 58 minutes earlier than at Savannah River. The Coast Guard has reported that St. Andrew Sound's inlet from the ocean has shoaled to 4 feet at its southern entrance. The buoys are often off-station in this area due to heavy seas. Knowledgeable locals advise against using this inlet to approach Jekyll Sound, and you are far wiser to use the big ship entrance of St. Simons Sound just a few miles to your north.

To continue south on the ICW after transiting Jekyll Creek, give a wide berth to Jekyll Point, with its light and green can. The point continues to build out. You can see the remains of a sunken shrimp boat at low tide close inshore of flashing green "29." Set your course for flashing red "32," the more easterly of two red lighted buoys far out in the sound. The markers in the sound can be hard to spot from a distance. Green can "29A" marks the end of a shoal in the seaward part of St. Andrew Sound; this point continues to build out.

If timed correctly, you will have a fair current on the ICW from about Mile 685 to a little past Mile 700. Otherwise, the current will be going with you in one direction and against you when you make the turn at red flashing buoy "32" (Mile 689), with seas behaving accordingly.

Flashing green "31" marks the breakers to the northwest of flashing red "32." This area of shallow water and breakers is marked by the two green floating aids ("31" and "31A") but is slowly building southward, and the strip of deep water marked by flashing red "32" has narrowed. Inside the flashing red "30" and "32," the bottom not only shoals but also shelters the sunken remains of old wrecks. A shoal has built out approximately 150 feet east of red buoy "32." Once you round flashing red buoy "32," you can safely head into the wide entrance of the Cumberland River and southward down the ICW.

Study the NOAA charts for this area carefully before transiting this area. Specific navigational suggestions and directions can be found on the Waterway Explorer (waterwayguide.com).

GOIN' ASHORE: JEKYLL ISLAND, GA

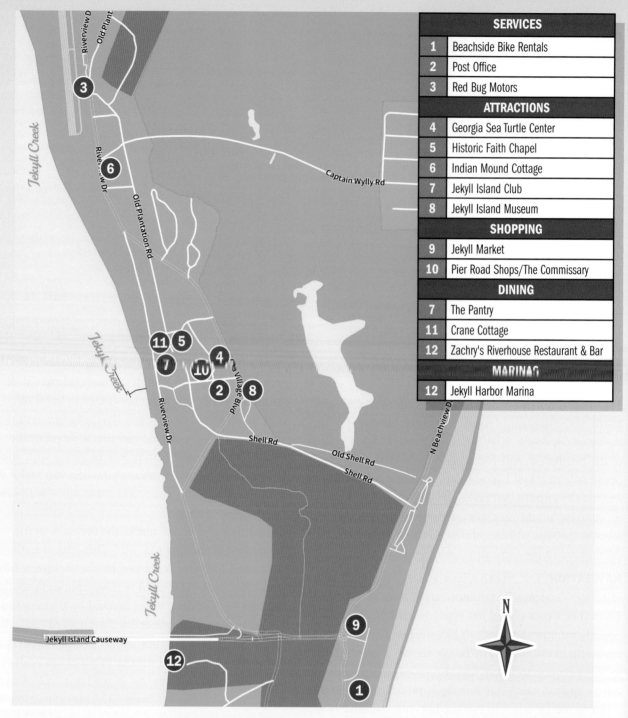

SERVICES	
1	Beachside Bike Rentals
2	Post Office
3	Red Bug Motors
ATTRACTIONS	
4	Georgia Sea Turtle Center
5	Historic Faith Chapel
6	Indian Mound Cottage
7	Jekyll Island Club
8	Jekyll Island Museum
SHOPPING	
9	Jekyll Market
10	Pier Road Shops/The Commissary
DINING	
7	The Pantry
11	Crane Cottage
12	Zachry's Riverhouse Restaurant & Bar
MARINA	
12	Jekyll Harbor Marina

Few places on earth are more inviting than Jekyll Island. From early settlers to America's social elite to today's young explorers, the story of this Georgia barrier island has captured imaginations for generations. Jekyll Island is a beautiful blend of serenity and discovery. Every path leads to a unique experience–majestic forests, saltwater marsh, wide-open beaches, historic ruins or opulent cottages. Jekyll Island has a rich history layered with a legacy of luxury in balance with nature. Start your exploration at the Jekyll Island Museum, then hop on the trolley tour for an even deeper glimpse into the island's history.

Attractions: Guests will find an array of artifacts, exhibits and tour opportunities at the free Jekyll Island Museum at 100 Stable Rd. (912-635-4036) was renovated in 2018 and reopened in 2019 and it is now open daily from 9:00

a.m. to 5:00 p.m. A guided tram tour is the perfect way to experience the Jekyll Island Club. Fifty-three prominent Jekyll Island Club members created an exclusive Gilded Era island retreat for family and friends on Georgia's coast. These empire builders shaped our nation's future. The tours run daily at 11:00 a.m., 1:00 p.m. and 3:00 p.m. You can also grab a bike from one of the many rental stands to explore the 5,700-acre island.

Pay a call at William and Almira Rockefeller's spacious vacation home on Jekyll Island, which they enjoyed "more than any other." The Rockefellers remained devoted to the Jekyll Island Club for 36 years. Visit their period-restored cottage (Indian Mound) and discover the family's affection for this island getaway. Tours offered on the hour, daily from 10:00 a.m. to 4:00 p.m. (371 Riverview Dr.).

Enjoy the charming Historic Faith Chapel, which Club Member Frederic Baker wanted to be "worthy of the island." Delight in the architectural whimsy of its animal carvings, terra cotta gargoyles, and Tiffany and Armstrong stained glass windows. Located at 375 Riverview Dr. Open daily, 8:00 a.m. to 10:00 a.m. for contemplation or take a tour (included with purchase of museum tour or tickets sold separately) daily from 10:00 a.m. to 4:00 p.m.

The Georgia Sea Turtle Center at 214 Stable Rd. is an education and rehabilitation facility that offers the public a chance to learn about sea turtles and see rehabilitation in action with a host of interactive exhibits and experiences. The center has year-round programs and is open daily from 9:00 a.m. to 5:00 p.m.

Getting around by car is possible, but in keeping with the preservation efforts, try riding a bicycle from Beachside Bike Rentals (60 S. Beachview Dr., 912-635-9801) or an open-air electric car from Red Bug Motors (500 Riverview Dr., 912-635-9330).

Some type of festival or sporting event takes place every month on Jekyll Island, including the New Year's Bluegrass Festival in late December/early January, the Beach Music Festival in August, the Wild Georgia Shrimp Festival in September and Holiday in History during the month of December. In addition, the Jekyll Island Museum has special themed historical tours, and the Jekyll Island Club Hotel hosts a series of lectures on historical, environmental and economic issues.

Shopping: The Jekyll Market (912-635-2253) is at 11 Main St. The Flash Food Convenience Store is at 50 Ben Fortson Pkwy. (912-635-2244); a Dairy Queen Grill & Chill (912-635-2573) is located in the same building. The Pier Road Shops in the Historic District include gift, art and clothing shops, including The Commissary (24 Pier Rd., 912-635-2878), a treasure trove of Georgia food products–including jams, jellies, sauces and Georgia peach and Vidalia onion items–and regional cookbooks.

Dining: Zachry's Riverhouse Restaurant & Bar (1 Harbor Rd., 912-319-2174) is adjacent to Jekyll Harbor Marina serving burgers, sandwiches and seafood.

The Victorian Sunday Brunch in the Grand Dining Room at Jekyll Island Club (912-635-5155) is a scene for social gatherings and gourmet southern Georgia dining. The expansive Sunday brunch is served from 10:45 a.m. until 2:00 p.m. See the menu on the dining section of their website. (Note: Reservations are recommended for dinner in the Grand Dining Room and gentlemen are requested to wear jackets and dresses for the ladies. You are in the south, after all…) Also at the hotel, The Pantry (912-635-5203) offers fresh-baked muffins and pastries as well as deli sandwiches, homemade soups, pizza and frozen yogurt.

The Crane Cottage (912-635-5200) in the Historic District has closed their dining room indefinitely. Call 855-535-9547 for free transportation to Crane Cottage or the Jekyll Island Club Hotel for room accommodations.

Dungeness Ruins on Cumberland island

■ CUMBERLAND ISLAND

Cumberland River and Dividings–
ICW Mile 690 to Mile 711

NAVIGATION: Use NOAA Chart 11503. Heading south into the Cumberland River, you will pass two markers at the northern tip of Little Cumberland Island: flashing green "33" on the northern tip and green daybeacon "33A" just beyond. Signs on Little Cumberland Island warn against any landings as this is a wildlife sanctuary, although there is a large house visible on the St. Andrew Sound shore of Little Cumberland Island.

The ICW route becomes progressively more complicated as it approaches the Cumberland Dividings Channel and Cumberland Sound. This whole route is subject to shoaling. You must favor the green side of the channel and proceed with extreme caution from red daybeacon "58A" to just south of flashing red daybeacon "64." Severe shoaling extends from the west bank into the channel much farther than indicated on the NOAA charts. Favor the green side from green daybeacon "59A" until flashing green "63A" for reported 12-foot MLW depths all the way through. Stay at least 200 feet off the reds. At Mile 703, the deep but unmarked Brickhill River joins the ICW route above Cumberland Sound at flashing red "60A." Markers are frequently missing in this area.

⚠ When passing from Cumberland Dividings into Cumberland Sound, there is a tricky spot in the ICW channel just south of green daybeacon "75" (Mile 707.8 just east of Kings Bay). Heading south, alter course westward to favor red daybeacon "76," leaving it close to starboard and then continue south in the channel, avoiding the charted 4- to 5-foot-deep shoal to starboard. Also be sure to leave green daybeacon "79" well to port heading south. This area was being dredged at press time (summer 2019), which should alleviate these issues.

Anchorage: On the Cumberland River, in the bight just east of flashing green "37" at Mile 693, you will find a fair-weather anchorage protected only from east and southeast winds. Avoid the shoal marked by flashing green daybeacon "37" and drop the hook in about 10 feet MLW. This anchorage is away from the Cumberland River traffic but gets uncomfortable with wind from any direction except east. Keep an eye out for wild horses on the shore here. While this anchorage is very exposed, it is a convenient place to stage before crossing St. Andrew Sound on a favorable tide

Other anchorages (all with good holding in mud) are on Floyd Creek (north of Mile 695.6, at least 17 feet MLW), Shellbine Creek (west of Mile 698, at least 9 feet MLW) and Brickhill River North (east of Mile 696, at least 14 feet MLW).

Delaroche Creek at Mile 702 has anchorage up to the first bend to the north and good holding in 12- to 18-foot MLW depths with mud bottom. Stay well off the ICW to avoid traffic from barges and speeding powerboats.

On the Brickhill River, 1.5 miles northeast of the ICW, you can anchor in 9 to 20 feet MLW just north of the Plum Orchard Plantation dock on Cumberland Island. Plum Orchard, one of the Carnegie family estates, was built in 1898. Dinghy ashore and you will be rewarded with a walk among huge live oaks draped with Spanish moss and a view of the well-preserved mansion. If you are fortunate, you may encounter a family of wild horses grazing on the lawn or alligators swimming in the anchorage. (No swimming!) The area where the Brickhill River meets Cumberland Dividings is subject to shoaling. Enter the Brickhill River slowly and watch the depth sounder. We have received reports of just 2 feet MLW mid-channel at the entrance to the river.

South of the Brickhill River, you can anchor in the Crooked River west of the ICW, with charted depths of 8 to 13 feet MLW at Mile 703.8. Here you will find soft mud, so anchor accordingly.

Side Trip: Cumberland Island

NAVIGATION: Use NOAA Charts 11503. Use the Savannah River Entrance Tide Table. For Brunswick, East River high tide, add 59 minutes; for low tide, add 51 minutes. Cumberland Island, behind which the ICW route winds for more than 20 miles, was once the center of controversy over development plans. It achieved its protected status as a National Seashore decades ago, ensuring that most of the island will remain in its primitive state. No road or causeway from the mainland will ever be constructed. Public land acquisition continues today, and the federal government owns approximately 85 percent of the island. Most visitors arrive via ferry service from St. Marys, a 45-minute trip.

However you arrive, all you will find is 50 miles of maritime forest trails, undeveloped beaches, wide marshes and more than 150 wild horses that have survived here in the wild since the Spanish originally set them free. Dungeness, ruins of the Carnegie family mansion, is a good spot for viewing some of the horses roaming freely. You will need insect repellent in the spring, summer, and fall.

Dockage: Limited daytime dockage is available at the Sea Camp dock on a floating pier maintained by the National Park Service. Head east near Mile 711 in the vicinity of flashing red "34," and then proceed north along the shore of Cumberland Island, following the eastern branch of Cumberland Sound, about 1.25 miles to the Sea Camp Dock and Visitor Center. The ferry from St. Marys occupies the major portion of the dock, and the National Park Service boats take most of the inside section. That leaves room for dinghies on the outside docking area aft of the ferry. After hours, there is more space. There are no power or water hookups, but this is an excellent base from which to explore the island. Visit nps.gov/cuis for more information.

It is an easy 0.50-mile hike east to the beach, and a little more than 1 mile south to the ruins of Dungeness. (Private boats may not dock at the National Park Service's Dungeness dock.) The privately-owned Greyfield Inn may have limited dockage available for its overnight guests (904-261-6408). The circa 1900 estate is now an upscale all-inclusive inn. It is mostly accessed by a private ferry from Fernandina Beach.

Anchorage: You can anchor near the Sea Camp Dock, where holding is good in 10 to 22 feet MLW. Mind the 7- to 9-foot tides and consider the effects of reversing current in the narrow channel. There is a long southwest exposure here, and the anchorage can become uncomfortable in wind-against-tide situations.

This anchorage is often very crowded during warm weekends and during spring and fall transient seasons. You can dinghy into the National Park Service Sea Camp Dock and go ashore while waiting for weather to make passage from the St. Marys River Entrance.

St. Marys River, GA

ST. MARYS			Dockage			Supplies		Services			
	Largest Vessel Accommodated	VHF Channel Monitored	Transient Berths / Total Berths	Approach / Dockside Depth (reported)	Floating Docks	Gas / Diesel	Groceries, Ice, Marine Supplies, Snacks	Repairs: Hull, Engine, Propeller	Lift (tonnage), Crane, Rail	Min/Max Amps	Laundry, Pool, Showers, Courtesy Car	Pump-Out Station	Nearby: Grocery Store, Motel, Restaurant
1. St. Marys Boat Service WiFi 904-219-2869	65	–	–	5/5	–	–	M	HEP	L50,C12	30/30	LS	–	R

🖵 Internet Access WiFi Wireless Internet Access WG Waterway Guide Cruising Club Partner onSpot dockside WiFi facility
See WaterwayGuide.com for current rates, fuel prices, web site addresses, and other up-to-the-minute information. *(Information in the table is provided by the facilities.)*

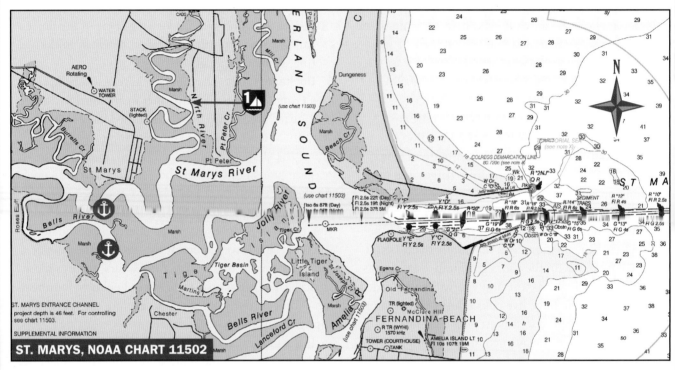

ST. MARYS, NOAA CHART 11502

■ CUMBERLAND SOUND

ICW Mile 711 to Mile 716

The complications of Cumberland Sound are compounded by the activity at the Navy's Kings Bay Submarine Base, home to six Trident-class submarines. Frequent changing of the navigational aids and nearly constant dredging operations make navigation challenging. Be sure to use the latest edition of NOAA Chart 11503, as many marks have been renumbered.

NAVIGATION: Use NOAA Charts 11503. The Cumberland Sound Range starts at Mile 705. Take time here to sort out the mosaic of lights, markers and ranges now serving the huge government installation on Kings Bay at Mile 708. This stretch is well marked and sufficiently deep, but watch the depth sounder.

Shoaling also exists near the range markers northwest of Drum Point Island.

⚠ The ICW fronts the Kings Bay Naval Submarine Base near Mile 708, and Navy security patrols carefully monitor traffic from both directions, especially when submarines are passing through Cumberland Sound and the St. Marys River Entrance. Kings Bay, and the area west of the ICW channel here, are strictly off limits to cruising skippers. No-Wake Zones have been established in this vicinity and are strictly enforced.

The patrol boats will ask you to move outside of the ICW channel if a submarine is in the vicinity and there is plenty of water off of the main channel. Patrol boats respond on VHF Channel 16. The submarines travel at high speeds in open water, creating very large wakes.

St. Marys Waterfront

St. Marys River (Cumberland Sound) Entrance–Mile 714

St. Marys is a relatively easy entry and exit point, conveniently located just off the ICW. The short 20-nm offshore jump from here to the St. Johns River at Mayport (near Jacksonville) or to the inlet at St. Augustine bypasses the sometimes shallow, shifting channels at Nassau Sound. If you are on a northerly leg to St. Simons Island, you can cut out the meandering shallows found in Cumberland Sound and Jekyll Creek. Both the St. Johns Entrance Channel and the St. Simons Inlet involve long entry channels and strong currents to return to the ICW so be careful and try to plan exits and entries with a slack current or fair tide. (See the Inlets section at the front of this guide for more information.)

NAVIGATION: Use NOAA Chart 11503. The St. Marys River Entrance is deep, wide, jettied and is well marked, but exercise caution when going through, as there are some shoal sections to the north of the channel inside the jetties. The current in this inlet is very strong and dictates appropriate boat handling to compensate. Slower boats are well advised to time their passages for slack water or a favorable tide.

The active Kings Bay Naval Submarine Base continues to be the reason for the frequent dredging and renumbering of buoys, beginning where the ICW joins the head of Cumberland Sound and continuing to the ocean inlet. The channel is consequently quite deep and wide. The St. Marys Entrance Channel buoys, offshore of the entrance, were eliminated several years ago. The buoy that formerly was "10" is now flashing red buoy "2," and every buoy in Cumberland Sound up to the head of Kings Bay was renumbered accordingly. ICW daybeacon numbering remains unchanged. Older charts may not show this change. Remember, the ICW daybeacons all have a yellow square or yellow triangle to designate them as ICW markers.

Side Trip: St. Marys, GA

The ferry that takes visitors to Cumberland Island leaves from St. Marys. Buy tickets at the Cumberland Island Visitor Center at 113 St. Marys St. (912-882-4336). The ferry makes several trips a day from the waterfront, running daily March through November. December through February finds a reduced schedule of Thursday through Monday.

This area has experienced several hurricanes over the past few years, which has left few choices for dockage and made the anchorage very popular. Despite the lack of services, St. Marys remains a "cruiser friendly" location. There is even a "Cruisers Net" at 8:00 a.m.

GOIN' ASHORE: ST. MARYS, GA

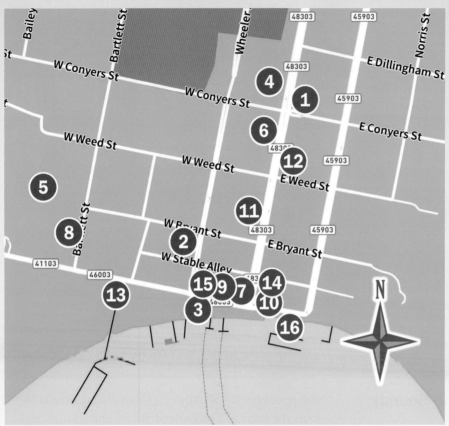

	SERVICES
1	Visitor Information
	ATTRACTIONS
2	Cumberland Island National Seashore Museum
3	Cumberland Island National Seashore Visitor Center
4	First Presbyterian Church
5	Oak Grove Cemetery
6	Orange Hall Museum
7	Riverview Hotel
8	St. Marys History Walk
9	St. Marys Submarine Museum
	SHOPPING
10	Market on the Square
11	Once Upon a Bookseller
	DINING
7	Captain Seagle's Restaurant
12	Cedar Oak Café
13	Lang's Marina Restaurant
14	Pauly's Café
15	Riverside Café
	MARINAS
16	Lang's Marina

St. Marys has more to it than meets the eye. It is one of the oldest cities in the United States. It sits aside the St. Marys River, looking the part of a fishing village with a dash of charm–lovely Victorian homes, inns, restaurants and shops. But the "Gateway to Cumberland Island" is quickly growing, like every other town along the ICW, in large part because St. Marys enjoys the added economic benefit of having Kings Bay Submarine Base nearby. Wars and their aftermaths, in fact, have been a historical constant, shaping life in St. Marys since its beginnings.

St. Marys sits on Buttermilk Bluff, the site of an old Indian village. Although shelled by Union gunboats, the town survived the Civil War and by the 1870s, was prospering as a seaport. Besides the British, early settlers included Acadian French, who landed at St. Marys in 1791. The Kings Bay Naval Submarine Base opened in 1979. This is home to most of the Trident nuclear missile submarines based on the east coast. It also hosts British nuclear subs from time to time.

Attractions: The Welcome Center at 400 Osborne St. (800-868-8687) can provide maps and brochures of the historic downtown and other attractions. It is also home to the Georgia Radio Museum (free admission). Strolling along the wide, cabbage palm and oak-lined streets is a pleasant way to check out the Colonial, antebellum and Victorian homes, several of which are now inns. Among them is the circa 1830-38 Orange Hall Museum (311 Osborne St., 912-576-3644), so-named for a large sour-orange grove behind the house, which is an architectural showcase of Greek Revival style. The First Presbyterian Church (110 W. Conyers St.), built in 1808, is believed to be the second oldest church in Georgia.

The Cumberland Island National Seashore Museum (129 Osborne St., 912-882-4335) was opened in 2001 to house a collection of artifacts in a climate-controlled atmosphere. A small portion of the items are on exhibit, including a Native American Indian canoe, pottery and arrowheads, as well as old black-and-white photos of people who lived on the island in the late 1800s and early 1900s. The displays are worth a visit.

The ferry that takes visitors to Cumberland Island leaves from St. Marys. Buy tickets at the Cumberland Island Visitor Center at 113 St. Marys St. (912-882-4336). The ferry makes several trips a day from the waterfront, running daily March through November. December through February finds a reduced schedule of Thursday through Monday. Nature lovers might see wild horses in the marshes in addition to mink, armadillos, alligators and deer. You can also explore the ruins of Dungeness, the old Carnegie Estate.

At the St. Marys Submarine Museum at 102 W. St. Marys St. (912-882-2782), you can learn everything you ever wanted to know about the underwater machines and check out the working periscope. Also, take a walk through the St. Marys History Walk (located across the street from Lang's Marina West) or 1788 Oak Grove Cemetery (corner of Bartlett and Weed Streets), where you can find much history of the area. It is believed that graves of veterans representing every war fought in and by America are there. For more ghost hunting, check into the Riverview Hotel (105 Osborne St.), built in 1916 and renovated in the 1970s, which some say has a resident ghost.

St. Marys Railroad Express (1000 Osborne St., 912-200-5235) offers train rides through scenic woodlands and marshlands (seasonal) with a variety of themed excursions. See the schedule at stmarysrailroad.com. A free railroad museum is open during train events with scale model trains.

Shopping: Shops in St. Marys are small and delightful. For provisioning, you will need to head west a few miles near I-95. But do check out the local stores on Osborne and St. Marys Streets, especially Once Upon a Bookseller (207 Osborne St., 912-882-7350), with a collection of NOAA charts. Be sure to visit The Market on the Square (100 Osborne St., 912-882-2215) for delicious fudge. There are several nice B&B's in town, should you decide to stay a few days.

Bulldog's Discount Liquor (1101 Osborne St., 912-576-5002) has a wide variety of beer, wine and spirits.

Dining: Lang's Marina Restaurant (307 W. St. Marys St., 912-882-4432) is on the water and has fresh-from-the-water fried shrimp. Pauly's Café, a small eatery near the waterfront, gets rave reviews (102 Osborne St., 912-882-3944). In the Riverview Hotel (105 Osborne St., 912-882-3242), Captain Seagle's Restaurant has seafood and steaks, while Riverside Café (106 St. Marys St., 912-882-3466) overlooks the harbor. Cedar Oak Café (304 Osborne St., 912-882-9555) serves breakfast, lunch and great coffee.

The Riverview Hotel and many of the local businesses, along with many of the residents, have organized a Thanksgiving Dinner for cruising boats since 2001. Each year it has grown in popularity, and last year more than 100 boats attended. The town provides and cooks all of the turkeys and ham, and the boaters bring the side dishes like salads, veggies and dessert. All of the paper goods are provided. This is a "don't-miss" event if you are in the area.

daily on VHF Channel 68. During the net, you can get information about town activities and announcements along with help, if needed, and also make arrangements for transportation.

NAVIGATION: Use NOAA Chart 11503. The charted and well marked St. Marys River enters Cumberland Sound from the west. Favor the center of the river and take flashing green "3" wide to starboard. Follow the markers to avoid extensive shoaling of the west bank from red daybeacon "6" to flashing red "10." An unmarked red nun buoy is between red daybeacons "6" and "8" to mark the shoal encroaching the channel from the west bank. Temporary (uncharted) red nun buoy "6A" has been added to assist with navigation.

Dockage: This area has been assaulted by several hurricanes over the past few years (most notedly Hurricanes Irma in 2017 and Matthew in 2016), which has left few choices for dockage. One victim of note was the town dock in St. Marys, which remained closed at press time (summer 2019) with no indication of a reopening date. When open, this will accommodate a few 35-foot vessels for a 6 hour period. Overnight dockage is not allowed.

The full-service St. Mary's Boat Service on the North River offers boat repairs of all kinds. They allow do-it-yourself repairs or can provide contract professionals to assist you. They report 5-foot approach and dockside depths. Call ahead.

Anchorage: There is a substantial anchorage area in front of the town with 8- to 13-foot MLW depths. Tidal currents run swiftly here, so keep that in mind when dropping anchor and be sure to set your anchor well.

■ NEXT STOP

Fernandina Beach at Mile 716.5 is the next town to the south on the ICW once you leave the St. Marys River area. *Waterway Guide's* Southern edition will get you from Fernandina Beach to the Florida Keys, where you can set off for the islands (and switch to the Bahamas edition of the *Waterway Guide*), or continue on to Tampa and then the Big Bend to Mobile, AL, on the Gulf Coast (covered in *Waterway Guide's* new Western Gulf edition).

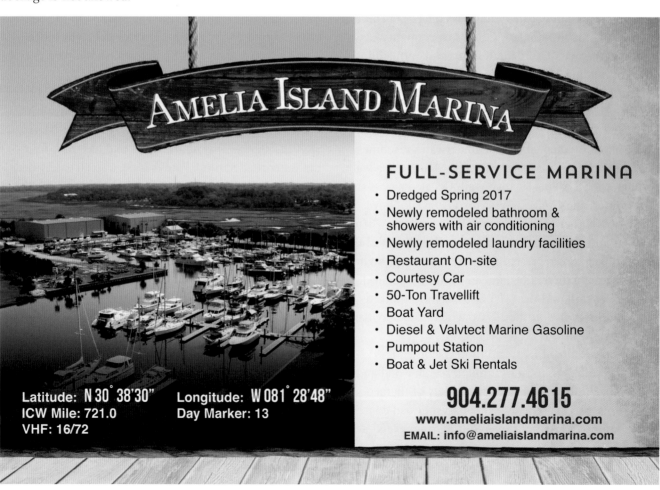

Marina/Sponsor Index

Sponsors are listed in **BOLD**.

MARINA/SPONSOR INDEX

MARINA/SPONSOR INDEX

Subject Index

Most relevant pages are listed in **BOLD**.

SUBJECT INDEX

Goin' Ashore Index

Inlets Index